SQUARE DANCE CALLING
An Old Art for a New Century

Also by Tony Parkes
> Contra Dance Calling: A Basic Text
> Shadrack's Delight and Other Dances
> Son of Shadrack and Other Dances

Recordings featuring Tony Parkes
> Kitchen Junket (with Yankee Ingenuity)
> Maritime Dance Party (with Gerry Robichaud)
> Heatin' Up the Hall (with Yankee Ingenuity)
> More Down East Fiddling (with Gerry Robichaud)
> Shadrack's Delight and Other Dances
> Supplements to Square Dance Calling (*in preparation*)

SQUARE DANCE CALLING

An Old Art for a New Century

Tony Parkes

Hands Four Books
Bedford, Massachusetts

Printed on acid-free paper

ISBN 978-0-9632880-4-2

Library of Congress Control Number: 2021951504

Copyright © 2021 by Tony Parkes. All rights reserved. No part of this book may be reproduced in any form or by any means now known or to be invented without written permission of the author, except as provided under the Copyright Act. For information address Hands Four Productions, P.O. Box 641, Bedford, Massachusetts 01730. www.hands4.com

Cover design by Ellie Erhart   www.ellieerhart.com
Photo of author by Doug Plummer   www.dougplummer.com

Because of the dynamic nature of the Internet, any Web addresses or links contained in this book may have changed since publication and may no longer be valid.

The mention of a product, trademarked or otherwise, in this book does not constitute an endorsement. The description of a product does not necessarily apply to other products from the same manufacturer.

See last page for country of manufacture

1.1

*To the glory of God
and the memory of Ted Sannella
(1928–1995)
caller, choreographer, mentor, friend
this book is gratefully dedicated*

Contents

Introduction	ix
Part One: Theory	**1**
1: Starting Out	3
2: History	9
3: Philosophy	33
Part Two: Delivery	**47**
4: Musical Structure	49
5: Dance Structure	63
6: Wording	73
7: Voice Technique	81
8: Calling Breaks	87
9: Patter	97
10: Programming	109
11: Teaching	117
12: Working with Music	129
13: Different Groups	143
14: Exploring	161
Part Three: Material	**181**
15: Basic Movements	183
16: Circles	249
17: Easy Squares	269
18: The Middle Ground	285
19: Visiting Squares	313
20: Singing Calls	331
21: Fancy Figures	355
22: Silly Stuff	367
23: Them's the Breaks	379
Glossary	403
Resources	461
Index	501

Introduction

The square dance is one of the most accessible dance forms, and potentially one of the most enjoyable. It affords the chance of moving to music without learning a lot of fancy footwork or body positions. In its most traditional forms, it has a natural exuberance that is almost irresistibly infectious. It enables its devotees to meet, greet, smile at, and even touch one another in relative safety – a precious privilege in a society where people hold aloof due not only to fear, but also to preoccupation with solitary pursuits. It promotes physical fitness and fosters teamwork and a sense of equality. Its multicultural origins make it an ideal recreation for the America of tomorrow as well as today.

During the 19th century, square dances developed into the forms that are more or less familiar to us today. In the 20th, square dancing became a recreation for many and a dedicated hobby for some. It is my hope that in the 21st, these dances can gain a new lease on life and continue to give people joy.

Ever since the nationwide square dance fad of the late 1940s, there has been a steady outpouring of books, magazines, and recordings on the subject. If we consider the traditional dance forms, we find that most publications are of one of two types. Most of those intended for the dancer comprise entry-level instruction, often advising the reader to seek a professional caller in order to advance further. Those aimed at the caller consist mainly of dance material, perhaps with a few tips on delivery. There have been very few books on the subject of the traditional caller's art since Rickey Holden's seminal booklet *The Square Dance Caller* in 1951. In a mere 48 pages Rickey managed to touch on every important aspect of calling and teaching.

The present book is an attempt to fill the void. Into it I have distilled over half a century's experience, including the things I know now that I wish I had known in 1964. (It should come as no surprise that I learned many of them the hard way.) I have tried to include everything a beginning caller might want to know today.

Most of the good books of traditional square dance material are out of print. Although many are readily available (some as free downloads), not everyone has the skill to select suitable dances from them. Therefore, I have supplemented my advice with a collection of the dances I use and enjoy myself. The calls are arranged in tabular form so that you can see exactly how the words fit the structure of the music, even if the call is not intended to be sung. Timing is the aspect of my calling that has brought the most compliments; I trust I have provided enough information, between the prose and the call charts, to enable a serious student to deliver the calls as I do. (Of course, anyone serious about calling will, perhaps without realizing it at first, quickly develop a unique personal style.)

I begin with a brief look at the history of the square dance and some thoughts on dance philosophy and the ethics of calling. I hope you will read this section; it will benefit you in the long run, though its benefits may not be as concrete or obvious as those of the rest of the book. The middle section concerns the technical skills involved in using one's brain and voice to deliver information to a group of dancers, such that they will know immediately what you mean and can follow your instructions with little or no mishap. The dance descriptions and call charts follow, sorted by formation, difficulty, and other factors. At the end are a glossary of terms, one of the most comprehensive available, and an annotated list of helpful books and recordings.

As many readers will be aware, I have written a similar book on contra dance calling. It contains a brief section on squares, because I feel that the two forms belong together. But the forms of the square dance and the styles of calling them are much more varied than the contra dance repertoire. Clearly they deserve a book of their own. There is some overlap between the two volumes; I have chosen to repeat myself at times, rather than force the reader to acquire both books. However, repeating every relevant point would have made this one unwieldy. Therefore, I have gone into detail on topics that seem particularly germane to the art of calling squares, while treating more briefly those things of more general interest, of which I have written more fully in the contra book.

There is some intentional repetition in this book: The same point may be made in different chapters. After an initial reading, the book is more likely to be consulted a chapter at a time, and I wanted to ensure that certain points that touch on different aspects of calling would be seen, no matter which aspect the reader might be considering.

There are very few diagrams here; including one for each dance would have doubled the size of the book without providing a commensurate amount of help. Some of the titles in the bibliography contain excellent diagrams. Of course, video recordings are by far the best way (short of live observation and participation) to get the feel of how a dance goes. Video clips of squares from various regional traditions (including some of the figures in this book) are available on YouTube; many are from the Square Dance History Project, and I anticipate that they will be available for some time to come.

One of the things I love about traditional square dancing is that it is not at all standardized. If you are part of a local dance scene, by all means keep doing things your way. The suggestions I have made in this book on style and terminology are primarily intended for leaders who have no existing local tradition to draw on. I would be sorry to see a rigid structure grow up around the points I make here.

Many contra dancers, and even some contra callers, are convinced that they dislike squares. I firmly believe this is due to a vicious cycle: Few present-day callers on the contra circuit have the background or training to appreciate squares and to teach and call them well. In presenting squares, they find themselves at the beginning of a learning curve; they choose dances that are too easy or too hard for their group, and they spend too much or too little time on the walkthrough. As a result, the dancers associate squares with an unpleasant time. Some callers will persevere and improve, but many will continue to fumble or will give up on squares. It is up to callers to break this cycle by learning to teach effectively and by acquiring a repertoire large enough that they can select an appropriate dance for any group. I pray that this book will be a means to that end.

The old-time callers were notorious for jealously guarding their little black books of calls. It was even said that if a caller was about to present a complicated or flashy new dance and saw a rival coming in the door, he would instead call a dance that everyone knew. In writing this book I have tried not to be "that guy," not to hold back any trade secrets. You will not get a predigested list of what dances to use, and in what order, because everyone's tastes are different. I have given you my favorite dances of many types, which are suitable for varying situations; I trust you to use your judgment in selecting them. I have had a long, fulfilling career and have benefited from the kindness of many people; I feel it is high time for me to "pay it forward."

It is my sincere hope that you learn something from this book, and that you enjoy the learning process as much as I have enjoyed the process of writing it.

Acknowledgments

I am, of course, indebted to all the generous men and women who taught and encouraged me in my pursuit of excellence and effectiveness. Their names appear in the front of *Contra Dance Calling*. The present volume is a distillation of their knowledge and wisdom; it would be hard to single any of them out as a greater influence than the others, with the possible exception of Ted Sannella, to whom the book is dedicated.

Several people contributed in some degree to the book's conception and gestation. For many insights into the caller's art as seen from other traditions than mine, I am indebted to my fellow "core consultants" to the Square Dance History Project: Bob Dalsemer, Larry Edelman, Phil Jamison, Bill Litchman, and Jim Mayo. Phil in particular informed my thinking about the African roots of calling, giving me the benefit of yet unpublished research. Richard Powers was of great help in shepherding me through the intricacies of 18th- and 19th-century dance history; he stressed the importance of consulting primary sources and pointed me to many. David Millstone, the creator and curator of the History Project, whose tastes coincide with mine to an uncanny extent, was a constant source of encouragement. Finally, my wife Beth provided technical help and emotional support in equal measure. Without her, the book would have been several years later and several shades weaker.

PART ONE
Theory

1
Starting Out

Welcome to the world of calling square dances! For more than half a century I've found it to be challenging but exhilarating – and ultimately very satisfying to the soul. In this book I'll do all I can to help you find your place in this world and develop the skills and attitude that will enable you to succeed.

Of course, the best way to become a caller is to dance for years, absorbing words and concepts from experienced callers. But if seasoned callers are scarce in your area, you can still make a go of it if you're willing to do a lot of reading and listening – not just to me, but to three generations' worth of talented leaders.

Should You Call?

If you are just starting to call, or you have a strong desire to do so, I suggest you do a bit of soul-searching. There are three general requirements for success as a caller: talent, technical knowledge, and a sense of dance history. Given a bit of talent to start with, all three can be developed with time and practice.

Talent

Talent is a gift from God. The best attitude toward your own talent is to be thankful for it, not overly proud or arrogant about the talent you've been handed, but not apologetic either: It's just a given. A caller needs a bit of many different talents; no one starts out with a full measure of each one, but we have the ability to develop them. Here's my list; feel free to add to it:

- Self-confidence
- Patience
- Good judgment
- Emotional balance
- A sense of rhythm and timing
- A pleasant speaking and/or singing voice
- Good diction
- Musical ability
- Good memory
- A sense of humor
- Spatial sense (see below)
- A love of people and a desire to see them happy
- A love of traditional dance and a desire to share it
- A delight in bringing order out of chaos
- Perseverance in the face of disappointment and frustration

By spatial sense, I mean the ability to see what's happening on the floor, how each call changes the shape of the set and the positions of the people – both when visualizing a dance at home and when calling to actual dancers. Lloyd Shaw (1939, pp. 40–41) was convinced that some people lack this sense, just as some people are color-blind or have trouble with musical pitches – and that many of them try to become dancers or callers.

A sense of humor includes the ability to laugh at yourself, and to laugh with, not at, your dancers when it seems appropriate. It's closely related to patience and emotional balance. A little levity at the right time, provided it's free of malice, can help to defuse the situation and keep tempers from rising.

Again, no one has all of these to the same degree. If you feel you lack most of them, you might reconsider your decision to be a caller. But on the whole, if you enjoy what you're doing, your dancers will too, and they'll be inclined to be patient with you as you learn and grow.

Technical Knowledge

The technical principles involved in calling, particularly traditional calling, are few but important. They will require much practice at the outset, but eventually your responses will become second nature. At that point you can go on autopilot from a technical standpoint (both your material and your delivery of it) and use your conscious mind to focus on the people who are present and their particular needs.

If you are under pressure to learn calling in a short time – if you're a teacher or recreation leader scheduled to present square dancing next season – you will have to make a decision. If you have a couple of months to prepare, you must make time to study, listen, and practice just about every day. If your time is even shorter, I suggest you focus on learning the basic principles of square dancing (if you don't already know them) and honing your teaching ability; you can use recordings with calls until you acquire the additional skills needed for calling.

Perspective

Studying square dance books, magazines, and recordings will not only help you develop your technical skills but also give you a sense of historical and cultural perspective. You may be able to avoid some classic mistakes if you look at what's worked and what hasn't in the past. Studying dance history is sure to give you a sense of the dedication that past leaders have had, and heighten your feeling that the dance is worth preserving.

First Steps

Make sure you know how to dance before you try to call. You should be able to respond as a dancer to all the calls you plan to use. I recommend two years of dancing (or one year of intensive dancing) before calling, except in an emergency (you've moved to an area that has no dancing, or the only caller in town has moved away, or you're a schoolteacher ordered to lead a semester of dance).

Regardless of your experience level, you should keep dancing even after you've begun to think like a caller. You'll be constantly reminded of how much fun it is, and you'll get valuable insights into the dancers' viewpoint. Visit dances other than your favorite local ones whenever you get a chance; you can compare yourself with the callers there. Ask the experienced dancers if they think that night's caller is good, and why or why not.

As you dance, stay aware of what's happening in the set. What does each movement accomplish? Does it change your partner, your facing direction, the shape of the set? Notice how the figures fit the music. Try to pick out the first beat of each 8-beat phrase, and the beginning of the tune as it comes around again. If the local style is one in which the figures are synchronized with the music, notice whether the caller is timing, phrasing, and (if applicable) prompting correctly.

Listen to as many callers as you can, at dances and on recordings. Ask permission to record the callers at live dances; find historic field recordings on the Web; obtain some commercial recordings of known good callers (see the Resources section of this book). You can always learn a thing or two, even if it's how not to do something. Ask people you know, in person and online, whether a recorded caller is good or not.

Buy some recordings without calls. You can practice calling to them, and also study the structure and feel of various tune types. Some things can be better assimilated by listening than by reading: the difference between jigs and reels, the importance of the 8-beat phrase and the ability to find it.

Practicing at home is important, especially when you're starting out. There are many ways to do it: You can call along with a called commercial or field recording, using the calls as training wheels, then try calling the same dance to instrumental music. As soon as you feel confident enough, try calling some dances without any recorded calls to help you. Some people find it helps to dance with an imaginary set; some find it confusing. If you stand still, visualize a set of dancers in front of you. As you gain experience, they'll act more and more like real dancers. Record yourself and listen to the playback with a critical ear.

It's better to learn a few dances well than try to master too many at once. I recommend learning two or three square dance figures and one or two breaks at the outset. Call them repeatedly at home until you can do it without looking at the words. Be honest with yourself about whether you really know them. If you can summon the courage, ask a friend or family member to listen.

Be prepared to give a lot of time to practice and planning, at the start and later on. Experienced callers often spend more time programming a dance than calling it. (This will vary with the situation. If you're hired to call for non-dancers, you can – in fact, you should – draw your program from a short list of very easy material that you know inside out, which can be the same for any such group. People who dance weekly or even monthly will appreciate some variety from session to session; if you are their only caller, it behooves you to learn something new fairly often.)

Breaking In

Making the transition from imaginary dancers to live ones can be scary but rewarding. If there are existing dance series near you, attend regularly and get to know the callers, musicians, and organizers. Perhaps you can convince them to let you call a guest number. Make it one you know well, and make sure it's within the capabilities of the crowd. Practice walking it through as well as calling it to music. With hard work and a bit of luck, you may be offered a larger part of a program, maybe even an entire evening if you impress the organizers. (Note that if the evening is advertised as a contra dance, there may be resistance to your choosing a square. In such a case I recommend using a contra; calling contras is in some ways easier than calling squares, and it will help you develop many of the same skills.)

If there are no nearby dances, you may have to start one. It can be in a room of your house (or a friend's house) or a hall you can rent cheaply; maybe you can use a gym or multipurpose room at your school, workplace, or house of worship. You'll need some friends to help you: some to play the music, some to help set up if you're in a hall, and most of all, several who will commit to showing up and dancing. If you're new at this, admit it to your potential dancers. You can emphasize the positive aspects of being "all in this together." It's often easier for people to share a good time if they feel everyone is equal. You can even start by dancing to recordings of other callers, handling only the walkthroughs yourself. If there are other callers to share the workload, so much the better; you'll all get more dancing time, and you can get together the next day for a post-mortem. In some regions, small groups of callers, particularly newer callers, have agreed to meet regularly for practice and mutual support; they may run periodic public dances at which they call one or two numbers each.

Resist the temptation to add dances to your repertoire too quickly. In particular, avoid from the start the practice of reading your calls, which can easily become a habit. Looking at a card or a computer screen draws your focus from where it should be: on your dancers. And if you read your calls, you will probably never gain the assurance you'll need to present them well. Your uncertainty will be contagious, robbing your dancers of the joy of moving with confidence. Experienced callers agree that the better you know the pattern of a dance, the easier it will be to find the right words on the fly without having to memorize a particular set of words.

Once you know enough easy dances (really well) to get you through an evening, you can spread the word among your business and social circles that you're available to call at corporate, community and private parties. Again, be honest about your lack of experience, and be willing to work for little or no money at first. I guarantee that you'll learn more from such events than from anything else you do. (See "First-Timers" in Chapter 13 for tips on what to do with inexperienced dancers. There are descriptions and call charts for several easy dances in Chapters 16 and 17.)

You will undoubtedly get discouraged from time to time, both now and later. Nervousness is perfectly normal, especially at first; some callers never get over it completely. Mistakes are normal too; as the famous caller Ralph Page used to say, "The person who never makes a mistake is a person who never does anything." The secret is to let yourself feel the fear for a moment, then stop paying attention to it and forge ahead. The more you actually do – whether it's practicing at home or calling to real dancers – the more confident you'll feel about your next task, and so on. The confidence you build in yourself through experience is something you couldn't get in any other way

2
History

Where does square dancing come from? Many people have asked me this question, and understandably so: Squares (and contras, for that matter) seem so different from any dance forms that have been popular within living memory. We will probably never know as much as we would like to about the origins and development of the square dance. Much of the tradition has been oral; clues in printed and written sources have been few and far between. But thanks to recent research, we know more than we did 50 or 100 years ago.

Here is a brief summary of square dance history:

- For two centuries or more, Europeans danced not just in couples, but in cooperating groups of couples – circles, squares, and longways sets.
- These group dances came to North America with the European colonists in the 17th, 18th, and 19th centuries.
- The dances were modified by European-Americans and African-Americans, particularly during the 19th century, when calling the figures became customary. Informal versions evolved and existed side by side with the ballroom versions.
- When the dances fell out of favor in urban society (as all dances eventually do), they survived in socially conservative rural areas. Both formal and informal versions were done.
- The dances were "discovered" by educators in the early 20th century and taught in schools and settlement houses.
- Starting in the 1930s, a few charismatic leaders presented them to the general public, aided by the new mass media.
- After World War II, square dancing became a hobby on a widespread basis. For a few years around 1950 it was a national and even international craze.
- In the 1960s and 1970s the most popular style of square dancing became increasingly codified. A consortium of callers drew up lists of calls, with exact definitions, to be used and advertised at dance events.
- Starting around 1970, contra dancing became popular among Baby Boomers, then largely in their teens and twenties. Squares were also done at first, but their popularity has waned in most contra groups.
- There was a revival of interest in old-time squares in several regions, beginning in the 1990s and growing in the early 2000s.

Works cited in this chapter are listed beginning on page 30.

The last three subcultures mentioned – modern square dance, urban contra dance, and old-time square dance – are still in existence.

This chapter is not an attempt to document the origins and evolution of square dancing in every part of North America. I have focused on the regions and time periods that have exerted the greatest influence on present-day traditional-revival dancing, and which I feel will be the most interesting and useful to the tradition-minded caller.

Two major strains run through square dance history. One was a product of formal ballrooms and dancing masters, a recreation of literate people who kept written and printed records of their doings, and so we know a fair amount about what they did. The other was mainly an oral tradition, kept alive by farmers, ranchers, and other country folk. Until recently, few people bothered to do any serious research into its origins or its practice in surviving communities, and the work of those who did was often marred by preconceived notions. It appears also that government and academic bodies that were in a position to fund such research did not always put a high priority on documenting traditional dance.

In the last two or three decades, however, the tide has turned. Along with new interest (in cities and college towns in particular) in square and contra dancing as a recreation has come a new thirst for knowledge of its roots and a new openness toward original research. This research takes three forms: tracking down references to the dance and its music in books, magazines, newspapers, and diaries of a given period (in addition to audio and video recordings when available); visiting and recording dance events; and interviewing dancers, callers, musicians, and their descendants.

The Formal Tradition

For several centuries, Europeans were accustomed to dancing not just in couples but in groups of couples. This was certainly true in the ballrooms of the royal courts and the upper classes; it appears to have been true among country folk as well. The size and shape of these groups varied widely as fashions came and went, but by the 17th century if not earlier, the English and French were dancing in circles, squares, and lines of couples.

A book entitled *The English Dancing Master,* published in London by John Playford, appeared in 1651 and went through 17 ever-larger editions. Although there are earlier mentions of these group dances in literature, Playford is the oldest surviving collection with danceable descriptions. Presumably most of the dances are quite a bit older, as they are not presented as great innovations.

The first Playford edition contained 104 dances in various formations; only 3 were squares. Longways dances made up an increasing percentage of each successive edition. By the last edition (3 volumes, 1721–1728), 904 out of 918 dances were "longways for as many as will," the direct ancestor of our contras. (Squares and longways have vied for popular favor through the years, eclipsing each other by turns.)

These sequences were known in England as "country dances," implying that at least some of them had been borrowed from an existing oral tradition. It has been hypothesized that country dances are descended from the Morris dance, a group of English traditions that apparently date back to the 15th century. Certainly some Morris figures are similar to country dance figures, but the exact lines of transmission are a matter for speculation. Likewise, the theory that either Morris or country dance traditions are remnants of ancient religious rituals must be regarded as purely speculative.

In the late 17th century, country dances were introduced to the English court. Originally they were done at the end of the evening, after the more sedate French dances that were then in fashion. By the early 18th century they had replaced the French dances, which (at least at the hands of the English) had grown stuffy and boring. Even in France, country dances imported from England were allowed at balls under Louis XIV, but as in England, only at the end of the evening at first.

The French, rather than translate the expression "country dances" into *danses de campagne,* transliterated it into *contredanses.* Originally this name could refer to any group dance regardless of formation. The longways was *la contredanse anglaise;* the square was *la contredanse française.* Eventually the English borrowed the name back and corrupted it into "contra dances." Soon the term became reserved for longways sets, perhaps in the belief that "contra" meant "opposite to."

The first dance in square formation to gain lasting popularity in the French ballroom was the cotillion. Introduced in Paris in 1716, it made its way to England in the 1760s, and from there to America. It never reigned alone as the favorite dance form – it had to share honors with the longways – but it was the most popular square.

Many cotillions were written, each with two parts: the "changes," a series of simple movements (such as circles and stars) that were identical from one cotillion to the next, and the "figure," a chorus sequence that was unique to each cotillion. (This pattern can be seen in earlier country dances like *Sellenger's Round,* published by Playford in 1670.) The changes were short, lasting for 8 to 16 measures of music; a typical figure took 16 or more. The set would dance the first change (for example, all circle left and right), the figure, the second change, the figure, and so on through all the changes – all to a single piece of music. (There are many videos of reenactors dancing cotillions, some available free on YouTube.)

In the early 1800s the quadrille emerged as the successor to the cotillion. It consisted of half a dozen figures, similar to those in the cotillion; the changes were dispensed with. Each figure was danced to a different piece of music; eventually composers wrote special settings for quadrilles, and arrangers took melodies from opera, theater, and popular songs – just as present-day callers use the latest hit tunes for singing squares. At first the quadrilles as well as the cotillions incorporated fancy footwork; in the 1830s this was abandoned in favor of a walking step.

Many quadrilles were written during the 19th century, in Europe and America. One of the first and most popular was the *First Set* of 1816; it was later also termed the *Plain Quadrille.* (The latter name eventually became a generic term for any multi-part square in some regions, such as New England.) The *Lancers Quadrille* was introduced in 1817 and outlasted most of its relatives; the fifth figure is still danced in a few communities, sometimes as a singing square.

The quadrille soon replaced the cotillion as the square of choice, but three decades later its star began to fade. Dances for individual couples, such as the polka, waltz, and schottische, found favor in society (though some early critics thought them too intimate for public use) and began sharing ball programs with the quadrilles and an occasional contra. Dancing masters incorporated waltz and polka steps into the quadrilles, but in the end, that was not enough to save them.

During the second half of the 19th century, quadrilles waned in popularity while contra dances all but disappeared except in New England. A ball program of 1900 might consist primarily of couple dances, with at most three or four quadrilles out of two dozen dances. The *Lancers* and *Plain Quadrille* were the most popular; apparently the dancing public found their figures the most interesting. The *Caledonian Quadrille* (or simply "the Caledonians"), originally done to Scottish melodies, was the third most popular of these dances and occasionally turned up on late 19th-century programs.

After 1900 quadrilles were rare at formal balls. But they survived much longer in rural areas, primarily in the northern and eastern states and adjacent parts of Canada. (Very often one or two figures would be omitted, a practice that started in the mid-1800s if not earlier.) They formed a large part of what we think of as the eastern style of traditional square dance, and (along with their forebears, the cotillions) they are one of the two great ancestors of the western square dance, both traditional and modern.

Two defining characteristics of quadrille-type squares are, first, that they are made up of standard movements such as "ladies chain" and, second, that most of the action takes place across the set. Typically the head two couples will execute a sequence of basic movements, and then the side two couples will dance the same sequence. In some cotillions and quadrilles, when the heads initiate a figure, the sides are drawn into the action. There is even an occasional figure in which one or both head couples visit their way around the set. But the dance tradition that is made up almost entirely of visiting figures appears to come from another source (see the following section).

Note that the ancestors of our square dance cannot be divided neatly into urban and rural, or upper and lower class. Formal squares such as the cotillion and the quadrille could be found in ballrooms in even the smallest towns. Learning to dance was important to middle-class Americans who aspired to upward mobility. Dancing masters, some of them itinerant, catered to these eager prospects.

The term "cotillion" was revived in the mid-19th century to refer to a completely different type of dance – an icebreaker that was part dance, part game. In this form, also known as the German cotillion or simply the German, a handful of couples gathered in someone's home to sit in a circle or a hollow square. A leader or "conductor" announced a figure; chose one, two, or more couples to get up and perform it; and gave them brief instructions. Each figure involved choosing or exchanging partners, generally with much mirth and flirtation; some required elaborate props and many involved favors to be kept by the guests. This reuse of the word "cotillion," along with the fact that "quadrille" and "cotillion" were sometimes used interchangeably by early 19th-century writers, has caused a good deal of confusion among would-be dance historians.

The Informal Tradition

The other great forebear of today's squares is the visiting-couple or around-the-set tradition. Its origins are relatively obscure, as it appears to have been done primarily by ordinary workers, country folk, and pioneers. All these people, even if literate, were too busy scratching out a living to write down their doings. In addition, it may have seemed superfluous to spend time documenting something that "everybody knew." As a result, this tradition is largely oral. Some of its most significant developments occurred before the invention of audio and video recording, or even of photography, so the only evidence we have from that era comes from a few paintings and an occasional mention in a magazine article, a diary, or a book-length account of the author's travels.

The hallmark of the rural dance is the visit. Although some quadrilles included a visiting figure, the movements during the visit were typically standard ones such as circles, stars, chains, and "right and left." And the visit was the exception to the rule. In the rural tradition, circles and stars are done, but a great many visiting figures are unequal: An active couple traces a curving path around and between a standing couple. This visit may be done by one couple around a four-couple square or a circle of more than four couples; it can also be done in a large circle in which every other couple is active. The couples in this tradition are always numbered consecutively counterclockwise. (Some, though not all, quadrille teachers numbered the head couples 1 and 2 and the side couples 3 and 4.)

Because this tradition was mainly oral, we know little with certainty about its origins. The English folklorist Cecil Sharp, who visited Appalachia in 1917, assumed – with no evidence – that the dances he observed were not only centuries old but purely English. A few of the figures that Sharp and others have collected in the South have analogues in the English dances collected by Playford. However, the circular structure and many of the figures resemble Scottish and Irish dances more closely than English. This is understandable: Dance historian Phil Jamison (2015) points out that the Scots-Irish (immigrants from Northern Ireland and their descendants) made up the single largest ethnic group among early white settlers in Appalachia. Similarly, Hugh Thurston (1969) cites 1880 census statistics showing an overwhelming number of Irish immigrants to Kentucky and points out the similarity of the Appalachian dance to an Irish dance form known as the *rinncí fighte*. Jamison also sees African-American and Native American influences on southern dance, though there is less hard evidence for this than for the Scots-Irish connection. Unfortunately, we know little about what Black residents of the Appalachians were singing and dancing in the 19th and early 20th centuries, because few researchers cared to visit them; Cecil Sharp actually turned away from a Black settlement that he stumbled upon (Jamison 2015, pp. 70–71).

The dances were also likely shaped in part by contact with people of all races from outside the region. It is important to note that Appalachia was never as isolated an area as some writers claimed. In reality, there was extensive traffic, much of it by water, between Appalachia and the rest of the continent (Spalding 2014, Jamison 2015). Naturally, the farther from the main routes of commerce they lived, the more insular a community's culture would be. But many mountain dwellers would have been aware of current events, fashions, and arts such as music, dance, theater, and even opera. The myth of an ages-old dance form that survived, unaltered, into the 20th century is just that: a myth.

The visiting-couple figures appear to have established themselves in the southern Appalachian mountains and made their way through the Ozarks and the Great Plains to Texas and the Rockies with the European- and African-Americans who migrated west. At the same time, pioneers from the Northeast and the upper Midwest would have taken along their dance forms, primarily the cotillion and quadrille. Which dances a frontier town preferred would depend on where its settlers came from.

The Advent of Calling

And what of the caller – that combination of teacher, floor manager, and entertainer, whose personality dominates the dance?

The impetus for calling seems to have been the replacement of the cotillion by the quadrille as the fashionable square dance in the early 1800s. A cotillion, you will remember, alternated several simple changes, which all the dancers would have known or could easily pick up, with a unique figure that lasted for 16 or at most 32 measures of music. The length of the figure may have taxed the dancers' ability to commit a sequence to memory, but it could be done. There was no need for prompting the contra dances either, as until the mid-1800s only the top couple began the sequence; the couples near the bottom got to see it several times before they had to join in.

By contrast, a quadrille had five or six figures, each one different, with no common changes interspersed. The popular *First Set* had 208 measures to get through, not counting repeats. And there was not just one quadrille either: Dancing masters tried to outdo one another in introducing "new and original" sets of figures. Given the situation, it was logical for someone to call out the name or even the description of each movement just in time for the dancers to execute it.

Within a few years of the quadrille's introduction, authors of dance manuals were referring to the practice of calling as "the general custom" (Chivers 1821), "frequent" (Pollock 1828), and "usual" (Lowe 1831). Such a widely accepted and understood practice might have gone unmentioned by these writers, were it not that much of the calling was done in French; the writers urged their readers to learn the meaning of the most common French terms.

(Before the advent of calling as we know it, to "call" a dance meant to have the privilege of choosing the next dance to be done, an honor that rotated among the couples at a ball. But from the context, it is clear that the references above are to calling out the figures during a dance.)

It is interesting that the word "calling" was used by all these early writers, rather than the more sedate-sounding "prompting." We can only guess at what the first callers sounded like. In any case, the art quickly progressed from reminding dancers of a set routine to something more inventive. The last figure of many quadrilles was rather ordinary and anticlimactic; it became common for the caller (who could be a dance teacher or one of the musicians) to substitute a "fancy figure." The actress and abolitionist Fanny Kemble mentioned this practice in her journal (Butler 1835).

A fancy figure might be simply a more elaborate pre-written sequence, but in many cases it was evidently improvised. "[Quadrilles] consist of a number of figures, varying according to the fancy of different teachers, or as the leader of the orchestra may choose to call them" (*Ball-room* 1841). "The figures of these … dances are generally called out by the leader of the orchestra, as they occur in the sets; or, rather as they occur to his whim and fancy" (Durang 1848).

African roots?

To say that mid-19th-century callers improvised is not necessarily to say that they were indulging in the kind of free-wheeling patter or chanting that we know was prevalent two generations later. But it is entirely possible that the phenomenon of caller-as-entertainer appeared as early as calling itself, or nearly so.

The earliest definite allusion to calling I have seen comes from New Orleans in 1819. There, a visiting Englishman complained about a Black man who played the tambourine and called the figures "in a forced and vile voice" (Jamison 2015, p. 44). There are a few other references to Black callers in 19th-century America, and even more to Black dance musicians. This makes sense in the context of slavery and the status of African-Americans in general, as playing for dances was considered servants' work. Many dance musicians in 19th-century illustrations are Black, though their percentage diminishes as the century progresses. And when calling is mentioned in books of the period, the caller is usually one of the musicians.

Did African-Americans exert a major influence on the style of calling? The evidence is circumstantial, but there is a lot of it. Poetry was extremely popular among white society in 19th-century England and America, and it might have been natural for a prompting fiddler, even a white one, to take the rhythm and even the pitch of his prompts from the music. But there are African and African-American art forms that bear a strong resemblance to the kind of calling that we associate with country-style square dances – rhyming couplets, with extraneous and often humorous patter.

Rhythmic chanting, with or without percussion or other instruments, is part of many well-known African and African-American traditions. These include the craft of the *griots,* the oral historians of West Africa. There is a long tradition of call-and-response songs, as vehicles for worship or work, in many cultures of sub-

Saharan Africa; this tradition made its way to the Americas with enslaved Africans in the 17th and 18th centuries. Chanting in rhyming couplets can be heard in today's Black communities in everything from schoolyard games to street-corner insults. The practice has once again been developed into a complete art by today's rappers.

On many southern plantations, corn-shucking time was the occasion for an annual slave holiday of sorts. Captains were chosen to lead competing teams of shuckers by chanting. At night the captains would make ceremonial speeches, alternating praise with teasing of the plantation owner and his friends, and continue their banter as the dancing commenced (Abrahams 1992). In addition, after the white folks' ball was over, the Black musicians might play for the other slaves. The whites may or may not have had dancing lessons, but the Blacks certainly had not and needed the kind of quick instruction that a caller could give.

The percentage of Black callers at the beginning is unknown, but it has certainly diminished since then. It is hard to tell much from written reports. In writings from the late 1800s, the race of the caller is often not mentioned. This may be because most writers were white and tended to mention people's skin color only when it differed from their own. But it may also be because the phenomenon of Black callers was so commonplace that it needed no mention. Jamison (2015) cites several reminiscences by African-American callers and says that a few of the callers who made recordings in the 1920s were Black.

Did the white callers learn rhyming and patter from the Black ones, or did they develop it on their own? We will probably never know with certainty. But communication in 19th-century America was better than one might think. News may not have traveled in seconds or minutes as it does today, but it certainly spread across the country within days or, at most, weeks. As mentioned above, this was true even in rural Appalachia.

Through the 19th Century

As one might expect, there is much more documentation on what urban and even small-town middle- and upper-class people were dancing in the 19th century than on the activities of the rural and less-favored classes. Some is in the form of dance cards, on which a lady's partners signed their names opposite the dance numbers, so we know a lot about the actual programs. As mentioned earlier, quadrilles took over from contra dances and cotillions; in turn, the waltz, polka, and other couple dances gradually eclipsed the set dances. By 1900 the quadrilles on a ball program were notable for their scarcity.

Away from the ballrooms it was a different story. While printed evidence is harder to find, quite a bit has been unearthed recently. Although, as mentioned above, 19th-century writers often conflated cotillions and quadrilles, it seems likely that the less-favored and less-educated classes, who tend to be more conservative than "society" folks, held onto the 18th-century cotillion after it had disappeared from the ballroom. At any rate, the squares described in later books incorporate features of both the cotillions and the quadrilles. During the 19th century, the "across the set" figures must have blended with the visiting-couple figures to become the country-style square and circle dances that are familiar to us. Based on early-20th-century interviews with aging callers, it is safe to say that by the 1870s and 1880s these dances had assumed the form in which we know them. Aside from the occasional invention of a new figure, the rural square dance repertoire appears to have stayed fairly constant from then until the 1940s. In some areas, such as upstate New York, singing calls became popular in the early 20th century, but the figures remained largely the same.

These dances were done by farmers, ranchers, tradesmen, miners, and other working people, without any self-consciousness. They were simply enjoying the dance forms that were common in their communities. They certainly would not have said they were "square dancing" (the verb "to square dance" seems to have come into common use only with the rise of the hobby in the mid-20th century); they were just "dancing." But in the cities, an attitude was already arising that might be called the "oh, how quaint" approach to the country dance. As early as the 1880s, city dwellers were enjoying "country vacations," including barn dances, at boarding houses in New England and the mid-Atlantic states; well-to-do New Yorkers hosted "rustic balls" at their country estates (La Farge 1958). This attitude was to become widespread in the 20th century, as well-to-do city folk dressed in old clothes and wildly hopped and skipped around – even as rural communities kept engaging in what, to them, was a perfectly normal recreation.

Donning special costumes for the dance held a number of attractions. Throughout history, the wearing of disguises has enabled people to behave in ways that society would normally scorn or condemn, whether their acts were criminal, licentious, or merely humorous. Examples include blackface minstrelsy and children's Halloween costumes. In addition, country folk were often stereotyped as more honest and community-minded than "city slickers," if a bit naïve. In upstate New York in the 1920s and 1930s, prominent dance bands felt the need to dress up as "hillbillies" to appeal to their followers (Bronner 1987).

The cowboy in particular was viewed as the ideal American: hard-working and self-sufficient, with no need for government handouts at taxpayer expense. While this was never completely true, the image was cultivated by conservative forces as early as the 1870s and has pervaded American mythology ever since (Richardson 2014). In the French-speaking areas of eastern Canada, record companies have often marketed fiddle music as "western," even though the local tunes and style originated in the British Isles and developed in Quebec and the Maritime Provinces.

Religion had a huge influence on Americans' mores and behavior right from the start, but "the church" was far from a monolith. Some religious bodies forbade all dancing on the grounds that it inevitably led to debauchery; others encouraged it (under close supervision) as a relatively healthy social activity. The Mormons in particular did much to keep square dancing alive on their westward trek. In parts of the South and the Midwest where conservative Protestants dominated, a compromise was reached: Dancing to instrumental music was taboo (the fiddle in particular was condemned as "the devil's box"), but young people could perform the same figures to singing and clapping as long as they used a two-hand arm's-length swing and called it a "play" or a "game." Many play-party figures are similar or identical to singing square dance calls; researchers have been unable to determine which came first.

Speaking of music, the fiddle seems to have been the mainstay of dance accompaniment through the centuries, but the style of music changed midway through the 19th century. Till then the prevailing style had been English, quite melodious judging from surviving manuscripts, with no particular tune type favored. Time signatures varied, as did the number of parts in a tune and measures in each part. Immigrants from Scotland and Ireland, particularly following the Irish potato famine of the 1840s, appear to have had an overwhelming influence on country-dance music. The hard-driving reel in 2/4 meter became the dominant tune type; jigs in 6/8 were popular in some areas (New England, Missouri, much of Canada) but unknown in others. Rhythm was valued more than melody, especially when a solo fiddler was the only musician available. In the Northeast and other relatively literate areas, it was fashionable to play dance tunes "by the book," but in the rural South the tunes became simplified and streamlined as the "old-time" musical tradition developed. Old-time string band music derived part of its character from African-American players: Both the banjo and the practice of syncopation are derived from African traditions.

The Early 20th Century

There were three great revivals of set dancing in the United States during the 20th century:

- The introduction of folk dancing in American schools and social service organizations.
- The renewed interest in square dancing among Americans of all ages, culminating in the mid-century square dance boom.
- The revival of contra dances and their music, originally among the countercultural element of the post–World War II generation.

The first revival, at its peak between the 1890s and the 1920s, arose in an attempt to provide wholesome recreation for schoolchildren and immigrants. It began with English country dances and the folk dances of other countries, primarily from northern and western Europe, whose inhabitants were considered racially desirable and worthy of emulation. By 1920 some American dances were added, including New England contras and quadrilles.

Despite the country vacations and rustic balls mentioned above, educators apparently knew little and cared less about country-style square dancing. A notable exception during this period was the 1917 visit of Cecil Sharp from England to Kentucky and other parts of Appalachia, which led to his description of what he styled "the Running Set" in a volume of his *Country Dance Book*. (The so-called Running Set was simply one community's version of the southern mountain dance; many other versions have since been documented throughout the southern Appalachians and the Ozarks. Sharp may have heard someone say "Let's run a set," meaning "Let's dance," and mistaken the expression for a local name. The dance he witnessed in Kentucky was indeed done at a fast clip, but tempos varied from place to place in the mountains.)

In the mid-1920s, three books were published that sprang from the first great revival and marked the start of the second. Two of these, one from Iowa (Boyd and Dunlavy) and one from Michigan (Ryan), were of dances collected from old callers by schoolteachers and settlement workers; their content was subsequently copied by other writers, not always with credit. The third, entitled *Good Morning,* was the product of a New England dancing master, Benjamin Lovett; it had the cachet of being sponsored by the industrialist Henry Ford. Ford, a noted anti-Semite and a cultural reactionary in many ways, hated jazz and the output of Tin Pan Alley, which he saw as the work of Jewish composers determined to foist African and other non-Nordic idioms on an unsuspecting nation. For two decades he actively promoted 19th-century quadrilles, contras, and couple dances, calling them "the dances of the northern peoples." However unsavory his motives may have been, he achieved a measure of success, particularly in and around Detroit where schoolchildren danced to music played for them on the radio and Ford executives learned the old dances on pain of dismissal.

The Square Dance Boom

The second great revival, which led to the mid-century square dance boom, began at different times in different regions. In Texas, square dancing apparently went from a surviving folk art to a hobby without ever quite dying; dancers were organizing into clubs as early as 1935 (Holden 1992). Texas callers were reportedly creating new figures and "hashing" old ones before callers elsewhere got the idea. In Canada, George Wade's Cornhuskers were touring, broadcasting, and recording in the 1930s; they found a ready audience in the thousands of rural Canadians with whom the old dances had never lost favor.

The northeastern United States was not far behind Texas and Canada. The first two branches of what is now the Country Dance and Song Society, in New York and Boston, both founded in 1915 to promote English dancing, added American squares and contras to their repertoire in the 1930s. In New England, city folk who had taken up the newly popular sport of skiing were looking for evening entertainment in the days before floodlit slopes and après-ski lounges. They discovered the local country dances, became infatuated, and organized their own dance series in cities like Boston, often hiring the callers they had enjoyed up north. Chief among those was Ralph Page of New Hampshire, whose insistence on courteous and sober dancing earned him the favor of town fathers who had suspended their local dances due to excessive drinking and rowdiness.

Other regions soon followed suit. In some communities an old-time caller might be persuaded to come out of retirement, or at least to pass his knowledge on to someone younger. In areas with highly active school programs, the first revival led straight into the second. During the 1930s the growth of interest in the old dances picked up speed; after World War II it accelerated nearly beyond belief. By 1950 square dancing had become a national craze. Within a year or two it had spread to England and Australia.

There were several reasons for this second revival. Starting around the 1920s, thanks to improved recordings and the new medium of radio, many people heard "hillbilly" and "cowboy" music for the first time. (Record companies were very selective in what they issued, leaving much good music unpublished or completely undocumented, but to hear rural artists at all was a novelty for many people.) Country radio shows, which attracted large theater and home audiences, were titled "barn dances" and often featured fiddle music with shouted calls. The same music and calls were made available on records (Phil Jamison has recently catalogued these and made audio files available online). Western movies promoted the romanticized image of the 19th-century cowboy; actor-singers like Gene Autry and Roy Rogers (himself a former caller) became matinee idols. Not infrequently, such a film would include a square dance scene. Hollywood stars hired western bands and callers for their lavish parties, and magazines like *Life* were there to snap photos and tell the world. Callers and folk dance teachers appeared at huge events like the New York World's Fair of 1939–1940. (Ed Durlacher of Long Island, who called at that fair, went on to conduct huge open dances in New York's Central Park, with thousands of people on the floor.) Sometimes the dancing was strictly audience participation, but often a troupe of trained and costumed dancers would perform for the crowd, perhaps splitting up and taking partners from the audience for a simple dance afterward.

The best-known performing square dance troupe was probably the Cheyenne Mountain Dancers. This teenage group, affectionately known as "Pappy's Kids," was the brainchild of Dr. Lloyd Shaw, a school superintendent from Colorado Springs who had incorporated dance into his school system at all levels. Beginning in the 1930s, the Kids took their program of varied American dance forms to school and civic auditoriums across the country, and Shaw, who had already made a name among his fellow educators, became well-known to the general public. He published a book-length collection, *Cowboy Dances,* in 1939 and hosted weeklong institutes that attracted hundreds of established and budding dance teachers and callers. (The institutes continued past Shaw's death in 1958; a foundation was established in his name and still runs dance camps and issues recordings.)

Singing squares – that is, dance routines done to popular melodies that the dancers would recognize – came into their own in the 1930s. Their increased popularity seems to have coincided with the development of the electronic public address system, although some singing calls appear to date back to the advent of play-party games in the 19th century. In some areas, such as New England, New Jersey, and upstate New York, singing calls became the predominant form of square dance; elsewhere they were used occasionally to spice up a program. By 1950, at the peak of the square dance revival, singing squares were done almost everywhere; by the 1960s, a standard club "tip" (of which there were about eight in an evening) comprised one patter and one singing call.

The war probably slowed the growth of large-scale square dance programs, though it did give rise to an extensive network of USO dances for servicemen. But after 1945 the nation made up for lost time. Soldiers and sailors came home, got married, bought the new tract houses, and looked for things to do in their free time. It seemed as though everyone wanted to become a square dancer, to dress up like a cowboy or a southern belle. In many cities, whenever the recreation department announced a square dance class, people stood in line around the block to sign up. A typical class of six once-weekly sessions attracted 100, 200, or even more if the hall could hold them; at times multiple gymnasiums were pressed into service. Clubs were quickly formed to absorb the graduates; some were open to all comers (though adult married couples were usually preferred), while others were "invitation only." While club structure and callers' repertoire could vary, a constant was "no alcohol": In order to gain entrée to school gyms and church halls, square dancers made it known that their dances were "dry" and fought the image of the moonshine-fueled barn dance, sending letters of complaint when beer companies ran advertisements with a square dance theme.

The widespread interest in square dancing prompted some to wonder how they could profit from it. It became possible for someone in a built-up area to make a living as a caller; in two years, the number of full-timers quintupled (Holden 1951). Almost every major book publisher and record company issued square dance titles; in addition, dozens of small businesses were formed to make nothing but square dance records and instruction sheets. Square dance dresses became a profitable business for a few entrepreneurial seamstresses and a lucrative sideline for sellers of western shirts, hats, and boots.

Contests for dancers and callers were fairly common in the early to mid-20th century, particularly in the Southwest. Competition teams of dancers were assembled, trained, and maintained for years by prominent callers (whose prominence was partly due to their teams). Around 1950, Lloyd Shaw and other influential leaders spoke out against contests, and most of the competition teams became exhibition teams. (Square dance contests have persisted in parts of Canada, and recently the modern square dance movement has reintroduced an element of competition in an attempt to attract teenagers.)

Until around 1950 most square dance groups employed live musicians: perhaps a solo pianist or fiddler for classes, a three-piece band for parties, a larger band for a festival. The use of recorded music began in classes and local clubs and eventually spread to include most larger events as well. Reasons included the improved quality of recordings and playback equipment; the proliferation of singing calls, requiring musicians to learn dozens of new tunes; the scarcity of musicians in some areas; and the desire of clubs to economize (and perhaps of callers to keep more of the gate receipts). The claim has been made that live musicians "priced themselves out of the market." If that is true, I suspect it was partly because musicians were relegated to the background behind increasingly flashy callers and decided that if they couldn't get recognition or respect, they wanted more money.

Both the style of dress and the style of dancing evolved as the network of square dance clubs became a going concern. As skirts became shorter among the general public, square dance fashions followed suit. The ankle-length skirts of 1950 gave way to the knee-length (and even shorter) skirts of the 1960s. Petticoats became fuller and more multi-layered until the skirt was apt to lie horizontally atop them. When hemlines in general came down in the 1970s, square dance dresses stayed at knee length. Eventually, many female dancers complained that the short skirts were unflattering to mature women and should not be an essential part of the dress code; the narrower, ankle-length "prairie skirt" was accepted as an alternative.

As for dancing style, in the late 1940s the average tempo of western square dance music, measured in beats per minute, was in the 130s and even the 140s. This is borne out both by written observations and by the majority of recordings made at the time. The dancers practically ran their way through the figures, judging by the few contemporary films available. During the 1950s, as the original cohort of club members aged, the tempos were reduced to around 130 and the dancers were encouraged to shuffle their feet. Today there is less emphasis on shuffling, but the tempos have remained fairly consistent.

Modern Square Dance Evolves

In 1950 there were still several distinct, identifiable regional square dance styles in the United States and Canada. At first the clubs in each area tended to follow the local tradition for at least some of the dances in an evening, but increasingly the "western" or "cowboy" style promoted by Lloyd Shaw became the dominant one. Shaw was hoping that this style, a blend of the quadrille and visiting-couple traditions, could become the Great American Folk Dance. But while western square dancing indeed took the nation by storm, it evolved over the next two decades into a form that Shaw never envisioned.

Modern "western" square dancing did not emerge, full-blown, all at once. For the first few years of the nationwide square dance boom, the material being called and danced was largely traditional. At the Santa Monica Diamond Jubilee in 1950, still the largest single evening in square dance history, most of the 36 numbers called to 15,000 dancers were decades old, and the few newer ones could hardly be told from the "oldies." Most figures employed circles, stars, arches, and curving "chase" paths, with an occasional chain or right and left through.

Most of the other distinguishing features of the modern scene – couples as the norm, the dress code, the structure of clubs and federations – were in place years before the choreography underwent any substantial change. As late as the mid-1960s, it was possible for someone with a solid background in traditional squares to attend a club and join in the dancing without having taken a "western" class. Only a handful of basic movements beyond the traditional corpus were universally accepted by club dancers; anything more required a walkthrough or a workshop.

But the shape of the dances was changing. Increasingly during the 1950s, callers disdained the visiting-couple figures, even when modified to keep more dancers moving. The new fashion was to manipulate dancers within a grid framework; at first, some figures included curving paths within the grid, but eventually most paths were straight, with right-angle turns to change direction. Ironically, the swooping circular figures, which Lloyd Shaw felt gave the western dance its character, were lost, and modern squares looked like formal quadrilles more than anything – except that the close relation of figure to musical phrase was no longer honored. Post-1960 modern square dancing is western in name only.

One reason for discarding the older figures was that each one was a unique set of movements; either the dancers had to memorize it or the caller had to walk it through. Callers discovered that they could add to their reputation and income by composing new figures, but if those also required extensive teaching, the load on dancers' and callers' brains would become untenable. The answer was to break every figure down into its component moves, teach only those moves that could be used in multiple dances, and discard the rest. This plan worked for a short time, but almost immediately callers began devising new "basic" movements, increasing the time needed for new dancers to learn enough to join a club.

During the transition from traditional to modern choreography, two opposing schools of thought emerged. One held that the way to capture and retain people's interest in square dancing was to make it as fast-paced and complex as possible. The unquestioned leader of this faction was Les Gotcher, a Texan transplanted to southern California. Gotcher had been a cowhand; he looked and sounded like Hollywood's idea of a caller, which got him cast in several western films. The other contingent believed in keeping the prevailing level of square dancing accessible to anyone willing to take a few lessons. Its leaders were Lloyd Shaw, whose watchword was "Keep it clean, keep it simple, keep it folk"; Bob Osgood, editor of *Sets in Order* magazine, who was an unabashed Shaw disciple; and Ed Gilmore, who campaigned for "comfortable dancing in the proper spirit." The dispute descended into name-calling and, reportedly, backstabbing. In a second great irony, although Shaw is revered in the modern square dance world and Gotcher is largely forgotten, it was Gotcher's ideas that won out. Today's "modern" square dance programs consist entirely of hash; there is nothing "simple" or "folk" about them. And while officially there are relatively accessible levels of achievement, there is nearly universal pressure to progress to a level ("Plus") that, if it is to be learned thoroughly, requires about two years of instruction and practice. To make things worse, most dancers are pushed through this program in less than a year; many leave the activity due to burnout.

The period of greatest interest and participation in square dancing was roughly from 1948 to 1952. During those years, thousands of people were dancing entry-level material in public parks and even the organized clubs were doing largely traditional figures – most of which were relatively easy, or they wouldn't have survived among the common folk. To the extent that improvisatory calling existed, the callers were working with a very limited number of basic movements – about the same number as callers in the folk-revival scene use today. As choreography evolved, with the number of basic movements and therefore the number of required lessons increasing, modern square dancing morphed from an international craze to a fairly insular hobby.

As the repertoire expanded, there was increasing agitation for a list of truly basic movements whose mastery would enable newcomers to dance almost anywhere. Bob Osgood in *Sets in Order* published a list of 20 basics which was revised several times through the 1950s and 1960s, but codifying these proved insufficient to stem the tide of new moves. Several leaders at various times proposed creating a square dance program, fixed at about 20 basics, that would be promoted as an alternative to the standard club level. Most of these programs failed to win widespread favor, but it is interesting to note that nearly all of them drew primarily on the traditional repertoire for their basic moves and suggested dance routines.

At first, the majority of influential callers opposed attempts at legislating which moves must be learned and how they were to be done, at least beyond the regional level. Ed Gilmore's assertion was typical: "Square dancing is a folk activity and no folk activity can be directed from headquarters" (*Sets in Order,* Oct. 1950). But as more and more new moves were invented, with no two callers using exactly the same list, the nationally respected leaders decided there was a need for some mechanism to regulate the flow of "new basics" to the clubs, as well as some means of communication among callers. In 1974, after several preliminary meetings, a group of callers from the Osgood-Gilmore faction formed Callerlab, the International Association of Square Dance Callers, using the American Medical Association as a partial model. They formulated a code of ethics and several lists of calls, which ultimately developed into the present "programs" of Basic, Mainstream, Plus, Advanced 1 and 2, and Challenge 1 through 4. Dance organizers were urged to advertise a program name for every event, and callers were admonished to use only the moves on that program's list and the ones below it.

Over the decades since its emergence, interest in modern square dancing has fallen off, first gradually, then more rapidly as its practitioners have aged out without attracting enough newcomers to replace them. Many vendors of clothing, recordings, and equipment have gone out of business. Recording companies in particular have been hit hard by the ease of making perfect copies at home, a problem felt in the international folk dance hobby as well. Attendance at the National Square Dance Convention, which averaged around 20,000 for many years, has hovered below 4,000 recently.

Concerned leaders are experimenting with new ways to attract prospective dancers and reduce the learning curve, including a "multi-cycle" method of overlapping series of lessons and still another attempt at a dance program using a relatively small number of basic moves. An increasing number of clubs are relaxing their dress codes and using more modern music in order to counteract the image of square dancing as stuck in the 1950s. At press time it is too soon to know whether these efforts will keep modern square dancing viable.

The New England Scene

In the early 1950s, a few New England callers were determined to buck the tide of "western style" square dancing, which was already growing too complex for a new dancer to pick up without taking lessons. Far from clinging to single-visiting-couple or simple across-the-set routines, they sought to modernize traditional New England style along relatively conservative lines, preserving the phrasing while modifying the figures to keep more dancers active. Ralph Page was fond of saying "Don't hate a dance just because it's new, and don't love a dance just because it's old; it takes more than age to make a dance good or bad." Many of the squares that Page recorded and presented at dance camps involved the whole set, not just one or two couples at a time.

The traditionalist group included a number of callers scattered around New England who had been running dances for many years, and also several young Boston-area callers who were followers of Page. The most influential of the latter proved to be Ted Sannella, who showed a great gift, not only for calling but for composing dances and for mentoring and encouraging new callers (including the present author). He conducted many dance series in and around Boston that usually included international folk dances as well as squares and contras; some of these series lasted for decades.

By dint of hard work and persistence, the tradition-minded New England callers had gained some ground by the 1970s. Some of them dared to dream that their gently modernized form of square dancing would surpass modern "western" style in popularity. However, some of their gains in the realm of squares were all but lost in the contra dance revival that began around that time. They were heartened by the renewed attention paid to contras, which had been extinct or nearly so in most areas, but dismayed by the shift away from squares.

The Contra Revival

This surge of interest in contras marked the third great revival of the 20th century. It began in the 1960s when a young New England caller named Dudley Laufman, who had danced with Ralph Page, developed an enthusiastic following among high school and college students. They flocked to the many series, primarily in New Hampshire, where Laufman presided (the kids called them "Dudley dances"), sometimes attending several in one week. Somehow, although Laufman used both squares and contras, this phenomenon acquired the name "contra dancing" – perhaps to make it clear that this was neither the regimented square dancing that some people remembered from grade school nor the equally rigid modern "western" style that had crowded out traditional squares, even in most of the Northeast. (Until around 1970, events were termed "square dances" – even in New England, even if contras made up half or more of the program.) The style at Dudley dances was loose and free-swinging, but it was anchored in the strong connection of the dance to the musical phrase, which kept it from getting completely out of control.

As Dudley's followers traveled to attend college or settle down in a job, they took the dances with them. Some learned to play the old tunes that Dudley's band, the Canterbury Country Orchestra, had revived; some took up calling; most were content to dance and perhaps help organize the evenings. Contra groups appeared in cities and college towns from coast to coast. When dance historian David Millstone was preparing his 2007 documentary film on Laufman, he discovered that with few exceptions, these new contra dance centers were started by callers who learned either first- or second-hand from Dudley.

During the 1970s and 1980s the burgeoning contra scene developed a personality of its own. It was populated largely by Baby Boomers, by then in their twenties and thirties, who made it into a combination of workout gym and singles club. Callers devised new dance routines that kept everyone moving, unlike most of the traditional contras. Dancers, especially the men, tended to dress down rather than up; T-shirts and shorts became common attire.

Even though the first wave of callers and organizers had probably danced squares with Dudley, it was the contras that attracted the most interest. Some of the new groups never did squares at all; even where squares started out on a nearly equal footing with contras, they often disappeared over the years. Eventually, even the dance series that had been established before the "Dudley revival," and that originally programmed one or more sets of squares for every contra, were either discontinued or converted to all-contra dances.

In squares and contras alike, the choreography has changed as the prevailing milieu for the activity has changed (in the words of Dart 1992) from *community dances* (gatherings of family and neighbors, where dancing was one of several forms of socializing) to *dance communities* (gatherings of people, often not close neighbors, who seek one another out on the basis of a single shared interest). When dancing becomes a hobby, its devotees are likely to prefer choreography that keeps everyone moving and poses at least some degree of mental challenge. This shift in the purpose of dancing, and therefore in the priorities of the dancers, has played out in the evolution of modern square dancing, and again in the rise of what has been called "modern urban" contra dancing.

Squares Make a Comeback

By 1990 squares were looked on in most contra groups as an invasive species, whereas an older New Englander or Southerner would have seen them as an endangered species. (In reality, contras were the invasive species in some areas, replacing the local square dance style.) At some dances there were even groans or boos when a square was announced. This was the diametric opposite of the situation in the 1950s, when some square dance callers begged their dancers to try contras. Those dancers complained that contras were too easy or too hard (depending on which ones the caller presented) and that they took too long to set up – the same complaints that contra dancers made about squares two generations later.

In a pair of provocative articles in the *Old-Time Herald* in 1987 and 2004 titled "Dare To Be Square," caller and folklorist Phil Jamison wrote that contra dancing had become over-regimented and contra dancers snobbish. He pointed out that the square and longways formations had battled for popularity for centuries – with the implication that neither form was superior – and encouraged contra dancers to try the free-wheeling southern sets. Jamison and others organized weekends under the Dare To Be Square banner, focusing on southern music and dance forms. There is probably no way to determine how many of those attending were current or former contra dancers, but at one such gathering in 2011, with a staff of six callers including this author, approximately 50 of the 70 participants were callers themselves. Many were from the contra dance scene and expressed great interest in taking squares back to their home groups. (While most Dare To Be Square staff callers have been those who work in the southern mountain style, the callers at the 2011 weekend represented five different regional traditions as well as modern square dancing.)

Whether or not it was due to the efforts of Jamison and his colleagues, there has been a thawing of attitudes toward squares among contra dancers and leaders in the new century. Prominent traveling contra callers include squares in their programs; callers who specialize in squares are increasingly being hired outside their home areas. Workshops on squares at camps and festivals often draw enthusiastic crowds.

In addition, a loose network of exclusively square dance events has appeared nationwide, originating in the old-time music community. (Old-time is a traditional southern string band style that pre-dates bluegrass; in fact, bluegrass arose from it.) Callers Sandy Bradley and Bill Martin promoted squares in the Pacific Northwest in the 1970s and 1990s; several dozen Dare To Be Square weekends have been held across the continent starting in the early 2000s; there are weekly or monthly series on both coasts and in between. Alcohol is available at many of these events; some are held in bars, others have a "bring your own" policy. Occasionally a modern square dance group will protest the existence of a "wet" event that styles itself a square dance, but the presence of alcohol does not seem to have fostered an unduly rowdy atmosphere.

Finally, there are areas in the United States and Canada where a square dance tradition has survived – where dancers, callers, and musicians are unaware of (or have chosen to ignore) the national and international networks such as the Country Dance and Song Society, Dare To Be Square, and the modern square dance scene. Each area has its own repertoire of figures and basic movements, its body language and footwork, its tunes and playing style, and (in most cases) its calling style. (In some areas, such as Nova Scotia's Cape Breton Island, the figures are memorized and there are no calls.) There are doubtless areas that have escaped the notice of researchers, but the known ones include parts of the Ozarks and southern Appalachians, northern and central New England, and parts of Pennsylvania and central New York. (Sadly, the rich Texas square dance tradition appears to have died out completely.) In addition to Cape Breton, Canadian areas include Ontario, Quebec, and the Prairie Provinces, where the Métis, people of mixed indigenous and European ancestry, have evolved a unique style drawing elements from both cultures.

Square dancing will probably never again be a nationwide craze as it was around 1950; history seldom repeats itself exactly. And it may look very different 50 or 100 years from now. But it will survive in some form as long as people have the urge to connect with their fellow human beings and share the joy of moving to music.

Cross-Currents and Standardization

Cross-currents have always been with us. In language, in clothing styles, perhaps most of all in cuisine, wherever people of different cultures mingle, they will absorb one another's ideas. This is certainly true of dance forms: As noted above, traditional square dancing as we know it today is the product of at least three centuries of social interchange between Black and white people, Native Americans and colonizers, French and Scots-Irish cohorts, urban and rural communities. Much of this interchange was not documented at the time it took place; we will probably never be able to reconstruct square dancing's family tree to our satisfaction.

By 1940 (just before the boom years), folklorists had documented half a dozen regional square dance styles in the United States and Canada. Each was of course a hybrid of older traditions, but each was clearly identifiable as distinct from other current styles. Such features as the type of music played, the favored tempo, prompting or cadence calling, the use or nonuse of patter, the preference for across-the-set or around-the-set figures, and the dominance of the ballroom swing or one- and two-hand turns gave each style its own personality.

Starting in the 1940s and increasingly in the 1950s, a virtual community of square dance enthusiasts arose. They took advantage of advances in transportation and communication to share their knowledge and to dance and call at events outside their own regions. This led first to spontaneous cross-currents, with callers learning figures from other traditions; then to regional standardization, with leaders in a city or state agreeing on how moves should be done; and finally to international standardization, as Callerlab published precise definitions of each call. Of course, many leaders opted to work outside the modern square dance scene. But even among traditionalists there has been some homogenization, as dance enthusiasts continue to travel and share ideas. Not only has each local style been influenced by the others; material written during the boom years is now used by callers at traditional-revival dances – and sometimes even at "survival" dances.

Standardization has its advantages, and is probably inevitable in a widely shared hobby. But I must confess that I value the joy of encountering regional variations. I would hate to live in a land where frying was the only acceptable way to cook chicken – not because I dislike fried food, but because there are so many other wonderful recipes. In the same spirit, I rejoice when I hear of a community that has its own way of dancing squares or similar group dances.

The Styles Converge

A new style of recreational square dancing has been developing that draws the best features from many of the broadly defined styles of the past.

From southern mountain and traditional western styles:

- The exuberance, fast tempo, and circular "swoopy" figures
- The colorful patter (influenced during the 1920s and '30s by radio barn dance programs and the associated recordings)

From New England / northeastern style:

- The close connection between the dance and its music
- The energetic but smooth buzz-step swings
- The squared-off grid-type figures (elegant when done well)
- The rich tradition of singing calls

From early modern ("transitional") square dancing (c. 1945–1955):

- The move toward all-active choreography
- The emphasis on doing as much as possible with existing basics
- The bringing together of singing and patter styles
- The free-wheeling allemande breaks

From later modern square dancing (c. 1955 on):

- The playfulness of callers' improvising and dancers' matching wits with the caller
- The kaleidoscopic/origami-like shifting of set shapes and facing direction/orientation

This new style is not uniform across the continent; each caller's delivery and choice of material depends on what that caller has been exposed to. Callers are being influenced by styles other than their own, whether they know it or not, in delivery technique and in choice of material. Most callers now learn much of their style and repertoire from books and recordings – and even in the case of callers at surviving traditional dances who learned from live role models, it is likely that those role models were influenced by sources outside their local tradition (see "Cross-Currents" above).

Is there an appropriate name for this developing eclectic style? I have heard it called "fast squares," which I think is too limiting because high speed is not its most attractive or essential feature. I have also heard it called "southern squares," which is historically incorrect: There is already an established southern style, which is still being danced. Perhaps a better name is "neo-traditional," as the style clearly owes more to the various regional traditions than to modern square dancing, but is not exactly like any of them.

Can this emerging style avoid the excesses of the modern square dance movement and the contra dance revival? Modern square dancing ultimately lost not only the swooping circular figures but also the joy of moving to music that those patterns fostered. The brisk walk, almost a run, was reduced to a shuffle as the patterns became more angular and cerebral – and as the original cohort of dancers got older. (The simple and free-wheeling traditional couple dances suffered a similar fate; the "rounds" that now accompany modern squares are complex in design. They are danced with feet close to the floor, and a "cuer" keeps up a constant stream of instructions that are not in rhythm, making it hard to hear and enjoy the music.) The number of lessons required to join a square dance club has grown from six to 30 or 40, even as Americans have grown reluctant to commit large portions of their leisure time to learning. Ironically, even though modern square dancing has many more movements to learn than any of the traditional styles, in practice it generally has less variety. This is because certain sequences of moves are in fashion at any given time and most callers tend to stick with them.

Contra dancing has avoided some of these problems, due to its strong connection with its music and to the custom of walking every number through before dancing it. But in recent years many new moves have appeared in contra choreography, nearly tripling the number of terms. It remains to be seen if other moves will be discarded to make room for the new ones, or if dancers will be expected to retain a bigger body of knowledge. Also, as mentioned above, contra dancers have come to prefer a steady diet of contras, with a waltz or two thrown in. (The waltzes provide musical contrast and the opportunity to dance romantically, but most contra dancers have no waltz training and are unable to waltz smoothly.) Some contra dancers claim to want variety in programming, but only within duple formation and with two swings in every dance; this makes it an increasing challenge for a caller to provide variety without incorporating new movements.

Only time will tell whether traditional squares will maintain their character, stay accessible to the average person, and hold their place as part of our rich and varied dance heritage. I dare to hope that if properly nurtured, the emerging eclectic style can become the Great American Folk Dance that Lloyd Shaw hoped western squares would be.

Works Cited

Abrahams, Roger D. *Singing the Master: The Emergence of African American Culture in the Plantation South*. New York: Pantheon Books, 1992.

The Ball-Room Instructer. New York: Huestis & Craft, 1841.

Boyd, Neva L., and Tressie M. Dunlavy. *Old Square Dances of America*. Chicago: Recreation Training School of Chicago, 1925.

Bronner, Simon J. *Old-Time Music Makers of New York State*. Syracuse, NY: Syracuse University Press, 1987.

Butler, Frances Anne (Fanny Kemble). *Journal of a Residence in America*. Paris: A. and W. Galignani and Co., 1835.

Chivers, G.M.S. *The Dancers' Guide*. London: T. Denham, c. 1821.

Dart, Mary McNab. "Contra Dance Choreography: A Reflection of Social Change." Ph.D. dissertation, University of Indiana, 1992. Available at **cdss.org**.

Durang, Charles. *The Dancer's Own Book and Ball-Room Companion.* Philadelphia: Fisher & Brother, 1848.

Ford, Mr. & Mrs. Henry [actually by Benjamin B. Lovett and Charlotte Lovett]. *Good Morning.* Dearborn, MI: Dearborn Publishing Co., 1926.

Holden, Rickey. *The Square Dance Caller.* San Antonio, TX: The author, 1951, p. 41.

Jamison, Phil. "Community Dances in the Eighties: Dare To Be Square!" and "Old-Time Square Dancing in the 21st Century: Dare to be Square!" *The Old-Time Herald,* vol. 1, no. 6 (1987) and vol. 9, no. 3 (2004). Available at **philjamison.com**.

Jamison, Phil. *Hoedowns, Reels, and Frolics: Roots and Branches of Southern Appalachian Dance.* Urbana, Chicago, and Springfield, IL: University of Illinois Press, 2015. Supplementary material available at **philjamison.com**.

La Farge, Rod. "Social Dancing in America." *American Squares,* January 1958, p. 6. Available at **newsquaremusic.com/ASDindexUNH.html**.

Lowe, The Messrs. *Lowes' Ball-Conductor and Assembly Guide.* 3rd edition. Edinburgh, 1831.

Pollock, J.S. *La Terpsichore Moderne.* London, c. 1828.

Richardson, Heather Cox. *To Make Men Free: A History of the Republican Party.* New York: Basic Books, 2014, pp. 86–90.

Ryan, Grace L. *Dances of Our Pioneers.* New York: A.S. Barnes and Co., 1926.

Sharp, Cecil J., and Maud Karpeles. *The Country Dance Book, Part V, Containing the Running Set.* London: Novello and Company, Ltd., 1918.

Shaw, Lloyd. *Cowboy Dances: A Collection of Western Square Dances.* Caldwell, ID: The Caxton Printers, Ltd., 1939.

Spalding, Susan Eike. *Appalachian Dance: Creativity and Continuity in Six Communities.* Urbana, Chicago, and Springfield, IL: University of Illinois Press, 2014.

3
Philosophy

I hope you don't skip this chapter or this section in your haste to see what's included under Material and Delivery. Before we delve into the mechanics of calling, I want to spend a little time on the less tangible aspects of the art.

Why Call?

Why do you call? If you're not yet a caller, why do you want to call?

Let's start with another question: What is a caller?

Some books and articles on calling take a mechanistic view of the practice. The author of one generally excellent book (King 1972) says "A caller tells square dancers what to do while they are dancing." He explicitly sweeps broader views aside as being irrelevant to his purpose, which is to teach the technical skills involved in calling. Other writers focus more on the social and emotional benefits of calling, both to the caller and to the dancers.

It seems obvious to me that this is not an either-or situation. A caller needs to pay attention to the technical aspects of the craft, and while one is doing so, a definition like King's is useful. But the broader view is also important. By telling the dancers what to do – with technical excellence, one hopes – the caller is giving them an opportunity to connect with one another in a positive, non-threatening way. In the dance, people can touch one another both physically and emotionally, experience the joy of moving to music, and keep a folk art alive and growing. More and more, people tend to keep to themselves; afraid of intimacy, they rely on technology for entertainment and for seemingly safe communication. In such a society, a skill such as calling square dances is more needed than ever.

There is an old story, made famous by Peter Drucker in *The Practice of Management* (1954): A traveler encountered three stonecutters and asked them what they were doing. The first said "Making a living," the second said "Being the best stonecutter I can be," and the third said "Building a cathedral." Yes, a caller tells people what to do, and should do it well, but for me that's too narrow a vision. We need to keep our "cathedral" in mind.

The truly great teachers of callers have always emphasized both the technical skills and the broader requirements of calling. Lloyd Shaw of Colorado, one of the most influential caller coaches of all time, held that the three pillars of calling from the technical standpoint were clarity, rhythm, and command, but he spent a goodly amount of time expounding on the need to keep the dance activity accessssible to the greatest possible number of people. Likewise, Ed Durlacher of New York stressed the technical requirements in his calling course, but throughout his career, by precept and example, he made it clear that he believed square dancing was a recreation for the masses, not just a chosen few.

As a caller, you will need to exercise multiple layers of consciousness. On one level, you need to focus on the timing and phrasing of your calls and their relation to the music. On a separate level, you need to be aware of the positions of the dancers in the set and their relation to one another, and of how each call changes things. And at the highest level, you should be thinking of the dancers' emotional well-being, and even of the health of the entire square dance activity.

This book deals with the technical skills involved in calling at greater length than the "people skills." This is partly because I feel I have more to say about the technical skills, which I believe I have mastered, than the people skills, which I am definitely still working on. Then too, the interpersonal skills are not unique to calling and have been dealt with by authors writing for a more general audience. But I urge you to keep in mind that both sets of skills are essential.

A few years ago, when I began working on this book, I heard war headlines on the radio and thought once again about the significance of what I do as a caller. For most of my career I have justified the time and energy I spend on calling by equating myself to a USO entertainer performing for the troops: giving the people who are out on the front lines, trying to make the world a better place, a chance to refresh their minds and spirits. But I always assumed that the work of those people was far more important than mine. Lately I've come to believe calling has a more direct benefit to the world than I had thought: I'm making an important change for the better too. "The most radical thing we can do is introduce people to each other" (Rosabeth Moss Kanter of Harvard Business School). We callers are facilitating a high-touch activity in a high-tech world, counteracting the effects of "bowling alone" (to borrow the title of Robert Putnam's 2000 book).

In addition, the caller is a link in the great chain of people who have kept a valuable tradition alive and will continue to do so as long as the human race endures. Larry Edelman, at a Dare To Be Square event in 2013, spoke about his apprenticeship with Jerry Goodwin, a second-generation caller in West Virginia and Pennsylvania. Larry observed that the rich repertoire of Goodwin's father would have been lost if Goodwin had not passed it on to Larry or someone like him. In the same way, Larry hopes to be a link between Goodwin and newer callers who will preserve these dances for future generations.

Dance, like other performing arts, is ephemeral: Although it can be described in words to some extent and can now be preserved in video recordings, it truly exists only while people are doing it. This fleeting quality gives dance a romantic air, akin to the feeling one gets on vacation: Photographs can serve as reminders of a cherished walk along a city riverbank by night, but can never take the place of the actual experience. In today's society many of us try to record all our experiences, often detracting from their live quality. A social activity like square dancing lets us relax and savor the moment. Once again, callers are providing a valuable service to the world.

Herding Cats

Some major shifts have occurred in the past few decades. Until around the time of the Second World War, most events that included group dancing to a caller were *community dances*; that is, they were gatherings of relations, friends, and neighbors – people who knew one another, lived in a small geographic area, and were likely to see one another frequently as they went about their daily occupations. A Saturday night party might include songs, games, and the serving of a substantial meal in addition to dances, and there was always ample time to chat. Dancing was important, but it was a vehicle for socializing rather than an end in itself. In addition, the repertoire of dances was probably small and everyone knew them; there was little or no need for teaching (and even, in some cases, for calling).

By the late 20th century, the vast majority of Americans were living in cities, perhaps far from their extended family and not knowing their neighbors. Other forms of recreation and entertainment were seriously competing for people's attention. As Mary Dart (1992) has pointed out, the prevailing model has changed from community dances to *dance communities*: groups, tied by neither kinship nor close geography, that come together mainly in order to dance. In several regions, friends-and-family parties have been supplanted by public dance halls as the venue for square dances.

What this means for you as a caller is that you will nearly always be expected to take a group of people of varying ages, abilities, and attitudes, who may not know one another, and make them into a cohesive whole – a community of sorts, if only for two or three hours. This requires a kind of alchemy that defies most attempts to reduce it to a formula.

In centuries past, the jobs were separate: A dancing master taught the steps and figures in advance; a prompter reminded the dancers during the ball; one or more floor managers enforced proper behavior. Today, the jobs are combined: Particularly in the traditional dance world, where series of lessons are rare, you will need to be teacher, caller, and floor manager in one. Calling skills can be worked on at home; teaching skills can at least be thought about in advance. But dealing with a diverse group of dancers – encouraging the shyer ones, keeping the more exuberant ones down to a dull roar, and everything in between – can only be learned by doing.

Leadership

As a caller, you will have the power to change lives. I have seen people who attended dances over a period of years develop their social skills to an astonishing degree, almost certainly due in part to the inclusive, nurturing atmosphere fostered by the caller. You can change lives for the worse, too, if you're not careful; a single offhand remark can destroy someone's shaky confidence. With power comes responsibility. Remember that the dancers will see you as an authority, no matter how little experience you may have.

Although few callers have training in theology or counseling, a caller is perforce a spiritual leader of sorts, in the sense of being a source of values. Like it or not, your own values will show in the way you act toward your dancers. It behooves you, then, to examine those values periodically and decide whether you are comfortable with them. This is true whether you subscribe to an established system of religious thought or are working out your own set of beliefs and ethics.

Two principles common to many belief systems are, on one hand, the inherent worth and equality of every individual and, on the other, the value and necessity of community. Square dancing provides a venue where those sometimes conflicting priorities can both be honored and put in balance. The dance will fall apart without cooperation among the dancers, or the three-way teamwork of the dancers, the musicians, and the caller. At the same time, each person's effort is equally essential to the success of the whole. Overall, the well-being of the dancers – as individuals and as a group – is more important than the particular art form that brings them together, or the degree of perfection achieved in pursuing that form.

Leadership includes shaping a community in healthy ways. In every generation there is at least one danger to be addressed. Sometimes it's rowdiness. In the early to mid-20th century, dances in parts of New England and the other northeastern states were marred by excessive drinking, roughness, and even fighting. Some were closed down by local authorities; to tame the others took a good deal of authoritarianism. Happily, that kind of gathering is largely a thing of the past. Larry Jennings, a Boston-area dance organizer in the late 20th century, spoke of country dancing as "an exercise in controlled abandon." The dancers (unless they are all but lifeless) will provide the abandon; it is your job as the caller to exert some measure of control. Together, you and they will find the balance between those states.

Calling is a delicate balance between giving the dancers what they think they want and giving them what you think they need. This applies to the amount of control you exert on behavior as well as the type of material you present. You can get away with doing a lot of things your way if you can keep the dancers happy.

If you are able to connect with your dancers beyond teaching them and calling to them – if you can get to know some of them as individuals, as your personality and your available time allow – so much the better. But even if you don't, you will affect their lives – hopefully for the good – just by providing a place for them to re-create and to connect with one another.

Mistakes

As I mentioned in Chapter 1, mistakes are normal. This applies both to callers and to dancers. If you make a mistake – say you tell the dancers to go the wrong way during the walkthrough, or omit an essential line while calling – you need to admit it, without fuss or defensiveness, then do whatever is needed to set matters right and go on from there.

If one or more dancers make a mistake, the best course of action depends on how many have gone wrong and how far the dance has progressed. The most important thing is to maintain an atmosphere of patience and tolerance, which the dancers will then extend to one another. Absolute perfection should not be your goal unless you are training an exhibition group. To some extent, it can be helpful in the long run to let dancers make and correct their own mistakes.

If several dancers have clearly misunderstood you during a walkthrough, you can put the sets back where they were before the trouble started, then teach the part in question again, using different words. If the problem occurs early in a number, it may be best to stop the music, smooth out the rough spot, and start the dance again. If the number is nearly over, press on to the finish, then take stock. In a class or workshop, you may want to go over the troublesome portion again, or present another dance that incorporates it. At a party, the next dance on the program should be one that you know is within the dancers' ability.

No matter who actually made a mistake, it is an axiom of the trade that the caller should take responsibility for it. Frankly, a dancer mistake is quite likely, though not certain, to be your fault in reality: Either you chose too tricky a dance for the group and the moment, or you didn't teach it clearly enough. If you take the blame, especially if you can do it with a touch of humor, your dancers will think well of you for it. (And of course you should never try to cover your own mistake by claiming it was the dancers' fault. No one is expecting you to be perfect, but the dancers have a right to expect honesty.)

If one or more particular dancers are having trouble, avoid singling them out if possible. If the group is large enough, addressing your correction to the dancers in general may allow the source of the problem to go unnoticed; if not, at least the dancers will respect you for your tact. If you must address someone directly, do it gently and diplomatically. Sarcasm and ridicule will alienate all of your dancers, not just those who were your target.

Always remember that absolute perfection is not the goal. It's all right to polish a routine – more so for exhibition groups than for general dancing – but it's unrealistic and unkind to insist on error-free performance. A good dancer is not one who never makes a mistake, but one who knows how to recover after making one. Bruce Johnson, a master caller, used to say "It's the recoveries that count." That goes for callers too; in fact, it's true in the rest of life as much as in dancing.

Professionalism

Many callers, whether full-time or part-time, do their dance work on a free-lance basis. To someone working for wages or a salary, self-employment may look like the ultimate in personal freedom. In reality, its challenges are no less than those of an employee, just different. Instead of a single boss, you have dozens or even hundreds over the space of a few years. Every organizer of a dance series, festival, or party is an employer whom you must please in order to receive praise, referrals, and repeat business – or, in extreme cases, to get paid without difficulty.

For this reason, you will do well to cultivate professional habits from the start. I had to learn this the hard way. Early in my career I often failed to allow enough travel time to my calling jobs; several of my log sheets show that someone else called the first dance of the evening in my absence. And I failed to develop a foolproof system for adding dates to my calendar, resulting in embarrassing incidents of double-booking.

So do as I say, not as I did. As soon as you become aware of a calling opportunity, whether you or the organizer initiates the conversation, put everything in a form you can refer to later. If someone at a dance asks you if you are free on a future date, say yes only if you can access your master calendar on the spot. Otherwise, ask all inquirers to phone or email you later – or, better still, get their contact information and make the next move yourself.

Once the transaction is under way, be sure you and the client agree on the details. What is the date? The starting and ending time? Who is providing the sound system? If there is a brief lesson before a public dance, who is expected to teach it? At a private party, how much time within the total is allotted for the dancing? Will you be fed? If so, will you eat what the guests do, or sandwiches in the kitchen?

Above all, make sure there are no unanswered questions about money. Will you be paid a flat fee, a percentage of the gate, or a combination? With a live band, how are the shares determined? Will you get a share of the band's pay or a separate fee? Will you receive a deposit? What is the cancellation policy? Is the deposit refundable? Under what conditions? When will you receive the balance of your pay? Will you be paid in cash, by check, or through direct deposit?

How much money should you ask for? It depends on your level of experience, the type of event, and supply and demand within your area. With a dance group, you may have little choice; many groups have a set fee or structure. For private parties, once you are skilled enough to work successfully with non-dancers, I suggest you charge at least as much as the average DJ in your city or region. Many event planners will respect a vendor who charges more than rock bottom. I also suggest you think of your rate for corporate and private events as your regular rate; you can always give a discount to nonprofit groups. But do learn to value your time, including the time you spend in preparation and travel.

Should you use a written contract, and should you ask for a deposit? For private and corporate parties I generally do. Some dance groups have their own contract form and written guidelines; others are more casual, relying on a verbal agreement. But make sure you are comfortable with the terms and reasonably certain that you and the client understand them in the same way.

Always allow plenty of time to get to the venue, including a cushion to allow for traffic congestion. Aim to arrive at least 30 minutes before starting time, more if you are bringing sound. Your car should have plenty of fuel or be fully charged. If you are providing sound, you should be confident that the system is in working order; carry a good heavy extension cord plus spare cables and fuses.

When you arrive, check in with the host or organizer. At a non-dancer event, ask about the length of your sets and the number and length of breaks. Be friendly with the arriving dancers or party guests, but allow time for your set-up tasks. From the moment you arrive to the moment you leave, your professionalism – or lack of it – is on display. You will need to cultivate the ability to be positive and patient while staying in charge of the proceedings.

Once you have spoken with the host and the sound is set up, find a quiet spot where you can be alone, even if it has to be the restroom. Take time to calm yourself before you go onstage. Now is the time for prayer or meditation, if that is part of your spiritual practice. If not, take a few deep breaths, stand up straight, and focus on relaxing. I find that this makes a big difference in my ability to cope with the challenges of a public event, especially if, despite all my precautions, I am running late.

I should add that part of professionalism is staying as healthy as possible, which includes eating well and getting adequate rest. As each calling date approaches, be honest in assessing your physical condition. I once called an evening too soon after undergoing surgery; in retrospect, I am fairly sure the client thought I was drunk. I got that date through an agent who never gave me another job. (This is a good reason for staying on good terms with other callers: You never know when you may need a substitute.)

At the end of the event, keep your wits about you. More than once the organizer has neglected to pay me until I spoke up. If you have done your job well, the host will probably thank you profusely and even offer you a return engagement. If you have your calendar and are awake enough to discuss dates, well and good; otherwise, at least make sure the host has your contact information. Business cards are a must for the working caller, even in this electronic age.

At non-dancer parties, you are likely to be offered a cash tip. Whether you accept it is up to you. If I am working alone, I make it clear that I was not expecting more money than we contracted for, but if they press the tip on me, I accept gracefully. Tipping makes some people feel good; having a gift rejected can hurt. If there is a band, often I am handed a large tip that is intended for all of us. In that case I put up no resistance; it wouldn't be fair to the band. I have learned to take small bills with me in case I am given a $100 bill after I have written the checks for the band.

Showmanship

You may be wondering what a section on showmanship is doing in a book on traditional calling. The word may conjure up images of a modern square dance caller, dressed like a rhinestone cowboy, working the crowd like a televangelist and manipulating the music level (via a thumbwheel on the microphone) to whip the dancers into a frenzy. That's one extreme of showmanship, certainly – and I suspect that not many readers of this book will wish to emulate it. But imagine for a minute the other extreme: Someone in street clothes, perhaps faded and patched (or even ripped), acting apologetic about asking for the dancers' attention at all. You may think that this is a ridiculous image, that no one would approach calling like that. Trust me; I've seen it happen.

Don't be afraid of showmanship. Your calling persona doesn't have to be an elaborate act, but at a minimum, it should be a projection of your own best self. Decide how you want to come across: bluff and hearty? more laid-back and nurturing? Then, especially if it's laid-back, bump it up a notch so it will "read" in a large room or hall, just as actors do. You need to love what you're doing, love dancing, be passionate about it, and let your passion show.

How you dress is up to you, but at a minimum your clothing should be neat and clean. I like to dress at least one level fancier than I expect dancers to dress. Not only does it set a good example, it also makes me easy to identify if anyone wants or needs to speak to me. (However, I must confess that at private parties, given many non-dancers' ideas of what constitutes suitable square dance attire, I am often the least flashily dressed person in the room.)

When I began calling in my teens, I was painfully shy – one might even say pathologically shy. I was certainly the last person anyone would have expected to climb onto a stage and order a hundred dancers around. But the idea of calling to a large group was actually less frightening to me than the thought of interacting with one, two, or a dozen people as individuals. (Asking a girl to dance wasn't scary, because it was quick and simple and expected, and I never found girls repulsive at any age; but I always had trouble keeping a conversation going afterward.) To the extent that I did find being onstage intimidating, I told myself that this was not the real me; this was an act that I was putting on, just as I had put on the character of the Boatswain in *H.M.S. Pinafore* in eighth grade.

Over the years, I noticed three things happening. First, the caller persona became more and more a part of what I perceived as the real me. Second, I started to develop the confidence to deal with other people as individuals instead of a faceless mob. Third, I quit taking it personally when the dancers on the floor didn't act exactly like the dancers in my head. (At the same time, their dancing grew closer to my ideal, due to my improving skills in teaching and giving effectively worded and timed calls.)

If you're shy, it may help you to do as I did and consider your calling an act, at least at first. If you do all the things you should be doing to enable the dancers' success – thinking about your words beforehand and delivering them clearly and positively – you'll be employing effective showmanship.

Many things that contribute to showmanship are simply aspects of skilled calling. These include blending with the music instead of fighting it; keeping your voice and energy up; and ending each dance exactly with the music, whether live or recorded. They are dealt with in Part Two of this book.

But at all cost, avoid sounding apologetic, no matter how nervous or uncertain of yourself you may feel. When the dancers walk into the hall, they are entering into an unwritten contract with you: You agree to give them a good time to the best of your ability, and they agree to do whatever you tell them to. The more confident you sound, the easier they will find it to follow your instructions.

Ethical Decisions

You need to decide, before the issue arises, how far you want to go toward certain attitudes – and conversely, how much you want to actively discourage them on the part of others. I refer to such things as using sexist patter; telling jokes (on or off the platform) that some might perceive as demeaning; and letting issues of politics, race, or religion intrude on the dance. I would particularly caution against assuming that everyone in the room shares your political or religious views. I have been on the wrong end of this, and it's not fun.

One decision to make regards the kind of material you are comfortable using. Sexist patter I have mentioned above (and discuss further in Chapter 9). If you use singing squares, the question arises of what songs you feel are appropriate. Years ago I resolved not to use Dixie because of its close association with racism. At the same time I decided that, in fairness, neither should I use Marching Through Georgia, historically one of the most popular singing-call tunes, because it commemorates an act that would now be considered a war crime. Some singing squares are set to songs by Stephen Foster and others that extol life on the old plantation, making slavery sound fairly innocuous. You will have to make up your own mind as to which ones, if any, to use. I have also decided not to use any songs that glorify drunkenness or adultery, as many country hits have done. Note that this does not preclude using songs that mention drinking or "the way of a man with a maid," which are normal parts of the human condition. But I avoid songs that are known for sexually suggestive or explicit lyrics, even if those lines have been replaced by dance commands.

At some point you will probably be faced with questions of commercialism. This word was used pejoratively during the square dance boom of the 1950s to imply that certain people or entities were profiting unduly from something that should be a community-based activity. Here I am not speaking of your own commercialism; you are providing a service that has taken some effort, and you are entitled to whatever monetary return you can get. What I have in mind is an event organizer who sees square dancing as a corny relic of the past that is nonetheless useful as a colorful addition to a large money-making enterprise. You need to feel comfortable about the way your activity is being presented, and also about the financial structure of the event and the use to which the money will be put.

You will undoubtedly be asked, now and then, to contribute your services with no compensation. You will have to decide each case on its merits: To what cause is the admission money going? Obviously, if the event is for the benefit of a caller or musician who has had equipment stolen or has otherwise fallen on hard times, it is fitting, as well as traditional, for the community to pitch in. But if the cause is unrelated to music and dance or any of your other interests, and no one you know personally is involved, you should think twice before agreeing. If you are new to calling and feel you need every opportunity, these offers will be particularly tempting. But keep in mind that if you get a reputation for doing non-paying jobs, many people will expect you to do the same for them.

My own policy on unpaid work, evolved over the years, distinguishes between *benefits* and *fundraisers*. If a church hosts an event to help its medical mission in Haiti, it's a benefit. If a church hosts an event to replace its own roof, it's a fundraiser, and I'm less likely to say yes (unless it's my church). Whether it's a benefit or a fundraiser, my one hard and fast rule is that no one but the stated cause is getting any money from the event. If food is served, for example, it must be donated, not provided by a paid caterer. (I make an exception for the New England Folk Festival, which pays its sound contractor as well as the obligatory police and medics, because it provides public visibility for the folk music and dance community and has showcased many rising performers, including me in my early days. But I have declined invitations from similar events outside my area.)

Obviously, you should accept only the types of calling job that you're comfortable with. Your comfort zone will likely expand as you gain experience; you may want to try stretching it deliberately from time to time. But if, after serious thought, you just can't see yourself providing a successful party for children, or senior citizens, or people who have been consuming a lot of alcohol, it's better to decline an invitation. If you particularly dislike the kind of party where everyone dresses like farmers or cowhands and there are haybales, wagon wheels, and other bits of "country" on display, you'll need to develop a talent for sniffing it out during your initial negotiations with the organizers.

You will definitely need to formulate a policy regarding alcohol. The movement that became modern square dancing adhered to the rule "No drinking before or during a dance." This was an attempt to combat the image of the hill-country dance with its jug of moonshine, and to ensure a welcome from schools and churches that were often the cheapest sources of dancing space. The present-day contra dance network has, by and large, followed this policy. However, the square dance events connected with the old-time music scene are often held in bars, and the dancers there are generally not discouraged from buying and consuming alcoholic drinks. In my limited experience with this culture, the availability of alcohol has not created problems on the dance floor, but a "wet" event always has the potential to pose a greater challenge to the caller than a "dry" one. Private or corporate parties are more unpredictable than events aimed at dancers. Some callers refuse to take any booking where alcohol will be served; some charge a higher rate for wet events. I charge top dollar for most private parties, wet or dry; at wet events, I have found that keeping the dances simple and keeping everyone moving usually forestalls any problems.

Another issue involving ethics has to do with toxic behavior and the way you and the dance organizers deal with it. This is discussed under "Exploitation" at the end of this chapter.

Humility

Keep your ego in check. True, you need to appear confident and in control of the situation when you're onstage. And presumably you know more about your subject than the dancers do. But you and the dancers will both be better off if your confidence is tempered by a healthy dose of humility. "Whoever would be great among you must be your servant" (Mark 10:43). The more you do with the good of your dancers and the whole activity in mind, the better off everyone will be and the better they'll think of you for it. There's nothing wrong with promoting yourself, but when you do it's well to focus on what you can do for dancers, musicians, and organizers, rather than on how great you are.

Don't fall into the trap of believing all your dancers' compliments. Many of the people you call for will develop their dancing skills; some will bloom socially. Often they will give you the credit for these transformations when a good part of the effort was their own. It is generally better to accept a compliment graciously than to turn it aside, but that doesn't mean you should believe it completely.

Similarly, learn to put dancer criticism in perspective. Listening is an important part of communication, and people who talk for a living often don't do enough of it. Callers get less direct feedback than some other professionals; many dancers will keep their thoughts to themselves. A few, however, will seize every chance to express their opinion of your style, your choice of material, the hall acoustics, the sound system's quality and settings, and every other factor of an event. Learn to distinguish between mere letting off steam and constructive suggestions.

If something in your calling life goes very wrong, resist the temptation to blame other people, or even circumstances beyond your control, before working out just what happened and why. Maybe you brought it on yourself.

Perfectionism

At first you may get frustrated when the dancers on the floor don't perform exactly like the ones in your head. You may feel angry and be tempted to vent your frustration over the microphone. Resist the urge. Over time two things will happen: The discrepancy will bother you less, and the gap will actually narrow because your skills will improve – you'll get better at choosing material to fit the dancers' ability, and you'll know how to teach and call it more effectively.

In the same way, dancers may become frustrated when they have trouble with a sequence; they may express their frustration in various ways, including outbursts of temper. It's part of the caller's job to reduce the anxiety level. Of course this can sometimes be done by teaching so well that the problem doesn't arise, but if it does, the caller can de-escalate the situation by refusing to buy into the tension and adopting a soothing tone instead. The group can be reminded that "it's only a dance" and the world won't come to an end if their execution is not perfect. Further, the caller stands ready to help them succeed by any means possible.

Attitudes – Yours and Theirs

People's tastes differ; that's the way life is, and in the words of the old saw, there's no accounting for tastes. But it is always regrettable when people with differing opinions come to blows, literal or figurative, about them.

You will be more effective as a leader if you teach and call only dances you like. But you, and ultimately your dancers, will have a richer experience if you learn to like as many different dance forms as you can. If there are forms, such as couple dancing or international folk dancing, that you find you don't have time to develop expertise in, encourage your dancers to learn them from others. In fact, your dancers will profit from dancing squares to other callers, just as you will profit from listening and dancing to as many callers as possible.

Remember that your dancers are looking to you for leadership. You really do have the power to shape their attitudes, though it may be hard to believe it when the occasional opinionated dancer tries to shape yours. If you regularly include mixers in your programs and emphasize their positive aspects, the vast majority of your dancers will join in. The same can be said of any dance form that you are enthusiastic about.

One of your biggest challenges as a leader will probably be convincing the more experienced dancers to maintain a welcoming atmosphere. A certain percentage of them will tend to choose and accept as partners only people they know to be equally skilled. One such dancer told me, "I want every dance in the evening to be a peak experience, and the only way I can ensure that is to book ahead." Some people may be beyond your ability to change. But I urge you to keep encouraging the old hands to remember what it felt like to be new, and to spend some of their dance time paying it forward by making the new folks feel welcome. Dancers' satisfaction is important, but so is the long-term health of the activity.

You may not always realize how closely your attitudes may be mirrored by your dancers. If you regard beginners as a necessary evil, your experienced dancers will too. You may not be able to coerce your more snobbish dancers into softening their attitude, but you can avoid modeling behavior that you deplore in others. Unchecked snobbery will destroy any group in time.

Tolerance

Just as there are many styles of music, many types of faith community, and many ways of cooking the same basic ingredients, there are many traditions that come under the general head of "square dancing." Some people prefer four-couple squares, some prefer longways or big circles. Some callers sing all their numbers, some chant them, some aren't musical at all. Some synchronize the dance figures with the musical phrases, some don't. Some groups prefer variety or complexity, some enjoy the same half-dozen dances every time they meet. Some want beer or liquor at their events, some keep their dances dry.

I want to go on record as advocating tolerance between groups that appear to have differing priorities. There are whole networks of groups that do things I don't enjoy – primarily focusing on complexity for its own sake, which more or less forces them to be exclusive – but I try to live and let live. I firmly believe that the more we can see one another as working for the same goal – bringing people together and helping them experience joy – the better off we'll all be.

Once again, remember that you are a public figure. Whatever you say within earshot of an audience will be heard and repeated. I strongly urge you to avoid criticizing other callers to anyone, except possibly your spouse or partner at home. I would also try hard not to complain publicly about other aspects of dance events, whether or not you are on the staff, whether they be one-nighters, series, camps, or festivals. If there is something about an event that you don't like or you think would better be done differently, find ways to give constructive criticism to those who are in a position to consider it. Complaining in public will swiftly get you branded as "the caller who doesn't have a good word to say about anybody."

This applies in particular to your attitude toward other callers' and organizers' series in your area. No matter what you think of them, speaking ill of them or refusing to tell your dancers of their existence will only hurt your reputation. If you encourage your dancers to sample other callers, they will respect you as a generous soul – and, provided you are constantly working to improve your skills, most of them will remain loyal to you. Every caller's long-time dancers tend to think he or she is the best around.

Tolerance is essential within a group as well as between groups. Inevitably, as a group of devotees of any activity stays together for any length of time, the gap widens between what a newcomer knows and what the original members know – not only in memorized facts but also in physical skills, such as posture and reaction time. The gap is obviously wider in modern square dancing, with its long list of movements to be learned, but even in a tradition with a limited number of moves there is a gap. (There will also be tension between hobby dancers who constantly want something new and social dancers who like comfort and familiarity.) Any group that wishes to survive must find a way to attract newcomers, make them feel welcome, and nurture them as they catch up with the "old hands." As attendance grows, this becomes increasingly difficult but also increasingly essential. The larger the dance, the less likely it is to be perceived as a true community, and the more incumbent it is on the regulars to combat the image of cliquishness.

Exploitation

One kind of trouble that has surely been part of country dancing throughout its history, but has only recently been addressed to any extent, occurs when one dancer makes another one feel uncomfortable, by rough handling, inappropriate touching, or unwanted romantic overtures. Dealing with this kind of behavior is more challenging in a dance group than in some other interest groups. Physical connection is an essential part of ballroom and country dancing, and for many people, one of the most treasured parts. Banning physical touch may be feasible in an office setting, but in a dance group it is obviously out of the question.

The greatest imperative about harassment is to acknowledge that it happens and be prepared to deal with it. Those who complain should be listened to and taken seriously. The accused should not be confronted immediately; singling out an individual publicly for anything – problem behavior or dancing errors – is counterproductive. But they should not be let off with a shrug and a line such as "Boys will be boys"; this was the prevailing attitude in many groups for decades.

An increasing number of dance organizers have adopted codes of conduct, spelling out unacceptable behavior and a grievance procedure. As a caller, busy on the platform most of the time, you are unlikely to be the one to whom an aggrieved dancer chooses to speak. But it will contribute to a healthy series if you confer with the organizers beforehand about your part in fostering the right atmosphere. Often the caller is given a statement to read to the group, such as "One of our goals is for everyone to feel comfortable. If at any time you are made uncomfortable, we encourage you to talk to one of our committee members (who are wearing special nametags and/or will raise their hands at this point)."

The increasing sensitivity to predatory behavior has effected a change in country dance etiquette. For many years the rule was "If you decline a request to dance, it is rude to accept one from a different person." Dancers, callers, and organizers increasingly feel that, because some people are given to rough handling or unwanted words or touches, it is unfair to insist that someone who wishes to avoid such a person must sit out the dance.

The idea that communication is key, and that weighty decisions are best made collaboratively, applies to physical safety and other issues aside from harassment. A dance community needs to agree on which actions are acceptable and which are not. As an example, the governing board of one dance hall voted to outlaw aerial moves (lifting dancers off their feet), common in swing dancing and recently imported into contra dancing. With a firm policy in place, signs can be posted and callers can announce the rule without having to take the blame for it.

A final word relating to exploitation: You are likely to find that your position as a performer and an authority has an aphrodisiac effect on some of the people who attend your dances. Most will simply gaze up at you, but a few will try for closer contact. They may arrange to be near you whenever you are off the platform, attempt to converse with you as often as possible, and even ask you to spend time with them away from the dance. If the feeling is mutual and neither of you is partnered, you can proceed as you would with any other attraction, while trying hard to discern whether the other person is acting mainly out of genuine friendship or hero worship. If you do not reciprocate the feelings, you have the job of dissuading the person gently. If either or both of you already have partners, it is imperative to keep things on the level of friendship or, if that proves impossible, to avoid communicating entirely. The risk of destroying relationships, and even lives, is too great. Finally, if you, partnered or not, find yourself deliberately taking advantage of someone's admiration by pursuing an exploitive relationship, please get professional help right away.

* * *

This concludes the section on theory. I hope you will return to it periodically, even as you study the mechanics of calling and build your repertoire of material. These principles are important, and they can be easy to forget when you are busy learning and practicing your trade.

PART TWO
Delivery

4

Musical Structure

You don't need to be a musician to be an effective caller (although any musical training you have is an added asset). But you do need to know something about the structure of square dance music. This knowledge will enable you to blend with the music rather than fighting it, and to satisfy your dancers in a deep way, even though they may not be aware of what you're doing. (There will be more to say about music later; see Chapter 12.)

Tune Structure

Square dance tunes vary more than tunes used for contra dancing, but they have certain properties in common. They are played at a constant, fairly brisk tempo, ranging from about 112 to 150 downbeats per minute. Most tunes are in 2/4 meter (usually spoken of as "2/4 time"); that is, there are two beats to a measure, and each beat is worth one quarter note (though the fiddler may play two eighth notes, four sixteenth notes, or any combination of these on any given beat).

A few tunes are in meters other than 2/4. In the northeastern United States, much of Canada, and a few other areas, it is common to hear tunes in 6/8; these are most often termed jigs. For practical purposes they may be thought of as having two beats to a measure. Many marches and singing squares are written in 4/4, with four beats to the measure. (See Chapter 12 for more about tune types.)

Most traditional dance tunes have two strains, known as the "A" and "B" parts. In the vast majority of tunes, each part is 8 measures or 16 beats in length. Each strain is normally played twice, for a sequence of AABB that is 32 measures or 64 beats long. The individual parts are known as A.1, A.2, B.1, and B.2. (Some tunes of this length, particularly marches and popular songs, have different musical patterns, such as AABA and ABCD, but for square dance purposes they may be thought of as AABB tunes.)

In New England style, many square dance figures are also 32 measures (64 beats or steps) long, as are nearly all contra dance routines. With experience a caller develops the ability to tell subconsciously how far the tune has progressed, which may help in keeping the parts of a New England square synchronized with the corresponding parts of the tune (see "Phrasing" below).

In other regional styles, such as southern mountain, Texas, and traditional western, start-to-finish synchronization of dance to tune is less common. Perhaps because of this, musicians' dance repertoire in those areas often includes tunes with structures other than the one described above. Some tunes have "A" and "B" parts of half the usual length: 4 measures or 8 beats. When played AABB, such a tune will be only 16 measures or 32 beats long; to someone used to the New England norm, it may sound as if the tune is being played ABAB. But because southern and western callers traditionally ignored any phrase longer than 4 measures, they were not bothered by this. (See also "Regional tune structure" in Chapter 12.)

Some tunes are "crooked"; that is, there are more or fewer than the usual number of beats in the "A" part, the "B" part, or both. (Some musicians play crooked versions of tunes that are also played "square.") Obviously, crooked tunes are not used for dancing in areas where the callers work within the musical phrase.

A few tunes are longer than the standard. Most of these are half again as long, having three strains and 48 measures or 96 beats, and are notated AABBCC. Some square dance figures are this long, and a caller who phrases start-to-finish can achieve a nice effect by matching a long figure with a long tune. (See "Long figures" under "Phrasing" below for more on this.)

One more word on tune sequences: You will occasionally hear musicians, live or recorded, play a particular tune using an unusual sequence, such as AAB. Don't assume that every band plays that tune identically.

Rhythm

In square dance usage, rhythm generally refers to the steady sequence of downbeats, to which the dancers are expected to synchronize their dancing. It should go without saying that the caller should synchronize the call to the beat as well, putting the accented words or syllables on the downbeats. But occasionally someone who can't hear the downbeat will attempt calling, with unfortunate results. It is almost impossible to call on the upbeat intentionally; the only way to do it is to be oblivious of the beat altogether. Callers who don't hear the beat are more likely to rush the beat than to call consistently on the upbeat; through pure coincidence they will be now on, now off the beat. If this happens, the dancers will have to choose, consciously or not, between following the caller's beat and following the musical beat. Inability to detect the beat, after repeated attempts, is one of the very few faults that should disqualify someone from calling.

In the vast majority of square dance traditions, dancers take one step on each downbeat. In some parts of Texas, most dancers used a two-step through the mid-20th century. Some dancers in the Ozarks and southern Appalachians have used a form of percussive dancing or stepdancing – variously referred to as clogging, jigging, buckdancing, or flatfooting – while executing square dance figures. However, it was apparently more common in those regions to walk the figures; freestyle stepdancing was generally done solo on the sidelines during sets or to music played between sets.

Most people can easily hear and respond to the downbeat, which is generally played in the low or bass notes: the pianist's left hand, the guitarist's thumb, or the string bass, tuba, or bass guitar. With an average group, you will probably not need to mention that one beat equals one step. If your group has trouble finding the downbeat, you may need to talk a little about it, and also make sure that your music (live or recorded) has a downbeat that is easy to hear. (But beware of music with too much downbeat and not enough upbeat; the music needs to lift the dancers, not hammer them into the ground like tent pegs.)

The speed or tempo of square dance music has varied from age to age and from region to region. What types of swings are used in a local style, and how often, has a lot to do with the favored tempo. Judging from recordings and mentions in books and magazines over the past century, the Northeast has consistently favored slower tempos, on average, than other regions – about 112 to 128 beats per minute for both squares and contras. Tempos have tended to run higher in the West – say 128 to 136 – with the two-step areas of Texas coming in a bit slower, around 120 to 128. The fastest tempos are heard in the southern Appalachians and the Ozarks, ranging from 130 to 150. If you are creating your own tradition, be sure your musicians play (or you have adjusted your recorded music to run) at a tempo with which you and your dancers are comfortable.

Calling in rhythm with the music will help the dancers find the beat, and it will make your calls more pleasing to the ear. See Chapter 7 for more about this.

Timing

Timing and phrasing are basic to the mechanics of effective calling. They are different things, but they're very closely related. Timing is allowing the correct number of beats for the dancers to execute each movement; phrasing is allowing those correctly timed movements to coincide with the phrases of the tune. Phrasing is more critical in some styles (such as New England) than others, but correct timing is important in any style.

Each basic dance movement requires a certain number of steps to perform comfortably. Some movements can be done in fewer steps, but forcing dancers to do so will make them feel rushed. Most movements that have stood the test of time can be danced in multiples of 4 steps, making them easy to fit to music. It is possible to time a dance correctly without phrasing the movements, but many callers – particularly those with experience prompting contras and New England squares – find it easier to phrase than not to.

It is important to know the number of steps required for the most common basic movements. Ideally you should assimilate this knowledge to the point where you can call without thinking consciously about those numbers. Otherwise you run the risk of giving your calls in too-quick succession, in effect asking your dancers to do the impossible. Even a few commercial recording callers have been guilty of this: The most common fault is to stack the calls (give one right after another) for two or more movements that each take 8 steps to dance but only 4 beats to call. Stacking calls is acceptable in a singing square in order to let the caller, and perhaps the dancers, sing the last part of the song. This is done by giving the final calls of the figure or break, such as "do-si-do and promenade," just before changing from commands to lyrics. If the dancers are unfamiliar with this practice, the caller must explain that they will be given enough time to execute each movement. The kind of stacking that is unacceptable never gives the dancers time to catch up; it's a form of clipped timing (see below).

Of course, instead of learning how many steps each movement takes, you can memorize all your calls, learning an exact set of words for each dance. Some callers, particularly schoolteachers who are new to square dancing or musicians who call only occasionally, have done this. But if you skip a line by accident, you won't know how to recover. And because there are so few truly basic movements, it is just as easy to memorize their timing as it would be to memorize words for a handful of dances. Even with singing squares, whose words are more or less set by tradition, you will feel more secure if you understand the timing of the moves and know how to recover if necessary.

If you have danced for a year or two before starting to call (as I strongly recommend), you have probably begun to develop a feel for timing. As you study the timing of the basic moves, you may find that you know a lot of this information even though you may never have consciously thought about it.

Note that timing has nothing to do with the speed, or tempo, of the music. The tempo can be quite slow, and the timing of a dance will still be too fast if you are not allowing people the full number of beats to dance each movement. Conversely, a fast tempo can be quite comfortable if you use proper timing (assuming the dancers are physically fit and can adjust their stride to the speed of the music).

In general, the timings given here are minimums – the least number of steps that dancers can take and still execute the movements comfortably. It is not good practice to cut the timing of a move below this number – with one exception (see the next paragraph). However, there may be times when you will want to allow *more* than the minimum. When working with senior citizens, or with beginning dancers of any age, it is wise to pay close attention to their reaction time – that is, the lag between the time you give a call and the time they start to execute it – as well as the number of steps they take to complete each movement and be ready for the next one.

The exception to the rule of adhering to the minimum timing for a movement comes when the dancers are close together and/or already in motion. For instance, a pass through takes 4 beats for two facing couples starting from their home positions – but only 2 or 3 beats for two couples who are making their way across the set, are moving at full speed, and are nose to nose when the call is given. Similarly, a do-si-do from a standing start takes 8 beats, and it normally takes at least 2 beats to move between partner and corner. But once the dancers are in motion, two allemandes and a do-si-do can easily be done in 16 beats. (See "Retrophrasing" below for more on this.)

Split timing and clipped timing

Two phenomena that need to be distinguished from each other are split timing and clipped timing. The first can be useful; the second is to be avoided.

Split timing means combining a movement that is longer than the musical phrase with one that is shorter, so that after the two movements the dancers will be back on phrase. For example, a caller can follow a grand right and left halfway around, which takes at least 10 beats to dance comfortably, with a partner do-si-

Chapter 4: Musical Structure 53

do, which can be executed in 6 beats if the dancers are close together and already in motion. Those two movements can be danced comfortably during one 16-beat phrase of music. In extreme cases, the dancing of a movement can straddle two 16-beat phrases, using part of each, but this requires consummate skill from the caller. (Of course, the phenomenon will not bother a caller who chooses not to phrase more than 1–4; see "Phrasing" below.)

Clipped timing means allowing the dancers too few beats to complete each movement without rushing. Western callers in the 1950s and 1960s commonly allowed just 5 or 6 beats for a right and left through or a ladies chain, and sometimes only 4. A caller who phrases start-to-finish with the tune (1–64; see "Phrasing" below) will automatically avoid this; even if you phrase only within the "A" or "B" part (1–16), you are unlikely to clip the timing.

* * *

The table on the next two pages lists the basic movements you are most likely to encounter in the eclectic style of square dancing that I refer to as neo-traditional, with the generally accepted number of steps required to dance each one. (See the Glossary in the back of the book for definitions of any terms that may be unfamiliar to you.)

Timing of Common Square Dance Movements

		Beats
Allemande	*See* Hand turn	
Arch and dive		2–4
Backtrack		2–4
Balance (incl. in a wave)	Once	4
	Repeated or double	8
Bend the line		4*
Box the gnat		4*
California twirl		4*
Chain	*See* Ladies chain	
Circle	Four people halfway	4
	Four people 3/4 around	6–8
	Four people once around	8
	Six people halfway	6–8
	Six people 3/4 around	8–12
	Six people once around	12–16
	Eight people halfway	8
	Eight people 3/4 around	12
	Eight people once around	16
Circle to a line		8
Courtesy turn		4
Cross trail	Simply cross paths	2–4
	Pass through and cross	4–6
Dive through		2–4
Do paso		12–16
Do-si-do	Back to back	6–8
	Various hand-turn series	12–24 (often 16)
Ends turn in		4
Forward and back		8
Four ladies chain		8–10
Four ladies chain 3/4		12
Gents chain	*Same as* Ladies chain	
Grand right and left	Six people once around	16
	Eight people halfway	10–12
	Eight people once around	20–24
Grand square	(including reverse)	32

Chapter 4: Musical Structure

		Beats
Half promenade		8
Half sashay		2–4*
Hand turn	Halfway	4
	3/4 around	4–8
	Once around	4–8
	Once and a quarter	8
	Once and a half	8
	Twice around	8–12
Hey	For three	12–16
	For four	16
Honor		4–8
Ladies chain		8
Ladies chain 3/4		10–12
Ladies grand chain	*See* Four ladies chain	
Lead right		4
Pass through		4
Promenade (couples)	Halfway around	8
	3/4 around	12–16
	Once around	16
Right and left through		8
Rollaway		2–4*
Sashay or **Slide**		Varies
Single file promenade	Four people inside, once	8
	Eight people halfway	8
	Eight people once around	16
Square through	Four hands	10–12
	Three hands	8
Star	Four people once around	8
Star promenade	Four couples once around	12
Star through		4*
Swing		Flexible; 4–16
Turn alone (U turn back)		2–4
Twirl to swap (all kinds)		4*
Weave the ring	Eight people halfway	10–12
Wheel around		4*

*Often "stolen" from the time allotted to other movements.

Phrasing

To recap, timing is allowing the dancers enough time to get through the moves comfortably, whether or not those moves have any relation to the music (other than the basic beat). Phrasing is synchronizing the moves, your calls, or both with the groups of 4, 8, 16, and 64 beats that are known as phrases.

If you plan to call in what I term neo-traditional style, you will probably want to phrase as much of the time as possible. It is possible to call any square without phrasing, since the caller tells the dancers what to do throughout. But anyone accustomed to calling contra dances will almost certainly find it more satisfying to phrase the squares.

Not all callers agree on the importance or desirability of calling to the phrase. I emphasize it in this book for several reasons:

- I'm saturated in it – those of us who learned to call that way find it easier to phrase than not to.
- Many people, even first-timers, instinctively move with the phrase if you let them.
- Starting and ending movements, figures, even whole dances with the phrase is intensely satisfying to many dancers, even if they aren't aware of the reason.
- Most callers in what I term neo-traditional style (which is often closely associated with contra dancing) use it as their default.
- It's better to learn rules first and then decide to bend or break them on purpose, just as budding artists are encouraged to learn to draw a horse that looks like a horse before trying abstract art.
- It's easier to ensure comfortable timing of the dancers' movements if you let the music guide you. If you try to time correctly without phrasing, you take on the added task of always starting the next call (with no help from the music) two beats before the dancers have finished the preceding move.

Regarding people's tendency to dance in phrase, there is usually no need to mention that your calls are related to the musical phrase. If you just put the calls in the right place, at a one-nighter or a lesson, the dancers are likely to feel the phrase and move accordingly. On occasion, if I sense that people are not completely relaxed, I may say "I only tell you *what* to do; the music tells you *when*."

How much to phrase?

Rickey Holden, one of the first to write about calling technique (1951), distinguished three types of phrasing:

- 1–64: making an entire figure or break begin and end with a 64-beat tune
- 1–16: making a series of movements or a series of calls coincide with a 16-beat "A" or "B" part of a tune
- 1–4: beginning each 4-beat call line on the first or fifth beat of an 8-beat musical subphrase

Chapter 4: Musical Structure   57

Holden separates this classification from the question of whether the call should come before or during the movement it applies to. I deal with the latter issue in Chapter 6.

Phrasing 1–64

If you have done any contra dance calling, you know that almost all contra dance sequences are 64 steps in length, and that contra dance tunes have 64 beats. Moreover, contras' component movements nearly always fit into the 16-beat divisions of the tune. As mentioned above, Holden refers to this marriage of dance and music as "phrasing 1–64."

Many squares in what is generally known as New England style follow the same rules as contras: Each figure or break is 64 beats or steps in length, and the calls are given in advance to let the dancers begin each part of the dance with the phrase. One difference is that in a contra, the caller will often reduce the number of spoken commands as the dancers memorize a sequence. This is possible because almost every contra sequence is repeated in identical form throughout. It is not practical to diminish the calls of most squares, even in New England style, because there are usually minor variations in the figure (such as giving directions alternately to the heads and sides) and because breaks are almost always interspersed with the figures. Expert callers working with skilled dancers often improvise their breaks, but even if the same break is used throughout a square, it makes the dance harder than a contra for the dancers to memorize.

Long figures: phrasing 1–96

The term "1–64" presupposes a tune of standard length: 32 measures (64 beats or steps), usually played AABB. As mentioned above under "Tune Structure," some dance tunes are longer by half, with 48 measures or 96 beats. Such tunes are not used for contra dances, and should not be used for 32-measure squares. However, many enjoyable square dance figures are longer than 32 measures. The majority of these are 48 measures long or can be adapted to that length by adding or subtracting movements (see Chapter 14 for hints on adapting dances). There are several ways to synchronize the movements of such a figure with the music:

1. Use a tune of that length (which generally has three parts, played AABBCC). This is generally the most satisfying approach for caller and dancers alike.
2. Get the band to play extra parts of a standard tune (such as AABBAB). Many musicians dislike doing this, as it requires them to focus on where they are in the tune, something that is normally automatic.
3. Use a standard (AABB) tune and start the first figure on an "A" part, the second figure on a "B" part, and so on. In other words, the music for the first figure will run AABBAA, for the second BBAABB, etc. This is my preferred method when the musicians know no 48-measure tunes.
4. Use a standard (AABB) tune, start each figure on an "A" part, and insert a 16-measure (32-beat) break after every figure. The figure will occupy

AABBAA and the break will use the remaining BB. This was a common practice of Ted Sannella, who often used a grand square for the break. A loosely timed sequence of allemande left, grand right and left halfway, and promenade home will occupy the same amount of music.

Phrasing 1–16

Alternative 3 above hints at a practice that appears to have been common during the square dance boom of the late 1940s and early 1950s: starting each segment of a figure with a musical "A" or "B" part but not attempting to line up the figure with the beginning and end of the tune. Holden refers to this as "phrasing 1–16." It can be particularly helpful in several cases:

- Some figures from the '40s and '50s are of irregular length (not 64 or 96 steps); phrasing 1–16 will give the satisfaction of dancing on the phrase without worrying about finding the beginning of the tune.
- With a group of dancers who enjoy being challenged, a caller who is phrasing 1–16 can insert a zero movement (see Chapter 14) into a figure on the fly.
- If the dancers are falling behind due to age or inexperience, the caller can let the phrasing slip without having to omit any movements, as would be necessary in order to stay within a 64-beat tune. (See below for further discussion of slipped phrases.)

Phrasing 1–4

The most minimal kind of phrasing is what Holden terms "phrasing 1–4." This is common in southern mountain style, in which the figures generally take an indeterminate number of steps to execute. (In contrast to quadrille-derived movements, such as right and left through, that position the dancers precisely, southern style favors figures in which the dancers describe circular paths around and between one another. It is often hard to tell where one movement of a southern figure ends and the next move begins.) A southern-style caller will give the name of a figure, either on the last four beats of the preceding phrase or the first four beats of the phrase on which it is to be danced (see the discussion of prompting vs. cadence calling in Chapter 6). The dancers will then execute the figure at a comfortable speed while the caller either fills in with patter or falls silent (the latter is common if the caller is dancing, as is traditional in some communities). Phrasing 1–4 was also common in the West and Southwest during the square dance boom.

When phrasing 1–4, it is possible to begin a 4-beat call on other than the first beat of a 4-beat phrase, as heard on many commercial recordings made during the 1940s and 1950s. On some of these recordings the caller habitually starts calling one beat before or after the phrase begins (that is, 4-1-2-3 or 2-3-4-1); on others the calls appear to have no relation to the music other than that the syllables generally fall on the downbeats, as they should. To my ear, placing four-beat calls on the phrases (1-2-3-4) is the method most pleasing to the ear and least confusing to the dancers. However, if a figure contains movements (such as certain hand or arm turns) that are most comfortably danced in 6 beats, it will be necessary at times to fall silent for 2 beats and deliver the following call on 3-4-1-2, returning as soon as possible to the 1-2-3-4 norm.

Slipped phrases

Inevitably, there will be occasions when the dancers take longer to execute a movement than you expected. This is particularly true if most or all of them are quite young or old, or if they are dancing for the first time. There may be a delay of 2 to 4 beats after the end of your command before they start to move. And once under way, they may need to take more steps than average to get through the movement. When this happens, you will need to realize that the timing has slipped. Your task then is to decide quickly between two options: You can omit one or more movements in an attempt to preserve the overall phrasing of the figure or break. Or you can let the phrasing slip as well as the timing, giving up the idea of synchronizing the entire dance with the tune.

With dances that depend on tight phrasing for much of their effect, such as singing calls and quadrille-type squares, be prepared to leave out "zero" movements or combinations – that is, parts of a routine that return all dancers to where they began that part – in order to get the dancers back on phrase. This can be an attractive alternative to letting the phrasing slip when the dancers have fallen behind. Doing it, of course, requires you to know which calls are zeroes and which are an integral part of the routine (see Chapter 14). It could even be argued that it's better to walk through only the key moves rather than a whole routine, to avoid training the dancers to expect a certain order of calls and then not giving it to them. The argument continues that if you use fewer moves than you walked through, you risk making the dancers feel inadequate, as if they didn't live up to your expectations. I think this may be true for some but by no means all groups of dancers; I recommend using your judgment here, as everywhere.

If the dance is less closely tied to the music, in tradition or in your mind, it may be better to keep all the movements and let the phrasing loosen up. Just make sure to keep phrasing 1–4, and get back to phrasing 1–16 as soon as you can. If you want to restore the 1–64 phrasing, figure out where you are in the tune and pad out with "filler" moves like do-si-do, swing, or promenade until you reach the end of an AABB round. This may cause the dance to need more music than it would have, so make sure the band knows that you may ask them to play longer than you originally intended. (If you work with recorded music, it will pay to determine in advance which dances are apt to be troublesome enough to your group that the phrasing is likely to slip. For such a number you can choose a recording that is longer than the dance. If all goes well and the dance ends before the recording, you can simply cut the volume when the dance is finished.)

One advantage of squares over contras is that you *can* let the phrasing slip. In squares, the caller is expected to call throughout because the pattern doesn't repeat exactly; therefore, the caller can reset the phrasing to let people catch up, then re-reset (if desired) to get back on the phrase if it looks as if the dancers can keep up. With a sequence like "Heads pass through, separate around one, into the middle with a right-hand star, [nearly] once around and look for your corner, allemande left," you can adjust the time allowed for each move depending on how long it takes the dancers to get to the star, then to find the corner. (If you stopped to analyze that sequence, you will have noticed that it doesn't match everyone with their own corner unless you call "Head ladies chain" first. See *Around One to a Star* in Chapter 20 for the complete figure.)

I am almost always willing to let the phrasing slip – not just in squares but in whole-set longways, phrased circles, and so on – when I work with anyone other than dance hobbyists. This includes children, seniors, people who have been drinking, and of course people with various mental and physical challenges. If you anticipate such a situation, it will help if you choose music whose phrasing is fairly subtle. For example, most Scottish country dance recordings are very sharply phrased, which is why they have been widely used for contras, but it makes them a poor choice if you think you may need to sacrifice perfect phrasing.

Note that allowing the phrasing to slip should be done only if you judge, in a specific instance, that the dancers are having trouble keeping up with you. This is different from making a habit of getting your timing from the dancers, which is something to avoid. If you wait for them to finish each movement before calling the next one, they will come to a halt between moves and will get increasingly farther behind the music. You need to deliver each call in its proper time, trusting that the dancers will execute it with the phrase. Only if they repeatedly fail to do so should you begin remedial action as outlined above.

Which is worse, to let the phrasing slip or to stop the music? It depends on a number of factors. If you judge, early in a routine, that the dancers will have real trouble keeping up, it may be better to stop the music and reteach any troublesome spots. If the trouble appears less serious, or if the number is almost finished, it is better to keep going and minimize any feeling of failure on the dancers' part.

Closely related to slipped phrasing is a question many authors have tried to answer: "If the sets aren't all moving together, which set should I cater to?" The answer depends on how closely to the music you are phrasing, and also on what percentage of the sets are falling behind. If you are phrasing 1–64, synchronizing the figures and breaks completely with the start and end of the tune, the music will determine the correct timing. The dancers are unlikely to rush the call for more than a few beats; they are much more likely to fall behind, for any of a number of reasons. You can follow the guidance above on slipped phrases; in addition, if a large percentage of dancers are having trouble keeping up, the figure may be too advanced for them or you may not have done an adequate job of teaching it. Don't beat yourself up over it, but do make notes and be ready to change the rest of your program. If you are phrasing less than 1–64 or not at all, you will need to use your judgment as to which sets to watch most closely, remembering that you must always lead, not follow the dancers.

Chapter 4: Musical Structure

Retro-phrasing

When I added some "transitional" squares to my repertoire – figures from the mid-1950s, when traditional western style was evolving into modern square dancing – I found myself instinctively trying to time my calls so that the dancers could dance with the phrase. I certainly wanted them to surge into a forward and back on beat 1 of a 4-beat phrase, at the very least; beat 1 of an 8-beat phrase was even better.

Almost any square dance figure or break can be analyzed for timing; that is, the routine can be broken down into its component movements, and the number of steps needed to execute each movement comfortably can be determined. (This is harder, though still possible, with things like stars and single file promenades. The challenge increases if four dancers are starring while the others are promenading.) Then a set of words can be devised that will cue the dancers before each movement, allowing them to dance to the musical phrase. (See Chapter 14 for more on analyzing and adapting dances.)

Remember that, as mentioned above under "Timing," certain movements may require fewer steps if the dancers are already in motion and are close to one another when the call is given. For instance, although a do-si-do with the opposite from a squared set will take at least 8 steps, a do-si-do when partners meet in a grand right and left can be done in 6 steps. I mention this again here because in retro-phrasing a traditional western or transitional square, it is particularly important to preserve the constant forward motion that gives those styles their character. The dancers should never have the sensation of coming to a momentary halt until the figure is over and they are back at home with their partner. Such halts are likely to occur if you allow 8 steps for every do-si-do in the belief that this is the correct procedure because the music is written in multiples of 8 beats. (In many of the older singing calls, 8 steps are allowed for every hand turn and do-si-do, but dancers in communities where these calls are popular have learned to stretch these movements to use up the music. That practice is part of a long-cherished tradition, but it would be out of character in a 1950s western square.) To tighten the timing where necessary and still keep dance and music together as much as possible, a 6-beat move can be paired with a 10-beat move as mentioned above under "Split phrasing."

Retro-phrasing allows dancers who are used to contras and New England squares to dance western squares comfortably, while it enables the caller to add patter for the sake of color and excitement. Further, I believe that it does not violate the spirit of western style. (Southern mountain style, whose structure is looser than those of other regions, is less susceptible to this treatment.) In the early 1950s, the two national square dance magazines printed articles by advocates and opponents of phrasing in western and southwestern calling. The advocates maintained that phrasing would improve one's calling regardless of style, while the opponents said phrasing was not traditional in their style and would change its character. The sides never reached agreement, but the advocates made a case for phrasing that many considered persuasive and showed how it could be done.

* * *

Here is a square dance figure, taken from Chapter 17, giving the number of beats (steps) required for each movement and showing how the movements fit the phrases of the music. Note that this dance is phrased 1–64; that is, once through the figure equals once through a standard (AABB) tune.

Ladies Chain

(The Dance Movements)

Square dance figure, corner progression

A.1	Head ladies chain across	8 beats
	Chain back	8 beats
A.2	Side ladies chain across	8 beats
	Chain back	8 beats
B.1	All do-si-do corner	8 beats
	All swing corner	8 beats
B.2	Promenade corner to gent's place	16 beats

SEQUENCE: Head ladies then side ladies (twice); side ladies then head ladies (twice).

If you are unfamiliar with the concept of phrasing 1–64, I suggest that you try dancing this figure in your home with imaginary people (don't worry about calling yet). You can take the part of a lady or a gent. If you have no suitable recorded music, you can sing, whistle, or hum Jingle Bells, which is exactly the right length and similar in structure to most fiddle tunes.

I also suggest you obtain a few recordings of dance tunes without calls. (Many are available as inexpensive downloads; see the Resources section.) Make sure you can identify the four parts of each tune. If you want a challenge, turn the volume down for several seconds, then turn it back up and try to spot the next "A" or "B" part. If you plan to use music in 6/8 meter (jigs) in your calling, add at least one recorded example to your library.

5
Dance Structure

When dancers are doing a square, they don't have to worry about the structure of the dance. All they need to know is their role (lady or gent, or equivalent terms), their position (couple number and head or side), and what movement they are expected to do next. Any other thoughts about the dance are the responsibility of the caller. A large part of the caller's job is to tell the dancers what to do, just before they do it. To accomplish this successfully, the caller needs to be thoroughly familiar with how square dances are put together.

Building Blocks

First, let's agree on terminology. The smallest unit of square dance construction is the *basic movement*. Sometimes abbreviated to "basic" or "move," it is a series of footsteps, often with accompanying handholds, that take a dancer, a couple, or a group of couples from one point in the set to another. (A few basics, such as swing or forward and back, have the dancers finish where they started. Other basics, such as promenade, may or may not return the dancers to their starting position.) Basics are usually short, taking 4, 8, 16, or a similar number of beats to perform. They are combined in various orders to make figures and breaks. (The most commonly used basics are discussed in depth in Chapter 15.)

A *figure* is a combination of basic movements that is intended to give dancers a satisfying experience. It usually lasts between once and twice through a 32-measure (64-beat) tune. Some figures result in a change of partners, shifting either the ladies or the gents one place to the right or left. Such a figure may be done twice with the head couples leading, then twice with the sides leading, so that partners are reunited after the fourth time through. Other partner-change figures begin with all four ladies, gents, or couples active, and are done the same way four times. Figures that do not change partners are sometimes referred to as "keepers"; they may start with one couple leading, or heads and sides may take turns starting the figure. In a pre-planned dance with its own name, such as *Duck for the Oyster,* the name always refers to the figure.

A *break* is a combination of basics that is inserted in a dance between the figures. Traditionally it serves to activate all the dancers if only some were involved in the figure, or to let the dancers relax if the figure was complicated. The calls in a break are usually addressed to all four ladies, gents, or couples at once. The break is generally (though not always) easier than the figure it accompanies. One inviolable rule is that the break never results in a permanent partner change; each dancer has the same partner after the break as before it, although a few breaks involve a series of quick and temporary partner changes. (Some authors give introductions and endings their own categories; to me they are simply special subclasses of breaks.)

The next larger unit of construction is the *complete dance,* done to one musical number (a single tune or a medley) and made up of figures (usually four) interspersed with breaks. There are usually opening and closing breaks; there may be a single middle break after two figures have been danced, or a break after every round of the figure. In the Northeast this unit was traditionally known as a "change," and three changes, danced with the same partner to three different pieces of music, constituted a "set." Neo-traditional style has retained this usage of "set" but not of "change." In some areas of the West the single dance number was known as a "tip" (the name may refer to an old custom of paying the musicians a small amount before or after each number); in modern square dancing it is termed a "call," and two calls – one patter and one singing – make up one tip.

The number of complete dances in a *set* has varied through the years. In the 18th-century cotillion, units similar to what we would now call figures and breaks alternated many times through one long selection of music. The 19th-century quadrille was a set of five or six figures, each danced to its own piece of music with pauses in between. Most quadrille figures were short and did not include breaks. The country-style square dance that evolved during the 19th century, and has continued to evolve since, has varied considerably in its structure from one region to the next and even from town to town. In the southern mountains the band may play for ten minutes or more without stopping, while the dancers do a long series of figures. In other parts of the United States and Canada the usual sequence is two or three separate dances in a row. Many (but not all) areas that used to do three are now doing two, often because the dancers wish to change partners more often or to do other forms such as couple dancing or contras more of the time.

In parts of the Northeast, selecting appropriate figures for the first, second, and third change in a set has become a fine art. Often the first change will be a fairly leisurely figure involving quadrille-derived movements, such as right and left through and ladies chain, that start and end with the dancers in a normal squared set, though some may have exchanged places. The second change may be a visiting-couple figure or some other type that takes dancers farther from their home positions. The third change is also known as a "breakdown," as is the tune type used for it; it generally requires more energy from dancers and musicians alike. A breakdown traditionally has all four couples active at once and involves a partner change; many breakdown figures could just as easily be done in a big circle of couples, and in some communities they are danced that way. This gives them the feel of a mixer, although in most cases the dance is continued until original partners are reunited.

Orientation

Caller and dancers alike need to be familiar with the basic nomenclature of a square dance set. The most common type of set comprises four couples; when all are "at home," each couple stands on one side of a hollow square, facing its opposite couple. In each couple, partners stand side by side, with their backs to a wall of the room – a different wall for each couple. A square should be small enough that the dancers can comfortably join hands in a circle without taking more than one step forward from their home positions; for adults this will be 6 to 8 feet across. (Some authors give a dimension of 10 or 12 feet, which includes a safety zone where dancers can promenade outside the square without colliding with dancers from other sets.)

The lady stands on the right side of each couple, the gent on the left. (See Chapter 13 for alternatives to the terms "lady" and "gent.") Adjacent dancers from different couples are corners: Your corner is the person on the other side of you from your partner when all are at home. To be specific: If you are a lady, your partner is on your left and your corner on your right; if you are a gent, your partner is on your right and your corner on your left. (For dancers who are facing out of the set, the directions are reversed; in general, a corner is the lady clockwise from a gent or the gent counterclockwise from a lady.) Your opposite is the person directly across from you when you're at home (and in some other temporary formations); in a squared set it will be someone playing the opposite gender role.

There is one other person with whom a dancer may be called to interact. For each gent, it is the lady of the couple on his right; for each lady, it is the gent of the couple on her left. Since the calls were traditionally addressed to the gents, this person has long been known as the "right-hand lady." For anyone wishing to make use of this relationship and wanting a gender-neutral term, I suggest "next-door neighbor." It has the same accents and number of syllables as "right-hand lady" and may be dropped into any traditional call without hurting the scansion.

Note that in some squares you may be expected to regard as your partner the person currently standing where you would expect to find your partner; likewise with your corner. (The caller may tell the dancers "We dance places, not faces.") This is true at the end of any figure with an obvious partner change; it may also be true in the middle of a complex figure. This is the opposite of the rule in contra dances, where "partner" always refers to the person with whom you entered the particular dance number.

The couples' positions are numbered as follows: Couple 1 has its back to the music, or to a designated "head of the hall" if the music is not clearly at one end of the room. (Before the era of amplification, in some communities where each square had its own caller, the first couple faced the music. This enabled the callers, who customarily danced in first position, to communicate with the musicians.) Couple 2 stands to the right of Couple 1. Couple 3 faces Couple 1, and Couple 4 is to the left of Couple 1. Couples 1 and 3, who face each other across the set, are often referred to as the head couples or heads (or formerly in some areas, the first four). Couples 2 and 4, who also face each other, are the side couples or sides (in some areas, the side four, or very rarely the second four).

Incidentally, the present-day couple nomenclature preserves elements of both of the great ancestors of square dancing. The couple numbering comes from dance traditions in which most figures had couples visit their way around a square or circular set. The names "heads" and "sides" come from the 19th-century quadrille, in which opposite couples often worked together. In some (though not all) quadrilles, the head couples were numbered "one" and "two," with the second couple standing across from the first. The third couple was to the right of the first; the fourth, then as now, was to the left.

Note that the definition of a call does not change simply because the dancers are away from home. Any two facing couples can do a right and left through, and an allemande left may be done at any place in the set as long as all the dancers are adjacent to their corner.

Types of Square

Square dance figures are often classified by the number and identity of the dancers who begin them.

One person start: normally the first lady or gent. The simplest such figure – one of the simplest squares of all – is an old singing call, *Spanish Cavalier,* in which the first lady goes to each gent and swings him, returning home to swing her partner after each "visiting swing." Other examples include a family of figures in which the active dancer does a series of hand turns with various people, such as *Ladies' Whirligig* (see Chapter 22).

Two people start: the head ladies or head gents, or in some old figures, the first lady and her opposite gent or the first gent and his opposite lady. The two active people may dance with each other in the center, or they may each lead to their right-hand couple to dance with one or both of its members.

One couple start. This is the largest and most varied category of figures. It includes the following types:

Divide the ring – the active couple dances through the center and between the opposite couple, separating and traveling one of several possible distances. In perhaps the oldest of these figures, the active dancers travel all the way home. In a few figures, the active couple travels only a short distance after splitting the opposite couple and forms a line of four with them.

Visiting couple with only foursomes – one of the oldest forms; the active couple visits each other couple in turn, dancing the same four-person figure with each, or (since the mid-20th century) a different such figure with each. A break is called after each couple has completed its circuit.

Cumulative visiting – the active couple leads to the right-hand couple and dances a four-person figure; those two couples lead to the next couple and dance a six-person adaptation of the same figure; those three couples lead to the last and dance an eight-person version. Examples are *Grapevine Twist, Lady Round Two,* and *Swing Like Thunder* (all included in Chapter 19).

Three-couple figures – the active couple leads to the right-hand couple, and those two couples plus the original left-hand couple dance back and forth across the set. Such figures include *Dip and Dive Six* (see Chapter 19), *Right and Left Six,* and *Three Ladies Chain.*

Lines of three – the active couple visits around the set and, by taking and leaving people, sets up a formation with two facing lines of three people and two

Chapter 5: Dance Structure

facing single people. The simplest such figure is known as *Forward Six (and Pass Right Through)*; there are many variations, of which the best known is *Right Hand High, Left Hand Low* (see Chapter 19).

Two couples start. This category also includes several subgroups:

Heads (or sides) dance together across the set, as in many 19th-century quadrille figures.

Heads face diagonally toward their right-hand (and/or left-hand) couple and dance a series of movements with them.

Heads pass through each other and dance around the outside. This is a logical development from the one-couple "divide the ring" group.

Heads go forward to meet their opposite person, then all turn to face their corner. This and the "heads pass through" group marked the beginning of modern grid-type square dance choreography around 1950. One of the best known such figures is *Chicken Plucker,* in which all four couples shuttle back and forth across the set.

Heads lead to their right-hand couple and circle four, then the circles open into two facing lines of four people at the sides. The best known such figure is *The Rout(e),* a series of chains that send the ladies around the set (see Chapter 18).

All four ladies, gents, or couples start. This type of figure may include a star in the center, a single file promenade around the outside, or both. Most breaks are of this type; the oldest and simplest is the grand right and left, with or without trimmings such as an allemande left before it or a promenade afterward. Many breaks include a series of hand turns. Innumerable variations on the grand right and left have been devised, some of which are known as the Allemande Alphabet. The oldest of these consist of a grand right and left interrupted by stars, hand turns, and/or balances.

How to let more people move more of the time

In some regions, callers kept the square dance alive for decades using only plain visiting-couple figures and a single break: allemande left, grand right and left halfway, meet your own and promenade home. The dance was one component among many in a social evening; people danced as a natural outgrowth of the urge to connect, not as a hobby in itself. They felt no more need to learn new dances than to write new verses to Happy Birthday or For He's a Jolly Good Fellow.

Ever since the great square dance revival began in earnest in the 1940s, some dancers have complained that too many of the traditional figures allowed only two couples to dance at a time, while the other two stood idle. Several ways have been devised of adapting such figures to allow more people to dance more of the time:

- Change a foursomes-only visiting figure to a cumulative figure. One of the first figures to be treated in this way was probably *Bird in the Cage.*
- Call both head couples out to the right at once in a visiting figure. (Some recording callers of the 1940s and 1950s did this frequently, perhaps partly to fit a "complete" dance on a 10-inch disc.) From there, the active couples may meet in the center to dance the figure together, or they may pass

beyond each other and proceed directly to their left-hand couple. Rickey Holden pointed out that if they meet in the center, the figure must be symmetrical, with both couples doing exactly the same thing.
- Let Couple 1 dance with Couple 2 and then Couple 3 in the usual way; when Couple 1 gets to Couple 4, have Couples 2 and 3 dance the same figure with each other. This practice is or was traditional in many areas. Calls for it have included "On both corners" and "Everybody dance"; in some communities the dancers did it without needing a call. The practice is different from the follow-up (described below) in that a break is called after each couple's turn. Sometimes, after doing the main figure, the two groups of four people (1 and 4, 2 and 3) form circles and do a "bouquet waltz," the circles revolving counterclockwise around each other while rotating clockwise.
- Call a follow-up: When Couple 1 gets to Couple 4, have Couple 2 lead out to Couple 3 and begin visiting completely around the set. Each couple leads out as soon as its right-hand couple is free to accept it; there is no break or chorus until all four couples have gone around.
- A hybrid of the last two methods described above, used by some callers in the 1940s, is to call Couple 1 out, have Couple 2 follow up and go all the way around (visiting all three other couples), and then call a break. Then Couple 3 starts, Couple 4 follows up, and all dance a final break.
- Change an across-the-set (quadrille-type) figure to a diagonal figure, with each active couple dancing with its right-hand couple.

Note that it may not always be desirable to keep everyone moving as much as possible. Guests at a non-dancer party, who are unaccustomed to exerting the energy required in square dancing, may appreciate figures in which half the people move and half look on. Some senior citizens may prefer to be active only half the time, and if the weather is hot and humid, dancers of any description may want less activity than usual. As with so many aspects of calling and facilitating a dance event, you will need to use your judgment.

It should also be noted that at a traditional dance, seldom are the "inactive" couples completely still. They may mark time in place, using as much or as little effort as they wish; the more energetic folks may choose to dance percussively. And of course they must often "counter-dance," moving a step or two this way or that to accommodate the actives. A good dancer can do this gracefully, tracing a circular path that lets active and inactive orbit a central point. Even at a party geared to first-timers, the inactive dancers would be well advised to think of themselves as participants and stay alert.

How to deal with uneven numbers of couples

One of the few criticisms of squares that I consider well-founded is that their form is rigid: If the number of couples wishing to dance is not an exact multiple of four, anywhere from one to three couples must sit out. But there are ways around this.

Chapter 5: Dance Structure 69

- If there are, say, 10 couples, you can have them form two sets of 5 couples each. You can have each couple visit around the set, doing two-couple figures or, better yet, a cumulative figure.
- With 6 or 18 couples, you can make 6-couple sets; you can then call Couples 1 and 4 out at the same time. (With 12 couples, of course, you can make regular squares.)
- If you lack only one couple to complete one of the sets, you can ask a set of stronger dancers to do the figure with an imaginary fourth couple. This can be fun in its own way.
- With any number of couples, you can always use Sicilian or southern-style two-couple sets, either arranged in a big circle or scattered around the floor. (I suggest the scatter formation if there are fewer than half a dozen foursomes.) If there is an odd number of couples, one couple will be left out, but it will be a different couple each time.

Constructing a Sequence

The figure

The first step in constructing a complete square dance is to choose a figure and make sure you are thoroughly familiar with it. Who begins the figure? Does it result in a change of partners? Your aim should be to ensure that every person in the set gets an equal amount of dancing overall, no matter how many or few people are dancing at a given moment.

If one couple begins the figure, of course it should be called once for each couple. If two facing couples begin, it should be called twice for the heads and twice for the sides. You will need to examine the figure and mark each point where the call is directed to the heads or the sides. In the repetitions of the figure when the sides begin, every reference to "heads" must be changed to "sides." If, in the figure as written with the heads leading, there are references to "sides," they must be changed to "heads" when the sides lead. This may be intimidating at first, but experience with figures of this type will result in more comfort with the process.

If the figure includes a partner change, it should be called twice in a row for the heads, then twice for the sides (HHSS). If instead it is called for the heads and sides alternately (HSHS), assuming the ladies go to their new partner's place each time, the original head ladies will lead the figure four times and the other two ladies not at all. (You can also use HSSH order, giving the ladies rather than the gents two consecutive turns at being active. The fact that HSSH "works" is worth remembering; if you inadvertently call the first two figures HS, you can recover by calling SH after the middle break.)

If, on the other hand, the figure is a "keeper," it is better to call it in HSHS order to avoid the monotony of two absolutely identical figures in a row. Some callers, if they sense that the dancers would appreciate it, will add more repetitions of a "keeper": for instance, HSHSHS. This can be done if the figure is particularly satisfying, or if the dancers have had trouble with it the first few times.

A few figures written and published in the late 20th century have a change of partners between pairs of adjacent couples (for instance, Couples 1 and 2 exchange partners, as do Couples 3 and 4). This puts the dancers who do the moving, usually the ladies, "out of sequence"; that is, they are arranged in numerical order clockwise around the set while their partners remain in order counterclockwise. This creates a dilemma: If the figure is called in HSHS order, two ladies never get to lead. In HHSS order, no one ever gets to dance with the opposite. HSSH order likewise gives each dancer only three of the four possible partners. For this reason, I avoid calling figures of this type. (Some such figures can be modified by changing or swapping movements to produce a more conventional progression of partners.)

Another type of figure needs a special caution: A figure in which only one couple is active, and which also contains a partner change, must be called at least twice for each couple. (Some figures, particularly of the "divide the ring" family, were traditionally called four times in a row for each couple. In the 1940s, to forestall dancer boredom, many callers cut this structure from four to two times per couple.) If a single-couple figure with a corner progression (that is, each gent takes his corner to his home position) is called only once for each couple, the first lady will be active all four times and no other lady will get to lead the figure.

Adding breaks

Once a figure is settled on and analyzed, the next step is to choose one or more breaks and decide where to insert them. You can use the same break throughout a square sequence, as the old-time callers did. You can modify the opening and closing breaks, perhaps adding "honors" on the first phrase of the introduction and the last phrase of the ending, or "forward and back, forward and shout" at the end. You can even call a different break each time you insert one, though I urge you to keep the breaks simple if you do this.

Recording technology may have influenced the length and structure of square dances in the mid-20th century. Until around 1950 it was usual to insert a break after each couple's turn at the figure. Assuming each figure or break to be around 32 measures in length (once through a typical dance tune), this would take at least nine times through the tune, or about four and a half minutes. Such a dance would fit on one side of a 12-inch 78 rpm disc, but not on a 10-inch side. The 10-inch records were much more popular with callers than the comparatively bulky and fragile 12-inch discs. In order to fit a complete dance on each side of a 10-inch record, callers had to call two figures in a row before inserting a break: introduction, figure for Couples 1 and 2 (or twice for heads), middle break, figure for Couples 3 and 4 (or twice for sides), closing break. This became the standard sequence for singing squares.

How many breaks should you put into a dance? If you are presenting only one square at a time, you can probably afford to call a break after each figure. Likewise, if your breaks are half a tune in length, or if you are phrasing only 1–4 or 1–16 and your breaks are short, you can use a lot of them without making the

Chapter 5: Dance Structure 71

dance feel overly long. On the other hand, if you are calling two or more squares in a row, you will do better to use only three breaks per number – especially if you are working with contra dancers who may not be sold on the merits of squares.

Speaking of sequences, one of the most common caller errors is losing track of how many times you have already called the figure. I can vouch for this, both from my own experience and from observation of other callers. In a partner-changing dance, it helps to note who is dancing with whom in the set nearest you, but it is easy to forget to do this. My impression is that dancers will forgive such a lapse if you don't do it too often.

* * *

It is possible, of course, to write your own figures and breaks, or even to improvise them on the fly, as modern square dance callers do. I like to have my figures worked out in advance, but I frequently improvise combinations of moves for my breaks – sometimes to the point where I literally don't know what command I'm going to give until two beats (one second) before I speak the words. There is more on calling breaks in Chapter 8. Writing your own material and improvising or "hashing" calls are treated in Chapter 14.

6

Wording

One of the most basic questions about calling is exactly when to deliver the commands – the standardized words or phrases that translate into dance movements. To put it another way, the dancers know *what* to do because they have learned what the key words mean, but only the timing of your words can tell them *when* to do it.

Wording questions are of two types. One is where to place the four-beat call lines in relation to the music and in relation to the dance movements. This includes the age-old question of whether to prompt the calls or deliver them as the dancers execute them; this is discussed in detail below. The second question is where to place the commands or key words within each call line. The answer depends in part on how the first question is dealt with; therefore, the topic is addressed throughout the chapter as well as separately at the end.

Music plays an important part in the equation. Exactly how the calls relate to the music depends on the regional style, both of music and of dance.

Placing the Call Lines

By long tradition, square dance calls are delivered in lines of four strong beats – most often, though not always, in rhyming couplets. This does not mean that every line, or even every beat, must contain an equal number of syllables. We are not composing poetry with rigid rules of scansion; what matters is the steady beat. (For more on this, see Chapter 9, Patter.)

Square dance music is played in phrases that are multiples of four beats. A perceived phrase may be 8, 16, 32, or 64 beats in length, but good dance musicians always provide punctuation that distinguishes the groups of four beats from one another. If you start a piece of recorded dance music playing with the volume all the way down, then increase the volume to the point where you can hear it, you should be able to identify the phrases fairly quickly. The chord changes will help, but even where the chord remains the same for several beats, there should be a bit of extra emphasis on the first beat of each phrase.

Because dance calls and dance music both come in groups of four beats, it stands to reason that the calls, for the maximum pleasing effect, should be synchronized with the music. That is, the 1-2-3-4 of each call line should coincide with the 1-2-3-4 of a musical phrase. This is the caller's responsibility rather than the musicians', because the musicians are playing continuously while the caller is speaking at intervals, based on how long the dancers take to execute the movements. Whether the calls are given before or during the movements to which they apply, they must blend rhythmically with the music – even though they must stand out from the music in terms of loudness.

73

Prompting

In some regional traditions, square dance calls are customarily given ahead of the musical phrase, so that the dancers can step out on the first beat of the new phrase, as in contra dances and 19th-century quadrilles. This practice is known as prompting.

Prompting is an exception to the general rule that calls are given in four beats. Many prompts take three beats, two beats, or occasionally just one beat to deliver. But the caller who prompts must still keep the four-beat phrase in mind; although the calls may or may not begin on the first beat of a phrase, they should always end on the fourth beat.

In a prompted call, the last syllable of each command should be spoken on the beat just before the dancers are expected to begin performing the called-for movement. The number of beats needed for each command, hence how early each command must be started, depends on how many words and syllables it takes to speak it. As you gain experience, you will develop the ability to sense, a second or two in advance, how many syllables your next call will consist of, and therefore on which beat of the 8-beat phrase to start that call. I think of this as "backing the call up to the end of the phrase."

Here's how it works. Let's say you want the dancers to swing their corners. Your dancers are experienced enough that their reaction time is minimal, and they are rather expecting a corner swing at this point in the music (say, starting 24 beats before the end of the tune: 8 for the swing and 16 – the entire B.2 music – for a promenade). You decide to call simply "Corner swing." The call has three syllables and can be given on two downbeats. Therefore it should go on the last two beats of the first 8-beat half of the B.1 music:

B.1:	—	—	—	—
	—	—	<u>Cor</u>ner	<u>swing</u>

If this is not the first time through the figure, and therefore the corner in question is not the original corner, you may want to call the dancers' attention to that fact by inserting the word "new." You could say it on the downbeat before "corner," but I would be more likely to put it on the upbeat and give it a little extra emphasis (indicated by the italic type):

B.1:	—	—	—	—
	—	— *New*	<u>cor</u>ner	<u>swing</u>

Now suppose you are calling the same dance to a group of newer dancers who need more time to process each call. You decide to start the call sooner:

B.1:	—	—	—	—
	<u>Swing</u> the	<u>cor</u>ner,	<u>cor</u>ner	<u>swing</u>

Chapter 6: Wording 75

In each of these three cases, you have "backed" the call against the end of the phrase, continuing to speak until its final beat. Let me emphasize again that this is the ideal way to deliver prompted calls. If you were to call a corner swing thus:

B.1:	—	—	—	—
	<u>Swing</u> your	<u>cor</u>ner	—	—

there is a good chance that some of your dancers would try to start the swing a couple of beats too soon, giving them a less satisfying experience. If the call preceding the swing is something like "Forward eight and back," it is physically possible for dancers to cut the move short and start swinging early. But not only is it less satisfying in itself; if some dancers are "jumping the gun" while others wait for the new phrase, the result is chaos. Note that the issue here is not just that "Swing your corner" is spoken early, but also that nothing is spoken on the last two beats of the phrase. Key words can be given early if most dancers in a group are inexperienced, but I recommend continuing to speak until the end of each phrase (see "Placing the Key Words" below for more on this).

By now you will have noticed that the length of a command – how many words and syllables it contains, how long it takes to deliver it – has no relation to the length of time it takes the dancers to execute the corresponding movement. "<u>Do</u>-si-<u>do</u> your <u>cor</u>ners <u>all</u>" takes four downbeats to speak, but the dancers cannot perform the move in that amount of time. This is why it is crucial to know how long each common movement lasts (see the timing chart in Chapter 4). It is easy for a caller to reel off a series of instructions that is impossible to dance.

Cadence calling

In dance traditions where prompting is not the norm, the calls are given on the phrase, each call beginning on the first beat of an 8- or 16-beat phrase. This is sometimes referred to as cadence calling.

Here is an example of a cadence call, a visiting-couple figure that has been done to many tunes over the years, often as a singing call.

A.1:	First <u>cou</u>ple	<u>right</u> and	<u>cir</u>cle	four,
	<u>cir</u>cle	four hands	round	— You
	<u>do</u>-si-	<u>do</u> your	<u>op</u>po-	site
	<u>all</u> the	way a-	round	— You
A.2:	<u>do</u>-si-	<u>do</u> your	<u>part</u>ner	— and
	then you	<u>swing</u> her	too	— You
	<u>swing</u> her	high and	<u>swing</u> her	low,
	<u>swing</u> her,	<u>yes</u>, you	<u>do</u>	—

Except for a single "swing" prompt midway through A.2, every call in this fragment is delivered while the dancers are executing the called move.

If you are used to prompted calls, as a caller, a dancer, or both, you may be wondering how the dancers deal with cadence calls. Rickey Holden (1951) wrote that in a theoretical ideal world, the music, the call, and the dancers' movement would all start together on the first beat of each phrase. This seems impossible unless the dancers know in advance what movements the caller will direct them to do – which would obviate the need for a caller.

What happens in practice is, first, that often the dancers *do* know what call is coming next. This is because the square dance repertoire in many communities is made up of a dozen or so figures that are relatively simple, are done the same way every time, and are therefore easily memorized by the dancers. Second, these figures are generally timed loosely enough that a dancer unfamiliar with them can start each movement a couple of beats late (that is, after hearing the call or part of it) and still end with the phrase. An example of such loose timing is "do-si-do your opposite" followed by "do-si-do your partner" in the fragment above, with 8 beats allowed for each do-si-do. Seasoned dancers in a traditional community will head for their opposite as soon as they hear the first "do," if not before. But even dancers less sure of themselves and the figure can start moving on the second "do" and still have time to complete both moves in the 14 remaining beats.

The oldest singing squares (from the 1930s or earlier) rely heavily on cadence calling. Square dancers before around 1950 were either members of a community with a limited repertoire as described above, or members of a square dance club who had taken lessons that usually included the best-known singing calls. In either case the dancers could respond quickly, though not instantly, to a cadence call. Beginning in the 1950s, some choreographers created singing squares that included prompted calls as well as cadence calls. This appears to have been done in response to an increasingly common scenario: With hundreds of singing squares being written, it was likely that a hall full of experienced dancers would encounter a singing call that was totally unfamiliar to them. Field recordings from the 1950s show callers walking their dancers through the newest singing squares, even if they were not in the habit of using walkthroughs for patter calls or "hash."

Ed Durlacher of New York, one of the most influential callers of the square dance revival, took a hybrid approach to the question. He used cadence calling for all of his figures, whether sung to the tune of a popular song or chanted to fiddle music. This was in keeping with the northeastern tradition of a limited repertoire of figures known to all the participants. But he prompted his breaks, as he liked to vary the order of the movements in his breaks, never letting the dancers know what was coming until two beats before they had to respond. He believed that, as a rule, both figures and breaks should be danced on the phrase, but he always walked the dancers through the figure and almost never walked through the breaks. (See Chapter 8 for more on the philosophy of using breaks.)

By contrast, Ted Sannella prompted not only his breaks but his figures (except for the very few singing calls he used). Like Durlacher, he used walkthroughs as the norm, but his figures were on average more intricate than Durlacher's and less tied to the musical phrase. (By that, I mean that each 16-beat component of a typical Durlacher figure, in a way, felt complete in itself, much like the parts of a classic contra dance. Sannella's figures felt more like modern contras: Although he allowed the correct number of beats for each move, the moves were not necessarily grouped obviously into 16-beat segments that coincided with the parts of the tune.)

Prompt, then patter

For those callers who enjoy calling patter on the musical phrase, but who prefer to let the dancers know the movements in advance, a combination method suggests itself:

1. Give a short call at the end of the preceding phrase. This call may contain the name of a movement (such as "promenade"), part of a name (such as "go forward"), or, if it will be clear to the dancers what is coming, one or more "lead-in" words that don't mention the movement (such as "everybody go" before a forward and back).
2. Deliver a couplet of patter on the 1–8 phrase during which the dancers are executing the movement.

Here is a fragment of *Squareback Reel* (from Chapter 18) containing three examples of this:

	sepa-	rate, go a-	round just	one, squeeze
	into a	line of	four, go	forward
B.1:	Up to the	middle and	back to the	ring
	— Hey	now, the	corner	swing
	Swing on the	corner,	swing around	all and
	prome-	nade, go	round the	hall
B.2:	Prome-	nade, go	two by	two
	All the way a-	round, just	me and	you

The second "Swing" and the second "Promenade" are also examples of trailing patter (see Chapter 9). Among the uses of trailing patter are, first, to reassure dancers that they are doing the right thing, and second, to give a "delayed prompt" to any dancers who did not process your first utterance of a command.

I suspect that most callers who consider phrasing important have used this technique at times, but some have made extensive use of it, notably Dick Leger in the 1960s and 1970s (see in particular his LP, *Phrase Craze Squares*).

"Prompt, then patter" is a helpful technique for the neo-traditional caller. It's one way to make a phrased dance feel like a traditional western square.

Placing the Key Words

Now we come to the second question of placement: where within each four-beat call line to put the key words – the words that actually cause the dancers to react. These are, by and large, "code words": The dancers have been trained to recognize certain words or phrases, such as "do-si-do" or "star," as commands to do a specific thing in a specific way.

An experienced dancer will usually start to execute a command about two beats after hearing it, or as soon as he or she has finished the preceding movement. A dancer trained in the New England tradition, in which most movements begin and end with a musical phrase, will generally try to execute each call starting on the first beat of a phrase. (If you want a particular movement to begin in mid-phrase, you must make your intentions clear during a walkthrough as well as during the dance.)

Therefore, if you are phrasing the movements and prompting your calls, the key words in most cases should be placed close to the end of the phrase. If you are calling consistently in 4-beat lines, the key words should go near the end of a line, as in "the corner swing" in this fragment:

B.1:	<u>Up</u> to the	<u>mid</u>dle and	<u>back</u> to the	<u>ring</u>
	— Hey	<u>now</u>, the	<u>cor</u>ner	<u>swing</u>

Newer dancers, as mentioned above under "Prompting," are likely to react more slowly to commands. If a group is made up primarily of dancers with little or no experience, you may find that you need to place the key words sooner in your call lines – perhaps four beats ahead of the desired motion, rather than two. If, in addition, you keep speaking until the last beat of the line, you are less likely to confuse any experienced dancers present than if you stop speaking early.

B.1:	<u>Up</u> to the	<u>mid</u>dle and	<u>then</u> back	<u>down</u>
	<u>Swing</u> the	<u>cor</u>ner	<u>round</u> and	<u>round</u>

One of the most common points at which a quick decision must be made is the moment just before partners meet in a grand right and left. This is particularly true if the dancers have been taught that any move may come next: do-si-do, swing, promenade, or one of the many variations on the grand right and left. At this point many callers have a habit of leaving the key words of the next call until partners are face to face. If the dancers must hesitate, not yet knowing what to do next, the caller has let them down.

The following examples illustrate different points at which you may insert the same call. It is impossible to tell you when to use each example, because dancers do not always execute a grand right and left at the same speed. You will have to watch your dancers and develop the ability to spot the moment when partners are about 2 to 4 beats away from meeting.

Chapter 6: Wording

| <u>Hand</u> over | <u>hand</u> a- | <u>round</u> you | <u>go</u> and |
| <u>meet</u> your | <u>own</u> with a | <u>do</u>-si- | <u>do</u> |

| <u>Hand</u> over | <u>hand</u> a- | <u>round</u> you | <u>go</u> and |
| <u>do</u>-si- | <u>do</u> when you | <u>meet</u> your | <u>beau</u> |

The more unusual the next call is, the more crucial it is to deliver it in plenty of time for the dancers to process and react to it. In the case of the traditional variations on the grand right and left, the caller customarily warned the dancers of what was coming by using leading patter (see Chapter 9).

Last, but by no means least, remember in most cases to say "who" before "what." As an example, it is better to say "On the corner, do-si-do" than "Do-si-do your corner." The "who" words allow the dancers to reorient themselves to face a new direction if necessary before they hear "what" they are supposed to do next. The only exception comes when the dancers are already facing the desired person or direction and there will be no ambiguity if you simply give the name of the next movement.

* * *

Please keep in mind that, perhaps more than any other calling skill, this is not something that can be mastered overnight. Even after years of practice, no one does it to perfection all the time. But the more you work at it, the better your batting average will be – and the more often you do it well, the more fun your dancers will have.

7
Voice Technique

Square dancing is a folk activity, and it can be argued that calling dances should be spontaneous. The image of the country caller doesn't conjure up thoughts of voice lessons. But you can bet that the old-time callers – be they farmers, cowhands, or full-time dancing masters – knew how to breathe, how to project (without amplification!), and how to care for their voices. If they hadn't developed these skills, they wouldn't have lasted long in the trade.

I feel that calling should *appear* spontaneous, but there are a few things the caller can do – behind the scenes, as it were – to avoid certain problems and increase everyone's enjoyment of the dance. A good way to learn is to record yourself and listen with a critical ear. I also recommend recording other callers, if there are any around and they give permission, and listening to them along with commercial recordings of callers who are generally considered good (see the Resources section for recommendations).

Voice technique breaks down into

- Artistic delivery of the calls: rhythm, timing and phrasing, musical pitch
- Physical delivery of the sound: tone production, projection, diction, emphasis, microphone technique, care of the voice

Rhythm

Calling in strict rhythm is the norm for squares, though exceptions can certainly be found on vintage recordings. To a new caller or one with a contra dance background it may feel stilted at first; you may think you will be less obtrusive if you give instructions in the cadences of natural speech. But it actually sounds more natural, and pleasing to the dancers, to keep time with the music. If you speak as you would in normal conversation, you will be off the beat much of the time, and the dancers will be forced to choose between stepping to your beat and stepping to the band's beat. If you call in rhythm, you become part of the band – the percussion section for sure, and even the melody section if you deliver your words on musical pitches.

Conversely, even if your words consistently fall on the beat, there is a danger of sounding too regular and precise, potentially boring your dancers or putting them to sleep mentally. An effective caller not only varies the volume and pitch of the words (see "Emphasis" below) but puts an occasional word just before or after the beat in the style of a jazz musician. The best way to get acquainted with this aspect of the art is to listen attentively to recordings of great callers of the past (again, see the Resources section).

In a similar vein, it is important to avoid letting the volume and pitch of your voice drop toward the end of each call line, the way you might at the end of an ordinary sentence. Again, it may feel stilted at first because of its unfamiliarity; it may feel as if your last word is sticking out like the proverbial sore thumb. But if you drop your voice, your dancers are extremely likely to mishear or entirely miss the command words you worked so hard to put in the right place.

Timing and Phrasing

These have as much to do with musical structure and choreography as with voice, and they are discussed from that standpoint in Chapter 4. But the question of when to deliver your commands can be considered part of vocal technique. If you are prompting a command, it's important to give the call on the "5-6-7-8" of an 8-beat musical phrase if the movement begins with the next phrase, or the "1-2-3-4" if the next move begins on the fifth beat. First of all, it sounds better; it's the principle of calling in rhythm, taken to its logical conclusion. It helps the dancers to move out on the first beat of the phrase. This enables them to dance to the phrase, the most satisfying way to dance, and it reassures them that they're in the right place at the right time. It can heighten your awareness of the timing and phrasing of the dance movements and help you allow the correct number of beats for each move. It can even improve your breath control; if your calls coincide with the phrases, you will probably find yourself breathing naturally after each phrase, just as you would when singing a song.

Musical Pitch

Some callers have an excellent sense of pitch, whether they were born with it or developed it over time. They don't necessarily have what is called "absolute pitch" (or popularly "perfect pitch"), which is the ability to identify the pitch of a note or the key of a musical selection. But they have "relative pitch": Once the music is playing, they can pitch their voice to any note of the scale being used. If you are one of these fortunate people, you have multiple choices for delivering your calls. The most elaborate technique is to get to know the chord progression of each tune and pitch your voice on a note that harmonizes with the chord currently being played. (See "Keys" in Chapter 12 for more on this.) Some tunes lend themselves to making up countermelodies, so that not only are you harmonizing with the chords, but your notes add up to a cohesive whole with a story line of its own. A simpler method is to call mainly on one note, jumping to others from time to time to break the monotony. If you have trouble staying on pitch, it's better to speak your calls. Even if singing the calls comes naturally to you, you may want to speak an occasional word to get the dancers' attention for a tricky spot in the dance. (For the sake of variety I use a combination of styles, going from speaking to mainly-one-note to harmonizing. Some dances feel right to me in one of those styles over the others.)

Note that in calling a singing square you don't have to stick to the melody throughout; indeed, your delivery can be more effective if you vary your technique as described above.

Tone Production and Projection

Take a full breath before each line of the call. This will give you what singers call "breath support"; it will sound better, be more physically satisfying, and put less strain on your voice. Be sure to breathe from your diaphragm: The belly, more than the rib cage, should move in and out as you inhale and exhale. You should feel a buzzing sensation in your "mask" (your nose and sinuses) when you produce a tone; the buzz will move upward and forward as the pitch rises. Even when you speak a word instead of singing or chanting it, the sound will be in a low, middle, or high part of your range and you should feel the buzz.

If this is completely new to you, or if you have trouble understanding it, you may well benefit from a few voice lessons. Ask your friends who sing to recommend a voice teacher; be sure to let your friends and any prospective teacher know what you hope to accomplish. A grand operatic technique may get in the way of your delivery; a teacher who specializes in light opera and musical theater is likely to be a good fit.

Diction

Another important quality that needs to be cultivated is diction, also known as enunciation. Except for an intentional elision here and there (such as the dropped "g" in "pattin' on the ground"), an effective caller pronounces every letter in every word, giving special attention to consonants. Just as with the practice of calling in rhythm, you may think this sounds stilted. But diction is like stage makeup: It needs to be exaggerated in order to seem natural at a distance. Without makeup, an actor's face would look almost like a blank tan or brown circle to the people in the last row. Similarly, with less than perfect diction, your words will sound slurred to the dancers in the back of the hall. They'll enjoy dancing more if they can instantly tell one call from another. Again, recording yourself will give you an idea of how you're doing (for this purpose it may be useful to record from the back of the hall to pick up what the dancers are hearing over the sound system).

Emphasis

It's more fun to listen or dance to a caller who varies the pitch and volume of the words than one who calls in a monotone. Some of the variety in your delivery will come naturally if you let your love of the dance, and your excitement at sharing it, show in your voice. But there is one function of vocal variety that is important enough to cultivate deliberately: emphasizing the key words of the call.

Some of the words in a call are more essential than others. The key words are the ones that the dancers have learned to react to – the "code words" that have a special square dance meaning, over and above their meaning in everyday English. Others may be "helping words"; they may clarify things for the dancers or reassure them that they're in the right place or going the right way. Or they may be patter, added to fill out the meter of a line, give color or humor to the call, or both.

Common sense dictates that the key words be the easiest to hear, the helping words next, and the patter kept in the background. For example, in the call

> Circle to the right, go the other way back
> Same old train on the eastbound track

the key words are "circle" and "right," which should be emphasized above the rest of the call. "The other way back" can be thought of as helping words (since they can reassure dancers that they heard the command correctly) and can well get some secondary emphasis. (If the line were "The other way back, you circle right," the situation would be reversed: The first words would be key and "circle right" would be helping words.) The second line is pure patter and should be kept subordinate.

You can emphasize a key word or phrase in one of two ways: by raising your voice in pitch or by raising it in volume. (In reading aloud or public speaking, you can draw attention to a passage by lowering your voice as well, but this is impractical at a dance due to the music and the noise of the crowd.) Normally you will probably find yourself doing a little of both at once: raising both the pitch and the volume of your voice slightly. When you consciously decide to stress a key word more than usual, it's good to raise pitch sometimes and volume at other times, for variety's sake. Here, as in every aspect of calling, it helps to get the opinion of trusted friends and to listen to recordings of yourself.

Microphone Technique

The microphone is an amazing instrument, and a godsend to those with small voices; but large or small, it must be used correctly. You need to let the mic do the work: Trust it, don't shout into it. But not all the work: Don't whisper or mumble and expect the mic to fix your calls before they get to the dancers' ears. You need to find a middle ground, projecting your voice as if you were talking without a mic to someone 10 to 20 feet away.

The best distance between the mic and your mouth varies slightly, depending on the type of mic and your style of delivery, but it's usually most effective for the mic to be an inch or two from your mouth. Amplified sound drops off quickly as your distance from the mic increases. But holding the mic too close has its own problems: Directional mics, which are otherwise the best type for callers, display something called "proximity effect": They overemphasize the low frequencies or bass notes when held closer than an inch. This makes the caller's voice sound muddy and can obscure the words of the call and even the walkthrough.

Note that the "hotter" the mic – that is, the more sensitive that particular mic is and the higher the "gain" or "trim" control on the amplifier is set – the greater the danger of feedback (the well-known howl or squeal caused by the mic

Chapter 7: Voice Technique 85

"hearing" the sound from a loudspeaker and amplifying it again and again). If you keep the mic within an inch or two of your mouth and avoid getting in front of the speakers, you should be able to get enough sound from a normally projected voice.

Most caller mics are directional; you need to talk into the end of such a mic, not above and across it. A common occurrence is for the caller to hand the mic at announcement time to the club president, who holds it vertically – perhaps even down at chest level – and talks over it, so that very little of the sound gets picked up. An inexperienced sound person may try to compensate by raising the volume control, and feedback is nearly inevitable. It's better to take time in advance to find out who will be making announcements and instructing them in proper mic technique if necessary.

To make your voice both pleasant and intelligible, you or the sound operator will probably need to use some equalization ("EQ"). In my experience, most callers, both male and female, in most halls will need to boost the high frequencies and cut back the low ones. Assuming that the EQ knobs point to 12 o'clock when they are set for "flat" response (neither boosting nor cutting), I suggest moving the high control forward to 2 o'clock and the low control back to 10 o'clock for a low voice. For a higher voice, try setting the high knob at 1 o'clock and the low one at 11 o'clock. These are only starting points; you will want to listen and adjust as necessary.

Most sound systems now include a third EQ knob on each channel to control the middle frequencies. A midrange boost on the mic channel can make the caller's voice stand out from the music, but this effect can be overdone. If the midrange is set too high, the upper and lower frequencies can seem to fade away by comparison, making you sound as if you're calling over an old-fashioned telephone. Again, any changes should be made sparingly. (Many microphones sold for vocal use have a midrange boost built in.)

As for volume, obviously you need to be not only heard but understood throughout the hall. But the music is an essential part of traditional dancing and needs to be heard too. The music volume should be high enough that the dancers can appreciate the music and hear the beat, the phrase, and the melody. But it must be low enough that the calls are clear, and that the sum of the music and calls is not painful.

Remember that a sound system, including your mic, is a tool to make your work easier. Your goal should be to develop enough skill at using the mic and the controls that it becomes second nature, that you can stop worrying about whether the dancers can hear you and spend your energy on helping them have fun.

For more about choosing and operating a sound system, see Chapter 8 of *Contra Dance Calling* and Bob Mills's booklet *All Mixed Up*, which is now available free online (see the Resources section).

Care of the Voice

Your voice is your instrument. It is as crucial to your performing as musicians' instruments are to theirs – and unlike fiddlers and pianists, you only get one. It behooves you to take the best care of it you can.

For your general health as well as your voice, it is important to drink lots of water – ideally every day, but especially the one or two days before a dance. I don't recommend "cramming" water – neglecting it for days and then trying to compensate – but it's probably better than nothing.

Never force your voice; in particular, avoid long conversations in noisy places where you can barely hear yourself and so speak louder than normal without realizing it. Unfortunately, this includes dance halls, corridors, and cafeterias at festivals, where some of the best human connections are made. But do be careful, even as you cultivate your friendships.

Get in the habit of warming your voice up before using it. This is essential for singing, but it's helpful even if you'll "only" be speaking your calls. You can use some or all of the following exercises to warm up and also to cool down after performing. The exercises can also be used regularly – anywhere from three times a week to every day – to strengthen your voice.

- Lip rolls – make a "brrrr" sound, like a motorboat or a Bronx cheer without any tongue. You can do this without producing a tone; do it on a monotone; waver between two notes; or do arpeggios (go up and down the notes of a chord, as in "say can you see" in The Star-Spangled Banner).
- Humming – again, you can do this on one note, waver between two, or do arpeggios. By humming on high notes and on low notes, you can get acquainted with what singers call "head voice" and "chest voice."
- Make an "oo" sound. Do low notes and high notes, then try going up the scale.
- Do the same thing with an "ah" sound.
- Try some sighs – "ahhhh" – starting high and ending low. Do some in head voice, some in chest voice, then do big ones that go from head to chest.
- The leaf blower – try (gently) to say "V" and "oooo" at the same time. Waver as you did with lip rolls and humming. This is very soothing, good for cooling down after a warm-up or a performance.

These suggestions are adapted from the work of voice teacher Shelley Kristen; I recommend her *Total Warm-Up* CD or download, which will lead you through these and other exercises (see the Resources section).

One last suggestion: Good posture is essential, not just for enabling proper vocal technique, but for building your confidence as well.

8
Calling Breaks

Contra dancing is currently such a popular and widespread hobby that there are several hundred contra callers in the United States and Canada – possibly more than traditional and neo-traditional square callers combined. Many of these contra callers would love to add squares to their repertoire, but find themselves intimidated by the challenge of dealing with breaks.

A contra dance consists of a single figure that is almost always 32 measures (64 beats or steps) in length and is danced and called the same way each time (there are a very few modern exceptions where two slightly differing figures are done in alternation). In contrast, most squares have a figure of that length, or even longer, which must be changed slightly with each repetition, plus a number of breaks ranging from one (called several times) to three or even five.

What is it about breaks that scares even experienced contra callers? The idea that breaks must be either memorized or ad-libbed. If they are to be memorized, that can nearly double the amount of material a caller must commit to memory. If they are to be ad-libbed, that adds a new item to the list of a caller's required skills.

If you are interested in calling squares but nervous about using breaks confidently and effectively, my advice is to start as simply as possible. Either memorize one or two easy breaks, or start to improvise by playing with a limited number of basic movements – or both. Remember that learning breaks, like learning anything, is a process. You won't be as polished at first as you will later, but the only way to get better is with experience – that is, by getting out there and doing.

Break History

In areas where squares survived as a community recreation (rather than a hobby), most callers used one standard break in all their squares. It was almost always a grand right and left, usually with the same or nearly the same trimmings each time. For instance, in some areas an allemande left preceded the grand right and left, while in others the dancers simply gave right hand to their partners. In much of the Northeast and in eastern Canada, a grand right and left (or in Canada, "grand chain") was and is all the way around, starting and ending in home position. The next call is often a partner swing and/or a promenade all the way around. In other regions, it was and is common for the grand right and left to end when partners meet across the set; in many areas a promenade home is automatic at this point, whereas in others the caller can specify a do-si-do or swing first.

The "hashed" or "tricky" school of break calling can be traced back to the mid- to late 19th century (see Chapter 22 for examples). I suspect that ever since then, there have been callers who enjoyed the feeling of competition with the dancers and invested the extra time and effort to master ad-libbing their breaks. Ralph

Page made this practice famous in the 1940s and 1950s; Ted Sannella and his disciples carried on the tradition. By the 1970s in the Boston area, it was accepted that although the figure of each square was composed in advance and called essentially the same way four times, the breaks were always improvised.

In the style that began as traditional western and evolved into modern square dancing, the first "fancy" breaks were variations on the grand right and left. Usually a regular grand right and left was called, then the variation was invoked when partners met across from home. Some of the breaks are so old that their origins are unknown; these include the turn back, the elbow swing, and the double elbow. (Descriptions of many of these are included under "Grand Right and Left" in Chapter 15.) Lloyd Shaw started the modern trend, perhaps inadvertently, by writing Allemande Thar around 1938. It was simply a grand right and left interrupted by a special kind of star (later named a "thar star") in which the gents moved backward while the ladies moved forward. Ray Smith wrote Allemande O (grand right and left interrupted by do paso) in 1947, clearly inspired by Allemande Thar. In 1948 Jack Hoheisal combined the two as Allemande Left and Away You Go (the interruption consisted of a do paso followed by a thar star), and the floodgates were opened: Many more breaks were written in imitation of the first three until there was a sizable list, which quickly became known as the Allemande Alphabet. Each one used "leading patter": The last letter or word of the first call line rhymed with the directional command in the second line, warning dancers of what was coming.

In the 1950s callers started "hashing" the breaks as never before, combining small pieces of several existing breaks into new sequences. Some of those pieces resulted in partner changes, requiring the caller to follow them with other fragments in order to reunite partners. An entire patter call might be constructed entirely of partial breaks, with nothing that would traditionally be termed a figure. Some of the new blends were given titles and published; others were ad-libbed and perhaps never called again in that exact order. Most of the early modern breaks are forgotten, but some, such as Allemande Thar, have survived in both the modern and neo-traditional scenes.

Break Theory

Traditionally, the break is directed to all the dancers at once; it's a breather between repetitions of the figure.

A break should

- be simpler than the figure, except possibly in conjunction with a very simple figure called to sophisticated dancers.
- use different movements and patterns (such as stars) than the figure.
- not result in a permanent change of partners (although there are a few breaks, particularly popular in the Southwest during the boom years, that consist of four partner changes in succession).

Opinion is split on whether movements should flow smoothly or it is permissible for the caller to call any move at any time, as in the game-like dance known as the *Merry-Go-Round* (see Chapter 22). Even in that dance, most callers are careful to alternate right-hand and left-hand turns, though they may call for two or more consecutive swings with different people.

Types of Break

The introduction should always be simpler than the figure (or else, as Ralph Page said, it's not an introduction). It often begins with "Honor your partner, honor your corner" during the A.1 section of the first playing of the tune. (Some callers prefer to let the band play the entire A.1 before starting the call, to give the dancers more of a feel for the music. This is easy enough to do, as the introduction is usually improvised and does not need to take up all 64 beats of a standard tune.)

An introduction can be made up of smoothly flowing basic movements, or can be mildly tricky (circle right instead of left, or swing various unexpected people, returning to partner). That kind of trickiness can be useful to the caller: It can help build rapport with the dancers (if done with good humor and not overdone), and it can serve as a quick check of the acoustics and the dancers' reaction time. With this knowledge gained, the caller is able to modify word placement and other aspects of delivery, or to alter the subsequent breaks or even the figure (not to mention the rest of the program) to suit the dancers' ability.

If finding the corner on the fly will be important in the figure, be sure to have the dancers do something with their corner during the introduction. (Neglecting to do this has been one of my most frequent mistakes over the years.)

The middle break is optional. It can be called after each time through the figure, or only after the first two times, depending on the length and complexity of both the figure and the break. It can be identical to the introduction, or slightly more complex.

If the figure involves a partner change, be careful not to disorient the dancers during the middle break. For example, if you call a grand right and left, be sure the dancers know to end with their current, not their original, partner. If the dancers have had trouble with other material or you know they are inexperienced, it is safer to avoid middle breaks that separate them from their partners.

The ending can be identical to the middle break, or nearly so. Some endings are simply generic breaks with "Honor your partner, there you stand" or similar words added at the end. But callers will often change the movements in the B.2 music to one of these:

- A series of honors to partner and corner, and sometimes the opposite and the right-hand lady (next-door neighbor)
- All forward and back twice (the second time presumably with a yell)
- Promenade "right off the floor" (if this is the last in a group of squares with the same partner)

Some callers have become well-known for frequently prolonging the ending of a square beyond a single time through the tune, particularly if the energy level is high among the dancers and the band. One prominent example was Ted Sannella, who may have gotten the idea from Ralph Page. Such extended endings are always improvised to some extent, although the caller may simply be combining several memorized "modules."

Teaching and Walkthroughs

Should the break be walked through? In my opinion, normally, no.

If the dancers are new to squares (or to dancing in general), I prefer to avoid using grand right and left in the first one or two squares, and to improvise breaks that include only circles, stars, forward and back, do-si-do, swing (or hand/arm turn if they haven't learned to swing), and promenade. I warn the dancers that I will be using sequences they haven't walked through, but I reassure them that the sequences will consist entirely of movements they know and that they will be quite capable of following any sequence I give them.

If I am going to use grand right and left with a group of new dancers, I prefer to introduce it in a big circle (such as *Lucky Seven*), as it's easier to find the next person when the dancer's track doesn't curve as sharply as it does in a square. Once they know the move, I may use it in squares, probably with a quick walkthrough to let them get used to the sharper curve. Of course, it helps to tell the dancers in advance that the person they start with is the person they will end with, whether on the opposite side of the set or in their home position.

With experienced square dancers, I like to improvise breaks that use the basic movements they already know, rather than use a tricky pre-planned break that requires a walkthrough. There are two exceptions: I may use a set break (such as Allemande Thar) with an extremely simple main figure, and I may use relatively complex breaks at a workshop in the middle of a dance camp or festival. If I have taught a set break at a daytime workshop, I may call it with little or no teaching (or even warning) that evening if I'm sure of the dancers' ability. But I seldom pair a break and figure that will both require teaching in detail.

Some contra callers, when they present a square, choose a fancy break and teach it in addition to the figure. They may do this as a way of making their one allowed square dance last longer than three minutes, or they may be afraid of boring their dancers with easy breaks. In both cases I think it backfires: Contra dancers have an overall impression of squares (beyond the absolute easiest ones) as taking too long to teach relative to the time spent dancing. My advice to contra callers: When you present squares at open dances, concentrate on figures; save the breaks for workshops.

Learning to Call Breaks

If you are new to squares, I suggest that you memorize a handful of breaks – perhaps as few as one or two, probably not more than half a dozen at the outset.

The introduction is usually simpler than the midpoint and closing breaks, and the same introduction may be used with many different dances. Other breaks can be used interchangeably; each one can serve as both the middle break and the closing break in a given dance.

Just as with figures, it is better to know a few breaks well than to try to learn too many too soon. Don't immediately try to memorize all the breaks that are printed in this or any other book. Of course, breaks are different from figures (and contra dances) in that they don't have to be memorized and called the same way each time. But if you decide to try ad-libbing, make a short list of building blocks that you can choose from when you get to each part of the tune.

For instance, if you are at the end of B.1 and the dancers have just promenaded home, you can choose one of these for B.2:

- Balance and swing partner
- Four ladies chain over and back
- Allemande left corner, swing partner
- All forward and back twice (particularly good at the end of a square)

Working with planned breaks

Go through your source material and look for breaks that appeal to you. Your sources can include books, syllabi, magazines, websites, and notes you have taken at other callers' dances. When you've found a few breaks you like, you can begin sorting them into categories: easy, moderate, tricky; good for introductions, middle breaks, or endings.

Improvising breaks (particularly with phrased squares)

Get to know common combinations of moves, and how long each one takes. Learn to sense how much time is left in the current round of the tune, and call a combination that's the right length to get you to the end of the tune (or more than one combination if a lot of time is left).

Try to maintain smooth flow (unless you're being deliberately tricky – which you should do sparingly if at all). Follow counterclockwise moves (such as allemande left) with clockwise moves (such as do-si-do, swing, or allemande right). Avoid a right shoulder do-si-do with corner followed by another one with partner. (Note that in regions where do-si-do corner then partner was traditional, one or the other do-si-do was understood to be left shoulder.)

If you choose to ad-lib or "hash" a break, I suggest ending it with a familiar sequence such as "allemande left, grand right and left, promenade." For several decades this has been the standard sequence following a totally hashed figure in modern square dancing; it lets the dancers relax a little after having to concentrate.

The promenade is unusual among movements, in that it has a prescribed ending point – the dancers' home position – but its timing varies depending on where in the set it begins. If the dancers are at home when you call "Swing your corner and promenade," it will take them 16 beats or more after the swing, as the promenade will be a little more than once around. But if they are across from home – say they have met their partner in a grand right and left – a promenade will take only 8 beats. (See "Writing Your Own" in Chapter 14 for a discussion of how promenade length affects singing-call choreography and word metering.)

If you ad-lib your breaks as a matter of course, you will develop the ability to "see ahead" – to know at what point in the music the promenade will end. You can then plan your other calls around it; for instance, you can insert a do-si-do before an 8-beat promenade. If you are past the point of no return – if you have already called the promenade and now see that it will end with 8 beats of the tune still to go – you can call "All eight to the middle and back" as the dancers are finishing the promenade. (If the next figure begins with a forward and back, it will be better to find another way to end the break.)

On the other hand, you may realize with a sinking feeling that, with only 8 beats left in the tune, you have just called a promenade with the dancers starting at home – which will take 16 beats. This means that the promenade will "slop over" from one chorus to the next; the second half of the promenade will take up the first 8 beats of the new chorus. Most callers develop the necessary skill to avoid this gaffe early in their career, but lapses of mind are always possible even with long experience. There are two ways to recover from such a lapse, assuming you desire to stay in sync with the 64-beat tune; both require acute presence of mind, honed by experience. One is to improvise another 56 beats of break following the 8 beats that complete the promenade; the other is to compress the next figure into 56 beats by omitting moves, substituting shorter moves, or allowing fewer beats for some moves.

Pairing Breaks with Figures

Many callers have asked me for advice in deciding which break to use with a given figure. Following are some general principles:

- Avoid duplication. If the figure is based on stars, avoid them in the break; likewise with chains. One break, formerly popular in the Southwest, alternates "all circle left" with "corner swing" four times; use it with a "keeper" figure, not one with a partner change.
- Avoid immediate repetition. If the figure begins with heads or sides promenading, don't call a promenade at the end of the opener or middle break. With such a figure, if you use a promenade in the break, put it in B.1; then for B.2 use something like "forward and back" twice or "allemande left (or do-si-do) corner, swing partner." Similarly, if the figure starts with some dancers going forward and back, avoid that movement at the end of a preceding break.
- Keep the break simpler than the figure in most of the squares you call. If you have a favorite tricky break, pair it with the simplest figure you know – one that barely needs a walkthrough – or save it for a workshop.

Chapter 8: Calling Breaks 93

Rarely is a break identified with a particular figure, except in the case of some classic singing calls whose breaks are as traditional as their figures. But many singing calls have no specific break, and others whose creators devised breaks for them have come down to us without those breaks.

Sample Breaks

Chapter 23 contains call charts for a few breaks, showing one possible wording. Below are some more breaks in outline form, for you to call in your own words. (Remember that you can take pieces of these or any breaks and combine them in new ways.) A wealth of additional breaks can be found in Hinds 1997 and Sannella 2005 (see the Resources section).

Introductions:
A.1   Bow to partner, bow to corner
A.2   Circle left once around
B.1   Balance & swing partner
B.2   Promenade

A.1   Bow to partner, bow to corner
A.2   Circle left halfway, circle right halfway
B.1   Allemande left corner, swing partner
B.2   Promenade

Multipurpose breaks:
A.1   Circle left halfway, circle right halfway
A.2   Allemande left corner, do-si-do partner
B.1   Gents star left, swing partner
B.2   Promenade

A.1   Circle left once around
A.2   Circle right once around (or all forward & back twice)
B.1   Allemande left corner, grand right & left
B.2   Do-si-do partner, promenade home

A.1   Four ladies (or gents) promenade inside, swing partner
A.2   Circle left halfway, circle right halfway
B.1   Allemande left corner, grand right & left
B.2   Do-si-do partner, promenade home

A.1   Allemande left corner, allemande right partner, allemande left corner
A.2   Grand right & left all the way (takes 20–24 beats)
B.1   Continue grand right & left, swing partner at home
B.2   Promenade once around

A.1	Allemande left corner, start a grand right & left
A.2	Continue the grand right & left all the way
B.1	Balance (or do-si-do) & swing partner
B.2	Promenade once around

A.1	All forward & back, circle right halfway
A.2	Allemande left corner, allemande right partner, allemande left corner
B.1	Grand right & left halfway, do-si-do partner at home
B.2	Promenade once around

A.1	Allemande left corner, grand right & left halfway
A.2	Around your own & the other way home, right hand pull by partner at home
B.1	Allemande left corner, swing partner
B.2	Promenade

A.1	Allemande left corner, grand right & left halfway
A.2	Do-si-do partner, allemande left corner
B.1	Grand right & left halfway (to home), swing partner
B.2	Promenade

A.1	Circle left once around
A.2	Do-si-do corner, turn partner left twice around
B.1	Four ladies chain over & back
B.2	Keep partner, promenade

A.1	Sides face partner, grand square
A.2	Reverse
B.1	Four ladies chain over & back
B.2	Keep partner, promenade

A.1	Circle left halfway, heads right & left through
A.2	Circle left halfway, sides right & left through (all are across from home)
B.1	Allemande left corner, grand right & left halfway (to home)
B.2	Balance & swing partner (or do-si-do & swing if you see they won't get home in time to balance on the downbeat)

A.1	Four ladies chain, all promenade halfway (gents are now across from home, ladies are home)
A.2	Four ladies chain, all promenade halfway (all are now home with partner)
B.1	Allemande left corner, allemande right partner, allemande left corner
B.2	Balance & swing partner

Chapter 8: Calling Breaks

A.1 Circle left halfway, circle right halfway
 (or heads forward & back, sides forward & back)
A.2 Head ladies chain, side ladies chain,
 head ladies chain back, side ladies chain back
 (chains overlap; one pair of ladies is crossing
 while the others courtesy turn)
B.1 Do-si-do corner, turn partner left & hold on
 (Timing is fudged; side ladies will be turning on first 4 beats of B.1)
B.2 Promenade

Recommended for an ending, but can be a middle break:
A.1 Allemande left corner, allemande right partner, allemande left corner
A.2 Grand right & left, do-si-do partner
B.1 Swing partner, promenade home
B.2 All forward & back twice

9
Patter

When members of the non-dancing public think about square dancing, the aspect that is usually uppermost in their mind is patter – the strings of words that the caller chants rhythmically, often in rhyming couplets. When the guests arrive at a corporate, civic, or family barn dance, I can often overhear their first reaction to the idea of square dancing. They will turn to one another and intone "Swing your partner round and round" or "Do-si-do and a hi-de-ho" or some such line. If they square danced in school, they have probably forgotten all the movements and figures; if their only exposure to it was through movies or television, they probably never noticed the specifics of the dance. But the patter stays with them.

Long before square dance calling was born, "patter" meant fast talking. (Merriam-Webster says the verb dates from the 14th century and the noun from 1758.) The word comes from the Latin *paternoster* ("Our Father") and originally referred to some priests' practice of reciting prayers at breakneck speed. Later its meaning was extended to include fast singing, as in "Largo al factotum" in Rossini's *Barber of Seville* and "A modern major-general" in Gilbert and Sullivan's *Pirates of Penzance*. Patter can also refer to the rapid speech of a magician, salesman, or carnival barker who uses it to distract his audience from his true intentions. Used by the dance caller, however, patter is perfectly innocent; there is hardly any misdirection involved.

There are sporadic references to extraneous words or nonsense syllables in 19th-century descriptions of calling. (See Chapter 2 for the possibility of African-American influence on calling.) By the early 20th century, judging from several printed collections, patter had become an integral part of the square dance in the West and Southwest. The recordings of string bands with calls issued commercially in the 1920s and '30s included a fair amount of patter. As with records, so with radio: Beth Tolman and Ralph Page (1937) credited radio barn dance programs for the popularity of the "rhyming caller" in New England. When square dancing became a national craze after World War II, the caller's patter was one of many colorful features that attracted the public. As modern square dancing developed, the use of patter diminished as the lack of walkthroughs made it more crucial for the dancers to hear the key command words. Patter is still alive and well, however, at surviving and revived traditional dances.

The caller's patter serves several purposes at once. On the most obvious level, it adds color to the proceedings and raises the energy level of the dance. It enables the caller to blend with the music, hopefully in a way that adds to it rather than detracting. But it is also a tool that can be used to the dancers' benefit. At the very least, it adds rhythm to the caller's voice, which can help the dancers find the beat and the phrase and reassure them that they are dancing correctly. By filling in the space between directive calls, it can help the caller adhere to correct and comfortable timing of the dancers' movements. In addition, by careful choice of words, a caller can telegraph the next movement to the dancers, and by careful placement of words within the phrase, the caller can give the dancers as much or as little warning as seems necessary (see also Chapter 6).

Note that patter does not necessarily follow the rules of scansion associated with classic poetry. In order to scan, lines of poetry must have the same number of syllables, and often (but not always) the accents fall at the same points within each line, as in Rudyard Kipling's poem "If" (which is often quoted as an example of a quality needed by callers):

> If you can keep your head when all about you
> Are losing theirs and blaming it on you…

In a square dance call, the steady rhythm of the downbeat is of prime importance. One, two, three, or four syllables may be fitted to each beat:

> Allemande left with your left hand (3, 2, 2, 1)
> A right to your honey and a right and left grand (3, 4, 3, 1,
>   not counting the initial "A")

Calling shares this property with rap, and also with instrumental music. Consider any fiddle tune: On each beat of a 2/4 tune, there may be a quarter note, two eighth notes, four sixteenth notes, or any combination that adds up to a quarter note (such as one eighth note and two sixteenth notes). You can probably guess that you don't have to match your syllables to the fiddler's note lengths.

There is a wealth of patter for the interested caller to choose from. Patter can be deliberately evocative of a culture, such as farming, ranching, logging, or railroading. Or it can be more generic, referring to aspects of the dance (two by two, big foot/little foot). A clever caller can make up rhymes about the dancers who are present that night.

Sexist Patter

In former times, a lot of patter was notably sexist. Sexism took two forms: first, referring repeatedly to the women as "girls" or "that pretty little thing," and second, addressing most calls to the men and leaving the women to discern whether they had to do the same thing, the opposite thing, or nothing at all. The first is a matter of taste, but the second can cause problems on the dance floor. To take a simple real-life example, I was once at a large dance, aimed at first-timers, where the caller said "Head couples go forward and back… now do-si-do the opposite lady." Not illogically, one of the head ladies in my set tried to do-si-do her opposite lady, who was busy do-si-doing her opposite gent as the caller intended. This occurred during the walkthrough, so there was time to sort things out, but it illustrated the drawbacks of this type of call.

In fairness, it should be noted that the custom of addressing calls to the men may have originated at least partially out of courtesy. In the 19th century, when the art of calling first developed, it was considered the height of presumption for a man to speak directly to a woman he had not been formally introduced to. Addressing the lady's male escort was the proper course, even to ask her for a dance. But of course this courtesy was rooted in sexism – the belief that, in some sense, a woman was a man's property and could not speak for herself. At any rate, this calling custom has clearly outlived any usefulness it may have had.

In my experience, both kinds of sexism have diminished over the past few decades, particularly in revival groups. There should be no trouble avoiding sexist patter, even in traditional dances and in singing calls from the 1950s: The English language has a wealth of rhyming words, and it should be easy to replace a problematic word or couplet. To take just one example, Ed Gilmore's recording of his dance *Back Away* includes the couplet "Forward eight and back to the world, forward again and face your girl." This is easily altered to "Forward eight and back to place, forward again and partners face" without changing the meaning.

Patter can get edgy, even when the caller gives both sexes equal time. Ralph Page used to call things like "Swing that old man standing there, Run your fingers through his hair" and "Give him a kiss, gals, if you dare." Such calls may be all right at a week-long camp, particularly toward the end when people know one another and the caller has had a chance to take the pulse of the group. They are generally not a good idea at a normal public dance; many dance series have had problems with individuals who didn't respect other dancers' personal boundaries (see Chapter 3). As with every aspect of calling, good judgment is needed.

Note that the use or nonuse of sexist patter of any kind is a separate issue from the use of gendered or gender-neutral terms for the two roles in a dancing couple. The latter is discussed in Chapter 13.

Leading and Trailing Patter

Frank Kaltman, an influential caller and record producer of the boom era, divided patter into two types, which he named "leading patter" and "trailing patter." Trailing patter, as the name implies, comes after a command. It serves primarily to add color, but it can also help a caller keep track of timing or help the dancers keep in time with the beat. Some trailing patter can serve as post-command assurance, letting dancers know they're doing the right thing.

> Swing your partner round and round
> Any old way but upside down
>
> Promenade your partners all
> Take a little walk around the hall

Leading patter, on the other hand, performs a specific and often important function. In a couplet of leading patter, the first line ends with a rhyming word that gives the dancers a clue to the next movement, even before they hear the actual command in the second line.

> Forward eight and back with you
> Forward again and pass through

> Forward eight and back like that
> Right to your opposite, box the gnat

Some completely pre-written breaks have an accepted set of words that incorporates leading patter.

> Allemande left and Allemande Thar
> Go right and left and form a star

> Allemande left in the Alamo Style
> Right to your partner, balance awhile

And several traditional sequences have a leading-patter couplet that is widely, if not exclusively, used.

> Corn in the crib and wheat in the sack
> Meet your own and turn right back

> Rope your cow and brand your calf
> Meet your own with a once and a half

Naturally, there are many sets of words for any given figure or break. In some cases it seems as if no two callers' wordings are alike. In other cases there is a wording that works so well that it has been adopted by nearly everyone who calls that figure. It is up to you to decide whether a set of words works for you. This decision will come partly as a matter of taste, partly from experience calling the figure and watching the dancers' response.

Patter vs. Prompting and Singing

Many of the 1950-era books state that there are three calling styles: prompt, patter, and singing. Certainly the singing call can be distinguished from any other type by its adherence to the melody, and often some of the lyrics, of a popular song. But I think the line between prompting and patter is fuzzier than is often believed. Even the line between prompting and singing may be misplaced. It depends partly on what is meant by prompting. If the word is used to mean a spare style of calling in which only the actual commands are given, the trichotomy makes sense. But I submit that the crucial aspect of prompting is the one suggested by the name itself: the delivering of the command before the dancers are expected to follow it. In the style of dancing dealt with in most of this book, this means giving the command just ahead of the musical phrase.

If this idea is carried to its logical conclusion, prompting ceases to be a calling style and becomes a desirable trait that can be applied to any style. We might say that the caller-of-few-words is using a "command call" rather than a "prompt call." If so, we can say that a command call can be prompted, as in a contra or a New England–style square, or not prompted, that is, delivered starting on the first beat of the musical phrase, as is done by some callers of southern sets. Likewise, a patter call can be prompted ahead of the phrase or called with the phrase, depending on where the caller places the commands. And even a singing call can be prompted or not, again depending on the placement of the key words.

If you are new to calling squares, I encourage you to find your own style, one that makes you comfortable. If you are not trying to preserve or recreate a particular regional tradition, I think you and your dancers will be happiest if you choose to incorporate prompts in most of your figures and breaks. (See Chapter 6 for tips on using prompts and patter in the same dance.) Conversely, even if you don't plan to use a lot of patter or think of yourself as a patter caller, remember that calls always sound better when delivered in rhythm with the music (as discussed in Chapter 7).

A word of caution: In any kind of patter, leading or trailing, it is important to avoid using "code words" – words that the dancers have learned to associate with a basic movement – unless you mean for them to execute that movement. In some cases, it can even be hazardous to speak the name of a basic twice in a row if you only want the dancers to do it once. The example in Chapter 6 of prompting a promenade, and then repeating the word, is an exception: The dancers are beginning a long movement that is normally done only once, and the second "promenade" merely reassures them that they are doing the right thing. But if they hear a call such as "do-si-do" twice in quick succession, they may look around for a second person to do it with.

Remember that not every call line needs to be part of a rhyming couplet. In the 1950s it was fashionable for callers to write, learn, and use patter calls consisting of uninterrupted couplets. This style can be heard to advantage in field recordings of Bruce Johnson (see the Resources section). Its greatest drawback is the difficulty of repeatedly placing the command words in exactly the right place to cue the dancers, although it can be done. And although the constant stream of couplets can impress the dancers at first, it can get stale if continued for an entire number. Then, too, it can be hard to adapt such a call if the dancers are late or lost. If you use one or two couplets during the "meat" of the figure and another during the promenade, the dancers will get the impression that you were rhyming throughout, just as the audience sees only what the magician wants them to see.

6/8 Patter

In most regions of the United States, the tunes used for square dancing are exclusively in simple meters such as 2/4 and 4/4: Each beat can be divided into two. However, in the northeastern United States and eastern Canada, dance musicians also play tunes in 6/8 time. This is a compound meter: There are two beats to a measure, and each beat is divided into three.

Calling to 6/8 music presents a special challenge to the patter caller. In simple meter, there is room for up to four syllables to be spoken during each beat:

<u>Cir</u>cle to the <u>right</u>, go the <u>oth</u>er way <u>around</u> (4, 3, 4, 1)

In 6/8 time, there is room for only three:

<u>Cir</u>cle <u>right</u>, the <u>oth</u>er way <u>round</u> (2, 2, 3, 1)

Note that patter which works with 6/8 can also be used with 2/4, but the converse is not necessarily true. Patter designed for 2/4 must be scrutinized, and where there are four syllables on a beat, the wording must be modified to fit 6/8.

Callers in Ontario, where it is traditional to play 6/8 music for the first change in a set of squares, have developed 6/8 patter to a fine art:

<u>All</u> the way <u>there</u> and <u>all</u> the way <u>back</u>
And <u>all</u> the way <u>back</u> on the <u>same</u> **old** <u>track</u>

Throw <u>up</u> your <u>chin</u>, throw <u>out</u> your <u>chest</u>
<u>Bust</u> the <u>but</u>tons right <u>off</u> your <u>vest</u>
<u>Kick</u> the <u>plaster</u> <u>off</u> the <u>wall</u>
And <u>promenade</u> with the <u>belle</u> of the <u>ball</u>

Also from Ontario comes the practice of including syllables for their sound rather than their sense:

<u>Down</u> the <u>center</u>, <u>cast</u> off <u>four</u>
And you <u>doodely-do</u> as you <u>did</u> be<u>fore</u>
(Fred Townsend)

<u>Step</u> right <u>up</u> ag'in, <u>over</u> ag'in-ag'in
<u>Once</u> and-a <u>once</u> and-a <u>once</u> and ag'in-ag'in
(Fred Townsend)

<u>Alle</u>mande a <u>shoe</u>pac, <u>all</u> around the <u>hay</u>stack
<u>I</u> chaw, <u>you</u> chaw, <u>all</u> chaw <u>hay</u>
(George Wade)

* * *

Here are some of my favorite snippets of patter. A few are original with me, but most were "researched" from other callers; I have given credit where a rhyme is associated with a particular caller. Some couplets that go well with a specific dance are included in the call charts in Part Three. (See page 181 for a key to the typography.)

<u>Bow</u> to your <u>partner</u>, <u>corners</u> <u>all</u>
<u>Cir</u>cle to the <u>left</u>, go <u>round</u> the <u>hall</u>

Honor your partner, corners salute
All join hands, go lickety scoot
(from Ontario; works well with 6/8 music; works only if dancers know this means circle left)

Circle to the right, go the other way back
Same old train on the eastbound track

(from a circle)
Hi, ho, here we go
Partner left, do paso
(Earl Johnston; can be modified for use with a back-to-back do-si-do)

Go into the middle and you come back out
(wait four beats)
Do it again with a great big shout
(Ted Sannella)

You join your hands and forward all
(wait four beats)
Once again for the good of the hall
(from Ontario; works well with 6/8 music)

Swing your partner round and round
Any old way but upside down

You swing yours and I'll swing mine
And promenade, go down the line

Swing 'em once, swing 'em twice
And promenade, now ain't that nice

The big ones swing and the little ones too
And promenade, that's what you do
(Lawrence Loy; also a favorite of Ted Sannella)

Promenade, around you go
Not too fast, not too slow
(Carson Robison)

Promenade with your boots and spurs
Lift your feet, don't step on hers
(Carson Robison)

Promenade around the square
All the way back home from there

Promenade, go round the town
Keep that calico off the ground
(i.e. don't let the lady's dress drag on the dusty floor)

Promenade, go down the line
All the way around and you keep in time
(Near-rhymes, which I find irritating in country songs,
don't bother me here because they go by so fast.)

Promenade, go round the ring
While the roosters crow and the bluebirds sing

Promenade, go round the ring
While the geese fly over, goin' high on the wing
(Marvin Shilling)

Promenade, go all the way around
With a big foot, a little foot, a-pattin' on the ground
(Ed Gilmore)

Promenade, go round the hall
With the short one, fat one, skinny one, tall
(Ed Gilmore)

Promenade, go round the room
Two by two like a bride and groom

Promenade, go side by side
All the way around like a groom and bride

Promenade, go round the set
Two by two, we're not through yet
(good for the end of the middle break)

Promenade, go round the barn
One more time won't do no harm
(L.D. Keller)
(good just before the last figure)

Promenade and head for home
I sure do hope you've got your own
(for the last figure of a change-partner dance)

The ace is high, the deuce is low
Promenade eight and home you go

Cross the ceiling, down the wall
All the way around and-a home you-all

Eggs in the basket, chicken in the pan
Everybody dance just as pretty as you can
(L.D. Keller)
(non-directive; use as trailing patter after prompting a promenade)

Visiting-couple figures:

> Lead right on to the next old two
> Circle up four is what you do
> (Bill Ohse)

> (when the active couple has visited all the others)
> Now you're home and now you're straight
> All join hands and circle up eight
> (Bill Ohse)

Do-si-do (hand-turn type):

> (The first line is always something like
> Break that ring with a do-si-do
> or
> Your partner left for a do-si-do;
> the last line is
> One more change and on you go
> or
> One more change and home you go)

> Do-si high and a do-si low
> And a do-si 'round on a heel and toe
> (L.D. Keller)

> Do-si lady and a do-si gent
> Do-si lady and on we went
> Do-si lady and a do-si-do
> One more change and on you go
> (Lloyd Shaw)

> Do-si lady and a do-si gent
> I came here with the best intent
> Now my windshield's smashed and my fender's bent
> (Charley Thomas)

> Do-si lady and a do-si gent
> Here comes the landlord, pay the rent
> (Rickey Holden)

> Don't ask me, 'cause I don't know
> I never could figure out a do-si-do
> (Rickey Holden)

> Do-si-do like shuckin' corn
> The old cow bawled when the calf was born
> The hens they cackle and the roosters crow
> Another little doe and home you go
> (Jim Williamson)

Allemande left:

> Allemande left with your left hand
> Right to your partner, right and left grand

> Allemande left like the hinge on a gate
> Right to your partner, right and left eight

> Allemande left your corners all
> Grand right and left, go round the hall
> (works well with 6/8 music)

During a grand right and left:

> Hand over hand and heel over heel
> The longer you dance, well, the better you feel

> Hand over foot and-a heel o-ver toe
> The more you dance, well, the less I know
> (Gib Gilbert)

> Grand old right and left you go
> Walk on your heel and on your toe
> (Ed Gilmore)

> Halfway round that ring you fly
> Hand over hand and don't ask why

> Right and left with the folks you know
> It's hello Mary! Hiya Joe!
> (Lee Helsel)

> – Here's Sal and here comes Sue
> And here's the gal that came with you

> Here's Sal, where's Kate?
> I don't know, just promenade eight
> (Joe Lewis)

Grand right and left variations:

> Meet your honey and kiss her on the chin
> And you turn right back and do it a-g'in
> (Carl Journell)
> (The direction is not to kiss again but to reverse direction in a grand right and left. This may be a softened version of "kick her on the shin.")

> There's a train a-comin' down the track
> Meet your partner, turn right back
> Steamboat comin' round the bend
> Meet your honey, turn back again

> Rope your yearling, brand your calf
> Meet your own with a once and a half
>
> Meet your honey right down by the pike
> With a once and a half and treat 'em all alike

Ending a square:

> Bow to your partner, corners all
> [Wave to your opposite across the hall]
> And that's the end of this old call
>
> Bow to your partner, corners too
> [Wave to the folks across from you]
> That's the end, that's it, we're through

If you plan to call another change immediately:

> Bow to your partner, corners all
> And hold your sets for one more call

If this was the last change of a set:

> Promenade right off the floor
> That's all there is, there ain't no more

After calling a final promenade:

> You know where, I don't care
> Take 'em out and give 'em air
>
> You know where, I don't care
> Take your honey to an easy chair

If this was the last dance of the evening:

> Now hang up the fiddle and you clear the floor
> Now blow out the lights and you lock the door
> And you promenade, boys, and you take 'em a-**way**
> We'll dance again some other day
> (Butch Nelson)

10
Programming

Programming is the craft of choosing dances to fill an event, whether it be an hour-long workshop, an entire evening, or a dance camp or festival. It is an art in itself, and the skills it demands of the caller are slightly different from those involved in teaching a dance or delivering the calls.

Let me begin with two general principles that apply to square dance programming.

"Square Dancing" Isn't All Squares

Few evenings billed as "square dances" were, or are, made up entirely of four-couple squares. At surviving traditional dances, usually the local favorite style of couple dance was and is interspersed, often in a sequence of three dances for individual couples (perhaps a foxtrot, polka, and waltz) followed by a set of three squares. At revival dances, squares may be alternated with contras and/or international folk and novelty dances. And a typical party for people with no dance experience may consist primarily of circles, "line" (modern solo) dances, and whole-set longways like the *Virginia Reel,* with few if any true squares included.

Similarly, in modern square dancing, the most popular format is a "tip" of two squares followed by two round dances. Opinion in the modern square dance world is split between those who favor rounds and those who would rather simply rest between squares. I believe the aversion to rounds stems from the change they have undergone since the 1940s. Before that time, a typical country-style couple dance consisted of a few walking and/or sliding steps followed by a few measures of a turning waltz or polka; the whole was repeated several times. During the square dance revival of the 1950s, many new rounds were composed and the average round dance became increasingly complex. Steps from ballroom and eventually Latin dance were introduced, and it became necessary to "cue" each dance throughout. Round dancing has become a skill set that requires a dedicated set of lessons in addition to (or, for some people, instead of) square dance lessons. I suspect the majority of modern square dancers would accept rounds if they were simpler, more like the couple dances that were apparently done in the old West.

The most obvious reason for avoiding an all-square event is the rigid structure of squares. A square, almost by definition, is a dance for four couples. Some squares can be adapted for more or fewer couples, but the square formation is less accommodating than other shapes. Anyone who has been to more than a few square dance events is familiar with the caller's incessant cry for "one more couple over here." If one or two couples are sitting out for their own sufficient reasons, the pressure to join a set can lead to bad feelings all around. (See Chapter 5 for tips on using squares with uneven numbers of couples.)

109

For this reason, I highly recommend learning a variety of dances in various formations, particularly circles and whole-set longways, in addition to squares. (Circles include southern sets and progressive circles as well as mixers. Other alternatives to squares that provide variety without excluding as many people include four-by-fours, which can be run with an odd number of lines if necessary, and of course contras if the group knows their structure.) The feeling of creating something together – caller, musicians, and dancers – is more important than the exact structure of the dance or the degree of conformance to past norms. The more different dance types you know, the more flexibility you will have in shaping your events and keeping your dancers happy.

There is a wealth of material available, in print and on recordings, for the caller who wishes to learn dances other than squares and contras. Some of the best is published by the artists and producers listed under "Especially for Children and First-Timers" in the Resources section.

The Hardest Stuff Goes in the Middle

No matter how easy or difficult the program, no matter how high or low the energy level, this is a nearly inviolable principle of dance programming: The hardest stuff goes in the middle. It is crucial to start and end an event with material you are sure the dancers can do with little or no teaching. This is equally true of a party for first-timers and an evening advertised as challenging.

At the beginning of an event, you seldom have an exact idea of the group's ability. Even at a weekly or monthly series, the percentage of first-time dancers tends to fluctuate from one event to the next. That being so, even the experienced dancers will appreciate some fairly easy dances that will help the newcomers get up to speed.

Toward the end of the evening, both physical and mental fatigue are almost certain to set in. Dancers may wish to ignore their physical symptoms in order to enjoy a last high-energy dance or two, but the chances are that their brains will refuse to remain receptive to extended teaching.

Therefore... the hardest stuff goes in the middle.

This is fairly obvious if you are programming a whole evening for newcomers or a mixed-level group, but it is also true of events billed as "challenging" or "for experienced dancers only," and even of workshops that are only 60 or 90 minutes long. Experienced dancers will appreciate a well-shaped evening just as much as less seasoned dancers will. And at a workshop, with time for only a handful of dances, you need to capture and hold people's interest with your first selection. Better make it one that you know you can "sell" to just about any group.

Remember that "the hardest" is a relative term. "Easy," "middling," and "hard" mean different things to different people. If you are coming to square dance calling from the "urban" or "aerobic" contra dance scene, you may have a certain idea of what constitutes an easy or difficult dance. It is dangerous to assume that one scale of difficulty is appropriate for all occasions. The danger is even greater if you are calling to newer dancers and have little experience with such situations. It is important to read the crowd constantly, looking for signs of confusion.

There is one important exception to the "hardest in the middle" rule. If an appreciable number of first-timers enter the hall around intermission time (as commonly happens at dances in summer resort areas), common sense dictates that the first dance or two after the break should be easy enough for newcomers to grasp. This assumes that they are dispersed among the regulars; in my experience this will get them acclimated more effectively than a quick tutorial during the break. If the number of new folks is very high (say one-third of the crowd), I will start from scratch with a big circle after the break. I find that the experienced dancers realize what I am up to and appreciate my forestalling later trouble.

Caller William Watson advocates a "sawtooth" approach to programming an evening, alternating slightly harder and easier dances so that anyone overly challenged or bored by one dance will find the next one more to their liking. But like most callers, he gradually increases the overall level of difficulty until the halfway point, then decreases it.

What Do People Want?

Just about the first thing you need to do in planning a program – be it for a one-nighter, a single evening of a series, a strategy for an entire series, or all or part of a weekend or week-long camp or festival – is ascertain what the guests want to get out of their experience.

Do they want to learn to dance?
Do they want to make new friends and/or find a romantic partner?
Do they want a relaxing place to socialize with current and new friends?
Do they want aerobic exercise?
More than one of the above?

The ideal program will look different in each case, although there will be some similarities.

The more the organizers and the attenders want dancing to be the vehicle of a social occasion, as opposed to a hobby pursued for its own sake, the easier the dances can be – in fact, the easier they should be.

Assessing a Single Dance

In the 1950s, as modern square dancing developed, some callers measured their success by their ability to "stop the floor"; that is, to call sequences that were so hard to follow that most of the squares broke down. Ed Gilmore, a top-tier California caller of the time, was famous for saying "Any idiot can stop the floor; it takes a caller to keep them dancing." In traditional calling, we don't *try* to stop the floor, but our choice of material may occasionally have that unintended effect.

The first step in programming is to assess the difficulty of each figure or break in your repertoire. (If you are new to squares or to country dancing in general, I highly recommend that you do this when you add each routine to your repertoire

– although obviously you will be unable at that time to consider a specific audience for it.) Difficulty depends on several factors:

- The number of basic movements it uses
- The number and nature of transitions between moves
- How far from home it takes the dancers
- Whether it is likely to disorient them
- Whether the timing is loose or tight
- Perhaps most important, the dancers' specific experience

An important factor that makes material easy or hard is how familiar dancers are with it. Have they learned those basics? Have they seen these transitions? *Queen's Quadrille* (see Chapter 18) is entry-level easy for contra dancers, but I wouldn't use it at a non-dancer party: It's based on two basic movements (right and left through, ladies chain) that both require a fair amount of teaching and, moreover, are easily confused with each other.

With all these factors considered, you can label the dance "easy" (suitable for beginning or once-a-year dancers), "intermediate" (appropriate at a series where most dancers have some experience), or "advanced" (to be used only at workshop sessions). If your dances are on index cards, you can put the degree of difficulty in an upper corner; once you have more than a few of each type, it will pay to create lists for the various levels. A borderline dance can be put on two lists, or on one list with a notation such as "L.I." for "low intermediate."

Note that if you are presenting squares to contra dancers who may have little or no experience with them, any given square will be more challenging than a contra that uses the same movements and transitions. See "Contra Dancers" in Chapter 13 for more about this phenomenon.

Guest Set

When you are asked to call a single square or two at a multi-caller event, you have one shot at success. There will be no chance to redeem yourself if you flop. Therefore it is best to underestimate the crowd's ability slightly and/or use a dance you *know* you can put across because you have done so before. Resist the urge to show off with a complicated dance; as Ralph Page said, the dancers are not the least bit interested in how much you know. If your repertoire is big enough, I suggest choosing two or three dances for each one you are expected to call. It is wise in any situation to have more material prepared than you'll end up using.

Arrive at the event early enough to spend some time reading the room, either while dancing or from the sidelines. Take note of other callers' choice of material, their teaching, their delivery of the calls, their mic technique, the acoustics of the hall, whether the sound operator (if any) is on top of any problems. Watch the dancers' reaction to all this; try to gauge their average level of experience and ability and the percentage of newcomers. This will help you decide which of your alternatives to go with. Arriving early will also let you see whether any of your chosen numbers get used by others; this will narrow down your choices for you.

Full Evening

Particularly when you are a newer caller, it is wise to pick multiple dances for each time slot in an evening, just as you would for a guest set. Sizing up the crowd is an ongoing process; you should be ready to raise or lower the level of difficulty on the fly. Admittedly, it can be hard to please both new and experienced dancers; a time-tested approach is to choose dances that are "easy but different." Variety can be fun in itself, and it can be used as a substitute for difficulty in keeping experienced dancers interested at an event with many newcomers. If the evening is part of a series that you attend regularly, it should be fairly easy to pick material that is seldom if ever used there. As always, you should call dances you know and like, but learn to like as much as you can.

There are two sets of factors to take into account when programming an evening. The first set comprises the various characteristics of the dances in your repertoire.

- Shape of the set: contra, square, big circle, progressive circle, four-by-four, scatter mixer, whole-set longways, trio (dance for three people), couple dance (choreographed or freestyle)
- Dominant pattern: circles, stars, lines, grids, quadrille movements across the set or diagonally
- Music: tempo, mood, meter (2/4, 4/4, 6/8), ethnicity (New England, southern, Scottish, Irish, Cape Breton, Québécois, fusion)
- Level of difficulty: number and type of movements, transitions, timing, forgiveness
- Mixers and partner-change squares vs. lots of partner interaction
- Energy level: depends partly on tempo, partly on whether everyone moves constantly

The second set of factors is external to the dances, involving the people and the venue.

- Age: Watch out for very young or old folks. People in their teens and early twenties will probably have energy to burn.
- Experience level: This can be hard to predict beforehand, even at a series.
- Attitude: Are they there to learn? Have fun? Get drunk?
- Gender balance: Will you need to modify terminology? Use trio dances? Not use certain dances with a strong flavor of courtship/flirtation, such as *Rose and the Thorn* (Chapter 22)?
- Couple/single status: If they're all singles, I use lots of mixers including scatters, also dances with lots of interaction with non-partners. If they're all couples, I use few if any mixers and provide lots of partner interaction.
- Hall size and shape: In many halls, some formations work better than others.
- Floor condition: A sticky or slippery floor can affect my idea of a suitable tempo. The same floor's condition can change from event to event.

- Crowding or lack of it: There are lots of good dances for either situation. (If the hall is vastly bigger than needed, shorten it by placing a row of chairs across the floor to create a new "foot.")
- Number of people: Try to have as low a percentage as possible sitting out; certain formations (notably progressive circles) require a minimum number to "work."
- Weather: Extremes of heat, cold, and humidity should suggest raising or lowering the energy level.
- Religious beliefs: Some conservative groups that wouldn't want to host a rock dance will accept square dancing if there's not much physical contact (elbow swings are good).

Pacing

It is almost impossible to maintain a constant level of difficulty or energy throughout an evening. Fortunately, it isn't really desirable.

The level of difficulty should rise during the first half of the evening, then fall during the second half. (Remember: The hardest stuff goes in the middle, when people are warmed up physically and mentally and have not yet begun to fade.) Taken as a whole, the level of energy or excitement should rise during the first half and again during the second half (it will drop during intermission). But it is possible to "play" with the dancers by raising or lowering the energy at various points within each half.

Interpersonal energy is a significant component of the overall energy at a dance. Toward the beginning of an evening, many of the crowd are likely to be assessing their fellow dancers and deciding which ones to approach as potential partners. To that end, I always include at least one circle mixer in the first half, and the squares and other group dances in that half feature lots of interaction with corners, neighbors, and other non-partners. Later in the evening, when people are likely to have settled on one or a few favored companions, I program dances that let them spend plenty of time with their partner.

Keep It Simple

Starting in the late 1960s, when I began calling complete evenings fairly frequently, I have kept a log of my programs. Each page contains a list of the dances I presented and the tunes used; in many cases there are notes on how well the dances were received, particularly if a dance was new to me or harder than usual for that group. When I look back over the first few years of these logs, I am struck by how complicated the dances were, on average, for any given situation. This was true both at non-dancer events and at series with a high percentage of regulars. One reason is that I was not yet skilled at discerning the right level of material for a group; I was in love with squares of all kinds and I was sure I could make my dancers love them too. (This was not a case of convincing contra dancers to accept squares; in fact, it was the other way around as I tried to "sell" the few

Chapter 10: Programming

contras I taught to casual square dancers who knew nothing of contras.) Another reason for my heavy use of middling-to-advanced material is that I didn't know many really easy dances. It is much harder to write a distinctive, interesting easy dance than a more advanced one; many of my current easy favorites were not in general circulation or had yet to be written.

All this is to say that unless you are leading a workshop specifically aimed at, and advertised to, experienced dancers who want an extra challenge, it pays to keep your material relatively simple. I firmly believe that most people who take up, or might be persuaded to take up, folk dancing of any kind as a recreation will get more satisfaction out of learning simple dances thoroughly and doing them well than from trying to learn every dance that's invented and never quite mastering any of them. There will always be a small percentage of dancers who are ready and eager to go on to tougher things; there will just as surely be a cadre of callers who are willing and able to cater to them. You may be one of those callers, now or in the future – but keep in mind that the majority of dancers you encounter will be happier with a less challenging diet.

The "dance camp romance" is a well-known phenomenon: The romantic setting of a camp, perhaps with an open-air dance pavilion, can make the partner of the moment look like the love of one's life. It can work that way with dance figures too: Learning an intricate routine in a set of seasoned dancers may convince you that it will be a hit with your home crowd. Be aware of the danger, and analyze a figure ruthlessly before deciding whether it's a good fit for your group.

In general, beware of using a dance just because you're fond of it. True, you should like everything you use, but each dance is appropriate in some cases and not others. The dancers' ability, and the other variables in the lists above, should always be uppermost in your mind.

Remember, too, that repetition is not always bad. This goes for repeating a move or a combination of moves within an evening, and for repeating a dance that you called to the same group at a recent meeting. People enjoy dancing familiar material.

11
Teaching

Teaching dancers is an essential skill for every caller in the traditional-revival scene. There may still be some "survival" dances in isolated areas – that is, places where square dancing never died out – at which all the dancers know the caller's entire repertoire and no real teaching is necessary. But even there, an astute caller will scan the room for unfamiliar faces and will throw in a more or less detailed walkthrough as needed. And most callers, throughout their careers, will face a variety of events where the proportion of novices may range from 10 or 20 percent all the way up to 100 percent.

You might think that because the caller's most distinctive function is to tell the dancers what to do, using a specialized language, it follows that a good caller is automatically a good teacher. Not so! In reality, calling and teaching involve two different sets of skills. Mastering the technical and human-relations aspects of calling, important as they are, does not make one an effective teacher.

The worst square dance teachers I have encountered went to one of two extremes: They explained things either too carefully or not at all.

I once attended an annual dance for the families of a small town. Some of the guests were regular square or contra dancers, but many danced only once a year. Toward the end of the evening, the caller did a fairly good job of teaching a *Virginia Reel,* though he could have used fewer words and been at least as effective while taking less time. The *Virginia Reel* is one of my favorite dances to end an evening with, and I thought he was going to sign off with it. But the hall's curfew had not yet come and some dancers wanted more, so he lined them up again and launched into a contra dance. Teaching a single contra dance at an event is not an efficient use of time, because it takes a while for people to understand the progression. Most of the dancers were unfamiliar with the contra set-up, and the caller had chosen a dance with several moves he had not yet used. The result was that he had to explain each move several times, struggling to find different ways to say the same thing, and the group spent much more time walking through the routine than dancing it to music. It was also too late in the evening to introduce a complicated dance. After the energy of the *Virginia Reel,* it was anticlimactic.

At the other extreme, I have vivid memories of two callers who failed their teaching duties completely. In both cases their *modus operandi* was to recite the calls in order, as they would deliver them to music, and expect this to serve as a walkthrough. One caller used the sequence "allemande left your corner, grand right and left, and promenade" at a non-dancer event without ever mentioning that the person you meet with the right hand, both at home and halfway around, is your partner. He had not used either allemande left or grand right and left that evening, let alone together. Most experts agree that their combination is disorienting and the two movements should be introduced separately.

The other caller was running a public dance in a city park with a mixture of first-timers and long-time dancers. He used a singing square with a partner change that went "swing your corner, allemande left [new corner], come back and promenade [the one you swung]." The man to my left kept trying to go into a grand right and left; when I tried to correct him, he said "Don't tell me what to do; I was square dancing before you were born." He insisted that allemande left is always followed by grand right and left. Others in our set were trying to allemande left the same person they had swung. The caller, an inadequately trained park employee, was no help at all; his only course was to repeat the calls. Obviously he had never truly assimilated their meaning or thought about how to explain them.

These errors may seem poles apart, but they represent two sides of the same coin. In each of these cases, the caller failed to analyze the routine in advance, take note of the movements and transitions that were likely to cause trouble, and think of multiple ways to describe them. These callers also may have exercised poor judgment by choosing dances that were too complex for the dancers' ability at that point in the evening. It may be that the same dance would have been a success if taught more effectively or if preceded by other dances that presented some of the concepts.

By telling you what not to do, I've just broken one of my own cardinal rules: Always be positive. But I wanted to emphasize the danger inherent in focusing solely on delivering the calls, to the neglect of the teaching function.

Admittedly there is a delicate balance between overteaching and underteaching. Dick Leger, who coached hundreds of calling students, said that good teachers are hard to find. My hope is that with the advice in this book and some serious practice, you will be one of them.

Your first teaching efforts will almost certainly be less than ideal; you may find it hard to get your dancers through any but the easiest material. Don't be discouraged! As you develop your teaching skills, you will probably find that you can bring a group up to speed on any given dance in less time than when you first tried calling. You will also, as I did, cultivate a sense of what is appropriate for a given group.

One of your most crucial tasks is to get and maintain people's confidence. This is equally true at a party for non-dancers, an ongoing series, or an out-and-out teaching session. You can do this by being confident yourself – or faking confidence at first if you don't feel it. Your choice of words, your tone of voice, even your posture should say that you know what you're doing. More than that, it should say that your job is to keep everyone comfortable throughout the learning process, and that you are determined not to let them down.

The following tips will serve you well in any teaching situation, from non-dancer parties to advanced workshops:

- Keep people winning – give them bite-sized doses of learning to let them succeed most of the time.
- Keep them moving – say as little as possible before you tell them to do something.
- Be positive – tell them what they're doing right. Tell them what to do, rather than what not to do. Not only is it easier on their egos, it's less confusing.

Choosing Material

As seen in the reminiscences above, the teaching process begins before the dancers arrive at the hall. The first step for the caller is to choose material that this group of dancers will be able to learn quickly and easily.

- What do these dancers know in the way of square dance fundamentals?
- Are they acquainted with the square formation and the most basic of the basic movements?
- Can they handle the transition from an allemande left to a grand right and left?
- Are they comfortable with a change of partners, even a temporary one?

It may be that you don't know the capabilities of a group before you meet them. If the event is a corporate, civic, or private party, you can safely assume that most of the guests will have no square dance experience; if there are a few seasoned dancers, it's likely that they will understand your position and will be good sports, joining in the dance and helping the first-timers. You will almost certainly need to start from scratch, getting everyone up in a big circle and running through half a dozen of the easiest moves (see "A Teaching Order" below). A progressive circle, with couple facing couple around the rim, works well for the second dance. By the time they form squares, the guests should know most of the moves you plan to use; you only need to give the names of the positions – corner, opposite, heads, sides. Squares can be alternated with circle mixers and whole-set longways. (See "First-Timers" in Chapter 13 for more on non-dancer events, including several methods of forming squares.)

If, on the other hand, you are asked to call at an evening that is part of a series, one that hopes to attract experienced dancers but is always open to newcomers, you may not know the proportion of one to the other until you have put them through their paces. You can sometimes get an idea of the mix before the dance begins (assuming a fair number of dancers arrive early) by asking the organizers, who may know many attenders by sight, or by engaging some folks in conversation and overhearing the conversations of others.

If a majority of those present are new to square dancing, you can begin much as you would at a party aimed at non-dancers, though if one of the stated goals of the series is to attain a moderate level of competence, you may want to introduce a few more movements than you would at a one-nighter. You will probably want to explain how to "give weight." You will definitely want to teach the swing, as it is such a part of traditional square dancing and so many figures include it. But here, as always, you should avoid giving people too much to digest at one time.

A rule that applies across the board, to first-timers and ongoing groups: Give the dancers only what they need *now*. For example, if you have just moved them from a big circle into squares, let them do the moves they already know a few times before telling them about heads and sides. Similarly, if the first dance in square formation uses only "heads and sides" movements, there is no need to mention couple numbers. Each dance as you go through the evening should introduce only one substantial movement that is new to the dancers. If you have a favorite dance that you really want to share with a group, work up to it with dances that each present one element of your favorite.

It is important to watch the dancers constantly for signs of overload or frustration. If they have trouble with a dance, don't abandon it partway through unless all is chaos. But do present a more straightforward one immediately afterward. (Remember, keep them winning.)

One often overlooked point is that prior experience with other dance forms does not necessarily provide an advantage in learning to square dance. Most forms of dance that are popular in North America today – ballroom dance, international folk dance, country line dance – are based primarily on footwork. Squares and contras, although they involve very little footwork beyond walking, require dancers to change their facing direction and the person they are working with frequently – sometimes as often as every two or three seconds. Some people find this skill set easier to acquire than footwork, but some find it harder.

When to Teach

Should there be a dedicated teaching session before a dance party, or should all of your teaching be done during the event, before each dance number? There are reasoned arguments for both approaches. Some dance organizers schedule half an hour of instruction before the dance officially starts, believing that this will attract would-be dancers who might feel intimidated by the thought of jumping unprepared into an unfamiliar skill set. Such a session has been quite successful in some dance communities. It needs to be heavily advertised, as first-timers often deliberately arrive late to ensure that the party will be in progress. At least a few regular dancers need to support the effort by attending the session and making themselves available to fill in sets and (if the teacher desires) serve as role models.

If I am asked to teach at a preliminary session (sometimes a series has a regular local instructor), I never try to present all the movements I plan to use that night. I feel that doing so would overload the newcomers' brains and thus be a waste of time, worse than no session at all. Instead, I concentrate on getting them comfortable with the formations – circle, square, and longways – and focus on posture, the dance-walk, and "giving weight." I make sure to spend time on the three moves – hand turn, balance, and swing – where giving weight is a major factor. But I explain that giving weight is important even in such "basic basics" as circling and going forward and back.

Most dance series manage without a separate session, relying on the walkthroughs for instruction as needed. If anything, this approach requires even more cooperation from the regular dancers, as all of them – not just a few early birds – will be affected by the newcomers' lack of skill and orientation. However, a caller who is a good teacher can bring the beginners up to speed while keeping the regulars entertained.

At parties for non-dancers, I ask the sponsors not to advertise a separate time for teaching. The material I use at such events is so easy, and my walkthroughs are so streamlined, that there is little need for more instruction. Also, if the guests arrive at various times, I feel it is not my place to disapprove. This is their party, not mine. Fortunately, most of the entry-level dances I use do not depend for their success on guests having participated in earlier ones. But there are nearly always people in the last set who *were* in earlier sets; they will help smooth the way for those who are getting up for the first time.

The Walkthrough

One of the features of traditional square dancing that its adherents count as an asset is that, in most cases, dance events are open to all comers. Even where instruction is made available, in a pre-dance lesson or a short series of lessons, newcomers are generally not required to take it. Therefore, it is the custom to walk the dancers through most figures before the music starts.

Make sure you have the dancers' attention before you attempt to teach. After they have formed sets, they may want to socialize a bit with their neighbors. I generally give them a minute or two to do this, having learned that it saves time in the long run. The surest way to get them listening is to tell them to do something physical. In a modern contra dance this is likely to be "Take hands four from the top." With squares you can say "Join hands all the way around and spread out as far as you can"; this also serves the purpose of distributing the sets evenly through the dancing space. "Now take two steps forward, drop hands and stay close to your partner" will produce comfortably sized squares and ensure a buffer zone between sets.

The words you choose in a walkthrough will depend on the dancers' knowledge base. If they know a basic movement well, it will probably suffice to speak the name of the move. If you are presenting a move to them for the first time, obviously you will have to describe it. If it is a complex move, such as right and left through, you will need to break it down into components, walking through a piece at a time. It often helps to tell the dancers, before they move, where they will be at the end of a basic or a part of one.

It is important to vary the tone of your voice when you walk dancers through a move or a figure. They need to know that when you describe something in a conversational tone, they should stand still and listen. Only when you speak in a voice of command should they move. This doesn't mean that you should bark your words like a drill sergeant, but your tone should make it clear that you want the dancers to act. It should be very clear at what moment they should join hands, drop hands, turn to face a different person, and the like. You can often forestall errors by catching the dancers with your voice before they have a chance to go the wrong way. The most successful walkthroughs occur when everyone to whom the call applies is following it at the same time.

A helpful criterion for choosing dances, which I got from the great caller and caller-mentor Don Armstrong, is that the walkthrough should be shorter than the dance. A square dance figure is generally called four times, requiring a total of roughly two to three minutes. If the dancers can't be walked through such a figure in less than three minutes, it is probably an inappropriate figure to use with that group at that time. It may be that later in the program the same group can learn it within that time frame.

Ed Durlacher, who called to thousands of dancers at a time in New York City parks, had an even stricter rule: He programmed only dances he knew he could teach in two minutes. This assumed a floor of dancers who knew do-si-do (back to back), swing, promenade, and the names of the positions (such as partner, corner, heads, sides, and couple numbers).

Note that when I refer to walking through a figure, I normally mean once for the head couples and possibly once for the sides. It may not be necessary to give the sides a walkthrough if the figure is fairly straightforward. Note also that because it takes longer to teach a move such as right and left through than to dance it, the dancers must already know the other moves in the figure if the walkthrough is to take less time than the dance. (This goes back to "Choosing Material": introduce only one new element at a time.)

However, you should not be afraid to repeat a walkthrough when you feel a need. Repetition is often a key to learning. It may feel like an alien concept to you if your experience is mainly in contra groups with 80 percent regulars at every event, where second walkthroughs are frowned on. Remember that in a contra the routine is done 15 or more times, so that anyone who failed to get through the walkthrough comfortably has a good chance of succeeding during the dance. In a square, there are normally only three or four chances to get it right; you can improve the odds of success by making sure most of the dancers understand the moves and transitions before the music starts.

(With squares and contras alike, but more crucially with squares, repetition from one dance number to another is as important as repetition within a number. It can pay big dividends if, after teaching and calling a move like right and left through, you use it in another routine the same night.)

I don't advocate teaching square dance breaks in most situations, but if you choose to walk through a break, again the teaching should take less time than the dancing. In most squares there are at least three opportunities to insert a break; if the same break is used each time, the total time spent dancing it will be about a minute and a half. As breaks are addressed to the entire set, not just one or two couples, it should be easy to keep the teaching time below this amount.

If you are teaching primarily basic movements rather than complete routines, and your dancers are responding well, dancing in phrase and exhibiting quick reaction time, you should be able to call an occasional square without a walk-through. This requires building a solid level of trust between you and the dancers: They need to trust that you will give them the directions they need at just the right time and not try to trick them, and you need to trust that they will listen to your calls and be serious about the business of having fun. There is no shame if you decide that a group can't handle this, but there is an extra measure of joy and satisfaction in this kind of "working without a net."

If you are handed the task of "teaching a group to square dance," perhaps in a school setting, you may need to spend more time teaching a dance than calling it to music *the first time you present it*. But in a case like this, which assumes a course of instruction that spans many days, you should definitely use each dance more than once, preferably several times. This will enable you to polish it and eventually let the dancers relax and enjoy doing dances they know well.

The warm walkthrough

If you want to cut to a bare minimum the time spent in teaching moves and sequences without music, you can use a technique sometimes termed a "warm walkthrough." To do this, start the music playing at less than full volume, then give your instructions to the dancers as if there were no music, letting them take as many steps as needed to complete each movement. Repeat short sequences such as "allemande left your corner, do-si-do your partner," getting closer to normal timing of call and movement with each repetition.

This teaching method is common in modern square dancing, where callers typically employ recorded music and pay little attention to the musical phrase. But it can be a useful stepping stone on the way to traditional timing and phrasing. It may be harder to implement with live music because even with the sound system off, the music may be too loud for the dancers to disregard the phrases.

A somewhat similar method, used by teachers of English country dance and international folk dance, is to instruct a single phrase of a dance, perhaps walk it through without music, then have the group do only that part to the music. The first part is repeated if necessary to smooth out the dancers' technique, then the same procedure is followed with the second part, and so on. This requires patient musicians or an elaborate playback setup with recorded music. (You could simply use the pause control if you were sure you wanted to play each part only once.)

Demonstrations

It has long been said that a picture is worth a thousand words, and demonstrating a move seems like an ideal way of getting people to understand what they need to do. But demonstrations have their drawbacks.

I make very little use of demonstrations at most of my calling events. The reasons vary: At a party for non-dancers, of course there is usually no one who knows the moves and can help me show them. If my wife Beth is with me, we may demonstrate a do-si-do while the dancers are in a big circle; but most of the time I work alone and have to rely on verbal descriptions.

At an event where the dancers vary in experience and ability, I am reluctant to single out one set for a demonstration. It is all too easy to pick a set where one or more people are unsure of themselves and will not take kindly to being put on display. If I feel that a demonstration is the best teaching method for the moment, I am careful to choose dancers who I am reasonably sure will succeed – folks I know personally or people who have been listening and moving well so far.

There are also the questions of how well the demonstration set can be seen and how well I can be heard. Using a wireless microphone has solved the latter issue; having one I can wear on my head leaves both hands free so I can join the set myself. As for visibility, the larger the group and the hall, the harder it can be to see the demo set – but the more helpful it may be to use one. Demonstrating is much more easily done from the center of a large circle than after the dancers have formed squares, but sometimes the need for a demonstration arises during the walkthrough of a square. At the huge square dance in Washington, DC, held in a very reverberant hall, the organizers have found that using a demonstration set and having everyone else squat down or move back is the only practical way to get the attention of 200 or more people, most of whom have little or no experience.

Music in a Teaching Context

The most important thing I can say about music as it applies to teaching is that the dancers should be allowed to move to music almost immediately in any teaching session. During the session, they should not be required to go without music for more than a short time.

I have copies of several books and pamphlets published in the 1940s and '50s on the subject of teaching square dance. Some of them advocate starting the first session of a class by walking the dancers repeatedly through "allemande left and grand right and left" without music. One author suggests drilling this and other combinations for 45 minutes before any music is used! I strenuously disagree with this approach, and I feel sure that every working caller nowadays would join me. Not only is it more enjoyable to move with music than without, but newcomers are far more likely to assimilate the nuances of good dance technique when they can hear the beat and be inspired by the melody and harmony to lift their chests and their souls.

My practice with learners is always to start the music within about 60 seconds of getting them in a circle. From then on, I normally introduce only one complex move or two simple ones in each new dance so that walkthroughs are kept to a minimum. As mentioned in Chapter 10, the hardest material should go in the middle of the time slot, whether that be a one-hour class or a three-hour dance. By the middle of a session, I have earned enough trust that I can afford to take the time to teach something tricky but fun.

In practical terms, if you are running a session devoted primarily to teaching, you will need either recorded music or one or more musicians who are willing to stand by while you explain and walk through movements (although, as noted above, such periods should be brief) and to stop, restart, and repeat passages as needed. If the group and the room are relatively small, you may be able to get by with a solo fiddler; many fiddlers are good at emphasizing the rhythm, particularly the crucial upbeat, as well as the melody. A pianist who understands the folk idiom can also be effective; with a piano you can get both melody and chords.

The first thing required of the dancers, beyond listening quietly to your instructions, is that they hear the basic beat of the music and take one step on each downbeat. But don't worry if a few people can't find the beat, as long as they can get from Point A to Point B along with the group. This is not to say that stepping to the beat is unimportant or that the whole group should be allowed to ignore the beat, just that perfection is not required. In my experience, most people learn fairly quickly to recognize and respond to the beat. And the rare person who continues to have trouble is usually not a hindrance to the group.

Regarding tempo, there are two schools of thought when working with new dancers – or, for that matter, any dancers who appear unable to keep up with normal tempo and timing. You can reduce the tempo, slowing the music as much as you think necessary. Or you can allow extra time for the dancers to complete their movements. Which route to follow depends on your goals: If you are presenting tightly phrased dances and you want the dancers to stick with the phrase, naturally you will drop the tempo rather than let the phrasing slip. If you are teaching dances that are freer in form, such as southern visiting figures, it may be better to keep the tempo up and wait to give the next call until the dancers are nearly done with the last one. I like to use a normal, or close to normal, tempo whenever possible, to maintain the forward momentum of the dance.

A Teaching Order

I have no desire to codify anything about traditional square dancing; a large part of its charm is that it varies from place to place. But the following lists may be helpful to callers with little or no experience in organizing a teaching session. I have used bullets rather than numbers because I don't want these lists to be viewed as the only, or even the best, order of teaching. What works for me may not work for you.

For once-a-year dancers

Here is a list of the terms I use at a typical non-dancer event or "one-night stand," in the order in which I introduce them. You should not feel any obligation to use them all. The list is based on my presenting six or more different dance numbers, but first-time dancers are often satisfied with three or even two. In such a case I open with a big circle, close with the *Virginia Reel* (with or without the "reel"), and possibly teach one other dance, such as a simpler longways or a circle mixer, in between.

- Formation: big circle
  - Naming: partner and corner
  - Circle left, circle right
  - Forward and back
  - Arm (elbow) turns
    (in lieu of hand turns and ballroom swing)
  - Do-si-do
  - Promenade
- Formation: progressive circle (circle contra)
  - Naming: neighbor
  - Star right, star left
  - Pass through
- Formation: square
  - Review: partner and corner
  - Naming: opposite, heads, sides
  - Figure type: heads or sides across set
  - Naming: couple numbers
  - Figure type: visiting-couple
- Review: big circle
  - Figure type: circle mixer
- Formation: longways
  - Naming: head or first couple, head, foot, up, down
  - Figure type: whole-set longways (one couple active)
  - Slide (chassez/sashay)

Additional teaching can be limited to moves that occur in the dances you present, such as two-hand turn, various kinds of arches, visiting-couple figures, cast off, and big circle (grand march) figures. I seldom use grand right and left with first-timers; when I do, it is always in a big circle. I never combine allemande left with grand right and left at a one-nighter. For eager learners, you can choose a move (such as ladies chain) from the "ongoing" list below, but make it the focus of a dance rather than expecting them to remember it later. As mentioned above, no more than one substantial move or two very simple ones should be introduced per dance.

For ongoing learning

With a group that is interested in really learning to dance, I start with the one-nighter list (more or less), but with:

- More emphasis on posture and giving weight
- Hand turns instead of elbow turns
  (and get them used to using either hand with any person)
- Ballroom swing (walk-around and/or buzz step) taught fairly early
  (to enable use of many popular dances without modification)

Chapter 11: Teaching *127*

I may also take time to say a few words of reassurance before we begin. (I do this at one-nighters too, but much more briefly.) I tell the dancers that I will only be giving them directions I know they can follow. I encourage them to keep calm, not to panic and start grabbing and pulling. If they get totally lost, I suggest that they put both hands about chest-high in front of them (as if starting an allemande); that way someone can offer a hand and gently steer them.

I also tell the dancers that if they become aware that they are behind the rest of their set, they should not try to catch up by doing all the moves they missed. Instead, they should look for an obvious hole in the formation – a gap in a line of four, or a person alone when the others are swinging someone – and fill it. Chances are that that's where they belong. I tell them "It's more fun to dance with the 'wrong' people than it is to stand still."

Once the dancers have done the entry-level movements, I will teach the following, in very approximate order:

- Grand right and left
(teach alone, before combining with allemande left)
- Balance
- Visiting-couple progression: one couple lead to the right
(if not done earlier)
- Split/separate
(teach them to listen and not assume how far to travel)
- Star promenade
- Single file promenade
(including turn out from a couple promenade or star promenade)
- Turn alone (U turn back)
- Wheel around / courtesy turn
- Ladies chain
- Half promenade
- Right and left through (I find teaching half promenade first helps)
- Circle to a line
- Grand square
- Weave the ring
- Four ladies chain
- Balance in a wave
- Bend the line
- Box the gnat
- Twirl to swap (California twirl)
- Half sashay and/or rollaway
- Cross trail
- Square through
- Star through
- Complete breaks that appeal to you
(I like Allemande Thar, Alamo Style, Triple Allemande)

How far down this list you go will depend on your assessment of the group's capacity to learn and how much time you will be spending with them. I would certainly not expect most groups to learn every move on the list, even over a course of several lessons. The moves near the bottom of the list should be introduced only if you want to present a dance that includes them.

It is perfectly all right to use a dance containing a movement that is not on the lists above or any other list you may have found or compiled yourself. But I would not expect dancers to remember such a move and be able to do it at a subsequent session without re-teaching it. Many good squares, particularly visiting-couple figures, have a unique move, and many of those moves are a lot of fun to do. But I would hate to see dancers required to know all of them in order to be considered competent. As long as walkthroughs are the custom in our branch of the activity, let's use them to teach unusual moves and thereby minimize the number of things our dancers need to know by heart.

* * *

Other comments on teaching appear under "First-Timers" in Chapter 13 and under each basic movement discussed in Chapter 15.

12

Working with Music

We are in a new Golden Age of square dance music. There is a concerted effort to preserve old tunes and regional styles of playing; musicians who are familiar with the tunes and styles are working hard to pass this knowledge on. In addition, people of all ages are playing dance music because they love it; they are developing new styles, incorporating elements of other musical genres.

Tune Types

Just about every square dance tune (aside from waltz quadrilles and other novelty squares using couple dance music) can be placed in one of three categories: reels in 2/4 time, jigs in 6/8 time, or marches and songs in 4/4 time.

Reels

Whether it is termed a reel, a breakdown, a hoedown, or a hornpipe, the tune in 2/4 meter is the quintessential square dance music. The "2/4" time signature, found at the beginning of each tune's written music, means that there are two beats to a measure and each beat is worth one quarter note. On any given beat the fiddler may play one quarter note, two eighth notes, four sixteenth notes, or any combination totaling one quarter note. Of course the dancers are not aware of the lines between measures that are visible on the sheet music; even so, there is a definite "one-two" pulse throughout the music that would be missed if some measures had a different number of beats.

In Scottish and Irish music a distinction is made between true reels and other 2/4 tunes, but in US and Canadian square dance music any tune in 2/4 is usually termed a reel. "Breakdown" and "hoedown" are names given to 2/4 tunes played in southern mountain style, which are generally less sharply phrased than northern reels. Hornpipes were originally in slower, "swung" or "dotted" time, and in English and Irish music they are still played that way. But in the Scottish and American traditions, hornpipes are almost indistinguishable from well-phrased reels. A few hornpipes, such as Durang's and Fisher's, are often heard even in southern fiddling.

Jigs

Tunes in 6/8 meter are usually termed jigs, though in Missouri they may be referred to as quadrilles (this is a throwback to the 19th-century quadrille, whose first figure was usually in 6/8). Nominally each measure of 6/8 has six beats, each worth an eighth note, just as the name implies. But in square dance use, 6/8 tunes are thought of as having two beats to the measure, just like 2/4. The difference is that in 6/8 each beat contains three rapid sub-pulses, giving the music a unique triple-within-double feeling. A few marches and singing squares are also in 6/8.

Marches and songs

A few march tunes in 4/4 meter are used for square dancing, and if a grand march is included in an evening's program, of course its tunes are quite likely to be marches. In addition, most songs that have been adapted for use as singing squares are in 4/4. As the numbers imply, there are four beats to a 4/4 measure, each worth a quarter note. The distinction between 2/4 and 4/4 time is of little importance to the caller, as for square dance purposes the tempo of the beats is identical in the two meters. The only difference a caller is likely to notice is that the phrases of a 4/4 tune, both melodically and harmonically, are twice as long as in a 2/4 tune. A march or song in 4/4 is also less likely to have passages of short quick eighth or sixteenth notes than a 2/4 tune.

Most 4/4 songs used as singing squares have a smooth, even feel, because each quarter-note beat is divided into two eighth notes of identical length. But a few are in "swing" rhythm, with each beat made up of a dotted (extended) eighth note and a sixteenth note. This uneven division gives such tunes a "bouncy" feel.

Tune Personalities

Every tune is unique in some way. Even though the same tune can feel very different when played by two different bands, each tune has characteristics that give it a distinct personality. The "feel" of various tunes can be sorted into categories in many ways; a broad dichotomy I find useful is "straight-ahead tunes" versus "tunes that tell a story."

"Straight-ahead tunes," to me, are tunes in which the pitch range of the melody and the number of notes in a measure are fairly constant within the "A" part, and also within the "B" part. (In most square dance tunes, one part is pitched higher than the other, although the parts are usually in the same key.) They often give the impression that melody is subdued in favor of rhythm, even if the melody instruments are playing at full volume. One time through the tune leads into the next with no drop in energy. Such tunes often use only two chords and have few chord changes. Examples are Irish reels like Drowsy Maggie and southern breakdowns like Mississippi Sawyer. These tunes work well with dances, such as southern mountain visiting-couple figures, that are not designed to begin and end with the tune. They are also good for a calling style that uses continuous patter a sizable amount of the time.

"Tunes that tell a story" have a distinct beginning, middle, and end. The pitches of their melodies are often more varied, and there is a definite feeling of closure at the end of each time through. Several chords are likely to be used, and chord changes are relatively frequent. Listeners, whether dancing or not, are likely to be more aware of the music when these tunes are used. Examples are East Tennessee Blues and Ragtime Annie. The best kind of dance to pair with such a tune is designed to fit the musical phrases exactly: to coincide with once through the tune (or one and a half times for a longer figure). Callers with a spare prompting style will enjoy working with these tunes; callers who use a lot of patter may find them a challenge, but the result can be pleasing.

Some callers find that one or the other of these tune types suits their personal style, no matter what kind of square they are calling. You will need to find your own preferences as you gain experience.

Keys

The key in which a tune is played is extremely important in a singing square. Even in patter calling to fiddle tunes, the key can affect a caller's delivery for better or worse. Many patter callers instinctively pitch their voice on one note of the chord that is being played; for instance, with a "tonic" or "home" chord, which is made up of the first, third, and fifth notes of the scale, calling on any of those three pitches will produce a pleasing effect. Most callers who harmonize in this way find some keys more comfortable than others; I can call in G at any time, but in A only after my voice has warmed up.

Each key has its own personality, at least to my ear. This may not be true of all music, but it is certainly true of square and contra dance music when the fiddle is the primary melody instrument. Tunes in different keys have different percentages of notes on "open" (unfingered) strings. The more open-string notes in a tune, the brighter the sound.

- For fiddle tunes, G is straightforward and often a bit laid-back; I often ask the band for a tune in G for the first dance of the evening, or for a challenging square when I don't want the music to overpower the calls.
- D is joyous and carefree ("gay" in the old sense of the word). Many of my favorite tunes are in D.
- A is forceful, hard-driving, at times almost harsh, due largely to the amount of time the fiddler plays on open strings; it's a good choice when you think a dance is high-energy or you want to make it so.
- E is extremely bright; it's used primarily in alternation with A in two-key tunes.
- C is a mellower version of D; F is a mellower version of G.
- B flat is more formal, with military echoes, as it's associated more with brass than strings; only skilled fiddlers tend to play in B flat because a high percentage of its notes need to be fingered.
- E flat is darker than B flat. There are E flat tunes meant for show, but I know of no dance tunes in E flat.

Most tunes used for squares are in major keys. Many Irish tunes are in A minor or E minor; they are used frequently for contras but have not been popular for squares. (The traditions that govern square dance music were in place before the North American revival of Irish music in the mid- to late 20th century, which coincided in large part with the contra dance revival.)

Some tunes have an "A" part in one key and a "B" part in another. (They are sometimes known as "cotillions," presumably because 18th-century cotillion music was often written in multiple keys.) In the most common two-key tune type, the "tonic" (the "do" or first note of the scale) of one key is the "dominant" (the "so" or fifth) of the other. Common combinations are D–A, G–D, and A–E. (In some other tunes, one key is the relative minor of the other.) When the key changes to the one I have given first in each combination, it can feel as if the tune is "coming home." Musicians' opinion is divided over which part such a tune should end on. One fiddler of my acquaintance always refused to end a two-key tune with the "B" part if the transition to the "A" part felt like "coming home." This was a source of irritation to callers who, not surprisingly, claimed the right to decide when to end the number. You and your musicians will have to come to an understanding about this.

For non-singing squares, you will want to develop a calling style that either lets you blend with the music or keeps you from fighting it. If you speak your calls without regard to pitch, you can call to music in any key. If you tend to call on one or more musical pitches as described above, make sure you are blending with the chords and not clashing. You may need to enlist the help of a friend to double-check this. (Most people have a range of an octave or more, which is enough to let them call on at least one note of any chord used in any key; but not everyone can consistently find the right note.)

When it comes to singing squares, the caller needs to discuss the key of each song with the musicians (or choose a recording in a comfortable key). Some keys are easier to play in than others, and the band's favored key may or may not be your best key. One or both of you may need to compromise. (See Chapter 20 for a discussion of singing calls, including how to choose a key.)

Intangibles

Certain characteristics are desirable, even essential, in square dance music whether it is live or recorded. If you work with live musicians, you can try to convey to them the points made here, or you can look for musicians who agree on their importance and strive to produce them. In the case of recorded music, all you can do is select tracks that embody the qualities you desire. Fortunately, there are plenty of recordings, old and new, that should match your requirements.

Lift

The quality that separates great dance music from merely good, or worse, is something I call "lift." Like many subtleties in art and life, it is easier to spot it than to define it. You may not have thought about it consciously, with or without a name. But I am sure that if you heard examples of music with and without it, you could identify them quickly.

After pondering the question for many years, I have decided that lift is largely a matter of balance. The rhythm players need to give nearly equal weight to the downbeat and the upbeat. The upbeat needs to be cut fairly short, not held too long. Both rhythm and melody players should give the upbeat a slight extra punch, but not so much that all one can hear is the backbeat, as is true of many square dance recordings of the 1960s. In the case of music played for phrased dances, the first and last downbeats of each 16-count phrase should get a bit of extra emphasis.

The most likely place to hear dance music devoid of lift is from musicians who are new to the genre. They may be able to play with accurate pitch and hold a steady tempo, but perhaps they have not heard fiddle tunes played idiomatically and are reading the notes from a printed page. Their most common error is to hold onto the upbeat too long. If you are helping classically trained musicians discover dance music, it is essential to provide them with recordings of tunes in your preferred style, played in a way that will inspire dancers.

Drive

A distinctive feature of southern mountain dancing, and to a lesser extent traditional western square dancing, is the constant forward impetus that the music gives the dancers. To some extent this is a function of the fast tempos that are customary in those regions, but the amount of "drive" can be raised or lowered by a skilled fiddler who varies the strength of the upbeat compared to the downbeat. I find that the key of the tune also affects the sense of drive. This may have to do with the amount of time the fiddler spends playing on open strings; that is, strings that are not held down by the fingers of the left hand so that the sound "rings" more. Tunes in the key of A, on average, seem to me to have more drive than tunes in G or D – or at least seem more susceptible to a more driving treatment.

Remember that a given tune can be played in more than one regional style. Soldier's Joy, for instance, is known throughout the United States and Canada, as well as England, Scotland, Ireland, and some Scandinavian countries, and is naturally played in slightly differing versions. Even within one region, a tune can be played with more or less lift or drive. It pays a caller to get to know how the local musicians play the tunes in their repertoire.

Live Music

Until around 1940, square dance music meant live music. Recordings of dance tunes, with and without calls, had been produced since the early 1900s, but they were made to entertain people sitting at home. The record players of the time were inadequate, in both fidelity and volume, to provide music at a noisy public dance. Every square dance event featured a live band, ranging from two pieces to eight or ten. Even the few classes that were run at that time had at least a fiddler or pianist, and sometimes both.

Since then, recordings and playback systems have improved greatly, and canned music is now standard for many types of dance, including modern square dance. But dancers and organizers in the traditional and neo-traditional scene have continued to insist on live music. Without it, they feel, a vital part of the equation is missing. The caller may tell the dancers *what* to do, but the music tells them *when* (if the dance is phrased) and *how* (in terms of tempo, style, and energy).

The primary advantages of live music are these:

- Immediacy – the musicians are in the room with the dancers, producing a three-dimensional sound that it would be impractical to duplicate with recordings.
- Spontaneity – the musicians are receiving energy from the dancers and caller, as well as giving it to them. Seasoned musicians will play elaborate arrangements or improvise new ones.
- Flexibility – a live band can make a dance longer or shorter at the caller's on-the-spot request, play a medley, change keys, or play a special sequence of verses and choruses for a favorite singing square.

For the caller, working with live music requires "people skills" and significant time and energy, both before and during dance events. But nearly every caller who has tried it feels that the rewards are well worth the effort.

Musicians are people

The key to working with musicians is communication based on mutual respect. They are not jukeboxes or Victrolas that can crank out perfect music on demand. Neither are they your slaves: Although, as was mentioned in Chapter 2, dance musicians used to be hired or enslaved servants, that dynamic is happily a thing of the past. You are an expert in your field; they are experts in theirs. As lyricist Gilbert once said to composer Sullivan, you must approach one another as master and master.

It helps to remember that you and the band have a common purpose: to give the dancers a good time while having fun yourselves. The more you can find ways of cooperating and avoid working at cross-purposes, the happier you and your dancers will be.

When you are on stage, you can set the tone for your relationship by standing next to the band, rather than in front of them. If you go down to the dance floor to demonstrate a move, you may have to turn your back to the band at times, but if you are generally on good terms with them, this should not be a problem.

If you work regularly with one band, of course you will want to get together periodically to discuss strategy, hear any new tunes in their repertoire, and listen to them practice. Far from resenting criticism, the bands I have worked with have appreciated hearing a caller's perspective.

If you have hired or been paired with a band new to you, I suggest meeting with them before the event. If this is impractical, you and the band should plan to arrive at the hall at least half an hour before the sound check, to go over the program. The band should show you a copy of their tune list; if you want specific tunes for some of your dances, you can make it known while encouraging them to play their favorite tunes for the rest of the program.

The musicians' experience level will affect the dynamic between you and the band. Less experienced musicians may want a fair amount of guidance from you, including tune suggestions. Seasoned musicians are more likely to want to choose the tunes themselves. If you and they listen to each other with a view to looking at things from each other's viewpoint, you should be able to arrive at a procedure that works for all of you.

Whether or not the band has a formal leader, there is usually one member who is used to being a liaison with the caller. This is the person to establish eye contact with; make sure you stand where you can easily see each other.

To start each dance, some bands will wait for you to tap out your desired tempo. Others will start playing as soon as you indicate you are ready for music. If you know their tempos to be steady and within your acceptable range, this should not pose a problem. Otherwise, it will pay to discuss the issue beforehand.

The typical square dance band has a preferred type of introduction for its tunes. The most common one for non-singing calls is "four potatoes": 4 beats' worth of fiddle shuffles or piano chords. This should be more than adequate for most callers, as square dances do not have to start at the beginning of the tune as contras do (as discussed further under "Recorded Music" below). For singing calls, the normal custom is to play the last 8 beats of the song as an introduction, but "four potatoes" will work if the caller is not taken by surprise.

You and the band will need to agree on some signals. The most important are "one more time" (usually an index finger held up) and "going out" (a foot lifted from the floor or a raised fist – "no fingers" equals "no more times"). Old-time bands (see the next section) are generally comfortable stopping at the end of any phrase. Contra-focused bands that plan their tunes to work up to a climax often want a "two more" signal, or at least to be alerted early to "one more." However, if "one more" is given too early in the tune, it can be unclear whether the current playing of the tune is the "one more" or the next to last time. The accepted place for the "one more" signal (and the "going out" signal) is the beginning of the last part of the tune (usually B.2).

The normal "going out" signal means "Going out at the end of this time through the tune." You may also feel the need of a signal for "Emergency on the floor – stop the music right now" (perhaps a chopping motion on your neck). But with luck and developing skills, you should seldom have occasion to use it.

There are no standard signals for "faster," "slower," "louder," or "softer." If you want some, you will have to work them out with the band.

Be sure to introduce the band at least once, perhaps just before intermission. The musicians need to hear applause at some point that they can be sure is directed solely to them.

Band styles

Most present-day square dance bands can be sorted into two broad categories: old-time southern on the one hand and contra-focused on the other. The latter group includes bands that play in New England, Québécois, Irish or other Celtic, or a combination of styles.

Contra-focused bands are used to having the caller drop out after two or three minutes, allowing the dancers to hear the music unencumbered by vocals. If you like to use a lot of patter, an old-time southern band may be a better fit for you. In my experience, old-time musicians tend to think of a square dance set as just another jam session; they are unlikely to become upset if the dancers are not focusing primarily on the music.

The repertoires of the two types of band tend to differ one from the other. Many tunes in the contra repertoire are what I call "tunes that tell a story" (see "Tune Personalities" above), with an easily discernible beginning, middle, and end. This is appropriate for contras, whose figures nearly always begin and end with the tune. It may also be appropriate for squares that are synchronized with the music in that way.

Conversely, many old-time tunes are what I think of as "straight-ahead tunes," particularly as played by musicians who prefer that genre. This repertoire and method of playing are well suited to southern sets and traditional western squares: In those dance types, the figures are seldom aligned completely with the music. The end of a figure may fall anywhere in the tune, so it would be obtrusive to have strong punctuation at the end of each musical chorus (AABB or equivalent).

If you have one or more favorite tunes that you would like a band to play, be aware that the two types of musicians generally learn tunes differently. Old-time southern players pick up most of their tunes by ear from other musicians, either in person or via audio or video recordings. If you are not a musician yourself, you will probably need to find a recording of your desired tune played the way you like it. Many contra-focused musicians read music; quite a few are classically trained. They may be open to learning your favorite tunes from sheet music; indeed, they may well own copies of the standard tune books. However, a well-played dance tune has nuances that cannot be learned from the printed page: idiosyncrasies of bowing, notes extended or cut shorter than their printed value would suggest. Even if your musicians are able and willing to read, you will be happier with the results if you can provide them with a good recording as well.

Regional tune structure

Speaking of AABB, most contra-focused bands will devote the vast majority of their repertoire (aside from waltzes and other couple dances) to 32-measure (64-beat) tunes. Most of these will have the form of AABB; a few will have other sequences, such as ABCB or ABCD, but the overall length of a chorus will be the same. If you call primarily New England squares and/or contras, this repertoire should suit you well. (A few phrased squares take 48 measures or 96 beats, and there are some good AABBCC tunes to match them, as discussed under "Phrasing" in Chapter 4.)

Old-time southern music is less uniform in structure. AABB is the most common sequence, but certain tunes are traditionally played AAB, ABB, or ABAB, among other possibilities. Then too, some southern tunes have parts that are only 4 measures (8 beats) long. When such a tune is played AABB, it will sound like ABAB to a northern ear. (On some commercial recordings made for square dancing, such tunes are played AAAABBBB in order to fit the expected 32-measure length, but this can produce a monotonous sound.)

Finally, some southern tunes are commonly played "crooked"; that is, the "A" and/or "B" parts are one or more beats longer or shorter than expected, often amounting to an odd number. (The custom is also practiced in Quebec and among the Métis people of western Canada.) This is likely to get in the way of your calling if you are used to thinking in multiples of 8 beats. Some crooked tunes can also be played "square" (with strict 8-beat phrases), but certain tunes are always or nearly always played crooked. If the use of crooked tunes would bother you, you will need to let the band know this. When I work with musicians who enjoy playing crooked tunes, I encourage them to do so apart from my dance sets – during the sound check; as part of a concert during intermission; or, in the case of private parties, as background music during social hour or dinner.

Changing tunes

Most old-time southern bands, in my experience, prefer to stick with one tune throughout a dance number. Bands in other styles, especially if they play for contra dancing, may be accustomed to playing medleys of two or three tunes. This has become popular since the 1970s as the urban contra dance scene developed its distinctive personality. Today's contra callers tend to stop prompting after a few rounds to let the dancers focus on the music. And a typical contra number lasts 15 to 18 times through the AABB sequence, and sometimes even longer. These factors have made tune changes not only desirable but almost essential from the musicians' viewpoint. Playing one tune repeatedly can lead to cramped fingers, aside from any boredom that may set in.

No matter what style your musicians play, you will need to tell them the length of any squares you plan to use. The shortest common type of square is phrased, each figure and break written to fit one playing of an AABB tune. With four figures and three breaks (at the beginning, middle, and end), such a dance will run seven times through the tune. Many if not most bands will be happy to play a single tune that long. (Note that a contra-focused band will still want to know how many times they will be playing the tune, as they may want to swap leads and build to a climax.) If they would rather use two tunes, the change should come just before or after the middle break; that is, after three or four times through the first tune. If you are thinking of prolonging the ending break past a single AABB, any tune change should be postponed until after the middle break, or the band may end up playing the second tune much longer than the first.

As mentioned in Chapter 4, you may be willing to let the phrasing of a dance slip in certain situations. Your musicians should be aware that this may happen. If there is a high probability that the dancers will have trouble keeping up with standard timing – if you know this from having worked with them previously, or if they are seniors, people with disabilities, or the like – it is doubly important to impress on the band that statements about the length of a dance are merely estimates.

If you plan to run your square longer than seven or eight times through a standard tune, you should let the band have a rough idea of length and give them the option of switching tunes. An old-time southern band, as I have said, will probably play one tune throughout – unless your dance will be much longer than normal. I usually end non-dancer parties with the *Virginia Reel,* and if the group and the space are large enough, I always dissolve the sets into a big circle and do a few figures in that formation, ending with a spiral into the middle. This takes at least twice as long as a typical square in any style, and I warn the band of this and suggest they think of several tunes to change to if they get tired or uncomfortable.

Finding a band

If you are not acquainted with any bands or musicians in your area, the first thing to do is to contact the organizers of local contra dance or traditional square dance series, if there are any. The next step is to determine which local music store caters to acoustic musicians: guitarists, banjoists, fiddlers, and so forth. The owner or one of the employees may know of people who might be interested in playing for dances (they may even be interested themselves). If not, they may have a bulletin board on which you can leave a request for interested parties to contact you.

You can also reach out to local music schools or the music departments of high schools and colleges. You may find young people who are unfamiliar with the square dance idiom but are skilled on their instruments and willing to try anything. In such a case, make sure you have some excellent recordings to give an idea of how the music should be played.

If you have a choice of instruments, get at least one fiddler. The fiddle is the quintessential square dance instrument for a reason – actually for multiple reasons. Alone among the usual folk instruments, the fiddle's notes can be extended indefinitely (rather than fading quickly), so that a good fiddler can really make the instrument "sing." And good bowing technique can emphasize the downbeats and upbeats, particularly the latter, well enough that a solo fiddle can provide both melody and rhythm.

However, a good rhythm player can give the music a fuller sound and take some pressure off the fiddler. The most common rhythm instruments are guitar (for old-time southern music) and piano (for New England and Québécois styles). The various types of accordion – piano accordion, button accordion, and concertina – can also provide a punchy rhythm, but they also normally play melody too, with a penetrating sound that not everyone enjoys; fiddlers and "box" players do not always get along.

The banjo is one of my favorite square dance instruments; it provides a percussive contrast to the fiddle's smoothness. Old-time players generally use a five-string banjo and favor a finger-picking style that produces a relatively gentle sound like rippling water. Bands in other styles may include a tenor banjo with four strings, played with a plectrum (a flat pick brushed across multiple strings at once) to give the louder, "punchy" sound associated with Dixieland jazz.

Wind instruments are traditional in Irish and New England dance music, harking back in the latter case to the quadrille bands of the late 19th and early 20th centuries. The flute, clarinet, and pennywhistle are often heard; clarinetists may provide a few jazz licks. Trumpets, trombones, and saxophones are occasionally found in larger bands.

For some extra punch at the low end of the rhythm section, a bassist is preferable to a drummer. A bass provides a variety of musical notes as well as a beat, and is less likely to be played too showily for your or the dancers' taste. But a sensitive player can add a dimension to the music with a drum set or a bodhran (an Irish hand-held drum played with a double-ended beater).

Singing squares

Squares with singing calls were extremely popular in most regions during the 1950s, and in the modern square dance scene they constitute half the numbers in an evening. But currently, few bands in the neo-traditional scene are used to playing them. Unless you are unusually fortunate, you will need to provide your band with resources for any singing squares you want to use. As with other kinds of dance music, you are better off if you can furnish at least one good recording in addition to printed music. (Singing calls are covered in more depth in Chapter 20; sources for singing call music are listed in the Resources section.)

If you enjoy singing some of your calls to popular songs, I encourage you to find musicians who enjoy playing them, or to try developing a taste for them among your dance musician friends. Some of my most pleasurable moments have come when bands took a Dixieland jazz approach to singing squares, the lead players taking turns on melody and improvising within the strict tempo of the square dance.

Recorded Music

Happily, live music is the norm in both of the present-day "traditional revival" square dance scenes – the one growing within the contra dance world and the one originating in the old-time string band scene. Still, there are situations in which recorded music may be worth considering. A newly formed dance group may rely on recordings until a suitable pool of musicians can be located and, if necessary, trained. A caller conducting a class may not have the budget for good live music, and if a group requires extensive teaching, musicians may not want to sit around between numbers. (I suggest that if a teaching series uses recorded music, a live band be hired for the final session.)

There are other uses for recorded dance music. If you have musicians who are technically competent and willing to play for you but are unfamiliar with any traditional tunes, good recordings can provide them with the notes and the desired style of playing. You can use recordings to practice calling at home. And if you have a sizable collection of recorded music, you can use it to try dance figures with different tunes, looking for a good fit.

For those callers willing to work with recordings at least occasionally, the current scene could hardly be more favorable. Several albums and individual tracks of excellent square dance music have been released in recent years and are available as CDs, downloads, or both. In addition, some of the best instrumental recordings of the 1950s have been reissued; the sound quality is not always ideal, but the musicianship and enthusiasm of the players shine through. And with today's technology, out-of-print recordings can be converted to computer files, cleaned up, lengthened if necessary, and made faster or slower.

I encourage you to be choosy when selecting recorded music. To compensate for the lack of immediacy and connection with the dancers, the musicianship on a recording needs to be excellent. There are many tracks that would be adequate as live performances but fall short as recordings for one reason or another – thin instrumentation, too many wrong notes, slightly uneven rhythm, or simply a lack of that nearly intangible quality, "lift." As so many good tracks, both new and old, are currently available, there is no need to settle for less than the best.

Media

The state of audio technology has been evolving so quickly that it is hazardous to describe current equipment, let alone make recommendations. Digital downloads appear to be the choice of a majority of users, but folk artists still sell CDs at their concerts and dances. Single dance tracks are increasingly available only as downloads, even tracks that were originally issued on vinyl discs in the 1950s. Remember that tracks can be transferred between CDs and computer files, in both directions, fairly easily at home. Just remember that if a track is commercially available, it is only fair to purchase a copy rather than get it from a friend.

My most emphatic piece of advice to users of recordings is to take two sources of music to every event. CD players do not always operate flawlessly; neither do music-playing software programs. And laptops and other devices are notorious for crashing at inopportune times. Even if both sources are of the same type – two CD players or two digital devices – the odds are against both of them failing on the same night.

Looping

Until recently, if a recording was shorter than the caller's intended dance, the only recourse was to set the needle back (or the equivalent in other media), requiring the caller to find the beat and the phrase again. Sometimes the caller got lucky, hitting the beginning of a phrase and synchronizing the call instantly. More often there was a definite break in the rhythm, throwing the dancers off their stride. (When this happened, Ed Gilmore used to follow his next call, such as "promenade," by chanting "with a broken leg.")

Happily, this sort of stumble is a thing of the past. Shorter tracks can be lengthened at home and fixed as such in the caller's electronic files. Also, music-playing software programs have a "loop" feature (as do CD players made for DJs): The caller can set a point at which the player will jump from a later passage of the track to an earlier one. The loop will be in effect until the caller disengages it. The starting and ending points of the loop can be fine-tuned so that the tempo will remain constant without an audible break. (Hint: The point between complete AABB choruses is not always the best point at which to create a loop.)

Know your tracks

It is important to listen all the way through every track you intend to use. On many fiddle tune recordings made in the 1950s, even those released by prominent square dance labels, the musicians add or omit an "A" or "B" part from time to time. Obviously, such a track cannot be used for a phrased 64-beat dance without modification. In the case of a singing square, make sure you know the sequence of musical verses and choruses. Is the same music (usually the chorus of the original song) used seven times in a row without variation? Or is there a pattern of verse-chorus or verse-verse-chorus? Are the last 8 beats of the song repeated as a tag? (One singing-call record popular in the 1950s had tags at the end of the figures but not the breaks.) If the track is a copy made from a vinyl record, it may have one or more skips. If it was created from a tape, there may be a dropout. You will need to check before you add the track to your working list of files.

The length of each track should help you decide which track to use for a given dance. Although, as noted above, it is now possible to lengthen a track, there are many wonderful recordings that I feel should not be extended or looped. This is because the musicians play the tune differently each time, working up to a climax of energy. The lead instrument may change with each chorus; the lead or other instruments may improvise harmonies. If the track is altered so that one or more distinctive choruses are repeated, the buildup of energy is less effective.

Therefore, it is good to make a list of tracks that run the right number of times for the various dance types in your repertoire. I have several favorites that run 6 x 32 measures; they are ideal for whole-set longways with six couples (a common number for this dance type). Tracks that run 7 x 32 are good for typical phrased squares with three breaks. Some squares have a double-length figure that feels complete without breaks; such dances work well with 8 x 32 tracks. If a visiting-couple figure takes 2 x 32 for each active couple, you may want to insert some breaks; look for 10 x 32 if you use an introduction and an ending, 11 x 32 if you also add a middle break. And so forth.

Some of my records, after the seventh full time, end with only part of the tune; with such a record I can extend my ending break. (When I add a track to my working list, I rename the file, adding after the title the number of times through the tune. A few tracks have earned numbers like 7.5 or 7.75.)

On quite a few recordings made in the 1940s and '50s, the musicians dive right into the tune without playing a 4-beat or 8-beat introduction. This has been a headache for contra callers: They need to deliver their first call before the tune starts, but their dancers should ideally hear the tempo before stepping out. It is much less of a problem with squares, as the dancers' first move does not have to start with the tune. Many callers are in the habit of letting the first 16 beats (A.1) go by before they speak, or of calling "honors" during that music. Starting with A.2, they will then improvise an opening break that requires only 48 beats (24 measures: ABB). The lack of an introduction is also less of a problem with digital media than with vinyl, as there is typically no lag between pressing "play" and hearing the music. At worst the lag is short and predictable, not the guessing game required by a vinyl record's lead-in area.

Your software or CD player will have a digital timer, which can be set to show elapsed time or time remaining. The latter is the more useful setting for callers, as it gives you an idea of how many times through the tune you have left to work with. Remember that at dance tempo, once through an AABB tune takes 30 seconds or a little more. If the timer reads 1:40, you can be fairly sure that you have 3 x 32 measures left and can call, say, two more figures and an ending.

Honor the music

In the modern square dance world, because the dancers typically have no idea what the next call will be, it is imperative that the caller's every word be crystal-clear. Modern callers therefore tend to choose recordings with lead instruments other than fiddles, and they keep the volume of the music so low that it can be hard to hear anything but the basic beat. (Most sound systems designed for that market include a music volume control mounted on the microphone, so the caller can lower the music for tricky spots in the choreography and raise it for excitement when the dancers make it all the way to an allemande left. The technique can be effective when done subtly, but it is easy to overdo, going from near-silence to an overwhelming bass beat.)

As a tradition-based caller, you are not laboring under the same constraint; your dancers probably have some idea of what is coming. I encourage you to honor the music by keeping the melody and harmony audible. As mentioned above, the fiddle is the mainstay of traditional square dance music in nearly every region. It contributes in no small measure to the strong personality of our beloved dance form. For the sake of tradition and the enjoyment of the dancers, I urge you to "let the fiddles sing."

I mention this in connection with using recordings because that is where you have the most control over the music, but it should be kept in mind with live music as well. No matter who mixes the sound – you, the band, a sound technician, or a combination – the music should always be given its due.

13

Different Groups

Historically, the normal square dance group has consisted primarily of adult mixed couples; many books and articles from the 1950s on teaching and calling presuppose such a group. ("Normal" here means "most common," with no moral or pathological implications.) However, many of your opportunities to call are likely to be with groups that depart from the norm in one way or another. In working with some demographic groups, you will need to modify your approach; with others you may wish to modify the dances themselves. This chapter discusses some of the more frequently encountered examples.

In General

First, here are some points that apply to many kinds of group.

In every case you will need to discern whether the people present are interested in square dancing as something to be learned well and perhaps adopted as a long-term hobby, or simply as a vehicle for socializing. Of course dance hobbyists use it as a social vehicle too; the question is whether or not each group you encounter can be expected to retain anything you tell and show them beyond the present event. (The first section below, "First-Timers," deals with groups that are not inclined to learn anything permanently.)

Note that "square dancing" does not have to mean four-couple squares. Squares will not be the best choice for some groups for various reasons, including short attention spans and small numbers. Even though having a home position is a seeming advantage of the square formation, it is outweighed for some people by the complexity of remembering which role they must play next. The same infectious energy and feeling of accomplishment can be achieved with big circles, progressive circles, southern sets, scatter promenades, and whole-set longways. In most of these formations, there are no more than two roles that dancers must learn: active and inactive. Many dances are even simpler in structure, with all couples doing the same thing or with a single active couple in the set. (See "Especially for Children and First-Timers" in the Resources section for a list of materials that include many circles, whole-set longways, and other easy dances.)

If your dance experience has been primarily in the world of contra dancing with everyone moving most of the time, don't assume that every dancer or potential dancer will prefer that level of activity. Many people are content with moving only about half the time; urban contra dancing and modern square dancing may be too intense for them. Visiting-couple squares and simple square figures using half a dozen basic moves, as well as whole-set longways, are ideal for groups in many demographic categories.

143

Another word of advice that applies particularly to experienced contra dance callers, though other callers will also benefit from it: It is allowable – in some cases it is desirable – to let the phrasing slip; that is, to give dancers extra time to complete some movements, even if it means the move takes up part of the next musical phrase. It is also permissible to omit from a routine one or more of the moves you were planning to do, in order to finish with the music. This is likely to be an attractive option when working with children, seniors, or people with disabilities. Slipped phrases are discussed more fully in Chapter 4.

As mentioned in Chapter 11, dance teachers are divided on whether to reduce the tempo as an alternative to allowing extra time. For me it depends on the group and the material. I have done one, the other, or a little of both as the occasion seemed to demand. However, I would caution against slowing the tempo down too far; there comes a point where the energy is lost.

Don't be afraid to adapt material, especially to simplify a dance for wider use or to provide non-gendered alternatives. With regard to the latter, sometimes a dance will be entirely gender-free, not even requiring neutral terms to replace "ladies" and "gents," except for one movement, for which a substitute is easily found. (See Chapter 14 for pointers on adapting dances and creating your own.)

First-Timers

For every person who joins a square dance club or regularly attends a public dance series, there are probably half a dozen who dance only once a year – or once in a lifetime – at an event designed especially for non-dancers. Such events have long been known in the calling trade as "one-night stands," with no contempt intended. (Dudley Laufman calls them "onesies.") Other names have been used, such as "party nights" and "fun nights"; the latter name is often adopted by square dance clubs who hold entry-level parties in the hope of recruiting new members.

The most important point for a caller to bear in mind about these events is that, except for dance-club-sponsored "fun nights," the guests are not there to learn to dance; they are there to be entertained. (Dudley says "Don't call them beginners; they're not beginning anything.") If you are calling at a country club, a fraternal order, or a similar organization, you are the entertainment for that night. Last month's meeting was a Las Vegas night; next month's may be a scavenger hunt. Your "barn dance" or "hoedown" should be as self-contained an event as those other nights.

It is an old axiom that the less experienced the dancers are, the more experienced their caller should be. Similarly, the less confident the dancers are, the more confident the caller needs to be. For non-dancer parties in particular, it will pay to memorize a few easy dances and polish your delivery of both the walkthrough and the calls. Your confidence will build that of the dancers.

Here more than anywhere, it pays to have a wide repertoire of dances in various formations and to resist the temptation to overweight the program with squares, no matter how much you love them and enjoy calling them. I always plan to use squares at one-nighters, provided the numbers "work out" (leaving as small

Chapter 13: Different Groups   *145*

a percentage of the group as possible sitting out). However, even when I don't use squares, I take charge of the proceedings more like a square dance caller than a present-day contra caller. (Many contra callers feel that their job is to get out of the way of the music as soon as the dancers can manage without them.) And I never plan to use contras at a non-dancer party; having tried it a few times, I find that learning a contra dance involves too many unfamiliar concepts for most groups to assimilate quickly. Both squares and contras have a learning curve; I choose not to present both in the same evening. And I have chosen to go with squares over contras, because they are so iconic in American culture and because they have a home position to retreat to in case of trouble.

Occasionally you will encounter a small group of people at a one-nighter who have extensive experience with modern square dancing, urban contra dancing, or some other sophisticated genre. This will obviously be the case if a dance group is sponsoring the night, but even at non-dance-related events a few dancers may attend in the hope of making converts. They may approach you with a request to announce their own events and/or to call some harder material just for their sub-group. The implication is that the rest of the guests are "not really square (or contra) dancing" and should be shown what "real" dancing is like and told where they can learn it. If you believe, as I do, that easy dancing is real dancing, my advice is to resist, politely but firmly, any effort to co-opt your event. If you wish, you can call a dance "for those who know how" and mention that lessons are available, but it should be your choice, and you should speak in your own words.

Above all, don't let dance hobbyists talk you into raising the difficulty level of the dances you call for the whole group. You are responsible for the success of the evening, and your judgment alone should determine what material is appropriate. If you present a couple of easy dances and you sense that the majority of guests would like a bit more challenge, your repertoire should be large enough that you can raise the level one notch. But again, it should be your decision.

How many basic movements should you use at this sort of party? In my opinion, as few as possible. I use circle, forward and back, do-si-do, arm turns, promenade, and star. Some of the dances I use have one additional move, such as pass through, separate, arch and dive, or sashay. If a group is responding well, I may use grand right and left, but usually only in a big circle, where the dancers' path is less sharply curved and easier to discern than in a square. I see no need to use ladies chain, right and left through, or the combination of allemande left and grand right and left; there is more than enough good dance material to call a full evening without introducing those terms. (See Chapter 11 for a fuller list of basics in a suggested teaching order.)

The swing in ballroom or similar position is, for me, the move that separates the non-dancer party from the first night of an ongoing dance class or series. A ballroom swing requires skill and practice: The dancers must learn through experience how to "give weight" or match the pull of their arms with their partner's pull. Normally this takes a full evening if not more, and for this reason I use only an elbow swing at one-nighters.

The two-hand swing is the next easiest for most people to learn, although it takes a bit of practice to do smoothly. You can choose to teach an elbow swing, a two-hand swing, or both, depending on the atmosphere that exists and the one you want to promote. Many teachers in the past taught the straight-arm hold to children (each person's right arm braced against the other's shoulder); it minimizes physical contact, but by the same token it is easy for dancers to lose control and even fly apart.

There are many ways to start the dance portion of a non-dancer party. Here are four of them:

1. Get people in a big circle with a partner and walk through "circle left, circle right, forward and back." (Some callers see no point in walking through anything that easy, but Beth and I have our reasons. The walkthrough takes only 20 seconds and can give a much-needed dose of reassurance. It also lets us model a good dance-walk, making it less likely that the dancers will get out of control in the circles and promenades.) All the other moves – arm turns, do-si-do, promenade – can be taught on the fly while the music is playing, if you like. (The big circle is no time to worry about phrasing 1–64, and even phrasing 1–16 may not always be practicable; I do try to prompt so that the dancers' movements coincide with the 8-beat phrases.)

2. Get couples in a big circle and don't walk through anything – just start the music and call. This is basically the "warm walkthrough" method mentioned in Chapter 11. Movements like "circle left" and "forward and back" can be called without explanation; with moves like do-si-do, arm turns, and promenade, you can talk the dancers through the parts of a move and then tell them its name. (One way to introduce a promenade is to have the dancers circle left, then right, then drop hands and keep going in single file, then have the gents or left-hand people move up alongside their partner on the inside.)

3. Do a snake dance around the hall, picking up bystanders as you pass them. You can also begin with a big circle, no partner needed. In either case, you can use a few of the ideas mentioned for the grand march in Chapter 16. End with a spiral into the center and out again. (The spiral is also an effective way to end the evening; after the *Virginia Reel,* I get everyone in a big circle, call a few moves, and end by leading a spiral. I would be unlikely to use two spirals in an evening, although repetition is not always bad.)

4. If no one is with a partner, start the music and have people clap their hands, stomp their feet, elbow swing the nearest person, swing the other way around, swing a new person, etc., then tell them to find a few other pairs and make a small circle (one of several such circles around the dance space). I have done this at high school dances where I knew from experience that the dancers were likely to get out of control if I put them in a single large circle.

There are also several ways to form squares:

- With the dancers in a big circle, select four couples to go into the center and form a square, then tell everyone else "Make yourselves look like that."
- From a big circle, teach and call a progressive circle (couple facing couple). At the end, tell each foursome to find another foursome and make a circle of eight people.
- In a big circle, have the dancers promenade as couples, then tell each couple to attach itself to another couple in a line of four and keep moving around the hall. Next, tell each line of four to find another line and promenade by eights. Have each line of eight find an open spot on the floor and form a circle.
- Many authors have included the Platoons figure of the grand march (see Chapter 16) on this list. It is certainly impressive at a ball, for dancers and spectators alike, but it strikes me as too elaborate and time-consuming for a teaching situation.

When sets of eight people are formed, I suggest giving a few calls like circle, forward and back, do-si-do, arm turns, and promenade to get the dancers comfortable in their groups, even before having them align their set with the walls. Terms such as heads, sides, and couple numbers should be introduced only when a particular dance requires them.

If a group shows signs of being hard to control, it is important to maintain continuity. Be ready at all times with the next thing to say, the next dance to present, the next recording to use. If you have a live band, they must understand that they need to start playing immediately on your signal. Be prepared to hold the dancers' attention continuously until break time; in the case of children and adolescents, it is often better to run a single, relatively short session with no break.

The availability of alcoholic beverages can be a complicating factor at a dance party. Some callers will not accept a booking for an event at which alcohol will be served; others report that they double their asking price if the party is to be "wet." I have been successful most of the time in keeping such parties from getting out of hand; the secret is to use material that is as elementary as possible and keeps everyone in motion most of the time.

Repetition, which can work against you with hobby dancers, can be an asset at a one-nighter. If the crowd enjoys a dance early in the evening, the same dance, or one with only a minor alteration, can be done to different music later. Non-dancers have very different standards from those of regular dancers; learning a single new move can be a major achievement, and you can score points by celebrating it as such.

Likewise, casual dancers are much less demanding than hobby dancers about the length of a program. Regular dancers usually prefer two to three hours of nearly nonstop dancing, with at most one break at the halfway point. (They can always sit out a number if they want less activity.) First-timers are often content with two or three separate half-hour sets; breaks can range from 10 to 20 minutes, depending on the guests' physical condition and desire to socialize sitting down. Occasionally a group will disperse after your initial big circle, not because they disliked it but because it was enough exercise for the time being. At several of my one-nighters, the only dances I called were the big circle and the *Virginia Reel*; in one or two cases the big circle was all the group wanted. You may feel in such a case that you didn't earn your keep, but the organizers nearly always think they got their money's worth. Of course, you need to keep reading the crowd and checking in with the organizers throughout your time slot, to ensure that everyone is happy with the pacing of the event.

Children

Square dancing and its related forms are often thought of as ideal for children. They are certainly a splendid form of exercise and foster a cooperative spirit. But they are, at heart, an adult pastime; in many communities they have served as an important vehicle of courtship. My concern over their use with children is not that the dances are inappropriate for young people; they are certainly tamer than some other dance styles. My concern is that they are supremely appropriate for adults, and it is cause for regret when teenagers and older folks write off square dancing as "kid stuff" because they did it in grade school.

This is not to say that squares and other traditional dances should never be taught to school-age children. There are several ways in which any negative results can be avoided or at least mitigated. But great skill and patience are crucial.

In the best of all possible worlds, folk dancing – including squares and contras – is something enjoyed by many of the adults in a community, and even those who choose not to participate view it as one among many valid forms of recreation. This state of affairs is healthy in itself, and it is the most favorable environment for introducing dance to children. It is true that they may still turn away from it when they reach adolescence, but if they see local adults engaging in it, they are less likely to consider it permanently beneath them. And a certain percentage, no matter how small, may return to it in the future.

With or without adult acceptance of these dances, it takes a skilled and sensitive teacher to present them successfully to children. In my view, the ideal person for the job is one who can readily establish rapport with children; this is more crucial than knowledge of the dance, which can be acquired fairly quickly if need be. It helps, of course, if the teacher has also developed a love for traditional dance and its music. Any negative feelings toward either the students or the dance material will transfer to the group in short order.

Two important factors in teaching dance to children are attitude and timing. The dance should be presented as an additional way to have fun, not as a drill. Although there is obviously a structure to squares and similar dances, and one hopes that the children's execution will get more precise with repetition, insisting on perfection at any price is likely to sour them on the whole activity. As for timing, both the time of day and the children's age should be taken into account.

Dancing is often best introduced in the classroom rather than the gym, perhaps at the end of the morning or the end of the day, when the children are becoming restless from sitting. And I would rather see the first dances – probably easy circles from this and other countries – presented in the early grades, with dances more sophisticated (both choreographically and socially) saved for later. The worst possible scenario is to introduce square dancing in middle school or junior high, when children are the most reluctant to socialize with the opposite sex, let alone touch them. By senior high, many young people have come to emulate adults in certain ways, including the ability to laugh at themselves; square and contra dancing is often an attractive recreation for this age group. And older teens, along with college students, tend to have energy to burn and are likely to enjoy the "all active" dances that other groups may find too strenuous.

Seniors

As Americans' lifespans increase and more senior centers and retirement communities are built, older adults are becoming a significant market for the dance caller. Many seniors are as mentally alert as ever and will welcome dance material that challenges their intellect. To accommodate their physical needs, tempos can be slowed slightly, long swings avoided, and rest periods increased. If singing squares or other strongly phrased dances are used, the figures may have to be modified so that fewer movements than usual are done during each 64-beat chorus. The alternative is to start calling the dance as written and discover the hard way that the dancers cannot keep up; this is disconcerting for the caller and demoralizing for the dancers.

Many groups of post-retirement age consist primarily or entirely of women. The additional challenges of calling to such groups are dealt with below under "Same-Sex Couples."

Special Needs

People of all ages with physical or mental challenges can nearly always learn and enjoy some form of group dance. My experience with such people has not been extensive, but many leaders have evolved techniques for working with them, and some have specialized in this area.

If you do not seek out "special" groups, your exposure will likely come in one of two ways: A group may approach you for a session, or individuals with various challenges may attend a "normal" group and expect to participate to a greater or lesser extent.

If an organizer approaches you, you will have to decide whether to take on the assignment or, perhaps, refer the group to another caller, based on the length of your relevant experience and your willingness to learn as you go. In the case of individuals, I have found that an average "normal" group can absorb one or two people who have little or no sight or hearing, or have difficulty walking. In my experience, the abler dancers always look out for them and help them through the figures. More than once I have seen a wheelchair user join in a big circle and keep up with the dancers on foot.

Dance groups exist in many areas in which all the dancers are in wheelchairs. These are of two types: Either the dancers propel themselves or each dancer has a "pusher." With self-propelling dancers, it will probably be necessary to modify at least the timing of some sequences, and possibly to modify movements or substitute some moves for others. With pushed chairs, you can likely use most routines intact, though some sequences will take more beats of music to execute.

With a group some or all of whom have lost (or never had) the use of their legs, you can call "seated square dances." Doing this requires devising substitutes for each movement you plan to use. For example, on the call "Circle left," the dancers (seated in a circle, with or without a table in the middle) can join hands, lean their bodies to the left, and gently bounce their hands up and down in time to the music. Several callers have developed quite a list of movements, notably Fred Wersan, whose work can be seen on YouTube. Seated square dances can also be used with an audience in theater seating, perhaps as one part of a concert where normal dancing would be impractical. One caller, when hired for a dinner-dance, uses the form when the guests have finished dinner but are still at their tables, to prove that they can follow the sort of directions that will be used later.

English Learners

You may be asked to call for a group of people for whom English is not the primary language. It may be a church with a large immigrant population or a group of foreign exchange students at a high school. If you are fortunate, there will be an equal number of native English speakers, but this is not always the case.

There are several things you can do to increase your chances of success at such an event:

- Use demonstrations for most or all of the dances, before the walkthrough.
- Avoid ordinal numbers ("first couple," "second couple," etc.) in favor of cardinal numbers ("Couple 1," "Couple 2," etc.), which are among the first things people learn in a new language.
- Use primarily moves, like circles and stars, in which people are physically connected and can help steer one another in the right direction.
- When teaching, keep your language plain; avoid figures of speech, slang, and similar idioms that the group may not understand quickly.
- Make your calls brief; avoid patter and extraneous language.

You may want to try different ways of wording the same instruction, watching people's reactions to the various options. When one set of words appears to elicit greater understanding than the others, it is wise to stick with it.

People of Color

In the past two years, prompted by a series of tragic events, white Americans have come to a heightened awareness of the pervasive bias in this country against people of color, particularly African-Americans. Groups dedicated to Anglo-American dance, whose membership is overwhelmingly white, are searching for ways to encourage a more diverse constituency. Dance teachers are taking their expertise to schools and community centers in marginalized neighborhoods.

Based on my half-century of experience, I have some thoughts and suggestions on this topic:

1. Don't assume that Black people or any other non-white group won't find square dancing attractive. I have called at grade schools in Boston's historically Black and Hispanic neighborhoods, and the students were as enthusiastic about the dances as any other group I have worked with. Some years ago I arranged to call a series of three open dances at a local outdoor center and got different people each time. On the second date, everyone who showed up was Black. I assumed they were looking for a different event, due to my preconceived notion that people of color would find square dancing too regimented in comparison with modern freestyle dancing. They assured me that they had come to square dance, and we had a great time.
2. Don't let anyone tell you that square dancing is racist. While it is true that Henry Ford was active in promoting 19th-century dance forms and that some of his motives were unsavory, that should not impugn country dance as an art form. In reality, today's square dancing is a blend of traditions from many cultures. The craft of calling in particular appears to have been influenced by Black musicians beginning in the early 1800s (see Chapter 2). Today's students will enjoy learning of our dance form's multicultural origins.
3. Obviously, acknowledging their ancestors' role in shaping our activity will not by itself attract people of color to our present-day groups. On the question of how to diversify our dancing, I say: Look to the schools. Dancing as done by adults is an intimate activity and one of the last places where the effects of racial enmity will fade away. Where children of all ethnic backgrounds go to school together, increasingly they are making friends across racial lines. When dancing is included in the grade school curriculum, they think nothing of holding hands with their classmates. Skin color is becoming like hair and eye color: a difference to celebrate rather than fear and hate. The process is slow, frustratingly so at times, but I believe acceptance will win in the end.

Contra Dancers

The present-day contra dance circuit is perhaps the largest single arena for the caller who wants to do something with neo-traditional squares. Contra dancers have several reasons to be receptive to squares, particularly phrased ones. Unfortunately, many contra dancers come to the floor with a strong bias against squares. Some of them may have unpleasant memories of compulsory dancing in school. Some may have suffered through long-drawn-out teaching sessions with callers who were new to squares themselves. But the odds are that at least some of the people at a contra dance event will think they dislike all squares.

At the 2010 Ralph Page Dance Legacy Weekend I led a callers' discussion on using squares with contra dancers. I prepared a handout listing the good and bad points of squares, primarily from a dancer's point of view. Here are the lists, augmented by contributions from the discussion group.

What are the appealing qualities of squares?

- Squares offer the satisfaction of a small group of people working together to create something that has a beginning, middle, and end. (Contras feel more like an open house – "Come when you can, leave when you must." Each type of dance has its appeal.)
- A four-couple set offers more choreographic possibilities than the two-couple minor set of a typical contra.
- The caller has more influence on the flavor of the experience. (Some will see this as a plus, others as a minus, but a skilled and sensitive caller can be a force for good.)
- The interaction of caller, musicians, and dancers is truly three-way – the caller isn't trying to bow out of the equation.
- Breaks let the caller play with the dancers and keep them on their toes (as do hashed figures, within reason).
- There is the potential for ecstasy when everything clicks, as well as the hilarity of a real meltdown.
- They can be done with a group too small for a viable contra line.
- The caller can alter the timing and phrasing to let dancers catch up in case of trouble.
- They can open up a band's repertoire – some tunes, such as 48-measure tunes and crooked tunes, can be used for at least some squares but not (as a rule) for contras.
- Having a home position lets dancers regroup if they're lost, and it gives a feeling of accomplishment at the end of the number.

What do contra dancers dislike about squares?

- They are less inclusive: They need exact numbers, and dancers can't jump in after a set has started.

- They require too much dependence on the caller – some dancers would rather tune out the calls and get/stay in their own mental groove.
- Dancers who can't find a place must sit out for 10 minutes. (I advise against using squares if a high percentage of your group will be left out – 5 out of 61 is probably OK, 5 out of 21 is probably not.)
- Some callers choose squares that are too easy for the group.
- Some callers choose squares that are complex and/or have moves unfamiliar to contra dancers, requiring overly long teaching and walkthroughs.
- Some squares leave people standing still too much of the time.
- They are harder than contras to call well, which leads to frequent bad calling.
- Many squares favored by contra callers have a partner change, which means that the dancers are with their chosen partner less than half the time.
- Because each set's complement of people is fixed, a dancer having trouble affects the same other dancers longer than in a contra. Similarly, any sets having trouble (usually the ones in the back of the hall) can flounder throughout, partly because it can be hard for the caller to watch all the sets at once.

From the caller's point of view, squares are more challenging to call than contras, due to the presence of breaks, the need to vary the wording of figures, and more split phrasing, on average, than in contras. But they can be more rewarding to call than contras: Varying the calls and dealing with tricky timing and phrasing can give the satisfaction of a difficult job done well.

A good dance contains a three-way exchange of energy among the musicians, the caller, and the dancers. Squares give you a chance to take your place as part of that trinity without apology. In some traditions, such as those of Cape Breton Island and parts of Appalachia, there is little or no calling; but in most the caller is a vital part of the shared energy. "Getting into a groove" is as real a possibility with squares as with contras; it's just a different groove.

If you are going to win over a crowd of diehard contra dancers:

- Squares need to be enough like contras that the walkthroughs won't be too long and contra dancers won't see squares as totally alien.
- Squares need to be enough unlike contras to justify including them in a contra program. If your squares feel too much like contras, why bother?

Here are some suggestions on choosing squares for contra dancers:

- Keep most people moving most of the time.
- Use mainly basic movements that dancers will know from doing contras.
- Use only one or two unfamiliar things per square, and learn to teach them carefully but quickly.

- Use choreography that would be difficult or impossible to include in a contra (four ladies or gents chain, grand right and left, grand square).
- At least one square per set or per evening should be a "keeper," which brings original partners together at the end of every figure (not just the fourth).
- Breaks should be interesting but not impossibly fast or confusing.
- Don't teach an unfamiliar figure and an unfamiliar break to be done during the same 4- to 6-minute piece of music – the walkthrough will be longer than the dance.

Remember that any given square is likely to give more trouble than a contra using the same movements and transitions. In a contra there are multiple chances to sort things out, helped by different neighbors each time. In a square there are only four chances to get the figure right; each couple leads the figure only once or twice, and the number of people available for help is small and static.

If you are going to include squares in an evening of contra dances, I suggest that you present at least two. Groups that accept squares at all will usually be amenable to this. If the organizers resist the idea of more than one, you can explain that doing a single square gives you only one chance to guess the dancers' ability. If they still resist, you will have to decide whether it is worth using squares at all that night.

It is up to you, in consultation with the organizers, to decide whether to call two squares in succession to the same sets, or to call one square at a time to different sets. Calling two together reduces the time spent on forming sets, but it increases the time during which dancers not in the squares must sit out (unless you invite them to "cut in" after the first number). In any event, I don't recommend using any squares at a contra dance when attendance is below about 40 people unless there is a clear desire for squares on the dancers' part. Any squares should be placed roughly in the middle of the first and/or second half of the evening so that there will be contras before and after them.

Never try to force or fool contra dancers into doing squares (as by letting them form contra lines and then giving them instructions that regroup them). If they come into the hall with a strong bias against squares, it will strengthen their dislike, and if they lack such a bias, you won't need to coerce them.

If a group wishing to hire you is firmly opposed to doing squares, you can probably provide some variety by using dances in other formations that work much like contras. These include circle mixers, triplets (longways for three couples), and, if the group is large enough, progressive circles (or southern sets, which are really a type of progressive circle) and four-face-four dances. Four-face-fours in particular offer the chance to include four-couple choreography without keeping each group of four couples together for the duration; further, the minimum unit is only two couples (with an odd number of lines, the extra line waits one turn and comes right back in). Whole-set longways, like triplets, share their basic formation with contras but have some of the feeling of creating something in a small group that is one of the hallmarks of squares. Southern sets and other progressive circles keep everyone moving, and again the minimum unit is only two couples; an extra couple can be allowed if all dancers understand that a different couple will be "extra" after each progression.

Same-Sex Couples and Gender-Free Dancing

There are three broad categories of group in which male-female couples are not the norm. They are dealt with together here because they present similar challenges to the caller.

The first type of group consists primarily or entirely of members of one sex. Because men in many cultures are not socialized to dance together, such a group will usually be female. Girl Scout events (other than father-daughter dances) are one example. Dance classes in retirement centers and other groups of older adults are often predominantly female, partly because women tend to live longer than men and partly because the men are more reluctant to dance.

The second type of group consists of children and young teenagers who are not comfortable taking partners of the opposite sex. Parents and teachers are increasingly reluctant to insist on boy-girl couples, and left to their own devices, many young people will adopt same-sex pairings.

The third type of group is organized to do what is commonly referred to as "gender-free" dancing – short for "gender-role-free," although, as will be seen, there are still two roles in each couple. Most such groups are founded and run by members of the LGBTQ (lesbian/gay/bisexual/transgender/queer or questioning) community, though "straight" people are usually welcome to attend. In contrast to the single-sex group, at a gender-free dance one may see same-sex couples, mixed couples dancing the traditional roles, and mixed couples dancing the opposite roles. An increasing number of dancers enjoy swapping roles back and forth during a single dance number. All this can be disorienting to a caller who is used to getting visual cues from the apparent sex of the dancers as to whether they are in the right place. With practice, however, a caller can learn to get along without such cues.

There are four ways to approach calling to a group in which same-sex couples predominate:

1. Use only dances in which both members of each couple do exactly the same thing (or a mirror image of the same thing) at all times, so that naming the roles is unnecessary.
2. Refer to the dancers as "ladies" and "gents" or similar names denoting traditional sex roles.
3. Devise new names for the two roles.
4. Refer to the dancers according to their position in the set and in the room.

The first approach, using only dances that are truly gender-free, is the easiest once you have assembled a repertoire, but it requires some forethought in choosing material. Many relatively simple dances are gender-free, although comparatively few are squares. In whole-set longways, which should be in every caller's repertoire, partners often mirror each other's moves, with no reference to gender. In squares and big circles, where the starting formation has partners side by side, it may be necessary to distinguish the right-hand person from the left-hand person – but it may not. In some circle mixers, such as those with a transition from a grand right and left to a promenade, it may be impossible to teach the sequence effectively without naming the roles. But in others, the routine may aim dancers at their new partners with no need to differentiate roles except to emphasize that dancers should keep facing in their current direction. Similarly, you should examine each square to determine whether naming roles is necessary.

In addition to true gender-free dances, there are numerous routines in which only one or two movements are "gendered." These moves can usually be replaced without too much difficulty. A sequence of "ladies forward and back" followed by "gents forward and back" can be changed to "heads forward and back" and "sides forward and back" (or, in a formation with no heads or sides, "all forward and back" twice). A ladies chain over and back can be changed to right- and left-hand stars, or to some other 16-beat movement. (See "Modifying dances" below, as well as Chapter 14, for more on adapting dances.)

The second approach, using "ladies" and "gents" or similar words, has been widely used for many years, with varying degrees of success. In the past, all-female groups have generally accepted this terminology, while predominantly male groups have not. There has evidently been a greater social stigma attached to boys acting as girls (except for comic effect) than to girls acting as boys. In any case, there is more resistance to the use of such terms than there used to be.

This leads to the third approach, inventing new names for the roles. In the past 30 years or so, this has become the prevailing method of dealing with the issue. Many different names have been tried. Some leaders have used "ones/twos" or "rights/lefts"; the problem with those terms is that they already occur, with different meanings, in many dance routines. More common are names like "lions/tigers" or "moons/stars." With such neutral names, it can be a challenge to remember which name refers to which role. (To the dancers it doesn't matter, but the caller must keep track of everyone.) It helps to pick a name for the right-hand person that begins with "R" (such as "reds/greens" or "rabbits/squirrels") or has a lot of R's (such as "farmers/cowhands").

Another helpful practice is to use terms that have the same number of syllables as "ladies" and "gents." This not only helps the caller (and perhaps some dancers) remember which role is which, but also enables the caller to adapt traditional patter calls easily. My wife Beth uses "birdies" and "crows," from the dance *Bird in the Cage* (see Chapter 19). In recent years several LGBTQ-sponsored dance series, and even some "traditional" series, have adopted "robins" and "larks." (Some series experimented with "follows/leads" or "rubies/jets"; I believe all such series have switched to "robins/larks." "Robins" was changed from "ravens" when it was learned that the latter word has strong connotations – some positive, some negative – for many indigenous people of the Northwest.)

At present, "robins" and "larks" have been adopted by less than 10 percent of contra dance series; I know of no old-time square dance series that have made the change. Time will tell whether the terms will gain wider acceptance, or whether a new set of words will eclipse them in turn. This book uses "ladies" and "gents" because they are still the most widely used terms by far. Change is an intrinsic part of a living tradition, and I am open to change, but I am not convinced that "robins" and "larks" will ultimately prevail. (For one thing, their vowel sounds are similar enough to cause confusion in a noisy hall.) Feelings have sometimes run high among both advocates and opponents of change. As with any controversy, resolution can come only from open dialogue, with each side willing to listen thoughtfully to the other.

In addition to new names, the roles can be distinguished by articles of clothing such as armbands, vests, neckties, or loose cloth yokes. Typically only one member of a couple is so equipped; in a single-sex group it will be the one playing the "opposite" role, and in a gender-free group it is usually the one playing the "gent." Chris Ricciotti, a pioneer in the gender-free dance field, referred to the roles for many years as "armbands" and "bare-arms" – although the armbands were eventually replaced by short clip-on ribbons, and the increasingly common practice of swapping roles during a dance made even the ribbons problematic. Hats are less practical than armbands or yokes; they come off easily, they can muss the hair, and they are sometimes suspected as a carrier of head lice.

There is a fourth approach to the question of gender, one that avoids the use of either old or new terms for the roles. It is known as "positional calling" or "global terminology." It refers to dancers by their position in the set relative to one another and the walls of the room, with no reference to gender roles even by non-gendered names. It has been used by some English and Scottish country dance groups since the 1970s; some contra dance callers are now experimenting with it. I know of no one who has attempted it with squares.

Modifying dances

As noted above, a dance routine that includes one or two sex-role-defined movements can often be modified to eliminate them. This is often done when working with children and families. Some callers, for either ideological or practical reasons, may want to go further toward eliminating movements in which the sexes do quite different things. Usually this involves movements in which the gent leads the lady, such as the swing and the movements using promenade position (promenade, ladies chain, right and left through). There are ways to modify some of these moves to make the two parts similar and enable partners to dance together without leading or following.

- The swing can be modified to a "unisex" handhold (see Chapter 15), or a simple two-hand swing (or elbow swing) can be used.
- For promenades, the "front skaters'" position can be used: right hands joined in front of the right-hand person, left hands joined in front of the left-hand person. This hold is standard in modern square dancing and is customary in traditional dancing as practiced in some localities.

- The right and left through can be danced as it is in some parts of northern New England: After the pass through, adjacent dancers put their near arms behind each other's back for the couple turn (or simply keep their near shoulders adjacent as if they were glued together).
- In the ladies chain, the "courtesy turn" in promenade position can be changed to an open left-hand turn (which was apparently the original styling). A few people have objected to the chain altogether, resenting the implication that the woman has to be handed in and out of any movement she makes on her own. Some dances can be modified for such a group by replacing the ladies chain with another movement; other dances will have to be left out of the repertoire. But most groups will accept the ladies chain as part of the folklore of country dancing – particularly if a "gents chain" is used occasionally.

Modern Square Dancers

From the viewpoint of the traditional caller, modern square dancers constitute a "special" group; that is, a group of people who must be dealt with slightly differently than the average adult. Callers unfamiliar with the modern square dance network are likely to be surprised by some of the responses of its devotees.

Traditional callers may encounter modern square dancers in several settings. Often a small number will show up at a traditional dance, either by mistake or for a change of pace. Occasionally a traditional caller will be asked to lead a workshop at a modern square dance festival or convention. And any caller who accepts private bookings will occasionally find that a percentage of the crowd are modern square dancers who have come to help (and possibly recruit) the beginners.

Modern square dancers have a different body of knowledge than either non-dancers or experienced traditional dancers. And they will respond to the calls and music in quite different ways than a traditional dancer would.

A dancer whose experience has been with phrased choreography will listen to the call, which is given at the end of a musical phrase, and step out boldly on the first beat of the next phrase. An experienced dancer will do this even if the caller is unseasoned or careless and gives the call at the wrong place in the music. But a modern square dancer has been taught to follow the caller, not the music.

Most modern square dancers will rush through a ladies chain or a right and left through in 5 or 6 steps. If they have not heard the next call by the time they finish, they will come to a dead stop. You will probably need to encourage them to "use up the music," to time their movements so that they begin and end with the changes in the music. There is no need to burden the dancers with a long explanation of phrasing; a simple reminder that this isn't a race will usually suffice. ("There are no prizes for finishing first – one of the nicest things about country dancing is that everybody wins!")

The swing can also be problematic. Modern callers hardly ever use it except as a means of changing partners in singing squares, and allow very little time for it even then. As a result, modern square dancers have evolved a move that consists of a swing about once around, followed by a twirl for the lady under the gent's arm as the couple begins to move in promenade direction. A mere reminder to use up the music will probably not be enough in this case. It may help to say "Swing twice around" if the swing is to take 8 beats. If most or all of the group are modern square dancers, it will also help if you limit swings to that 8-beat length. A "balance and swing" can be changed to "do-si-do and swing."

The basic dance step is another point of difference. Whereas most traditional dancers take relatively long steps, with the feet leaving the floor, modern square dancers are taught to take short shuffling steps. The body is held more erect than in traditional styles, which usually favor a slight forward lean. The short steps, erect posture, and lack of giving weight make it hard for modern dancers to get through certain sequences, such as a series of quick hand turns, in the music normally allotted. This means that you may find the same dancers taking too much time for some moves and too little time for others.

I should mention that in many years of working with modern square dancers, I have found that they are much more receptive to the idea of phrased dancing in contras than in squares. Contras seem different enough from anything they are used to that they are willing to play by a new set of rules. As soon as they are back in square formation, their normal habits return: Even if the music is sharply phrased, they cut corners and rush the timing of the movements for fear the caller will give the next call before they are ready. This can pose a challenge if you are presenting phrased squares; if you are calling southern or traditional western figures, it is less likely to be a problem.

One more point to be aware of is that modern square dancers are conditioned to respond to code words rather than plain English; every movement they are expected to do has a standard name that is always used. (This conditioning is done so that the dancers can enjoy an entire evening without any walkthroughs.) If you call "ladies chain" they will do it immediately, but if you call "two ladies turn by the right hand round" they will take an extra beat or two to think about what the words mean. If you call to a group of modern dancers, it will be to your advantage to obtain a list of the moves they have learned; then you can deliver your calls using the standard terms they know. If you want them to do something that can't be described using terms familiar to them, pick a name for it and try to use the same wording each time you come to it.

14
Exploring

Throughout this book I have endeavored to make it clear that any serious study or analytical thinking in connection with calling is entirely optional. At the end of his small but invaluable book, *The Square Dance Caller* (1951), my role model Rickey Holden wrote "Probably the best rule for success is to forget completely the foregoing package of words and just git out an' call."

Nevertheless, some people in any field enjoy pondering the fine points more than others. This fact has inspired writers through the ages to set down millions of words on every topic imaginable in pursuit of influence, fame, or fortune. Two millennia ago a sage, weary of the constant deluge, wrote "Of making many books there is no end" (Ecclesiastes 12:12). But such sentiments have done nothing to stem the flow.

If you are inclined to "just git out an' call," more power to you; most traditional callers probably do just that. But if you derive pleasure or edification from thinking about it while offstage, I salute you as a kindred spirit and hope to be of service to you. The greater part of this book is an attempt to describe the mechanics of calling in a way that will be helpful to readers of an analytical frame of mind. It is in the same spirit that I offer the following chapter to anyone who wishes to explore the less-traveled roads of callerdom.

There are at least three avenues to explore beyond the basic set of skills required to teach and call a standard dance:

- Adapting other composers' material to suit your taste and the needs of your group
- Writing original dances, with standard basics and/or your own ideas
- Ad-libbing or "hashing" calls, using basics known to your dancers

Adapting Dances

The easiest way to start exploring is to adapt other people's routines to suit your personal preferences. Adaptation can be taken to various degrees. You can change only the words of a sequence, keeping all the movements as they are. You can change one or two movements in an otherwise ideal figure, perhaps because you dislike a certain move or would rather not add it to the list of things your dancers must know. At the other extreme, you can take an attractive string of two or three moves from the middle of a figure and discard the rest, devising new ways to get in and out of the part you like. At that point you have crossed the line into writing your own material and ought to give the figure a new name. (Some writers choose a name that is somehow related to the name of the older dance.)

This is as good a place as any to state unequivocally that using other writers' material is not only permissible but expected of you. I was recently asked about this by a new caller whose experience was in other branches of the performing arts, where authors jealously guarded their creations. Composers of square and contra dance routines almost invariably dedicate their works to the public, sometimes explicitly. And the Copyright Office has ruled that social dances, including square dances and other folk dances, are not copyrightable (Compendium of U.S. Copyright Office Practices, 3rd edition (2014, revised 2021), Chapter 800, Section 805.5(B)(2)). Obviously, this cuts both ways: You must reconcile yourself to the fact that any benefit you get from creating your own material will be to your reputation, not your bank account.

Changing words

It is almost a given that you will develop your own wording for every figure and break that you use – if not immediately, then gradually as you use it repeatedly and grow more comfortable with it. You may find yourself totally comfortable with a sequence but less so with the set of words you inherited from a book, a recording, or a fellow caller. If you are so inclined, you can sit down and brainstorm new words for an entire sequence. More likely, inspiration will hit you as you are calling it, a word or a phrase at a time. You may not recall the new words after the evening is over (this is one good reason for recording yourself), but chances are that they will come to you again the next time you use the sequence. If you can remember them when you have pen and paper or computer access, by all means jot them down; but if you use the sequence regularly, you may not need notes to jog your memory.

Changing moves

You will probably be motivated to change one or more movements in some of the figures you learn. Many figures are likely to appeal to you in nearly their entirety, but one basic move will bother you. It may be that you feel the move is always awkward, or perhaps it strikes you as awkward in this context. Or you may not wish to introduce it to your dancers at the moment; it may be the only move that uses gender roles in an otherwise gender-neutral sequence, or it may just be one thing too many for the dancers to learn right now.

Luckily, many basic square dance movements can be substituted one for another. This is particularly true in the easier figures and breaks, as their moves seldom take dancers very far from their starting point.

There are two kinds of movements you should be familiar with if you want to adapt dance material: zeroes and equivalents. Both terms were devised by callers in the modern square dance network; not surprisingly, they are even more useful for writing your own dances and for ad-libbing your calls.

A zero is a move or combination of moves that begin and end with the dancers in the same spots. A forward and back is a zero; so is a do-si-do. Some elementary zero combinations are a circle left followed by a circle right, and a ladies chain

Chapter 14: Exploring 163

(or right and left through) over and back. More intricate zeroes are not as easy for the dancers to detect; a modern caller hopes they won't. There are also fractional zeroes, sequences that must be called two or three times in a row before they "zero out." These were originally known as double and triple zeroes, but the trend is to term them half zeroes and one-third zeroes.

An *equivalent* is a move or combination that leaves the dancers in the same positions as another (usually simple and well-known) movement. As an example using traditional basics, "heads right and left through" followed by "sides right and left through" is equivalent to "all circle left halfway." Equivalents may differ from each other in which hands they leave free, or in how much momentum each dancer has and in which direction.

Sometimes it takes two new movements to produce the effect of one old one, or vice versa. Let's take two examples of movements whose introduction changed the feel of square dancing: "Heads square through" can be replaced with "Heads swing your opposite, then face the sides." "Heads star through" can be changed to "Heads swing your opposite, then face the middle." Both of these suggested sequences were common ways to get the active couples to face the desired direction before "square through" and "star through" were introduced.

As you can see, an equivalent does not have to take the same number of beats or steps as the movement it replaces. (In the first example above, a circle half takes 8 beats whereas a pair of right and left throughs takes 16, or 12 if called so that they overlap.) This fact can be useful in adapting or constructing a sequence: An equivalent can be substituted for another move or moves specifically in order to lengthen or shorten the sequence to fit the music. This will be discussed further in the next section, "Adding and subtracting moves."

For now, let's assume that you want to get rid of an unwanted move while keeping the total number of beats or steps the same. To do this, look at what the move accomplishes. To take one of the simplest examples, imagine a dance with a right and left through followed by a right and left back. The repeated move takes 16 beats of music and returns the dancers to the place where they began that move. If your dancers don't know the right and left through and you would rather not teach it at this point in the evening (or at all), but they do know the ladies chain, you can change the call to a ladies chain over and back. (All the sequences in this and the next paragraph happen to be zeroes, but they are dealt with here in their function as equivalents.)

The substituted sequence does not have to take the dancers to all the same spots as the original sequence, as long as it ends in the same place. Say that you dislike the element of "leading" and "following" in the ladies chain, or think your dancers may object to it. If a dance includes a chain over and back, you can substitute any 16-beat combination that starts and ends with the dancers in the same place. Examples for two facing couples are a circle four to the left followed by a circle right, and a right-hand star followed by a left-hand star. Depending on the context, you may be able to use moves for all eight dancers where the original sequence had moves for only four.

While all this may seem obvious, it is important to understand the principle, as it applies to more complex situations as well. Let's look at Jerry Helt's classic figure *Queen's Quadrille,* which has been widely used by both modern and neo-traditional callers. To begin, the head couples do a right and left through followed by a ladies chain; the sides then do the same two moves. The result is that the ladies are home again but the gents are across from home. (To end the figure, all circle left, swing the present corner – who is the original next-door neighbor – and promenade to the gent's home place. Call charts for the complete figure appear in Chapters 18 and 20.)

Let's suppose once more that you would rather not introduce the right and left through at this time. As there is no "easy out" in this figure – that is, each movement alters the dancers' relationships in a new way – we will look at the right and left through itself. What does it do? It moves two facing couples to the opposite side of the set. Well, we can get them to the same spot with a half promenade; that is, a promenade inside the set, ending with a "wheel around" or "courtesy turn" to face the center. (The half promenade can be useful as a stepping stone in teaching the right and left through.)

If a dance uses chains that are not in pairs, you will have to work harder to eliminate them. As will be discussed later under "Writing Your Own," a chain at one point in a figure often has to be "canceled" by a second one later, or else the ladies will be "out of sequence" (in numerical order clockwise when the gents are in order counterclockwise). When this happens, it complicates the task of getting everyone home again.

Adding and subtracting moves

There are many square dance figures in books and magazines from the 1950s that lend themselves to the style of calling that I have termed "neo-traditional." Some can be used as they appear, but many need to be modified for best results. One of the most common issues is that a figure will take more or fewer than 64 beats to dance if each basic movement is allowed a comfortable number of steps. As discussed in Chapter 4, some moves will require fewer than the "textbook" number of steps when the dancers are close together and already in motion. But there is an optimum timing below which a sequence should not be called, and the clever rhyming couplets in the magazines often allow too little time for some of the moves. Their authors frequently made sounding good their top priority, without making sure that the "key" or "command" words came at the right time.

Assuming you prefer to synchronize your dances with the phrases of the music, these are the steps required to make such a routine usable:

- List its basic moves in order, using standard terminology and disregarding the printed wording.
- Look for moves you don't wish to use, and change them to equivalent moves or combinations of moves. Don't worry if the new moves take more or fewer steps than the old ones.
- After each move, put the number of steps it is generally considered to take.

- Scrutinize these numbers, looking for spots where they may be wrong in this context.
  - They may be too large if the dancers are close together and already in motion.
  - They may be too small if two moves in succession are tightly timed (for example, four ladies grand chain done twice).
- Adjust the numbers so that the dancers will not have to speed up or pause. It will help if you dance the routine yourself at normal tempo, alone or with others.
- Write out the routine from the dancers' point of view: the dance movements next to the "A" and "B" parts of the music, at the point where the dancers would do them (not where you would call them).
- Add the numbers of steps.
  - If they total 64 (or 96), you can use the routine as it stands, each figure coinciding with once (or one and a half times) through a standard tune.
  - If they total too few, you can insert additional moves to equal 64 (or your desired number).
  - If they total too many, you can either look for moves that can be eliminated or add moves to equal the next higher length.
- Write out your revised routine, again using standard terminology.
- Finally, devise a set of words you are comfortable with, using basic prompts, patter, or some of each.

A recording with calls can be treated in the same way as a printed dance. Of course, you will first need to transcribe the wording, pausing the playback frequently in order to make an accurate copy.

If you don't care too much about synchronizing figures completely with the tune ("phrasing 1–64"; see Chapter 4), your task is easier. All you need concern yourself with is ensuring that each routine (figure or break) begins at the start of an "A" or "B" part and finishes with the end of such a part ("phrasing 1–16").

Inserting or deleting movements is fairly easy. There are points in nearly every routine at which a forward and back can be added or eliminated. The same is true of swings. Working on your material at home, you may not be sure which version of a dance you prefer. The only sure way to decide is to try different versions on live dancers, either paying customers or volunteers in your living room. This is admittedly a lot of work, but it will pay off in dancer satisfaction.

Playing with singing calls

One activity that is relatively easy for a caller with some experience is to create a "new" singing square by pairing an existing figure with a favorite song. This constitutes a kind of halfway point between adapting others' material and writing your own.

You can start with a ready-made figure that you learned from a book or from another caller. A good one to start with is Jerry Helt's *Queen's Quadrille* (included in Chapters 18 and 20), which is easy to memorize and easy to call. Tod Whittemore created two of his famous yodeling calls using a simplified version of Ted Sannella's *Do-si-do and Face the Sides* (Sannella 1982) and *Ted's Presque Isle Eight* (Sannella 1996).

Osgood 1969 includes several singing squares arranged by Ed Gilmore especially for that book, printed with carefully metered wording. Gilmore had been calling at least some of those figures for decades, fitting them to new songs every few years. If you have the inclination and understanding, you can do the same. You will find a few generic figures in Chapter 20 and a list of popular song titles in the Resources section.

Diagrams and Checkers

It helps immeasurably to be able to visualize the dancers' positions at any given point and their movement from one position to the next. This is true for writing your own dances and "hashing" or improvising routines (both below), and it can also help when you adapt existing material (above).

Two aids to visualization are diagrams and physical objects. The latter can be checkers, coins, playing cards, salt and pepper shakers, or custom-made dolls. They let you move quickly and easily between positions, but they have no memory. Unless you snap a picture of each step in a routine (and immediately label it so you know what move you just "called"), you will have no record of what happened. All you will know with certainty is whether the routine "works out" at the end; that is, whether the dancers are all with their partners and all "in sequence" (see below).

I recommend adopting a system of diagrams and developing the ability to work with them. Here are two possible systems:

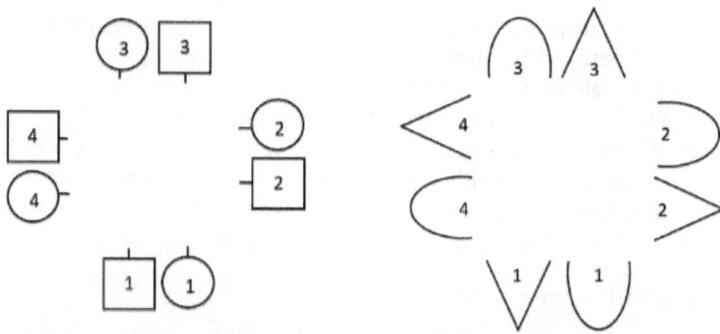

The system on the left is a common one, but I prefer the one on the right (used by Jay King and Don Beck) because it is easier to draw quickly. If the dancers look to you as if they are facing out of the set, you must be thinking of the angled lines as arrows; try imagining them as open arms.

If you draw a new diagram every time one or more dancers' position changes, and label it with the name of the move that was just done, you will end up with a complete record of where your make-believe dancers went. You can follow each dancer as he or she progresses around or across the square. I assure you that making a practice of this will give you a better sense of what happens during a dance. Remember, though, that you will still need to analyze each routine for smooth flow, alternating use of hands, and the like, and to check its timing and (if it is important to you) phrasing.

Writing Your Own

If you decide to try writing your own square dance figure, you will need to choose one of two broad categories. One is a sequence of basic movements (such as ladies chain) that are known and accepted in the dance community; each move is called separately, using a name familiar to the dancers. The other, termed a "unique" or "dominant" figure, usually has one or more active couples trace a curving path around and through the standing couples. Most unique dances are visiting-couple figures, though a few have the active dancers work through the center of the set (as in some versions of the dance *Figure Eight*). Typically a unique figure is called using a series of traditional phrases that appear in no other dance and that give little or no information about the movements (such as "Duck for the oyster, dig for the clam" or "Chase the rabbit, chase the squirrel").

It takes a lot of creativity to concoct a brand-new unique figure. If you choose this path, you can either make yourself thoroughly familiar with the existing repertoire of such dances (there are several sources, in print and online) or let your imagination run wild, with little heed to what has been done before. (You probably know at least a few such figures, such as *Duck for the Oyster,* which will give you a broad idea. Several are included in Chapter 19.)

Rather than create a dance out of nothing, most choreographers opt for figures composed of existing basics. Here again you can study the material that already exists or strike out on your own, but at least you will have a standard vocabulary to work with.

Where to begin

If you choose to study what has been done before, I suggest you begin by reading Chapter 5, which describes the various formations that choreographers have used. Within most formations, you can decide whether you want all eight dancers to become active quickly or limit the action to one or two couples. Both types of dance have their advantages; which type you favor will depend largely on your intended audience.

One way to write a dance is to think of a "gimmick" or specific effect and then find appropriate movements to precede and/or follow it. For example, when I began writing the figure that became *Duck Through and Swing* (see Chapter 18), I had a certain effect in mind: I wanted lines of four, facing out, to execute "ends turn in" (as in Ed Gilmore's classic dance by that name, included in Chapter 21) and immediately find their next partner – or, the fourth time through, their original partner. I started with this effect and worked backwards, figuring out which moves I needed to use to get the dancers into the right arrangement of partners and gender roles when they formed their lines of four.

You can also start with an ordinary basic move and see what can comfortably precede and follow it. When I wrote my first contra, *Shadrack's Delight*, I was playing around with the modern square dance move "swing through." I liked its flow, but I was stymied by the fact that it takes 6 steps or beats, an awkward number to fit to music that is written in 4s and 8s. Squeezing it into 4 beats would create a rat race; stretching it to 8 beats would require the formal timing of a 19th-century quadrille, which wasn't what I was looking for. My solution was to put 4-count balances between the turns, as in the Alamo Style break. A turn halfway around in 4 beats is fairly loose timing, but combined with getting set for the next balance it feels right. I noticed that the gents were approaching their partners with 8 beats left in the phrase, making a swing the obvious choice for the next move. From there I added movements that gave a traditional feel while keeping everyone moving, which had been my overall goal for the sequence.

It is an intrinsic part of effective calling to be aware of what each call accomplishes and how long it takes the dancers to execute, but it is supremely important when you are putting together your own figure or break. One example that gives even experienced callers trouble is the grand right and left into a promenade. Many callers enjoy writing singing squares that let the caller (and the dancers if they wish) sing the original lyrics of the song during the last 16 beats of the chorus. This means that the directive calls should be finished before the last 16 beats – specifically, at the end of the phrase that would be termed B.1 in a fiddle tune. Many singing calls end each break with a promenade after a grand right and left. But starting from home, four hands' worth of a grand right and left puts everyone across from home. So 16 beats is too much time for the promenade, because the dancers need to go only halfway around the set. One solution is to write in some movements toward the beginning of the tune that put the dancers across from home when the grand right and left begins. The standard break for *Trail of the Lonesome Pine* does this with a circle left halfway.

Variety

Variety is often cited as one of the most desirable qualities in a caller's repertoire or an evening's program. There are several ways to provide it. You can vary the energy level from one dance number to the next. You can vary the amount of physical contact between the dancers, going from a martial feeling to a romantic mood. You can vary the formations used – circles, stars, lines, grids. You can vary the dance types – circles, squares, longways sets, couple dances. I mention this here because in composing routines you can try to capture a specific mood, perhaps one embodied in too few of the dances you already use. Or you can incorporate several formations in one number, as Ted Sannella did in his classic square *Do-si-do and Face the Sides* (see Chapter 18).

Smooth flow

Smooth body flow was not always considered essential as square dance choreography developed. Most routines incorporated several points at which the dancers returned home and their motion came to a temporary halt. (An example, still found in many figures, is a courtesy turn with partner followed by a corner do-si-do or allemande left.) But I recommend making smooth flow one of your criteria if you choose to create your own sequences.

Examples of good flow:

- A circle right into an allemande left
- A circle left into a right-hand turn with either partner or corner
- A corner do-si-do into a ladies' left-hand star
- A partner do-si-do into a gents' left-hand star
- A corner see-saw into a gents' right-hand star
- A partner see-saw into a ladies' right-hand star

Note that after a do-si-do or see-saw, all eight dancers have both hands free, but the star mentioned above is the smoother option because the designated dancers can continue their clockwise or counterclockwise motion by moving forward into the star. On the other hand (pun intended), one of Ed Gilmore's favorite singing-call figures included a corner do-si-do followed by a gents' left-hand star. To make this a smooth transition, the gents need to "follow their nose"; that is, to walk forward around their corner rather than finish the do-si-do by walking backward as usual.

After you have devised a complete figure or break, it is a good idea to take a step back mentally and consider it as a whole. Does each movement flow smoothly into the next? Is there a consistent overall mood? Will the dancers feel as though they have "gone somewhere" when they are finished? Working with the same few building blocks, it is possible to write either a cohesive, satisfying routine or one that feels like a mere bunch of basics strung together. You should use the same criteria to judge your own work as you can (and should) use to decide whether to add an existing dance to your repertoire.

In and out of sequence

Sequence is a concept that choreographers became aware of during the great square dance revival. If the four couples, ladies, or gents are in numerical order counterclockwise around the set, they are said to be in sequence. If they are in numerical order clockwise, they are out of sequence. This is true no matter what formation they may be in or which direction they are facing. If you draw a diagram of eight dancers at a given point in a routine, you can see at a glance whether they are in or out of sequence.

In most traditional figures and many newer ones, sequence is not an issue because no one ever gets out of sequence. Visiting figures are not generally thought of as subject to the rules of sequence; any departure from the original configuration of the set is remedied when the active couple returns home. Figures in which opposite couples work together, however, must be looked at case by case. In many such dances, if the heads do something, the sides do the same thing immediately afterward. But some figures start with only the heads (or sides) doing a right and left through, which puts the couples out of sequence. If a promenade is called at that point, when two couples get home the others will be across from home. Getting everyone back in sequence can be done in several ways; the variety of methods is what gives each dance its unique personality.

If you want to use ladies chain in your choreography, beware of getting the ladies out of sequence. If this happens and is not nullified before the end of the figure, there is no way to accomplish both of two things that are generally accepted as desirable: first, to let every gent dance with all four ladies (and vice versa), and second, to give everyone an equal amount of time as an active dancer.

Box formation

As you experiment with choreography, take special note of the "box" formation, where two couples (say the sides) are at home and the other two (say the heads) are back to back in the center, each inside couple facing an outside couple. This is one of the key formations in modern square dancing: It is only a short distance from home position, and the simplest arrangement from which to call an allemande left. Typically, from box formation, the active and inactive couples pass back and forth along an east-west or north-south traffic lane.

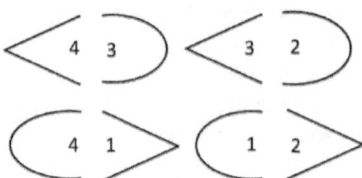

There are two general ways to get the dancers into a box formation. The one most commonly used in the modern scene is to move the active couples in a grid pattern. The first movement is often the equivalent of having the heads step forward and face their corner. The result is shown in the diagram above; you can see that each head dancer is next to his or her opposite. After several moves, the simplest grid routine returns the dancers to this position for an allemande left. If certain rules are followed, the caller can be sure that whenever the gents are in sequence, the ladies are too.

Some equivalents of "Heads step forward and face your corner" are:

- Heads do-si-do opposite, then stay in the middle and face the sides
- Heads swing the opposite, put the lady on the right and face the sides
- Heads right and left through, pass through, separate around one, come into the middle and pass through
- Heads square through four hands (they will have their right hand free)

- Heads pass through, separate around one, come into the middle and square through three hands (they will have their left hand free, ready for an allemande left)

The other way to set up a box formation is to have the heads (or sides) lead to the right as couples, so that Couple 1 is facing Couple 2 and 3 is facing 4. This set-up is rare in modern square dancing, but of course "Heads lead right" is a mainstay of traditional dance, and you may be tempted to start with it when devising your own material. Because the dancers in all four couples are next to their partner, this arrangement "looks right" on paper, and it is easy to assume that all kinds of grid movements may be called from here. But note an important point: In a box formation where all partners are together, if the gents are in sequence, the ladies are out of sequence, and vice versa. This means that an allemande left cannot be called where you might expect, because only half the dancers will be facing their corner.

It is actually quite easy to avoid getting "caught" by this phenomenon. Simply have the head ladies chain before calling the head couples out to their right. The heads will now be with their opposite rather than their partner as they move across the set, just as if you had kept them in a grid from the start.

In general, if you are writing a figure and find that some dancers are not where you want them at the end, you can often solve the problem by inserting one or two moves at the beginning. To take *Duck Through and Swing* as an example again, I discovered that I needed to put the couples out of sequence in order to get the ending I wanted. The simplest way to do this was to have either the heads or the sides do a right and left through. I made the routine more interesting by having the other pair do a right and left over and back at almost the same time, a trick I learned from Ted Sannella.

New movements

You may be tempted to try writing new "basic" movements, especially after you have played around with the existing ones for a while. By all means experiment, and feel free to use your creations with live dancers. But be sure to work out a way to explain clearly what you mean, and don't expect it to become something that all dancers must learn. Lloyd Shaw, a pioneer of the 20th-century square dance boom, wrote several figures and breaks that could not be called using existing terminology. But he had a solid grounding in traditional style before he started innovating. Even so, only one of his creations, the Allemande Thar break, has stayed with us.

Don't feel you have to write material just to give dancers something new. Remember that every movement, every dance will be new to those who haven't encountered it before. As for the most experienced dancers in your group, there is plenty of good material out there for you to draw on. Experiment if you want to, but test your material – your own creations and those of others – and be ready to revise or discard it if it proves awkward or unsatisfying.

My strongest word of advice, if you are bent on writing your own material, is to dance and call as often as you can. The more experience you get, the more in tune with tradition your creations will become, and the better they're likely to be.

Hash and Near-Hash

Hash as practiced in the modern square dance scene is an art in itself. Its defining characteristic is that the dancers never know exactly what call is coming next. It seems as if the caller is ad-libbing completely, putting sequences together on the fly. Sometimes this is true, or nearly so, but most hash callers memorize at least a few short combinations, and all operate according to some important established rules.

As a neo-traditional caller, you will probably not wish to improvise your calls as a matter of course. (Old-time southern callers often improvise, but only to the extent of choosing which of several existing figures to call next.) I explain a bit about modern hash here because studying the elementary principles of choreographic management has made me a more effective caller and choreographer within my chosen sphere. If you are of an analytic turn of mind, this may be true for you too.

All-out hash calling requires the caller to keep track of where the dancers are in the square, while continuing to time the calls properly. But even with simple routines that you can easily memorize, it will help your calling if you can follow the dancers from one position to the next. You're less likely to forget a line if you're actively thinking about what the words mean to the dancers.

I begin with a brief history of hash, noting the successive stages that led to today's free-wheeling improvisation. You may wish to explore the possibilities of one or more of these intermediate stages, as I have.

Based on passing references in dance manuals, diaries, and other printed sources, it seems clear that many 19th-century callers improvised at least some of their routines. Ralph Page, who was active from the 1930s to the 1980s, enjoyed ad-libbing his breaks and occasionally called an entire "confusion square," in which the dancers had no idea what his next command would be. Ted Sannella carried on the tradition of improvised breaks in phrased New England squares; he rarely ad-libbed a whole square except for his trademark *Merry-Go-Round* and an occasional round of Continuous Ninepin (see Chapter 22 for both).

The importance of allemande left

In written records of country-style square dances dating back to the early 1900s, the most widely encountered chorus sequence is "Allemande left your corner, right hand to your partner, grand right and left." What caused it to become the standard across the continent is unknown, but it was collected in the Midwest and the Southwest early in the century, and in the Northeast in the 1930s. Eastern callers generally expected the dancers to continue the grand right and left all the way around the set until they regained their home positions; a promenade full around might or might not be called at that point. In western regions the custom was for partners to promenade home upon meeting halfway around.

When square dancing became a hobby and then a craze, two phenomena occurred in succession, both involving the allemande left and grand right and left. First, callers began devising "breaks" or choruses that were more complex than the standard sequence. Second, the allemande left and its following movements changed from a free-standing chorus to an integral part of the figure.

Allemande breaks – By the 1930s a number of variations on the grand right and left had appeared. Typically a caller would bring them into play when partners met across from home in a normal grand right and left. The earliest were Once and a Half (turn partner by the right, the next person by the left, and so on until partners meet at home); Double Elbow (turn partner by the right, then left, and do the same with each person you meet); and the grand right and left interrupted by balances that ultimately took the name of Alamo Style. Another pre-1950s break was the Grand Sashay: do-si-do partner, then pass by the right hand or right shoulder; see-saw the next, then pass by the left; and so on to home.

In 1938 Lloyd Shaw unwittingly started a trend when he devised Allemande Thar, originally for his teenage performing group. This is a grand right and left interrupted twice by a special kind of star; the word "thar" is leading patter to alert the dancers of what is coming. Shaw released the break to the public in 1946. It was wildly popular from the beginning; the "thar star" has become a standard "basic" in modern square dancing. Also, it inspired several imitations, including Allemande O (interrupted twice by a do paso) and Away You Go (do paso leading into a thar star). By the early 1950s, choreographers were trying to outdo one another in creating complex combinations of stars and hand turns; the collection was dubbed the Allemande Alphabet.

Surprise allemande left – Originally, as mentioned above, the standard chorus of allemande left and grand right and left was self-contained. Dancers would do the main figure of the dance; whether that was a visiting-couple figure or used some other structure, the dancers would always end each couple's or pair's turn by coming home and squaring their set. The allemande left that began the chorus was always done from home positions.

In the early 1950s this began to change. Callers devised routines that integrated an allemande left with the figure. One of the first was Ed Gilmore's *Ends Turn In* (see Chapter 21), published in 1952, in which the two active couples circled in the center, then passed through to face their original corners. Eventually every newly composed figure was expected to lead to a "surprise" allemande left; callers looked for new ways to mix the dancers so thoroughly that the sight of their corner was unexpected. As choreography became more challenging, it was logical for the allemande left, the start of the standard chorus, to become the point for release of tension. It has become the custom for the dancers to whoop on the call of "allemande left" – partly in appreciation of the caller's cleverness in mixing and unmixing them, but mainly, I think, because the improvisatory nature of modern calling forces them to keep quiet during most of the dance.

Hashing breaks

Some of the breaks in the Allemande Alphabet were complex enough to confuse even experienced dancers, but typically they were planned in advance and memorized (or read) by the caller. By the mid-1950s callers were hashing their breaks completely, improvising a new sequence every time they began a tip. (Most of these hashed breaks were made up entirely of hand turns, hand pulls around the set, and stars for the ladies or the gents.) More conservative leaders complained that this practice violated the principle that a break should be easier than the figures, a chance for the dancers to relax between bouts of harder work. But challenging the dancers' mental capability was increasingly seen as desirable.

Hashing figures

The logical next step from hashing breaks was hashing figures. The earliest attempt at providing extra variety was probably the "medley change": a visiting-couple dance in which Couple 1 did one figure (say *Bird in the Cage*) with the other three couples; then after a chorus, Couple 2 did a different figure (say *Duck for the Oyster*); and so on for Couples 3 and 4. The process could be carried to extremes by having each active couple do three different figures, one with each receiving couple; with experienced dancers, callers could choose any figure in their repertoire without advance warning. (Southern mountain dancing as practiced in some communities works like this; the repertoire of figures is usually small.) Lloyd Shaw favored medleys for exhibition and contest work, to forestall boredom on the part of the audience as well as the dancers.

Another kind of hashing was the practice of changing the ending of established figures. A caller might call a figure "by the book" once or twice, then vary it by altering the last few calls or adding a short sequence. As an example, the end of Ed Gilmore's *Lazy H* (see Chapter 21) has four dancers passing through in the center and meeting their corners for an allemande left (similarly to *Ends Turn In*). Gilmore would call it that way two or three times, then change it to "Pass through, split the outside two, go around one, come into the middle with a right-hand star, go once around to the corner, allemande left." This was a convenient way of satisfying dancers' desire for "more" by using well-known basic moves in new combinations.

By the mid- to late 1960s, most modern square dance callers were hashing their patter calls completely; that is, calling strings of basic movements in an order unknown to their dancers. They would not necessarily call the same sequence to the side couples as they had just called to the heads. Singing calls were generally choreographed in advance, usually by the callers who recorded them, though some astute and talented callers devised their own routines to suit the needs of their dancers. But in later years this custom fell by the wayside; for several decades now, singing calls have consisted entirely of nondescript strings of calls. In fact, they are almost identical to patter calls, except for their constrained length and an obligatory partner change with each repetition of the figure.

Keeping track

Modern square dance callers often speak of "choreographic management" – that is, keeping track of their dancers. This is important in their style of dance because most sequences are assembled on the fly and the dancers never know exactly what is coming next. As will be seen below, callers have several ways of keeping track. Some come close to pure improvisation, but most make use of one or more shortcuts.

As with the idea of hash in general, it is not at all necessary for a tradition-minded caller to know any methods of tracking the dancers. But spending a little time studying them can deepen your understanding of choreography – and possibly give you some tools that may come in handy once in a while.

Choreographic management can be done in any of the following ways:

Reading

It is, of course, possible to read a dance aloud from start to finish, using an index card, a sheet of paper, or an electronic device. Every writer who mentions this possibility has warned against the practice. Looking at the words takes the caller's focus off the dancers, breaking a crucial part of the three-way connection between the caller, the dancers, and the music. A caller who reads is likely to miss a sign of incipient trouble on the floor; conversely, shifting one's attention to the dancers can lead to losing one's place in the text, possibly skipping a line or two. Relying on a printed text is often the mark of a newer caller who has not taken the time to learn what each call accomplishes, and who therefore has trouble interpreting the shifting patterns on the floor.

In present-day contra dancing, many callers carry the directions for hundreds of dances and may not be able to memorize them all. I have misgivings about claiming imperfectly learned dances as part of one's repertoire, but this seems to be the current norm. I always advise contra callers to refresh their memory with the card during the walkthrough, if they must, but then to avoid looking at it while calling the dance to music.

In old-time and neo-traditional square dancing, callers typically have a much smaller repertoire than in modern contra dancing – dozens of figures rather than hundreds. Whether you are new to squares or an old hand at them, I urge you to expand your repertoire at a pace that lets you become completely familiar with each dance. This will allow you to keep your focus on the dancers, where it belongs. In addition, the added confidence that comes from thoroughly knowing your material will show in your voice, making you a more effective and attractive caller.

Memory

In the days when dancing in squares was not a hobby but a normal part of everyday life, most callers probably delivered all their material from memory. Depending on the region, a typical caller might know anywhere from half a dozen to 20 or 30 "changes" or figures – not a burdensome number to memorize over a few years of apprenticeship. As for breaks, most callers used only one or two;

even in areas where varying the break was popular, there were a mere half dozen, mostly variations on the grand right and left. Many callers kept a "little black book"; some wrote down whole figures, others merely listed titles. But I sincerely doubt that any of them looked at the book while calling.

Memorizing entire poems and essays used to be part of the school curriculum; for better or worse, this is largely no longer true. But the human brain is capable of more along these lines than we tend to give it credit for nowadays. If you have never learned a dance by heart, I encourage you to commit one or two figures and at least one break to memory. I believe the feeling of confidence and satisfaction that this produces will give you a taste for more.

Sight

"Sight calling" has been a catchphrase in the modern square dance scene since the 1950s. The term can mean a number of things; the differences are more of degree than of kind. In its ultimate form, sight calling comprises two steps. The first is to deliver unplanned calls to the dancers in a steady stream, the only constraint being that each call must be possible – and, ideally, comfortable – for the dancers to execute after the preceding one. The second step is to discern where the dancers are in relation to one another, and to call movements that will "resolve the square"; that is, to get the dancers "in sequence" (see above) and between their partner and their corner. From there they can be directed to their corner for an allemande left, or straight to their partner to begin a grand right and left.

If this sounds complicated, it is. In order to deliver free-wheeling calls, a caller must know what each call accomplishes, how many steps it requires, and which calls can comfortably follow it. In order to resolve the square, the caller must have memorized the appearance of four dancers in at least one set – typically the original Gent 1, his partner, his corner (Lady 4) and her partner. Most sight callers do this for multiple squares, in case one square breaks down or deliberately switches partners. (This memorization is easier in a subculture where people tend to dance with the same partner all evening and often wear matching outfits.) Because nearly all modern square dance choreography is symmetrical, the caller knows that if Couples 1 and 4 are positioned to do an allemande left, so are Couples 2 and 3. As Jay King (1972) wrote, a sight caller is by no means taking the easy way out, as an excellent memory is needed for preliminary work and for choosing dancers to watch.

Although I have never called at the rarefied heights of full-fledged modern callers, I do use a rudimentary form of sight calling during my square breaks, which I usually improvise. At the start of a break I will note the appearance of one couple in the set nearest me, then make sure to reunite them by the end of the break if the choreography separates them. (Because I keep my breaks relatively simple, I seldom need to worry about getting the dancers "out of sequence.") I also use "sight timing" during the grand right and left: Regardless of the number of steps it takes in theory to go halfway or all the way, I watch the members of a key couple as they make their way around the set, and deliver the next call (such as "swing") just before they meet.

Mental image

The "mental image" method is similar to sight calling, with this difference: Instead of watching actual key dancers in one or more squares, the caller visualizes a few dancers (say Gent 1 and his partner and corner) going through the movements. The caller watches the real dancers, but only to double-check their reaction to the calls so as to give the next one at the proper time. Those who prefer this method believe it to be the best of all worlds, freeing the caller from having to memorize either the sequence or the dancers' appearance.

Drawing diagrams is an important part of learning mental imagery. Although, as noted above, I have never taken hash calling to its extremes, I can vouch for the fact that diagramming sequences – my own and those of others – has improved my understanding of what each call accomplishes, and has suggested new possibilities. Many of my published original squares occurred to me because of the work I had put into diagramming.

Modules

The use of modules is a kind of halfway point between memorizing and freewheeling. A module is a short sequence of movements, readily memorized, that takes dancers from one standard formation to another. A caller can string any number of modules together to form a complete dance. The process is much like playing dominoes: One must be sure to match the formation at the start of each new module with that at the end of the preceding one.

There are three kinds of modules:

Set-ups – modules that start with the dancers at home. Examples using traditional basics are "Heads lead to the right, circle four; head gents break to a line of four" and "Heads forward and back, swing your opposite; put the lady on the right and face the sides." The latter example ends in what a modern caller would term a "box" formation (discussed under "Writing Your Own" above).

Main or intermediate modules – those that neither start nor end with the dancers at home. One or more of these are inserted between a set-up and a get-out to form a dance. A traditional example that could follow the second set-up above is "Circle four [with the side couple], split those two and separate around one to a line of four." This takes the dancers from a box formation to a line formation. A module that changes the formation like this is known as a *conversion module*; a module that starts and ends with dancers in the same relative places is a *zero*, as mentioned under "Adapting Dances" at the beginning of this chapter.

Get-outs – modules that end with the dancers "in sequence" and usually either meeting their corner (for an allemande left or, in singing calls, a swing) or facing their partner (for a grand right and left). A get-out could conceivably end with the dancers "squared up" at home or approaching partners to swing at home; the latter is not typically used in modern square dancing but could be employed to advantage by a neo-traditional caller.

Keep in mind the concept of *equivalents,* as described under "Adapting Dances." Note that an equivalent for a given move can be another single move, a pair of moves, or a lengthy module containing several moves.

I should mention here that a typical modern hash dance, which lasts about 4 to 8 minutes, contains multiple "sub-dances" that begin at home and end with an allemande left or other resolution. The caller can vary the length of such a sub-dance, making it shorter if the dancers are known beginners or are having trouble, or longer to give the dancers the extra challenge of staying with the caller for an extended period. This is an outgrowth of the traditional practice of calling four figures, each starting and ending at home and each usually followed by an allemande left.

What I do

For choreographic management in my calling of squares, which draws from both traditional and modern wisdom, I use a combination of long-term memory, short-term memory, and in-the-moment awareness. I focus on such things as:

- The appearance and clothing of key dancers (to help me keep track of how far partners are from each other)
- The number of times I've called the figure so far (to help me pace my energy, and to let me know when to insert breaks)
- Whether the dancers are at home or across from home when it's time for a promenade
- How many steps until partners meet in a grand right and left
- How much music is left in the chorus when partners meet (so I can decide how many moves to use from the grand right and left to the end of the chorus)

Final thoughts on hash

After reading this far, you are likely to know whether the idea of calling hash appeals to you. If it doesn't, that's perfectly all right; hashing calls, particularly figures, is not a part of most regional traditions, and an old-time or neo-traditional caller can become quite popular and successful without it. If it does appeal to you, you can explore this area of calling as much or as little as you wish – there is no "right" amount, no ideal percentage of your repertoire that should be hashed.

But in a general recreational square dance program, hash should be used very sparingly if at all. Even with experienced dancers who enjoy a challenge, I believe the healthiest approach is to provide a solid diet of classic dances – squares, contras, mixers, couple dances, maybe no-partner dances – in addition to the "seasoning" of hash and tricky stuff.

If you get the urge to experiment with hash, you can ease into it. Here are a few suggested steps:

- Adopt a system of symbols to represent the eight dancers of a square, as discussed above.
- Draw diagrams of a short sequence of calls. Be sure to make a new diagram each time one or more dancers move to a new position. (For example, a forward and back or a do-si-do does not require a new diagram, but a pass

through or a right and left through does.) Continue diagramming all the way to a resolution (everyone with partner, or approaching corner for an allemande left).
- Repeat the process for other sequences. Be sure you understand what each move does to the shape of the set and the relative positions of the dancers.
- Once you have absorbed this knowledge (what each move accomplishes) to the point where you no longer have to think about it consciously, you can try calling standard basic movements to live dancers in any order. Your only "hard" constraint is that each move must be possible after the preceding one (you can't call a right and left through unless you have at least one pair of facing couples). Of course, there are also the "soft" constraints that everyone get an equal amount of time in motion and that the sequences be enjoyable.

If doing this whets your appetite for more, you can choose and memorize a few simple modules – set-ups, zeroes, get-outs. This will greatly expand your effectiveness: Not only will your repertoire increase, but the confidence that comes from mastering the material will improve your delivery, even of standard figures.

One very important point is that hash calls must be prompted. This does not necessarily mean that each call must come at the end of a musical phrase, as in a contra dance – only that it must come two beats before the dancers finish the preceding move. Cadence calls – that is, calls delivered at the same time as the dancers are executing them, as in some singing squares – are useless if the dancers have no idea what is coming. The "prompt, then patter" method described in Chapter 6 is permissible in calling hash; it is especially good if you are doing phrased hash. Even if you are not phrasing the whole dance, there will almost certainly be portions you can phrase.

While I would never suggest that every caller needs to learn to use hash, I greatly prefer hashing my breaks. It cuts teaching time compared to presenting a complete break with every figure. I think it also makes for better dancers; they quickly realize they must listen carefully, and their reaction time improves – qualities that will help them even when they are dancing familiar material. Because breaks are traditionally simpler than figures, improvising them is a fairly easily learned skill.

If you are improvising breaks for the first time, use only calls that direct dancers to work with their partner and corner; this will keep them "at home" for practical purposes, no matter how far they get from their original side of the square. Once you are comfortable doing this, you can add movements that send dancers to their opposite, either for a brief interaction (such as a courtesy turn or a single hand turn) or to claim the opposite as a temporary partner. Eventually you can add the next-door neighbor to the mix – in which case you will be employing more hashing than I generally use, even after half a century.

One caution: If you are calling a figure that includes a partner change, be extremely careful during any break other than the introduction and ending – that is, any break that does not start and finish with original partners together. Dancers with little experience doing squares will have enough trouble remembering who their current partner is, without having to identify a new corner, opposite, or neighbor on the fly. And the average crowd at an open dance will contain enough such dancers to ensure that hashing a middle break will "stop the floor." If the figure is a "keeper," on the other hand, you can indulge in a certain amount of experimentation, always watching the dancers for signs of frustration.

If you have what it takes to go further, you'll know.

PART THREE
Material

Key to typography of call charts

A dash (–) indicates a downbeat where the caller is silent.

An <u>underlined</u> word or syllable is to be spoken on the downbeat. (The underlines do not indicate the words to be emphasized.)

Words given no special treatment are to be spoken as naturally as possible within the beat structure.

A word in *italic* type is to be given extra emphasis.

A word in **bold** type is to be spoken slightly earlier than it would otherwise be (for instance, if it is the first word printed on a downbeat, it is to be spoken just ahead of the downbeat).

Call lines in (parentheses) are helping words or patter and may be omitted.

A line in [*brackets and italics*] is not part of the spoken call; it often indicates the start of a break.

15

Basic Movements

Because neo-traditional square dancing is a grassroots activity with no governing body, there is no official list of movements that are to be considered basic or that every accomplished dancer must know. In this chapter I have enlarged upon the definitions of the movements that I believe are used most often by neo-traditional callers. If others are in common use in your area, you will of course teach them; it is my hope that most if not all of them are defined in the Glossary.

The basics appear in the approximate order in which I would introduce them to a group. (This order does not include variations, such as the breaks described in the section on the grand right and left.) Note that in traditional and neo-traditional dancing, where most dances are set routines rather than hash, it is customary to present basics by choosing figures that include them, rather than teaching them out of context and using them in drills.

I have not attempted, either here or in the Glossary, to define every two-couple figure used in the southern mountains or other areas where visiting-couple dances are common. Many of them can be found in the books described in the Resources section, particularly those dealing with southern dancing.

Before the Basics

Square dancing is more than the sum of its parts. Knowing and assimilating certain principles of good dancing is as important as learning the basic movements. If you are working with people who dance as a hobby or clearly intend to do so, I encourage you to develop good habits in them, by teaching and by example. At a non-dancer event, you will probably not want to say much about these points, but you will do well to stay aware of them yourself. (These matters are discussed at greater length in *Contra Dance Calling,* Chapters 5 and 11.)

Courtesy

In the context of a dance, the Golden Rule dictates courtesy toward your partner, the other dancers in your set, the other sets on the floor, and the band and caller. This is a group activity; what each person does affects everyone in the room, for better or worse. Good dancers are aware of those around them, and are always looking for ways to make them feel more comfortable, and to make the set feel like a team. (Note that this does not always mean correcting other dancers.)

The dance-walk

The basic step for square dancing in most regions is a walk, one step for each downbeat. But dancing is different from walking down the street, at least the way many people do the latter. The weight should be kept forward, over the balls of the feet, rather than back on the heels. Each walking step should begin directly below the body, and the foot should push back; the feet should never reach forward. When not moving, the weight should be balanced over both feet so the dancer can change direction instantly.

The style of walking differs slightly between regions. Dancers in southern mountain style tend to lean forward a bit more than northeastern dancers, with traditional western style somewhere in between. The faster the tempo, the more important it is to keep the body under control; sometimes taking shorter steps can help with this.

First-time dancers often ask "Which foot should I start on?" Most of the time one foot is as good as the other. Given that the only basics where it definitely matters begin on the right foot (the buzz-step swing and, in most areas, the balance), I have developed the habit of starting all my movements on that foot. Interestingly, some 19th-century dance manuals specify the right foot.

Giving weight

A principle common to contra dancing, English country dancing, and traditional square dancing in just about every region is that of giving weight. This means putting just enough spring in one's arms to match the resistance of one's partner or neighbors. Giving weight applies not only to swings and other kinds of turns but to circles as well. The "pull by" in the grand right and left and some versions of the right and left through needs a bit of resistance, although it should not be done roughly or jerkily. Even in movements where two or more people are moving side by side, such as the promenade or forward and back, dancers should support their own arms and not rely on their neighbors to do it for them.

Transitions

Getting from one movement to the next is as essential a skill as executing the movements themselves. The nature of the transitions in a routine can affect its difficulty just as surely as the number and complexity of the movements. Transitions are slightly less crucial in squares than in contras, where they can affect the dancers' ability to remember a routine after the caller has quit prompting it, but they are still important. Under each basic in this chapter, the most common transitions to and from other moves are discussed.

Naming and Numbering

By far the most common square set comprises four couples, each standing on one side of an imaginary square with their backs to one of the walls of the room. The person on the right in each couple is termed the lady; the person on the left is the gent. (See "Same-Sex Couples and Gender-Free Dancing" in Chapter 13 for a discussion of alternative terms.)

Chapter 15: Basic Movements 185

In nearly all places where American square dancing is done, Couple 1 have their backs to the music. (If the source of the music is not obviously on one side of the room, the caller will designate a "head of the hall.") In a few areas where each set customarily had its own caller, notably Chicago in the first half of the 20th century, Couple 1 faced the band for better communication with the musicians.

In most present-day square dance communities, the couples are numbered counterclockwise: Couple 2 is to the right of Couple 1; Couple 3 is to the right of Couple 2 and across from Couple 1; Couple 4 is to the right of Couple 3, to the left of Couple 1, and across from Couple 2. Couples 1 and 3 are known as the head couples or the heads (in older parlance, the head and foot or the first four). Couples 2 and 4 are the side couples or the sides (in older terms, the side four or rarely the second four).

This numbering is a product of the circular or around-the-set tradition, in which most dances were visiting-couple figures. Some (though not all) 19th-century dance manuals placed Couple 2 across from Couple 1 for quadrilles, which consisted largely of across-the-set figures. A few dance communities apparently kept the latter numbering through the early 20th century. (Curiously, Tolman and Page 1937, the bible of New England dance for decades, does not specify couple numbering, referring only to head, foot, and side couples.)

If you are dancing the part of a lady: When all are in home positions, the person on your left is your partner; the person on your right is your corner; the person directly across from you is your opposite gent or simply your opposite; the gent in the next couple to your left is your left-hand gent (or "next-door neighbor").

If you are dancing the part of a gent: When all are in home positions, the person on your right is your partner; the person on your left is your corner; the person directly across from you is your opposite lady or simply your opposite; the lady in the next couple to your right is your right-hand lady (or "next-door neighbor").

In many square dances, one's partner at any given time may not always be one's original partner. For one thing, some figures incorporate a partner change, with one role (usually the gents) maintaining their home place and the other role ending each repetition of the figure on their new partner's side of the square. This is most often accomplished by having the dancers swing their corner or their next-door neighbor (who becomes their partner during the swing) and promenade to the gent's (or occasionally the lady's) home place. In addition, at certain moments in some complex figures the caller may refer to the lady currently on one's right, or the gent on one's left, as a partner. Before calling such a figure, or calling any partner-change dance to an inexperienced crowd, it is well to caution that "we dance places, not faces." This differs from the rule in contra dances, where one's partner never changes during a musical number.

Circle

Done by

Three or more dancers who are already in a more or less circular group. The most common numbers are four and eight, but circles of six are used in cumulative visiting-couple dances, and odd numbers of circling dancers are seen occasionally (as in the dance *Bird in the Cage*).

Description

The dancers join adjacent hands to form a circle, all facing the center. They turn their bodies to face diagonally either left or right, and using the basic dance-walk, they move in the direction they are facing, staying on the rim of the circle and keeping its size constant. If no direction is specified, a circle moves to the dancers' left (clockwise).

Result

The dancers are in a group similar to their starting formation. They may or may not be in their original places, but they are all in the same positions relative to one another.

Teaching Technique

The circle is deceptively simple in appearance. It's really a demanding movement, easy to spoil by indifferent dancing, and how you teach it can make or break an evening. I always start a pre-dance lesson, or the first dance of an event for non-dancers, by going over the fine points of the circle. Some of those points may not need to be mentioned explicitly, but they should all at least be modeled.

Make sure the circle is as perfectly round as it can get without browbeating the dancers; that is, any obvious corners should be smoothed out, and people should all be roughly the same distance apart. (The latter goal can be a challenge if most people are entering the dance area from one side of the room.) Arms should be bent, with elbows pointing down and hands about shoulder-high to the shorter dancers. To avoid endless false moves when taking hands, the traditional rule is "Gents' palms up, ladies' palms down." Some groups that de-emphasize gender roles have modified this to "Right palm up, left palm down."

Giving weight is as important in a circle as in any other move, if not more so. The precise amount of resistance needed will vary between different people; it requires judgment from the dancers that comes with experience, but you can help beginners make a start by telling them to put some spring in their arms.

Variations

Some dancers, especially those with experience in international folk dancing or modern square dancing, will do a "grapevine" step while circling. This involves crossing alternately in front and behind with the trailing foot (the right foot in a circle to the left) while rotating the upper body from side to side. If everyone in a circle does the grapevine at once, it can be fun (as in those Israeli dances where it's the prescribed step), but many people feel that it spoils the sense of strong connection in a square or contra dance circle. And if some of the dancers are doing it and some are not, the result is a shambles!

Transitions

When coming into a circle, dancers need to anticipate the movement enough to let them join hands strongly at the beginning of the circle. This means allowing one or two beats at the end of the preceding move to release hands and reorient themselves.

A circle can be followed by almost any other movement. Because each dancer has two strong connections, it's easy to use either hand and arm as a springboard into the next move. For example, the gent's right arm and the lady's left arm together can send the lady into a ladies chain.

Historical Notes

The ring of dancers with joined hands must be one of the oldest movements in the history of group dancing. It's an obvious formation, and it puts everyone on an equal footing.

Since the earliest days of printed dance descriptions, "four hands around" has meant "four people circle"; likewise for six or eight. This is, of course, not a reference to the number of literal hands, but the same idiom as in the nautical expression "all hands and the cook." To get a laugh from the dancers, a caller will sometimes get literal partway through a number, calling "Join sixteen hands and circle to the left."

Timing

Four people can circle once around in 8 beats, halfway in 4 beats. Eight people can go once around in 16 beats, halfway in 8 beats. Six people can go once around, or eight people three-quarters around, in 12 beats.

Note that a circle to the left followed by a circle right is an undemanding movement: Even if they don't get as far in the first circle as the caller intends, the dancers will end up at home if they go an equal distance to the left and the right. However, a circle four once around followed by some other movement (such as a pass through) can be quite demanding; when walking through such a sequence it is important to pause the action after the circle and make sure the dancers have gone all the way around and know which way to face.

Forward and Back

Done by

Any number of dancers in a circle, or any number of adjacent dancers facing a similar number (occasionally any number of dancers facing no one).

Description

Adjacent dancers join nearest hands. They move into the center of the circle, or toward the facing dancers, by taking three steps forward and closing the free foot (that is, stepping on it or touching it next to the other foot). They then return to their starting point by taking three steps backward and closing the free foot.

Result

All dancers are in their original places. Forward and back is used primarily as a "gathering" movement, to emphasize the unity of the set or to make sure the dancers are oriented before the next move.

Teaching Technique

As with the circle, there's more here than meets the eye. Forward and back is a powerful figure if it's done well, and a mess if it's not.

When the move is done in lines, caution the dancers to keep their lines straight, staying aware of the people next to them as well as the one they're facing. In a circle, encourage them all to move in at the same rate, taking steps of equal length. In either formation, make sure they allow the full 8 beats.

Variations

Some dancers enjoy swinging their free foot forward on the fourth beat (in the circle dance *La Bastringue,* this is traditional). A dancer at the end of a line will often clap the free hand, pattycake style, with the facing dancer on the fourth beat.

Transitions

For transitions into the forward and back, the most important thing is for the dancers to finish the preceding movement in time to begin going forward on the first beat of the new phrase of music. The caller can help by choosing a preceding move that the dancers can readily finish on time, and by metering the words of the call in a way that will allow them so to finish.

If the following movement requires facing dancers to be fairly close together, they can "fudge" the forward and back by taking smaller steps on the way back than on the trip forward.

Chapter 15: Basic Movements

Timing

In most forms of traditional dancing, forward and back always takes a full 8 beats. In modern square dancing, it is most often done in 4 beats (2 forward, 2 back), partly because callers typically do not allow enough time for an 8-beat move. In addition, modern callers often call "Forward and back" without ensuring that the call ends with a phrase of music to enable the dancers to begin the move with the new phrase. This makes it unlikely that all the dancers will start going forward on the same beat, making forward and back an unsatisfying movement. A neo-traditional caller who wants a 4-beat move should always so indicate, either during the walkthrough or by including the word "balance" during the dance.

Do-si-do (back to back)

Done by

Any two dancers who are adjacent (such as partners or corners) or facing each other (such as across the square) with no intervening dancers.

Description

The dancers face each other, if they were not already doing so. They both move forward, keeping to the left so that their right shoulders are adjacent, until they have passed each other. Without turning, they move to their right to pass back to back (whence the name, a fractured version of the French "dos à dos"). They now move backward, keeping to the right so that their left shoulders are adjacent, until they are in their starting positions. In the standard version of the do-si-do, each dancer continues to face in his or her original direction throughout the maneuver.

Result

Both dancers are in their starting positions. They are facing each other unless the next call sends them to another person or location in the set.

Teaching Technique

Many people have trouble telling their right side from their left. It often helps to have the dancers shake hands with the person they're facing, and then to say *"On that side,* go around each other – now come back on the other side." A demonstration, if practical in the venue, should make it clear.

With first-timers in particular, I generally avoid using the words "back to back." Even if they have seen a do-si-do at some point in their lives, they may not connect it with what they are being asked to do. If told that "do-si-do" means "back to back," they may oblige by doing just that: standing back to back with their partner.

Variations

In many illustrations and films, the dancers fold their arms in front of their chests while doing the do-si-do. When I first encountered square dancing in grade school, we were taught to do so. I have been unable to determine the origin of this practice. Phil Jamison (2015) points out that Elizabeth Burchenal, an early 20th-century teacher of contras and squares, also taught dances from Finland and Russia that include the posture. Burchenal was a major influence on Lloyd Shaw, apparently sparking his initial interest in dance education, but Shaw's teenage performing group never adopted the folded-arms posture, judging from their photographs and films.

I have heard that schoolteachers taught the folded-arms do-si-do to keep children from pawing and poking one another. Whatever its origins, I believe that most dancers through history have simply let their arms swing freely at their sides. (Another stylized form, popular in the 1950s, is for the gents to place their hands on their back trouser pockets, palm out, while the ladies hold their skirts and swish them from side to side.)

Enthusiastic dancers at all levels of experience enjoy spinning (usually counterclockwise, or to their own left) as they go around each other. This is not unduly disconcerting to most callers, as the dancers must stay fairly controlled in order to keep their own balance. Those who opt to spin should remember to end the move facing in the correct direction, which is critical in some figures.

Certain variations may be specified by the caller. One is a do-si-do once and a quarter into an ocean wave. Another is a do-si-do once and a half; this is equivalent to a pass through in its effect, and may be used instead of a pass through in order to fill out an 8-beat phrase when fitting a dance to music. When one couple is facing another couple, the caller may direct the dancers to do a "couple do-si-do": Each couple acts as an individual, perhaps with arms around each other's waist. If a couple do-si-do is not specified, the dancers move independently, no matter how many adjacent people are facing a like number.

A left-shoulder do-si-do may be called, with all directions reversed. In modern square dancing this is known as a "see-saw." The name comes from a sequence that was described by Herb Greggerson in 1939 and was popular in the West and Southwest in the 1940s: "All around your left-hand lady" followed by "See-saw your pretty little taw." Originally, the ladies went forward and back twice while the gents walked in a figure-eight path around their corner and then their partner, passing behind each lady first. By the 1950s it had degenerated into a corner do-si-do and a partner see-saw.

Transitions

Since the do-si-do is a "no hands" movement, most transitions into and out of it are relatively smooth. A do-si-do can be followed by a right-hand turn with the same person (continuing the clockwise body flow) or a left-hand turn with a different person (resulting in a figure-eight track). If the dancers are in the habit of spinning, any do-si-do that must end facing a precise direction (such as a do-si-do into a wave) demands a careful walkthrough.

Many older routines call for a do-si-do with the corner followed by one with the partner (or vice versa). If both movements are done starting with the right shoulder, the body flow is somewhat awkward. In regions where this sequence was or is common, it was/is an unwritten rule that one of the moves should be a left-shoulder do-si-do. In New York state and Ontario, the left-shoulder move is done with the corner. In the Southwest, as mentioned above, a common sequence was "all around your corner, see-saw your partner," which was roughly equivalent to a right-shoulder do-si-do with corner and a left-shoulder one with partner.

Historical Notes

The name "do-si-do" comes from "dos à dos," which is French for "back to back." In French "dos à dos" is pronounced "doze-ah-doe"; presumably the 19th-century dancing masters in England and America pronounced it that way. The "do-si-do" spelling undoubtedly stems from the common pronunciation of "doe-see-doe"; the latter presumably comes from the rural habit of changing final "ah" to "ee," as in "Pour me full of ice cream sodies" (Woody Guthrie, "Mail Myself to You").

There is another family of movements with the same name: See "Do-si-do (hand turns)" later in this chapter. One name for two very different moves would appear to be the potential source of much confusion, but in fact there was little or no confusion until the start of the square dance boom. This is because in each region where both movements were danced, only one of them bore the name of "do-si-do," the other being known by some other name. It was only when people began studying square dance traditions, and traveling from one region to another to dance, that major confusion started. More will be said about this under "Do-si-do (hand turns)"; what is relevant here is that Lloyd Shaw, who described both movements in his seminal 1939 book *Cowboy Dances,* urged callers to pronounce the back-to-back movement "doe-sah-doe" to distinguish it from the hand-turn "doe-see-doe." (He spelled the latter move "docey-doe," but of course the distinction doesn't come through in speech.) As Shaw was an extremely influential leader in the development of modern square dancing, his advice was taken; book authors and magazine editors began spelling the back-to-back move "do-sa-do."

To muddy the waters even further, many callers since the 1950s have taken to pronouncing the back-to-back movement "doe-sigh-doe," possibly thinking that "sah" (in "doe-sah-doe") must be a southern corruption of "sigh" (as "mah" is of "my" in "Shet mah mouth"). Some of these callers use the "do-sa-do" spelling, some use "do-si-do."

My suggestion, now that all forms of the hand-turn movement have died out or are known by other names, is to spell and pronounce the back-to-back movement any way you like. I spell it "do-si-do" (or "dosido" when jotting notes) and generally pronounce it "doe-suh-doe," with very little time given to the "suh."

Timing

In regions where the dance movements were strictly synchronized with the musical phrases, a do-si-do traditionally required 8 beats. However, two dancers who are close to each other and already in motion can execute the movement comfortably in 6 steps. In many modern phrased squares, the do-si-do shares a 16-beat phrase with two other moves, usually hand turns (such as "allemande left your corner, do-si-do your partner, allemande left your corner again"), giving each move an allotment of 5 to 6 beats. The moves typically flow well, and the dancers don't feel rushed. Similarly, a grand right and left halfway (10 steps) can be paired with a partner do-si-do in a 16-beat phrase.

Chapter 15: Basic Movements 193

Star

Done by

Three or more dancers who are in a more or less circular group. Four is the most common number.

Description

The dancers extend their right or left arms toward the center of the group and make contact in one of two ways (see below). They move forward around their extended hands (clockwise in the case of a right-hand star), usually once around. Right or left hands are nearly always specified, but if not, a right-hand star is generally understood.

Wrist star or *box star*: This works with any number of dancers. Each person holds the wrist of the one directly in front of him or her as they face around the group. For everyone's comfort, the thumb should be held next to one's own fingers, not used to grip the other person's wrist.

Hands across: There must be an even number of dancers. Each person joins right or left hands with the dancer who is directly across the center of the group. In a four-person mixed star, the gents usually join hands above the ladies' hands. Elbows are slightly bent, and the dancers give weight (pull gently toward themselves) as they go around.

Result

After the usual once-around star, all the dancers are in their starting position. Their facing direction depends on what call is given next.

Teaching Technique

The star is one of the easiest movements for new dancers to understand. Giving weight is an issue, particularly in the hands-across version; ideally the dancers will have been exposed to the concept in learning to circle and go forward and back. In a wrist star, dancers should be told to *rest* their hand on the wrist ahead of them, rather than *grasping* with the thumb. I also encourage new dancers, after extending their arm, to start moving before trying to make contact; that way they can be certain who is ahead of them.

Variations

Which type of star is used will depend largely on what is traditional in the area, and to some extent on what is traditional or seems to work well in a specific figure. If you are starting a dance community from scratch, I recommend using the wrist star as the default: It allows a strong connection with relatively little skill, and it works with odd as well as even numbers of dancers. However, if two people are directed to drop out of a star and the other two are to start a chain, it is smoother to begin by taking hands across.

The modern square dancing world recognizes a two-person star. By this is meant a hand turn using the "hands up" position that is the prevailing style in the neo-traditional scene. (Most hand turns in modern square dancing are done with a forearm hold.) Obviously, a star for two would be a redundant definition in traditional or neo-traditional dancing.

Transitions

The transition out of a star can be challenging to the average dancer, who must, while in motion, spot the location of the next person to engage with. In a star full around, at least, there is usually enough time for this if the dancers are warned ahead of time that it takes some anticipation. Fractional stars, particularly if less than a full revolution, are much more challenging due to the high probability of disorientation. An important caution is that when two of the starring dancers are facing toward their next person, the other two dancers have passed theirs if the star handhold is maintained. Experienced dancers know to begin dissolving the star as they approach their destination.

A transition *into* a star is fairly straightforward, unless of course the transition is *from* another star.

Timing

For four people once around (the most common usage), 8 beats. Fractional stars take relatively less time. For an eight-person star (which is something of a novelty), allow 8 beats to go halfway, 16 beats to go all the way around.

Pass Through

Done by

Any number of dancers, facing a similar number. (Theoretically, pass through may be done by two solo dancers, but the term "cross over" is more commonly used in that case.)

Description

Each dancer moves forward four steps, keeping to the left and passing right shoulders with the opposite dancer.

Result

Each dancer has exchanged places with the opposite dancer and is back to back with that dancer. The movement ends at this point and must be followed by another call, such as "turn alone" or "separate."

Teaching Technique

Pass through is the most straightforward of the basic movements, figuratively and literally. I present it early in a teaching session or a non-dancer event because I always follow the initial big circle with a progressive circle (if there are enough dancers). Pass through is the simplest and most common means of progression in such circles.

Be aware that many dancers will try to turn immediately after a pass through, either individually (about-face) or in tandem with an adjacent dancer (usually to the right). This is more true in squares than in progressive circles; presumably, when they find themselves facing out of the set, they feel something must be wrong. You can forestall this by warning them that they will only be taking four steps and stopping, or by telling them firmly and clearly, before they finish passing through, what you want them to do next.

Variations

A pass through by the left shoulder is possible but almost unheard of. A caller may specify it in very unusual circumstances, such as in a sequence of "pass through, turn alone, now pass through the other way back." In general, the traffic rule in squares is to keep left when individuals pass and to keep right when couples pass (as in a half promenade).

Transitions

Most transitions into and out of the pass through are easy. An exception is a circle left for four people followed by a pass through: The dancers must quickly change from all facing slightly to the left to facing one of the adjacent dancers, which means two people must look to their right. All four must then adjust themselves so that the person they face is slightly to their right rather than directly opposite. Once dancers have mastered this combination, it can be quite satisfying, as the dancers help to propel each other through just before releasing hands.

Timing

Usually 4 beats. In a fast-moving figure, a pass through can sometimes be seen as taking only 2 beats. In progressive circle dances, 8 beats are often allowed for "pass through and on to the next." This timing may seem unduly loose, but I find that beginners appreciate the extra time to reorient themselves with a new facing couple, especially if the sets are spread out. (For experienced dancers, a pass through in a progressive circle may be replaced with one of several other movements; see Chapter 16.)

Hand Turn (Allemande)

Special Note

There are different ways to execute this movement. I have chosen the "hands up" or "arm wrestling" hold (sometimes called a "pigeon wing" hold) as the default; it is universal in present-day contra dancing and prevalent in the neo-traditional squares that are done in conjunction with contras. If a different hold is standard in your area, you will of course teach accordingly. (See "Variations" below for two other common holds.)

Done by

Any two adjacent dancers (such as partners or corners).

Description

The dancers face each other, if they were not already doing so. They move toward each other until they are about three feet apart. (The distance will vary depending on the timing of the move; see "Timing" below.) They join either right or left hands as directed by the call, as if they were arm wrestling with their elbows resting on a table: Hands are joined chest- to shoulder-high, wrists straight, elbows bent and pointing downward. Fingers are cupped around the other person's hand; thumbs are usually grasping each other. (Dancers concerned about thumb injuries can keep their thumb against their own index finger, relying on the cupped fingers to maintain the hold.) Both dancers "give weight," pulling toward themselves just enough to provide a degree of resistance without leaning backward or turning the move into a tug-of-war. Using a normal dance-walk (not a sashay or a buzz step), they move forward around each other as far as the call dictates, usually between halfway around and twice around. The center of the turn is the joined hands; both dancers travel an equal distance. Feet and body should face in the direction the dancer is moving in, not toward the other dancer. Heads are often turned to look the other dancer in the eye. The dancers finish as directed by the call, either moving toward someone else or backing away to face each other.

Result

The two dancers are still adjacent. They may be in their original places (in the case of a turn once around), in each other's original place (after a turn halfway or once and a half), or anywhere in between. They may be facing each other or, more likely, facing away from each other in preparation for their next move.

It is my impression, as both a well-traveled dancer and a well-read student of dance history, that calling a hand turn an "allemande" implies that the dancers are to leave the one they turned and go to someone else for their next move. This is certainly true of the common "allemande left" into a grand right and left. (Of course, many other hand turns are followed by a move with someone else – but not all.) In the common combination "allemande left and promenade," it is definitely understood that the two moves are done with two different people. This is true even if these two calls follow a command to swing the corner, who becomes the new partner. In that case the allemande is done with the *next* corner; the dancers return to the one they swung for the promenade. Failure to explain this adequately can lead to confusion and contention on the dance floor. (If the caller desires the two moves to be done with the same person, it is clearer to call "Turn by the left, keep this one and promenade." The term "roll promenade," popular in the 1950s, was intended to apply to this combination.)

Another source of contention is the failure of some dancers to understand that the allemande left is not always followed by a grand right and left. Other following calls may be rarely or never used in some dance communities, but they are certainly possible.

Teaching Technique

This is one of three basic movements involving a degree of "giving weight" that makes it hard for a beginner to comprehend from watching others do it. In a teaching session, I always spend extra time on the hand turn (along with the balance and the swing). In a small group, the leader can dance with each person; with a larger group, it will be necessary to describe the feel of this movement. Encourage your dancers to gauge the amount of force required, which will vary with each combination of two people.

You are strongly advised to teach the allemande and the grand right and left separately. Judging from the literature of the boom years, the combination of these two movements has been the source of more dancer confusion than any other single factor in teaching squares. Further comments on this issue are included under "Grand Right and Left" below.

Variations

Some dancers habitually do "hands up" turns with a sharply bent wrist, forcing the other dancer to do likewise. Or worse, they make contact not with the hand but with the inside of the wrist, an area of delicate bones and blood vessels. The best defense against the bent wrist is to keep one's own wrist straight; the only sure defense against the wrist-to-wrist hold is a limp arm. A third variation that gives me trouble as a dancer is to keep the fingers straight and rely on palm-to-palm pressure to maintain contact; I find that I can't reciprocate without inducing shaking in my forearm. If the other dancer objects to my wrapping my fingers around their hand, I have no choice but to withdraw my hand and walk the expected floor track hands-free.

There are two other common holds in addition to "hands up":

Handshake – In some dance communities, such as upstate New York and parts of the South, hand turns are done with a handshake hold; in these areas either more time is allowed for each turn or the turns are executed at a relatively fast clip. As modern square dancing began evolving out of traditional western style, the handshake hold was used at first – in fact, the standard allemande left with the corner included a "float out" to arm's length midway through the movement.

Forearm – Since the 1960s the standard modern square dance practice has been to do all turns with a forearm hold: Forearms are adjacent and horizontal, and each dancer presses his or her hand against the other's arm just below the elbow. It is considered bad form to grasp with the thumb, which should be held alongside the index finger. Note that "giving weight" is not a factor in a forearm turn; both dancers hold their body erect and support their own weight.

Transitions

Most dances that include hand turns pose no problems of physical awkwardness; the turns flow smoothly from one to the next (right hand to left hand, for example). The primary challenge for most dancers will be orienting themselves after each turn, noting which way to face and what dancer to interact with next.

For the transition from an allemande left with one person to a promenade with another, see below under "Promenade."

Historical Notes

One might think the name "allemande" to be a corruption of "à la main," French for "by the hand." Ralph Page used this supposed derivation to argue for a handhold and against a forearm hold. However, I think the similarity is a coincidence. "Allemande" is the French word for "German," and there is a long history of dances and dance movements named "allemande." One of the best known among historical dance teachers and hobbyists has two dancers, (say) right shoulders adjacent, extend their right arm behind each other's back and put their own left hand behind their own back to receive the other's right hand.

The transcriber of the calls in the Nebraska Folklore Pamphlets of the 1930s (collected in Welsch 1966) consistently wrote "all the men left." Whether the informant callers actually pronounced the command this way, or the transcriber only thought they did, can only be guessed at. It is a logical bit of folk etymology, as the men do indeed go to their left to execute this movement from home.

At least two writers in the 1940s claimed that the word "allemande" signifies "foreign man" and that "you cannot allemande your partner." This would have been news to the thousands of dancers in upstate New York, New England, and Ontario who were accustomed to following the call "Allemande left your corner, allemande right your partner, allemande left your corner again."

According to Rod La Farge, the standard interpretation of "allemande left" in northern New Jersey in the 1940s was a left elbow swing with the corner, often several times around. (North Jersey square dancing was apparently quite energetic: La Farge also wrote that in the grand right and left the gents twirled each lady they met.) California caller Mildred Buhler claimed (in *Let's Dance,* August 1949) that Ralph Page reported the use of an elbow hook for the allemande left in his section of New England. Even if Page was merely observing, not advocating, I find this hard to believe, based on the rest of the literature. Buhler may have been confused by the picture in *The Country Dance Book* (Tolman and Page 1937, p. 33) showing two people with linked elbows and captioned "allemande left," directly above text that clearly defined the move as a hand turn.

Timing

Varies from dance to dance, depending on both the number of revolutions and the speed desired by the caller or choreographer. Pre-revival dances often allowed 8 beats for a turn once around, which would have been executed sedately (or with footwork) at arm's length. The average timing in neo-traditional squares appears to be 8 beats to turn once and a half, 5 to 6 beats to turn once. In order to keep the dance movements synchronized with the musical phrases, three movements (hand turns and/or do-si-dos) are often called for within one 16-beat phrase. Good dancers will adapt their style to each routine by adjusting the angle of their bent arms: sharper for fast turns, less so for leisurely ones.

See under "Grand Right and Left" later in this chapter for the specific challenge of timing an allemande left followed by that movement.

Chapter 15: Basic Movements 201

Swing

Done by

Any two dancers who are adjacent (such as partners or corners) or facing each other (such as across the square) with no intervening dancers.

Description

The dancers face each other, if they were not already doing so. They move forward, keeping to the left, until they are almost (but not quite) alongside each other. (The other dancer should be on a right diagonal, about one foot away.) They are still facing in opposite directions: If one dancer's toes are pointing north, the other's are pointing south. They hold each other in one of several ways (described below) and revolve clockwise as a unit, using either a normal dance-walk (one step to each musical downbeat) or a "buzz" step (two steps to each downbeat). One dancer may walk and the other may buzz with no ill effects. (In western Texas and other parts of the Southwest in the mid-20th century, it was the fashion to use a two-step for all square dance movements, including the swing.)

The buzz step: On each downbeat, both dancers step solidly on the right foot, with the little toe toward the other's little toe and almost touching it. On each upbeat or slightly after it, both dancers step lightly on the left foot, taking body weight for a split second, with the toe of the left foot roughly in line with the heel of the right. The next step on the right foot is well ahead of the left, and so on. The motion has been compared to riding a scooter or playing at being a galloping horse, but the steps are smaller and more controlled than either of these images would imply. The scooter analogy is particularly misleading because in a swing the right foot must be picked up and set down in a slightly different place, pointing in a new direction, whereas on a scooter it never leaves the footboard. The word "pivot" is also misleading because it too implies that the right foot stays in one place. Mary Ann Herman used to tell her dancers to pretend they had a pebble in their left shoe, causing them to limp around their partner.

The ballroom hold: This is similar to a waltz position except that the dancers are on a diagonal rather than face to face. The gent's right arm encircles the lady, with his right hand flat on the middle of her back. The lady rests her left arm on the gent's right arm, with her left hand pressed against his upper arm or shoulder, depending on the length of her arm. (She should resist the temptation to grasp his arm with her thumb.) The gent's left hand (palm up) holds the lady's right hand (palm down), their arms forming a half circle. In crowded halls, this handhold may be modified, the dancers reaching halfway up each other's arm and holding on with cupped fingers (again, not grasping with the thumb).

Unisex holds: This is sometimes used when both people are of the same sex, although some dancers prefer the ballroom hold regardless of whom they are swinging. There are two variations: (1) Each dancer puts the right arm around the other's back or waist and rests the left arm on the other's right arm. In other words, each dancer's right arm does the part of the gent's right arm in the ballroom hold, while each dancer's left arm does the part of the lady's left arm. (2) Each dancer's right arm encircles the other dancer, with the right hand flat on the back of the other's waist. Left hands are joined between the dancers, underneath their right arms.

The straight-arm hold: This is invariably done with the buzz step. It is similar to the second unisex hold except that instead of encircling the other's waist, each dancer's right hand is cupped on the other's right shoulder, so that right arms are straight and parallel. This hold is often taught in elementary schools to enable children to learn to swing without having to touch each other more intimately. It is admittedly easier to learn the buzz step in this position, since dancers can focus on the footwork without worrying about the precise curve of their arms (and are far enough apart that their feet are unlikely to become tangled). But many callers discourage it because it takes up more space than other holds, and many sequences in neo-traditional dancing require compact sets. It is also less secure than other holds, as neither dancer has a hand or arm behind the other; if hands are moist, the dancers can easily lose their grip and fly apart, colliding with a post or another person. In addition, dancers using this hold are often tempted to tilt their heads back at an extreme angle, risking a head-to-head collision with someone in another set.

A few sources describe a hold that is a hybrid of the straight-arm and the second unisex hold: The gent's right arm is around the lady's waist, while her right arm is straight and her right hand is on his right shoulder. As in those other holds, left hands are joined underneath. One or another of these left-hand holds is occasionally termed "the buzz-step hold," implying (without evidence) that it is the oldest or the most common handhold for the buzz-step swing.

In any of these holds except the straight-arm, the strongest connection should be the right hand on the other dancer's back: the right hand of the gent in the ballroom hold or of both dancers in the unisex hold. Each dancer pulls toward himself or herself with the right hand, and at the same time, each dancer who is being so held pushes back with the whole upper body against the other dancer's right hand. If the dancers lean their bodies back, it should be at only a slight angle. Knees should be slightly bent, and steps with both feet should be small and close to the floor.

The two-hand swing: This movement pre-dates the ballroom hold; it was used in the 18th-century cotillion and the 19th-century quadrille. In the country-style square dancing that developed during the 19th century, its most common use was apparently as a substitute for other forms of swinging in regions where conservative churches exerted some influence on the form of the dance but did not ban it outright. I believe it was and is done most often with a dance-walk rather than a buzz step. (Indeed, many southern dance communities have favored a fast tempo that would make the buzz step uncomfortable.) The dancers extend both arms, usually straight across but occasionally with arms crossed at the hands. Traditionally the gent extends his hands palm up and the lady takes them with her palms down. The dancers pull away from each other as they go around; as with the straight-arm hold, they must guard against losing their grip and flying apart.

Result

In most neo-traditional choreography (as well as most contra dances written since about 1970), the two dancers end side by side, the lady on the gent's right, facing in a direction specified by the call. In some older routines (both squares and contras), they return to their starting position, facing each other.

To end a swing side by side, the gent comes to a smooth, controlled stop facing in the required direction and carefully straightens and extends his right arm to the side, letting the lady "unroll" until she is at his right, facing in the same direction as he. If the dancers are to back away from each other instead, they must both be careful to end the swing with their backs to their own desired position, and must not release the hold until they are sure they are in control of their own bodies.

More than any other movement, the swing is done for the joy of the dance rather than to propel dancers from one point to another. However, many present-day choreographers use the swing as a positioning device, taking advantage of the modern custom of ending most swings side by side with the lady on the right.

Teaching Technique

The swing, particularly with the buzz step, takes more effort to learn than any other movement in square dancing. If you are leading a 15- or 30-minute teaching session before an evening dance, it's a good idea to set aside a large portion of the time to deal with the swing. (Many of the other basics can be learned on the fly and need not be covered in a pre-dance session.)

In my experience, the swing marks the dividing line between a session for beginning square dancers and a "one-night stand," a private or community party whose guests have never square danced and may never do so again. The buzz-step swing is the heart and soul of northeastern square dancing, as well as contra dancing, and must be taught to anyone who intends to take up such dancing as a hobby. But at a party for folks who dance no more than once a year, an elbow swing provides much of the fun without a long learning curve. If the group wants to go further that night, a walk-around swing using a ballroom or unisex hold can be taught fairly quickly.

One way to teach the buzz step to new dancers is to have them join hands in a large circle and move to the left, crossing the right foot slightly over the left foot. You can begin by having them move their feet at a walking tempo, taking one step for each imagined beat of music. Then gradually increase the speed of your cadence until they are moving at close to an actual buzz-step tempo (two steps to a beat). Once they have an idea of the footwork, they can pair off, join both hands with a partner, and turn clockwise, pulling away from each other while using the buzz step. When they have the feel of "giving weight," they are ready to try one of the conventional handholds.

To teach the ballroom and unisex holds, I prefer to demonstrate them rather than try to explain them solely in words. Points to emphasize include the push-and-pull exchange of weight, the need for bent knees and small steps, and the comfortable way to end a swing (gent stops first).

No one can assimilate all these points the first time they try the swing, and even if they could, it's not enough to know what to do – it takes practice. Encourage the newcomers to keep trying. Remind them that everything comes more easily with time. And provide plenty of opportunities for them to change partners, so they don't get stuck in a rut with the same person.

Transitions

As noted above, most swings end with the dancers side by side, lady on the right. The lady's right hand and the gent's left hand are released first; then, as the lady continues turning to face the same way as the gent, she removes her left hand from his arm or shoulder. He catches her left hand either with his right hand (for a circle, forward and back, or ladies chain) or with his left hand (for a promenade). If the call following the swing sends the dancers to someone else – to do an allemande left, for example – the gent releases the lady completely just before she reaches the next person. She executes either a right-face half turn or a once-and-a-half spin, and ends facing the new person, ready for the next call.

Transitions from a unisex hold are similar in that the dancer playing the part of the gent stops revolving first. But the hold numbered "2" above poses a slight problem for the person playing the lady, who must extricate the right arm from the sandwich formed by the partner's left arm and body. Many dancers prefer the hold numbered "1" for its ease of getting into and out of position.

In areas where the two-hand swing is commonly employed, the dancers are often called upon to leave each other and go to the next adjacent person for another swing or some other move. They usually break their handhold when each dancer is facing in the direction he or she must travel to reach the next person (remember, the other swinger is offset to one's right and so is not in one's way).

A common instance of two successive swings is the sequence of "swing your opposite, swing your own" that is often used as a kind of subchorus after two-couple figures in southern mountain dancing. Doing it well requires a good deal of both physical and mental skill. Modern square dancing may require more memorization than traditional, on the part of dancers and caller alike. But traditional dancing, particularly in southern and old western styles, requires the dancers to create their own transitions; there are no official, precise definitions of where each movement starts or ends, or which wall a dancer should be facing at a given time.

"Swing your opposite across the hall" was a favorite call in the West and Southwest, usually part of an introduction or other break; Ralph Page also used it frequently. The call was understood to be directed to the gents; to avoid collisions, each gent must keep to his own left, letting the gent of the couple on his left cross in front of him.

Historical Notes

It is hard to say with any certainty just when the ballroom hold supplanted the two-hand hold as the most popular position for turning or swinging, or when the buzz step became popular. The ballroom hold would naturally not have been used until the waltz and polka were introduced; those couple dances were considered highly improper by many at first, and the relatively conservative communities that clung to the quadrille through the late 19th century were likely to frown on such intimacy even after the waltz had been accepted in high society.

In parts of the South, the ballroom swing never did replace the two-hand hold. In the West and Southwest, the position for swinging apparently depended on whether a woman liked and trusted the man in question. An old call, "Meet your honey and pat her on the head, if she don't like biscuit, give her cornbread," supposedly refers to the two swing positions. Biscuits made with refined wheat flour were a Sunday treat; cornbread was the everyday staple. So a "biscuit swing," with the gent's arm around the lady's waist, was something special, to be allowed only if the girl liked you. The term "biscuit swing" lasted into the 1950s; it was sometimes used after a series of one-hand turns (known as "swings" in the Southwest) to make it clear that the next move was different.

As for the buzz step, there are many theories but little solid information. The step appears in the dances of many European nations, from Ireland to Hungary; it is described, for example, in a Danish book of 1830. It is possible that immigrants from one or more of those countries exerted their influence in the mid- to late 19th century, as the cotillion, quadrille, and Celtic dances were evolving into the American square dance. An English dancing master named Edward Scott mentioned the buzz step in 1887 and described it in 1892. By the early 20th century it was an established part of tradition; Grace Ryan (1926) and Benjamin Lovett, writing for Henry Ford (also 1926), both describe it, though Lovett seems to prefer a walk-around swing with a two-hand hold. Boyd and Dunlavy (1925) do not mention any footwork, but they refer to the movement as a "swing" rather than a "turn" and observe that a skillful couple may swing three or four times – all of which leads me to think that "buzzing" was not unknown in the Iowa of their day.

Timing

The swing is a flexible movement, both in the time allotted to it and in the speed at which the dancers choose to execute it. The usual length of a swing varies by region: In the southern mountains and in traditional Texas style, as well as in modern square dancing, 4-beat swings are common, with 8-beat swings a possibility. In New England and other northern regions, swings range from 8 to 16 beats; a common combination is a 4-beat balance and a 12-beat swing, as in contra dancing. In Quebec, 16 beats is a bare minimum, with many swings lasting longer.

As for speed, different couples in the same set may choose to revolve once around in every 4 beats, every 3 beats, or even every 2 beats. Note that dancers don't consciously think about these numbers; they simply set their speed based on their experience level and the mood of the moment. As long as a couple can end a swing at the right time, facing in the correct direction, the speed of rotation doesn't matter. And it's worth repeating that one person can walk around while the other is buzz-stepping, as long as both are moving at the same speed.

Promenade

Done by
Two adjacent dancers playing opposite gender roles.

Description
The dancers turn (if necessary) so that they are side by side, with the lady on the gent's right. They take hands in one of several "promenade positions" (see below) and travel around a square set or a big circle (counterclockwise unless otherwise specified) or along or across a longways set as directed by the call. If they meet another couple traveling in the opposite direction, they keep to their own right as they pass.

Result
The vast majority of promenades are used to return couples to their home positions (or, in the case of figures with a partner change, to the gents' or ladies' positions). A promenade called with no qualifying language is understood to end at home. Couples may be directed to promenade halfway or three-quarters (or some other fraction) of the way around the set. The call to promenade may be directed to one active couple, as in "First couple promenade around the outside (or inside)." The head or side couples may be directed to promenade while the other two couples do something else or stand still; if the latter, the inactive couples may need to move inward or outward to let the active couples go by.

In the case of a promenade to home places that is shorter than halfway around the set, particularly if it is only a quarter way around, it is customary on reaching home to go all the way around from there without stopping, unless the caller clearly indicates that there is not enough time. In case of ambiguity, Couple 1 makes the decision.

Positions

1. *Front skaters'* (or simply "skaters' "): Right hands are joined in front of the lady, left hands are joined in front of the gent, waist high or a bit higher. (Each dancer's arms are not crossed in front of him or her, though beginners seeing other dancers in this position may try to copy it by crossing their own arms.) In most regions, right arms are above left; in parts of Texas until the 1950s, left arms were on top.

2. *Back skaters', New England,* or *courtesy turn*: Left hands are joined in front of the gent, usually at the height of his chest. The gent puts his right arm around the lady's waist; she usually places her right hand just behind her hipbone, palm out, for the gent to hold with his right hand. Some exhibition groups use this position, but with the lady's right hand holding her skirt (and moving it back and forth).

3. *Over the shoulder, varsovienne,* or *courting*: Left hands are joined as in #2. The gent puts his right arm around the lady's shoulders; she raises her right hand, palm forward, and he wraps the fingers of his right hand around hers.

4. *Half shoulder-waist*: As the name implies, the gent puts his right arm around the lady's waist and she rests her left hand on his right arm or shoulder (wherever it falls comfortably).

5. *Escort*: The gent bends his right elbow outward and the lady holds his right arm with her left hand.

6. *Ballroom*: In a few areas, when "promenade" is called, the dancers respond by taking a closed ballroom position (as for a square dance swing, but face to face rather than offset) and doing a turning two-step or polka around the set.

Which position is the right one? It depends largely on local custom. When I toured the West Coast in the 1980s, most of the dancers in Portland, Oregon used position #1, whereas in Seattle, Washington they used position #3. It can also depend on context: A given position may be more comfortable after some preceding moves but less so after others. The same dancer may use different promenade holds in different situations. A couple's choice of hold does not affect the other couples, as everyone is moving in the same direction at the same speed, regardless of hold. I have seen squares in which three or even four different holds were used at the same time.

Teaching Technique

The promenade is a simple movement requiring little teaching. When working with first-time dancers, I introduce it from a big circle by calling a circle to the left, reversing it into a single file promenade, and having the original left-hand person in each couple step up alongside partner on the inside.

Any hand position is easier to demonstrate than to describe in words. If the room is too crowded for easy demonstration from the center, you can assume the handhold with a partner on stage. If you are teaching the front skaters' position without a demonstration, it is best to avoid speaking of "crossed hands": The dancers are likely to cross their own arms. A more effective wording, once the dancers are facing in the right direction, is "Shake hands and hold on; now shake left hands under the right hands."

Variations

Most of the following variations are prescribed by the caller, rather than spontaneously executed by the dancers (but see the comment at the end of "Star promenade" below).

Half promenade: From a squared set, two facing couples (heads or sides) promenade across, keeping to their own right but staying within the boundary created by the standing couples. (As mentioned above under "Pass Through," the traffic rule in squares is to keep left when individuals pass but to keep right when couples pass.) Upon reaching the opposite side, each couple executes a "courtesy turn": Without altering their handhold, the gent backs around as the lady moves forward in a half circle, the pivot point being between the two dancers. Each couple ends in the opposite couple's place, facing across the set toward the other couple.

Single file promenade: Any number of dancers can be directed to walk on a circular track without taking hands. The call can be directed to four dancers (usually the ladies or gents) or to all eight. If fewer than eight are involved, they can be told to promenade inside or outside the other dancers. Like a couple promenade, a single file promenade is to the right (counterclockwise) unless otherwise specified.

Star promenade: Each couple assumes half shoulder-waist position (#4 above) and faces around the set (usually counterclockwise to start). The four dancers nearest the center form a star with their free hands (usually with a wrist hold) and all move forward in the direction they are facing until the next call is given. On the call "Inside out and outside in," the star is released, each couple pivots halfway around (or once and a half) to face the other direction, and the new center dancers form a star. In some areas, every time a promenade is called, the dancers execute a star promenade, stopping at home. (In such areas, a hands-across hold is more common than a wrist hold; sometimes the gents do not touch hands at all, but simply extend their left arm into the center.)

Transitions

From a swing into a promenade with the same person: Both dancers release hands, the gent comes to a stop facing in the desired direction as the lady lets her momentum carry her another half revolution, and they take hands in promenade position. Seasoned dancers find this "let go and catch" very satisfying, though it takes a bit of practice and mutual trust.

From a grand right and left into a promenade: Because the promenade is usually in the direction the gent was traveling in, the lady must make an about-face turn to get into promenade position; she usually does this after right hands have been joined. Whether she turns to her right or her left depends in part on what handhold is used for the promenade. Where position #1 is standard, most ladies turn right; indeed, in modern square dancing the lady typically makes an additional full right-face turn under the gent's arm. In areas that favor position #2, many experienced dancers turn left. Into position #3, right-face turns appear to be more common, but left-face turns work as well.

From a corner allemande left to a partner promenade: This is a frequently used combination in partner-change dances; after a swing with the new partner, a common call is "Allemande left, just one, just one, and promenade the one you swung." The transition to the promenade is similar to that from a grand right and left (above).

From a promenade to a squared set: At the end of a promenade home, many couples balance apart and nod to each other before facing the center of the square. In modern square dancing, the lady makes a full right-face turn under the joined right hands; often the couple will clap their outside hands (gent's left, lady's right) together before settling down.

In most figures involving a partner change, the promenade is traditionally to the gent's home place. The main exception is that when the gent effects the change by passing his partner and swinging the next (his right-hand lady or "next-door neighbor"), the promenade is often done to the lady's place to better fit the music. (One old example, which has 19th-century roots in the *Caledonians* and the *Irish Quadrille,* is a semi-singing call to the tune of Irish Washerwoman: "All four gents to the right of the ring, first you balance, then you swing. After the swing, remember the call, you take that lady and promenade all.") During the walk-through of a partner-change dance, the caller should specify where the promenade is to end.

Historical Notes

At first, English-speaking dancing masters pronounced "promenade" in more or less French fashion, rhyming it with "act of God." Comedian Cal Stewart in his character of Uncle Josh Weathersby was rhyming it with "window shade" as early as 1901. There was a long period of overlap between the two choices; some callers still pronounced it the old way on recordings made in the 1940s. Since 1950, if not earlier, a consensus has formed around the long "a."

In southern California at the beginning of the square dance boom, it was customary for couples reaching home to balance out and swing after the lady's right-face twirl. On some recordings from that era, although the caller does not specify a swing at the end of a promenade home, his next call begins "One and three, when you finish your swing…"

Timing

A promenade once around a square set takes 16 beats; a promenade halfway around or a half promenade across the inside takes 8 beats. A three-quarter promenade nominally takes 12 beats, although 16 are often allowed to let the active couples maneuver around the standing couples. A single file promenade for four dancers around the inside takes 8 beats; a single file promenade for all eight dancers takes 8 beats to go halfway, 16 to go all the way.

Comment

The couple promenade is an easy, relatively long movement with a definite stopping point, so it can be useful if the dancers are having trouble keeping up with the caller or finding their proper places. The caller can insert a promenade to give the dancers a familiar move and allow them time to recover and regroup.

Grand Right and Left

Special Note

In Canada this movement is commonly called "grand chain." It is the same movement described here and bears no relation to "ladies (gents) grand chain," which is also called "four ladies (gents) chain."

Done by

Four couples in a square, or any number of couples in a big circle; occasionally three couples in a subset of a square.

Description

From normal couples (facing the center, lady on gent's right), all dancers turn to face partner. Ladies are now facing clockwise, gents counterclockwise around the rim of the set; this is known as "the right way." All join right hands with partner as if for a handshake and move forward, passing partner and releasing hands to avoid being forced by the handhold to turn around. Continuing in their starting direction, they join left hands with the next person they meet and move past him or her, releasing hands. All continue moving in this direction, joining right and left hands alternately with each person they pass, until partners meet again or until otherwise directed.

Result

In a square, the action stops with all dancers facing partner. In parts of the US Northeast and eastern Canada, the grand right and left – usually called "grand chain" in Canada – is understood to be all the way around the square: The first time partners meet on the opposite side from home, they give right hands and pass by, continuing the movement until they are home again. In the US West and Southwest and in modern square dancing, the movement ends the first time partners meet.

In a big circle, it is the caller's choice whether or not a grand right and left will reunite partners. In some circle mixers, the grand right and left is the means of changing partners.

Teaching Technique

The grand right and left is one of the most challenging basic movements to teach. The difficulty is multiplied if the move is preceded by an allemande left with the corner. It is tempting to present this combination early in a session, as it is by far the most common "break" or chorus in most styles of square dancing. However, I would strongly advise against doing so at all in the first session with a group, unless the task is to teach a set routine to an exhibition team. In my experience, the allemande left is disorienting in itself: Some people will return to partners while others will travel beyond their corner. When the dancers are expected to follow the allemande left immediately with a move in which they are not supposed to turn at all, confusion reigns.

I suggest that at a non-dancer event or the first session of a teaching series, hand or arm turns be kept separate from the grand right and left. If the latter move is used at all, doing it in a big circle will make it easier to comprehend, as the curve of the dancers' path will be less extreme. In a four-couple square, the curve of the path is sharp enough to disorient new dancers: Are they supposed to go straight or to turn? The correct path feels like a little of both. Depending on how well the dancers do in the circle, you may or may not want to use grand right and left in a square later.

Variations

In some regions at some points in time, it was standard for each gent to turn under his arm each lady he met in the grand right and left. This is workable only if everyone does it; if some are twirling and some are trying to move ahead without twirling, the gents in the latter group will be presented with the ladies' backs rather than their fronts.

There are countless variations on the grand right and left. As with the promenade, most of them are prescribed by the caller. The simplest is

Weave the ring: The dancers follow the path of a grand right and left without taking hands; they pass partner by the right shoulder, the next person by the left shoulder, and so on until partners meet again.

The next three variations are additions rather than substitutions: The dancers execute a normal grand right and left until they meet partners across from home, then they do a series of moves that are elaborations on the grand right and left, usually moving in their normal direction, until they are home with partners again.

Once and a half or *grand allemande*: Upon meeting across from home, partners do a right-hand or right-elbow turn. After moving about once and a quarter around each other, they release their hold and travel in normal grand right and left direction to the next person. With this person, they do a left-hand or left-elbow turn about once and a quarter, then travel on to turn the next by the right and the one after that by the left. This brings them home to face partner, ready for the next call.

Double elbow: Upon meeting across from home, partners do a "catch all eight": turn by the right halfway, then change hands and turn by the left until they can travel to the next person. They repeat the identical movement – half by the right, back by the left – with each of the next three people in turn. This brings them home to face partner, ready for the next call.

Grand Sashay or *Grand Do-si-do*: Upon meeting across from home, partners execute a right shoulder do-si-do. They then pass each other by the right shoulder (in some areas taking right hands briefly) and travel to the next person for a left shoulder do-si-do and a left hand or shoulder pass. They repeat these moves with the next two people – one by the right, the other by the left – to return home. The name Grand Sashay was given in 1948 by Rickey Holden; "sashay" was one term used for the back to back movement in the Southwest, where the name "do-si-do" was reserved for a series of hand turns.

Grand ballonet or *Alamo Style*: This is usually called when the dancers are at home, rather than being added to a grand right and left. After doing an allemande left, the dancers retain the left-hand hold with the corner and give right hand to partner to form an eight-person circle with gents facing the center and ladies facing out. Elbows should be bent, hands chest-high. All do a 4-beat forward and back balance, the arms acting as springs. All release the left hand and turn halfway by the right in four steps, giving left hand to the next person but retaining right hands with partner. Ladies are now facing in, gents out. All balance, then turn halfway by the left to a new person. They repeat the balance and turn with two more people to reach partner again. If they started from home, they are now across from home. Any call may be used here that would be appropriate after a grand right and left: do-si-do, right-hand turn, swing, promenade, or even a grand right and left. (The original name appears to have been "grand ballonet"; the move was popularized in 1948 by Rickey Holden, who named it "Alamo Style" as he was teaching in San Antonio at the time.) This break may be prompted or cadence called; the chart in Chapter 23 gives examples of both.

A few grand right and left variations require the dancers to move in the opposite direction to their normal path; this is often called "the wrong way" with no negative connotation, just as in sewing directions the side of the fabric that will be unseen in the finished garment is called "the wrong side."

Turn back or *grand right and wrong* (in New England, *around your own and the other way home*): Upon meeting across from home, partners turn halfway around by the right hand, using their local customary hand or arm hold for turns. They are now facing "the wrong way": gents clockwise, ladies counterclockwise. They execute a grand right and left in this direction, passing partner and giving left hand to the next person they meet, and so on around until partners meet again. At this point the caller may have them do a common move like do-si-do or swing, or may say "Turn back again, you're still going wrong," in which case partners turn by the right halfway and do a normal grand right and left. (See Chapter 23 for a call chart of an ending break featuring two turn backs.)

For an extra bit of challenge, a caller can direct only certain couples (heads or Couple 1, for example) to turn back, so that some of the hand passes will be between dancers playing the same gender role. The normal sequence for this variation is to call heads and then sides, or to call one couple at a time, to turn back on successive repetitions until everyone has been called. Note that partners are reunited after every four passes, so the sequence can be ended at any time (with a swing or other move); there is no need to get everyone going "the right way" again.

Grand left and right (in Ontario, *left grand chain*): This starts with a left-hand pass; in my experience it is called when dancers are facing their corner, often following an allemande left with the corner and an allemande right with partner.

One of the first phenomena in the development of modern square dancing was the creation of "allemande breaks," which combined a grand right and left with one or more other moves. Many had a distinctive line of leading patter to warn the dancers of what was coming, as seen in the examples below. So many were written that the genre was dubbed the Allemande Alphabet. Most are long forgotten, but a handful have stood the test of time. (Call charts for a few are included in Chapter 23.)

Allemande Thar (occasionally called *Allemande R*): This is a grand right and left interrupted by stars. The dancers do an allemande left with their corner, give right hand to partner and pass straight by as in grand right and left, and join left hands or forearms (depending on the area) with the next person. These pairs turn halfway by the left and retain this hold, and the gents (who are now on the inside) join right hands in a wrist star. This formation travels a few steps, with the gents walking backward and the ladies forward. On the call "Shoot the star," the gents release their right hands and each pair turns halfway by the left to face in grand right and left direction (as if they had just done an allemande left). All repeat the right-hand pass with the next person and the half left-hand turn into a "thar star" with the person after that. Another "shoot the star" (left-hand turn with the present co-worker) will have original partners facing, ready for the next call. This break was devised by Lloyd Shaw in 1938; after using it with his exhibition dancers, he taught it at his summer institutes starting in 1946. By all accounts it was the first new break written in the modern era. Shaw encouraged his student callers to be creative, but later came to rue the proliferation of hashed breaks and figures. See Chapter 23 for a call chart.

Throw in the clutch and *slip the clutch*: These calls date from the peak of the square dance boom, after callers had begun "hashing the breaks"; that is, combining bits of more than one established break. Soon after Allemande Thar (above) was released, callers started directing dancers to "turn by the left *like* an Allemande Thar": to form a "thar star" without going through the allemande left and the right-hand pass. The transition out of this star, like the one into it, had to be chosen and announced by the caller. On the call "throw in the clutch," introduced by Fenton Jones in 1949, left hands or forearms were released; the gents retained their star and began walking forward (clockwise) while the ladies continued moving forward (counterclockwise). The caller told the dancers how far to travel and whom to meet. From a thar star, "slip the clutch" was a direction for all dancers to release the left hand and immediately give it to the next person they faced.

Allemande O: This is a grand right and left interrupted by iterations of the do paso (which equals one change of the Texas do-si-do; see the discussion of hand-turn do-si-dos later in this chapter). The dancers do an allemande left with their corner, give right hand to partner and pass straight by, and join left hands or forearms (depending on the area) with the next person. They now perform a do paso, remembering that the person they begin it with becomes a temporary partner: They turn this person by the left, new corner by the right, new partner left again. In a do paso this third move can be a plain turn or a courtesy turn, depending on what call is to follow; in this case it is a plain turn that functions like an allemande left (as "shoot the star" does in Allemande Thar), sending the dancers in grand right and left direction. They give right hand to a new person, pass straight by, join left hands or forearms with the next person, and perform another do paso. The final turn by the left sends them toward their original partner. This break was devised by Ray Smith in 1947. (Note: Some neo-traditional callers have taken to calling "Allemande left with an Allemande O" and instructing the dancers to pass their partners and do an eastern [back to back] do-si-do with the next.)

Away You Go: This is a combination of "Allemande Thar" and "Allemande O." The dancers do an allemande left with their corner, give right hand to partner and pass by, and start a do paso with the next person, who becomes a temporary partner. The turns are new partner left, new corner right, new partner left again. The third turn starts a "thar star" with the gents forming a right-hand wrist star and backing up as the ladies go forward. On "Shoot the star" the gents release right hands, pairs turn half by the left, and all proceed in grand right and left direction to repeat the entire sequence: pass the next person by the right hand, start a do paso with the next, use the third turn to go into a thar star, and shoot that star to face original partner. The combination was devised by Jack Hoheisal in 1948.

Triple Allemande: The dancers start an allemande left with their corner, but when they have turned halfway around, the ladies form a right-hand star in the center and travel forward (clockwise) while the gents promenade in single file around the rim of the set (counterclockwise). In 4 to 6 beats they will meet their original corners again; they turn the corner left halfway and the gents form a right-hand star and travel clockwise while the ladies promenade in single file counterclockwise. In another 4 to 6 beats they will meet corners and do a full allemande left into a grand right and left starting with partners. This break was devised by Vera Holleuffer in 1945. See Chapter 23 for a call chart.

Transitions

The most common lead-in to a grand right and left is from an allemande left with the corner. This is perfectly straightforward: Corners release left hands or arms, and each dancer looks, and moves, toward partner. In some traditions, the allemande left is not used, and partners simply face each other to begin the grand right and left.

Most transitions from the grand right and left are also easy. As the dancers have their right hand free, a smooth transition requires the next movement to be right-handed or clockwise. A do-si-do (back to back) or a swing is ideal.

For transitions from a grand right and left to various promenade positions, see under "Promenade" earlier in this chapter.

Historical Notes

Just as the allemande left does not always lead into a grand right and left, the latter movement is not always preceded by an allemande left. From the available literature, it appears that the grand right and left by itself (often termed "grand chain" or "right and left all round") was commonly used as a chorus in 19th-century formal squares before anyone thought of combining it with allemande left. The combination is mentioned in an 1898 poem and a 1903 magazine article; by the 1920s it had become standard.

In the Northeast during the 1970s, when squares were still an integral part of the then-new contra dance revival, it was common after an allemande left for the dancers to execute an uncalled forward-and-back balance with their partner before moving into a grand right and left. Callers had varying opinions of this practice; some allowed time for it, some actively discouraged it. Now that squares are less often danced in contra groups, there are fewer unwritten traditions connected with them, and dancers are more apt to do just what the caller says – no more, no less.

Timing

On average, it takes about two and a half beats to meet and pass each person. A grand right and left halfway around a four-couple square takes about 10 beats. There are several ways that a break incorporating this movement can be fitted to 32 beats of music (half of a standard fiddle tune, comprising two "A" parts or two "B" parts). A common one is to combine an allemande left (6 to 8 beats), a grand right and left halfway (10 to 12 beats), and a promenade home. With partner twirls at the start and/or the end of the promenade, the whole thing will take about 32 beats. If the dancers do the first two moves snappily and meet their partners when a full 16 beats are left in the tune, the caller can insert a do-si-do before the promenade (assuming the dancers are not accustomed to executing promenade flourishes). But if the figure following this break is close-timed and possibly disorienting, it is best to omit the do-si-do in order to allow extra time at the end of the break for the dancers to "settle down" at home, rather than to expect them to perform each move in the textbook number of beats.

Balance

Done by

Any two adjacent dancers.

Description

The dancers face each other. According to local custom or the context of the routine, they either join right hands, join both hands straight across, or support their own weight without taking hands. In four beats of music, they move slightly from their starting position and then return to it. This is done in one of several ways, again depending on context or local custom.

Forward-and-back balance

Beat 1: Step forward on the right foot, keeping body weight over it, and almost immediately bring the left foot up to the right foot.

Beat 2: Touch the left foot to the floor next to the right foot, without taking weight.

Beat 3: Step backward on the left foot, keeping body weight over it, and almost immediately bring the right foot back to the left foot.

Beat 4: Touch the right foot to the floor next to the left foot, without taking weight.

Sideways or step-swing balance

Beat 1: Step to the right on the right foot, keeping body weight over it, and begin to sweep the left foot across in front of the right foot.

Beat 2: Hop on the right foot, continuing to sweep the left foot across in front.

Beats 3 & 4: Repeat the action of beats 1 & 2, but starting with the left foot.

Either of these balances may be done with as much or as little energy as the dancers care to put into it. The hop may amount to a mere raising and lowering of the heel while the toe stays in contact with the floor. If the dancers are holding hands, they may pull together on beat 1 and push apart on beat 3.

Result

The dancers are still facing each other. The next call almost always directs them to dance together again. They will naturally use their hands (if joined) to pull each other into a do-si-do or swing.

Teaching Technique

The balance is one of a very few square dance movements that use footwork other than the basic walking step (others are the swing and the sashay). Like the swing and the hand turn, it can't be fathomed just by watching and should receive special attention during teaching sessions.

A key element of the forward-and-back balance in particular is the action of the hands and arms. In the present-day contra dance world, most balances are of this type, and the pulling together and pushing away is, in my mind, more essential to the dynamics of the dance than is the footwork.

Dancers should keep their weight (as always) over the balls of their feet, rather than kicking their feet out in front of their bodies. This should be modeled whenever it seems necessary to emphasize the point.

Variations

The balance probably has more variations than any other square or contra dance movement. One researcher found 50 without half trying! (Ralph Piper in *Fiddle and Squares* [Wisconsin], Feb. 1952; reprinted in *Northern Junket,* vol. 5, no. 1, March 1955.)

In a very few areas, it has become customary to balance starting on the left foot. These areas include southern New Hampshire, long a hotbed of contra dancing, and parts of Illinois and Indiana, possibly influenced by émigrés from New Hampshire.

In parts of the West and Southwest during the square dance revival, the call "balance" meant to take a couple of steps away from one's partner and then dance forward, usually into a swing. In some areas the motion of the balance was completely lost and the call "balance to the next" or "balance home" merely meant "proceed to the next" or "go home."

Transitions

As noted above, the balance is usually followed by a swing or a do-si-do with the same person. Such a transition is easy: The dancers simply use their hands (if joined) to pull each other into the next move. In the case of a swing, they let go just in time to assume the new handhold.

Transitions *into* the balance can be challenging for the dancer. "Balance and swing" is less common in squares than in contra dances, but if this combination is used, the balance must be danced on the specific beats assigned to it or it loses its whole point. Even in square dance traditions where the dance and the music are nominally fully synchronized, in practice most moves can be fudged: The dancers can speed up or cut corners to get to the right place if they miss the first couple of beats. Not so with the balance; the rule here is "Better never than late." This being so, dancers should learn to end their moves comfortably by the end of the preceding phrase if they suspect that a balance is coming.

Timing

4 beats for a normal balance, 8 beats if repeated (sometimes called a double balance).

Twirl to Swap

Done by

Two adjacent dancers playing opposite gender roles.

Description

The dancers join hands (one hand each; see below for which hands) and raise them above their heads. They exchange places, stepping out of each other's way only as much as necessary, with the lady moving under the raised hands. The handhold needs to be supportive but flexible; the most effective method is for both dancers to curl their fingers about halfway to a closed fist and bear firmly against each other's hand without grabbing. During most of the move, the gent's hand will probably be outside the lady's, with the palm of his hand against the back of hers forming a ball-and-socket joint.

Facing (box the gnat): Both dancers use their right hand. The gent takes four steps in a clockwise semicircle, keeping to his left, as the lady takes four steps in a tighter counterclockwise semicircle. For both dancers, the first two steps are somewhat forward and the last two are somewhat backward. The same move done with left hands is called "box the flea" or "swat the flea."

Side by side (California twirl or frontier whirl): The dancers, starting with the lady on the gent's right side, use their adjacent hands (gent's right and lady's left). They move as in box the gnat, except that all the steps are forward.

Hybrid (star through): The dancers face each other and join hands (gent's right and lady's left), often by touching palms. As they cross to each other's place in four steps, the gent makes a quarter right-face turn while the lady (under the raised arms) makes a quarter left-face turn.

Result

In each of these moves, the dancers have exchanged places. After a box the gnat, they are again facing each other. After a California twirl, they are again side by side, lady on the right, but facing opposite to their starting direction. After a star through, they are side by side, lady on the right; if the gent was facing north and the lady south, both are now facing east.

Teaching Technique

All of these moves are much easier to learn from a demonstration than from a verbal description. If you want your dancers to master all of them, I suggest teaching the moves at widely separated points in time to avoid confusion.

The star through is particularly hard for dancers new to it because the choice of hands is not intuitive; there is no easy way to remember which hand to use.

Historical Notes

"Box the gnat" was originally a complete figure, with a call that ran "Box the gnat, box the flea, box that pretty girl back to me." The hands used and the direction traveled in the moves varied by region. I was once told by a colleague that "box the gnat" was a corruption of an old French dance term, "bauxinet"; but apparently no one can confirm that such a term was ever in use.

The move now generally called "California twirl" was traditionally known in some regions as a simple or single dishrag turn. In 1951 Ed Gilmore used a similar move done with the lady on the gent's left and named it "California whirl"; two years later Jim York named the "normal" couple move "California twirl." The latter call proved to be the more popular one. To avoid confusion, there was an attempt to rename the standard California twirl a "frontier whirl." This attempt appears to have been abandoned, as the current literature from Callerlab (the closest thing to an official arbiter of modern square dancing) uses only the name "California twirl." (Another and perhaps better name for the mirror-image version is "turn your corner under.")

"Star through" was introduced in 1960 by Ed Michl of Ohio. Almost simultaneously, the same movement was introduced by Frank Lane of Colorado under the name "snaparoo." After some discussion, Lane agreed to withdraw his choice of name. Presumably the name "star through" alludes to the fact that when two facing couples execute the move, their raised hands appear to form a star.

Transitions

In a sense, each of these movements is itself a transition, as it is usually done to change a couple's facing direction and/or relative positions to get them in place for a following movement. The various moves have evolved in order to achieve the smoothest possible transition between certain other moves.

It should be noted that when partners meet in a grand right and left, box the gnat (provided the dancers know the move) can be a less confusing way to reverse direction than a hand turn, as there is no ambiguity about how far to turn.

Timing

Usually 4 beats. In practice, the time for a twirl or turn-under is often "stolen"; that is, no time is allowed for it by the caller, and the dancers must compensate by executing the preceding and following moves in fewer beats than usual.

Ladies Chain

Done by

Two facing couples, each with the lady on the gent's right.

Description

The two ladies move forward, joining right hands as if for a handshake. They pass each other, release hands, and approach their opposite gent. Each gent moves a step to his right, begins rotating in place to his left, and receives the approaching lady's left hand (palm down) with his left hand (palm up) as if for a promenade. The gent puts his right arm around the lady's waist and she joins her right hand with his, completing a back skaters' promenade position (see more comments under "Promenade" above). The two dancers, side by side, pivot counterclockwise, the lady moving forward and the gent backward, until they are facing the couple they chained with.

The pivot in promenade position is often termed a "courtesy turn," though this name is seldom used in calling. The turn has been part of the chain for decades, but apparently it was not thought of as a discrete movement until 1952, when it was named by Jack McKay. The courtesy turn is also the last part of the right and left through and the do paso, although in the latter movement it may be replaced by a left-hand turn depending on what is to follow.

In the courtesy turn the gent should refrain from pushing the lady around with his right arm. If he does any leading, it should take the form of a very gentle pull with his left hand.

Result

The couples are again facing each other. The ladies have exchanged places; the gents are in their starting position.

Teaching Technique

Relating the unknown to the known is good teaching. The dancers will grasp the ladies chain quickly if they see how much of it is simply a promenade.

A three-part process works well in teaching the ladies chain:

1. Have facing couples assume back skaters' promenade position and pivot in place until couples are facing each other again. This will give the ladies an idea of what to do when they reach the opposite gent.
2. Have the ladies take two steps forward and turn to face their partners (the ladies are now back to back in the center). Then have partners join left hands and go into the courtesy turn.
3. After warning the dancers that the first courtesy turn will not be with partner, have first the head ladies, then the sides, chain over and back.

If Step 1 is used without Step 2, the dancers are likely to have trouble figuring out how to get side by side for the turn.

Variations

Many dancers, particularly present-day contra dancers, prefer to omit the courtesy turn, substituting a move in which the lady turns under the gent's raised arm or spins one or more times as the gent supports her by keeping his left arm raised. Any of these variations is often referred to as a "twirl," whether or not the lady actually spins.

The twirl in lieu of a courtesy turn can be the subject of controversy, for two reasons: First, enough dancers prefer the twirl that it has become more than a variation, though not yet the standard; and second, many dancers do not enjoy twirling or being twirled. Many leaders suggest that the twirl be used only between "mutually consenting adults." The lady, who must work harder and risks getting dizzy, is generally conceded the privilege of choosing to twirl or not. She indicates her preference by raising her left arm (for a twirl) or keeping it down (for a courtesy turn) as the gent takes her left hand.

If a twirl is indicated, the gent should turn left-face, constantly facing the lady and keeping his raised left arm steady as the lady spins clockwise beneath it (rather than "cranking" her). The lady should keep her feet under her and take small steps, to avoid colliding with other dancers. As in any twirl, hands should form a ball-and-socket joint.

Other variations on the chain are prescribed by the caller, rather than spontaneously executed by the dancers:

Power turn: At the end of a chain, the dancers continue their courtesy turn until they are facing away from the couple they chained with. This call is given only when there are dancers behind the ones who are chaining. The term was introduced by Kathy Anderson in the 1980s, but the movement was used earlier and called directively: "Ladies chain, turn 'em around and chain [for instance] with the couple behind you."

Four ladies chain (ladies grand chain): From a square set, the four ladies form a right-hand star in the center and move forward, turning the star halfway around until they can give left hand to the opposite gent and execute a courtesy turn. In some areas the ladies use a wrist star, in others they hold their palms together shoulder-high.

Ladies chain three-quarters: This can be done by two or four ladies. It is simpler with four ladies, who merely turn their star an extra place around the square for a courtesy turn with the gent who was their corner at the start of the move. When two ladies chain three-quarters, either their destination must be empty of ladies or, if there is already a lady there, the gent must put the approaching lady somewhere else. A common call here is for the gent to do a courtesy turn with the new lady (his partner must step to her right to get out of the way) followed by a rollaway to put the new lady on his left.

Gents chain: The gents chain appears to have been a very rare movement throughout the history of square dances, going back to the 18th-century cotillion and the 19th-century quadrille. The term is used in some 19th-century dance manuals, but I have yet to find one where it is defined. Lacking printed evidence, it is anybody's guess whether the gents were supposed to take right or left hands in passing. Present-day contra dance callers appear to have standardized on a gents chain that is a mirror image of a ladies chain: The gents give left hands in passing and go into a mirror courtesy turn, with all handholds reversed and the ladies backing around as the gents go forward.

Transitions

Problems are more likely to arise after a ladies chain than before it. From a courtesy turn, any following move will be awkward if the couple hold onto each other too long. From a twirl, it is crucial for both dancers to be aware of the direction they need to face next and "put on the brakes" rather than letting the lady careen wildly like the spinning top in the table game of skittles.

From either ending, the gent can quickly release the lady's left hand from his left and catch it with his right hand, ready to help her into the next move (such as a circle or a forward and back).

See "Right and Left Through" below for the special case of ladies chain preceded or followed by that movement.

Historical Notes

It appears that instead of a courtesy turn as we know it, the second half of this movement was originally an open left-hand turn. It is described that way in dance manuals as late as the 1920s (Boyd and Dunlavy 1925, Ford 1926, Ryan 1926).

In the 19th century generally, and halfway into the 20th in New England, "ladies chain" meant a round trip – chain to the opposite, then back to partner – and a single exchange must be called a "ladies half chain." Now that the single exchange is commonly used as a choreographic device, it has taken the name "ladies chain," and a "chain back" must be made explicit.

Timing

For a two ladies (or gents) chain, 8 beats, of which 4 are allotted to the ladies crossing and 4 to the courtesy turn or twirl. A chain with a power turn is frequently allowed only 8 beats, the dancers being expected to turn faster than usual (hence the name). A four ladies chain can be done in 8 beats if the set is kept compact and all the dancers move with determination; otherwise it takes about 10. A three-quarter chain requires 10 to 12 beats.

Right and Left Through

Done by

Two facing couples, each with the lady on the gent's right.

Description

The dancers execute a pass through, each person keeping to the left and passing right shoulders with the opposite dancer. (In some areas, opposites join right hands briefly as they pass.) They are now facing away from the couple they are working with. Each couple now assumes a back skaters' promenade position: left hands joined in front of the gent, gent's right arm around lady's waist, lady's right hand at her right hip to receive gent's right hand. Thus attached, they pivot counterclockwise as a unit (lady forward, gent backward), remaining side by side, halfway around to face the opposite couple again.

The pivot in promenade position is often referred to as a "courtesy turn"; see the comments under "Ladies Chain" above.

Result

The two couples have exchanged places. Dancers are with the partner they started the movement with, side by side, lady on the right.

Teaching Technique

The right and left through gets my vote for the most difficult move to teach. It's a compound movement: The dancers go straight ahead and then turn, and they turn in a way they couldn't have predicted. A common error is for the lady to turn solo to her right after the pass through.

In areas where the dancers give right hands in passing, they must be sure to release right hands as soon as they are abreast of their opposites. If they hold on too long, they may find themselves pulled around to face the direction they came from; this will be especially disorienting to new dancers.

You can avoid a deal of trouble by waiting to use the right and left through until you have taught the promenade, ladies chain, and pass through. Then every part of the new move can be related to something the group already knows. When I teach right and left through to new dancers, whether in a progressive circle, a square, or a contra line, I now walk them through two half promenades with the facing couple first. I then tell them that the next thing they will do is almost the same, except that instead of keeping to their right as a couple, they will let go of their partner and "melt" through the other two.

This is one move that benefits greatly from the technique of telling the dancers where they will end up before having them move. If they know that they are about to exchange places with the facing couple, and that the lady will still be on the right, they will be more confident – and also able to recover quickly if they do go astray.

The timing of your instructions is critical. Just as the dancers are finishing the pass through, tell them firmly to stop. Then have them take promenade position and hold still as you tell them which way to turn. This should keep the ladies from attempting a solo right turn, or any of the dancers from turning in place to face the opposite couple.

Variations

The most common variation on the right and left through is the replacement of the courtesy turn with a twirl. The discussion of twirls under "Ladies Chain" above applies to this move as well.

Whether or not the dancers give right hands on the initial pass depends largely on local custom. My impression is that hands are being used in an increasing number of areas where contra dances and neo-traditional squares are done. (In the modern square dance world, the taking of right hands became universal in the 1950s.) The right and left through is probably a descendant of an English country dance movement (see "Historical Notes" below), so the use of hands is historically appropriate.

In contra dances a "right and left" is often called when two gents are facing two ladies. The traffic pattern is the same as described above. Right hands are not given on the pass; the pivot is counterclockwise, with the left-hand person in each pair moving backward. Instead of taking promenade position, the pair may put nearest arms around each other's shoulders or waist, or they may move without touching, staying side by side as if their shoulders were glued together. There is no reason why this type of right and left should not be used in a square, provided the dancers are familiar with it and are aware that it may be called for.

In some dance communities, past and present, the movements done on the call "right and left" are identical to "pass through, cross trail, and turn alone" (see the end of this chapter for "Cross Trail").

All four couples right and left through: This was done in the 1950s as a novelty, apparently just to prove it could be done. All pass right shoulders with corner, give right hand to the next (original opposite) and pass by, pass left shoulders with the next, and courtesy turn with partner across from home.

Transitions

For the transition from a circle of four into a right and left through, see under "Pass Through" above. For transitions out of the courtesy turn, see under "Ladies Chain" above.

Although in theory the courtesy turns are identical in ladies chain and right and left through, in practice they often differ slightly. The pivot point is supposed to be between the lady and the gent, and both dancers should move an equal distance. This standard is usually observed in right and left through, but in ladies chain the gent frequently stays on or near one spot on the floor, making the lady travel farther and faster than he does. This means that a ladies chain followed by a right and left through is awkward for the lady, who must slow down in order to pass through at the same speed as the gent beside her. A right and left through followed by a ladies chain is smoother, as the lady must accelerate into the chain, always easier than braking.

Historical Notes

The right and left through as we do it today is the product of many decades of evolution. Apparently the original form was similar to what is now termed a square through: a miniature grand chain with the gents traveling clockwise and the ladies counterclockwise (the reverse of our common grand right and left). In the case of two facing couples, the sequence was right hand to opposite, left to partner, right to opposite, left to partner, while following one's nose around a small imaginary square. Unlike the modern square through, the dancers were not expected to pull straight by the last hand, but generally returned to their places, facing the center of the set. (In English country dancing this movement is known as "four changes of a circular hey with hands.")

By the late 19th century, the left-hand pass had become a left-hand turn, with the gentleman helping his partner around to face the center. As with the ladies chain, this turn was similar to a modern courtesy turn but without the gent's right arm around the lady's waist; it was being so described as late as the 1920s.

As with ladies chain, "right and left" meant a round trip (ending in starting place) throughout the 19th century and, in New England, halfway into the 20th. In that era, a single exchange must be called a "half right and left."

The terms "pass through" and "right and left through" were not fully standardized until the early 1950s. "Right and left through" could mean what we now call "pass through" (that is, the crossing move without the turn). The context of the dance determined whether or not the turn was required. There were even cases in which one couple turned and the other did not, such as "Circle four halfway round, right and left through and on to the next," a common ending for visiting-couple figures in parts of the Northeast. Just about everywhere, either the dancers knew what was coming or the caller explained the routine before the music started.

Since the early 1950s, most callers (in both the traditional and the modern square dance worlds) have agreed that "right and left through" includes a turn back but "pass through" does not. There is also near-universal agreement that "right and left through" means a single exchange of couples, and "right and left back," if desired, must be explicitly called for.

Timing

8 beats, of which 4 are allotted to the pass through and 4 to the courtesy turn or twirl.

Rollaway

Done by

A couple (one lady and one gent) standing side by side, holding nearest hands. The most common rollaway begins with the lady on the gent's right.

Description

In the most common version, the lady does a rolling turn in front of the gent, ending on his left side, while the gent moves sideways to his right into the lady's starting place. At the midpoint of the turn, the lady is facing the gent, directly in front of him, and both hands are joined straight across for a split second.

Result

The two dancers have exchanged places, but the couple is standing on the same spot, facing the same direction as before.

Teaching Technique

This move is much easier to learn from a demonstration than from a verbal description. It is important, though, to emphasize the necessity of "giving weight" – putting springy resistance in both dancers' arms – as without this counterforce the move will take longer than the allotted time and will be unsatisfying to dance.

Variations

Although the most common type of rollaway is as described above, with the lady rolling from the gent's right to his left, a "corner rollaway" may be called for: The lady rolls to her right in front of her current corner gent to end on his right side. The gent may also be directed to do the rolling. Of course, the caller must be crystal clear as to who is to roll, and in which direction.

Transitions

It is important, in incorporating this move into a routine, to avoid combinations that would require an awkward change of body flow. One pleasing transition used in contra dancing is from "roll the gents to the left" to a ladies chain with the opposite couple. Conversely, a corner rollaway in which the lady rolls to her right should never be followed by a ladies chain.

Historical Notes

The rollaway is the most recent addition to a family of movements called "sashay." The word is a corruption of the French *chassez*, the imperative of *chasser*, "to hunt" or "to chase." In the original *chassez*, the action is suited to the word: One foot chases the other as the dancers slide sideways.

In American square dancing, the most common call involving this move was a visiting-couple figure: From a circle of two or more couples, the call was "Sashay partners halfway round" (with each lady passing to the left in front of her partner) followed by "Re-sashay, go all the way round" (with the lady passing to the right in front of him, to the left behind him, and to the right behind him again, ending where she began). Eventually the sliding step disappeared and the figure was walked like most square dance moves.

The half sashay was borrowed from this complete figure to become a basic building block of "hashed" figures. Often, for added spice with experienced dancers, a caller would start a sequence by having the heads do a half sashay at home, which meant each dancer would thereafter be going through movements normally done by the opposite gender role.

In the mid-20th century it was decided that a rolling motion would allow smoother transitions than a simple sideways exchange of partners. In 1950 Ed Gilmore coined the term "rollaway with a half sashay." For a few years there was an attempt to distinguish between "rollaway" (from a courtesy turn or star promenade) and "whirlaway" (starting with nearest hands joined), but "rollaway" is now the common term for any move of this type.

Timing

4 beats. In some fast-moving routines, no time is allotted to the rollaway; the dancers must "steal" the time from the preceding and following movements.

Lead Right

Done by

One or two active couples, each with an inactive couple to its right.

Description

Each active couple moves from its starting position (usually home place) in a curving path, forward and to the right, to face its right-hand couple.

Result

The inactive couples have not moved; the active couples are facing their inactive couple squarely. If two opposite active couples (heads or sides) lead right, those active couples will be back to back in the center of the set.

Variations

A lead to the left is possible but is extremely rare. Lloyd Shaw was fond of telling the story of a visiting caller who was laughed out of the hall by Shaw's teenage dancers for calling Couple 1 out to the left.

It is important to understand the difference between *lead right* and *face right*. If the heads are directed to face right, they simply pivot slightly in place, as a couple, until they are at a 45-degree angle, facing the sides, who will pivot slightly to the left to face the heads. The heads are still the active couples, but all four couples have adjusted an equal amount to change their facing direction. Any movements they execute (such as ladies chain or right and left through) will be done diagonally.

Transitions

A lead right is most often followed by a circle four to the left. This is true in single visiting-couple figures, where Couple 1 leads to Couple 2, and in two-couple-active dances, where the heads lead to the sides.

Timing

4 beats to lead to the right. If a circle of four follows, the timing of the circle is normal: 4 beats to circle halfway, 8 beats to circle once around. For another common combination, see "Circle to a Line" below.

Circle to a Line

Done by

Usually two groups of two couples, each with one active and one inactive couple.

Description

After leading to the right, each active couple joins hands in a ring with its inactive couple. The four people circle left. When the circle has gone halfway around, so that the active couple is on the outside of the set facing in, the active gent releases the inactive lady from his left hand and moves in a straight path to his left, still facing across the set. The other three people open the circle into a line, facing across the set toward the other line. If the heads are the active couples, the lines form at the sides, and vice versa.

Result

The dancers are in two lines of four, facing the other line across the set. Each line comprises two couples side by side, each with original partner. An active gent is at the left end of each line, close to his home side of the set. An inactive lady is at the right end of each line; the inactive couple is facing in its original direction, but standing slightly to the right of its home place to accommodate the active couple. (The dancers should adjust their position during this move so that the resulting lines are directly across from each other.)

Teaching Technique

Although this is not an extremely complex figure, it is definitely not for absolute beginners. It will need careful explanation and the caller's constant attention during the walkthrough. A demonstration will be helpful if there is a set familiar with the move. The same pair of active couples may need two or three walkthroughs in order to feel comfortable with the combination. Also, this move should be walked through with the other pair of couples active, as the active and inactive roles feel completely different.

Variations

Among experienced dancers, it is customary for the inactive lady, rather than moving backward to form the right end of the line, to make a left-face turn under an arch formed by her raised left arm and her partner's right arm. By doing so, she can be moving forward to her right to pull her end of the line straight.

Transitions

The call following this movement is almost invariably "Forward eight and back." See the comment under "Timing" below.

Chapter 15: Basic Movements 231

Historical Notes

The most common use of circle to a line is in setting up the formation for *The Rout(e)*. This figure, which is included in Chapter 18, seems to be a rather late addition to the traditional repertoire; it does not appear in widely circulated collections of dances until the 1940s. There is a figure in 19th-century quadrille books that incorporates the ladies chains around the set that are the distinctive feature of *The Rout(e)*, but it uses a different method of forming the lines of four.

Timing

In theory it should take 8 beats from the time the circles are formed until the lines have been stretched out straight, or 12 beats including the initial "lead to the right." In practice, only 8 beats are commonly allowed for "lead right and circle to a line"; the dancers begin going forward (the next call almost always being "Forward eight and back") while they are still straightening out the line.

Bend the Line

Done by

A line of four people, all facing the same direction.

Description

The two people closest to the center of the line release their handhold. Each pair of people pivots one-quarter, the end person moving forward and the center person backward; the pivot point is between the two people working together.

Result

The line has become two facing couples. If the line was facing north or south, the couples are facing east and west. If two facing lines of four execute a "bend the line," the result is two new lines of four, each couple having acquired a new neighboring couple. If the original lines were facing north and south, the new lines are facing east and west.

Teaching Technique

This is one of the easiest movements for dancers to understand; it even has a name that describes the move well. As always, it may help to tell the dancers where they will be at the conclusion of the move.

Variations

It is possible for a line of six or eight people to bend, with the pivot points being at the center of each half. Obviously such a move can take place only in an asymmetrical figure; most such figures are generally thought of as gimmicks. Perhaps the most common use is in sequences designed to put all eight dancers in a line facing the stage. The music is stopped and announcements are made. Afterward, the music starts again and the caller says something like "Bend the big line."

Historical Notes

According to Rickey Holden (1962), this movement was named in 1957 by Bill Hansen (famous as the author of "square through," introduced the same year). However, many square and contra dances incorporated the move before that date, using calls such as "Break in the middle and face those two" or "Turn and face the other two."

Timing

Nominally 4 beats, but the time is often "stolen" from the preceding and following movements.

Arch and Dive

Done by

Various numbers of couples, with at least one couple to make an arch and at least one person to dive through it.

Description

The details will depend on the specific routine, but in general two designated adjacent people join nearest hands and raise their arms to create an arch; one person or couple, facing those making the arch, moves forward, bending head and upper body as needed while going under the arch, and follows the next call. Those making the arch may or may not be expected to move forward as the diving person or couple passes between them.

The most common use of this maneuver, apart from specific named dances, is in the movement that was known as "inside arch and outside under" until the 1950s, when it was dubbed "dive through." It is called to four couples arranged such that two couples are back to back in the center of the square, each face to face with an outside couple. (This is sometimes known as "box formation"; see Chapter 14.) On the call, each inside couple joins near hands, forms an arch, and moves forward over the outside couple as the latter moves forward under the arch. After a dive through, the arching couple, now facing out of the set, is expected to do an automatic California twirl to face in, keeping the lady on the gent's right.

Result

After a dive through, the original outside couples will be in the center face to face; each original inside couple will be on the outside facing in, behind a new inside couple. The result in other cases involving arch-and-dive maneuvers will depend on the specific routine. If a couple making an arch ends up facing in, they are not expected to do a California twirl.

Teaching Technique

This is one of the most straightforward movements for teacher and dancers alike. The teacher must make it clear where the sequence is to start and finish, particularly which direction everyone must face at the end.

Variations

The most popular square using this move is probably *Dip and Dive Six,* also known as *Inside Arch and Outside Under.* The figure has been known and loved for years across North America; it was traditionally done to jigs in Ontario, to reels in the West, and in the East to the song Red Wing. (See Chapter 19 for the Ontario version.) Couple 1 leads to the right and circles halfway around with Couple 2; this aligns three couples facing east-west, with Couple 2 in the middle.

From here the rules are: If you're in the middle you make an arch and move forward; if you're facing an arch you go under it; if you find yourself facing out, you do a California twirl to face in. The action continues until both side couples have crossed the set twice to end at home. Couple 1 now goes to Couple 3, circles half, dives through, and leads to Couple 4 to set up the three-couple formation again (with the same couples as before: 1, 2, and 4). There is a variant, from Quebec I believe, in which the three-couple routine is done on the diagonal and Couple 3 is involved more of the time. The couples that work together are first 1, 2, and 3; then 1, 3, and 4; and finally 1, 4, and 2. In each case the two couples listed first begin the action by circling.

Transitions

As with the movement itself, transitions are relatively straightforward. I would caution against calling a dive through immediately following a courtesy turn, as the dancers (particularly the arching couples) need to have near hands joined at the very start of the arch-and-dive motion.

Timing

A single pass (one couple arching, one diving) takes 4 beats. In practice, a number of short, straight moves, some of which involve arching and diving, are often done in a total number of beats that breaks down to only 2 or 3 beats per move. For example, one complete cross of the set in *Dip and Dive Six,* including a dive, an arch, and a California twirl, can be done in about 8 beats.

Grand Square

Done by

An entire square of dancers (four couples).

Description

Starting from home, each dancer will walk in a square path around his or her corner, while the corner walks around him or her. However, corners will take no notice of each other; each dancer will be looking only to partner and opposite for guidance. Everyone will face inward at all times; no one will turn their back on the set.

The heads start by facing across the set toward their opposites, as they would do on the call "Square your sets." They take 3 steps forward to meet their opposites, then turn one-quarter in place to face their partners. Side by side with their opposites, they take 3 steps backward, away from their partners, and turn one-quarter to face their opposites. They take 3 steps backward, away from their opposites, and turn one-quarter to face their partners. Finally, they take 3 steps forward to meet their partners at home.

The sides start by facing their partners (a common prompting call is "Sides face, grand square"). They take 3 steps backward, away from their partners, then turn one-quarter to face their opposites. They take 3 steps forward to meet their opposites, then turn one-quarter to face their partners. Side by side with their opposites, they take 3 steps forward to meet their partners, then turn one-quarter to face their opposites. Finally, side by side with their partners, they take 3 steps backward to end at home.

To recap:

> Heads go forward, back, back, forward.
> Sides go back, forward, forward, back.

This sequence is usually followed by the call "Reverse." At this point the heads should be facing their partners and the sides should be facing across toward their opposites. Without turning initially, the heads execute the sides' first part, and the sides do the heads' first part, once more ending at home.

Teaching Technique

The time-honored method for teaching the grand square is to have the sides move out of the set, then instruct and drill the heads in their part of the routine. Once the heads appear to know what to do, they move out and the sides learn their part. Finally all eight dancers practice their parts at once.

In my experience, it is not worth the extra time it takes to teach the parts separately. If the move is explained clearly and walked through slowly, with pauses at the turns, all eight dancers can be led to understand this movement in little more than half the time.

My preferred method involves informing the dancers of three ground rules:

- Everyone face your partner, nose to nose. When you are this close to someone, you will always take three steps backward.
- Everyone face across, toward your opposite. You will always be facing either your partner or your opposite. You will never turn your back on anyone.
- When you are as far away from someone as you are now from your opposite, you will always take three steps forward.

Recap: When you're close you back away; when you're apart you go forward.

I now have the sides face their partners and tell the heads to keep facing across. I then have the dancers move 3 steps at a time, pausing to tell them to turn and face the other person they are working with. I repeat the 3 steps and a pause until everyone is again home. Often, if the dancers are moving well, I do not have them reverse the movement at this point, but save the reverse as a surprise. If there is some confusion, I may repeat the first half, including the pauses.

When I am satisfied that the dancers will be able to do the movement successfully, I use the following cadence calls without music (the parts of the tune are shown here for clarity):

Beats:	1	2	3	4
Intro:	Sides	face,	grand	square
A.1:	One,	two,	three, turn a	quarter, go
	One,	two,	three, turn a	quarter, go
	One,	two,	three, turn a	quarter, go
	One,	two, *don't*	turn, re-	verse, go
A.2:	One,	two,	three,	turn,
	One,	two,	three,	turn,
	One,	two,	three,	turn,
	One,	two,	three, you're	home!

If the dancers are moving well through the first half, I accelerate the tempo during the second half to show them how easy the movement is once they know what to do. Sometimes I say "Are you home?" instead of "You're home!" if I think they will respond with a cheer.

Variations

A common practice, particularly in the modern square dance world, is to encourage the dancers to take two walking steps, then three small steps in place while turning, rather than three steps and a single-step turn, on each side of their little square. The cadence call for this is "One, two, cha-cha-cha." The set must be compact in order for this to work.

Regrettably, many modern square dancers do not do the grand square to the phrases of the music. Instead, they take three beats to walk each side of their small square, cutting across the phrase, for a total of 12 beats. They swing their partner once around to use up the final 4 beats of the phrase. The second half, or reverse, is treated in the same way.

Several variations on the grand square have been devised, some too complex (and rarely done even in modern square dancing) to warrant mention here. The simplest is to call "Heads face, grand square," whereupon the sides go forward and the heads face their partners and back away.

Grand slide: The dancers follow the path of a normal grand square but remain facing in the same direction throughout. As usual, the sides start by facing partner and the heads by facing across the set. When the dancers would normally turn a quarter, they instead use a sliding step (two slow slides or four quick ones) to move laterally to the next corner of their small square. The movement was named by Chip Hendrickson in 1967; it may actually be easier than the normal version for new dancers to understand.

An experienced caller can have fun with reasonably confident dancers by varying the directions for the grand square. Note that most of these variations will be disorienting, as the dancers will not have someone doing the mirror image of their part.

- Just the ladies grand square.
- Just the gents grand square.
- Ladies face, grand square. (This means the ladies face toward their partners and begin by backing away, but the gents face across the set and begin by going forward.)
- Gents face, grand square. (The gents face toward partner and back away while the ladies face across and go forward.)
- Head gents take their corner lady into the middle and back (this is to alert the dancers that the grand square will be on the diagonal); the others face, grand square (side gents and head ladies, who are corners, face each other and back away).

There are "gimmicky" sequences in which the dancers are first rearranged, by means of ladies chains and other movements, so that a partial grand square (say 8 steps) will bring corners or partners together, to the dancers' surprise and, hopefully, delight.

In a double grand square, done in a double or "royal" set with two couples on each side, each couple will play the role of a single dancer in a normal grand square. The right-hand couple on each side acts as a lady, the left-hand couple as a gent. The movement may be done in two ways:

1. Each couple keeps near arm around each other's waist throughout the movement. Each couple pivots one-quarter as a unit on reaching a corner of its small square. This version is probably easier for most dancers to comprehend.

2. Each person acts independently. On the call "Sides face," instead of facing partner, both members of each right-hand side couple face left and both members of each left-hand side couple face right. To begin the movement, the heads move forward, side by side with partner (and the adjacent head couple), and the sides move backward, one partner behind the other. At each corner of the small square, every dancer turns a quarter in place individually. Each couple will alternate being side by side with being one behind the other. This version may take a little extra time to learn, but it is very impressive when done as an exhibition.

Transitions

Leading into a grand square, it is important to give the dancers time to anticipate the movement. This is particularly true if they have little experience with squares, even if they are seasoned contra dancers. If the timing of the preceding sequence (figure or break) is so tight that they can barely reach home by the end of the tune, they will have trouble orienting themselves even if you call "Sides face, grand square" at the proper time.

Leading out of a grand square, two couples are approaching and facing partner and the other two are facing across (having just backed into place). If I am ending a break with a grand square and the following figure starts with a pair of couples moving forward, I like to tailor the grand square to flow into the next move. If two couples are going to promenade, I use the version of the grand square that ends with them facing across: the normal "Sides face" for the heads, or "Heads face" for the sides. If the active couples will be going forward and back, I use the version that ends with them facing partner: "Heads face" for the heads, "Sides face" for the sides. This is to avoid their going backward for 4 beats and immediately forward and back again.

Historical Notes

The grand square appears in the dance *Hunsdon House,* in the 17th-century book *The English Dancing Master,* published by John Playford. In the 19th century it was used as a chorus (or, as we would now say, a break) in various quadrilles; in several books it was given as an alternative to the grand chain (grand right and left) in Figure 5 of the *Lancers,* the most popular of the quadrilles.

Around 1950 a routine featuring this movement became popular under the name *Grand Square Quadrille* or simply *Grand Square.* In it, the grand square alternates with a series of straight and diagonal chains and other maneuvers. In modern square dancing, the grand square is often used as the first half of a singing call break, in order to let the caller (and possibly the dancers) sing the opening lyrics of the original song.

Timing

16 beats for each half of the grand square, or 32 beats for the whole thing. The movement is best danced in total synchronization with the phrases of the music;

that is, not only should each 4 steps coincide with a 4-beat musical half phrase, but the entire movement should be fitted to the two "A" parts, or the two "B" parts, of a standard tune (or the first or second half of a 64-beat singing call).

Wheel Around

Done by

Any number of couples, each couple acting independently of the others. The most common application is during a couple promenade.

Description

Each couple stops its forward motion and pivots halfway around counter-clockwise, the lady moving forward and the gent backward. The pivot point is between the two dancers.

Result

The couple is facing in the opposite direction from where they started. If the lady was on her partner's right (as is usual), she is still on his right.

Note that if just the heads (or sides) wheel around from a promenade, the dancers are effectively in facing lines of four. From here, any moves can be done that could follow "heads lead right and circle four, head gents break to a line."

Teaching Technique

This movement is easy to understand. As with all couple pivots, it should be emphasized that both dancers move an equal distance; the gent should not stand on a fixed spot and expect the lady to do all the traveling.

Variations

If the members of a couple are of the same gender, the rule holds that the right-hand person moves forward and the left-hand person backward. However, in the case of mixed couples with the lady on the left, the direction of the pivot is reversed to clockwise so that the lady can move forward.

A similar movement, *backtrack,* is less commonly used than wheel around. In a couple backtrack, each dancer turns individually, so that if the lady was on the right to begin, she ends on the left. In a promenade around the set, this may be thought of as "staying in your traffic lane." The backtrack is done without releasing handholds. If the dancers are promenading in front skaters' position, they turn toward each other to backtrack; if they are in back skaters' or varsovienne position, both dancers make a right-face turn.

Note that "backtrack" can also be called from a single file promenade, in which case the designated dancers make a solo turn away from the center of the set to reverse their direction. Typically the call "backtrack" implies that the dancers who turn around will be traveling some distance; if they are to move only from their current partner to the one behind, the call "roll back" is more common.

Chapter 15: Basic Movements 241

Transitions

Transitions to and from a wheel around or a couple backtrack should be easy, as couples will be promenading before, and possibly after, the movement. If a different call is to follow the turn, the couple simply release their handholds.

Timing

4 beats, often "stolen" in fast sequences.

Do-si-do (hand turns)

Done by

Two or more couples in a circle. Some variants can be done only by two couples; others can be done by any number of couples. In the case of three or more couples, each dancer will work only with his or her own partner and corner.

Description and Variations

There are several traditional versions of the hand-turn do-si-do. At the end of most versions, partners approach each other and execute either a courtesy turn or a left-hand (or left-arm) turn, depending on the next call.

Do paso: This is the simplest version; it can be done by any number of couples. Each dancer faces partner and turns him or her by the left hand or arm, goes to corner and turns by the right, and returns to partner for a courtesy turn or a regular turn by the left (depending on the next call).

Texas do-si-do: In Dallas and in states bordering Texas, this was identical to the do paso (see "Historical Notes" below for the story of the various names). In West Texas it was understood that the dancers were to repeat the pattern of partner left, corner right, until the caller said "One more change and on [or home] you go." West Texas callers developed elaborate and prolonged patter to recite while the dancers continued their figure-eight maneuvering (Holden 1951). On the call "One more change," the usual rule was "If you are with or just leaving partner, go to corner, back to partner and stop. If you are with or just leaving corner, go back to partner and stop" (Holden, booklet for Folkraft record album F-15, 1949).

Grange do-si-do: This is done by two couples. Each dancer turns the opposite by the right, partner by the left, opposite by the right, and does a courtesy turn or a left-hand turn with partner. I am not sure the name "Grange do-si-do" was ever used in calling, though it appears in the explanation of the move in some texts. (See "Historical Notes" below for other names.)

Northern, cowboy, or Lloyd Shaw do-si-do (docey-doe): This can be done only by two couples. From a circle of four, the two ladies exchange places, either by releasing both hands and passing left shoulders or by doing a rollaway to the right in front of their opposite gent. In either case, the dancers then turn partner by the left, corner by the right, and return to partner for a courtesy turn.

Result

The couples are again in a circle, partners reunited. If the next call is "On to the next," a promenade, a chain, or something similar, the couples have done a courtesy turn and are ready to move as a couple or to send the lady in the desired direction. If the next call does not keep partners together, they do a plain left-hand (or left-arm) turn instead of the courtesy turn and are ready to move away from each other.

Teaching Technique

Each variant of this do-si-do must be carefully taught as a unique sequence; some thought must be given to which name to use (see "Historical Notes" below). If the move will be used in the context of hash (sequences of calls that the dancers do not know in advance), the dancers must be taught both possible endings – courtesy turn and plain turn – and be ready to judge which one to use, depending on the following call (which should be delivered before they complete this move). If the do-si-do will be used in only one context, the dancers can be taught a single way of ending it.

Historical Notes

The hand-turn do-si-do has been known by various names and served various purposes. In some dance communities, mainly in the South, it constitutes a visiting-couple figure in its own right, usually followed by a swing with the opposite (in the circle of four) and one with partner. In other parts of the South, and in traditional western style, it is done as a subchorus following certain visiting-couple figures. (In the northeastern US and eastern Canada, where the hand-turn do-si-do by any name is all but unknown, the same visiting figures may be followed by "circle four halfway, pass through to the next [or to home]" or "circle half, inactive couple arch, active couple duck through to the next [or to home].")

It is not certain how a term meaning "back to back" came to be used to denote a sequence of hand turns. There are, however, some intermediate forms that suggest that the process may have been gradual. At one time in at least one area, from a circle of four it was customary to call "Ladies do-si-do," whereupon the ladies would release both hands and cross the circle to face out – which put the ladies back to back. At that point the ladies might take the nearest hand of the gents on both sides, creating a new circle with the ladies facing out and the gents in (as in "do-si-ballonet," described in Shaw 1939 and also done in Ontario). Whether or not this new circle had been created, the four dancers would then start a series of hand turns. Eventually, the theory goes, the back-to-backness of the ladies was no longer noticed and the hand turns became the distinguishing feature of the sequence, but the "do-si-do" name was retained.

Another theory holds that the name stems from the fact that in most four-person versions of this movement the gents are momentarily back to back as they reach behind each other's back to find the next lady. Rickey Holden has suggested that the name was influenced by *dos y dos* (Spanish for "two and two"); this seems possible but unlikely to me, as the name "do-si-do" was used for hand-turn sequences over a wide swath of what is now the United States, including areas far from Spanish-speaking regions.

Turning from the name to the history of the move itself, I believe that the oldest form of the hand-turn do-si-do is likely the one described above as the Grange do-si-do. Most people are right-handed and a movement starting with the right hand seems more intuitive to me. This version has also been known in various regions as the Georgia rang tang, Georgy Alabam, reel the set, and run the reel, among other names. In 1949 Jim York of California popularized it as the Suzy Q, taking the name from a ballroom dance step of the 1930s in which dancers must twist their bodies back and forth.

Assuming the Grange do-si-do to be the oldest form, its initial right-hand turn was modified or eliminated in many areas during the late 19th and early 20th centuries. In Texas it disappeared entirely; the Texas do-si-do consists of partner left, corner right, partner left (repeated at the caller's will in West Texas). Farther north, the initial turn with the opposite became a hands-free maneuver; Boyd and Dunlavy (1925) describe it as a pass through by couples, while Shaw (1939) has the ladies passing left shoulders as they cross the circle. All agree that partners join left hands after this, but the two sources cited here emphasize that this "partner left" is more a pull-by than a full turn.

The Texas do-si-do is certainly the simplest form of this move. When square dancing became a widely popular hobby and callers' repertoires were heavily affected by cross-currents, the Texas version might have been expected to become the standard do-si-do. However, Lloyd Shaw, who was extremely influential through his books and institutes, preferred the more complicated version he had encountered in Colorado or neighboring states, and promoted it as the standard. (He spelled it "docey-doe," but of course the distinction is not apparent in spoken calls.) Shaw dubbed the Texas version "do paso," presumably in reference to the city of El Paso, home of influential caller Herb Greggerson. (Merriam-Webster, which spells it "do-pas-so," suggests the term is a blend of "do-si-do" and "pass," but I know of no one in the square dance world who believes this.) The term appears once in Shaw's 1939 book *Cowboy Dances* with no definition or explanation; Ralph McNair, another Colorado caller, may have been the first to describe it in print (1941). Texans resented the name when it attained widespread currency in the late 1940s, but it has become the accepted term for the only form of hand-turn do-si-do that has remained in wide use.

As for Shaw's beloved "docey-doe," soon after his 1939 book was published, he changed the initial move from "ladies pass left shoulders" to "ladies roll to the right in front of their opposite gent" (though he never made the change in the book). Apparently his teenage performing group liked it that way; it is certainly smooth to do and attractive to watch. For better or worse, the Shaw docey-doe disappeared from recreational square dancing when the visiting-couple figures were dropped in the late 1950s. Since then it has been confined to exhibitions and the occasional workshop in historical styles.

Note that until square dancing became a hobby, nowhere was the term "do-si-do" used for more than one movement. In the East, "do-si-do" meant "two people circle each other, passing back to back"; if a hand-turn movement was traditional in an area, it was known by a completely different name, such as "Georgia rang tang" or "run the reel." In the West and Southwest, where "do-si-do" meant a hand-turn movement, the back-to-back movement was known by some other name, such as "do-si," "sashay," or "all around" and "see-saw." Confusion arose when square dance enthusiasts from different regions began communicating, with each region insisting that its do-si-do was the true one and that other movements needed other names.

Interestingly, the floor track of "all around corner, see-saw partner" as it was done in most areas is identical to that of a do paso or Texas do-si-do. This suggests another possible origin for the practice of naming a hand-turn movement "do-si-do": Could "all around" and "see-saw" have been originally called in the eastern manner as "do-si-do," and could dancers have started using hands while executing those moves?

If you want to use a hand-turn do-si-do with your dancers, I suggest you choose one that you like and decide on a name for it. If, as most present-day callers do, you are using "do-si-do" to mean "back to back," I would avoid using that name for any other movement. I have attempted to teach a Texas do-si-do under that name (rather than "do paso") and found that dancers instinctively go into a back to back movement on the call "do-si-do." However, I have attained some success teaching the Lloyd Shaw two-couple docey-doe in a dedicated workshop, always using the warning call "Circle up four and make it go, Now break it all up with a docey-doe."

Timing

A do paso takes 12 to 16 beats, depending on how briskly it is danced and how far apart the dancers are at the start; a Grange do-si-do or a Lloyd Shaw-style docey-doe takes 16 beats when done briskly. A West Texas do-si-do lasts until the caller says "One more change and on (or home) you go."

Cross Trail

Done by

One or more couples (usually two), each side by side with partner, normally with the lady on the gent's right.

Description

The two members of a couple dance in a curving path, forward and toward each other, until their paths cross. The gent takes a shorter path to let the lady cross in front of him. (At some times and in some places this call directed facing couples to pass through and then cross; see "Historical Notes" below.)

Result

To an observer facing in the couple's original facing direction, the lady is now on the gent's left. Which way the two dancers face depends on the next called movement; the caller may direct them to turn alone (in which case they are expected to end facing opposite to their original direction) or to go to a dancer to the right or left of them (in which case they must make a 90-degree turn from their original direction).

Teaching Technique

The first step in teaching cross trail is to decide which definition to use (see "Historical Notes" below). During the walkthrough, it is important to tell the dancers, before they start to move, how far they are expected to travel and which way they should be facing after executing the movement.

Transitions

As this is a hands-free movement, transitions in and out of it should be smooth, although the changes of direction can be disorienting.

Historical Notes

This movement appeared (not necessarily under its eventual name) in a handful of dances around 1940; the first may have been *Corners of the World* by Pat Pattison. At first it was used simply to provide variety in the family of "pass through and around one" figures. In the early 1950s, when the "surprise allemande left" came into vogue, the cross trail became one of the most-used ways for dancers to get to their corners.

For a time in the early 1950s, there was disagreement as to whether the call "cross trail" should refer solely to the crossing maneuver or be called only to facing couples and include a pass through before the cross. There was an attempt to standardize "cross trail" to mean just the cross and "trail through" or "cross trail through" to mean pass through and cross. (In some areas "cross trail" meant what might better be termed "cross through": one couple split another, then only the splitting couple cross.) By the mid-1950s, however, the wording "trail through" had been discarded and "cross trail" was generally understood to mean pass through and cross.

Beginning in the 1970s, Callerlab (the *de facto* governing body of modern square dancing) has formulated precise definitions of the movements in each of its programs, including the exact starting and ending positions and facing directions for each dancer. The ending of "cross trail" is difficult to pinpoint because traditionally it depends on the next call. For this reason, the movement has been removed from the programs that most dancers do and relegated to the stratosphere.

To my mind, cross trail has a traditional feel even though it is a product of the subculture that became modern square dancing. I am happy to incorporate the move into neo-traditional dancing as I understand it. I suggest that for our purposes, the call "cross trail" should refer only to the crossing movement. This is because during the boom years, it was defined thus by roughly half of the callers who used the move, and also because I have observed that dancers tend to start crossing as soon as they hear the word "cross," even if the caller wants them to pass through first. Of course, callers should make it clear to their dancers how they want the move executed, particularly as it is currently uncommon outside the modern square dance world and likely to be unfamiliar to the dancers.

Timing

For the crossing move, allow 2 to 4 beats. For a pass through followed by a crossing move, 4 to 6 beats.

16
Circles

Circles are powerful. There is something special about a circle, be it a ring of solid matter, a ring of objects all alike, or a ring of people with joined hands. A circle symbolizes completeness, perfection, unity. Many cultures recognize this in one way or another; an impressive number reflect it in their dances. In some cities you can attend an evening of "sacred circle dances" from around the world.

Country dancing has included circles since the beginning of its recorded history. Besides having an appeal all their own, they provide the spice of variety to a dance party. Many callers make a point of programming at least one circle dance during an evening of squares or contras, and of course many southern Appalachian dance communities favor the circle for most or all of their programming.

The Big Circle

A time-tested way to begin a group's initial exposure to square dancing is to have them form a single circle of couples, all facing the center with hands joined. In each couple, the lady stands at the gent's right. If the room will not accommodate a single circle comfortably, two or more concentric circles may be formed. The instructions and calls will remain the same regardless of the number of circles. (If you are directing the formation of an inner circle, remember to take only about one-third of the couples from the outer circle, not one-half.)

There are many reasons for beginning with a circle:

- A circular formation, in which all positions are equal and each couple's movements identical, will give the group a feeling of solidarity. Individual dancers will not feel singled out.
- The joined hands of a circle give strong support to the individual. It is much easier to move in the right direction when one is physically connected to many other dancers, all going the same way.
- Because in a single circle there are no couple numbers or different roles to learn, a caller can get people moving to music in less time than with any other formation.
- A circle is ideal for teaching or demonstration from the floor. The leader can stand in the center or toward one side, or in smaller groups even join the circle, and still be visible to all.
- Circle dances are traditional in many regions of the continent and, as such, are part of our North American heritage. That they have stood the test of time speaks well of their constructive qualities.
- Any movement that is danced by two people can be taught in a big circle. This enables a new group to learn about half of the basic movements of

249

square dancing before having to deal with couple numbers, "heads" and "sides," or other nomenclature.
- From a single circle, the group can be easily moved into a progressive circle formation, where most of the remaining square dance basics can be taught.
- Most circles are mixers, changing partners for each round of the dance to avoid monotony. Dancing mixers will enable even the shyest members of a group to mingle with the crowd; it may also make it easier for some people to learn the basic moves, away from a constant partner who might be a source of embarrassment or encourage bad dancing habits.

At the end of a mixer, some callers make a point of asking the dancers to keep their current partner for the next dance. This practice has been advocated by many writers of books and articles, particularly at non-dancer events and the first few nights of a class. As noted above, it can make learning easier by separating partners who may be a bad influence on each other. If you choose to do this, however, I advise you to announce the fact clearly at the beginning of the mixer; some people may resent having the situation presented as a *fait accompli*. I would especially advise against trying this with experienced dancers; like it or not, many of them have a strong aversion to being told whom to dance with.

The Grand March

The grand march is a special form of big circle that is traditionally done at the beginning of formal balls, but can be adopted (and adapted as desired) as a part of any square dance. Some of its maneuvers are identical to certain big circle figures in southern mountain dancing.

The following are the most popular figures. Not all of them need be done at every party.

Promenade – A grand march always begins with a promenade by couples, normally counterclockwise around the hall. Usually a leading couple is designated and the other couples line up behind them. The caller may be in the leading couple or can direct traffic, either from the stage or near the leading couple or couples.

Follow the leader – If there are many children in the group, the leader may do things like hopping on one foot, jumping on both feet, or shuffling, and encourage the other couples to follow suit.

Arches or *London Bridge* – The leading couple turns (typically as individuals toward each other) to face the couples behind. The leading couple joins nearest hands to make an arch and walks forward, passing the arch over the other couples' heads. Each couple reaching the head of the formation makes a similar arch and follows the leaders. Typically, when the leaders reach the rear of the formation, they join the couples who are ducking under the arches; when they reach the head again, they continue marching in the original direction.

Open tunnel – This is Arches in reverse. The leaders turn around and bow their heads to indicate that the following couples should form arches. In this figure, the leading couple goes under all the other couples' arms. When the leaders reach the rear, they turn and form an arch themselves, traveling to the head behind all the other couples.

Over and under – This is a tricky figure, recommended only for dancers with some experience. The dancers must be forewarned of this figure, as there is no quick way to indicate what is wanted. The leaders turn around and duck under the first following couple, make an arch over the next, duck under the next, and so on. Each successive couple, on reaching the front, turns around and joins the motion, taking its cue from the approaching couple. The leaders can continue the motion until they have traveled in both directions and regained the head, or they can travel in only one direction, leading the group into a clockwise march, and choose another figure.

Columns – This works best with a large group. From a regular promenade, when the leaders have covered the distance across either the head or the foot of the dancing space, they double back to their left and lead the other couples across the hall again, parallel to the couples who are still promenading normally. The leaders cross back and forth several times to create parallel columns of couples, the rest of the group continuing to follow. When the leaders reach the end of the hall opposite to where they began this figure, they resume the regular promenade.

Zig-zag – If the floor is crowded with couples, this is a good way to make room for Platoons (below). From a regular promenade, when the leaders reach the foot of the hall, they march up the center. When they reach the head, they separate, the lady going to her right, the gent to his left; the other couples follow suit. Mirroring each other's movements, they travel back and forth in their own half of the hall. They must be careful not to get too close to the side walls, as they must leave room for couples to march in the next figure. When the leaders arrive at the foot again, they are ready for Platoons. (If the floor is not too crowded, it may be possible to go from a promenade to Platoons without interspersing a Zig-zag.)

Platoons – This is the defining figure of the grand march; in some communities the grand march consists solely of a promenade followed by Platoons. The leading couple marches up the center from the foot to the head; when they reach the head, they turn right, the next couple turns left, the next turns right, and so on. Couples proceed down the sides of the hall until the two halves of the group meet at the foot. The two leading couples link arms and march up the center four abreast; each successive pair of couples does likewise. At the head, the first four turn right, the next four left, and so on. The foursomes go down the sides until they meet at the foot and can form lines of eight people to march to the head.

The above description assumes that the leader is playing a lady's part and wishes to remain at one end of the front line. If the leader is playing a gent's part, the first couple or line should turn to the left each time. If the group is not familiar with grand marches, the leader may need to drop out, face the group, and direct traffic. It can also be helpful for another person, perhaps the leader's partner, to be stationed at the foot to help couples and lines find their counterpart.

The Platoon figure can be ended in a number of ways:

- The eights can alternate going to the right and the left and can form lines of sixteen people at the foot. The lines can be unwieldy, and of course the hall must be large enough to permit them to maneuver comfortably.
- The eights or sixteens can face the band and clap in rhythm, as a show of appreciation and a signal that the march is over and the band can stop playing.
- Each eightsome can find a spot on the floor, join hands in a circle, and form a square for the next dance. (As noted under "First-Timers" in Chapter 13, this is far from the quickest method of forming squares.)
- The eightsomes can align themselves down and across the hall; if all dancers then face their partner, four contra lines will be formed.
- The line at the head can lead a transition into the Serpentine (below).

Serpentine – From the Platoon figure, the line closest to the head begins. If the leader is still dancing, the leader's end will naturally be the head of the line; a leader who has dropped out may rejoin the line at either end. The line doubles back on itself, turning away from the music to face the second line. That line waits for the first line to pass by and then joins its trailing end. Each successive line joins the "snake" after it has passed in front of them. Once all the lines are joined together, the leader may cast out in any direction (provided there is enough space) or may lead the line into a circle in preparation for the Spiral.

Spiral – From a big circle, the leader retains his or her partner (if any), releases the other hand, and leads the dancers into the center in a spiral. The music may end when the spiral is wrapped as tightly as it will go, or the line may reverse direction and spiral outward into a circle again. A leader planning to reverse must allow extra room between coils of the spiral while proceeding into the center.

Note that some of these figures may be used apart from a formal setting. I usually end non-dancer parties with the *Virginia Reel*; when every couple has taken its turn, I often dissolve the longways sets into a single large circle and, to the same piece of music, lead the dancers through some concluding figures. The first two below do not lend themselves to elegant dancing but are ideal to end a barn dance:

Squeeze the balloon – From a big circle, the dancers at the head and foot of the hall move forward several steps, then back out. The dancers at the sides of the hall repeat the figure.

Basket – This requires dancers who are comfortable playing the two traditional gender roles, whether they are labeled "ladies" and "gents" or given other names. I usually prepare for this figure by having the ladies, then the gents, go forward and back. To begin the figure itself, the ladies take two steps forward and join hands in a circle while the gents join hands in an outer circle. The ladies circle left while the gents circle right (or vice versa) for about 16 beats, then reverse directions. When they approach their partner, they must keep their hands joined in the two separate circles. The gents make sure they are standing to the left of their partner, then raise their joined hands over the ladies' heads and bring them down in front of the ladies. In this "basket" formation, everyone travels to the left. (You may call for a buzz step if the dancers know it; I usually use this figure at non-dancer parties where I have not taught it.) On the call "Turn the basket inside out," the gents bring their arms up and over, then the ladies bring their arms up and over behind the gents, and all circle to the right. This concludes the Basket figure; I usually break it up with a partner swing.

Wind up the ball of yarn – This is the Spiral figure described above. If I am working without a partner, I lead into this figure from a "circle right," taking the hand of a lady and spiraling counterclockwise. With a partner, I would release my corner's hand and lead clockwise from a "circle left." A leader playing a lady's part would reverse the procedure.

Into the middle with a whoop and a holler – This explains itself; I generally follow it with "Do it again, just a little bit louder." Alternatively, I can call "Into the middle and make a little noise," then "Do it again and make a big one."

The Progressive Circle

The progressive circle (sometimes called a Sicilian circle from the name of a popular dance in this formation) is a hybrid between the big circle and the progressive longways or contra dance. In a progressive circle dance, the big circle is broken into smaller groups of facing dancers. Each group comprises either a couple, a trio, or a line of two couples facing a like number of people. One half of the group faces clockwise, the other counterclockwise. The couples or lines are arranged around the room like the spokes of a wheel; each half-group is back to back with half of another group.

The movements in a progressive circle are similar to those in a contra dance, and are done to tunes of the same length (32 measures; 64 beats or steps). In most such dances, the progression is accomplished during the last phrase of music, and is fairly straightforward: Unlike in many modern contra dances, it is obvious when the dancers move from one facing couple to the next.

There are several ways to accomplish this progression:

- Pass through – working as individuals, each person passes right shoulders with the opposite and continues forward to the next facing couple. This takes 8 steps or fewer, and is usually preceded by "forward and back." To use up more music, you can have the dancers pass through two or even three couples; if you are "hashing" your calls, you can vary the number.
- Arch and dive – one couple raises their joined hands and the other couple ducks through, both couples moving forward. This obviously requires the caller to number the couples "1" and "2" (and the dancers to remember their numbers). To use up a 16-beat phrase, multiple passes may be called (each couple goes over, then under, or vice versa, always moving forward) or the original two couples may arch and dive once, then move backward, reversing roles, and finally repeat their first pass to find a new couple.

- Zig and zag – each couple takes 4 steps diagonally forward and to the right, then 4 steps forward and to the left. This flows nicely into a circle left with the new couple. It is a useful alternative to "pass through" for large groups of new dancers; holding on to their partner may provide added confidence.
- Do-si-do once and a half – execute a do-si-do once around, then move forward, passing right shoulders, to the next couple. This may be done as individuals or as couples; the latter form fits a 16-beat phrase and has the same advantage as "zig and zag" of keeping partners connected.
- Promenade once and a half – keeping to the right, promenade once around the other couple, then move forward, still keeping right, to face the next couple. This is a traditional move that has largely been forgotten; it keeps partners connected but can be disorienting for new dancers due to the constant changes in facing direction.

There are definite advantages to using the progressive circle in teaching square dancing. In a progressive circle, the dancers can learn any of the movements that are done by two couples, without being distracted by the dancers in other groups. Also, unlike in squares, all the dancers at once can practice moves like ladies chain. The big-circle and progressive-circle sessions will give dancers the confidence they will need to move into squares and learn the few movements that require more than two couples.

A point of caution in using progressive circles is that they work best if there are enough dancers for at least half a dozen groups. Otherwise, the curve that the dancers must follow to reach the next couple will be so sharp that they may fail to see it and become disoriented. If a large crowd is split into two concentric circles, the same caution applies to the smaller circle in the middle. With two or more circles, there is a real danger of couples passing through and going on to a new couple in the wrong circle.

If there are too few dancers for a viable progressive circle and you wish to teach two-couple movements, you can form a straight line of couple-facing-couple subsets; this formation is identical to a duple improper contra dance with everyone facing neighbor. There will be neutral couples to deal with, but the formation still has advantages over squares if you want all the couples to practice moves like ladies chain simultaneously.

An alternative for a small number of dancers is the scatter promenade. Instead of being aligned around a larger circle, the two-couple subsets begin by standing anywhere on the dance floor; no couple needs to face in a specific direction relative to the walls of the room. After two couples have danced together for a while, instead of one of the means of progression listed above, you can call "Promenade anywhere on the floor." Each couple leaves its facing couple and can promenade clockwise, counterclockwise, straight across the middle of the floor, or in a curving path. (If you are phrasing 1–64, this promenade should coincide with the B.2 music.) During the promenade, the dancers are doing two things: avoiding collisions and looking for a new couple to dance with. One advantage of the scatter promenade is that each couple can potentially dance with all the other couples on the floor, rather than just half as in a standard progressive circle.

In recent years there has been a revival of the four-face-four progressive dance (sometimes called "mescolanze"), which some people feel combines the best features of squares and contras. Such dances are now usually done in lines up and down the hall, rather than in a circle; this makes better use of the floor space. It does require neutral couples at the ends as in a contra, but the minimum unit for joining such a dance is only two couples rather than four, as an odd number of lines is perfectly acceptable; a different line will be waiting out each round. Also, it is often possible for two waiting couples to dance all or part of the routine with each other, modifying it on the fly.

It is possible to transform a big circle into a progressive circle without stopping the music. From a couple promenade, for instance, you can call "Find another couple and promenade four by four," then have the groups of four people circle left and finally square off so that each couple is back to back with a couple in another group. The progressive circle can be dissolved into a single big circle near the end of the musical number; this big-to-small-to-big-circle sequence is one of the most common forms of the southern mountain dance.

Southern Sets

I am a great admirer of the southern mountain forms of group dancing. I say relatively little about them in this book, not because I consider them less worthy of attention than other forms, but because I lack the experience that would allow me to speak with authority about them. I commend them to your study and use.

You should be aware that a southern style dance is not a free-for-all. It may seem that way at first because of the fast tempo, but southern dancing at its best is quite controlled. (The faster the tempo, the shorter the steps need to be for good control.) Any style can be danced tightly or sloppily.

The structure of the southern dance varies widely from one community to the next, but apart from four-couple squares, the form includes a big circle, small circles of two couples each, or both. A common structure begins and ends in a big circle, with small-circle figures constituting the central part.

As mentioned above, many southern big-circle figures also appear in the grand march as done in other regions. (The Platoon figure is a notable exception; I have never encountered it outside the context of the grand march.) The southern small-circle setup is similar to the progressive circles described here, but typically the couples have their backs to the center and the wall, and the progression is accomplished by having the inside or "odd" couple move left to circle four with a new outside or "even" couple. (The facing directions are not always as exact as this, and in some communities the couples spontaneously choose one another, as in a scatter promenade, instead of being counted off.)

Whereas northern progressive circles usually comprise widely known basic movements like stars and chains, southern small-circle figures have unique names and unique patterns. Most if not all of them can be done as visiting-couple squares;

many, such as *Bird in the Cage* and *Lady Round the Lady,* are well-known in the latter form. A typical southern caller has a repertoire of a dozen or more small-circle figures and will call them in any order.

If the southern way of dancing appeals to you, I encourage you to learn more about it from leaders who are thoroughly steeped in its traditions. Books and videos are readily available, some online at no charge (see the Resources section).

* * *

Some basic routines in both big-circle and progressive-circle formations are given on the next few pages. In addition, you are encouraged when using both formations to ad-lib or "hash" your calls, using all the movements your dancers know. This is a good place for your first try at ad-libbing, as there are fewer factors to deal with than there are in squares. You can choose whether or not to use partner changes, based on your assessment of the group.

Many of the books listed in the Resources section contain circles, particularly those mentioned under "Especially for Children and First-Timers."

Ten Words of Advice to Callers
from Ralph Page

1. Don't drink on the job.
2. Be able to do the dances well yourself, for the better dancer you are, the better caller you ought to be.
3. Don't allow your parties to degenerate into brawls.
4. Keep your temper. Smile, even if it kills you to do so.
5. Have patience. Remember that you too had to learn.
6. Don't call dances that are beyond the ability of most of your dancers. They are not the least bit interested in how much you know.
7. Don't talk too much. People came to dance, not to listen to you chant a mess of doggerel.
8. Admit a mistake. Laugh at it, and don't let it get your goat. Remember this: The person who never makes a mistake is a person who never does anything.
9. Practice. Practice. Practice.
10. Never be satisfied with just getting by.

– *Northern Junket,* vol. 3, no. 11, March 1953

Circassian Circle

(author and date unknown)

This dance appears in my earlier book, *Contra Dance Calling,* but I had to include it here because it is the quintessential easy routine using square dance basics. In one form or another it has probably been around for a century or two. There is no single "right" way to call it; many versions exist, from different times and places. One common version starts with "all forward and back" twice followed by ladies, then gents going forward and back, although that makes for a lot of repetition in the first half. Traditionally a 16-beat swing occupies the entire B.1 music; the do-si-do makes the dance more appropriate for groups that have not yet learned to swing smoothly.

You may want to let people dance with their original partners the first time through the sequence. It can be frustrating to ask someone to dance and be separated right away by the caller. Groups that might be confused by the change in the routine, such as very young children, are probably not ready for mixers in the first place.

Some callers use this dance as a framework for improvisation. At non-dancer events I often improvise the opening big circle completely, but when I use a circle mixer I usually stick with the same sequence throughout.

Circassian Circle
(The Dance Movements)

Circle mixer, corner progression

Formation: Couples facing center in a single circle, lady on gent's right

A.1	All circle left	8 beats
	All circle right	8 beats
A.2	All forward and back	8 beats
	Forward and back again	8 beats
B.1	Do-si-do corner	8 beats
	Swing corner	8 beats
B.2	Promenade corner, who becomes new partner	16 beats

Repeat any number of times (I suggest 7 or 8, the length of many good instrumental square dance recordings).

Circassian Circle
(The Calls)

Beats:	1	2	3	4
Intro:	<u>All</u> join	<u>hands</u> and	<u>cir</u>cle	<u>left</u>
A.1:	—	—	—	—
	—	— And	<u>cir</u>cle to the	<u>right</u>
	<u>Eve</u>ry-	<u>bo</u>dy	<u>for</u>ward and	<u>back</u>
A.2:	—	—	—	—
	— Now	<u>do</u> that	<u>one</u> more	<u>time</u>
	<u>Face</u> your	<u>cor</u>ner,	<u>do</u>-si-	<u>do</u>
B.1:	—	—	—	—
	<u>Swing</u> with the	<u>cor</u>ner,	<u>cor</u>ner	<u>swing</u>
	—	—	—	— And
	<u>prome</u>-	<u>nade</u> a-	<u>round</u> the	<u>ring</u>
B.2:	—	—	—	—
	—	—	—	—
	—	—	<u>Face</u> the	<u>mid</u>dle,
	<u>join</u> your	<u>hands</u> and	<u>cir</u>cle	<u>left</u>

Lucky Circle with notes on Paul Jones

(adapted by Tony & Beth Parkes from the traditional *Lucky Seven*)

This is one of our favorite easy dances. We would use it at every non-dancer event, except that it requires two roles (traditionally "lady" and "gent"). This is not a problem in itself; the roles can easily be renamed. But in the heat of the dance, members of a group not paired off by gender can easily forget which role they started in.

There are several versions of *Lucky Seven*; most of them end with a 16-beat swing, and as the name implies, the dancers are supposed to swing the seventh person they meet in the grand right and left. Beth and I have found that a great many new dancers lose count or are hindered in their progress by those who have done so. To reduce frustration, we now tell the dancers simply to continue the grand right and left until the next musical phrase begins ("until the music changes"), then swing the person coming toward them. (As in any circle mixer, "lost and found" is in the middle.) We also substitute a pair of arm turns for the long swing, and we have eliminated an initial "circle left" and added a promenade. (A promenade leads more smoothly into a forward and back than into a circle left.)

Lucky Circle
(The Dance Movements)

Circle mixer, multiple progression

Formation: Couples facing center in a single circle, lady on gent's right

A.1	All forward and back	8 beats
	Forward and back again	8 beats
A.2	Face partner, grand right and left	16 beats
B.1	With the one you meet, right arm turn	8 beats
	Left arm turn the same person	8 beats
B.2	Promenade this new partner	16 beats

Repeat any number of times (I suggest 7 or 8, the length of many good instrumental square dance recordings). Note that if you use the traditional custom of swinging the seventh person met and the number of couples in the circle is a multiple of six, original partners will be reunited frequently. With a circle of exactly six couples, the dance will not be a mixer.

Lucky Circle
(The Calls)

Beats:	1	2	3	4
Intro:	<u>All</u> join	<u>hands</u>, go	<u>for</u>ward and	<u>back</u>
A.1:	—	—	—	—
	—	— <u>Now</u>	<u>do</u> it a-	<u>gain</u>
	—	—	<u>Face</u> your	<u>part</u>ner, right
	<u>hand</u> pull	<u>by</u>, grand	<u>right</u> and	<u>left</u>
A.2:	—	—	—	—
	—	—	—	—
	—	—	—	— With the
	<u>one</u> you	<u>meet</u>, turn a	<u>right</u> arm	<u>round</u>
B.1:	—	—	—	—
	— <u>Come</u>	<u>back</u> with a	<u>left</u> arm	<u>round</u>
	—	—	—	— And
	<u>prome</u>-	<u>nade</u> that	<u>one</u> you	<u>found</u>
B.2:	—	—	—	—
	—	—	—	—
	—	—	<u>Face</u> the	<u>middle</u>,
	<u>join</u> your	<u>hands</u>, go	<u>for</u>ward and	<u>back</u>

The traditional mixer *Paul Jones* is closely related to *Lucky Seven* and *Lucky Circle*, its chief difference being that the changes from one movement to the next come at unexpected times. In its most common version, couples in a big circle execute a circle left and a grand right and left. At a signal, all take the nearest approaching person in a ballroom hold and do some form of couple dance. The signal may be a whistle or noisemaker, or a spoken call such as "Dance with the nearest lady" or simply "Paul Jones!"

In the simplest version, the music stays in 2/4 time and the couple dance is a one-step. In another popular version, the couple dance is a waltz and the music alternates between march and waltz time. A more complex version uses a different couple dance each time: waltz, foxtrot, polka, swing, Latin.

Another way to vary the *Paul Jones* is to use several mixing figures in place of, or in addition to, the grand right and left. From a couple promenade, the ladies can turn around and move clockwise in single file as the gents keep moving counterclockwise (as in *Atlantic Mixer* on the next page). Or the ladies can take a few steps toward the center and form a circle facing out as the gents form a circle facing in. The dancers in both circles then travel to their own left, so that the circles are moving in opposite directions.

For another closely related dance, see the description of *Tucker's Waltz* under "Tucker" in the Glossary.

Atlantic Mixer

(author and date unclear)

According to the Society of Folk Dance Historians, this is a German dance, "introduced" in 1948 by A.J. Hildenbrand of Hamburg. It is unclear whether Hildenbrand originated it or was simply the first to present it to an American audience. I have danced it in many groups, and none of the leaders spoke about its origin. At a gathering in Minnesota, it was presented as the *Swede-Finn Mixer* and taught with the "A" and "B" parts reversed. Regardless of its origin, it certainly fits into the square and contra milieu well.

This has been a favorite of mine since I first danced it at Folk Dance House in my teens. A large part of the fun is the uncertainty of who will be your next partner, combined with the opportunity for flirting with the people passing by in the other circle.

In Germany the dance is done to a particular march tune with a bit of a polka flavor. Any number of 32-measure (64-beat) tunes in 2/4 or 4/4 meter will fit it nicely.

Atlantic Mixer
(The Dance Movements)

Circle mixer, multiple progression

Formation: Couples facing counterclockwise in a circle, lady on gent's right

A.1	All promenade	16 beats
A.2	Ladies reverse direction, gents keep going	16 beats
B.1	Turn someone by the right hand	8 beats
	Turn the same person by the left hand	8 beats
B.2	Swing that person, who becomes new partner	16 beats

Repeat any number of times (I suggest 7 or 8, the length of many good instrumental square dance recordings).

Atlantic Mixer
(The Calls)

Beats:	1	2	3	4
Intro:	Every-	body	prome-	nade
A.1:	—	—	—	—
	—	—	—	—
	—	—	—	—
	Ladies	turn, go the	other way	back
A.2:	Gents keep	going on the	same old	track
	—	—	—	—
	—	—	—	— Now
	find some-	one and	turn by the	right
B.1:	—	—	—	—
	—	— And	back by the	left
	—	—	—	—
	— Step	up and	swing 'em,	too
B.2:	—	—	—	—
	—	—	—	—
	—	—	Keep this	one and
	prome-	nade, a-	round you	run

Heel and Toe Mixer

(author and date unknown)

This classic mixer, also known as *Pattycake Polka,* straddles the borderline between square and contra dancing (very little footwork) and folk and couple dancing (lots of footwork). At one-nighters I sometimes prepare the dancers for the unusual steps by saying "This is the hardest thing we're going to do tonight." Of course it's not that hard, although it (along with the *Virginia Reel*) is likely to be the most physically strenuous part of the evening.

For the "heel and toe," both dancers extend their leg (gent's L, lady's R) to the side and plant the heel on the floor, toe pointing up, then bring the leg back and touch the toe next to the other foot. They can stand or hop on the other foot as they choose.

There are two versions of the clapping; which one to use depends on the type of tune played. Some prefer jigs, some prefer polkas or reels with a polka flavor.

Note that although the notation uses "lady" and "gent," this is one mixer that does not require terms for the two roles, as the progression does not depend on putting one person on the right of the other. At father-daughter dances we put the girls on the inside, "fenced in" by the adults.

Heel and Toe Mixer

(The Dance Movements)

Circle mixer, single progression

Formation: Couples facing partner in a circle, gent's back toward center (or gent facing counterclockwise, lady clockwise); ballroom hold or both hands joined straight across

A.1	Heel and toe twice (gents lead L foot, lady R foot); take 3 side-steps leading with same foot	8 beats
	Repeat all in opposite direction	8 beats
A.2	Clap with partner	8 beats
	6/8 music: together, R, tog, L, tog, both, tog, knees	
	2/4 music: right 3x, left 3x, both 3x, knees 3x	
	Turn partner by the right arm once around; move to next person on the left (or beyond partner) and assume ballroom or two-hand hold	8 beats

Repeat any number of times (7 or 8 times through a standard AABB tune will yield 14 or 16 times through the dance; you may want to run it shorter than that). Often the dance is started fairly slowly and the tempo is gradually increased.

Heel and Toe Mixer
(The Calls)

When done to music in 6/8 meter (jigs):

Beats:	1	2	3	4
Intro:	<u>All</u> get	<u>set</u> for the	<u>heel</u> and	<u>toe</u>
A.1:	<u>Heel</u>,	<u>toe</u>,	<u>heel</u>,	<u>toe</u>,
	<u>slide</u>,	<u>slide</u>,	<u>slide</u>, re-	verse
	<u>Heel</u>,	<u>toe</u>,	<u>heel</u>,	<u>toe</u>,
	<u>slide</u>,	<u>slide</u>,	<u>slide</u>,	<u>clap</u>! To-
A.2:	gether,	<u>right</u>, to-	gether,	<u>left</u>, to-
	gether,	<u>both</u>, to-	gether,	<u>knees</u>! Right
	<u>arm</u> a-	round	—	— Move
	<u>on</u> to the	<u>next</u> for the	<u>heel</u> and	<u>toe</u>

When done to music in 2/4 or 4/4 meter (polkas, reels):

Beats:	1	2	3	4
Intro:	<u>All</u> get	<u>set</u> for the	<u>heel</u> and	<u>toe</u>
A.1:	<u>Heel</u> and	<u>toe</u> and	<u>heel</u> and	<u>toe</u> and
	<u>slide</u>,	<u>slide</u>,	<u>slide</u>, re-	verse
	<u>Heel</u> and	<u>toe</u> and	<u>heel</u> and	<u>toe</u> and
	<u>slide</u>,	<u>slide</u>,	<u>slide</u>,	<u>clap</u>! It's a
A.2:	<u>right</u>, two,	<u>three</u> and a	<u>left</u>, two,	<u>three</u>, a
	<u>both</u>, two,	<u>three</u> and a	<u>knees</u>, two,	<u>three</u>! Right
	<u>arm</u> a-	round	—	— Move
	<u>on</u> to the	<u>next</u> for the	<u>heel</u> and	<u>toe</u>

Note that several of these directions are cadence calls (that is, given during the motion rather than before it). With footwork like this, I find that cadence calls are less confusing than prompts; they reassure the dancers that they are doing the right thing, and the routine is so short that the dancers can do without an advance reminder.

On the call "knees" the dancers actually slap their own thighs. However, "knees" is the traditional call. It's easier than "thighs" to say quickly, and perhaps it was at one time a more acceptable word to speak in polite company.

Sanita Hill Circle

(Ed Durlacher, 1949 or earlier)

This is another repeat from *Contra Dance Calling,* included here because it is the easiest set routine in a progressive circle, which in turn is the easiest vehicle for teaching many square dance basics. I routinely use this with complete beginners, right after the initial big circle. For years I thought I had invented the sequence, but it appears in Ed Durlacher's monumental book *Honor Your Partner* (1949) and on two recordings that Ed made at around that time.

The only trouble spot in this dance is the ending. In a crowded hall, the forward and back will be uncomfortable and a pass through from one subset to the next will take only about four steps. Making two circles of couples, one inside the other, will alleviate the crowding; but the inner circle must have enough subsets that the dancers can easily see where they are going next. You can also change the ending to one of the alternatives given in the introduction to this chapter.

Sanita Hill Circle
(The Dance Movements)

Progressive circle

Formation: Couple facing couple around a large circle, lady on gent's right

A.1	Circle left	8 beats
	Circle right	8 beats
A.2	Do-si-do opposite	8 beats
	Do-si-do partner	8 beats
B.1	Right-hand star	8 beats
	Left-hand star	8 beats
B.2	Forward and back	8 beats
	Pass through to the next couple	8 beats

Repeat any number of times (I suggest 7 or 8, the length of many good instrumental square dance recordings).

Sanita Hill Circle
(The Calls)

Beats:	1	2	3	4
Intro:	<u>Join</u>	<u>hands</u>,	<u>cir</u>cle	<u>left</u>
A.1:	—	—	—	—
	—	— And	<u>cir</u>cle	<u>right</u>
	—	—	—	—
	<u>With</u> your	<u>op</u>posite,	<u>do</u>-si-	<u>do</u>
A.2:	—	—	—	—
	<u>With</u> your	<u>part</u>ner,	<u>do</u>-si-	<u>do</u>
	—	—	—	—
	<u>Right</u> hands	<u>in</u>,	<u>right</u>-hand	<u>star</u>
B.1:	—	—	—	—
	<u>Change</u>	<u>hands</u>,	<u>left</u> hand	<u>back</u>
	—	—	—	— Take your
	<u>part</u>ner's	<u>hand</u>, go	<u>for</u>ward and	<u>back</u>
B.2:	—	—	—	—
	<u>For</u>ward a-	<u>gain</u> and	<u>pass</u>	<u>through</u>
	—	—	<u>On</u> to the	<u>next</u>,
	<u>join</u>	<u>hands</u>,	<u>cir</u>cle	<u>left</u>

Note: I usually use music in 6/8 meter for this dance, for contrast with the 2/4 music that I use for the initial big circle in an evening. The calls above are tailored for 6/8 music, with no more than three syllables per beat.

17
Easy Squares

If newcomers are to be convinced of the joys of square dancing, we need a good supply of figures that are easily taught and learned. Ideally, they should also flow smoothly and include what songwriters call a "hook": a distinctive feature that holds people's interest.

I have found it difficult to create a truly original figure that meets these criteria. Judging from the published work of others, I am not the only would-be dance composer in this situation. When I do run across an easy but interesting square, I treasure it as I would a gemstone or a piece of fine jewelry. Those included here are my all-time favorites; I use at least one or two of them at nearly all my non-dancer parties.

Visiting-couple figures are in Chapter 19. In general, I consider them a step up in difficulty from the dances in the present chapter. I have used them with first-time dancers, but numbering the couples adds one more thing to learn, and many people have trouble understanding the progression of the active couple's visit. If I do use a visiting square at a non-dancer event, it is always after I have called a figure I have classified here as easy, and only if the group has done that one without any problems.

Some of the singing calls in Chapter 20 can be classified as easy. One or two use movements I have excluded from the present chapter (such as ladies chain and right and left through) but are otherwise fairly straightforward.

Heads and Sides

(popularized by Ed Durlacher, 1940s; adapted by folk process)

Just about every caller (other than those who confine their repertoire to singing squares) has used some version of this dance. It's the quintessential "first square" on a program, a way for a caller to judge the dancers' ability to listen and respond to commands – particularly if the caller varies the order of the movements.

A wise caller will have sized up the crowd already, during a big circle and perhaps a progressive circle or whole-set longways, before presenting this dance or any other square. If the dancers had trouble mastering the earlier routines, the caller in *Heads and Sides* can use the same moves in the same order several times in a row. If everything went well and it appears that the dancers would welcome a challenge, it's easy to vary the moves as suggested below.

Heads and Sides
(The Dance Movements)

Square dance figure, no partner change

A.1	Head couples forward and back	8 beats
	Heads do-si-do the opposite (as individuals)	8 beats
A.2	Side couples forward and back	8 beats
	Sides do-si-do the opposite	8 beats
B.1	All allemande left (or left elbow turn) corner	8 beats
	Do-si-do partner	8 beats
B.2	All promenade partner	16 beats

SEQUENCE: Flexible. Because there is no partner change, I usually begin the second time through the figure with the side couples, resulting in a sequence of HSHS – which would be bad practice in a partner-change dance, as two of the ladies (or gents) would be active four times and the other two not at all. But in a "keeper" dance – particularly one like this, where the heads and the sides get an equal amount of activity – the order matters very little.

I often vary the movements in B.1, though I always have the dancers go to their corner first and their partner second. I might call a corner do-si-do and a partner left elbow turn. If the dancers are following really well, I sometimes change each do-si-do in the "A" parts to a circle four (to the left) with the opposite couple on the third and fourth time through the figure.

Heads and Sides
(The Calls)

Beats:	1	2	3	4
Intro:	Head	couples	forward and	back
A.1:	—	—	—	—
	With your	opposite,	do-si-	do
	—	—	—	—
	Side	couples	forward and	back
A.2:	—	—	—	—
	Forward a-	gain and	do-si-	do
	—	—	—	—
	Face your	corner,	allemande	left
B.1:	—	— Now	come back	home and
	do-si-	do, go a-	round your	own
	—	—	Keep your	partner,
	prome-	nade, go	all the way a-	round
B.2:	—	—	—	—
	—	—	—	—
	—	—	— This	time,
	Side	couples	forward and	back
A.1:	—	—	Forward a-	gain,
	Join your	hands and	circle	left
	—	— Now	back a-	way,
	Head	couples	forward and	back
A.2:	—	—	—	— Go
	into the	middle and	circle	left
	—	—	Every-	body
	face your	corner,	do-si-	do
B.1:	—	—	With your	partner,
	turn by the	left, left	hand a-	round
	—	—	Keep your	partner,
	prome-	nade, now	promenade	all
B.2:	—	—	—	—
	—	—	—	—
	—	—	—	—
	—	—	—	—

Note: To save space, I have changed "do-si-do opposite" to "circle four" in the second iteration of the figure above. In real life, I would do so starting with the third figure, if at all.

Heads Arch

(author unknown)

This dance has been printed in many books and magazines since 1950, and possibly earlier. In some versions the people who tunnel remain with their opposites long enough for all four couples to swing and promenade, then the entire figure is repeated to bring the tunnelers home.

I don't use this figure as often as other easy squares because it relies heavily on gender roles (by whatever name), and most of the groups I call for that would appreciate such an easy dance are difficult or impossible to arrange in gendered couples: Either the group is mostly women (or men), or it has a large number of children who are disinclined to take opposite-sex partners. Some figures can be called successfully using substitute terms for the roles, but I have had poor luck with this one. Your results may vary.

Heads Arch
(The Dance Movements)

Square dance figure, no partner change

A.1	Head couples forward and back	8 beats
	Forward, give both hands to opposite and form an arch	8 beats
A.2	Side ladies tunnel through (don't bump heads!)	8 beats
	Side ladies swing the opposite	8 beats
B.1	Side ladies tunnel home	8 beats
	All swing partner	8 beats
B.2	All promenade partner	16 beats

SEQUENCE: Heads arch and side ladies tunnel; sides arch and head ladies tunnel; heads arch and side gents tunnel; sides arch and head gents tunnel.

Heads Arch
(The Calls)

Beats:	1	2	3	4
Intro:	<u>Head</u> two	<u>coup</u>les	<u>for</u>ward and	<u>back</u>
A.1:	—	—	—	—
	<u>For</u>ward a-	<u>gain</u> with your	<u>hands</u> up	<u>high</u> and
	<u>build</u> an	<u>arch</u> a-	<u>gainst</u> the	<u>sky</u>
	<u>Side</u> two	<u>la</u>dies	<u>tun</u>nel	<u>through</u>
A.2:	—	—	—	— And
	<u>swing</u> the	<u>op</u>posite	<u>gent</u> you	<u>do</u>
	—	—	—	— The
	<u>same</u> two	<u>la</u>dies	<u>tun</u>nel	<u>home</u>
B.1:	—	—	—	— And
	<u>every</u>-	<u>bo</u>dy	<u>swing</u> your	<u>own</u>
	<u>You</u> swing	<u>yours</u> and	<u>I'll</u> swing	<u>mine</u> and
	<u>prome</u>-	<u>nade</u>, go	<u>down</u> the	<u>line</u>
B.2:	—	—	—	—
	—	—	—	—
	—	—	—	—
	<u>Side</u> two	<u>coup</u>les	<u>for</u>ward and	<u>back</u>

Crooked Stovepipe

(based on a traditional Canadian figure; popularized by Ralph Page, 1940s on)

This is perhaps the single most commonly called New England square; I have attended New England Folk Festivals where as many as five different callers used it in the same weekend. Ralph Page used it as the first square of many of his workshops and parties. It accustoms dancers to several traits of the New England style, including the close correlation between the movements and the music as well as the sense of playfulness in the caller's relation with the dancers.

In my experience, Ralph always called the figure for two facing ladies or gents. A similar Canadian figure, which may pre-date Ralph's calling career, has each lady and her opposite gent take the lead. At the French-American Victory Club of Waltham, Massachusetts in the 1970s, the second figure of the square set had the active lady swing her opposite gent, then swing her own partner in the center while the others circled around them.

This call was a quintessential example of Ralph's semi-singing style. Ralph delivered several of the lines as cadence calls (to be danced simultaneously with the call) rather than prompts; this is a common feature of pure singing squares. I have adjusted the phrasing and timing of the "A" parts into prompt style but left B.1 as a cadence call. I have also replaced a corner do-si-do (at the end of B.1) with a second allemande left for smoother flow.

Crooked Stovepipe
(The Dance Movements)

Square dance figure, no partner change

A.1	Head ladies forward and back	8 beats
	Head ladies swing in the center; the other six join hands around them and circle left once around	16 beats
A.2	(*preceding movement carries over to first half of A.2*)	
	All swing partner	8 beats
B.1	Allemande left corner, allemande right partner, allemande left corner again	16 beats
B.2	Do-si-do partner	8 beats
	Swing partner	8 beats

SEQUENCE: Head ladies; side ladies; head gents; side gents (Ralph had the gents "elbow reel" rather than "swing"); or each lady and her opposite gent.

Crooked Stovepipe
(The Calls)

Beats:	1	2	3	4
Intro:	<u>Head</u> two	<u>la</u>dies	<u>for</u>ward and	<u>back</u>
A.1:	—	—	—	—
	<u>For</u>ward a-	<u>gain</u> and the	<u>la</u>dies	<u>swing</u>
	<u>Six</u> hands	<u>round</u> them	<u>while</u> they	<u>swing</u>
	—	—	—	—
A.2:	<u>Once</u> a-	<u>round</u> till you	<u>get</u> back	<u>home</u> and
	<u>swing</u> your	<u>part</u>ner,	<u>swing</u> your	<u>own</u>
	—	—	—	— Now
	<u>square</u> your	<u>sets</u> and	<u>look</u> for the	<u>cor</u>ner
B.1:	<u>Alle</u>mande	<u>left</u> your	<u>cor</u>ner	— and
	<u>alle</u>mande	<u>right</u> your	<u>own</u>	— You
	<u>alle</u>mande	<u>left</u> your	<u>cor</u>ner a-	<u>gain</u> and
	<u>do</u>-si-	<u>do,</u> go	<u>round</u> your	<u>own</u>
B.2:	—	—	—	<u>Swing</u> your
	<u>part</u>ner	<u>there</u> at	<u>home</u>	—
	—	—	— And	<u>now</u> the
	<u>side</u> two	<u>la</u>dies	<u>for</u>ward and	<u>back</u>

Cumberland Square

(traditional English)

This is the most widely usable square I know of. The movements are easy and can be further simplified if necessary. Most importantly for many situations, there are no references to gender roles.

The "slide across" is traditionally done in ballroom (waltz) position, with the couple's joined hands pointing across the set, but it can also be done with each couple joining both hands and spreading their arms to form the shape of a kayak. In either case, each couple keeps to its own right in passing the opposite couple, then keeps to its right again in returning. When couples reverse direction, they do not turn around but simply look the other way. The footwork is seven sliding or "chassez/sashay" steps; encourage dancers to go as far as the seven slides will take them, rather than stop when they get to the opposite couple's place.

The "basket" is done with the same buzz step as a couple swing; all four dancers put their arms around their nearest neighbors' waists. The buzz step is a skill that takes practice; at one-nighters I usually substitute a "slipping circle" for the basket (the four dancers join hands and circle left, using a sliding step).

Cumberland Square
(The Dance Movements)

Complete square dance, no partner change

A.1	Head couples slide across	8 beats
	Slide back	8 beats
A.2	Side couples slide across	8 beats
	Slide back	8 beats
B.1	Heads right-hand star (traditionally hands across)	8 beats
	Left-hand star	8 beats
B.2	Sides right-hand star	8 beats
	Left-hand star	8 beats
A.1	Heads make a basket	16 beats
A.2	Sides make a basket	16 beats
B.1	All circle left once around (traditionally with a polka step)	16 beats
B.2	Promenade partner once around (same step)	16 beats

SEQUENCE: As many times as desired (traditionally twice); no breaks needed.

Cumberland Square
(The Calls)

Beats:	1	2	3	4
Intro:	Head	couples	slide a-	cross
A.1:	—	—	—	—
	—	— And	slide	back
	Side	couples	slide a-	cross
A.2:	—	—	—	—
	—	— You	slide	back
	Heads	— right	hands a-	cross
B.1:	—	—	—	—
	—	— Left	hands	back
	Sides	— right	hands a-	cross
B.2:	—	—	—	—
	—	— Left	hands	back
	Heads	make a	basket,	go!
A.1:	—	—	—	—
	—	—	—	—
	Sides	make a	basket,	now!
A.2:	—	—	—	—
	—	—	— Every-	body
	join	hands,	circle	left
B.1:	—	—	—	—
	—	—	—	— And
	prome-	nade your	partner	home
B.2:	—	—	—	—
	—	—	—	—
	Head	couples	slide a-	cross

Note that once through the figure is twice through a standard tune.

Kitchen Lancers

(adapted by folk process from Figure 5 of the *Lancers Quadrille* of c. 1817)

This is one of my all-time favorite squares. It's easy enough to use with first-timers (and indeed I use it at nearly every non-dancer party), but experienced square and/or contra dancers enjoy it too (they love to take shortcuts during the single file promenades). It makes no reference to gender roles except for the "B" parts, where you can speak of "the right-hand (or left-hand) people."

There are many versions of this figure. In a folk activity, there is no "right" or "wrong" version, so if you choose to adapt it further, you will be "right" too.

Note that in the column formation, the dancers will be facing a different wall each time. With new dancers (and sometimes even with experienced dancers) this can be disorienting. I always warn that the facing direction will change, and I often walk the start of the figure (setting up the column) for Couple 2.

Kitchen Lancers
(The Dance Movements)

Square dance figure, no partner change

A.1	Couple 1 promenade inside the set, ending at home facing out; sides fall in behind Couple 1	16 beats
A.2	All forward and back in column	8 beats
	All take 3 slides to own right, then 3 to own left	8 beats
B.1	Ladies promenade in single file around gents	16 beats
B.2	Gents promenade in single file around ladies	16 beats
C.1	All face partner, join hands in a line with neighbors; dance backward 3 steps, then forward	8 beats
	All swing partners to original place in square	8 beats
C.2	All join hands (in a circle), forward and back	8 beats
	All forward and back again	8 beats

SEQUENCE: Once for each couple.

Variation:

C.1	Couple 1 lead partner through center, others follow; separate and return to relative places in column (but a bit farther from partner than before); form two facing lines of four	16 beats
C.2	Join hands in line, forward and back	8 beats
	All swing partners to original place in square	8 beats

Kitchen Lancers
(The Calls)

Beats:	1	2	3	4
Intro:	—	—	Couple	One
	prome-	nade the	in-	side
A.1:	—	—	—	—
	When you're	home, face	out.	Sides
	— jump	in be-	hind	— and
	every-	body	forward and	back
A.2:	—	—	—	—
	Every-	body	slide to the	right
	—	— and	come on	back
	Ladies	— go	round the	gents
B.1:	—	—	—	—
	—	—	—	—
	—	—	—	—
	Gents	round the	ladies,	go
B.2:	—	—	—	—
	—	—	—	—
	—	— Now	face your	partner,
	every-	body	back a-	way (with a
C.1:	one,	two)	Forward a-	gain and
	swing your	partner	right back	home
	—	—	—	— All
	— join	hands, go	forward and	back
C.2:	—	—	—	—
	Do it a-	gain in the	same old	track
	—	—	Couple	Two
	prome-	nade the	in-	side

Just before press time, I discovered that Ralph Page published a version of this dance very close to the one given here (with the "C" parts as shown under "Variation") in his magazine *Northern Junket* (vol. 5, no. 3, October 1955, p. 37). He gave its name as *Canadian Lancers,* "obtained from Norman Lindsay, London, Ontario, who says this is a real old timer, close to 100 years old." That would date it to around 1860, during the original period of interest in the *Lancers*. Of course, there is no way to know when it was simplified from the formal figure.

Ladies Chain

(as called by Tony and Beth Parkes)

We developed this figure out of a perceived need for an elementary square with a partner change. We use it at some but by no means all of our one-nighters. At such parties we treat the ladies chain as a unique movement of this one dance (similar to the key sequence of *Duck for the Oyster*) rather than a "basic" which the dancers are expected to remember throughout the evening.

You may have noticed that the figure resembles the singing square *Just Because*. (All we eliminated was the quick changes of direction between partner and corner in B.1.) Actually it goes back to a 19th-century "fancy" (that is, non-standard) figure called "The Sociable," one of several that a prompter could substitute for one of the figures of the wildly popular *Plain Quadrille*. "The Sociable" and the fourth figure of *The Caledonians* (another popular 19th-century multi-figure quadrille) are the oldest partner-change squares I know of.

Ladies Chain
(The Dance Movements)

Square dance figure, corner progression

A.1	Head ladies chain across	8 beats
	Chain back	8 beats
A.2	Side ladies chain across	8 beats
	Chain back	8 beats
B.1	All do-si-do corner	8 beats
	All swing corner	8 beats
B.2	Promenade corner to gent's place	16 beats

SEQUENCE: Head ladies first (twice); side ladies first (twice).

Ladies Chain
(The Calls)

Beats:	1	2	3	4
Intro:	<u>Head</u> two	<u>la</u>dies	<u>chain</u> a-	<u>cross</u>
A.1:	—	—	—	—
	<u>Turn</u> a-	<u>round</u> and	<u>chain</u> on	<u>back</u>
	—	—	—	— Now the
	<u>side</u> two	<u>la</u>dies	<u>chain</u> a-	<u>cross</u>
A.2:	—	—	—	—
	<u>Chain</u> right	<u>back</u> in the	<u>same</u> old	<u>track</u>
	—	—	—	—
	<u>Face</u> your	<u>cor</u>ner,	<u>do</u>-si-	<u>do</u>
B.1:	—	—	—	—
	<u>Swing</u> the	<u>cor</u>ner,	<u>cor</u>ner	<u>swing</u>
	—	—	—	<u>Keep</u> 'em,
	<u>prome</u>-	<u>nade</u>, go a-	<u>round</u> the	<u>ring</u>
B.2:	—	—	—	—
	—	—	—	—
	—	—	—	— Now the
	<u>new</u> head	<u>la</u>dies	<u>chain</u> a-	<u>cross</u>

Six Pass Through

(assembled by Tony Parkes, 1970s, from parts by Dick Leger and Jerry Helt)

This has become one of my "go to" squares in situations where I need something easy but interesting for a mixed crowd of new and experienced dancers. I don't use it with groups made up entirely of first-timers, as even though it uses very few established basics, the quick changes of direction can be disorienting.

Dick Leger used the "A" parts as a break; I don't know whether he thought up the sequence himself, but knowing his inventive mind, I suspect he did; I had never encountered it before. I combined it with the "B" parts of Jerry Helt's classic *Queen's Quadrille* (see Chapters 18 and 20) to create a partner-change dance.

When the figure changes to "ladies take two gents," it can be disorienting. I leave it to you whether to warn the dancers of this before the music starts, though I usually do.

Six Pass Through
(The Dance Movements)

Square dance figure, corner progression

A.1	Head gents take two ladies, forward six and back	8 beats
	Same six pass through, turn alone	8 beats
A.2	Side gents take two ladies, forward six and back	8 beats
	Same six pass through, turn alone	8 beats
B.1	All circle left halfway	8 beats
	Swing corner	8 beats
B.2	Promenade to gent's place	16 beats

SEQUENCE: Head gents and side gents; side gents and head gents; head ladies and side ladies; new head ladies and "other two ladies."

Six Pass Through
(The Calls)

Beats:	1	2	3	4
Intro:	<u>Head</u> gents	<u>take</u> two	<u>ladies</u>	<u>for</u>ward
A.1:	<u>In</u>to the	<u>mid</u>dle and	<u>come</u> on	<u>back</u>
	— Same	people	pass	through
	—	— You	turn a-	**lone**, Side
	<u>gents</u> *you*	<u>take</u> two	<u>ladies</u>	<u>for</u>ward
A.2:	<u>In</u>to the	<u>mid</u>dle and	<u>back</u> you	<u>do</u>
	— Why	don't you	pass	through
	—	— Turn	<u>all</u> a-	**lone**, All
	— join	<u>hands</u> and	<u>circle</u>	<u>left</u>
B.1:	— Half-	<u>way</u> a-	<u>round</u> the	<u>ring</u> and
	swing with the	corner,	corner	swing
	—	—	<u>Keep</u> this	<u>one</u> and
	prome-	nade, now	have a little	fun
B.2:	—	—	—	—
	—	—	—	— Side
	<u>gents</u> *you*	<u>take</u> two	<u>ladies</u>	<u>for</u>ward

18
The Middle Ground

There are many more square dance figures at what I would term an intermediate level than there are particularly easy or hard ones. There is a perennial need for easy squares, but it is notoriously difficult to write a well-constructed, smooth-flowing figure suitable for the newest dancers. And although it is possible to devise a figure that will challenge even the most experienced dancers, a good deal of such a figure's difficulty stems from its novelty. Once a group of seasoned dancers is familiar with a figure, it becomes less difficult.

Note that I would classify most visiting-couple figures (see Chapter 19) as intermediate, although most of them can be taught successfully to beginning dancers who are willing to pay attention.

Deer Park Lancers

(George T. Sheldon, around 1890; adapted by Ralph Page and others)

This is one of my all-time favorite phrased squares. I included it in *Contra Dance Calling,* but it's too good to leave out of a book devoted to squares.

It began as Figure 1 of a Lancers that was mentioned in an 1890 newspaper and appeared in at least two dance manuals (F.L. Clendenen, *Fashionable Quadrille Call Book,* 1895; E.H. Kopp, *The American Prompter,* 1896). According to the late Ed Moody, a contemporary of Ralph Page, he and Ralph (and possibly others) modified it to let all eight dancers be active most of the time. When I started using it in the early 1970s, I added the do-si-do before what was otherwise a 16-beat swing. If your dancers are running late and the dip and dive overlaps into B.2, by all means omit the do-si-do.

For the dip and dive, everyone holds inside (nearest) hand with partner. The sides make an arch while the heads duck through, and each couple moves forward around the set, alternately going over and under, until four passes have been made. The positions at the start and end of the dip and dive are identical.

Deer Park Lancers
(The Dance Movements)

Square dance figure, no partner change

A.1	Head couples promenade outside (all the way around) and end at home, facing the right-hand side couple	16 beats
A.2	Two facing ladies chain (#1 with #2, #3 with #4)	8 beats
	Chain back to partner; keep facing that couple	8 beats
B.1	Sides arch, dip and dive (all the way around)	16 beats
B.2	Do-si-do (as individuals) with the same facing couple	8 beats
	Swing partner, ending in home position	8 beats

SEQUENCE: Heads promenade to right, sides arch first; heads promenade to left (then #1 dance with #4, #3 with #2), sides arch; sides promenade to right (then #2 dance with #3, #4 with #1), heads arch; sides promenade to left (then #2 dance with #1, #4 with #3), heads arch. When the active couples are working to their left, I like to replace ladies chain with right and left through and back – unless the group is relatively inexperienced and doesn't know right and left very well.

Deer Park Lancers
(The Calls)

Beats:	1	2	3	4
Intro:	<u>Heads</u>	<u>prome</u>-	<u>nade</u> out-	<u>side</u>
A.1:	—	—	—	—
	(<u>All</u> the	<u>way</u> a-	<u>round</u> the	<u>ring</u>)
	—	—	—	— With the
	<u>right</u>-hand	<u>couple</u> two	<u>ladies</u>	<u>chain</u>
A.2:	—	—	—	—
	—	— And	<u>chain</u> on	<u>back</u>
	—	—	<u>Face</u> that	<u>couple</u>,
	<u>sides</u>	<u>arch</u>,	<u>dip</u> and	<u>dive</u>
B.1:	—	—	—	—
	—	—	—	—
	—	—	—	— With the
	<u>couple</u> you	<u>meet</u>, do a	<u>do</u>-si-	<u>do</u>
B.2:	—	—	—	<u>Swing</u> your
	<u>partner</u>,	<u>right</u> back	<u>home</u> you	<u>know</u>
	—	— This	<u>time</u>,	<u>heads</u>
	<u>prome</u>-	<u>nade</u> to the	<u>left</u>,	<u>go</u> (The
A.1:	<u>wrong</u> way	<u>round</u> on a	<u>wrong</u> way	<u>track</u>,
	<u>all</u> the	<u>way</u> and	<u>don't</u> look	<u>back</u>)
	—	—	—	— With the
	<u>left</u>-hand	<u>couple</u> do a	<u>right</u> and left	<u>through</u>
A.2:	—	—	—	—
	— And a	<u>right</u> and left	<u>back</u> you	<u>do</u>
	—	—	<u>Face</u> them a-	<u>gain</u>,
	<u>sides</u>	<u>arch</u>,	<u>dip</u> and	<u>dive</u>
B.1:	—	—	—	—
	—	—	—	—
	—	—	—	—
	<u>Do</u>-si-	<u>do</u> the	<u>one</u> you	<u>meet</u>
B.2:	—	—	—	—
	<u>Right</u> back	<u>home</u> and	<u>swing</u> your	<u>sweet</u>
	—	—	—	—

[*First line of break goes here*]

If the dancers know the grand square, I like to include it in the opener, middle break, and ending.

Do-si-do and Face the Sides

(Ted Sannella, 1953)

This is another of my favorite almost-all-purpose squares; I use it with every kind of group except for all first-timers. As Ted pointed out, it's ideal for an exhibition before an audience because of its variety: It shifts from circles to lines to stars.

During the walkthrough, I emphasize that the dancers will be interacting with their corner at almost every point in the figure. During the dance, I like to call "At the head" rather than "Head couples" to begin the second time through the figure, because the original side ladies are now in the head positions.

When the sides are active, I call "split those two" to avoid the unpleasant connotations of "split the heads."

This was one of Ted's earliest compositions. I think you'll agree he scored a hit.

Do-si-do and Face the Sides
(The Dance Movements)

Square dance figure, corner progression

A.1	Head couples forward and back	8 beats
	Heads do-si-do the opposite; stay in the middle, turn away from partner, face the sides (all are now facing corner)	8 beats
A.2	Circle four to the left once around	8 beats
	Heads split the sides and separate around one person (their corner), then take hands with that person in a line of four (sides are still in original place)	8 beats
B.1	Lines of four forward and back	8 beats
	Center four (original sides the first time) right-hand star in the center	8 beats
B.2	Turn corner by the right hand, once and a half	8 beats
	The other four (heads the first time) right-hand star	8 beats
C.1	Balance and swing the corner	16 beats
C.2	Promenade to the gent's place	16 beats

SEQUENCE: Heads lead (twice); sides lead (twice).

Do-si-do and Face the Sides
(The Calls)

Beats:	1	2	3	4
Intro:	<u>Head</u>	<u>couples</u>	<u>for</u>ward and	<u>back</u>
A.1:	—	—	—	— Go
	<u>for</u>ward a-	<u>gain</u> and	<u>do</u>-si-	<u>do</u> your
	<u>op</u>posite;	— Turn a-	<u>way</u> from your	<u>part</u>ner,
	<u>face</u> the	<u>sides</u> and	<u>cir</u>cle	<u>four</u>
A.2:	—	— Go	<u>once</u> a-	<u>a</u>round and
	<u>when</u> you're	<u>there</u> you	<u>split</u> the	<u>sides</u>
	<u>Sep</u>a-	<u>rate</u>, go a-	<u>round</u> just	<u>one</u> to the
	<u>ends</u> of a	<u>line</u> of	<u>four</u>, go	<u>for</u>ward
B.1:	<u>Eight</u> to the	<u>mid</u>dle and	<u>back</u> to the	<u>bar</u>
	<u>Cen</u>ter	<u>four</u> *right-*	<u>hand</u>	<u>star</u>
	—	—	<u>Once</u> a-	<u>round</u>, turn
	<u>cor</u>ners	<u>all</u> by the	<u>left</u> hand	<u>round</u>
B.2:	—	— Once	<u>and</u> a	<u>half</u>, the
	<u>oth</u>er	<u>four</u> *right-*	<u>hand</u>	<u>star</u>
	<u>Once</u> a-	<u>round</u> but	<u>not</u> too	<u>far</u>, *two*
	<u>hands</u> to the	<u>cor</u>ner,	<u>bal</u>ance	<u>now</u>
C.1:	—	— And	<u>swing</u> 'em	<u>too</u>
	<u>You</u> swing	<u>me</u> and	<u>I'll</u> swing	<u>you</u>
	—	—	—	— And
	<u>prom</u>e-	<u>nade</u> all a-	<u>round</u> you	<u>do</u>
C.2:	—	—	—	—
	—	—	<u>Gent's</u>	<u>place</u>
	—	—	—	—
	<u>At</u> the	<u>head</u> go	<u>for</u>ward and	<u>back</u>

Note that this is a 48-measure dance. You can use a 48-measure (3-part) tune if the band knows one or you have a suitable recording. Otherwise you can do one of two things: either call each time through the figure while the tune runs AABBAA, then pad out with a 16-measure break to use up the BB, or else begin the second and fourth figures on the "B" music, so the heads (and later the sides) dance on AABBAA their first time and on BBAABB their second time.

Duck Through and Swing

(Tony Parkes, 1975)

    This is the square dance equivalent of my contra routine *Shadrack's Delight*: sheer beginner's luck, better than most of the figures I've written since. I wrote it backwards: I wanted to use Ed Gilmore's "arch in the middle and the ends turn in" and have it lead right into a swing. On the last repetition, I wanted to have original partners suddenly reunited for the swing. From there it was just a matter of figuring out what moves I needed to use, and in what order, to get everyone from home position to the correct lines of four.

    One night, shortly after I began using the figure, my band played the French-Canadian tune Growling Old Man and Grumbling Old Woman for it. It was a perfect match. We recorded the combination on our *Kitchen Junket* album, and I've never used another tune for the dance. (The track is now available as a download from the Lloyd Shaw Foundation; see the Resources section.)

    You might wonder why I classify this dance as "middling" and *Ends Turn In*, which may look simpler in some ways, as "fancy" (see Chapter 21). All I can say is that I have had more trouble with the latter figure. *Duck Through and Swing* usually goes smoothly if the group is familiar with its constituent moves; *Ends Turn In* has two transitions that often disorient dancers.

Duck Through and Swing

(The Dance Movements)

Square dance figure, next-door neighbor progression

A.1	Head couples right and left through		8 beats
	Side couples right and left through (on beats 5–12)		
	Head couples right and left back		8 beats
A.2	Head couples lead to the right, circle four about halfway around; head gents break with left hand, pull the circle out into a line at the side position		8 beats
	Lines go forward and back		8 beats
B.1	Pass through; lines join hands again		4 beats
	Center two people in each line make an arch; end people come around and duck through		4 beats
	Those who ducked swing the one they meet; those who made the arch swing the one they made it with (gents are home, swinging original next-door neighbor)		8 beats
B.2	Promenade to the gent's place (once around)		16 beats

SEQUENCE: Heads go first and lead right (twice), sides go first and lead right (twice). When sides lead, the lines are in the head positions.

Duck Through and Swing
(The Calls)

Beats:	1	2	3	4
Intro:	<u>Head</u> two	<u>couples</u>	<u>right</u> and left	<u>through</u>
A.1:	<u>Side</u> two	<u>couples</u>	<u>right</u> and left	<u>through</u>
	<u>Head</u> two	<u>couples</u>	<u>right</u> and left	<u>back</u>
	—	<u>Heads</u>	<u>lead</u> to the	<u>right</u>, to the
	<u>couple</u> on the	<u>right</u> and	<u>circle</u>	<u>four</u>
A.2:	—	— <u>Head</u>	<u>gents</u>	<u>break</u>, make
	<u>lines</u> at the	<u>side</u> of the	<u>set</u>, go	<u>forward</u>
	<u>Eight</u> to the	<u>middle</u> and	<u>back</u> with	<u>you</u>
	<u>Forward</u> a-	<u>gain</u> and	<u>pass</u>	<u>through</u>
B.1:	<u>Arch</u> in the	<u>middle</u> and the	<u>ends</u> duck	<u>in</u>
	<u>Swing</u> in the	<u>middle</u> and	<u>swing</u> **on** the	<u>end</u>
	—	—	—	— And
	<u>prome</u>-	<u>nade</u>, you've	<u>got</u> a new	<u>friend</u>
B.2:	—	—	—	—
	—	—	—	—
	<u>At</u> the	<u>head</u> go	<u>right</u> and left	<u>through</u>

I don't recommend using this figure with new dancers, or as a first or second square with people who are primarily used to contras; it contains too many unfamiliar movements and transitions.

Gents and Corners

(apparently by Ralph Page, 1953)

This is one of the most consistently popular New England squares. It originally saw print in *American Squares* magazine, attributed to Ralph Page. The popular Florida caller Don Armstrong toured the Northeast in 1955 and, shortly thereafter, published and recorded several squares by New England callers, some with credit, some with his own name attached. The figure given here was one of the latter, recorded as a singing call to the 1913 song On the Trail of the Lonesome Pine. The figure has seen wide use since then, in both singing and prompted forms. I do it both ways; when prompting it as shown here, I like to use music in 6/8 meter.

Note that the timing shown below for the end of A.2 and the first half of B.1 is approximate. The dance should be instructed and walked through without any reference to timing; the two allemandes and the do-si-do should be taught as one continuous combination. Even though the allemande left straddles the line between the "A" and "B" parts of the tune, the figure remains a dancer favorite.

Gents and Corners
(The Dance Movements)

Square dance figure, corner progression

A.1	Head gents take corner's nearest hand; those four go into the center and back	8 beats
	Same four circle left once around in center	8 beats
A.2	Same four left-hand star once around	8 beats
	All turn partner by right hand	4 beats
	Go to corner	2 beats
	Begin allemande left with corner	2 beats
B.1	Finish allemande left with corner	2 beats
	Do-si-do partner	6 beats
	Swing corner	8 beats
B.2	Promenade to the gent's place	16 beats

SEQUENCE: Head gents with corners (twice), side gents with corners (twice).

Gents and Corners
(The Calls)

Beats:	1	2	3	4
Intro:	—	—	— Head	gents
	take your	corner	lady	forward
A.1:	Into the	middle and	come on	back
	— Same	four,	circle	four, go
	once a-	round	—	— Left-
	hand	star, the	other way	back
A.2:	—	—	—	—
	—	Turn your	partner	right
	hand a-	round and	look for the	corner
	Allemande	left,	come back	home and
B.1:	do-si-	do your	partner	there
	—	— Your	corner	swing
	Swing the	corner,	swing around	all, and
	prome-	nade, go	round the	hall
B.2:	—	—	—	—
	—	—	—	—
	—	— Head	gents	take your
	new	corner	lady	forward

Hofbrau Square

(Jerry Helt, 1950s)

Ralph Page printed this dance in *Northern Junket* in 1959; I learned it from his calling in the 1960s. I've never seen it anywhere else.

For the sashays in C.1, Ralph had each couple move to the right in a straight line. I prefer to have the set join hands and sashay to the right around the circle. You can decide which way you prefer.

The figure is very satisfying to dance to the right sort of music: strong on melody, almost in 19th-century quadrille style. There is a double-length 6/8 tune from Quebec in the keys of A minor, C, and F that fits the dance like a glove.

Hofbrau Square
(The Dance Movements)

Square dance figure, corner progression

A.1	All circle left halfway	8 beats
	Head couples right and left through	8 beats
A.2	All circle left halfway	8 beats
	Side couples right and left through	8 beats
B.1	Four ladies grand chain	8 beats
	Head couples half promenade (inside the set)	8 beats
B.2	Four ladies grand chain	8 beats
	Side couples half promenade (all are now home)	8 beats
C.1	All balance in place (step right and swing left, then step left and swing right)	4 beats
	All sashay to the right (see discussion above)	4 beats
	All balance (left foot first) and sashay left to place	8 beats
C.2	Allemande left corner	6 beats
	Do-si-do partner	6 beats
	Four gents begin a left-hand star, three-quarters around	4 beats
D.1	Gents finish the star facing their corner	4 beats
	All balance corner	4 beats
	Swing corner	8 beats
D.2	Promenade once around to lady's place	16 beats

SEQUENCE: Heads go first (twice), sides go first (twice). Note that each time through the dance equals twice through a standard (AABB) tune; you can use a double-length tune or an 8 x 32 recording that plays four tunes twice each.

Hofbrau Square
(The Calls)

Beats:	1	2	3	4
Intro:	Join	hands,	circle	left
A.1:	—	— Go	halfway	round
	Head	couples	right and left	through
	—	—	—	All join
	hands a-	gain and	circle	left
A.2:	—	—	—	—
	Side	couples	right and left	through
	—	—	—	—
	Four	ladies	grand	chain
B.1:	—	—	—	—
	Heads	— half	prome-	nade
	In-	side, a-	cross you	go
	Four	ladies	grand	chain
B.2:	—	—	—	—
	Sides	— half	prome-	nade
	—	—	Now you're	home,
	every-	body	balance	right
C.1:	—	—	Slide	right
	—	—	Balance	left
	—	—	Slide	left
	On the	corner	allemande	left
C.2:	—	—	Come back	home and
	do-si-	do	—	— Four
	gents	— *left-*	hand	star
	Three-	quarters,	not too	far
D.1:	Find the	corner,	balance	there
	—	—	Corner	swing
	—	—	—	— And
	prome-	nade, go	round the	ring
D.2:	—	—	—	—
	—	—	Lady's	place
	—	—	—	All
	join	hands,	circle	left

Indiana

(Ed Gilmore, 1954)

From the viewpoint of a caller steeped in the New England style, Ed Gilmore of southern California was the greatest square dance choreographer of the 1950s. His creations are so well put together that each movement seems to flow inevitably out of the preceding one. Although, on the recorded evidence, he did not always allow a comfortable amount of time for each move, his figures adapt well to New England timing and phrasing.

The figure below, written as a singing call to the 1917 song Back Home Again in Indiana, has been given minor variations over the years, some of them by Gilmore himself. He often had the active couples star rather than circle before breaking to a line; see his *Starline* (in Chapter 21) for a dance whose entire personality depends on that transition.

Gilmore used this figure with songs other than Indiana. You are invited to set it to one of your favorite songs. (See Chapter 20 for more figures that lend themselves to this treatment.)

Indiana
(The Dance Movements)

Square dance figure, next-door neighbor progression

A.1	Head couples right and left through	8 beats
	Head couples lead to the right, circle four about halfway around; head gents break with left hand, pull the circle out into a line at the side position	8 beats
A.2	Lines go forward and back	8 beats
	All pass through and individually face to the left	8 beats
B.1	All promenade in single file halfway around (counterclockwise)	8 beats
	Ladies turn around, swing the gent behind them (original next-door neighbor)	8 beats
B.2	Promenade to the gent's place	16 beats

SEQUENCE: Heads start (twice), sides start (twice).

Indiana
(The Calls)

Beats:	1	2	3	4
Intro:	<u>Head</u>	<u>coup</u>les	<u>right</u> and left	<u>through</u>
A.1:	—	—	—	<u>Heads</u>
	<u>lead</u> to the	<u>right</u> and	<u>cir</u>cle	<u>four</u>
	—	—	— Head	<u>gents</u> break
	<u>out</u> to a	<u>line</u> at the	<u>side</u>, go	<u>for</u>ward
A.2:	<u>Eight</u> to the	<u>mid</u>dle and	<u>back</u> you	<u>do</u>
	<u>For</u>ward a-	<u>gain</u> and	<u>pass</u>	<u>through</u>
	—	<u>All</u>	<u>face</u> to the	<u>left</u>, go
	<u>sin</u>gle	<u>file</u> a-	<u>round</u> the	<u>set</u>
B.1:	—	—	—	— Now the
	<u>la</u>dies	<u>turn</u> and	<u>there</u> you	<u>swing</u>
	—	—	<u>Keep</u> this	<u>one</u> and
	<u>prome</u>-	<u>nade</u> a-	<u>round</u> you	<u>run</u>
B.2:	—	—	—	—
	—	—	Gent's	<u>place</u>
	—	—	—	— Now
	<u>at</u> the	<u>head</u> go	<u>right</u> and left	<u>through</u>

Joys of Wedlock

(Gene Gowing, before 1957; adapted by Tony Parkes)

This is a relatively easy figure in the quadrille tradition with a partner change but no swing. I like to use a three-part jig for music; there are many fine ones.

The sequence of ladies chains is identical to the basic figure of *The Rout(e)* (included in this chapter), but here it is "played straight"; there is no attempt to fool the dancers. (See the note at the end of *The Rout(e)* regarding the distance traveled in the courtesy turns.)

For the second "pass through," I like to specify a left-shoulder pass.

Joys of Wedlock
(The Dance Movements)

Square dance figure, corner progression

A.1	Head couples forward and back	8 beats
	Pass through, turn alone	8 beats
A.2	Pass through again, separate around one side person, and squeeze into the center of a line of four at the side (with original corner for a partner)	8 beats
	Lines forward and back	8 beats
B.1	Two ladies chain across the set	8 beats
	Two ladies chain along the line	8 beats
B.2	Two ladies chain across the set	8 beats
	Two ladies chain along the line	8 beats
C.1	Four gents right-hand star in the center	8 beats
	Left-hand star	8 beats
C.2	Gents pick up corner, star promenade to gent's place	12 beats
	Turn as a couple, gent backing up, lady going forward	4 beats

SEQUENCE: Heads start (twice), sides start (twice).

Joys of Wedlock
(The Calls)

Beats:	1	2	3	4
Intro:	<u>Head</u>	<u>cou</u>ples	<u>for</u>ward and	<u>back</u>
A.1:	—	—	—	—
	<u>For</u>ward a-	<u>gain</u> and	<u>pass</u>	<u>through</u>
	—	— Turn	<u>all</u> a-	<u>lone</u> and
	<u>pass</u>	<u>through</u> the	<u>oth</u>er way	<u>back</u>
A.2:	<u>Sep</u>a-	<u>rate</u>, go	<u>round</u>	<u>one</u>, squeeze
	<u>in</u>to a	<u>line</u> of	<u>four</u>, go	<u>for</u>ward
	<u>Eight</u> to the	<u>mid</u>dle and	<u>back</u> a-	<u>gain</u>,
	a<u>cross</u> the	<u>set</u>, two	<u>la</u>dies	<u>chain</u>
B.1:	—	—	—	—
	A<u>long</u> your	<u>line</u>, two	<u>la</u>dies	<u>chain</u>
	—	—	—	—
	A<u>cross</u> the	<u>set</u> you	<u>chain</u> a-	<u>gain</u>
B.2:	—	—	—	—
	<u>In</u> your	<u>line</u> chain	<u>one</u> more	<u>time</u>
	—	—	<u>Four</u>	<u>gents</u> go
	<u>in</u>to the	<u>mid</u>dle, *right*	<u>hand</u>	<u>star</u>
C.1:	—	—	—	—
	<u>Change</u>	<u>hands</u>, *left*	<u>hand</u>	<u>back</u>
	—	<u>Take</u> your	<u>cor</u>ners	<u>all</u> and
	<u>star</u> prome-	<u>nade</u>, go	<u>round</u> the	<u>hall</u>
C.2:	—	—	—	—
	—	— To the	<u>gent's</u>	<u>place</u>
	<u>Back</u> out	— with a	<u>full</u>	<u>turn</u> and
	<u>at</u> the	<u>head</u> go	<u>for</u>ward and	<u>back</u>

Note that this is a 48-measure dance. You can use a 48-measure (3-part) tune if the band knows one or you have a suitable recording. Otherwise you can do one of two things: either call each time through the figure while the tune runs AABBAA, then pad out with a 16-measure break to use up the BB, or else begin the second and fourth figures on the "B" music, so the heads (and later the sides) dance on AABBAA their first time and on BBAABB their second time.

I usually use music in 6/8 meter for this dance. The calls above are tailored for 6/8 music, with no more than three syllables per beat.

Queen's Quadrille & King's Quadrille

(Jerry Helt, around 1955; adapted by Tony Parkes, 1988)

These dances have both appeared in books of mine, but no comprehensive book on neo-traditional calling would be complete without them. *Queen's Quadrille* was much used as a change of pace in the modern square dance scene of the 1950s; its popularity may have been what caused modern callers to refer to any phrased, prompted square as a "quadrille." Despite being written by a Cincinnati caller, it makes a good introduction to New England basics as done in squares.

I make no claim of originality for *King's Quadrille*; doubtless many other callers have improvised the same sequence. My aim was to come close to the simplicity of *Queen's* while keeping all eight dancers in motion throughout.

Both of these figures, due to their straightforward routines, lend themselves to use as singing calls (see Chapter 20 for more examples, including one using *Queen's Quadrille,* and tips on constructing your own).

Queen's Quadrille
(The Dance Movements)

Square dance figure, next-door neighbor progression

A.1	Head couples right and left through	8 beats
	Same ladies chain	8 beats
A.2	Side couples right and left through	8 beats
	Same ladies chain	8 beats
B.1	All circle left halfway	8 beats
	Swing corner (original next-door neighbor)	8 beats
B.2	Promenade to gent's place	16 beats

SEQUENCE: Heads start (twice), sides start (twice).

King's Quadrille
(The Dance Movements)

Square dance figure, next-door neighbor progression

A.1	Heads face right, right and left through with the sides	8 beats
	Same ladies chain	8 beats
A.2	On the other diagonal, right and left through	8 beats
	Same ladies chain	8 beats

(The "B" parts, progression, and sequence are as in *Queen's Quadrille*.)

Queen's Quadrille
(The Calls)

Beats:	1	2	3	4
Intro:	<u>Head</u>	<u>coup</u>les	<u>right</u> and left	<u>through</u>
A.1:	—	—	—	—
	— <u>Same</u>	<u>la</u>dies	<u>chain</u> a-	<u>cross</u>
	—	—	—	—
	<u>Side</u>	<u>two</u> do a	<u>right</u> and left	<u>through</u>
A.2:	—	—	—	—
	<u>Same</u> two	<u>la</u>dies	<u>chain</u> you	<u>do</u>
	—	—	—	<u>All</u>
	<u>join</u>	<u>hands</u> and	<u>cir</u>cle	<u>left</u>
B.1:	— <u>Half</u>-	<u>way</u> a-	<u>round</u> the	<u>ring</u> and
	<u>swing</u> with the	<u>cor</u>ner,	<u>cor</u>ner	<u>swing</u>
	—	—	<u>Keep</u> this	<u>one</u> and
	<u>prome</u>-	<u>nade</u>, a-	<u>round</u> you	<u>run</u>
B.2:	—	—	—	—
	—	—	—	—
	—	—	—	—
	<u>At</u> the	<u>head</u>, do a	<u>right</u> and left	<u>through</u>

King's Quadrille
(The Calls)

Beats:	1	2	3	4
Intro:	<u>Heads</u> face	<u>right</u>, do a	<u>right</u> and left	<u>through</u>
A.1:	—	—	—	—
	<u>Face</u> 'em a-	<u>gain</u>, *those*	<u>la</u>dies	<u>chain</u>
	—	—	—	<u>Face</u> the
	<u>other</u>	<u>way</u>, do a	<u>right</u> and left	<u>through</u>
A.2:	—	—	—	— The
	<u>same</u> two	<u>la</u>dies	<u>chain</u> you	<u>do</u>
	—	—	<u>Face</u> the	<u>mid</u>dle,
	<u>all</u> join	<u>hands</u> and	<u>cir</u>cle	<u>left</u>

(Continue as in *Queen's Quadrille* above, starting at B.1.)

Right and Left Five

(as called by Tony Parkes)

I adapted this figure from a more complicated one that appears in some Ralph Page syllabi from the 1950s under the title *Forward Five*. This simpler version is just different enough from the norm to hold dancers' interest. It uses the key move of *Right Hand High, Left Hand Low* (see Chapter 19) in a routine that can be used with newer dancers who might be intimidated by that dance. (However, I would hesitate to use this figure if the dancers did not already know the courtesy turn.)

The call "right and left five" is not descriptive; the movement must be explained and walked through in advance.

Right and Left Five
(The Dance Movements)

Square dance figure, no partner change

A.1	All forward and back	8 beats
	Forward and back again; Gent 1 retains the hand of his corner (Lady 4) and brings her and Lady 1 home with him to stand in a line of three (all others back away to their home position)	8 beats
A.2	Head couples "right and left five": All heads and Lady 4 cross the set; the line of three makes two arches and Lady and Gent 3 duck under them	4 beats
	The line of three does a "right hand high, left hand low" while Couple 3 does a courtesy turn	4 beats
	Repeat the "right and left five" and the turns, ending at home	8 beats
B.1	Allemande left corner	6–8 beats
	Swing partner	8–10 beats
B.2	Promenade partner once around	16 beats

SEQUENCE: Gent 1 and heads; Gent 2 and sides; Gent 3 and heads; Gent 4 and sides.

Right and Left Five
(The Calls)

Beats:	1	2	3	4
Intro:	<u>All</u> join	<u>hands</u>, go	<u>for</u>ward and	<u>back</u>
A.1:	—	—	—	—
	<u>For</u>ward a- <u>bring</u> two <u>at</u> the	<u>gain</u> and <u>la</u>dies <u>head</u> do a	<u>Gent</u> Number <u>home</u> <u>right</u> and left	<u>One</u> you — Now <u>five</u>
A.2:	—	—	—	— Do a
	<u>right</u> and left	<u>back</u> and	<u>look</u> a-	<u>live</u>
	—	—	—	—
	<u>On</u> the	<u>cor</u>ner	<u>alle</u>mande	<u>left</u>
B.1:	—	— You	<u>come</u> back	<u>home</u> and
	<u>swing</u> your	<u>part</u>ner,	<u>swing</u> your	<u>own</u>
	—	—	<u>When</u> you're	<u>through</u> you
	<u>prome</u>-	<u>nade</u>, go	<u>two</u> by	<u>two</u>
B.2:	—	—	—	—
	—	—	—	—
	—	—	—	—
	<u>All</u> join	<u>hands</u>, go	<u>for</u>ward and	<u>back</u>

The Rout(e)

(author and date unknown)

The distinctive part of this figure, the series of ladies chains around the set, appears in 19th-century quadrille books, but the method of setting up the lines is quite different. As given here with "circle to a line," I have been unable to find it in printed sources earlier than the 1940s. It has been popular ever since.

I believe the title was originally *The Rout,* possibly named after a tune that was once used for it. The tune may have been named to commemorate a military rout, although one definition of "rout" is "a noisy party," which seems appropriate for a square dance. My guess is that the name was altered to *The Route* by someone in an area where the two words were pronounced alike.

There are different versions of this figure. Some western callers around 1950 prefaced it with "Heads promenade half, right and left through to home, head ladies chain over and back" before the head couples led out; after lines were formed they inserted a right and left through across and back before going into the chains.

Ralph Page was fond of hashing this figure, interspersing right and left throughs with the chains in seemingly random order. The secret is to pair "across" moves with "down" moves, and chains with right and lefts.

The Rout(e)
(The Dance Movements)

Square dance figure, no partner change

A.1	Head couples lead to right, circle four to the left about halfway around; head gents drop left hand, lead circle to a line of four in the side position (#1 and #2 in #2's position, #3 and #4 in #4's position)	8 beats
	Forward eight and back	8 beats
A.2	Two ladies chain across	8 beats
	Two ladies chain in line	8 beats
B.1	Two ladies chain across	8 beats
	Two ladies chain in line (to partner)	8 beats
B.2	Promenade partner once around	16 beats

SEQUENCE: Heads, sides; repeat all if desired, possibly with variations.

The Rout(e)
(The Calls)

Beats:	1	2	3	4
Intro:	—	—	— Head	couples
	<u>lead</u> to the	<u>right</u> and	<u>cir</u>cle	<u>four</u>
A.1:	—	—	Head gents	break, make
	lines	at the	side, go	forward
	Eight to the	middle and you	come on	back
	Across the	set, two	ladies	chain
A.2:	—	—	—	—
	Down the	line, two	ladies	chain
	—	—	—	—
	Across the	set, two	ladies	chain
B.1:	—	—	—	—
	Down the	line, two	ladies	chain
	—	— You've	got your	own, so
	prome-	nade once	round to	home
B.2:	—	—	—	—
	—	—	—	—
	—	—	Side	couples
	lead to the	right and	circle	four

Note that when the side couples lead the figure, the lines of four will be at the heads. "Across the set" will then be up and down the hall; I always warn the dancers of this, whether or not I choose to walk the sides through the figure. (I nearly always walk them through setting up the lines, though I often omit the chains.) When the heads are active, I sometimes use the phrase "down the line," but to avoid confusion, I avoid the word "down" when the sides are active, substituting "in your line" or "along your line."

A fine point: When the couples are reorienting from "chain across" to "chain in line" or vice versa, the courtesy turn will be farther than normal for two of the couples but shorter for the other two. The couples with the short turn have the option of going an additional time around.

Squareback Reel

(Roger Whynot, 1970s)

One of the callers who helped me when I was new to the Boston scene was Roger Whynot, who had recently moved to Massachusetts from Nova Scotia. At some point in the mid-1970s Roger challenged me to write a square beginning "Head couples pass through, turn alone." I had trouble thinking of anything interesting and asked him to tell me what he would do with the idea. In a short time he came up with the figure given here. He told me he had thought of it while driving home from a dance in his Volkswagen Squareback, so I suggested the title. (The Squareback was in one respect the ideal car for a traveling caller: It was a station wagon with its engine under the rear cargo floor, leaving both that floor and the space under the hood free – one for luggage, one for sound equipment.)

This is one of my favorite figures to use with moderately experienced groups, including those that know contras but not squares. When teaching it, I warn the dancers that they need to stay alert and keep listening because sometimes, after passing through, they will turn alone on the spot and sometimes they will separate and follow their nose (i.e. move forward) outward and around one inactive person.

I also warn the dancers that the person in their corner position when it comes time to swing will not be their original corner. More than in any other figure, I find myself saying "In squares we dance places, not faces."

Squareback Reel

(The Dance Movements)

Square dance figure, next-door neighbor progression

A.1	Head couples forward and back	8 beats
	Pass through, turn alone (facing center, lady on left)	8 beats
A.2	All join hands and circle left halfway	
	(two ladies are adjacent, two gents likewise; tell the dancers to trust you, they're in the right order)	8 beats
	Side couples pass through, separate around one, squeeze into the center of a line at the head	8 beats
B.1	Lines go forward and back	8 beats
	All swing current corner (original next-door neighbor)	8 beats
B.2	Promenade to the gent's place	16 beats

SEQUENCE: Heads start (twice), sides start (twice).

Squareback Reel
(The Calls)

Beats:	1	2	3	4
Intro:	<u>Head</u> two	<u>coup</u>les	<u>you</u> go	<u>for</u>ward
A.1:	<u>In</u>to the	<u>mid</u>dle and	<u>back</u> you	<u>do</u>
	<u>For</u>ward a-	<u>gain</u>, you	<u>pass</u>	<u>through</u>, now
	<u>turn</u> a-	<u>lone</u> and	<u>face</u> back	<u>in</u>, *all*
	— join	<u>hands</u> and	<u>circle</u> to the	<u>left</u>
A.2:	—	— Go	<u>half</u>way	<u>round</u>, now
	<u>side</u>	<u>coup</u>les	<u>pass</u>	<u>through</u> and
	<u>sepa</u>-	<u>rate</u>, go a-	<u>round</u> just	<u>one</u>, squeeze
	<u>in</u>to a	<u>line</u> of	<u>four</u>, go	<u>for</u>ward
B.1:	<u>Up</u> to the	<u>mid</u>dle and	<u>back</u> to the	<u>ring</u> and
	<u>swing</u> with the	<u>cor</u>ner,	<u>cor</u>ner	<u>swing</u>
	—	— New	<u>part</u>ners	<u>all</u>, hey,
	<u>prome</u>-	<u>nade</u>, go	<u>round</u> the	<u>hall</u>
B.2:	—	—	—	—
	—	—	Gent's	<u>place</u>
	—	—	—	— Now
	<u>at</u> the	<u>head</u> go	<u>for</u>ward and	<u>back</u>

Swing Two Ladies

(as called by Ralph Page, adapted by Ted Sannella)

I don't know whether Ralph originated this figure. Don Chambers used the key moves (B.1 and B.2 as given here) in New York City in 1946 (*American Squares,* February 1946, p. 1), but Ralph was well known by then and may have been Chambers' source. Ted added the do-si-do to smooth the transition into the basket. I always use music in 6/8 meter for this dance.

Swing Two Ladies
(The Dance Movements)

Square dance figure, no partner change

A.1	All join hands, go forward and back	8 beats
	Forward again; head gents bring partner and corner back to a line of three; side gents go home alone	8 beats
A.2	Head gents allemande right partner	~5 beats
	Head gents allemande left corner	~5 beats
	Head gents do-si-do partner	~6 beats
B.1	Each head gent with two ladies make a basket of three and circle left several times with a buzz step	16 beats
B.2	Same three people join hands and circle left until the side lady is as far as possible from her partner, but facing him	~8 beats
	Head couple make an arch and pop the side lady toward her partner	~4 beats
	All begin a swing with partner	4 beats
C.1	Continue the partner swing	8 beats
	All allemande left corner	8 beats
C.2	All promenade partner once around	16 beats

SEQUENCE: Head gents with two ladies; side gents with two ladies; head ladies with two gents; side ladies with two gents.

Swing Two Ladies
(The Calls)

Beats:	1	2	3	4
Intro:	<u>Join</u> your	<u>hands</u> and	<u>for</u>ward	<u>all</u>
A.1:	—	—	—	—
	<u>For</u>ward a-	<u>gain</u> and the	<u>head</u> two	<u>gents</u> bring
	<u>two</u> ladies	<u>home</u>. Head	<u>gents</u>	<u>turn</u> the
	<u>right</u>-hand	<u>la</u>dy a	<u>right</u>-hand	<u>round</u>
A.2:	<u>Left</u>-hand	<u>la</u>dy a	<u>left</u>-hand	<u>round</u>
	<u>Right</u>-hand	<u>la</u>dy a	<u>do</u>-si-	<u>do</u>
	<u>Put</u> your	<u>arms</u> a-	<u>round</u> their	<u>waists</u> and
	<u>swing</u> two	<u>la</u>dies a-	<u>round</u> in	<u>place</u>
B.1:	—	—	—	—
	—	—	—	— Now
	<u>break</u> it	<u>up</u> and	<u>circle</u>	<u>three</u>, the
B.2:	<u>same</u>	<u>three</u>	—	— You
	<u>pop</u> the	<u>cor</u>ner	<u>lady</u>	<u>home</u> and
	<u>every</u>-	<u>body</u>	<u>swing</u> your	<u>own</u>, you
	<u>swing</u> your	<u>part</u>ner	<u>all</u> a-	<u>lone</u>
C.1:	—	—	—	—
	<u>On</u> the	<u>cor</u>ner	<u>alle</u>mande	<u>left</u>
	—	— You	<u>come</u> back	<u>one</u> and
	<u>prome</u>-	<u>nade</u> the	<u>one</u> you	<u>swung</u>
C.2:	(Prom<u>e</u>nade	<u>one</u> and	<u>prome</u>nade	<u>all</u>, go
	<u>all</u> the way	<u>round</u> to your	<u>place</u> in the	<u>hall</u>)
	—	—	—	— You
	<u>join</u> your	<u>hands</u> and	<u>for</u>ward	<u>all</u>

Note that this is a 48-measure dance. You can use a 48-measure (3-part) tune if the band knows one or you have a suitable recording. Otherwise you can do one of two things: either call each time through the figure while the tune runs AABBAA, then pad out with a 16-measure break to use up the BB, or else begin the second and fourth figures on the "B" music, so the head gents (and later the head ladies) dance on AABBAA and the side gents (and the side ladies) dance on BBAABB.

Three Against One

(traditional)

There are many versions of this figure, which is also known as *Lady Go Halfway Round Again*. I learned the version given here from John Melish at the Farm and Wilderness Camps (Plymouth, Vermont) in the 1960s. I have never seen the do-si-do through two arches in any other source – written, oral, or recorded.

The figure has the feel of a southern or western visiting-couple dance, but I believe it to be adapted from a routine that appears frequently in 19th-century books of five-figure quadrilles. In Ontario they do a dance (sometimes known as *The Devil to Pay*) that is closer in form to that old quadrille figure, in which the two head ladies travel around the outside from one head gent to the other.

My wife Beth sometimes uses a mirror-image version of this figure, as shown on the lower half of the facing page. She will have each couple lead the dance both ways in succession (as shown here) or have Couples 1 and 2 do it the first way, in succession, and then have each of those two couples do the mirror version.

Three Against One
(The Dance Movements)

Square dance figure, no partner change

A.1	Couple 1 promenade all the way around the outside	16 beats
A.2	Lady 1 go halfway around the outside (counter-clockwise) and stand at the left side of Gent 3	8 beats
	The line of three and Gent 1 go forward and back	8 beats
B.1	The line of three make two arches; with the ladies going along for the ride, the two gents do-si-do, with Gent 1 going forward through the arch on his left and backward through the arch on his right	8 beats
	Gent 1 allemande right with Lady 2	5 beats
	Gent 1 begin an allemande left with Lady 4	3 beats
B.2	Finish the allemande left	2 beats
	Gent 1 and Lady 3 two-hand turn	6 beats
	Couple 1 swing, moving toward their home position	8 beats

SEQUENCE: Once with each couple leading. Optionally, each couple may do a mirror-image version, as shown on the lower half of the facing page.

Three Against One
(The Calls)

Beats:	1	2	3	4
Intro:	Cou<u>p</u>le	<u>One</u> you	<u>p</u>rome-	<u>n</u>ade <u>out</u>-
A.1:	<u>side</u>	— Go	<u>all</u> the way a-	<u>round</u> and the
	<u>rest</u> move	<u>in</u> and you	<u>give</u> them	room
	—	— Now the	<u>gent</u> stay	<u>put</u> but the
	<u>lady</u> go	<u>half</u>way	<u>round</u> a-	<u>gain</u> and
A.2:	<u>stand</u> in	<u>line</u> with	Cou<u>p</u>le	<u>Three</u>
	<u>At</u> the	<u>head</u>, go	<u>forward</u> and	<u>back</u>, it's
	<u>three</u> against	<u>one</u>	—	— Now
	<u>do</u>-si-	<u>do</u> and	<u>have</u> a little	<u>fun</u>
B.1:	—	—	—	— Now
	<u>Gent</u> Number	<u>One</u> go	<u>out</u> to the	<u>right</u>, turn the
	<u>right</u>-hand	<u>lady</u> with the	<u>right</u> hand	<u>round</u> and the
	<u>left</u>-hand	<u>lady</u> with the	<u>left</u> hand	<u>round</u>, now the
B.2:	<u>opposite</u>	<u>lady</u> with	<u>two</u> hands	<u>round</u>
	—	— Your	<u>partner</u>	<u>swing</u>
	<u>Take</u> her back	<u>home</u>, it's a	<u>traveling</u>	<u>swing</u> and
	Cou<u>p</u>le	<u>One</u> prome-	<u>nade</u> to the	<u>left</u>, to the
A.1:	<u>left</u>, to the	<u>left</u>, go the	<u>wrong</u> way	<u>round</u> and the
	<u>rest</u> move	<u>in</u> to the	<u>center</u> of the	<u>hall</u>
	—	— Now the	<u>lady</u> stay	<u>put</u> but the
	<u>gent</u> go	<u>half</u>way	<u>round</u> a-	<u>again</u> and
A.2:	<u>stand</u> in	<u>line</u> with	Cou<u>p</u>le	<u>Three</u>
	<u>At</u> the	<u>head</u>, go	<u>forward</u> and	<u>back</u>, it's
	<u>three</u> against	<u>one</u>	—	— Now
	<u>do</u>-si-	<u>do</u>, we're	<u>still</u> not	<u>done</u>
B.1:	—	—	—	— And
	<u>Lady</u> Number	<u>One</u> go	<u>out</u> to the	<u>right</u>, turn the
	<u>right</u>-hand	<u>gent</u> with the	<u>right</u> hand	<u>round</u> and the
	<u>left</u>-hand	<u>gent</u> with the	<u>left</u> hand	<u>round</u>, now the
B.2:	<u>opposite</u>	<u>gent</u> with	<u>two</u> hands	<u>round</u>
	—	— Now	<u>swing</u> your	<u>own</u>, you
	<u>swing</u> your	<u>partner</u>	<u>right</u> back	<u>home</u> and
	Cou<u>p</u>le	<u>Two</u> you	<u>p</u>rome-	<u>nade</u>

19
Visiting Squares

To some folks, visiting-couple figures are the quintessential square dances. Indeed, some people think traditional dancing includes nothing else. They are certainly iconic; in some communities they are indeed the only structural form of square, and in others they constitute the bulk of the repertoire.

A frequent criticism of visiting squares is that they leave half the set standing still. There are three answers to this. First, not everyone wants to be in motion all the time. Waiting for one's turn in a square is an opportunity to rest on one's feet, and in some cases to socialize. Second, those who desire more exercise can move gently back and forth in place or indulge in a bit of percussive dancing while they wait their turn. Third, several methods have been devised over the years to let more of the set participate in the action. They are outlined in Chapter 5; one of them (the cumulative method) is employed in a few dances in this chapter.

If you are new to visiting squares and enjoy the examples given here, I encourage you to explore the world of southern mountain dancing, where two-couple figures are the norm. (Indeed, in the widely used big circle / small circle structure, everyone is in motion at all times.) As mentioned in Chapter 16, several of the books in the Resources section deal with southern style; some are available as free downloads. There are also many fine dance-length recordings of southern music, for instructing and inspiring your musicians or for calling to in a pinch.

Bird in the Cage #1

(traditional, as called by Ed and Don Durlacher)

As with other visiting-couple squares, there are many versions of this figure. For completely new dancers I use the version given here as #1. If I think the dancers can manage the transition from an opposite swing to a partner swing well enough to enjoy it, I use the version on the next two-page spread (#2).

One attractive variation, which Larry Edelman learned from Jerry Goodwin of West Virginia and Pennsylvania, has the "bird" or "crow" retain both hand-holds and duck backward under his or her own left arm to move into the center with arms crossed, rather than let go and dance solo. (In other communities, the solo spot is an opportunity to dance percussively.) Another version has the active couple pick up each other couple, creating circles of six and then eight. One version of *Ladies' Whirligig* (see Chapter 22) ends each lady's turn with "bird in the cage and seven hands round" instead of having the lady swing someone.

In Canada and the North Central states, the gent is sometimes known as the "hawk" or "hawkie" instead of the "crow." In one Michigan book (Ryan 1926) the term is "hockey," perhaps due to a transcriber's error.

Bird in the Cage #1
(The Dance Movements)

Square dance figure, no partner change

A.1	Couple 1 lead to right, circle four with Couple 2	8 beats
	Lady 1 go to center of circle, the others keep circling	8 beats
A.2	Lady 1 rejoin circle, Gent 1 go to center	8 beats
	Couples 1 and 2 swing partner	8 beats
B.1	Couple 1 go to Couple 3 and circle four, #2 go home	8 beats
	Lady 1 go to center, others keep circling	8 beats
B.2	Lady 1 rejoin circle, Gent 1 go to center	8 beats
	Couples 1 and 3 swing partner	8 beats
A.1	Couple 1 go to Couple 4 and circle four, #3 go home	8 beats
	Lady 1 go to center, others keep circling	8 beats
A.2	Lady 1 rejoin circle, Gent 1 go to center	8 beats
	All go to home position and swing partner (right arm)	8 beats
B.1	Keep swinging partner	8 beats
	Swing the other way around (left arm)	8 beats
B.2	Promenade once around	16 beats

SEQUENCE: Once with each couple leading. Note that each couple's turn requires two playings of a standard (AABB) tune.

Bird in the Cage #1
(The Calls)

Beats:	1	2	3	4
Intro:	Couple	Number	One	go
A.1:	out to the	right and	circle	four
	Circle	left, go	round the	floor
	Bird in the	cage and	shut the	door, you
	Circle	three hands	round	— Now the
A.2:	bird hop	out and the	crow hop	in
	Caw!	Caw!	—	—
	Those two	couples	take a	swing
	Swing your	birdie a-	round	— It's
B.1:	on to the	next and	circle	four
	Circle	left in the	middle of the	floor
	Bird in the	cage and	shut the	door
	Circle	three hands	round	— Now the
B.2:	bird hop	out and the	crow hop	in
	Caw!	Caw!	—	—
	Those two	couples	take a	swing
	Swing your	birdie a-	round	— It's
A.1:	on to the	last and	circle	four
	Just the	same as you	did be-	fore
	Bird in the	cage and	shut the	door
	Circle	three hands	round	— Now the
A.2:	bird hop	out and the	crow hop	in
	With a	little	silly	grin
	Every-	body	home and	swing your
	partner	round and	round	—
B.1:	—	—	—	—
	— Now	swing the	other way	round
	—	—	—	— And
	prome-	nade, go	round the	town
B.2:	—	—	—	—
	—	—	—	—
	—	—	—	— And
	Couple	Number	Two	go

Bird in the Cage #2

(traditional; subchorus patter from Sandy Bradley)

This is the version I use when I think the group can handle it. It makes for a more interesting dance than Version #1 for dancers who have progressed beyond the initial learning stage. I have them swing in ballroom position (although a two-hand swing would also work); they need to end the first swing with the lady on the right so everyone is facing his or her partner, ready to move into the second swing. The smooth transition between the swings is one of the most satisfying features of the many visiting-couple figures that use the two swings as a sub-chorus. (A walk-around swing is traditional in many areas where these figures are common.)

Bird in the Cage #2
(The Dance Movements)

Square dance figure, no partner change

A.1	Couple 1 lead to right, circle four with Couple 2	~8 beats
	Lady 1 go to center of circle, the others keep circling	~8 beats
A.2	Lady 1 rejoin circle, Gent 1 go to center	~8 beats
	Couples 1 & 2 swing each other's partner	~8 beats
B.1	Same couples swing own partner	~8 beats
	Couple 1 lead to Couple 3 & repeat figure, #2 go home	
	Couple 1 lead to Couple 4 & repeat figure, #3 go home	
	All swing partner and (optional) promenade	

SEQUENCE: Once with each couple leading. Note that each couple's turn requires at least two and a half playings of a standard (AABB) tune.

(Continued from facing page)

A.1:	—	— Now	<u>ain't</u> that	<u>fine</u>, I'll
	<u>swing</u> my	<u>own</u> gal	<u>any</u> old	<u>time</u>
	<u>Every</u>-	<u>body</u>	<u>home</u> and	<u>swing</u>
	<u>Ev</u>erybody	<u>home</u> and	<u>ev</u>erybody	<u>swing</u>

You can use A.2 for a long swing and start the next couple on B.1, or you can insert a promenade on B.1 and either start the next couple on B.2 or insert a filler, such as "forward & back" twice, on B.2 and start the next couple on A.1.

Bird in the Cage #2
(The Calls)

Beats:	1	2	3	4
Intro:	<u>Coup</u>le Number	<u>One</u> go	<u>out</u> to the	<u>right</u> and
A.1:	<u>Cir</u>cle	<u>four</u>	—	— Put the
	<u>bird</u> in the	<u>cage</u> and	<u>cir</u>cle	<u>three</u>
	—	—	—	— Now the
	<u>bird</u> hop	<u>out</u> and the	<u>crow</u> hop	<u>in</u>
A.2:	—	—	—	— Now the
	<u>crow</u> hop	<u>out</u> and	<u>cir</u>cle a-	<u>gain</u>
	<u>Yours</u> is	<u>pret</u>ty and	<u>so</u> is	<u>mine</u>
	<u>I'll</u> swing	<u>yours</u> and	<u>you</u> swing	<u>mine</u>
B.1:	—	— Now	<u>ain't</u> that	<u>fine</u>, I'll
	<u>swing</u> my	<u>own</u> gal	<u>an</u>y old	<u>time</u>
	<u>Coup</u>le Number	<u>One</u> go	<u>on</u> to the	<u>next</u> and
	<u>cir</u>cle	<u>four</u>	—	—
B.2:	—	<u>Now</u> put the	<u>bird</u> in the	<u>cage</u> and
	<u>cir</u>cle	<u>three</u>	—	—
	—	— Now the	<u>bird</u> hop	<u>out</u> and the
	<u>crow</u> hop	<u>in</u>	—	—
A.1:	—	— Now the	<u>crow</u> hop	<u>out</u> and
	<u>cir</u>cle a-	<u>gain</u>	—	— Well,
	<u>yours</u> is	<u>pret</u>ty and	<u>so</u> is	<u>mine</u>
	<u>I'll</u> swing	<u>yours</u> and	<u>you</u> swing	<u>mine</u>
A.2:	—	— Now	<u>ain't</u> that	<u>fine</u>, I'll
	<u>swing</u> my	<u>own</u> gal	<u>an</u>y old	<u>time</u>
	<u>Coup</u>le Number	<u>One</u> go	<u>on</u> to the	<u>last</u> and
	<u>cir</u>cle	<u>four</u>	—	— Put the
B.1:	<u>bird</u> in the	<u>cage</u> and	<u>cir</u>cle	<u>three</u>
	—	—	—	— Now the
	<u>bird</u> hop	<u>out</u> and the	<u>crow</u> hop	<u>in</u> (He's a
	<u>pret</u>ty good	<u>bird</u> for the	<u>shape</u> he's	<u>in</u>)
B.2:	—	— Now the	<u>crow</u> hop	<u>out</u> and
	<u>cir</u>cle a-	<u>gain</u>	—	— Well,
	<u>yours</u> is	<u>pret</u>ty and	<u>so</u> is	<u>mine</u>
	<u>I'll</u> swing	<u>yours</u> and	<u>you</u> swing	<u>mine</u>

(*Continued on facing page*)

Dip and Dive Six

(traditional figure, as called in Ontario, Canada)

This is one of the true classics; you can find it almost anywhere. In the West it was often referred to as *Inside Arch and Outside Under*. Starting in the 1930s, many American callers did it as a singing square to the 1907 popular song Red Wing. In Ontario they do it as given here, always to jigs (tunes in 6/8 meter), which gives the patter a distinctive rat-a-tat-tat sound.

The ground rules: If you're in the center, make an arch. If you're facing an arch, duck under it. If you're facing out, turn as a couple (usually done with a "twirl to swap," also known as a single dishrag or California twirl) and face in again. Once it gets going, the pattern is "under, over, turn; under, over, turn."

Dip and Dive Six
(The Dance Movements)

Square dance figure, no partner change

A.1	Couple 1 lead to Couple 2, circle four to the left halfway (#1 is on outside, #2 is in center standing in front of #4)	8 beats
	Begin a "dip and dive" for three couples: #2 arch and #1 duck; #1 arch and #4 duck; #4 arch and #2 duck	8 beats
A.2	Continue the dip and dive: #2 arch and #1 duck; #1 arch and #4 duck; #4 arch and #2 duck	8 beats
	#2 arch; #1 duck to center and go to #3 (on their right); #1 and #3 circle four to the left halfway	8 beats
B.1	#3 arch; #1 duck to center and go to #4 (on their right); #1 and #4 circle four to the left halfway	8 beats
	Dip and dive again: #4 arch and #1 duck; #1 arch and #2 duck; #2 arch and #4 duck	8 beats
B.2	Continue: #4 arch and #1 duck; #1 arch and #2 duck; #2 arch and #4 duck	8 beats
	#4 arch; #1 duck and go home; all swing partner	8 beats
C.1	Continue the partner swing	8 beats
	Allemande left corner	8 beats
C.2	Promenade partner	16 beats

SEQUENCE: Once for each couple.

Dip and Dive Six
(The Calls)

Beats:	1	2	3	4
Intro:	First	couple	lead to the	right: You
A.1:	join your	hands and	circle a	half
	Inside	over, the	outside	under
	Dip and	dive on the	ocean	wave, it's
	all the way	there and	all the way	back and
A.2:	all the way	back on the	same old	track
	—	— Now	lead to the	next, you
	join your	hands and	circle a	half
	Inside	over, the	outside	under
B.1:	Lead to the	last and	circle a	half
	Inside	over, the	outside	under
	Dip and	dive and	go like	thunder
	Inside	high and the	outside	low, you
B.2:	dip, you	dive and a-	way you	go
	—	—	—	— Now
	head for	home and	swing your	own and
	every-	body	swing 'em at	home
C.1:	—	—	—	— Now
	on the	corner	allemande	left
	—	— You	come back	one and
	prome-	nade with the	one you	swung
C.2:	(Prome-	nade a-	round the	hall, go
	two by	two with the	belle of the	ball)
	—	—	—	— The
	second	couple	lead to the	right

Note that this is a 48-measure dance. You can use a 48-measure (3-part) tune if the band knows one or you have a suitable recording. Otherwise you can do one of two things: either have each couple dance its turn while the tune runs AABBAA, then pad out with a 16-measure break to use up the BB, or else begin each even-numbered couple's turn on the "B" music, so Couples 1 and 3 dance on AABBAA and Couples 2 and 4 on BBAABB.

Sometimes in the West the dance is shortened by having each "dip and dive" continue only until the sides have exchanged places. Sometimes the active couple does a different visiting figure and/or a docey-doe with the opposite couple.

Duck for the Oyster

(traditional)

This dance appears to be newer than many of the standard visiting-couple figures: The earliest references to it that I can find are from the late 1930s, whereas many other visiting figures were collected in the 1920s from callers who were old at the time, so presumably they date back to the late 19th century.

There are two ways to do "Duck through the hole in the old tin can"; the spoken call is identical for both. In the harder version, all hands stay joined. The active couple ducks through the other couple's arch, then the actives turn away from each other, raising their joined hands (his right, her left) while making sure those elbows are bent. The actives pass their joined hands over their own heads and keep turning until they face the other couple. The actives step apart and pull the other couple under the actives' raised arms. The inactives will find themselves turning toward each other, with their own joined hands in front of their faces; they should stay that way until they are pulled through, rather than trying to unwind first. Finally, the inactives raise their joined hands and turn away from each other, and the knot will unwind into a normal circle.

With a less capable group or a wide disparity in heights, I use a simplified version: The actives duck under, release their partner's hand (but the other three handholds in the circle are retained), turn away from each other, and each active moves around the outside of the foursome to his or her starting position, forcing the inactives to turn under their own arms to re-form the normal circle.

The timings given here for each movement are approximate. As the dance progresses and the dancers become familiar with the moves, they are likely to take less time to do each one, as is shown in the call chart on the facing page.

Duck for the Oyster
(The Dance Movements)

Square dance figure, no partner change

Couple 1 lead right, circle four halfway	8 beats
Couple 2 arch, Couple 1 duck under and back out	~6 beats
Couple 1 arch, Couple 2 duck under and back out	~6 beats
Couple 2 arch, Couple 1 duck under, turn away, and move outside #2 to re-form circle (see above)	~8 beats
Couple 2 arch, #1 duck under and go on to the next	~8 beats

SEQUENCE: Once with each couple leading. Note that each couple's turn requires nearly two playings of a standard (AABB) tune.

Duck for the Oyster
(The Calls)

Beats:	1	2	3	4
Intro:	Couple Number	One lead	out to the	right and
A.1:	circle	four for	half that	night
	Couple	One	duck for the	oyster
	—	—	Couple	Two
	dig for the	clam	—	— Now
A.2:	duck thru the	hole in the	old tin	can
	Turn a-	way,	pull 'em on	through
	—	— Now	one more	duck, go
	on to the	next and	circle	four
B.1:	Halfway	round in the	middle of the	floor and
	duck for the	oyster	—	— And
	Couple	Three	dig for the	clam
	—	— Now	duck thru the	hole in the
B.2:	old tin	can,	all the way	through
	—	— Now	one more	duck,
	on to the	last and	circle	four
	Halfway	round as you	did be-	fore and
A.1:	duck for the	oyster	—	— And
	dig for the	clam	—	— Now
	duck thru the	hole in the	old tin	can
	—	—	—	— Now
A.2:	one more	duck,	head for	home and
	every-	body	swing your	own
	—	—	—	—
	—	— Now	on the	corner
B.1:	Allemande	left with	your left	hand
	Right to your	partner,	right and left	grand
	Halfway	round the	ring you	go
	Meet your	partner,	do-si-	do
B.2:	Back to	back all a-	round you	do then
	prome-	nade, go	two by	two
	Right back	home and	Couple	Number
	Two	— lead	out to the	right

The final B.1 and B.2 can be altered at the caller's discretion; for example, B.1 could be a promenade and B.2 could be "forward and back" twice.

Grapevine Twist

(traditional; patter from Dick Kraus, Frank Kaltman, and others)

This is one of my favorite visiting squares, partly because of the unusual figure, partly because it's so much fun to call. I first encountered it in the 1960s, and I've been collecting patter for it ever since. On Yankee Ingenuity's second album (*Heatin' Up the Hall,* Varrick 038) you can hear me call it all the way through, with different patter for each couple. Note that I vary the ending: After the first couple's turn I call a partner swing as given here; the second time I have the dancers swing their corners, then their partners; the third time the ladies cross the set and swing their opposites, then return to their partners and swing; the fourth time the gents swing their right-hand ladies, then their partners.

There is another figure known as *Grapevine Twist* which is similar only in that it includes a line of dancers traveling on a circular path. From a circle of eight, the active gent drops his corner's hand and leads the others under successive arches. Both figures are included in Lloyd Shaw's *Cowboy Dances* (1939).

Grapevine Twist
(The Dance Movements)

Square dance figure, no partner change

A.1	Couple 1 lead right, split Couple 2 & go around Lady 2 (Couple 1 hold partner's hand, gent in the lead)	~8 beats
	Couple 1 loop clockwise in center (as if circling left with an imaginary couple)	~8 beats
A.2	Couple 1 split Couple 2 again & go around Gent 2	~4 beats
	Couples 1 & 2 circle left once around	~8 beats
	Gent 1 release left hand, line of four lead to Couple 3	~4 beats
B.1	Line of four split #3, around Lady 3, loop in center, split #3 again	~16 beats
B.2	Go around Gent 3; Couples 1, 2, & 3 circle left once	~16 beats
A.1	Gent 1 release left hand, line of six lead to Couple 4, split #4, around Lady 4, start loop in center	~16 beats
A.2	Finish loop in center, split #4 again, around Gent 4	~8 beats
	All circle left	~8 beats

[*Caller's choice from here*]

SEQUENCE: Once with each couple leading. Note that each couple's turn requires two playings of a standard (AABB) tune.

Grapevine Twist
(The Calls)

Beats:	1	2	3	4
Intro:	<u>Couple</u>	<u>One</u> lead	<u>out</u> to the	<u>right</u>
A.1:	<u>Take</u> your	<u>la</u>dy	<u>by</u> the	<u>wrist</u> and a-
	<u>round</u> that	<u>la</u>dy with a	<u>grape</u>vine	<u>twist</u>
	<u>Back</u> to the	<u>cen</u>ter with a	<u>whoa</u>-haw-	<u>gee</u> and a-
	<u>round</u> the	<u>gent</u> you	<u>did</u> not	<u>see</u>
A.2:	—	— Now	<u>circle</u>	<u>four</u>
	<u>Cir</u>cle to the	<u>left</u> at the	<u>side</u> of the	<u>floor</u>
	<u>First</u> gent	<u>break</u>, go	<u>on</u> to the	<u>next</u>
	<u>Take</u> your	<u>la</u>dy	<u>by</u> the	<u>wrist</u> and a-
B.1:	<u>round</u> that	<u>la</u>dy with a	<u>grape</u>vine	<u>twist</u>
	—	—	<u>Pret</u>ty little	<u>loop</u> in the
	<u>mid</u>dle of the	<u>square</u>	—	— And a-
	<u>round</u> the	<u>gent</u> who's	<u>stand</u>ing	<u>there</u>
B.2:	—	— Now	<u>circle</u>	<u>six</u>
	<u>Cir</u>cle to the	<u>left</u> and	<u>don't</u> get	<u>mixed</u>
	—	—	<u>First</u> gent	<u>break</u>, go
	<u>on</u> to the	<u>last</u> with the	<u>gent</u> in the	<u>lead</u>
A.1:	<u>Take</u> your	<u>la</u>dy	<u>by</u> the	<u>wrist</u> and a-
	<u>round</u> that	<u>la</u>dy with a	<u>grape</u>vine	<u>twist</u>
	—	— Come	<u>back</u> to the	<u>cen</u>ter on the
	<u>same</u> old	<u>track</u>	—	— And a-
A.2:	<u>round</u> the	<u>gent</u>, go	<u>clickety</u>	<u>clack</u>
	—	—	—	— Now
	<u>all</u> join	<u>hands</u> and	<u>circle</u>	<u>eight</u>
	<u>cir</u>cle to the	<u>left</u> by the	<u>gar</u>den	<u>gate</u> and
B.1:	<u>swing</u>	— your	<u>part</u>ners	<u>all</u>
	<u>Swing</u> 'em	<u>short</u> and	<u>swing</u> 'em	<u>tall</u>
	—	—	—	— And
	<u>prome</u>-	<u>nade</u>, go	<u>round</u> the	<u>hall</u>
B.2:	(<u>Prome</u>-	<u>nade</u> on the	<u>heel</u> and	<u>toe</u>
	<u>Get</u> back	<u>home</u> and	<u>don't</u> be	<u>slow</u>)
	—	—	<u>Sec</u>ond	<u>couple</u>,
	<u>Number</u>	<u>Two</u> go	<u>out</u> to the	<u>right</u>

Lady Round Two

(traditional)

Like *Grapevine Twist*, this dance is cumulative, but it has less potential for rowdiness because the dancers are in single file rather than holding hands. There are countless versions, with swings and/or reversals of direction at different points. I believe I learned this version from Gib Gilbert at the Lloyd Shaw Fellowship in Colorado Springs in the 1970s, though I may have altered it a little.

Lloyd Shaw in his book *Cowboy Dances* (1939) gives a different set of patter for a version of this figure:

> Around that couple with the lady in the lead
> Now the gent fall through and take the lead
> Now the lady fall through the old side door
> Now we'll all join hands and circle four

Lady Round Two
(The Dance Movements)

Square dance figure, no partner change

A.1	Couple 1 face right as individuals & go behind #2; Lady 1 goes behind Couple 2 & starts to pass in front of Gent 2; Gent 1 goes behind only Lady 2, comes into center, splitting #2, & takes lead away from his partner	~8 beats
	Couple 1, gent now in lead, go behind #2; repeat the first half of A.1 with gender roles reversed	~8 beats
A.2	Couples 1 & 2 swing partner	8 beats
	Couples 1 & 2 circle left once around	8 beats
B.1	Circle right about one-quarter; release hands	~4 beats
	Lady 1 lead Gent 1 & Couple 2 behind Couple 3; each lady goes behind two people, each gent cuts between #3 & steps in ahead of his partner; repeat pattern with gender roles reversed (start)	~12 beats
B.2	Finish pattern	~4 beats
	Couples 1, 2, & 3 swing partner, moving toward home	~12 beats
[etc.]	Circle six & repeat pattern with six people around #4	[etc.]

SEQUENCE: Once with each couple leading. Note that each couple's turn requires two playings of a standard (AABB) tune.

Lady Round Two
(The Calls)

Beats:	1	2	3	4
Intro:	—	—	<u>Coup</u>le	<u>One</u>
	<u>face</u> to the	<u>right</u>, go	<u>sing</u>le	<u>file</u>
A.1:	<u>La</u>dy round	<u>two</u> and the	<u>gent</u> cut	<u>through</u>, be-
	<u>hind</u> them	— Go	<u>round</u> a-	<u>gain</u> with the
	<u>gent</u> around	<u>two</u> and the	<u>la</u>dy cut	<u>through</u>
	<u>Swing</u> 'em on the	<u>in</u>side,	<u>out</u>side	<u>too</u>
A.2:	<u>Both</u>	<u>coup</u>les	<u>swing</u>	— Now
	<u>face</u> that	<u>couple</u> and you	<u>cir</u>cle	<u>four</u>
	<u>Cir</u>cle to the	<u>left</u>, go	<u>round</u> the	<u>floor</u>
	— To the	<u>right</u>, go the	<u>oth</u>er way	<u>back</u>. First
B.1:	<u>la</u>dy	<u>break</u>, go be-	<u>hind</u> the	<u>next</u>, it's
	<u>la</u>dy round	<u>two</u> and the	<u>gent</u> cut	<u>through</u>, next
	<u>la</u>dy round	<u>two</u> and the	<u>gent</u> cut	<u>through</u>, now the
	<u>gent</u> around	<u>two</u> and the	<u>la</u>dy cut	<u>through</u>
B.2:	<u>Swing</u> 'em on the	<u>in</u>side,	<u>out</u>side	<u>too</u>, three
	<u>coup</u>les	<u>swing</u> toward	<u>home</u>	—
	—	—	—	— Now
	<u>face</u> to the	<u>mid</u>dle and you	<u>cir</u>cle	<u>six</u>
A.1:	<u>Cir</u>cle to the	<u>left</u> like a-	<u>pick</u>in' up	<u>sticks</u>
	—	— Go the	<u>oth</u>er way	<u>back</u>. First
	<u>la</u>dy	<u>break</u>, go be-	<u>hind</u> the	<u>last</u>, it's
	<u>la</u>dy round	<u>two</u> and the	<u>gent</u> cut	<u>through</u>, next
A.2:	<u>la</u>dy round	<u>two</u> and the	<u>gent</u> cut	<u>through</u>
	—	—	—	— Now
	<u>gent</u> around	<u>two</u>,	<u>la</u>dy cut	<u>through</u>,
	<u>Swing</u> 'em on the	<u>in</u>side,	<u>out</u>side	<u>too</u>
B.1:	<u>Every</u>-	<u>bod</u>y	<u>home</u> and	<u>swing</u>
	<u>Ev</u>erybody	<u>home</u> and	<u>every</u>body	<u>swing</u>
	—	—	—	— And
	<u>prome</u>-	<u>nade</u>, go	<u>round</u> the	<u>ring</u>
B.2:	(<u>Prome</u>-	<u>nade</u> your	<u>part</u>ners	<u>all</u> and you
	<u>take</u> a little	<u>walk</u> all a-	<u>round</u> that	<u>hall</u>)
	—	—	<u>Coup</u>le	<u>Two</u>
	<u>face</u> to the	<u>right</u>, go	<u>sing</u>le	<u>file</u>

Right Hand High, Left Hand Low

(traditional)

There are several square dance figures that involve setting up two facing lines of three people; this is probably the best known and most popular.

It may help to tell the ladies that if they are on the right of a line of three when the formation is set up (at the end of A.2), they will be a right-hand lady (and make the arch) all four times the key movement is danced. If they are on the left, they will be a left-hand lady (and go under an arch) each time. (Each time a new couple leads the figure, the ladies will change from being on the right of the lines to being on the left, or vice versa.)

This figure is traditionally danced to a cadence call rather than a prompted call. The key movement is so distinctive, and repeated so many times, that this should not present a problem to the dancers.

Right Hand High, Left Hand Low
(The Dance Movements)

Square dance figure, no partner change

A.1	Couple 1 lead to Couple 2, circle four	8 beats
	Gent 1 lead to Couple 3 and circle three, leaving Lady 1 on the left of Couple 2 in a line of three	8 beats
A.2	Gent 1 transfer Lady 3 from his left to his right side; take her to Couple 4, leaving Gent 3 at home alone	8 beats
	Gent 1 circle four with Lady 3 and Couple 4, then leave them in a line of three (Lady 3 on the left of Couple 4) and go home alone	8 beats
B.1	Lines of three go forward and back	8 beats
	Head gents do-si-do while each side gent helps the two ladies to cross in front of him, the left-hand lady going under an arch made by gent and right-hand lady; each lady backs into place next to a head gent, who takes her hand as he backs up from his do-si-do	8 beats
B.2	Repeat B.1 (lines of three at the head, side gents alone)	16 beats
A.1	Repeat B.1	16 beats
A.2	Repeat B.2	16 beats
B.1	All swing partner (caller may choose another ending)	16 beats
B.2	All promenade partner	16 beats

SEQUENCE: Once with each couple leading. Note that each couple's turn requires two playings of a standard (AABB) tune.

Right Hand High, Left Hand Low
(The Calls)

Beats:	1	2	3	4
Intro:	<u>Couple</u>	<u>One</u> lead	<u>out</u> to the	<u>right</u> and
A.1:	<u>circle</u>	<u>four</u> with	<u>all</u> your	<u>might</u>
	<u>Leave</u> the	<u>lady</u>	<u>where</u> she	<u>be</u>
	<u>Gent</u> to the	<u>next</u> and	<u>circle</u>	<u>three</u>
	—	—	<u>Steal</u> that	<u>gal</u> like
A.2:	<u>hon</u>ey from a	<u>bee</u>,	<u>put</u> her on the	<u>right</u>,
	<u>take</u> her to the	<u>next</u> and	<u>circle</u>	<u>four</u>
	<u>Leave</u> her	<u>there</u>, go	<u>home</u> a-	<u>lone</u>
	<u>Read</u>y,	<u>side</u>	<u>six</u>	<u>go</u>
B.1:	<u>Forward</u>	<u>six</u> and	<u>back</u> you	<u>know</u>
	<u>Lone</u>some	<u>gents</u> do a	<u>do</u>-si-	<u>do</u>
	<u>Right</u> hand	<u>over</u>,	<u>left</u> hand	<u>under</u>
	<u>Ladies</u>	<u>cross</u> and	<u>go</u> like	<u>thunder</u>
B.2:	<u>Forward</u>	<u>six</u> and	<u>come</u> on	<u>back</u>
	<u>Lone</u>some	<u>gents</u> go	<u>back</u> to	<u>back</u>
	<u>Right</u> hand	<u>high</u> and the	<u>left</u> hand	<u>low</u>
	<u>Ladies</u>	<u>cross</u> and a-	<u>way</u> we	<u>go</u>
A.1:	<u>Forward</u>	<u>six</u> and	<u>then</u> back	<u>down</u>
	<u>Gents</u> do-	<u>si</u> in the	<u>middle</u> of	<u>town</u>
	<u>Right</u> hand	<u>over</u>,	<u>left</u> hand	<u>under</u>
	<u>Ladies</u>	<u>cross</u> and	<u>don't</u> you	<u>blunder</u>
A.2:	<u>Forward</u>	<u>six</u> and	<u>come</u> on	<u>back</u>
	<u>Lone</u>some	<u>gents</u> go	<u>back</u> to	<u>back</u>
	<u>Right</u> hand	<u>high</u> and the	<u>left</u> hand	<u>low</u>. Now
	<u>every</u>-	<u>body</u>	<u>swing</u> your	<u>own</u>
B.1:	(<u>Swing</u> your	<u>partner</u>	<u>round</u> and	<u>round</u>
	<u>Any</u> old	<u>way</u> but	<u>upside</u>	<u>down</u>)
	—	—	—	— And
	<u>prome</u>-	<u>nade</u>, go	<u>round</u> the	<u>town</u>
B.2:	(<u>Prome</u>-	<u>nade</u> a-	<u>round</u> you	<u>go</u>
	<u>Kickin'</u> on the	<u>heel</u> and	<u>on</u> the	<u>toe</u>)
	—	—	—	—
	<u>Couple</u>	<u>Two</u> lead	<u>out</u> to the	<u>right</u>

Swing Like Thunder

(traditional)

This was the favorite square at the Farm and Wilderness Camps (Plymouth, Vermont), where I fell in love with square dancing in the 1960s. The caller had to caution us not to let the girls' feet leave the floor. There are exhibition groups that lift the ladies, but it takes careful practice.

Swing Like Thunder
(The Dance Movements)

Square dance figure, no partner change

A.1	Couple 1 lead right, circle left with Couple 2	~8 beats
	Those ladies join both hands (straight across); gents join both hands below ladies' hands; ladies raise hands over gents' heads & lower them behind gents' backs; gents do same with their hands & ladies' backs	~8 beats
A.2	In this formation, four people circle left w/a buzz step	~12 beats
	Same four join hands in a ring & walk to the left (start)	~4 beats
B.1	Finish circling	~4 beats
	Gent 1 release left hand, add Couple 3 to the circle	~8 beats
	Three ladies join hands; gents join hands below; repeat "basket" maneuver (start)	~4 beats
B.2	Finish forming basket	~4 beats
	Six people circle left with a buzz step	~12 beats
A.1	Same six join hands in a ring & walk to the left	~8 beats
	Gent 1 release left hand, add Couple 4 to the circle	~8 beats
A.2	Four ladies join hands; gents join hands below; repeat "basket" maneuver	~8 beats
	All circle left with a buzz step (start)	~8 beats
B.1	Finish buzz-step in "basket" hold	~8 beats
	Break basket when close to home; swing partner	~8 beats
B.2	Promenade partner once around	16 beats

SEQUENCE: Once with each couple leading. Note that each couple's turn requires two playings of a standard (AABB) tune.

Swing Like Thunder
(The Calls)

	Beats: 1	2	3	4
Intro:	<u>Couple</u>	<u>One</u> lead	<u>out</u> to the	<u>right</u> and
A.1:	<u>circle</u>	<u>four</u> with	<u>all</u> your	<u>might</u>
	—	— And	<u>hands</u> a-	<u>cross</u>
	<u>Ladies</u>	<u>bow</u>,	**gents** bow	<u>under</u>
	<u>Hug</u> 'em up	<u>tight</u> and	<u>swing</u> like	<u>thunder</u>
A.2:	—	—	—	—
	—	—	—	— Now
	<u>break</u> it all	<u>up</u> and	<u>circle</u>	<u>four</u>, the
	<u>same</u>	<u>four</u>	—	— Now
B.1:	<u>pick</u> up	<u>two</u> and	<u>make</u> it	<u>six</u>
	<u>Circle</u> to the	<u>left</u> and	<u>don't</u> get	<u>mixed</u>
	—	— And	<u>hands</u> a-	<u>cross</u>
	<u>Ladies</u>	<u>bow</u>,	**gents** know	<u>how</u>
B.2:	<u>Hold</u> your	<u>holts</u> and	<u>get</u> there	<u>now</u>
	—	—	—	—
	—	—	—	— Now
	<u>break</u> it all	<u>up</u> and	<u>circle</u>	<u>six</u>, the
A.1:	<u>same</u>	<u>six</u>	—	— Now
	<u>pick</u> up	<u>two</u> and	<u>make</u> it	<u>eight</u>
	<u>Circle</u> a-	<u>round</u> by the	<u>garden</u>	<u>gate</u>
	—	— And	<u>hands</u> a-	<u>cross</u>
A.2:	<u>Ladies</u>	<u>bow</u>,	**gents** bow	<u>under</u>
	<u>One</u> more	<u>time</u> you	<u>swing</u> like	<u>thunder</u>
	—	—	—	—
	—	—	—	—
B.1:	<u>Every</u>-	<u>body</u>	<u>home</u> and	<u>swing</u>
	<u>Ev</u>erybody	<u>home</u> and	<u>everybody</u>	<u>swing</u>
	—	—	—	— And
	<u>prome</u>-	<u>nade</u>, go	<u>round</u> the	<u>ring</u>
B.2:	(<u>Prome</u>-	<u>nade</u>, a-	<u>round</u> you	<u>go</u> with the
	<u>right</u> foot	<u>high</u> and the	<u>left</u> foot	<u>low</u>)
	—	—	—	—
	<u>Couple</u>	<u>Two</u> lead	<u>out</u> to the	<u>right</u>

20

Singing Calls

A singing call is generally understood to be a dance done to the music of a song, as opposed to a fiddle tune or other instrumental music. Most callers, in choosing their singing-call repertoire, pick songs that their dancers are likely to know. A caller can use any of hundreds of existing routines or write an original one; some songs have had many different figures associated with them, and some figures have been done to multiple songs.

To construct a singing square, a sequence of dance calls is fitted to the melody of the song in place of its lyrics. Most dance writers try to preserve as much of the scansion as possible, but in order to include all of their desired moves, they may need to insert a patter-like passage of rapid syllables where the song has a few long notes. In most singing calls, the original lyrics are retained for about 16 beats at the end of the figure, and sometimes at the beginning of the break, to let the dancers sing along. Typical moves for this are a promenade to end the figure and a circle left or a grand square to open the break.

The prominence of singing calls in the repertoire varies widely by region. In the southern mountain tradition they are virtually unknown, although play-party games may be done using some of the same tunes. (Researchers have been unable to establish whether the first singing squares developed from play-party games or whether the latter were watered-down versions of the squares.) By contrast, at the surviving traditional square dances in New England, New York, and Pennsylvania, singing calls are the norm; some northeastern callers use them almost exclusively. Most other regions fall between these extremes.

Singing Call History

The first songs to be adapted into square dances were the popular songs of the mid-1800s (along with a few older ones like The Girl I Left Behind Me). Among the favorites were the compositions of Stephen Foster, such as Nellie Bly and Oh Susanna, and of some of Foster's contemporaries, such as Golden Slippers by James A. Bland and Darling Nellie Gray by Benjamin R. Hanby (who also wrote the Christmas song Up on the Housetop). This adapting was apparently done beginning in the late 19th century, well before electronic amplifiers reached the market. Grace Ryan, writing in 1926, treated singing calls as an established part of the Michigan tradition.

As callers and dancers warmed to them, especially in the Northeast, singing calls displaced the old quadrilles and contra dances. The availability of public address systems, starting in the 1920s, made the caller's job easier and undoubtedly contributed to this drastic shift in repertoire. By the 1930s, callers had added songs from the early 20th century, such as Red Wing (1907) and My Little Girl

(1915); by the 1940s, some callers were using songs currently popular on the radio in addition to old standards.

In the modern square dance scene, which developed from the traditional squares of the Midwest and Southwest, singing calls were a novelty at first. Many callers and dancers associated them with the East and with very easy choreography, which was not to their taste. Gradually singing calls were accepted in square dance clubs; new and more challenging ones were written. By 1960, if not before, the "tip" of one patter call and one singing call had become standard.

One reason for the proliferation of singing squares was the need for callers to "publish or perish": A caller could cement a local reputation and get noticed nationwide by writing and recording original dances. Singing calls were ideal for this purpose, as the blend of choreography with special music caused more of a stir than choreography alone. The larger square dance record companies maintained a stable of well-known, reliable callers; some smaller concerns opened their doors to just about anyone. It was an open secret that some callers paid for the privilege of appearing on a record label, perhaps by buying the entire pressing (minimum 500 copies) and hoping to resell the discs from the stage.

Starting around 1950, other genres were added to the repertoire of popular songs used for squares. The first new genre to be widely used was the one termed "hillbilly" at the time but eventually renamed country-and-western. Rock, jazz, blues, soul, and gospel have all taken their place in the square dance catalog. If a song is in 2/4 or 4/4 meter and played at anywhere near a march tempo (about 120 beats per minute), it is almost certain that it has been turned into a singing call, with at least one recording made. Some marches and other songs in 6/8 have been used as well. Even waltzes are not exempt from the square dance treatment: A waltz may be sped up to 6/8 (e.g. Take Me Out to the Ball Game) or stretched out to 4/4 (e.g. My Bonnie Lies Over the Ocean) to achieve the desired tempo.

The structure of singing calls, in both traditional and modern scenes, was at first not standardized. Songs of varying length were used, and different callers chose different sequences of verse and chorus for different choreography to the same song. Eventually, 32-measure songs (often in AABA form) came to predominate, with seven choruses (four figures plus opening, middle, and closing breaks) making up a dance. The second most common arrangement, made if a choreographer wants to use more than 32 measures of a song, is four times through the desired portion (perhaps 48 or even 64 measures); any break is integrated with the figure rather than requiring its own chorus.

Choreography

On average, singing calls tend to be simpler than patter calls. One reason is that in a singing square the caller cannot afford to let the phrasing slip. In a patter call, if dancers are falling behind, the caller can allow extra beats and carry movements over to the next part of the tune (say from B.2 to A.1). Singing calls are always designed to be synchronized completely with the music; if the dancers cannot keep up with the choreography, the only graceful course of action is to omit one or more moves on the fly so that the figure can end in a satisfying way.

It is also true that singing calls are not expected to be as complicated as patter calls. The singing call is usually done last in the tip; it is often seen as a reward for getting through the choreography of the patter call and a chance to relax and enjoy the music. Then, too, the fun of dancing – and perhaps singing along – to a familiar tune makes the experience more interesting. Dance figures that might feel too elementary for an experienced group when done to generic fiddle tunes can be supremely satisfying when paired with a well-loved song.

Like their musical structure, the choreographic structure of singing squares was not standardized until the 1950s. Some figures were led by a single couple; most of these did not have a partner change, for reasons explained in Chapter 5. Gradually it became the norm for dancers to change partners in singing calls, usually by swinging their corner when a patter figure would call for an allemande left. Most singing call figures are led twice by the head couples, then twice for the sides, although a few have all four couples doing the same things throughout.

Over the last few decades, the trend in the modern square dance scene has been to "hash" the singing as well as the patter calls. Modern singing call routines tend to be generic and interchangeable, with little if any attempt made to match the style of choreography to the mood of the music. Many modern callers will use a different routine for each of the four iterations of the figure if they know their dancers can handle it.

Call Timing

As discussed in Chapter 6, there is a dilemma connected with traditional patter calls: Should the directions be given in advance of the dancers' movements or during them? This dilemma is, if anything, more sharply apparent in singing calls, because (aside from one or two pickup notes) the lyrics of a song start on the first downbeat of the music. From an aesthetic point of view, cadence calls – calls delivered as the dancers are executing them – are more satisfying than prompts. And cadence calls are the natural result of substituting dance directions for song lyrics. But the dancers cannot begin moving on the first beat of the phrase if they have not yet heard the call and do not know what it will be.

With singing calls this problem can be addressed in two ways. The older approach, used universally from the late 1800s through the 1940s, was to use cadence calls and let the dancers fend for themselves. This was practicable for two reasons: First, the dancers in a given community were familiar with their caller's repertoire, which might include ten or twenty singing squares. The same dance was called to the same tune every time; when the title was announced or the music began, the dancers knew what figure was coming. Second, in regions where singing calls were popular, the timing of dance routines tended to be loose. Dance movements, such as do-si-do and ladies chain, were fitted to 8-beat and 16-beat phrases, even though they might take fewer steps to execute. Dancers could listen for the first syllables of the call, start executing the move on beat 3 or 4 of the phrase, and still finish on beat 8 or 16.

The other way to address the issue is to write a singing square in which at least some of the calls are given ahead of time. In recent decades, some creators have done just that. It can make for very smooth, comfortable dancing, but the practice has not made the older style obsolete. In most dance communities where singing calls are enjoyed, most numbers are constructed primarily with cadence calls.

Hybrid Calls

Two types of calls devised during the square dance boom incorporate some but not all of the singing square's distinctive qualities.

The *semi-singing call,* popularized by Ralph Page in the 1940s and Rod Linnell in the 1950s, is sung by the caller to a dance tune, such as a march or a two-step, rather than a song with lyrics. The caller may stick to the melody or harmonize with it. The figure may be newly written for the purpose or adapted from a traditional patter call; Linnell's version of the dance *Arkansas Traveler* to the Cape Breton jig Little Burnt Potato is an example of the latter. Most semi-singing figures that I have seen use cadence calls, in the manner of the older singing squares.

The *modern quadrille* (for lack of a better name) is popular as a change of pace with some callers in the modern square dance network. It consists of mainly traditional 8- and 16-beat movements, such as right and left through and ladies chain, danced to the music of a well-known song or march, but with the calls prompted rather than sung. Stars and Stripes Forever and the Colonel Bogey March are two favorite musical choices.

Writing Your Own

Creating a new singing call is one of the easier ways to explore square dance choreography. You can start by picking a popular song (a list of titles appears in the Resources section) and deciding how much of the music to use. For the choreography, you can choose an existing routine of the right length (the call charts in this chapter include some easy ones) or devise a new one, using the principles outlined in Chapter 14. Finally, write call lines to replace the song's lyrics, staying as close to the original scansion as you can.

Your creation will be more effective, and likely more popular, if the nature of the choreography matches the mood of the song. A military march suggests squared-off movements and single file promenades; a love song works well with lots of physical contact, such as star promenades and courtesy turns.

As you fit the dance directions to the notes in place of the lyrics, you will have to decide whether to use prompted calls, cadence calls, or a mixture of both. Presumably you will be letting your dancers walk through the figure and calling it without variations, so you can probably get away with cadence calls, as in most of the classic singing squares. (Note that in some older calls, such as *My Little*

Girl, half the calls work as prompts because the song is written that way, with many lyrics coming before the first beat of their line.) You can "cheat" a little on the timing of the calls in order to mimic the lyrics more closely, but all things being equal, it is better to give a command early than late.

What Key?

If you are going to include singing squares in your repertoire, of course, you will need to know what key you prefer for each one. You might think you have a single key that you find more comfortable than any other. For calls that are chanted or half-sung to fiddle tunes, this may be true; I've found that I prefer pitching my voice on the G below middle C most of the time, which works best if the tune is in the key of G. But in the case of actual songs, there is no such thing as a perfect key for a singer, one that will do for any song. The guiding factor is the range, from the lowest note to the highest, which is different for each song.

To take myself as an example: I have a low baritone voice, and my comfortable range extends from middle C to the C below it (one octave), plus a few extra notes at the bottom – down to the next A or even G. Many male callers have a similar range, give or take a few notes at each end. If Darling Nellie Gray is played in the key of C, it lies perfectly within my range: C to C. But if My Little Girl were played in C, it would be too high for me: Its range would be from D at the bottom to F at the top, several notes above middle C. That tune, for male callers, is most often played in G; that makes its range from low A to middle C – which coincides with my best range.

So you will need to examine each song you plan to use, find its highest and lowest notes, and figure out (perhaps with the help of a musician friend) what key will make its range most comfortable for you. If you can obtain one or more recordings of that song arranged for square dancing, you can often get a clue as to which key is most often used. Note that most singing calls are arranged for the average male voice; high tenors, and many if not most women, will need a key that is a musical fourth or fifth above the baritone's favorite key for that song. For instance, I call *Trail of the Lonesome Pine* in G, but my wife Beth calls it in D.

I should mention one more concept relevant to this discussion: tessitura. This is a musical term (Italian for "texture") for the strongest part of a singer's range or the part of a song's range where most of the notes fall. Tessitura can be more important than the highest and lowest notes in determining what key to use for a given song. Two songs can have the same nominal range (say low C to middle C, one octave), but if one song's melody is primarily in the lower part of that octave, certain singers will find that song more comfortable in a slightly higher key. If the other song lies mainly in the upper part of the octave, certain other singers will want to transpose the song to a lower key.

Of course, if only one or two notes in a song are uncomfortably high or low in a given key, you can speak the words that fall on those notes. You can also change a problematic note to a more comfortable note, as long as it doesn't clash with the chord that's being played.

A Trap to Avoid

Singing squares appear deceptively simple to call. After all, the wording of a classic singing call is already established; so is the music, both melody and chord progression. It would seem that all you need to do is memorize the words and melody; then, at a dance, simply sing the words on the correct pitches. If you are one of those fortunate folks who can carry a tune, you may think the singing call is not just the easiest kind of square to learn and use, but far and away the easiest.

This is not so, for many reasons. First, it is dangerous to assume that the timing and phrasing of an unfamiliar set of words are correct. You will need to analyze the construction of each new singing call for accuracy, just as you would for any square. Don't be afraid to adjust the wording, even of well-known and well-liked dances. Seldom do I add a singing square to my repertoire without altering or rearranging the words. Sometimes I find that the creator's original wording puts some of the key words too soon or too late for the dancers to respond smoothly. In other cases the wording has become corrupted over the years, and a little research reveals that the original words were more effective.

When you present a singing call to your dancers, remember that you are still giving directions, not just singing a song. Make sure the key words are crystal clear; you may need to emphasize them, just as you would with a patter call. Keep watching the dancers; if you see them beginning to fall behind, be prepared to alter the call – perhaps by omitting a movement or changing a 16-beat move to an 8-beat one that leaves the dancers in the same place.

When it comes to showmanship, singing squares are the icing on the cake. You can easily "wow" your dancers with them while having a lot of fun along the way. Just be sure you are giving the dancers the same smooth, comfortable, positive experience that you strive for with all your material. As always, keep them moving and keep them winning.

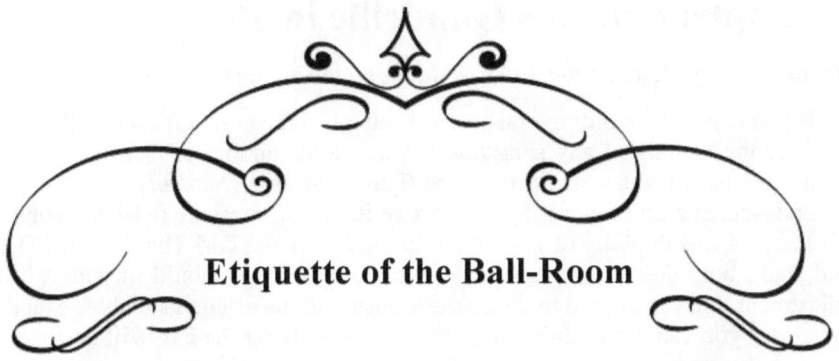

Etiquette of the Ball-Room

- Lead the lady through the quadrille; do not drag her, nor clasp her hand with unnecessary pressure, but just hold it daintily and respectfully.

- When a lady is standing in a quadrille, though not engaged in dancing, a gentleman not acquainted with her partner should not converse with her.

- When an unpracticed dancer makes a mistake, we may apprise him of his error; but it would be very impolite to have the air of giving him a lesson.

- Do not contend for position in a quadrille; if you cannot secure a head without altercation, accept a side in a quiet way, and show you are a gentleman.

- Persons should avoid attempting to take part in a dance, particularly a quadrille, unless they are familiar with the figures.

   – *Dick's Quadrille Call-Book* (1878)

Example: Queen's Quadrille in 4/4

(figure by Jerry Helt, around 1955; wording by the author)

If you adjust the wording of a phrased square, you can fit almost any figure or break to the melody of any song that has the same number of measures. As an example, I have taken a straightforward figure, *Queen's Quadrille* from Chapter 18, and written a set of words to fit (more or less) a 32-measure (64-beat) song in 4/4 meter. I was thinking of I Want a Girl (Just Like the Girl That Married Dear Old Dad), but other songs, such as Yankee Doodle Boy, should fit with a little adjustment. I have not tried to match the scansion of the original syllables exactly; the closer you can get to doing this, the more satisfying the call will be for you and your dancers.

For convenience, the dance movements of this figure are repeated below.

Queen's Quadrille
(The Dance Movements)

Square dance figure, next-door neighbor progression

A.1		Head couples right and left through	8 beats
		Same ladies chain	8 beats
A.2		Side couples right and left through	8 beats
		Same ladies chain	8 beats
B.1		All circle left halfway	8 beats
		Swing corner (original next-door neighbor)	8 beats
B.2		Promenade to gent's place	16 beats

SEQUENCE: Heads start (twice), sides start (twice).

Example: Queen's Quadrille in 4/4
(The Calls)

Beats:	1	2	3	4
Intro:	—	—	—	—
A.1:	<u>Head</u>	<u>cou</u>ples	<u>right</u> and left	<u>through</u>,
	<u>turn</u> a-	<u>round</u> as you	<u>al</u>ways	<u>do</u>,
	<u>same</u> two	<u>la</u>dies	<u>chain</u> a-	<u>cross</u> the
	<u>town</u>	—	—	<u>Sides</u>
A.2:	<u>right</u> and left	<u>through</u> a-	<u>cross</u> the	<u>square</u>,
	<u>turn</u> a-	<u>round</u> when	<u>you</u> get	<u>there</u>, those
	<u>la</u>dies	<u>chain</u> and	<u>turn</u> 'em	<u>left</u> a-
	<u>round</u>	—	— Join	<u>all</u> your
B.1:	<u>hands</u> and	<u>cir</u>cle	<u>left</u> a-	<u>round</u> that
	<u>big</u>	<u>old</u>	<u>ring</u>	—
	<u>Swing</u> your	<u>cor</u>ners	<u>all</u>, then	<u>prome</u>-
	<u>nade</u>	<u>and</u>	<u>sing</u>	—
B.2:	<u>I</u>	—	<u>want</u> a	<u>girl</u>
	<u>just</u>	—	<u>like</u> the	<u>girl</u> that
	<u>mar</u>-	<u>ried</u>	<u>dear</u>	<u>old</u>
	<u>Dad</u>	—	—	—

Around One to a Star

(as called by Dick Leger)

Dick Leger called, chose music, and composed dances primarily in the modern square dance network, but at heart he was a traditional New England caller. His dances were beautifully timed and phrased, and he enjoyed seeing how many different sequences he could devise using only the most basic of basics.

This is not an "all moving" routine; the inactive couples are not swept into the action until halfway through the figure. But they do need to pay attention sooner than that, as they must counter the active couples' "around one" motion to keep out of the way.

This figure is very closely timed; it can be done comfortably by experienced dancers but is probably not appropriate for beginners. If you like the first half but think your dancers will have trouble keeping up, you can loosen the timing as shown in the lower charts.

Around One to a Star

(The Dance Movements)

Square dance figure, corner progression

A.1	Head ladies chain across	8 beats
	Head couples forward and back	8 beats
A.2	Heads pass through	4 beats
	Separate around one	4 beats
	Into the center, right-hand star three-quarters around	6 beats
	Start an allemande left with corner (crosses the phrase)	2 beats
B.1	Finish the allemande left	2 beats
	Do-si-do partner	6 beats
	Swing corner	8 beats
B.2	Promenade to gent's place	16 beats

SEQUENCE: Heads start (twice), sides start (twice).

Easier variant, next-door neighbor progression

A.1	Head ladies chain across	8 beats
	Head couples forward and back	8 beats
A.2	Heads pass through	4 beats
	Separate around one	6 beats
	Into the center, right-hand star three-quarters around	6 beats
B.1	Allemande left corner, pass partner	8 beats
	Swing the next	8 beats
B.2	Promenade to gent's place	16 beats

Around One to a Star
(The Calls)

Beats:	1	2	3	4
Intro:	—	—	— Head	<u>la</u>dies
A.1:	<u>chain</u>	— a-	<u>cross</u> the	<u>ring</u> and
	<u>Couples</u>	<u>One</u> and	<u>Three</u>	<u>dance</u>
	<u>up</u> to the	<u>middle</u> and	<u>come</u> on	<u>back</u>
	— <u>Pass</u>	<u>through</u> for	<u>me</u>	— <u>Sepa</u>-
A.2:	<u>rate</u>, go	<u>round</u>	<u>one</u>,	<u>into</u> the
	<u>middle</u> with a	<u>right</u>-hand	<u>star</u>	—
	<u>To</u> the	<u>corner</u>,	<u>allemande</u>	<u>left</u>
	— <u>Come</u>	<u>on</u> back	<u>home</u> and	<u>do</u>-si-
B.1:	<u>do</u>	— <u>Go</u>	<u>back</u> to	<u>back</u> and
	<u>with</u> the	<u>corner</u>	<u>swing</u>	—
	— <u>You</u>	<u>swing</u> 'em	<u>round</u> and	<u>round</u>, then
	<u>prome</u>-	<u>nade</u> and	<u>sing</u>!	—
B.2:	[*Sing the last 16 beats of the original song*]			

Easier variant:

Intro:	—	—	— Head	<u>la</u>dies
A.1:	<u>chain</u>	— a-	<u>cross</u> the	<u>ring</u> and
	<u>Couples</u>	<u>One</u> and	<u>Three</u>	<u>dance</u>
	<u>up</u> to the	<u>middle</u> and	<u>come</u> on	<u>back</u>
	— <u>Pass</u>	<u>through</u> for	<u>me</u>	— <u>Sepa</u>-
A.2:	<u>rate</u>, go	<u>round</u>	<u>one</u> to the	<u>middle</u> and
	<u>star</u> with the	<u>old</u> right	<u>hand</u>	—
	—	<u>Find</u> the	<u>corner</u>	<u>and</u> you
	<u>go</u> left	<u>alle</u>-	<u>mande</u>	—
B.1:	<u>Pass</u> right	<u>by</u> your	<u>partner</u>	— and
	<u>with</u> the	<u>next</u> one	<u>swing</u>	—
	— <u>You</u>	<u>swing</u> 'em	<u>round</u> and	<u>round</u>, then
	<u>prome</u>-	<u>nade</u> and	<u>sing</u>!	—
B.2:	[*Sing the last 16 beats of the original song*]			

Crosstown

(as called by Don Durlacher and Dick Meyers)

This figure is fairly easy for newer dancers, as long as they understand the rule that the lady (or equivalent term) is on the right of each couple. I first danced this at Jones Beach around 1970 to the calling of Don Durlacher, who did it as a singing call to the tune of I Want a Girl (Just Like the Girl That Married Dear Old Dad). In 1978 Dick Meyers recorded it under the present title.

The secret is in the set-up. The "pass through, turn alone" inverts the active couples so that the gent is on the right of the lady. After both heads and sides have crossed the set, all four couples are once again "in sequence" (in numerical order counterclockwise). "New partner" in B.1 means the lady now on the gent's right, or the gent on the lady's left; the first time through the figure, this will be the original next-door neighbor (right-hand lady or left-hand gent).

Crosstown
(The Dance Movements)

Square dance figure, next-door neighbor progression

A.1	Head couples forward and back	8 beats
	Heads pass through, turn around alone	8 beats
A.2	Side couples forward and back	8 beats
	Sides pass through, turn around alone	8 beats
B.1	All circle left halfway around	8 beats
	Swing new partner	8 beats
B.2	Promenade to the gent's place	16 beats

SEQUENCE: Heads start (twice), sides start (twice).

Crosstown
(The Calls)

Beats:	1	2	3	4
Intro:	—	<u>Head</u>	<u>couples</u>	<u>forward</u>
A.1:	<u>Up</u> to the	<u>mid</u>dle and	<u>back</u> with	<u>you</u>
	Forward a-	<u>gain</u> and	<u>pass</u>	<u>through</u>
	— You	<u>turn</u> a-	<u>round</u>	<u>and</u>
	<u>wait</u>.	—	<u>Sides</u>	<u>forward</u>
A.2:	<u>Up</u> to the	<u>mid</u>dle and	<u>come</u> on	<u>back</u>
	Pass	<u>through</u> a-	<u>cross</u> the	<u>track</u>
	— You	<u>turn</u> a-	<u>round</u>.	<u>All</u>
	<u>join</u>	<u>hands</u>,	<u>circle</u>	<u>left</u>
B.1:	<u>Half</u>-	<u>way</u> a-	<u>round</u> and	<u>then</u> your
	new	partner	swing	—
	<u>Swing</u> 'em	<u>round</u> and	<u>round</u> and	prome-
	nade	that	<u>ring</u>.	Sing!
B.2:	[*Sing the last 16 beats of the original song*]			

Don's Easy Star

(Don Durlacher, around 1970)

This is one of several very easy routines that Don Durlacher used at the public dances at Jones Beach State Park, Long Island, New York, where he carried on the tradition started by his father Ed. I learned more from Don than from any other single source about crowd psychology and keeping things accessible to casual dancers.

It was this figure that inspired me to write *Star Breakdown* (1976), one of my most popular squares. At the time I wrote it, I was working a lot with experienced dancers and wanted a more tightly timed figure than Don's. There is a place for both types of dance; it depends on your audience.

I notated Don's figure slightly differently in *Shadrack's Delight* (1988). I may have remembered it incorrectly at that time, or Don may have used different versions of it through the years. The routine given here was transcribed from a field recording I made in 1970.

Don's Easy Star
(The Dance Movements)

Square dance figure, corner progression

A.1	Four ladies right-hand star once around	8 beats
	All do-si-do partner	8 beats
A.2	Four gents right-hand star once around	8 beats
	All turn partner by left hand, about once and a quarter	8 beats
B.1	Do-si-do corner	8 beats
	Swing corner	8 beats
B.2	Promenade to gent's place	16 beats

SEQUENCE: Four times through.

Don's Easy Star
(The Calls)

Beats:	1	2	3	4
Intro:	—	—	— Four	<u>la</u>dies
A.1:	<u>right</u>-	<u>hand</u>	<u>star</u>	<u>in</u> the
	<u>mid</u>dle	<u>of</u>	**town**	— You
	<u>do</u>-si-	<u>do</u> your	<u>part</u>ner,	— go
	<u>one</u> time	<u>a</u>-	**round**	— The
A.2:	<u>gents</u>	<u>star</u>	<u>right,</u>	— it's
	<u>once</u> a-	<u>round</u> you	<u>go</u>	— You
	<u>turn</u> your	<u>part</u>ner	<u>left,</u>	— your
	<u>cor</u>ner	<u>do</u>-si-	<u>do</u>	— Go
B.1:	<u>once</u> a-	<u>round</u> your	<u>cor</u>ner	— and
	<u>then</u> you	<u>swing</u> 'em	<u>too</u>	— You
	<u>swing</u> 'em	<u>and</u> you	<u>keep</u> 'em,	<u>prome</u>-
	<u>nade</u>	<u>you</u>	**do**	—
B.2:	[*Sing the last 16 beats of the original song*]			

Remember, words in bold type are to be spoken or sung just ahead of the beat. See page 181 for a complete key to the typography of the call charts.

Ed's Grand Chain

(Ed Gilmore, 1955)

It is quite possible that Ed Gilmore called this routine more often than any other. For the most part, each tip consisted of one patter call and one singing call, and Ed reused his singing-call figures more than he repeated his patter calls. Over the years, he set this one to several tunes, ranging from My Bonnie Lies Over the Ocean (stretched into 4/4 meter) to the current hit songs of his day.

The timing of A.1 is rather tight; it is a challenge to complete a four ladies chain in 8 steps, and two in a row are even harder to get through in 16. However, there is enough leeway in the next few moves to allow the dancers to recover.

Ed's Grand Chain
(The Dance Movements)

Square dance figure, corner progression

A.1	Four ladies chain across	8 beats
	Four ladies chain back	8 beats
A.2	All do-si-do corner	8 beats
	Four gents left-hand star in center	8 beats
B.1	All do-si-do partner	8 beats
	Swing corner	8 beats
B.2	Promenade to gent's place	16 beats

SEQUENCE: Four times through.

Ed's Grand Chain
(The Calls)

Beats:	1	2	3	4
Intro:	—	—	— Four	<u>l</u>adies
A.1:	<u>chain</u>	—	—	<u>and</u> you
	<u>turn</u> 'em	<u>a</u>-	**round**	<u>Chain</u> on
	<u>back</u>	—	—	<u>Don't</u> you
	<u>let</u> 'em	<u>fall</u>	**down**	—
A.2:	<u>Do</u>-si	<u>round</u> the	<u>cor</u>ner	— The
	<u>gents</u>	<u>star</u>	<u>left</u>	— In-
	<u>side</u> the	<u>ring</u> you	<u>go</u>	<u>Round</u> your
	<u>part</u>ner	<u>do</u>-si-	<u>do</u>	—
B.1:	<u>All</u> the	<u>way</u> a-	**round**	<u>then</u> the
	<u>cor</u>ner	<u>you</u>	**swing**	—
	<u>Keep</u> that	<u>new</u>	**one**,	<u>prome</u>-
	<u>nade</u> that	<u>old</u>	**ring**	—
B.2:	[*Sing the last 16 beats of the original song*]			

Remember, words in bold type are to be spoken or sung just ahead of the beat. See page 181 for a complete key to the typography of the call charts.

In the Good Old Summertime

(Don Durlacher, around 1970)

Here is another easy figure from the calling of Don Durlacher (see *Don's Easy Star* in this chapter). Don once told me that for newer dancers he preferred routines like this, where partners stay connected much of the time, to traditional "split the ring" figures. He said "I can call 'Lady go right, gent go left,' but what actually happens is that the woman goes to her right but the man wants to follow 'Mother' and goes to *his* right too."

This figure keeps partners together throughout the dance. Don liked to use several "keepers" before introducing squares with a partner change. If you wish, you may change the partner swing to a corner swing.

In the Good Old Summertime
(The Dance Movements)

Square dance figure, no partner change

A.1	Head couples forward and back	8 beats
	Heads promenade inside the set, halfway across (to opposite side) and wheel to the left	8 beats
A.2	Heads promenade outside the set, halfway (to home) and wheel to face the center	8 beats
	Four ladies promenade single file inside the set	8 beats
B.1	Do-si-do partner	8 beats
	Swing partner	8 beats
B.2	Promenade once around	16 beats

SEQUENCE: Heads lead and ladies promenade; sides lead and gents promenade; repeat for heads and ladies; repeat for sides and gents.

Note: If you alter this dance to include a partner change, you must call the heads twice in a row and the sides twice; otherwise two ladies will be active all four times and the other two not at all.

In the Good Old Summertime
(The Calls)

Beats:	1	2	3	4
Intro:	—	<u>One</u> and	<u>Three</u>	— <u>walk</u>
A.1:	<u>up</u> to the	<u>mid</u>dle and	<u>come</u> on	<u>back</u>
	— Prome-	nade a-	cross	—
	— Prome-	nade out-	<u>side</u> the	<u>ring</u> you
	<u>go</u>	—	When you're	<u>home</u>,
A.2:	— four	<u>la</u>dies	prome-	nade in-
	<u>side</u> the	<u>ring</u> you	go now	—
	<u>One</u>	time a-	<u>round</u>	— Your
	<u>part</u>ner	<u>do</u>-si-	<u>do</u>	—
B.1:	<u>All</u> the	<u>way</u> a-	<u>round</u>	<u>and</u>
	<u>swing</u>	<u>your</u>	<u>part</u>ner	— and
	<u>have</u>	— a	<u>ve</u>ry	<u>good</u>
	<u>time</u>	—	—	— You
B.2:	prome-	nade the	<u>ring</u>	— and
	<u>ev</u>ery-	<u>bod</u>y	<u>sing</u>!	<u>In</u> the
	<u>Good</u>	<u>Old</u>	<u>Sum</u>-	<u>mer</u>-
	<u>time</u>!	<u>Two</u> and	<u>Four</u>	— walk

Note: The original song was a waltz in 3/4 meter. For square dance purposes it was stretched to 4/4 and recorded that way on the Grenn label, which is presumably where Don Durlacher found it. The figure that came with the record was aimed at experienced modern square dancers. Such figures are not set in stone; except for a handful of classics like *My Little Girl* and *Trail of the Lonesome Pine,* there is nothing to keep you from setting a figure of your choice to a personal favorite tune.

Jingle Bells

(as called by Don Durlacher, 1962)

Jingle Bells has been used for square dancing since the 1940s if not earlier. Several different figures have been set to it, most of them fairly simple. This is one of the easiest, recorded by Don Durlacher and included in Honor Your Partner Album 20, *Holiday Dances*.

Note that some of the instructions are delivered as cadence calls, in the manner of many classic singing squares. Your dancers will need to know what is coming, unless you choose to rewrite the routine to use prompted calls throughout.

As with all these singing call figures, you may set this one to another song of your choice, changing the words as necessary, or use a different figure with Jingle Bells.

Jingle Bells
(The Dance Movements)

Square dance figure, corner progression

A.1	Head couples right and left through;	
	sides swing partner	8 beats
	Heads right and left back; sides may keep swinging	8 beats
A.2	Side couples right and left through;	
	heads swing partner	8 beats
	Sides right and left back; heads may keep swinging	8 beats
B.1	All join hands, go forward and back	8 beats
	Swing corner	8 beats
B.2	Promenade to gent's place	16 beats

SEQUENCE: Heads start (twice), sides start (twice).

Jingle Bells
(The Calls)

Beats:	1	2	3	4
Intro:	—	—	—	—
A.1:	<u>Head</u> two	<u>coup</u>les	<u>right</u> and left	<u>through</u>, the
	<u>side</u> two	<u>coup</u>les	<u>swing</u>	—
	<u>Right</u> and left	<u>back</u> and	<u>home</u> you	<u>go</u>,
	<u>hear</u> those	<u>sleigh</u> bells	<u>ring</u>	— The
A.2:	<u>side</u> two	<u>coup</u>les	<u>right</u> and left	<u>through</u>, the
	<u>head</u> two	<u>coup</u>les	<u>swing</u>	—
	<u>Right</u> and left	<u>back</u> and	<u>home</u> you	<u>go</u> and
	<u>listen</u>	<u>while</u> I	<u>sing</u>	— All
B.1:	<u>for</u>ward	<u>up</u> and	<u>come</u> on	<u>back</u> and
	<u>swing</u> your	<u>cor</u>ners	<u>all</u>	—
	<u>Swing</u> the	<u>cor</u>ner	<u>high</u> and	<u>low</u>, then
	<u>prome</u>-	<u>nade</u> the	<u>hall</u>,	<u>sing</u>!
B.2:	<u>Jin</u>gle	<u>bells</u>,	<u>jin</u>gle	<u>bells</u>,
	<u>jin</u>gle	<u>all</u> the	<u>way</u>,	—
	<u>Oh</u>, what	<u>fun</u> it	<u>is</u> to	<u>ride</u> in a
	<u>one</u>-horse	<u>o</u>pen	<u>sleigh</u>!	—

Whispering

(Ed Gilmore, 1955)

Here is another relaxing figure from Ed Gilmore using traditional basic movements. For his commercial recording of it, Ed set it to the 1920 popular song Whispering, but it would not surprise me if he used the same figure with various songs, as he did with some of his other figures. He also used different figures with the same song: He recorded a dance to Whispering again a few years later, using the then-new move "wheel and deal."

I believe the "promenade half" in A.2 was intended to be outside the square, but if you think your dancers may have trouble getting through it in time with the music, you may substitute a "half promenade" inside the set.

The "corner" in B.1 is the original next-door neighbor (the gent's right-hand lady or the lady's left-hand gent). To find this person after turning the opposite, the gents move clockwise and the ladies counterclockwise, as usual when going to the corner.

Whispering
(The Dance Movements)

Square dance figure, next-door neighbor progression

A.1	Four ladies chain across	8 beats
	Head couples right and left through	8 beats
A.2	Four ladies chain across	8 beats
	Side couples promenade halfway around	8 beats
B.1	Four gents right-hand star halfway	4 beats
	Turn opposite by left hand, once and a quarter	6 beats
	Swing corner (original next-door neighbor)	6 beats
B.2	Promenade to gent's place	16 beats

SEQUENCE: Heads right and left through first (twice), sides right and left through first (twice).

Chapter 20: Singing Calls

Whispering
(The Calls)

Beats:	1	2	3	4
Intro:	—	—	—	—
A.1:	<u>All</u> four <u>Couples</u> <u>right</u> and left <u>turn</u> 'em	<u>la</u>dies <u>One</u> and <u>through</u> a-<u>there</u> for	<u>chain</u> a-<u>Three</u> <u>cross</u> the me	<u>cross</u> and — Do a <u>set</u> and — Four
A.2:	<u>la</u>dies <u>Couples</u> <u>prome</u>-<u>All</u> four	<u>chain</u> right <u>Two</u> and <u>nade</u> half-<u>gents</u> you	<u>back</u> a-<u>Four</u> <u>way</u> to-<u>star</u> by the	<u>gain</u> and — You <u>night</u> <u>right</u>
B.1:	<u>Half</u>way <u>with</u> a <u>Swing</u> the <u>prome</u>-	<u>round</u> and <u>left</u> hand <u>cor</u>ner <u>nade</u> the	<u>turn</u> your <u>round</u> <u>high</u> and <u>town</u>	<u>op</u>posite — <u>low</u> and —
B.2:	[*Sing the last 16 beats of the original song*]			

21
Fancy Figures

The squares in this chapter are those I have found to take longer to teach than the ones in the preceding chapters. Either they have one or more points at which dancers tend to become disoriented, or they just have more components to learn and practice. Some have both characteristics.

This is a good place to remind you that except for a session advertised as a workshop, a figure should take less time to teach than it does to dance. I would not use any of the following figures at a normal open evening unless I had been calling to the group regularly. Even then, I would call several easier numbers, watching the dancers carefully and assessing their reaction time and knowledge of the basics, before attempting a "fancy figure." (Each easier number should include one of the movements used in the harder one.) Of course I would use a different dance if I thought my planned one would cause problems.

That said, mastering a tricky figure can give dancers a powerful feeling of accomplishment. Just be sure your dancers are willing to be challenged.

Birthday Contra Square

(Rod Linnell, 1964–65)

Rod Linnell of Maine was a contemporary of Ralph Page; they often worked together at dance camps. Rod was a choreographic genius who unfortunately died at age 59, at the height of his creativity. He had started to collect his dances in book form; Louise Winston completed the project (Linnell and Winston 1974).

Rod's best-known creations are probably his eight-couple squares known familiarly as "Rod's Quads," but he also devised some innovative contras and four-couple squares. The figure given here is one of my favorites.

Birthday Contra Square
(The Dance Movements)

Square dance figure, no partner change

A.1	Allemande left corner	8 beats
	Promenade partner halfway around	8 beats
A.2	Couple 1 promenade through the middle from opposite place to home place, to end facing out at home; the other couples follow Couple 1 into a column, all facing the same way (the order is 1, 4, 3, 2)	8 beats
	Finish the promenade; all face partner and back away	8 beats
B.1	Couples 1 and 3 ("actives") do-si-do partner	8 beats
	Same couples swing partner; end facing down (with backs to #1 position) with lady on gent's right	8 beats
B.2	Same couples go down the center; turn alone	8 beats
	Return and cast off (as in a contra dance)	8 beats
C.1	Facing couples right and left through	8 beats
	Right and left back	8 beats
C.2	Facing ladies chain (bringing partners together)	8 beats
	Same four people right-hand star, adjusting to drop off at their home position	8 beats

SEQUENCE: Couple 1 lead (order is 1, 4, 3, 2; actives are 1 and 3); Couple 2 lead (order is 2, 1, 4, 3; actives are 2 and 4); Couple 3 lead (order is 3, 2, 1, 4; actives are 3 and 1); Couple 4 lead (order is 4, 3, 2, 1; actives are 4 and 2). Note that "down the center" is always away from the leading couple's home position. This means that when Couple 3 leads, "down" will be toward the head of the hall. Rod enjoyed watching the confusion that this engendered.

Birthday Contra Square
(The Calls)

Beats:	1	2	3	4
Intro:	<u>On</u> the	<u>cor</u>ner	<u>alle</u>mande	<u>left</u>
A.1:	—	—	<u>Take</u> your	<u>own</u> and
	<u>prome</u>-	<u>nade</u>, a-	<u>round</u> you	<u>roam</u>, go
	<u>half</u>way	<u>round</u>	—	—
	<u>Couple</u>	<u>One</u> lead	<u>through</u> the	<u>middle</u>,
A.2:	<u>toward</u> your	<u>home</u>	—	—
	—	— Now	<u>face</u> your	<u>part</u>ner,
	<u>back</u> a-	<u>way</u>	—	—
	<u>One</u> and	<u>Three</u> you	<u>do</u>-si-	<u>do</u>
B.1:	—	—	—	—
	<u>Same</u>	<u>two</u> you	<u>swing</u> in the	<u>middle</u>
	—	—	—	—
	<u>Down</u> the	<u>center</u> go	<u>two</u> by	<u>two</u>
B.2:	—	—	—	—
	<u>Turn</u> a-	<u>lone</u> and	<u>come</u> **on**	<u>back</u>
	—	—	<u>Cast</u>	<u>off</u>, with the
	<u>couple</u> a-	<u>cross</u> go	<u>right</u> and left	<u>through</u>
C.1:	—	—	—	—
	<u>Turn</u> a-	<u>round</u> and a	<u>right</u> and left	<u>back</u>
	—	—	—	— The
	<u>same</u> two	<u>ladies</u>	<u>chain</u> a-	<u>cross</u>
C.2:	—	—	—	—
	<u>Same</u>	<u>four</u> *right*-	<u>hand</u>	<u>star</u>
	— Drop	<u>off</u> when	<u>you</u> get	<u>home</u> and
	<u>on</u> the	<u>cor</u>ner	<u>alle</u>mande	<u>left</u>

Note that this is a 48-measure dance. You can use a 48-measure (3-part) tune if the band knows one or you have a suitable recording. Otherwise you can do one of two things: either have each couple dance its turn while the tune runs AABBAA, then pad out with a 16-measure break (preferably starting with an allemande left) to use up the BB, or else begin each even-numbered couple's turn on the "B" music, so Couples 1 and 3 dance on AABBAA and Couples 2 and 4 on BBAABB. For this dance I generally use the last method, as the allemande left seems to flow well out of the right-hand star.

Ends Turn In

(Ed Gilmore, 1952; some patter from Sandy Bradley, 1970s)

Of all the callers in the West Coast square dance movement of the 1940s and '50s, Ed Gilmore was the closest to the current neo-traditional scene in terms of style and philosophy: He believed in comfortable, accessible dancing. He didn't always phrase completely in New England style, but he could when he wanted to; he used contras and quadrilles in his programs and recorded some of each.

Ends Turn In is his best-known creation. The key movement was considered a "basic" in recreational western style for several years; that is, it could be incorporated in other routines and the dancers were expected to be familiar with it.

This was one of the first squares in which the allemande left was integrated into the figure rather than occurring after all had returned home. It may be turned into a change-partner dance by substituting a corner swing for the allemande.

See *Duck Through and Swing* in Chapter 18 for an explanation of why I rate that figure as easier than this one.

Ends Turn In
(The Dance Movements)

Square dance figure, no partner change

A.1	Head couples forward and back	8 beats
	Heads forward, turn away from partner; with opposite, split the nearest side couple, then separate around one to stand next to corner at the end of a line of four at the side (close to own home position)	8 beats
A.2	Lines forward and back	8 beats
	Drop hands, pass through, join hands again; center two make an arch, ends turn in and duck to center (arching pair California twirl and face the center)	8 beats
B.1	Those in the center circle four to the left once around	8 beats
	Pass through (right shoulders with own partner), split the side couple, separate to the ends of a line of four	8 beats
B.2	Repeat A.2	16 beats
C.1	Those in the center circle four to the left once around	8 beats
	Pass through, allemande left corner	8 beats
C.2	All do-si-do partner at home	8 beats
	Swing partner	8 beats

SEQUENCE: As given here, alternate heads and sides leading; if inserting a partner change, call heads twice and sides twice (otherwise the same two ladies will be active every time).

Chapter 21: Fancy Figures

Ends Turn In
(The Calls)

Beats:	1	2	3	4
Intro:	<u>Head</u> two	<u>coup</u>les	<u>you</u> go	<u>for</u>ward
A.1:	<u>Up</u> to the	<u>mid</u>dle and	<u>back</u>	— Go
	<u>for</u>ward a-	<u>gain</u> but	<u>split</u> your	<u>cor</u>ner thru the
	<u>big</u> side	<u>door</u>, a-	<u>round</u> just	<u>one</u>, stand
	<u>close</u> to	*<u>home</u> in a*	<u>line</u> of	four
A.2:	<u>For</u>ward	<u>eight</u> and	<u>back</u> with	<u>you</u>, go
	<u>for</u>ward a-	<u>gain</u>, you	<u>pass</u>	<u>through</u>
	<u>Arch</u> in the	<u>mid</u>dle and the	<u>ends</u> turn	<u>in</u>, come
	<u>in</u>to the	<u>mid</u>dle and you	<u>cir</u>cle	<u>four</u>, go
B.1:	<u>one</u> full	<u>turn</u> in the	<u>mid</u>dle of the	<u>floor</u>
	—	— You	<u>pass</u>	<u>through</u>
	<u>Split</u> the	<u>out</u>side	<u>two</u>, go a-	<u>round</u> just
	<u>one</u> to a	<u>line</u> of	<u>four</u>, go	<u>for</u>ward
B.2:	<u>Eight</u> to the	<u>mid</u>dle and	<u>back</u> you	<u>do</u>, go
	<u>for</u>ward a-	<u>gain</u>, you	<u>pass</u>	<u>through</u>
	<u>Arch</u> in the	<u>mid</u>dle and the	<u>ends</u> turn	<u>in</u>, come
	<u>in</u>to the	<u>mid</u>dle and you	<u>cir</u>cle	<u>four</u>, go
C.1:	<u>once</u> a-	<u>round</u> as you	<u>did</u> be-	<u>fore</u>
	—	— Now	<u>pass</u>	<u>through</u>
	<u>Alle</u>mande	<u>left</u> your	<u>cor</u>ner	— You
	<u>come</u> back	<u>home</u> and	<u>do</u>-si-	<u>do</u>
C.2:	—	—	<u>Swing</u> your	<u>own</u>, you
	<u>swing</u> your	<u>part</u>ner	<u>there</u> at	<u>home</u>
	—	—	—	— Now the
	<u>side</u> two	<u>coup</u>les	<u>you</u> go	<u>for</u>ward

Note that this is a 48-measure dance. You can use a 48-measure (3-part) tune if the band knows one or you have a suitable recording. Otherwise you can do one of two things: either call each time through the figure while the tune runs AABBAA, then pad out with a 16-measure break to use up the BB, or else begin the second and fourth figures on the "B" music, so the first and third figures will be danced to AABBAA and the second and fourth figures to BBAABB.

Fiddle Faddle

(Jim York, 1950s)

Jim York was a contemporary of Ed Gilmore (see *Ends Turn In*) who was a little more daring in his choreography. Few of his dances have made it into the neo-traditional world, but *Fiddle Faddle* has become a classic. It's based on *Dallas Route* by Buck Benny, which in turn is a blend of *The Rout(e)* (see Chapter 18) and *Quarter Sashay* (aka *Forward Six and Fall Back Eight*). Jim York removed the Rout(e) chains and added a bit of *Texas Star*.

In B.2, if wheeling once and a half around in 8 beats is too demanding for your dancers, you may change it to a simple "wheel around" (halfway).

Fiddle Faddle

(The Dance Movements)

Square dance figure, no partner change

A.1	Couples 3 and 4 right and left through	8 beats
	#1 down center, split the opposite couple, around one to a line of four	8 beats
A.2	Line of four forward and back	8 beats
	Line slide or sidestep one-quarter to the right around the square, ending behind the couple in #4's place	8 beats
B.1	Ends of line take outside hand of couple in front of them; those six forward and back	8 beats
	Couple 2 down center, split the first couple they meet, around one to a line of four (in front of the other four)	8 beats
B.2	Two lines (facing same direction) forward and back	8 beats
	Center two in each line wheel around (gent backward, lady forward), once and a half to face the other way	8 beats
A.1	Four ladies right-hand star while gents left-hand star	8 beats
	Gents pick up partner, star promenade	8 beats
A.2	Each couple wheel once and a half (gent backward)	8 beats
	Star promenade the other way (ladies' right hands in center)	8 beats
B.1	All swing partner at home	16 beats
B.2	Promenade once around	16 beats

SEQUENCE: Couple 1 lead (3 & 4 right and left through); Couple 2 lead (4 & 1 right and left through); Couple 3 lead (1 & 2 right and left through); Couple 4 lead (2 & 3 right and left through). Note that each couple's turn requires two playings of a standard (AABB) tune.

Fiddle Faddle
(The Calls)

Beats:	1	2	3	4
Intro:	—	—	<u>Coup</u>les	<u>Three</u> and
	<u>Four</u>	— do a	<u>right</u> and left	<u>through</u>, that's
A.1:	<u>Three</u> and	<u>Four</u>	<u>right</u> and left	<u>through</u>
	<u>Couple</u>	<u>One</u> go	<u>down</u> the	<u>mid</u>dle and
	<u>split</u> the	<u>ring</u>, go a-	<u>round</u> just	<u>one</u>
	— Make a	<u>line</u> of	<u>four</u>, go	<u>forward</u>
A.2:	<u>Four</u> to the	<u>mid</u>dle and	<u>back</u> to-	<u>night</u>, that
	<u>line</u> of	<u>four</u>	<u>slide</u> to the	<u>right</u>
	<u>Around</u> to the	<u>right</u> and you	<u>pick</u> **up** the	<u>couple</u> in
	<u>front</u> of you	— go	<u>forward</u>	<u>six</u>
B.1:	<u>Up</u> to the	<u>mid</u>dle and	<u>back</u>	— Now
	<u>Couple</u>	<u>Two</u> go	<u>down</u> the	<u>mid</u>dle and
	<u>split</u> one	<u>couple</u>, go a-	<u>round</u> just	<u>one</u>
	— Two	<u>lines</u> of	<u>four</u> go	<u>forward</u>
B.2:	<u>Eight</u> to the	<u>mid</u>dle and	<u>then</u> back	<u>down</u>
	<u>Center</u>	<u>couples</u>	<u>wheel</u> a-	<u>round</u>
	<u>Once</u> and a	<u>half</u> in the	<u>middle</u> of	<u>town</u>
	<u>Gents</u> star	<u>left</u> and the	<u>ladies</u>	<u>right</u>
A.1:	<u>Once</u> a-	<u>round</u> in the	<u>middle</u> of the	<u>night</u>
	<u>Pick</u> **up** your	<u>lady</u> with an	<u>arm</u> a-	<u>round</u>
	<u>Star</u> prome-	<u>nade</u>, go	<u>round</u> the	<u>town</u>
	—	— Now the	<u>inside</u>	<u>out</u>, the
A.2:	<u>inside</u>	<u>out</u> and the	<u>outside</u>	<u>in</u>, turn
	<u>once</u> and a	<u>half</u>, we're	<u>gone</u> a-	<u>gain</u>
	<u>Ladies</u> star	<u>right</u>, take	<u>him</u> with	<u>you</u>
	—	—	<u>Get</u> back	<u>home</u> and
B.1:	<u>swing</u> your	<u>hon</u>ey and	<u>swing</u> your	<u>beau</u>
	<u>Swing</u> 'em	<u>fast</u> or	<u>swing</u> 'em	<u>slow</u>
	—	—	—	— And
	<u>prome</u>-	<u>nade</u>, all a-	<u>round</u> you	<u>go</u>
B.2:	—	—	—	—
	—	—	—	—
	—	— Now	<u>Coup</u>les	<u>Four</u> and
	<u>One</u>	— do a	<u>right</u> and left	<u>through</u>

Lazy H

(Ed Gilmore, 1950s)

Several of Ed Gilmore's signature dances were adaptations of older figures. This one is based on the traditional *Four in a Center Line* (described in Shaw 1939).

Variation 1: Replace the right and left through with a ladies chain over and back, with the ladies going through an arch made by the two people in the center of the line of four. I often use this when Couple 3 and Couple 4 lead the figure.

Variation 2: At the end of C.1, instead of passing through to an allemande left, the center four dancers pass through, separate around one standing person, and come into the middle for a right-hand star, which they turn until they meet corners for the allemande left. I use this during Couple 4's turn if the dancers have been following me well.

Lazy H
(The Dance Movements)

Square dance figure, no partner change

A.1	Couple 1 down the center, split the ring, separate around one to the ends of a line of four	8 beats
	Line of four go forward and back	8 beats
A.2	Forward again and stop in the center of the set	4 beats
	Sides right and left through, keeping to one side of the center line while their partners keep to the other side	8 beats
	Sides start a right and left back	4 beats
B.1	Sides finish the right and left back	4 beats
	Line of four back up four steps and arch in the middle	4 beats
	Ends of line turn in, duck through the arch, separate around two people to stand between the members of a side couple	8 beats
B.2	Lines of three go forward and back	8 beats
	Couple 3 down the center, separate around one person and squeeze in to make a line of four	8 beats
C.1	Lines of four go forward and back	8 beats
	Center four people right and left through	8 beats
C.2	Same four people pass through, allemande left corner	8 beats
	All swing partner at home	8 beats

SEQUENCE: Once with each couple leading (sides right and left through when a head couple leads, and vice versa).

Lazy H
(The Calls)

Beats:	1	2	3	4
Intro:	<u>Couple</u>	<u>One</u> go	<u>down</u> the	<u>cen</u>ter and
A.1:	<u>split</u> the	<u>ring</u>, go a-	<u>round</u> just	<u>one</u>
	— to a	<u>line</u> of	<u>four</u>, go	<u>for</u>ward
	<u>Four</u> to the	<u>mid</u>dle and	<u>four</u> fall	<u>back</u>
	<u>For</u>ward a-	<u>gain</u>,	**there** stand	<u>pat</u>
A.2:	<u>Side</u>	<u>cou</u>ples	<u>right</u> and left	<u>through</u>
	<u>Down</u> the	<u>mid</u>dle and you	<u>turn</u> 'em	<u>too</u>
	<u>Turn</u> right a-	<u>round</u> and a	<u>right</u> and left	<u>back</u>
	<u>Right</u> and left	<u>back</u> on the	<u>same</u> old	<u>track</u> and the
B.1:	<u>line</u> of	<u>four</u>,	<u>you</u> fall	<u>back</u>
	<u>Arch</u> in the	<u>mid</u>dle and the	<u>ends</u> duck	<u>through</u>
	<u>Sepa</u>-	<u>rate</u>, go a-	<u>round</u> just	<u>two</u>, be
	<u>tween</u> the	<u>sides</u> you	<u>stand</u>	— Go
B.2:	<u>for</u>ward	<u>six</u> and	<u>back</u> with	<u>you</u>, now
	<u>Couple</u>	<u>Three</u> go	<u>down</u> the	<u>mid</u>dle and
	<u>sepa</u>-	<u>rate</u>, go a-	<u>round</u> just	<u>one</u>
	— Two	<u>lines</u> of	<u>four</u>, go	<u>for</u>ward
C.1:	<u>Eight</u> to the	<u>mid</u>dle and	<u>back</u> with	<u>you</u>, now the
	<u>cen</u>ter	<u>four</u> do a	<u>right</u> and left	<u>through</u>
	—	— And you	<u>turn</u> 'em	<u>too</u>, now
	<u>face</u> them a-	<u>gain</u> and	<u>pass</u>	<u>through</u>
C.2:	<u>Alle</u>mande	<u>left</u> your	<u>cor</u>ner	— Come
	<u>swing</u> your	<u>part</u>ner,	<u>part</u>ner	<u>swing</u>
	—	— Now	<u>sett</u>le	<u>down</u> and
	<u>Couple</u>	<u>Two</u> go	<u>down</u> the	<u>cen</u>ter

Note that this is a 48-measure dance. You can use a 48-measure (3-part) tune if the band knows one or you have a suitable recording. Otherwise you can do one of two things: either have each couple dance its turn while the tune runs AABBAA, then pad out with a 16-measure break to use up the BB, or else begin each even-numbered couple's turn on the "B" music, so Couples 1 and 3 dance on AABBAA and Couples 2 and 4 on BBAABB.

Starline

(Ed Gilmore, 1950s)

This is one of several figures in Ed Gilmore's album *Square Dance Party* (Decca/MCA). I believe I was the first caller to reintroduce it to the neo-traditional dance world, starting in the 1970s. I've had overwhelmingly positive response to it wherever I've presented it. Both you and your dancers should be thoroughly comfortable with squares before trying this one.

Starline
(The Dance Movements)

Square dance figure, corner progression

A.1	Head couples lead to right, circle four to the left about halfway around; head gents drop left hand, lead circle to a line of four in the side position (#1 and #2 in #2's position, #3 and #4 in #4's position)	8 beats
	Lines of four go forward and back	8 beats
A.2	With the opposite couple (#1 with #4, #3 with #2), right-hand star about three-quarters around	6 beats
	Heads go into the center, left-hand star with each other once around	8 beats
	Heads return to the same side couple, begin another right-hand star about halfway around	2 beats
B.1	Finish the star; head gents lead other three to a line of four in the head position (#1 and #4 in #1's position, #3 and #2 in #3's position)	4 beats
	Lines of four go forward and back	8 beats
	With the new opposite couple (#1 with #2, #3 with #4), begin a right-hand star about three-quarters around	4 beats
B.2	Finish the star; heads left-hand star in center	10 beats
	Heads return to the same side couple, make another right-hand star about halfway around; head gents lead to a no-hands column (#1 and #2 in #4's position, #3 and #4 in #2's position)	6 beats
C.1	All promenade in single file to the left (clockwise) halfway around (all are near home position)	8 beats
	Ladies about-face, swing the gent behind them (corner)	8 beats
C.2	Promenade to the gent's place	16 beats

SEQUENCE: Heads lead, forming lines at the side in A.1 and the head in B.1 (twice); sides lead, forming lines at the head in A.1 and the side in B.1 (twice).

Starline
(The Calls)

Beats:	1	2	3	4
Intro:	Head two	couples	lead to the	right
A.1:	Circle	four at the	side of the	floor
	Head gents	break, make	lines of	four
	Up to the	middle and	back to the	bar, with the
	couple a-	cross, a	right-hand	star
A.2:	Heads to the	center with a	left-hand	star
	Sides	wait	where you	are. Come
	back to the	sides and	star some	more
	Head gents	lead to	lines of	four at the
B.1:	head	— Go	forward	eight
	Up to the	middle and	back to the	bar, with the
	couple a-	cross, a	right-hand	star
	Heads	in with a	left-hand	star
B.2:	Sides	wait	—	— Come
	back to the	sides and	star a	while
	Head gents	lead 'em	single	file
	One big	ring, go	'bout a	mile
C.1:	—	—	—	— Now the
	ladies	turn and	there you	swing
	—	—	—	— And
	prome-	nade, go	round the	ring
C.2:	—	—	—	—
	—	—	Gent's	place
	—	—	—	—
	At the	head, lead	out to the	right

Note that this is a 48-measure dance. You can use a 48-measure (3-part) tune if the band knows one or you have a suitable recording. Otherwise you can do one of two things: either call each time through the figure while the tune runs AABBAA, then pad out with a 16-measure break to use up the BB, or else begin the second and fourth figures on the "B" music, so the heads (and later the sides) dance on AABBAA their first time and on BBAABB their second time.

22
Silly Stuff

Sometimes a good laugh is the best medicine. Dancing is a recreation, after all, and while excessive clowning or rowdiness is likely to spoil the fun of the majority, a little lightheartedness can relieve the frustration and tension that are sometimes produced by taking things too seriously. I vividly remember one workshop at a dance weekend when mastery of a complicated figure was proving elusive, even after repeated walkthroughs, and tempers were running high. Suddenly the caller barked "And remember, it's more important to get it right than it is to have fun!" In a flash, the dancers realized they had indeed been operating under that notion; the resulting laugh broke the logjam, and the figure went smoothly.

In addition to witty observations, callers can leaven the proceedings by choosing dance material whose chief merit is its silliness. Sometimes the humor stems from improvisation on the caller's part; sometimes it is built into the design of a particular dance number. Patter, whether improvised or learned from an outside source, can lighten the atmosphere (or damage it if the patter is ill-chosen).

It is likely that callers have been improvising routines as long as there has been calling. There are references to improvisation in dance manuals of the 1840s (see Chapter 2). A generation later, William de Garmo, author of *The Dance of Society* (New York, 1875, p. 57n), took an apparently jaundiced view of the practice. After explaining, apparently somewhat reluctantly, that a certain call could be interpreted as meaning all or half of a figure, depending on the dance and the teacher, he wrote "This license is freely indulged in by prompters in New England to produce a 'variety of changes.' They seldom 'call' the figures of the quadrilles in their original form."

Humorous patter, too, has probably been around from the beginning. As early as 1862 it appeared in print: Elias Howe's *American Dancing Master and Ballroom Prompter* included a "Punch and Judy Set." Figure 2 went like this:

> First lady balance to right hand gentleman,
>   swing the gentleman with big feet...
> pass on and balance to the next gentleman,
>   swing the gentleman with the long nose...
> pass on and balance to the next gentleman,
>   swing the gentleman with the red hair...
> balance to partners, swing the best looking gentleman in the set [etc.]

Figure 4 has the gentlemen swing the lady with black eyes, the lady with curls, the lady with dimples in her cheek, and the most beautiful lady in the hall.

Ralph Page, the dean of New England callers in the mid-20th century, was famous for tricking his dancers by calling one movement when they were clearly expecting another. (In the 1957 syllabus of the Stockton Folk Dance Camp he wrote "You will find none of these surprise calls in your syllabus. If you know about it ahead of time it isn't a surprise.") He was especially fond of doing this during the introductory breaks of his squares – in part, no doubt, to size up the dancers and make sure they could hear him clearly. An example is "Bow to your partner; swing your partner; bow to your corner; swing your partner one more time." This practice did not originate with Page. In J.A. French's *Prompters' Hand Book* (Boston, 1893), which Ralph admitted to having studied when he was learning the trade, one of the quadrilles (p. 25f) includes the following calls:

All balance partner; turn (wait one bar) corners...

Later in the same figure, now that the dancers are wary of reacting too soon:

...all balance corner (wait one bar) turn (then say) why don't you turn...

Obviously, this sort of thing can be overdone. Dances that depend on a gimmick to hold interest should be used sparingly, like seasoning in food; one in an evening is probably more than enough. As for misleading calls, they should clearly be given in a lighthearted way. The last thing I want to do is betray the trust my dancers have in me, and that trust will vanish quickly if I make a habit of fooling them.

Following are a few dances that I would classify as "silly." I have not made call charts for them because most do not lend themselves to strict phrasing or a single set of call words – and because, before trying them, you should have attained a level of competence and confidence that will let you work "without a net." With some, executing them without a hitch can be a worthwhile challenge; with others, getting them wrong is practically their whole point. I leave it to you to decide which is which.

Birdie Fly Out

This gimmick is based on a version of *Bird in the Cage* that is different from both of the versions presented in Chapter 19; it is actually a variation of *Ladies' Whirligig* (see below). After the active lady has turned each of the gents, returning to her partner after each, she goes to the center while the other seven dancers join hands and circle left around her ("Bird in the cage and seven hands round"). At this point, the usual call is "Bird hop out and the crow hop in" (as with most versions of *Bird*). In this variation, on the call "Birdie fly out," the seven dancers stop circling and raise their joined hands, and the active lady dances out of her set and into another set of her choice. If a set is already occupied by a bird, she must continue searching until she finds a vacant cage. She then takes the place of the lady who left that set, swinging and promenading with the gent whose partner has "flown." This call may be used with any bird (lady) or crow (gent); the caller may choose whether to keep the dancers with their new partners at the end or tell everyone to fly home.

Cheat or Swing

There are several dances whose basic premise is that, at certain times, a dancer being approached for a swing has the option of turning away and refusing to swing. This idea goes back to the 19th century; *Dick's Quadrille Call-Book* (1878, p. 75) says "he or she may refuse to turn or be turned; may turn alone, or go and get any one else in the Quadrille to turn with." It is unclear whether "the Quadrille" meant one's own set or any set in the hall; the word was used in both senses.

McNair (1951, pp. 102ff) gives the title *Cheat or Swing* to a dance, which Sandy Bradley used to enjoy calling, in which the active couple proceeds around the set, picking up the other gents in turn as their ladies decide whether to swing one or none of them, and then dropping off the other gents to meet their partner at home ("She won't cheat, she'll swing her own").

In the dance of this type that has attained the most popularity in recent decades (see *Ladies' Whirligig* below), "cheat" is given a slightly different definition. When an active person (say a lady) is directed to cheat, she may not swing her partner but must swing someone else – in her set, in another set, or sitting out.

Intermingling Squares

In *Length of the Hall* (below) the dancers leave their original sets, but only to make a continuous round trip to both ends of the hall, returning immediately to their home places. There are other square dance forms that also require the sets to be aligned across and along the hall. Describing them in detail is beyond the scope of this book, but there is plenty of information available, much of it online, for the caller who wishes to explore them.

Grid Squares

This is a relatively recent addition to the multi-square family of dance forms, made popular by New Jersey contra caller Bob Isaacs. The form has much in common with present-day contra dance: There are several set routines, each with its own name. A typical routine has two alternating sequences, each lasting 32 measures of music (64 steps) like most contra dances. The dancers are taken from set to set but retain their partner throughout the dance; no attempt is made to return them to their original square.

Progressive Squares

Ed Gilmore of California popularized this form in the 1960s; Jerry Helt of Ohio made it a trademark throughout his calling career. It grew out of modern square dance, which it resembles: The dancers do not know what call is coming next; the caller may be improvising or calling a series of memorized modules. A distinctive feature is that when the dancers are facing away from the center of their set, those who can are directed to dance with a couple from an adjacent set. The caller's goal is to take the dancers as far away as possible from their partner and their original set, then to reunite couples and squares when the dancers are least expecting it. Typically no attempt is made to synchronize the movements with the phrases of the music (the caller's job is hard enough without that extra challenge).

Jerry Helt was fond of pretending to lose track of the dancers; he would stop the music and act as if he had brought everyone home. When the dancers informed him of his error, he would shrug and tell them to square up with their current partner, on the ground that it was more fun to dance with the "wrong" people than to stand still. He would then launch into a singing call, eventually reuniting everyone to wild acclaim. (Many stage magicians use this feigned-error routine, having discovered that audiences appreciate an effect more if it appears to have required serious effort.)

Exploding Squares

The Exploding Square was originally just one of Ed Gilmore's progressive square routines, named for the way each square appears to burst open. The effect is produced by having all four couples go forward and back, then immediately do a California twirl to migrate to the surrounding sets. (Other progressive squares start by forming lines of four and having the dancers pass through to new sets.) Over the years, "exploding squares" seems to have become a synonym for "progressive squares."

Ladies' Whirligig

This was Ralph Page's name for a dance that has probably existed nearly as long as dancing in squares. In its simplest form it goes like this:

> Lady 1 go out to the right
> Turn your right-hand gent with the right hand round
> Your partner left with the left hand round
> Opposite gent with the right hand round
> Back to your own with the other hand around
> Left-hand gent with the right hand round
> Partner left with the left hand round

From here, there are two main versions. One continues:

> Bird in the cage and seven hands round
> [*silence or patter for 4 beats*]
> Bird hop out and the crow [*gent*] hop in

and can conclude in any number of ways, such as

> Crow hop out with a left allemande

or

> Birdie to the center, swing your crow
> The rest join hands and around you go

The other version, which appears in Ralph Page's syllabus notes as *Whirligig and Cheat,* starts with the sequence of hand turns shown above, then has the active person cheat (leave partner). He or she must swing someone in the same set, in another set, or sitting out. The figure concludes with the actives returning home to swing partners.

Possible patter for this version includes

> Left-hand gent with the right hand round
> Partner left, you're leavin' town
> (from Sandy Bradley)

and

> That one lady cheat 'em and swing
> Anywhere else in the hall or the ring
> (from Louise Winston)

If a longer dance is desired, after each lady (and gent) has had a solo turn, the head and then the side ladies or gents may be called out; it is usual to end by calling all four ladies, then all four gents.

Over time, this dance evolved into *Merry-Go-Round* as called by Ted Sannella (see below). It is unclear how much hashing of this figure Ralph Page did (he certainly hashed several of his squares), but Ted certainly developed it to a fine art.

Length of the Hall

I was fortunate enough to dance this to Ralph Page's calling on more than one occasion. The basic movements used are common; the calls are simple, with barely anything to memorize. However, the dancers must be experienced enough to step out with confidence, and the caller must watch the dancers carefully to see when everyone is back home. It is much more effective to give the next call just before the dancers arrive at home than to wait until they stop moving.

This dance requires a number of square sets – at least four – aligned in both directions (across the hall and along the hall) in a grid pattern. Not all of the following moves need to be included.

> Head couples right and left through
> Right and left back
> Side couples right and left through
> Right and left back

The above calls, while not part of the main figure, are almost necessary for the dancers to "get their motors running."

> Heads right and left the length of the hall

Each head couple proceeds forward through all the possible sets, passing through each couple they meet. Opposites pass right shoulders without taking hands (this was Ralph Page's preferred style for the right and left through). A couple reaching the end of the hall does a courtesy turn to reverse direction and proceeds forward again. Each couple travels to both ends of the formation before returning to its starting place. The timing depends on the distance between squares; if that distance is roughly equal to the width of a set (about 8 feet), the average couple will take 6 to 8 steps to cross one set and cover the distance to the next.

> Sides right and left across the hall

Sides do likewise along their path. If memory serves, Ralph called a partner swing and promenade after every one or two figures.

> Head ladies chain the length of the hall
> [*separately*] Side ladies chain across the hall

To execute the continuous chain, the couples at the ends of the formation (i.e., those with no couple behind them) do a normal courtesy turn to reverse the lady's direction. All other couples do a courtesy turn halfway, so that in effect the gent is merely helping the lady to continue in the direction she was going in. The timing is the same for each chain: 8 steps, whether the courtesy turn is half or full. The dancers should adjust their stride to let the chains fit the musical phrases. The chains within the squares will alternate with the chains between sets. The ladies travel to both extremes of the grid before returning to their partners.

> Heads sashay the length of the hall
> [*separately*] Sides sashay across the hall

This is similar to the "slide across" in *Cumberland Square* (Chapter 17). The active couples face their partner and take a ballroom hold. Using a chassez or step-close, they proceed across the set, keeping to the right of the oncoming couple (the gents will pass back to back). They continue in the same direction, traveling to and through successive sets, until they reach the end of the formation. Without turning, they look over their other shoulder and reverse direction, again keeping to the right (the ladies will pass back to back). Again, each couple travels to both ends of its line of sets before arriving at home.

For many groups this will have been enough. But Ralph had more tricks up his sleeve:

> [*called without a pause*]
> Heads right and left the length of the hall
> Side ladies chain across the hall
> [*and similar combinations*]

This requires careful stepping on the dancers' part, and it is likely that the heads will finish before the sides, or vice versa. It depends partly on how many squares are lined up in each direction. The dancers doing "right and left" will travel faster than the ones chaining, as they are not doing a full right and left through except at the very ends, but only passing through each couple they meet.

When I danced this with Ralph, he finished by calling a sashay for both sets of couples at once. I cannot emphasize too strongly that this was a group of experienced adult dancers. Such a call is not appropriate with any group that has shown the faintest signs of rowdiness; there are several less hazardous ways to liven up a program.

Dip and dive (see Chapter 19 for a dance incorporating it) can be done the length of the hall. However, an even number of couples is required, as Lloyd Shaw (1939 and revised editions) learned the hard way.

Merry-Go-Round

Several square dance figures have been given this name through the years. The one that has become a solid favorite of hundreds of folk-revival dancers is an outgrowth of *Ladies' Whirligig* (see above). Ted Sannella learned the basic framework from Ralph Page and developed its calling into a fine art. It became Ted's showpiece; for many years he called it in the closing session of the New England Folk Festival.

Each lady in turn is "activated" and given a series of instructions to turn or swing various members of her set. Ted's custom was to deliver increasingly outlandish calls as the dance progressed: Lady 1's sequence often adhered closely to the first group of calls shown above under *Ladies' Whirligig*, with hand turns for all the gents. Ladies 2 and 3 might be instructed to turn some ladies as well as the gents, and possibly to swing a few people too. When it came to Lady 4, all bets were off: She would typically be directed to swing almost everyone in the set, including such luminaries as her "partner's corner's partner" and her "corner's partner's corner."

After the ladies have had their day in the sun, the gents may be called out. As with *Ladies' Whirligig*, two active people may be called out at once, and then all four ladies or gents.

If you want to try calling *Merry-Go-Round*, I advise you first to listen to an experienced caller doing it, either live or on a recording. Sannella 2005 includes two audio recordings of Ted calling it, along with printed transcripts, but to get the full effect you really ought to watch a video (lacking an opportunity to dance it yourself). Videos of Tony Saletan and the present author calling the dance on several occasions, including at least three New England Folk Festivals, have been uploaded to YouTube. (Try searching both for "merry-go-round" "square dance" and for "merry-go-round" "neffa".)

Ninepin

A "ninepin" is an extra dancer who stands in the middle of the square to begin the dance. *Ninepin* is in essence a game; the object is to avoid being left without a partner.

I know of two main versions of *Ninepin,* described below. Structured Ninepin requires the dancers to be comfortable with playing gender roles (by any name), but Continuous Ninepin can theoretically be used without regard to gender (though I have never seen it done). In either version, people must be willing to dance assertively. Any dancer who is diffident about seizing a partner when the time comes, or is even somewhat slow to do so, is likely to become a permanent ninepin.

Structured Ninepin

This is the version you will find in most books. The order of the movements may vary; a common sequence goes like this:

> Head couples slide across and back [*avoiding the ninepin*]
> Sides the same
> Heads right-hand star [*perhaps using the ninepin as a hub*]
>   and back by the left
> Sides the same
> Ninepin swing Number 1, Number 2, Number 3, Number 4

The ninepin swings, in turn, each dancer of the opposite gender role. It is possible to have ninepins of both kinds on the floor, but it is less awkward if all the ninepins are playing the same role. The latter case is more common, as this dance is usually chosen only if there is an obvious imbalance of the sexes.

> Now circle five and look alive

The ninepin and the other four dancers playing the same gender role go into the middle and form a ring. The caller can direct them, in any order, to circle left, circle right, and make a right-hand or left-hand star.

> Round and round and round and round and SWING!

You may choose to stop the music when you call "Swing!" Obviously, your musicians must be prepared to stop suddenly and all together. With recorded music, you may cut the volume or touch the pause control.

At this point, each of the five dancers in the center must try to swing someone on the outside of the set, eventually going "home" with them. Whoever fails to get a partner becomes the new ninepin. The routine is usually called about half a dozen times, stopping just before the dancers tire of the game.

Continuous Ninepin

This version, to the best of my knowledge, did not appear in 20th-century books (although there are numerous 19th-century references to a *Ninepin* with improvised calls); I danced it to Ralph Page's calling in the 1960s and 1970s. It is a potentially hilarious undertaking, but even more than the structured version, it requires the dancers to be determined and aggressive in seeking partners – but experienced enough to avoid injury.

The premise here is that the ninepin may cut in whenever the other dancers have both hands free, even if only for an instant. For example, the ninepin may not interfere with a hand turn, a swing, or a courtesy turn in progress. But during an allemande left with the corner, the ninepin (say a gent) may plant himself in Gent 1's home position, such that when Lady 1 leaves her corner she will meet the ninepin for the next call (which could be a swing or a grand right and left), while the current Gent 1, leaving his corner, will be presented not with his partner's face but with the ninepin's back.

The caller's imagination is key here. Of course the movements used must be familiar to the dancers, but they may be called in any order. I believe Ralph had the head or side couples do a lot of things like ladies chain and right and left through. There were certainly many "all-moving" calls like hand turns with partner and corner.

There are no explicit calls addressed to the ninepin, who as mentioned above may cut in at any time. As soon as a dancer finds himself displaced, he must repair to the center and look for a new opportunity. "Tagging back" – cutting out the person who has just cut you out – is not forbidden, but like all other moves in this dance, must be done with care to avoid physical harm.

Judging how long to run this dance-game is more difficult than with the structured variety. If the dancers are spirited in their cutting in (as they should be if you opt to use this dance), there will be many more than one or two cuts per minute. My advice is to run no longer than the longest of traditional structured patter squares – about five minutes, or ten times through a standard tune.

Rip and Snort

This is a fairly straightforward break, almost a basic movement; it is included in this chapter because of the way it is often used. From a circle, one couple is designated as active. The couple across from the active couple must raise their joined hands to form an arch. The active couple moves toward the opposite couple, bringing the adjacent dancers with them; all hands in the circle are retained at this point. The active couple ducks through the arch, releases partner's hand (all other hands are still joined), and separates: The lady moves to her right, the gent to his left, around the outside, still bringing the others with them. The active couple returns home to join partner's hand again; the opposite couple must turn under their own arms to reestablish the original circle.

A typical call is

> Couple 1 you rip and snort
> Down the middle and cut 'em off short
> Lady go right and gent go left
> When you're straight you circle to the left

or

Lady go gee and gent go haw
Circle to the left with your mother-in-law

(A circle left is not obligatory after a rip and snort, but it is probably the most common following call.)

I have seen rip and snort used in two primary ways. One is to call a rip and snort for each couple following its turn in a visiting-couple dance: figure for Couple 1, rip and snort for Couple 1, figure for Couple 2, and so on. The other is to wait until all four couples have led the figure and then call a series of "rips." This is where things can get silly: After all four couples have "ripped," the caller can say "The oldest couple rip and snort," "The youngest couple," etc. "The best-looking couple" often produces an effect similar to "All into the middle." If you think your group will tolerate it, you may call "The most sensuous couple" or a pithier equivalent. The finishing touch is

— — The *smartest* couple
allemande left on your left hand

to which the only appropriate follow-up is Bugs Bunny's "Ain't I a stinker?"

Rose and the Thorn (or A Rose Between Two Thorns)

This is also known as *The Fan Dance* or *The Hat Dance,* depending on the prop used; it is more game than dance. Three chairs are placed side by side at the head of the hall, facing down. The dancers form two lines at the sides of the hall, one of ladies and one of gentlemen. To begin, the lady and the two gents at the top of the lines sit in the chairs, the lady in the center. The band begins a waltz, which they play continuously (a polka or other couple dance tune can also be used). The lady is given a rose, a fan, a hat, or other prop. She flirts with both gents, seeming to offer the prop to each in turn, then changing her mind. Finally she gives the prop to one gent and dances down the center of the hall with the other; the two retire to the ends of the lines. The gent with the prop moves into the center chair; the next two ladies in line sit at his left and right, and he flirts with them, eventually giving the prop to one and dancing with the other. Normally the process is repeated until all have had a turn in the chairs. If the lines are very short, everyone may go through the process twice; if the lines are long, the game may be stopped after the band has played about five minutes.

I love this number because in a sense everyone wins: Either they are chosen or they get to do the choosing. I have used it only with groups that divide naturally into "ladies" and "gents," though I am told that others have had success with it in less binary groups.

Step Right Back & Shoot the Rooster

Step Right Back is a movement that is sometimes used as the key figure of a visiting-couple dance, but can be inserted any time a swing is called, provided the

Chapter 22: Silly Stuff

caller is not phrasing or has allowed for a long swing. It requires the dancers to use a ballroom hold for their swinging.

On the call "Step right back," each couple retains their handhold (lady's right in gent's left), releases their arm holds (lady's left on gent's arm, gent's right around lady's back), and backs away to arms' length. In most versions, they immediately return to ballroom hold and continue swinging. This is normally done twice, with the following call:

> Step right back and watch her smile
> Step right up and swing her awhile
> Step right back and watch her grin
> Step right up and swing her ag'in

A skilled couple can time their moves so that they are at arms' length on the words "smile" and "grin."

To make this a visiting figure, have Couple 1 lead to the right and circle four with Couple 2, then call the four lines above. From there, you have two options: Either call "Yours is fine but I'll swing mine" and have them swing their own partner before Couple 1 moves on to the next, or keep them with their new partners and have Gent 1 take Lady 2 with him. After Couple 1's turn, incorporating three swaps, everyone will have their original corner for a partner (the ladies will have moved one place to their right). Original partners will be reunited after all four couples have led the figure.

With so many repetitions of "step right back," you may want to vary the patter:

> Step right back and hear her laugh
> Step right up, swing once and a half
> Step right back and hear her roar
> Step right up and swing some more

> Step right back, her laughter grows
> Step right up and now propose
> Step right back, hear her guffaw
> That you won't like your mother-in-law
> (Charley Thomas)

"Shoot the rooster" is an addition to "step right back." It was shown to me by Gib Gilbert of Colorado in the 1970s; I have never encountered it elsewhere. On the call "shoot the rooster" and later "shoot the hen," the swinging dancers, now at arms' length, jump twice on both feet. The call goes as follows (4 beats to a line as usual):

> Step right back and shoot the rooster
> [Bang! Bang!] Swing her around just
> like you useter. Step right back and
> shoot the hen [Bang! Bang!]
> Step right up and swing her again.

Gib feigned reluctance to tell me of this break, saying he thought that, being from New England, I was too reserved to enjoy it. I hastened to assure him that I was not offended in the least. However, I have not made the move a regular part of my repertoire, largely because many of my constituents have been of an age when such an undertaking is hard on the shins. I have empathized with such folk increasingly over the years.

Turn Back from a Right and Left Grand

As mentioned in Chapter 15 under "Grand Right and Left," when partners meet in that movement, it is possible to direct just one couple, or just the heads or sides, to go "around your own and the other way home." This will cause people playing the same gender role to take hands; dancers are disoriented by this and the fact that some are going in an unfamiliar direction with fewer visual cues than usual.

23
Them's the Breaks

This chapter includes some introductions, middle breaks, and endings transcribed from my calling over the years. The patter was improvised on the spot, as were some but not all of the sequences. Also here are those of the standard "prefabricated" breaks that I thought would benefit most from call charts. More of my own breaks are in Chapter 8; several "prefab" breaks derived from the grand right and left are described in Chapter 15 under that movement.

Alamo Style

(named by Rickey Holden, 1948)

This break was apparently known as "grand ballonet" in at least some areas before Rickey Holden renamed it in a nod to San Antonio, where he was then living and calling for the recreation department. Under its new name it became popular across the continent in the 1950s. Unfortunately, it lost its charm when modern square dance callers lost the ability to make clear to the dancers where the balances should go in relation to the music. Tradition-based callers have kept it alive; seeing it done by a floor full of dancers in unison (as it was intended) has brought experienced modern callers to tears of joy.

The sequence is simply a grand right and left interrupted by a balance every time the dancers progress to a new person.

Alamo Style
(The Dance Movements)

Square dance break

A.1	Allemande left corner, using a hands-up hold; retaining corner's left hand, give right hand to partner (gents are facing in, ladies out)	8 beats
	All balance forward and back	4 beats
	Turn partner right halfway; retaining partner's right hand, give left hand to next person (ladies are facing in, gents out)	4 beats
A.2	Balance; turn by the left hand halfway to next person	8 beats
	Balance; turn by the right hand halfway to next	8 beats
B.1	Balance; turn by the left halfway to meet partner	8 beats

At this point, partners are facing each other halfway across the set from home, with half of B.1 and all of B.2 available if you are phrasing 1–64. The situation is the same as if partners were meeting after a grand right and left: You may call any combination of do-si-do, swing, or promenade, or you may send the dancers into a standard grand right and left. If you choose the latter move (which takes about 10 steps), the dancers will be home when they meet again, with just enough time for a 6-beat do-si-do and an 8-beat swing. This last sequence is shown on the facing page; the other possibilities should be easy to improvise.

Alamo Style
(The Calls)

Beats:	1	2	3	4
Intro:	—	—	<u>On</u> the	<u>cor</u>ner
A.1:	<u>Al</u>lemande	<u>left</u> in the	<u>A</u>lamo	<u>Style</u>, a
	<u>right</u> to your	<u>part</u>ner,	<u>bal</u>ance a	<u>while</u>
	<u>Bal</u>ance	<u>for</u>ward,	<u>bal</u>ance	<u>back</u>, right
	<u>hand</u> turn	<u>half</u>, go	<u>down</u> the	<u>track</u>
A.2:	<u>Bal</u>ance	<u>up</u> and you	<u>bal</u>ance	<u>down</u>
	<u>Turn</u> by the	<u>left</u> just	<u>half</u>way	<u>round</u>
	<u>Bal</u>ance	<u>to</u> and you	<u>bal</u>ance	<u>fro</u>
	<u>Turn</u> by the	<u>right</u> and	<u>don't</u> be	<u>slow</u>
B.1:	<u>Bal</u>ance a-	<u>gain</u> and	<u>don't</u> just	<u>stand</u>
	<u>Turn</u> by the	<u>left</u> to a	<u>right</u> and left	<u>grand</u>
	<u>Hand</u> over	<u>hand</u> a-	<u>round</u> you	<u>go</u>
	<u>Meet</u> your	<u>part</u>ner,	<u>do</u>-si-	<u>do</u>
B.2:	<u>Back</u> to	<u>back</u>, go	<u>all</u> the way a-	<u>round</u> and
	<u>swing</u> your	<u>part</u>ner	<u>up</u> and	<u>down</u>
	—	—	—	—

[*First line of the next figure goes here*]

Note that cadence calls are traditionally used with this break. If you wish, you may prompt it as follows:

A.1:	<u>Al</u>lemande	<u>left</u> in the	<u>A</u>lamo	<u>style</u>, a
	<u>right</u> to your	<u>part</u>ner,	<u>bal</u>ance a	<u>while</u>, go
	<u>for</u>ward	— Now	<u>turn</u> by the	<u>right</u>
	<u>Half</u>way	<u>round</u> and	<u>bal</u>ance a-	<u>gain</u>, go
A.2:	<u>for</u>ward	— Now	<u>turn</u> by the	<u>left</u>
	<u>Half</u>way	<u>round</u> and	<u>bal</u>ance a-	<u>gain</u>, go
	<u>for</u>ward	— Now	<u>turn</u> by the	<u>right</u>
	<u>Half</u>way	<u>round</u> and	<u>bal</u>ance a-	<u>gain</u>

and so on.

Allemande Thar

(Lloyd Shaw, 1938)

This is the granddaddy of modern square dance breaks. It appears to have been the first genuinely new idea since country-style square dancing (as practiced in the late 19th century) was introduced to the public by several authors in the 1920s. Lloyd Shaw devised it in 1938 but omitted it from his book *Cowboy Dances,* published the following year (which did contain four Shaw originals). Apparently he wanted to save it for his performing group. He finally released it for general use in 1946.

Like several older breaks, this amounts to an interrupted grand right and left. Every time you meet someone with your right hand, you keep it at handshake height and pull by, as in a standard grand right and left. But every time you meet someone with your left hand, you assume a hands-up hold (modern square dancers use a forearm hold) and turn halfway around. This puts the gents in the middle of the set; they form a right-hand wrist star and retain the lady's left hand. The whole formation now moves counterclockwise, the gents walking backward and the ladies forward. On "Shoot that star" or a similar call, the gents release their star and turn halfway with the lady to meet the next lady with the right hand, continuing in grand right and left direction. Twice through the sequence reunites partners: At that point, as in any such break, the caller may opt for a do-si-do, a swing, a promenade, a right-hand turn, or a standard grand right and left.

Allemande Thar

(The Dance Movements)

Square dance break

A.1	Allemande left corner	4–6 beats
	Right hand to partner, pull by	2–4 beats
	Turn next person by left hand, halfway around; gents form a right-hand star but keep the lady	4 beats
	In this formation, gents walk backward, ladies forward	4 beats
A.2	Repeat all of A.1, starting with a left-hand turn with the person currently held	16 beats
B.1	Turn the person you hold now, halfway round to meet partner with right hand (caller's choice from here)	4 beats

Allemande Thar
(The Calls)

Beats:	1	2	3	4
Intro:	—	—	<u>On</u> the	<u>cor</u>ner
A.1:	<u>Allemande</u>	<u>left</u> and	<u>Allemande</u>	<u>Thar</u>, go
	<u>right</u> and	<u>left</u> but	<u>not</u> too	<u>far</u> and the
	<u>gents</u> to the	<u>mid</u>dle with a	<u>right</u>-hand	<u>star</u>, you
	<u>back</u> it	<u>up</u> right	<u>where</u> you	<u>are</u>. Now
A.2:	<u>let</u> that	<u>star</u> thro' the	<u>heav</u>ens	<u>whirl</u>, a
	<u>right</u> and	<u>left</u> to a	<u>brand</u>-new	<u>girl</u>. Now the
	<u>gents</u> to the	<u>center</u> and	<u>star</u> once	<u>more</u>, you
	<u>back</u> it	<u>up</u> a-	<u>round</u> the	<u>floor</u>
B.1:	<u>Shoot</u> that	<u>star</u> and	<u>there's</u> your	<u>own</u>
	<u>Take</u> her by the	<u>hand</u> and	<u>promen</u>ade	<u>home</u>

Substitute your preferred last lines if you choose a movement other than promenade.

As with similar breaks that are shorter than 32 measures (64 beats), this can be used as an introduction, by calling honors during A.1 and starting the break with A.2, or as a middle break or ending, with most of B.1 and all of B.2 available for improvisation.

Triple Allemande

(Vera Holleuffer, 1945)

Vera Holleuffer of Palo Alto was one of the few female callers in California at the beginning of the square dance boom. She was a regular at Stockton Folk Dance Camp and developed a reputation for working with children and teachers of children. Judging by this original break, however, I think she could have made a name on her creativity.

This is one of my favorite "prefab" breaks, not least because it fits nicely into 8-beat phrases and takes up less than one playing of a standard tune. As with most breaks that are based on the grand right and left, how you end it is up to you. It can be used as an introduction, by calling honors during A.1 and starting the break with A.2, or as a middle break or ending as given here.

The break is easier for dancers to learn than it may look at first glance, because the allemande left is done with the same person every time. It should be pointed out that this person will appear quickly when the ladies and gents are traveling in opposite directions.

Triple Allemande
(The Dance Movements)

Square dance break

A.1	Allemande left corner about halfway	4 beats
	Ladies right-hand star while gents promenade in single file counterclockwise	6 beats
	Allemande left same corner about halfway	4 beats
	Gents right-hand star while ladies promenade in single file counterclockwise (start)	2 beats
A.2	Finish the gents' star and ladies' promenade	4 beats
	Allemande left same corner about three-quarters	4 beats
	Right hand to partner, grand right and left	8–10 beats
	(B.1 and B.2 ad lib.)	

Triple Allemande
(The Calls)

Beats:	1	2	3	4
Intro:	<u>All</u> get	<u>set</u> for the	<u>Triple</u> Alle-	<u>mande</u>
A.1:	<u>All</u>emande	<u>left</u>, four	<u>la</u>dies	<u>star</u>, gents
	<u>walk</u> to the	<u>right</u> out-	<u>side</u> the	<u>bar</u>, do an
	<u>alle</u>mande	<u>left</u> and the	<u>gents</u> you	<u>star</u>
	<u>La</u>dies	<u>walk</u> but	<u>not</u> too	<u>far</u>
A.2:	<u>All</u>emande	<u>left</u> on	<u>your</u> left	<u>hand</u>, a
	<u>right</u> to your	<u>honey</u> and a	<u>right</u> and left	<u>grand</u>
	(<u>Hand</u> over	<u>hand</u> and	<u>heel</u> over	<u>heel</u>, the
	<u>long</u>er you	<u>dance</u>, well the	<u>bett</u>er you	<u>feel</u>)

The grand right and left takes up the second half of A.2 (or of B.1 if you have used A.1 for honors), and possibly an additional 2 beats. When partners meet in the grand right and left, you may call a do-si-do, swing, promenade, or "around your own, the other way home."

Introduction: Sound Check

(as called by the author, in the style of Ted Sannella)

This is one of my favorite introductions. Its roots lie in the calling of Ralph Page and Ted Sannella. Ralph was fond of calling "Bow to your partner; swing your partner. Now bow to your corner; swing your partner one more time." This got an embarrassed laugh from the dancers, who were expecting to swing their corner. Ted used this gag too; once his dancers had gotten used to it, he continued to keep them on their toes by sometimes calling "Now bow to your corner; swing... your corner." I don't remember whether I heard the complete sequence, as given here, from Ted or devised the ending myself.

As this sequence relies for its effectiveness on the element of surprise, I have to be careful not to use it too often with the same dance group; you should be too.

During the promenade, I usually say, out of rhythm, "That's called a sound check." This gets a second laugh, but like the sequence itself, it can be overused.

Introduction: Sound Check
(The Dance Movements)

Square dance introduction

A.1	Wait 4 beats; honor partner	8 beats
	Swing partner	8 beats
A.2	Honor corner; wait 4 beats for next call	8 beats
	Swing corner	8 beats
B.1	Allemande left next corner (original opposite), once around	4 beats
	Turn original corner by the right, once and a half	8 beats
	Turn original partner by the left, once around	4 beats
B.2	Promenade partner once around	16 beats

Introduction: Sound Check
(The Calls)

Beats:	1	2	3	4
Intro:	—	—	—	—
A.1:	—	—	—	—
	<u>Bow</u> to your	<u>part</u>ner	—	—
	<u>Swing</u> your	<u>part</u>ner	—	—
	—	—	—	— Now
A.2:	<u>bow</u> to your	<u>cor</u>ner	—	— And
	<u>swing</u>....	— your	<u>cor</u>ner	—
	—	<u>With</u> your	<u>next</u>	<u>cor</u>ner,
	<u>alle</u>-	<u>mande</u>	<u>left</u>	— The
B.1:	<u>one</u> you just	<u>swung</u>,	<u>turn</u> by the	<u>right</u>
	<u>All</u> the way a-	<u>round</u>, a	<u>little</u> bit	<u>more</u>
	<u>Ori</u>ginal	<u>part</u>ner	<u>turn</u> by the	<u>left</u> and
	<u>prome</u>-	<u>nade</u>, go	<u>round</u> the	<u>set</u>
B.2:	—	—	—	—
	—	—	—	—
	—	— Now	<u>square</u> your	<u>sets</u>

[*First line of the next figure goes here*]

Break: No Promenade

(improvised by the author)

This is one of several breaks I used at the Dare To Be Square weekend held at the John C. Campbell Folk School, Brasstown, North Carolina in November 2011. This one was the middle break for *Squareback Reel* (see Chapter 18 for the figure).

As this break has no promenade, it can follow a figure that ends with one (as most figures do); more importantly, it can precede a figure that begins with a promenade, although this is not necessary.

I occasionally begin a break with a circle right, to surprise the dancers. This is a relatively innocuous surprise, as they can easily recover if they have begun circling left. Note that the allemande right with partner flows smoothly from the circle left that follows the circle right. This is the sort of thing to look for when improvising breaks: What is the most comfortable movement to put after the one the dancers are doing now?

Break: No Promenade
(The Dance Movements)

Square dance break (improvised)

A.1	All circle right, halfway around	8 beats
	All circle left, halfway around	8 beats
A.2	Allemande right partner	4 beats
	Allemande left corner	6 beats
	Do-si-do partner	6 beats
B.1	Four gents left-hand star, once around	8 beats
	Allemande right partner	6 beats
	Allemande left corner (start)	2 beats
B.2	Finish the allemande left	4 beats
	Swing partner	12 beats

Break: No Promenade
(The Calls)

Beats:	1	2	3	4
Intro:	<u>Cir</u>cle	— to the	<u>right</u>,	<u>go</u>!
A.1:	—	— [*falsetto*:]	<u>What</u> did he	<u>say</u>?
	<u>Cir</u>cle	<u>left</u>, go the	<u>oth</u>er	<u>way</u>
	—	—	<u>Turn</u> this	<u>part</u>ner
	<u>right</u> hand	<u>round</u>	—	—
A.2:	<u>Look</u> for the	<u>cor</u>ner,	<u>alle</u>mande	<u>left</u>
	— Come	<u>back</u> and	<u>do</u>-si-	<u>do</u> your
	<u>part</u>ner	—	— Four	<u>gents</u>
	<u>left</u> hands	<u>in</u>, a	<u>left</u>-hand	<u>star</u>
B.1:	<u>once</u> a-	<u>round</u>	—	<u>Turn</u> that
	<u>same</u>	<u>part</u>ner	<u>right</u> hand	<u>round</u>
	<u>Look</u> for the	<u>cor</u>ner,	<u>alle</u>-	<u>mande</u>
	<u>left</u>	—	—	<u>Swing</u> this
B.2:	<u>part</u>ner,	<u>eve</u>ry-	<u>bo</u>dy	<u>swing</u>
	—	—	—	—
	—	— Now	<u>square</u> your	<u>sets</u>

[*First line of the next figure goes here*]

Break: The Other Four Star

(as called by the author, in the style of Ted Sannella)

When calling a square that has a change of partners, it is often a good idea to keep the middle break simple. The dancers are with their original opposites, and too complex a break may disorient them. The grand right and left in particular can cause problems: Inexperienced and insecure dancers meeting their original partners may try to keep them.

Therefore, callers are always looking for middle breaks that are interesting but forgiving. This family is one of my favorites.

Most male callers probably start with the version that goes "Four ladies forward and back; four gents right-hand star." I certainly use that one, but I think the first one given below is especially nice: Not only does it give the ladies a chance to star, but the "do-si-do and a little bit more" flows beautifully out of the star and into the promenade.

The second example below adds the element of surprise. I'm pretty sure I got it from Ted Sannella.

Break: The Other Four Star
(The Dance Movements)

Square dance break

A.1	All circle left halfway	8 beats
	All circle right halfway	8 beats
A.2	Four gents forward and back	8 beats
	Four ladies right-hand star	8 beats
B.1	Four ladies left-hand star	8 beats
	Do-si-do partner, about once and a half	8 beats
B.2	Promenade partner once around	16 beats

Variation:

A.1	All circle left halfway	8 beats
	All circle right halfway	8 beats
A.2	One person from each couple go forward and back	8 beats
	The other four right-hand star	8 beats
B.1	The same four left-hand star	8 beats
	Swing partner	8 beats
B.2	Promenade partner once around	16 beats

Break: The Other Four Star
(The Calls)

Beats:	1	2	3	4
Intro:	<u>All</u> join	<u>hands</u> and	<u>circle</u>	<u>left</u>
A.1:	—	—	—	—
	— And the	<u>other</u> way	<u>back</u> to the	<u>right</u>
	—	—	—	—
	<u>Four</u>	<u>gents</u> go	<u>forward</u> and	<u>back</u>
A.2:	—	—	—	— Four
	<u>ladies</u>	— right-	<u>hand</u>	<u>star</u>
	(<u>All</u> the way a-	<u>round</u>, it's	<u>not</u> a	<u>chain</u>) Now
	<u>switch</u> hands	— and a	<u>left</u> hand	<u>back</u>
B.1:	—	— You	<u>come</u> back	<u>home</u> and
	<u>do</u>-si-	<u>do</u>, go	<u>round</u> your	<u>own</u>
	<u>Once</u> a-	<u>round</u> and a	<u>little</u> bit	<u>more</u> and
	<u>prome</u>-	<u>nade</u>, go	<u>round</u> the	<u>floor</u>
B.2:	—	—	—	—
	—	—	—	—
	—	—	—	—

[*First line of the next figure goes here*]

Variation:

Beats:	1	2	3	4
Intro:	<u>All</u> join	<u>hands</u> and	<u>circle</u>	<u>left</u>
A.1:	—	—	—	—
	<u>To</u> the	<u>right</u>, go the	<u>other</u> way	<u>back</u>
	—	<u>From</u> each	<u>couple</u>,	— one
	<u>person</u>	— go	<u>forward</u> and	<u>back</u>
A.2:	—	—	—	— The
	<u>other</u>	<u>four</u> right-	<u>hand</u>	<u>star</u>
	—	—	—	— Now
	<u>change</u>	<u>hands</u> and a	<u>left</u> hand	<u>back</u>
B.1:	—	— You	<u>come</u> back	<u>home</u> and
	<u>swing</u> your	<u>partner</u>,	<u>swing</u> your	<u>own</u>
	—	—	<u>When</u> you're	<u>through</u> you
	<u>prome</u>-	<u>nade</u>, go	<u>two</u> by	<u>two</u>
B.2:	[*Finish as above*]			

Break: Promenade First

(improvised by the author)

I used this as a middle break at Dare To Be Square 2011. As it begins with a promenade, it should be used following a figure that does not end with one. Also, this break does not end with a promenade, so it is appropriate for use preceding a figure that begins with one, although it can be used with almost any figure. The partner swing is a long one; the dancers at this event were all experienced and fond of swinging.

As with many of my breaks, I am fairly certain that I made this one up on the spot, not knowing exactly what I was going to call until I called it. If the thought of doing likewise intimidates you, remember that this skill, like any skill, comes gradually with practice.

Break: Promenade First
(The Dance Movements)

Square dance break (improvised)

A.1	Promenade partner once around	16 beats
A.2	Four ladies chain across	8 beats
	Four ladies chain back	8 beats
B.1	Do-si-do corner	6 beats
	See-saw (left shoulder do-si-do) partner	6 beats
	Allemande left corner (start)	4 beats
B.2	Finish the allemande left	2 beats
	Swing partner	14 beats

Break: Promenade First
(The Calls)

Beats:	1	2	3	4
Intro:	Prome-	nade, a-	round you	roam
A.1:	(Prome-	nade your	partners	all, go
	two by	two a-	round the	hall)
	—	—	—	— And
	all four	ladies	chain a-	cross
A.2:	—	— to your	opposite	gent
	Help them a-	round and	chain	back
	—	—	—	— Now
	look for the	corner,	do-si-	do
B.1:	—	—	— Left	shoulder
	round your	partner	—	—
	Allemande	left your	corner	—
	Come back	home and your	partner	swing
B.2:	Swing with the	great big	handsome	thing
	—	—	—	—
	—	—	—	—

[First line of the next figure goes here]

Break: Single File Twice

(origin uncertain)

I'm sure I heard someone call this sequence exactly as given here, but I'm not sure who. Dick Leger is a likely candidate, as he liked to explore what could be done with standard basics within the confines of the musical phrase. But I'm leaning toward Roger Whynot as my source; he was a great admirer of Leger, and I heard him call on many more occasions than Dick. The final couplet of patter is from Ed Gilmore; obviously, you can substitute any patter or use none at all.

As with all distinctive breaks, I try not to overuse this one, but I think it can stand more repetition than some that rely on an element of surprise.

If this sequence is used as a middle break, it is important to remind the dancers to remember who their current partner is. You can do this before or after the initial call to circle left.

Break: Single File Twice
(The Dance Movements)

Square dance break

A.1	All circle left halfway	8 beats
	All circle right, dropping hands to proceed in single file	8 beats
A.2	Ladies turn solo, right face, to proceed clockwise on the outside; gents keep going counterclockwise	8 beats
	Gents step in behind partner and all go clockwise	8 beats
B.1	Ladies turn solo, left face, to proceed counterclockwise on the outside; gents keep going clockwise	8 beats
	Gents step in behind partner; all go counterclockwise	8 beats
B.2	Gents step up next to partner, on her left; all promenade as couples once around	16 beats

Break: Single File Twice
(The Calls)

Beats:	1	2	3	4
Intro:	<u>All</u> join	<u>hands</u> and	<u>circ</u>le	<u>left</u>
A.1:	—	—	—	—
	— And the	<u>oth</u>er way	<u>back</u> to the	<u>right</u>, drop
	<u>hands</u>, go	<u>sin</u>gle	<u>file</u>	—
	<u>La</u>dies turn	<u>out</u>, go the	<u>oth</u>er way	<u>back</u>
A.2:	<u>Gents</u> keep	<u>go</u>ing on the	<u>same</u> old	<u>track</u>, now the
	<u>gents</u> step	<u>in</u> be-	<u>hind</u> your	<u>lady</u> and
	<u>fol</u>low her	—	— A-	<u>gain</u>,
	<u>la</u>dies turn	<u>out</u>, go the	<u>oth</u>er way	<u>back</u>
B.1:	<u>Gents</u> keep	<u>go</u>ing,	<u>same</u>	<u>track</u>
	<u>Gents</u> step	<u>in</u> be-	<u>hind</u> her a-	<u>gain</u> and
	<u>fol</u>low her	—	—	<u>Now</u> the
	<u>gents</u> move	<u>up</u> and	<u>prome</u>-	<u>nade</u>, (you go
B.2:	<u>two</u> by	<u>two</u>, now	<u>get</u> away	<u>round</u> with a
	<u>big</u> foot, a	<u>lit</u>tle foot, a-	<u>pattin</u>' on the	<u>ground</u>)
	—	—	—	—

[*First line of the next figure goes here*]

Break: Stars and Turns

(improvised by the author)

I used this as the middle break when I called *The Rout(e)* (see Chapter 18) at Dare To Be Square 2011. I rather assume I was making it up as I went along, as I often do. I may or may not have called these movements in the same order before.

This break is included here as an example of how 6-beat movements can flow into one another to constitute a smooth sequence using exactly 64 beats (once through a standard tune). You can learn a lot by comparing the notation below with the call chart on the facing page.

The ladies' first star does not have to go all the way around because they will return to their starting point with the second star.

Notice that some movements are danced across the phrase; if the calling is clear and assertive and the command words are put in the right place, the dancers are unlikely to notice. (However, I would be less likely to use this sort of break with "tunes that tell a story" than with "straight-ahead tunes.")

Break: Stars and Turns
(The Dance Movements)

Square dance break (improvised)

A.1	Do-si-do corner	6 beats
	See-saw (left shoulder do-si-do) partner	6 beats
	Four gents right-hand star, once around (start)	4 beats
A.2	Finish the star	4 beats
	Turn partner by left hand, once and a quarter	6 beats
	Turn corner by right hand, once around	6 beats
B.1	Turn partner by left hand, once around	6 beats
	Four ladies right-hand star	6 beats
	Ladies left-hand star (start)	4 beats
B.2	Finish the star	2 beats
	Do-si-do partner	6 beats
	Swing partner	8 beats

Break: Stars and Turns
(The Calls)

Beats:	1	2	3	4
Intro:	<u>Do</u>-si-	<u>do</u> your	<u>cor</u>ners	<u>all</u>
A.1:	—	—	— Left	<u>shoul</u>der
	<u>do</u>-si-	<u>do</u> your	<u>part</u>ner	— Four
	<u>gents</u>	— Right-	<u>hand</u>	<u>star</u>
	<u>Once</u> a-	<u>round</u> but	<u>not</u> too	<u>far</u>
A.2:	<u>Turn</u> your	<u>part</u>ner	<u>left</u>	—
	<u>Turn</u> your	<u>cor</u>ner	<u>by</u> the	<u>right</u>
	—	—	<u>Turn</u> your	<u>part</u>ner
	<u>by</u> the	<u>left</u>	—	— Four
B.1:	<u>la</u>dies	— <u>right</u>-	<u>hand</u>	<u>star</u>
	<u>in</u> the	<u>mid</u>dle	—	<u>Change</u>
	<u>hands</u>,	<u>left</u>-	<u>hand</u>	<u>star</u>
	<u>Get</u> back	<u>home</u>,	<u>do</u>-si-	<u>do</u> your
B.2:	<u>part</u>ner	—	—	— And
	<u>swing</u> your	<u>part</u>ner,	<u>part</u>ner	<u>swing</u>
	—	—	—	—

[*First line of the next figure goes here*]

Ending: Double Turn Back

(from the calling of Ed Gilmore)

Calling a turn back from a grand right and left has been traditional in country-style square dancing for many decades; Herb Greggerson of Texas and Lloyd Shaw of Colorado both mention it in their 1939 books. Ed Gilmore of California, who delighted in ringing all the possible changes on traditional figures, may not have been the first caller to incorporate a double turn back, but as a traveling caller and recording artist, he was in a position to influence the repertoire of hundreds of disciples.

This is probably my favorite ending, but like all unusual sequences, it should not be used too often.

Ending: Double Turn Back
(The Dance Movements)

Square dance ending

A.1	Allemande left corner	6 beats
	Right hand to partner, grand right and left halfway	10 beats
A.2	Turn partner by right halfway around	4 beats
	Grand right and left the wrong way	8 beats
	Turn partner by right halfway around	4 beats
B.1	Grand right and left in the normal direction	8 beats
	Promenade partner halfway to end at home	8 beats
B.2	Honor partner, corner, opposite	16 beats

Note: Some of these times are approximate. When one movement flows into another, it can be difficult to say when one ends and the next begins.

Ending: Double Turn Back
(The Calls)

Beats:	1	2	3	4
Intro:	<u>A</u>llemande	<u>left</u> with your	<u>cor</u>ners	<u>all</u>
A.1:	— Right	<u>hand</u> to your	<u>part</u>ner,	<u>grand</u>
	<u>right</u> and	<u>left</u>, go	<u>round</u> the	<u>land</u>
	—	—	—	— Go a-
	<u>round</u> your	<u>own</u> and the	<u>oth</u>er way	<u>home</u>, turn
A.2:	<u>half</u> by the	<u>right</u> go the	<u>oth</u>er way	<u>home</u>
	—	—	—	— When you
	<u>meet</u> this	<u>time</u>, turn	<u>back</u> a-	<u>gain</u>, you're
	<u>still</u>	<u>go</u>ing	<u>wrong</u>	— Well,
B.1:	<u>now</u> you're	<u>right</u> and you	<u>can't</u> go	<u>wrong</u>, gonna
	<u>meet</u> 'em this	<u>time</u> and	<u>prom</u>enade a-	<u>long</u>, you
	<u>prome</u>-	<u>nade</u>, go	<u>right</u> back	<u>home</u> and
	<u>stop</u> right	<u>there</u>, no	<u>more</u> to	<u>roam</u>, you
B.2:	<u>bow</u> to your	<u>part</u>ner	—	— And
	<u>bow</u> to your	<u>cor</u>ner	—	— You
	<u>wave</u> to your	<u>op</u>posite a-	<u>cross</u> the	<u>hall</u> and
	<u>that's</u> the	<u>end</u> of	<u>this</u> old	<u>call</u>

Alternatives to the last line:

	<u>hold</u> your	<u>sets</u> for	<u>one</u> more	<u>call</u>
	<u>that's</u> the	<u>end</u> of the	<u>sec</u>ond	<u>call</u>
	<u>that's</u> the	<u>end</u> of a	<u>mixed</u>-up	<u>call</u>

Ending: Pull the Corner By

(from the calling of Ed Gilmore)

Through the wonders of modern technology, I learned this break from Ed Gilmore, a master caller whom I never met. It appears on his Decca LP, *Square Dance Party,* which also contains *Fiddle Faddle* and several other enjoyable figures.

Ed used it as part of an introduction, going from the second swing into an allemande left and grand right and left. I have arranged it here as an ending because when timed comfortably it barely fits a 32-measure (64-beat) tune. If you are not phrasing 1–64 or are using a 48-measure tune, you will have more leeway to add to the sequence.

Ending: Pull the Corner By
(The Dance Movements)

Square dance ending

A.1	Allemande left corner	6 beats
	Turn partner by right once around	6 beats
	Left hand to corner, pull straight by	4 beats
A.2	Swing the next person (original opposite); end facing center, leaving lady on right of gent	8 beats
	Allemande left new corner (orig. next-door neighbor)	6 beats
	Turn current partner by right once around (start)	2 beats
B.1	Finish the right-hand turn	4 beats
	Left hand to corner, pull straight by	4 beats
	Swing original partner (roughly across from home)	8 beats
B.2	Promenade partner home	8 beats
	Honor partner and corner	8 beats

Ending: Pull the Corner By
(The Calls)

Beats:	1	2	3	4
Intro:	—	—	<u>On</u> the	<u>cor</u>ner
A.1:	<u>Alle</u>mande	<u>left</u> your	<u>cor</u>ner	— and
	alle<u>mande</u>	<u>right</u> your	<u>own</u>	— Give a
	<u>left</u> to the	<u>cor</u>ner and you	<u>pull</u> 'em on	<u>by</u>
	<u>Swing</u> the	<u>next</u> one	<u>on</u> the	<u>fly</u>
A.2:	<u>Swing</u> that	<u>new</u> one	<u>high</u> and	<u>low</u>, put the
	<u>lady</u> on the	<u>right</u> and	<u>don't</u> be	<u>slow</u>
	<u>Alle</u>mande	<u>left</u> new	<u>cor</u>ner	— and
	alle<u>mande</u>	<u>right</u> this	<u>part</u>ner	— Give a
B.1:	<u>left</u> to the	<u>cor</u>ner and you	<u>pull</u> 'em on	<u>by</u>
	<u>Swing</u> your	<u>part</u>ners	<u>way</u> up	<u>high</u>
	<u>Swing</u> your	<u>part</u>ner	<u>round</u> and	<u>round</u> and
	<u>prome</u>-	<u>nade</u> a-	<u>round</u> the	<u>town</u>
B.2:	<u>prome</u>-	<u>nade</u>, go	<u>right</u> back	<u>home</u> and
	<u>stop</u> right	<u>there</u>, no	<u>more</u> to	<u>roam</u>, gonna
	<u>bow</u> to your	<u>part</u>ners,	<u>cor</u>ners	<u>too</u>
	<u>That's</u> the	<u>end</u>, that's	<u>it</u>, we're	<u>through</u>

Glossary

This glossary contains most of the terms a caller of neo-traditional squares is likely to encounter; not all of them are used in the body of this book. I have attempted to include the majority of terms found in 20th-century books on traditional squares. In addition, I have included a handful of terms used chiefly in the world of modern square dancing; some are adaptable to neo-traditional choreography, some are of historical interest.

Many terms used in the definitions are themselves defined at their proper place. Browsing is strongly encouraged.

If you don't find a term here, it may be the name of a visiting-couple figure (of which there are dozens) or a modern square dance movement (of which there are literally thousands, although only a few hundred are in current use and most dancers know about 100).

Attributions of originator and date are taken from *Instant Hash* (Holden & Litman 1962), *The Handbook of Modern Square Dancing* by Jay King (1976), and a 1950 Rickey Holden syllabus (Square Dance History Project item #1304).

Entries marked with an asterisk (*) are treated more fully in Chapter 15. To save space, some points made in that chapter are not mentioned here.

"A" The first part of a square or contra dance tune, normally 16 beats (8 measures) in length and normally repeated.

A.1, A.2 The first and second playing of the "A" part of a tune.

AABB The standard pattern of most tunes used for square and contra dancing.

AABBCC The pattern of a three-part (48-measure or 96-beat) dance tune.

Across In a square, with or toward the person or couple that one is already facing, as in "Ladies chain across the set" in the dance *The Rout(e)*. In a progressive circle, toward the wall or the center of the circle, as opposed to "around."

Active couple The couple that initiates a figure.

Address An old word for **honor.**

Advanced In modern square dancing, the fourth of five programs a dancer may learn; divided into subgroups A1 and A2. Before the advent of Callerlab, "advanced" was a nebulous term indicating a more difficult level than the average club maintained, in number and/or usage of movements.

Alamo Style A break constituting a grand right and left interrupted by balances: All allemande left corner, retain the left-hand hold, and give right hand to partner to form a circle with gents facing in and ladies facing out ("Alamo ring"). All balance, turn by the right hand halfway, give left hand to the next person, balance again, turn by the left hand halfway, and so on until partners are reunited across the set from home position. At this point (as in a plain grand right and left) the caller may call a do-si-do, swing, promenade, or other movement. The term was introduced by Rickey Holden in 1948; according to Holden, the break already existed under the name "grand ballonet." It was also danced without a formal name in Iowa and Canada (*Sets in Order,* May 1950, p. 22). See Chapter 23 for a call chart.

All around the left-hand lady Originally, the ladies went forward and back while the gents danced in a clockwise loop around their corners, starting behind the ladies (outside the set) and returning in front of them (inside the set), always traveling forward. Modified during the 1950s into an ordinary right shoulder do-si-do with corner. Usually followed by **see-saw your pretty little taw.**

All eight chain A break from the "transitional" era, introduced in 1955 by Cleo Harden. All give right hand to corner, pass by, give left hand to original opposite, do a courtesy turn with them, and square the set. Ladies have moved one place to the right, gents one place to the left. Repeating the sequence will reunite partners across from home.

Allemande A **hand turn.** The word is not a corruption of the French "à la main" ("by the hand"); rather, it is the French word for "German."

Allemande A One of the earliest truly complex breaks, introduced in 1949 by Joel Orme. All do an allemande left with the corner, give right to partner, give left to the next person for a moment, and with that person do a half sashay and re-sashay full around. The four gents then make a right-hand star halfway across, turn the lady there (original corner) by the left, give right to new corner (original opposite), pull by, and swing the next (original right-hand lady). The break was usually called twice; to get everyone home with partner, "gents cross the set and swing the opposite" would be called between the two sequences or after the second one.

Allemande Alphabet An informal grouping of breaks whose calls started with "Allemande left and allemande [letter]." Modeled on Lloyd Shaw's Allemande Thar (sometimes called and written as "Allemande R") and Ray Smith's Allemande O, many were devised in the early 1950s. Some were fairly complex and perhaps not intended for widespread or long use, but written merely to fill out the alphabet. One wag wrote "Allemande left and Allemande W, there's no such call so don't let it trouble you."

Allemande left A left-hand turn, nearly always with corner. Usually, but not always, followed by a grand right and left starting with partner.

Allemande left just one A signal that the allemande left will not be followed by a grand right and left. Usually called after a corner swing that results in a change of partner; the allemande left is done with the new corner. The complete call is "Allemande left just one, And promenade the one you swung."

Allemande O A break consisting of a grand right and left interrupted by a do paso every time the dancers meet someone with a left hand (see Chapter 15 under grand right and left). Introduced in 1947 by Raymond Smith.

Allemande right A right-hand turn, often with partner, often following an allemande left with corner. Some sources suggest the term originally meant an allemande left with the (gent's) right-hand lady.

Allemande Thar A break constituting a grand right and left interrupted by stars: All allemande left corner, give right hand to partner and pass by, turn the next person by the left halfway around, retain the left-hand hold, and the gents form a right-hand star; the star turns, gents backing up and ladies going forward. On the call "Shoot the star," gents break the star and turn the same lady by the left halfway around, give right hand to the next person (in grand right and left direction) and pass by, turn the next person by the left halfway and form the "thar star" again. A second "shoot the star" will bring partners together, at which point (as in a plain grand right and left) the caller may call a do-si-do, swing, promenade, or other movement. Also known as Allemande R. Introduced in 1938 by Lloyd Shaw, Allemande Thar was perhaps the first term added to the square dance vocabulary in the modern era. Shaw later voiced concern about the proliferation of new material. See Chapter 23 for a call chart.

Allemande Whee A break, introduced in 1950 by Phil Monroe, who claimed to have devised it on the fly: "Allemande left and Allemande Whee, Go right and left and turn back three. Count them, folks, and have a little fun, One, two, three and turn back one." This should get everyone facing in grand right and left direction, toward their original corner; all turn corner once and a half to meet partner for a grand right and left. Also known as Allemande E.

Allemande X One of the simpler allemande breaks: "Allemande left with an Allemande X, Pass your partner, swing the next."

All the way around (1) In a hand turn or other circular move, an instruction to go once around. (2) In a grand right and left, an instruction to partners when they meet across from home to pass by the right hand and continue the movement until they are reunited at home.

Along the line Same as **in line.**

Angel In modern square dancing, a dancer who has taken a course of lessons and attends another similar class in order to assist the learners, particularly by filling places in square sets where needed.

Appalachian style See **Southern style.**

Arch* Two dancers raise their joined hands to let one or more other dancers pass under the space between them. In most squares the arching dancers are side by side and have only nearest hands joined; in a few dances (such as *Virginia Reel*) the arching dancers face each other and join both hands.

Arkansaw See **Girl from Arkansaw.**

Arky style In modern square dancing, a term indicating that some couples are "half-sashayed"; that is, the lady and gent have exchanged places. In such a sequence, dancers playing the same gender role will come in contact more than usual. The term comes from *Arkansas Star* (written by Cal Golden in 1950), a variation on *Texas Star* in which the heads or sides, rather than the gents, form the star that becomes the star promenade.

Arm turn (1) An **elbow swing** (definition 1). (2) In modern square dancing, a move that has largely supplanted the hand turn: Two dancers place their right (or left) forearms together so that each one's hand presses the other one's arm just below the elbow (never gripping with the thumb) and they move forward around each other.

Around In a progressive circle, toward the next group or subset (clockwise or counterclockwise around the large circle), as opposed to "across."

Around your own A New England call (in full, "Around your own and the other way home") for a **turn back** (definition 2) from a grand right and left.

Away You Go A break combining Allemande O and Allemande Thar. The gents lead into a thar star from the final left-hand turn in each do paso. Introduced by Jack Hoheisal in 1948.

"B" The second part of a square or contra dance tune, normally 16 beats (8 measures) in length and normally repeated.

B.1, B.2 The first and second playing of the "B" part of a tune.

Back In breaks derived from the grand right and left, the direction opposite to the one in which the dancers normally progress during that movement: "Back" is clockwise for the gents, counterclockwise for the ladies. The term is not an instruction to walk backward.

Back to back Just what it says. The most common example is for either the ladies or gents to move to the center and stand back to back while the other four dancers promenade single file around them. (In English country dancing, "back to back" is the equivalent of the American **do-si-do,** definition 1.)

Backtrack (1) From a single file promenade, the ladies or gents move "out" (away from the center of the set) and turn alone to move in the opposite direction. (2) From a couple promenade, the two dancers turn individually without dropping hands and promenade in the opposite direction; if the lady was on the gent's right, she is now on his left. If the dancers are in front skaters' position, they turn toward each other; if in back skaters' or varsovienne position, they both turn to their right. Compare **wheel around.**

Balance* In New England style, dance forward or to the (usually right) side for two beats, then return to place in two beats. Often during a sideways balance the free foot is swung across in front of the other leg (a step-swing balance). In other regional styles, can mean a quick bow or acknowledgment, especially before a swing; can also be a synonym for "travel" (for instance, after a round of visiting, "first couple balance home").

Balance four in line In a line of four people, alternately facing in opposite directions (now generally known as a wave), do a New England balance. The formation dates back at least to the first quadrilles of the early 19th century.

Balance in In southern style, often a synonym for "All forward and back."

Ball of yarn See **Wind up the ball of yarn.**

Ballonet Has various meanings, but most commonly refers to a balance in a circle with half the dancers facing in and half facing out. See also **do-si-ballonet.** (In recordings I have heard, the "t" is generally pronounced.)

Ballroom hold The most common swing position in many regions. Gent's right arm is around the lady's back; lady's left arm rests on gent's right arm; gent's left hand and lady's right hand are joined. Similar to the common waltz position, but partners should be offset so each person is slightly to his/her own left and perceives partner as being slightly to the right. Each person's feet should be clear of the other's, making it possible to use either a walking step or a buzz step without the feet getting tangled.

Banner raid A custom in modern square dancing designed to encourage inter-club visitation. Eight or more dancers from Club A attend an event run by Club B to earn the right to "steal" Club B's banner and display it in their hall. To retrieve the banner, Club B must reciprocate by visiting a Club A dance.

Bar A musical term. Strictly speaking, a bar is the vertical line that separates two measures, but in common parlance "bar" is used as a synonym for "measure" (as in "a 32-bar tune").

Barn dance (1) An evening with a more or less rustic flavor that includes several types of dancing, typically the local form of square or other group dancing alternating with the currently popular form(s) of freestyle couple dancing. Among present-day callers, the term is often used to mean an event at which the guests are not regular dancers and do not expect any particular form of square or contra dancing. See **one-night stand.** (2) A dance in slow 4/4 meter (schottische tempo), especially one of several short choreographed routines that have traditionally been danced between square sets.

Basic (1) A dance movement with a name to which dancers have been taught to respond. A dance figure is usually a sequence of basics. (2, *capital B*) In modern square dancing, the first of five programs a dancer may learn.

Basket A circle of dancers with arms interlaced, either in front or in back of their bodies. Each dancer holds the hands of the next-but-one on both sides. There are several ways of getting into position. Typically, dancers in a basket move to the left (clockwise), using a buzz step or a walking step.

Beat The fundamental unit of choreography. Movements are classified by the number of musical beats (downbeats) it takes to dance them. Normally, dancers will take one step on each beat, unless using a buzz step or a two-step.

Beau In some situations in modern square dancing, the person on the left-hand side of a couple or occupying the position historically taken by the gent.

Belle In some situations in modern square dancing, the person on the right-hand side of a couple or occupying the position historically taken by the lady.

Bend the line* The centermost dancers in a line release hands, and each half of the line pivots to face the other half. Named by Bill Hansen in 1957, though similar movements had long been done.

Big circle A circle of couples, all facing the center with partners side by side, as distinguished from a progressive circle or small circle.

Big circle figure One of several figures traditionally done by the entire group at the beginning and end of a southern set, with a series of small circle figures as the central part of the dance.

Big set Can mean a **big square** or a southern set that begins and ends in a **big circle.**

Big square A square set with multiple couples on each side, taking up the entire dancing space. If figures are to be danced by pairs of facing couples, the two head lines must have an equal number of couples, as must the two side lines. The formation has been observed in Prince Edward Island (Linnell & Winston 1974) and Quebec. Compare **double square, tandem square.**

Bird or **birdie**   The active lady in the dance *Bird in the Cage*. The corresponding name for the active gent is "crow." Some callers use "birdies" and "crows" as semi-gendered role terms at family dances.

Biscuit swing   A name for a swing in ballroom position. Used in the West and Southwest during the traditional and transitional eras. See "Historical Notes" under "Swing" in Chapter 15.

Bluegrass   A musical style, developed in the 1940s from blues, jazz, and old-time string band music, in which the players take turns on melody and often improvise as jazz musicians do. Although associated in the public mind with square dancing, it was developed for concert work; however, many recordings have since been made in bluegrass style for the square dance market.

Body   The **figure** of a square dance as distinguished from the **break.** The term was used in the early 1950s by Joe Lewis, who referred to breaks as "mixers."

Boomps-a-daisy   A call directing partners or corners to bump adjacent hips. Often delivered as "Clap your hands, slap your knees, boomps-a-daisy if you please." Can also indicate that partners are to stand back to back and bend quickly at the waist, using the resulting bump to propel them around the outside of the set. Probably derived from Hands, Knees, and Boomps-a-Daisy, a song and accompanying dance that was a fad in Great Britain in the 1930s. Also spelled bumps-a-daisy.

Boom years   The period following World War II when square dancing developed into a national craze in the United States and, to varying extents, in Canada, the United Kingdom, and Australia.

Bounce around   A regional name for a back to back **do-si-do** or an **all around** and **see-saw.** The call is "Bounce around your corner, bounce around your partner." Also known as dance around.

Bouquet waltz   Two circles of three or more people rotate clockwise while revolving around the other circle counterclockwise (the same traffic pattern followed by couples doing a freestyle waltz). The name may come from a mishearing of "pokey," which in turn may be a corruption of "polka."

Box formation   A square dance formation in which two couples are back to back in the center, each facing an outside couple that is facing in. The outside dancers are in their own or another couple's home position. The term is used primarily by modern square dance callers but can be useful in understanding neo-traditional choreography.

Box star   Another name for the wrist hold in a star.

Box the flea   A box the gnat done with left hands. Around 1960 some influential modern callers changed the term to "swat the flea" to keep dancers from automatically using right hands when they heard "Box."

Box the gnat*   Two facing dancers join right hands and exchange places (and facing directions), the lady going under the gent's arm. The term, common in modern square dancing, is sometimes used loosely by traditional callers to mean any kind of **twirl to swap.** (Until the early 1950s the term meant different types of turn-unders in different parts of the West.)

Bracket A name used in Australia for a set of dances (ballroom or square) done with the same partner.

Break (noun) A sequence called between square dance figures as a change of pace. Typically it is easier than the figure and involves the whole set; it never ends with a partner change. (In the 1950s there were complex breaks that changed partners, but they were always repeated, or another call was inserted, to reunite partners before the next figure.)

Break (verb) To release a handhold; the most common instances are an active gent dropping his left hand to let a couple into his circle, or to transform a circle into a straight line.

Break and trail In traditional western style, to release hands from a circle left and reverse direction into a single file promenade counterclockwise.

Break down Of a set, to have enough dancers out of place to make on-the-fly recovery impossible.

Breakdown (1) A lively dance tune in 2/4 meter, similar to a reel but with less clearly defined phrasing. Also known as a hoedown. (2) A square dance figure in which all four couples are active at once, traditionally the third and last number in a set of squares. A breakdown, almost by definition, involves a partner change; in some communities it is danced in a big circle, either as a mixer or until partners are reunited. (3) A set of three changes done with the same partner. This appears to be a rare usage (N. Roy Clifton of Toronto in the liner notes to his 1958 Folkways LP). (4) In the past, a form of percussive dance and also a group dance similar to a southern big set, both observed in African-American communities.

Break to a line See **circle to a line**.

Buckdancing A form of solo **percussive dance**.

Buckle up four Occasionally heard as a synonym for **circle four**.

Bull-by-the-tail A colloquial name for the **straight-arm hold**.

Bumps-a-daisy See **boomps-a-daisy**.

Butterfly whirl (1) A solo turn by a dancer who is part of a circle or a single file promenade. (2) A fast turn by a couple who are side by side with near arm around each other's waist. The context of the dance will dictate who backs up (usually the gent) and how far to turn.

Buzz step The usual footwork for a swing in eastern style; often used in other styles. On the downbeat, each dancer steps forward solidly on the right foot; on (or just after) the upbeat, each dancer steps lightly on the left foot just behind (and to the left of) the right foot. The action is akin to limping; many authors have compared it to riding a scooter, but this can make the dancers think they should keep their right foot on a single spot (impossible when two people are going around each other).

"C" The third part of a three-part (48-measure) dance tune, normally 16 beats (8 measures) in length and normally repeated.

C.1, C.2 The first and second playing of the "C" part of a tune.

Cadence call A call given on (rather than before) the musical phrase during which the dancers are expected to execute it. Obviously the dancers must be familiar with the routine. Common examples are the traditional calls for *Right Hand High, Left Hand Low* and the "one, two, three, turn" in the grand square.

California style A name used in the 1950s for square dancing as done in California, particularly southern California. It developed out of traditional western style, especially as interpreted by Lloyd Shaw, and exerted an increasing influence on square dancing nationwide. Around 1960 the term dropped out of use and was replaced by "modern western" or simply "modern."

California twirl* A lady and a gent, side by side with the lady on the right, join near hands, raise them, and move into each other's place, the lady going under the gent's arm. They end side by side, facing in the opposite direction. The lady is still on the gent's right. Named by Jim York in 1953; until then it was termed a "dishrag turn" or performed without a call in certain dances, such as *Dip and Dive Six*. In the late 1950s there was an attempt to rename this movement "frontier whirl," but the California name has persisted.

California whirl A mirror image of a California twirl (frontier whirl), done by a gent with the lady on his left (typically his corner in a big circle or when squared up at home). The term was coined by Ed Gilmore in 1951 and was current for a short time. It was dropped, no doubt, because the name was too similar to "California twirl" (which immediately gained acceptance); even when "frontier whirl" was proposed to replace the latter term, many dancers still remembered the old name. Also known as "turn your corner under."

Call As a noun, can mean an entire dance number, one line of a number, or a single basic movement.

Callerlab A professional organization of callers that, since the 1970s, has issued guidelines for modern square dance choreography, including precise definitions of each basic movement. Callerlab has grouped the movements into five programs for dancers to learn: Basic, Mainstream, Plus, Advanced (A1 and A2), and Challenge (C1 through C4). The current Basic program includes about twice as many named movements as the average neo-traditional caller uses.

Carry-o-swing A name for a **traveling swing.**

Cast off To separate from an adjacent active dancer and move around one or more inactive dancers to a new position. In a whole-set longways dance, the actives typically travel all the way to the foot, often with the other dancers following. In a contra dance, the actives usually each go around one inactive dancer to end next to him or her. The term was rarely used in squares until 1956, when California callers started using it from a line of four in preference to "break in the middle and hinge on the ends" (*Let's Dance,* Jan. 1957, p. 24).

Catch all eight Partners turn by the right hand about halfway around, then change hands (sometimes clapping once, on the fourth beat of the move) and turn by the left hand, either once or once and a half to another person as dictated by the next call.

Ceilidh A Gaelic word (pronounced "kay-lee") for a gathering with singing and/or dancing. In England, can be a synonym for **barn dance** (definition 1).

Glossary

Center The exact center of a square or circle, or the area inside a set as opposed to outside it.

Center(s) (1) The dancer(s) in the middle of a line of three or four, as distinguished from the ends. (2) The dancers or couples closest to the center of the set in any formation where this distinction can be made.

Chain See **gents chain, grand chain, ladies chain.**

Chaîne anglaise (French for "English chain") A 19th-century term for **right and left.**

Chain the route Another term for **rout(e) chain.**

Challenge In modern square dancing, the fifth and most complex program a dancer may learn; divided into subgroups numbered C1 through C4.

Change (1) A single call line (a rare usage). (2) The figure of a square dance (as in "Jim knows 30 different changes"). (3) An entire square (figures and breaks) done as one of a set of two or three. In Ontario the third change is called "the breakdown"; in Michigan it was known as "the jig figure" (Ryan 1926/1939); in New York state both terms have been used. (4) One iteration (partner left, corner right) of the Texas do-si-do, as in "One more change and on you go." (5) In English country dancing, one hand or shoulder pass in a hey.

Chant call A patter call in which every word is delivered on a musical pitch rather than spoken; loosely, any patter call.

Chassez The French term (pronounced "shassay") that was corrupted into **sashay.** The word is the imperative form of *chasser*, "to hunt" or "to chase," which aptly describes the step (one foot chases the other).

Cheat To refuse to swing the expected person, and often to swing someone else instead. Almost always done humorously in a context where it is socially acceptable, as in the dances *Cheat or Swing* and *Whirligig and Cheat.*

Chicken Plucker A figure written by Bill Shymkus in the mid-1950s, similar to Ed Gilmore's *Ends Turn In* but with a higher percentage of shuttling across the set, with no really inactive couples. Veteran caller Jim Mayo says it marked a major change in square dance choreography.

Chorus (1) Sometimes used as a synonym for **break.** (2) A musical term for the best-known portion of a popular song; hence, one playing of a singing-call tune (which usually coincides with the musical chorus); hence, one playing of a fiddle tune (as in "On this recording the banjo takes the lead on the third chorus").

Circle* As a noun, three or more dancers with hands joined to form a closed ring. As a verb, to travel to the left or right in such a ring. Circles traditionally move to the left (clockwise) if not otherwise specified.

Circle contra Another name for a **progressive circle.** Such a dance is a true contra in that the figure is repeated, move for move, an indefinite number of times, the dancers moving to a new neighbor couple each time.

Circle to a line* Two active couples lead to their right and circle with their right-hand couple; the active gents break with their left hand and lead their circle into a straight line in the inactive couple's position.

Class level In modern square dancing, a level of complexity that members of a learners' class can dance without much difficulty. A class level ball may be given for the learners from classes sponsored by one or more area clubs, using only the basic movements and concepts they have learned to that point.

Clipped timing Timing that does not allow enough beats for the dancers to execute one or more movements comfortably. Compare **split timing**.

Clog dancing or **clogging** A form of **percussive dance** that can be done by solo dancers or incorporated into group dance routines.

Closed dance See **open dance.**

Closed position A name used in ballroom dancing and round dancing for the hand-and-arm hold used in waltzing.

Club dancing or **club style** A common name for **modern square dancing,** which is nearly always organized into formal clubs (and associations or federations of clubs). Not commonly used by modern square dancers or callers, some of whom object to the term.

Club level In modern square dancing, a term used widely in the 1950s and '60s to mean the prevailing program done by fully qualified dancers at a given club, as opposed to "class level." The term was always ambiguous, as such programs varied from one area to the next; it fell out of use when the present five Callerlab programs were instituted.

Colorado-California style Another name for **California style,** referring to the tremendous influence that Coloradan Lloyd Shaw had on the development of recreational square dancing in southern California in the 1940s and early 1950s.

Command A word or group of words that tells the dancers what to do, using everyday English, standard basics with recognized names, or both.

Command call A **patter call** as opposed to a singing call. Appears to be the normal term in upstate New York; has been used elsewhere.

Community dance (1) An event or a series of events at which the public is welcome but a majority of people attending have some dance experience (as distinguished from a modern square dance club or a one-night stand). (2) A one-night stand as distinguished from an ongoing dance series. (Author's note: I can discern no consensus among dance leaders on the meaning of this term, and therefore I do not find it useful.)

Concept (1) A variation on a basic that the dancers will be able to associate with that basic once they have learned it. Four ladies chain is a concept of ladies chain. The term was apparently coined by educator Patricia Phillips and caller Dick Leger. (2) In modern square dancing, an instruction given before a call that affects how that call is to be danced (for example, "as couples" before a movement that is normally done by individuals).

Contra dance (1) A dance, done in a longways set, in which the set is divided into groups of two or three couples. In each group, one couple is active and progresses down the set; the others are inactive and progress up the set. The form survived in New England after it had died out elsewhere (roughly 1900–1950), and its present revival began in New England. (2) An evening of such dances, often mixed with other dance types (see **contra dancing**).

Glossary 413

Contra dancing As commonly used today, the entire activity that involves dancing contras, circles, and traditional squares. This activity was generally known as "square dancing" in New England until around 1970, when contras overtook squares in popularity.

Contra square (1) A dance routine that starts and ends in a square but puts the dancers in facing lines for a time, during which they execute moves similar to those in a contra dance. Compare **square contra.** (2) Occasionally used for the type of square that the speaker or writer would expect to encounter at a contra dance event, presumably one with New England movements, timing, and phrasing rather than an unphrased visiting-couple dance.

Contrary or **contrary partner** An old name for **opposite.**

Corner In a square or big circle, the lady clockwise from a gent or the gent counterclockwise from a lady. The term may originally have been "corner partner"; presumably that was too confusing.

Cotillion (1) A dance in square formation, popular in the 18th century; one of the chief ancestors of present-day squares. (2) In some areas, a fiddle tune whose "A" and "B" parts are in different keys; the term may be a holdover from the type of music played for the original (definition 1) cotillions. (3) In the late 19th century, a **German.** (4) A formal ball, especially one at which debutantes are presented. (#4 is the usual present-day definition outside the world of square dancing.)

Counter or **counter-dance** Of an inactive dancer, to move around one's own position in order to stay out of the actives' way.

Country dancing Can mean the activity that includes square and contra dancing; can also mean English group social dancing (traditional or historical) or country-and-western dancing (couple and line).

Couple Two people who have chosen to dance a set together, or two people who are together in a set after a partner change. In particular, one of the numbered pairs (Couple 1 through Couple 4) in a square. In some complex dances, "couple" can refer to a pair of people playing opposite gender roles who are together for a short time.

Couple dance Any dance, such as a waltz or polka, done by one or more couples independently (rather than in sets), whether they are doing a uniform routine (a "sequence dance" or "round dance") or improvising their own steps (a "freestyle dance"). Traditionally, most "square dance" evenings have consisted of set dances alternating with couple dances.

Couple numbering There have been several systems over the years for numbering the couples in a square. In the visiting-couple tradition, the couples are numbered counterclockwise so that Couple 2 is to Couple 1's right and Couple 3 is across from Couple 1. This system is all but universal in North American square dancing today. In the quadrille tradition, where opposite couples worked together much of the time, some but not all dancing masters put Couple 2 across from Couple 1; Couple 3 was to the right of Couple 1. This system apparently survived in isolated areas into the mid-20th century.

Couple up four A direction for two couples to join hands in a ring. Used particularly in southern style to mark the transition from big circle to small circle figures.

Courtesy turn A couple, side by side, assumes promenade position (definition 2) and turns as a unit (the gent or left-hand person moving backward, the other person forward) until the couple is facing into the set or facing an opposite couple. Usually done as the ending movement of a ladies chain, a right and left through, or a do paso. The name was coined in 1952 by Jack McKay, but of course the turn had been part of existing basics for decades.

Courting promenade See **promenade position** (definition 3).

Crooked tune A tune with more or fewer beats than the standard number (usually 16) in the "A" or "B" part or both. Not used for group dancing in regions (such as New England) where the dance movements are traditionally synchronized with the musical phrases.

Cross over To move from one side of a set to the opposite side, usually changing places with a facing person or couple. Can be done by individuals (as in the traditional singing call *Two Head Ladies Cross Over*) or by couples (as in Figure 1 of the *Lancers,* where one couple splits another as they cross).

Cross through Two people cross paths while splitting another couple.

Cross trail* Two people, side by side, cross paths and follow the next call. Typically the gent, on the left, lets the lady cross in front of him. Introduced around 1940, possibly as part of the dance *Corners of the World* by Pat Pattison. Often the call is understood to include a pass through before the crossing. This was not always so; in the early 1950s a distinction was being made in some regions between "trail through" (pass through, then cross) and "cross trail" (simply cross, or cross through). I suggest using "cross trail" to mean only the crossing move, specifying a pass through where needed. This is because many dancers instinctively start to cross as soon as they hear the call.

Crow The active gent in the dance *Bird in the Cage*. The corresponding name for the active lady is "bird" or "birdie." Some callers use "birdies" and "crows" as semi-gendered role terms at family dances.

Cue To **prompt** a dance; the term is standard in modern round dancing, where the prompter is known as a cuer.

Cut in To take the place of a dancer or couple, who must then leave the floor or cut in on someone else. The phenomenon of cutting in is well known in ballroom dancing. During the square dance boom, cutting in was done by couples: A couple from the sidelines would wait for a couple promenade to be called and insert itself into a set. The couple behind them would have to leave the set and, if they wished to keep dancing, find another square to cut into. The practice was observed and accepted in some but not all regions. Compare **ninepin, Tucker.**

Cut time A musical term for 2/2 meter (two half notes to a measure); usually shown in written music by a "c" with a line through it (like a "cents" sign) rather than "2 over 2." Cut time is functionally equivalent to 2/4 meter for square dance purposes. Fast passages will be written with eighth notes instead of sixteenth notes, but are played identically in both meters as long as the metronome speed is the same for a half note in 2/2 as for a quarter note in 2/4.

Cut timing   Another name for **clipped timing**.

Daisy chain   A break based on the grand right and left. Starting with partners, all dancers repeatedly go "forward two and back one" using hand pulls and hand turns halfway around to reverse direction. The second person met on the fourth "forward two" is original partner. Introduced by Paul Little in 1951.

Dance   As a noun, can mean a dance routine (such as a square figure or a complete sequence of figures and breaks), one number played by the band, a set of two or three numbers (usually squares) done with the same partner, or an entire event of dancing.

Dance around   A regional name for a **do-si-do** (definition 1) or an **all around** and **see-saw**. The call is "Dance around your corner, dance around your partner." Also known as bounce around.

Demonstration set   A set of dancers brought together to show how a movement or sequence of movements is done, after which all the dancers in the room do it. Compare **exhibition set**.

Descriptive calling   Same as **directive calling**.

Dip   Same as **duck**.

Dip and dive   To go alternately over and under other couples, making an arch and ducking through by turns. Can be done by three couples in line, four couples around a square, four couples per square moving the length of the hall, or all the couples in a progressive circle or a grand march. The name is odd, as "dip" and "dive" both mean "duck," but it is firmly set in tradition.

Directive calling (also **directional** or **descriptive calling**)   Calling that clearly tells dancers what to do, either because it is in everyday language (such as "go around two") or because it consists of accepted basics that the dancers have already learned. The term dates from the 1950s; at that time it was fashionable for callers to write new dances with patter that was colorful but did not always describe the movements clearly – perhaps in imitation of unique traditional calls like "bird in the cage" and "wave the ocean." A few respected callers editorialized against non-descriptive calling; by around 1960 the fad had blown over and the recent concoctions had largely vanished, but the traditional calls had disappeared along with them.

Dishrag turn   A turn that requires a dancer to go under one or both of his or her own arms. In a double dishrag, partners face, join both hands, and do a mirror-image turn all the way around, raising their arms over their heads and rolling back to back, until they are facing again. A single dishrag can be a similar move done with one pair of joined hands; it was also an older name for what is now known as a California twirl.

Dive   Same as **duck**.

Dive through*   From two facing couples, the one closer to the center of the set makes an arch with near hands. The one on the outside ducks under the arch, moving toward the center. The arching couple moves away from the center and does an automatic (i.e. uncalled) California twirl to face the center. The couples are now facing in the same direction, one behind the other.

Divide To move away from one's partner, typically around the outside (as in "Heads go forward, sides divide"), often until meeting one's opposite. In a grand square, the dividing couples face their partner and back away; in some other dances they turn away from partner and move forward. "Divide the ring" is a synonym for "split the ring."

Dixie chain A movement, introduced by Bill Owen and popular in modern square dancing in the late 1950s and early 1960s. Two couples, each in single file, approach each other and do a series of hand pulls; the first pair give right hands to start. Each person does two pulls. The movement ends with each couple, still in single file, facing away from the other couple. The next call was often "Lady go left and the gent go right."

Docey-doe Lloyd Shaw's preferred spelling for his favorite form of do-si-do (definition 2): From a circle of four people, the ladies change places (with either a left shoulder pass or a corner rollaway) so that partners are facing; then execute a do paso, but with the ladies covering more ground than the gents, who merely reach past each other to take the next lady's hand. Can be done only by two couples. Was used as a subchorus in visiting-couple figures in the 1940s and early 1950s; fell into disuse along with those figures in the late 1950s.

Dominant figure See **unique figure**.

Domino A word shouted by the caller to indicate the end of a number. It is particularly associated with the Québécois tradition, although I have heard it in recordings made in other regions (Texas bandleader Bob Wills used it). Phil Jamison spoke with a Quebec caller who believed it came from "Dominus vobiscum" ("The Lord be with you," part of many Christian liturgies). Sometimes "Domino" stands alone, sometimes it introduces a couplet: "Domino, les dames/femmes ont chaud" – literally, "Domino, the ladies/women are hot" (i.e., exhausted). Some present-day callers have altered this to "Domino, tout le monde ont chaud" – "Domino, everyone is hot." Compare **keno**.

Don't slow down During a promenade, particularly in modern square dancing, an instruction to keep moving without stopping at home. Usually followed by having the heads (or sides) wheel around to face the couple behind them and do a movement such as right and left through.

Do paso Lloyd Shaw's name for one iteration (partner left, corner right, partner left) of the Texas do-si-do. During the 1950s the name became standard worldwide, even in Texas as that state adopted California style.

Do-sa-do The standardized spelling of **dos-à-dos** or **do-si-do** (definition 1) in modern square dance usage.

Dos-à-dos The original French spelling of **do-si-do**. Quite early in the development of country-style square dancing, callers were pronouncing it "doe-see-doe." In the 1930s Lloyd Shaw recommended using it for the back to back movement and pronouncing it "doe-sah-doe" to distinguish it from the hand-turn do-si-do; book and magazine writers started spelling it "do-sa-do." The latter spelling has persisted, although in the modern scene all forms of hand-turn do-si-do have disappeared or been renamed so that there is no longer anything for the back to back move to be distinguished from.

Do-si The name for the do-si-do (definition 1) in some areas that used "do-si-do" to mean some form of hand-turn sequence (do-si-do, definition 2). See also **do-si your partner left.**

Do-si-ballonet A variation on the do-si-do (definition 2). From a circle of four, the two ladies cross, passing left shoulders, and join hands in a ring with ladies facing out and gents facing in. Partners are holding left hands; opposites are holding right hands. All balance forward and back, then turn partner half by the left to form a new ring with gents facing out and ladies in. All balance again, then turn opposite once by the right and give left to partner for a courtesy turn. Sometimes the left-hand turn with partner and the second balance are omitted.

Do-si-do* (1) Two facing dancers (or rarely two facing couples) move forward, passing right shoulders; move sideways to their right, passing back to back; and move backward to place, passing left shoulders. The name is a corruption of "dos-à-dos," French for "back to back." Note that in some regions where it is common to call a corner do-si-do followed by a partner do-si-do, one of those two movements is by custom done passing left shoulders first; this makes for a smoother transition between the two. Also known as bounce around or dance around. See **dos-à-dos** and Chapter 15 for more history. For variations see **all around the left-hand lady** and **see-saw your pretty little taw.** (2) Any of several compound movements comprising a series of hand turns. In some dance communities it constitutes a visiting-couple figure; in others it is done as a sub-chorus following other such figures. See **docey-doe, do paso, Grange do-si-do, Texas do-si-do.**

Do-si-do Kentucky style A break done in California around 1950, perhaps based on notes taken in Kentucky: From a circle of any number of couples, all turn corner by the right until the gents are facing out and ladies in, then give left to partner and the circle moves clockwise. Turn corner by the right again, then execute a do paso (partner left, corner right, partner left).

Do-si-do mountain style Called to a couple standing side by side, lady on the right, near hands joined. They raise their joined hands and the lady walks forward in a small circle around the gent, passing in front of him and behind his back and returning to her starting point. The lady may do a left-face spin as she progresses. Often called to two couples in a circle of four; the usual next move is to swing the opposite in that circle. Also called lasso. Sweep the floor is similar except that the gent kneels.

Do-si your lady A southern term for the move that became known nationwide as **do-si-do mountain style.** "Gents kneel and do-si your lady" is the same as **sweep the floor.**

Do-si your partner left (corner right) One form of call for the turns in the **Texas do-si-do.** Attested in the Houston area around 1950.

Double bow knot A variation on **right hand high, left hand low.** Three dancers in a line execute that movement but retain their handholds, and the center person turns under the arch so that all three are facing the other way. They then do "left hand high, right hand low" in the same manner to end by facing their original direction. Introduced by Lloyd Shaw in 1938.

Double dishrag See **dishrag turn.**

Double elbow A variation of the grand right and left: Partners do a catch all eight (turn half by the right, then turn by the left to meet the next person in normal grand right and left direction), then repeat the movement with each new person until partners meet again. Traditionally a caller would call for a plain grand right and left halfway around, then a double elbow when partners met.

Double pass through Two couples, one behind the other, face two couples similarly arranged. Everyone passes through both facing couples, so that each pair of couples ends facing away from the other pair. The term was apparently introduced by Madeline Allen in 1956; before that time, the same movement could be called as "pass through two (couples)."

Double square or **double quadrille** A dance with two adjacent couples on each side of a square. Typically each couple has its own identity, though it is possible to call a normal square routine to dancers in such a formation, with the right-hand couple taking the lady's part and the left-hand couple the gent's. Also called royal square. Compare **big square, tandem square.**

Double the dose An old call that, depending on the area, could direct the dancers to repeat the last movement called or, upon meeting partner in a grand right and left, to execute a **turn back** (definition 2), a **once and a half,** or a **double elbow.**

Down "When you come down" means "when you finish the movement you were just executing."

Downbeat The musical impulse that signals the dancers to take a step. See **beat.**

Down the line (1) Same as **in line.** (2) Occasionally used to direct dancers to move around the set in the same direction as their immediately preceding move, as in "Swing your corner... now swing the next one down the line."

Duck To bend over and move through an arch.

Duck and dive Same as **dip and dive.**

Duple minor A contra dance in which each minor set has two couples.

Eastern style (1) A style of traditional square dancing characterized by strong physical connection, relatively few basic movements, many dances made up entirely of standard basics (i.e. containing no unique figures), many relatively long buzz-step swings, and (often) complete synchronization with the musical phrase (beats 1–64 of the tune). (2) Used inaccurately, and often pejoratively, to refer to any square dance form other than modern square dancing, especially during the formative years of the latter (1945 through the 1960s). Even dances written by callers in the modern scene were referred to as "eastern style" once those dances had lost favor in that scene.

Eight chain through A modern square dance movement similar to a **right and left eight** except that instead of passing through as they meet each couple, the dancers give right hands and pull by the first person they meet, left hands with the next, and so on. Those facing out are supposed to do a courtesy turn, but in practice this is often simplified to a left-hand pull by. In the complete movement there are eight actions (pull by or courtesy turn) for each couple, but the caller may specify a different number of actions by calling, for instance, "eight chain three" or "eight chain four." Eight chain four is frequently used, as although it turns the set 180 degrees, it leaves all the dancers in the same positions relative to one another as when they started. Introduced by Ed Epperson in 1957.

Eight chain through formation Same as **box formation.**

Elbow swing (1) A fast turn by two dancers who link right (or left) elbows and move forward around each other. This movement appears to be derived from various rural traditions; it is used by many callers at one-night stands, both in strip the willow and in place of a standard square dance swing when they judge that the latter would take too much time to teach or would be viewed as too intimate. In dances that were popular in New England and the West and Southwest in the 1950s, it was used when the call was for two gents to swing each other. (2) A variation of the grand right and left: Partners link right elbows and turn about once and a quarter around until they can see the next person in grand right and left direction. They move forward to that person and turn by the left elbow a similar amount. They turn the next person by the right elbow, the next by the left, and meet partners to follow the next call. Traditionally a caller would call for a plain grand right and left halfway around, then an elbow swing when partners met. Also known as grand allemande, once and a half, or single elbow.

End ladies chain From two lines of four made up of normal couples, the ladies at the right end of each line chain diagonally through the center.

Ends The dancers at the ends of a line of three or more, as distinguished from the center or centers.

Ends turn in From a line of four facing out, the center two people make an arch; the end people move toward each other, duck through the arch, and follow the next call. Those who made the arch do an automatic (i.e. uncalled) California twirl to face in. Originally the key movement in a 1952 routine by Ed Gilmore (see Chapter 21), it was considered a "basic" in modern square dancing for several years. Compare **ends turn out.**

Ends turn out Similar to **ends turn in,** but called when one or more lines of four are facing in. Those who made the arch do not do a California twirl unless it is explicitly called.

Equivalent A movement or series of movements that has the same starting and ending positions as another movement, and so may be substituted for it. The term was first used widely by modern square dance callers, but the concept is useful for neo-traditional callers as well, particularly in making a figure easier or harder to suit the needs and desires of a group of dancers.

Even couple In southern mountain circle dancing, the couple that stays on the outside facing in and is visited by one odd couple after another.

Everybody dance In some communities, when Couple 1 has visited Couples 2 and 3 and gets to Couple 4, a signal for Couples 2 and 3 to face each other and do the same figure that 1 and 4 are doing. Same as "On both corners."

Exhibition set A set of dancers formed to show square dancing to a non-dancing audience. Often the line between this and a **demonstration set** is blurred when the exhibition dancers split up and take partners from the audience to shepherd them through an easy routine.

Exploding squares One form of **progressive squares** that begins with every couple doing a California twirl to face outward in their set, so that each square appears to burst open. The term was popularized by Jerry Helt, based on Ed Gilmore's work with progressive squares. Compare **grid square.**

Face right (left) The couples directed (say the heads) turn 45 degrees to face an adjacent couple, which must turn to face the active couple; neither couple leaves its home position. Distinguished from **lead** (verb).

Face to the middle A call used in the 1950s to direct four active dancers in the center of the set to change their facing direction from north-south to east-west. A non-intuitive call (since the dancers were facing the middle before and after the call), it was rendered obsolete by the introduction of star through.

Fancy figure In 19th-century quadrilles, a figure that contained an unusual move or sequence of moves. At the prompter's discretion, a fancy figure could be substituted for one of the normal figures of a plain quadrille, often the last.

Federation style A name for **modern square dancing.** Used by traditional dancers in Washington state, where modern square dance clubs are grouped into a state federation.

Fiddle tune A tune in brisk tempo, as a jig, reel, or breakdown, suitable for square dancing and traditionally played on the fiddle.

Fifty-fifty (1) Same as **half and half.** (2) Same as **split the pot.**

Figure A series of dance movements that forms a cohesive whole. In square dancing, a figure is generally considered the "main course" of a dance, as distinguished from the break. Some figures incorporate a partner change, in which either the ladies or the gents move one place around the set. Some, such as visiting-couple figures, give each couple in turn a chance to lead; such a figure rarely has a partner change.

Figure eight A dancer or a line of dancers moves in a figure-eight pattern, usually going around and/or through other dancers. There is no single standard definition of "figure eight"; there are at least three distinct figures by that name, none of which incorporates the "figure eight" of English country dancing and present-day contra dancing.

Filler Has been used at various times and places to mean patter, a square dance break, and probably other things.

First couple or **Couple 1** The couple that leads the figure first. Usually this is the couple nearest the head of the hall, but if each square has its own caller, he or she is likely to be in the first couple, and so it makes sense to have Couple 1 face the band to facilitate communication (as was formerly done in the Chicago area).

First four A term for the **head couples.** Used in the Southwest around 1950.

Flatfooting A form of solo **percussive dance.**

Flip record   A square dance record with called and instrumental versions of the same dance on opposite sides.

Flourish   A motion, such as a twirl, that is not part of a dance's choreography and may be omitted without detriment to the dance as a whole. Some flourishes are spontaneous, initiated by one member of a couple; others are done at specific points by most dancers in an area. One example is the lady's twirl under the gent's arm between a partner swing and a promenade, which is nearly universal in modern square dancing.

Follow (noun)   A gender-neutral term for the person taking the lady's role (the corresponding term for the gent's role is lead). Common in couple dancing, these terms are somewhat controversial in country dancing. See **gender-free**.

Foot   The side of the room opposite the obvious or designated head.

Foot couple   (1) In a whole-set longways dance, the couple farthest from the head. (2) An old name for the couple opposite Couple 1 in a square (Couple 2 in some 19th-century quadrilles, Couple 3 in most other traditions).

Forearm turn   An **arm turn** (definition 2).

Forward   In breaks derived from the grand right and left, the normal direction in which the dancers progress during that movement: clockwise for the ladies, counterclockwise for the gents.

Forward and back*   In most cases, the designated dancers take three steps forward and close the free foot, then take three steps back and close. Occasionally the term refers to a forward-and-back balance (one step forward and close, one step back and close).

Four-by-four   A modern term for a **mescolanze**. Also four-face-four.

Four-four (4/4) meter   A musical time signature in which there are four beats to a measure and a quarter note is worth one beat. Also known as common time and shown by a "c" in written music. In traditional dance music, 4/4 is typically used only for marches. Attempting to write reels and breakdowns in 4/4 often leads to errors in notation.

Four gents chain   Same as **gents grand chain**.

Four ladies chain   Same as **ladies grand chain**.

Four ladies chain in line   From a box formation, the ladies chain repeatedly (the center two couples alternating with the pairs of center/outside couples) until each lady has gone to both ends of the formation and returned to her starting position. As in three ladies chain, the center gents do not do a full courtesy turn but help each lady along without reversing her direction.

Four-leaf clover   (1) From a circle of two couples, the active couple ducks under the inactive couple's arch. The active dancers raise their joined hands and turn away from each other, then all four dancers lower their arms to stand in a circle with each dancer's arms crossed. Sometimes they circle left at this point. On "Break it" or a similar call, the active couple again raise their joined hands and pull the inactive couple between them. Finally, the inactives raise their hands and turn away from each other (or "unwind") so the four are in a normal circle again, all facing in. All hands remain joined throughout. This movement is an interrupted **roll the barrel.** (2) A couple promenade, in either direction, with the dancers in the center almost touching.

Fourth couple or **Couple 4**   The couple to the left of Couple 1. Typically the last couple to be called out to perform a visiting-couple figure. In areas where such figures made up most or all of the repertoire, the standard way to learn to dance was to take fourth position in a set.

Freestyle dance   A couple dance, such as a free waltz or polka, in which each couple determines the type and order of its steps. Compare **sequence dance.**

Frontier whirl   Another name for **California twirl,** suggested by Bruce Johnson in 1957 and promoted heavily for a while, possibly because it took less time to say and possibly to avoid the confusion of California twirl with California whirl. The term appears to have fallen into disuse.

Fudge   To break stride or cut corners in moving from one place to another, either to recover from a lapse of mind or to compensate for an awkward transition in the routine. The term is most commonly used in discussing couple dances or other dance styles involving footwork beyond walking.

Fun level   In modern square dancing, a program simple enough to be danced by people who have not taken a class. Some but not all traditional dance programs would qualify as fun level.

Fun night   A **one-night stand,** especially one sponsored by a square dance club in the hope of recruiting new learners and eventually members.

Gal from Arkansaw   See **girl from Arkansaw.**

Gather in six (or eight)   Another term for "**pick up two** and make it six (or eight)."

Gee-haw   Occasionally used as a synonym for grand right and left (e.g. "and now the old gee-haw"). From the old commands to horses or mules, "gee" (to turn or bear right) and "haw" (to turn or bear left).

Gender-free or **gender-neutral**   Of a dance event or series, using terminology that does not refer directly to gender. At an event featuring easy dances, it is often possible to avoid referring to gender roles at all. At an ongoing gender-free series, the two traditional roles (gents/ladies) are given new names. Currently the most popular set of terms appears to be larks/robins (recently changed from larks/ravens); an earlier pair was jets/rubies. Another set is leads/follows; this is frowned on by some who argue that there is very little leading and following in country dancing, and that flourishes can be initiated by either member of a couple.

Gent   The member of a couple who stands on the left side to begin the dance and traditionally leads the other member through certain movements. Anyone, irrespective of gender, may play the part of a gent.

Gents chain   Used but not defined in 19th-century call books; usually interpreted now as a left-hand pass for the gents. Each gent then takes promenade position (definition 2) with the opposite lady and moves forward (clockwise) around her as she turns almost in place. The motion is a mirror image of the ladies chain. Increasingly, the promenade position is also done in mirror image; that is, the lady's left arm goes around the gent's waist, rather than his right arm around her waist. Gents chain has been used in several recent contra dances, and I expect it to be reintroduced in squares any day now.

Gents grand chain Similar to **ladies grand chain:** The gents star in the center to the opposite lady, then turn with her as in a two gents chain.

Gents half chain See **half chain.**

Georgia rang tang A name for the **Grange do-si-do.** The name, probably originally confined to a limited geographic area, has become popular in neo-traditional style, possibly due to its oddity.

Georgy Alabam Another name for the **Grange do-si-do.**

German In the late 19th century, a dance party attended by friends and acquaintances, consisting of a number of partner-choosing games with props and favors. Often called **cotillion.**

Get-in Another name for **set-up.**

Get-out In modern square dancing, a combination of basics, often memorized by the caller, that will move the dancers from their current formation to a resolution (everyone "in sequence" with original partners; see **sequence,** definition 4). Compare **set-up.**

Gimmick A term, used primarily by callers among themselves, for a dance or part of a dance that has the feel of a game or a trick, often containing an element of surprise.

Girl from Arkansaw In the dance *Sally Goodin,* a gent's opposite lady (or corner lady in some regional variations). Compare **Grandmaw.**

Give weight To offer resistance to another dancer, usually by pulling slightly with the arm during a handhold (as in a circle or a hand turn).

Global terminology Another name for **positional calling.**

Goalposting A term for a type of figure in which four dancers stand still and the other four move around them with a series of "pass through and around one" sequences. Developed in the 1940s, it was an intermediate point between traditional curving paths and the grid choreography of modern square dancing.

Grand allemande Another name for **elbow swing** (definition 2).

Grand ballonet An older name for the break now known as **Alamo Style.**

Grand chain (1) The original name for **grand right and left;** still used in Canada and the British Isles. (2) See **ladies grand chain, gents grand chain.**

Grand chain eight (1) A synonym for **grand right and left,** used mainly in patter. (2) For a brief period in the 1950s, a synonym for **all eight chain.**

Grand Cuttyshaw A name, used by Rickey Holden around 1950, for the **Grange do-si-do.**

Grandmaw In the dance *Sally Goodin,* a gent's corner lady (or opposite lady in some regional variations). Compare **Girl from Arkansaw.**

Grand left and right A movement like **grand right and left,** but beginning with a left hand pass, often with corner. Compare **grand right and wrong.**

Grand march A series of marching and follow-the-leader movements executed by all the couples on the dance floor, usually done to open a formal ball.

Grand promenade A dance for groups of two couples forming lines of four around a big circle, all facing in promenade direction (counterclockwise). The term was used by Dick Leger (1960s–1990s), who hashed the calls and included frequent partner changes.

Grand reel A name for the **Grange do-si-do,** used in West Virginia.

Grand right and left* The most common chorus movement in square dancing, both traditional and modern. Partners face, join right hands as if for a handshake, then pass by each other to join left hands with the one they meet. They continue moving forward, taking right and left hands alternately with the people they meet, until the next call is given or until the default is reached. In Ontario and the northeastern US the default is to go all the way around the square, passing partner once by the right hand and continuing to home. In traditional western style and in modern square dancing the default is to stop when partners meet for the first time. Can also be done in a big circle; the distance traveled depends on the routine (the movement is used as the means of progression in some circle mixers).

Grand right and left direction Normally the ladies face to the left and travel clockwise, the gents face right and travel counterclockwise.

Grand right and wrong A grand right and left in the opposite direction; it can begin with a right hand to corner when the dancers are at home, or with a right hand to partner if they are facing the "wrong way." Also known as wrong way grand. Compare **grand left and right.**

Grand right eight A **grand right and left.** The term was used in the Southwest in the 1950s.

Grand Sashay A grand right and left interrupted by do-si-dos (definition 1). Partners face, do a right shoulder do-si-do, give right hands and pass by. With the next person they do a see-saw (left shoulder do-si-do), give left hands and pass by. They continue the pattern, usually until partners meet again. Named by Rickey Holden in 1948, though the sequence is certainly older.

Grand slide Dancers follow the traffic pattern of a grand square while facing the same direction throughout. When they cannot move forward or backward, they sashay (slide) to the next point. Introduced in 1967 by Chip Hendrickson.

Grand square* A well-known break that dates back several centuries. From a square, two couples (usually the sides) face partner while the others continue to face across the set (a common prompt is "Sides face, grand square"). Each dancer moves in a small square, one-quarter the size of the set; corners move around each other without ever interacting. All take three steps on each side of their small square, then turn a quarter on the fourth beat. The heads go forward to start, the sides backward. All are facing either partner or opposite throughout (and doing a mirror image of those dancers' parts); no one ever faces outward. The movement is almost always done twice, the second time with the heads' and sides' roles reversed.

Grange do-si-do Done by two facing couples: turn opposite by the right hand or arm, partner by the left, opposite by the right, and courtesy turn partner (or turn partner by the left, depending on the next call). Typically each turn lasts only long enough so the gents can reach behind each other's back to join hands with the next lady. The call was simply "do-si-do" (not "Grange do-si-do," which may have been a name given by a folklorist to distinguish it from other similar moves); in any given area before the 1940s revival, there would have been only one movement known as a do-si-do. Also known as Georgia rang tang, Georgy Alabam, Grand Cuttyshaw, reel a grand reel, reel away four, reel the set, run the reel, Suzy Q, etc. I believe this is most likely the original form of hand-turn do-si-do, as most people are right-handed and most dance movements that involve the hands begin with the right one.

Grapevine step A step used in circling: The dancers step to the side on the leading foot (the left foot if circling to the left) and cross alternately in front and behind with the trailing foot, producing a rotation of the upper body. Used extensively in international folk dancing; common among modern square dancers even when not taught to them in class.

Grapevine twist A figure in which two or more active dancers move in a curving path between and around other dancers. Lloyd Shaw (1939) described two completely different figures by this name (see Chapter 19 for one of them).

Grid pattern A type of square dance figure in which the dancers travel in straight paths aligned with the walls of the room, changing their facing directions by means of standard movements with accepted names. Most modern square dancing is made up of grid patterns (except for breaks that are based on circular patterns such as grand right and left and Allemande Thar).

Grid square One term for a dance done by a number of squares that are aligned in both directions with the other sets; dancers find themselves migrating between squares. The term has been popularized in recent years by Bob Isaacs, who has devised a series of such dances. Isaacs' routines are similar in form to contras: The pattern repeats, the movements are synchronized with the musical phrases, and returning all couples to their original places is not an objective. Compare **progressive squares, exploding squares.**

Group Sometimes used to mean one of the subsets in a progressive circle.

Gypsy Two dancers, keeping right (or left if specified) shoulders adjacent, dance around each other while maintaining eye contact. This movement was introduced from English country dance into contras around 1980 and has shown up in a few squares. Note that the term is considered offensive by some (though not all) of the Romani or Roma people (the ethnic group often called "Gypsies" by outsiders and by some Roma themselves), but no substitute term has attained widespread acceptance. "Right (left) shoulder round" currently appears to be the most promising candidate.

Half and half One term for the type of dance programming (round and square) common in parts of the Northeast, such as upstate New York.

Half chain A term used for a one-way (almost always ladies) chain in the days when "ladies chain" meant over and back. Half chains were all but unknown until the square dance revival of the 1940s, when callers began combining movements in new ways. There was a very short period of time when the call "half chain" was in use; by the mid-1950s "ladies chain" had come to mean a one-way trip everywhere except rural New England and possibly other parts of the Northeast.

Half promenade Two facing couples in promenade position exchange places within the bounds of the set, keeping to the right as they pass and doing, in effect, a courtesy turn to face each other again.

Half right and left A term, common until the mid-20th century, for a right and left through. In those days "right and left" meant over and back; if "over" only was desired, the "half" call must be used. Half right and left was rare; its most common usage was following a half promenade to fill out a 16-beat phrase.

Half sashay Partners, side by side, change places with a sliding or sideways walking step. Normally the lady moves from right to left in front of the gent as he moves from left to right. Originally the key move in the square figure *Sashay Partners Halfway Round*. Compare **rollaway**. See also **sashay**.

Half shoulder-waist position See **promenade position** (definition 4).

Halfway back A southern call for a circle to reverse direction. It may be a curtailment of "Halfway round and the other way back," and does not mean literally to travel half the distance of the original direction.

Hand turn* Two dancers join right (or left) hands, give weight, and move forward around each other. The next call or the context of the dance will indicate how far to travel. In many regions the prevailing style was to join hands at waist level as if for a handshake. In New England style and therefore in present-day contra dancing (which has greatly influenced neo-traditional squares), the default is to join hands chest-high as if for arm wrestling; wrists are kept straight, and bent elbows point toward the floor.

Hands across (1) One method of forming a star, common in southern mountain dancing and English country dancing: Each diagonally opposite pair of dancers (often two ladies or two gents) join right (or left) hands and give weight, bending the elbow slightly, as the four move forward around the hands. (2) A call from the figure *The Basket* or *Swing Like Thunder* (see Chapter 19), indicating that two facing ladies are to join both hands, or three or four ladies are to form a circle, as the gents do likewise.

Hands around A call indicating a circle. "Four hands around" is a call for four people to join hands and circle left. In this context "hand" means a person, as in "all hands and the cook," rather than a literal hand.

Harlem rosette A figure introduced in 1938 by Lloyd Shaw, who had seen dancers doing it in New York City's Harlem district. I had always assumed they were jitterbuggers, but Rod La Farge (in *Rosin the Bow,* March 1946) reported seeing the figure in a Caribbean quadrille done by Harlem dancers. From a line of two couples with gents in the center, the gents raise their joined left hands; the ladies, holding partner's near hand, duck under the gents' arch, make a left-face turn in place, and join right hands in the center. The formation rotates clockwise with a walking or buzz step. A grand Harlem rosette is similar, done by all four couples from a star promenade.

Hash As the name implies, a dance constructed by combining pieces of other dances. The oldest and simplest form of hash is a visiting-couple dance (sometimes called a "medley change") in which each couple does a different figure during its turn, or even a different figure with each couple it visits. Around 1950 callers began combining part of one break with part of another; the term "hashing the breaks" became common. Soon after that, they started hashing figures in the same way. Eventually the norm in modern square dancing became total hash, a sequence of short basic movements arranged to flow smoothly with no defining figure (and often improvised in real time by the caller).

Hawk or **hawkie** An alternative term for **crow,** used in Michigan and Ontario.

Head couple (1) In a whole-set longways dance, the couple nearest the head of the hall. In the vast majority of such dances, the head couple initiates the figure. (2) An old name for Couple 1 in a square. Where this term was in use, the couple opposite #1 was known as the foot couple.

Head couples (or **head four** or **heads**) Couple 1 and the opposite couple; the latter is now usually #3, but in some 19th-century quadrilles it was #2.

Head of the hall Most often, the side of the room where the band is (with recorded music, the side on which the loudspeakers are set up). If the band is in a corner or the room setup is otherwise ambiguous, the caller will designate one side of the room as the head.

Hey Three or four dancers (in squares, usually four), starting from a straight line, weave past one another until all have been to both ends of the line and have returned to their starting point. Who begins the hey, which way they face, and which shoulders they pass all depend on the specific figure. The hey disappeared from contra dances early in the 19th century but was revived in the 1970s and is now quite common. A square dance figure incorporating a series of heys was briefly popular in the 1950s; a few recent neo-traditional squares have featured the hey. In English country dancing there is also a circular hey, which may be done with or without hands; the version with hands is apparently the direct ancestor of our right and left through, and has also been adapted into modern square dancing as the square through.

Hey Ma! A phrase traditionally shouted by the caller to raise the dancers' energy level. The dancers are to respond by shouting "Hey Pa!" Also "Hi Ma, Hi Pa."

High level A term used in the 1950s to denote material too complicated for the average club dancer, done at advanced workshops or in closed groups.

Hip swing A swing using the ballroom hold, particularly a walk-around swing in which partners are side by side with right hips adjacent. The term was used in the Southwest in the 1950s, not in calling but in printed dance directions to distinguish the ballroom swing from one- and two-hand turns (often called "swings" in that region).

Hoedown (1) Same as **breakdown** (definition 1). (2) A party featuring square dances and/or similar group dances. (3) In some regions, a dance event sponsored by more than one club. (4) In the early days of the square dance boom, a term for a **medley change** or rudimentary **hash.**

Hold fast (1) In Atlantic Canada, a direction to join both hands with one's partner and dance percussively in place. (2) In Ontario, occasionally used by the caller to indicate the end of a change (definition 3) but not the end of the set (i.e., the dancers should remain in their places rather than clear the floor).

Home In a square, the dancers' starting position; in nearly all square dances, everyone returns home at the end, whether or not there are temporary partner changes along the way. In a longways or circle dance, there is no home position; each dancer is oriented in relation to partner and neighbor, regardless of where he or she is in the hall.

Home couple Occasionally used as a synonym for the couple being visited by an active couple.

Honor To acknowledge one's partner and/or corner at the start and end of a dance. Originally done as a deep bow and curtsy, in recent years it has degenerated into a casual nod.

Hornpipe A dance tune with very sharply defined phrases. Hornpipes were originally in slow tempo, similar to schottische tempo, and notated in either 2/4 or 4/4 meter. The English and Irish still play them that way, but the Scots and Americans now play them like reels; a fast hornpipe is usually written in 2/4.

Hot hash A nebulous and often derogatory term, current in the 1950s, for a style of calling that (according to its detractors) was deliberately flashy. Hot-hash callers not only hashed breaks and figures but supposedly tried to "stop the floor"; that is, to confuse the dancers enough to make them unable to continue following the call.

Hub The dancers in the center of a star promenade or a thar star.

In (1) Toward the center of a square or a big circle. (2) Occasionally, toward one's partner.

Inactive couple A couple that does not initiate a figure. Depending on the dance, an inactive couple may be in motion as much as the active couple, or nearly so.

Indian style A term for a single file promenade done by all eight dancers in a square set, each lady in front of her partner. The term, but not the movement, has fallen out of favor.

In line With the person or couple next to one, as in the call "Ladies chain in line" in the dance *The Rout(e)*.

In sequence See **sequence** (definition 4).

Inside arch and outside under (1) Another name for **dive through.** (2) Another name for the dance *Dip and Dive* (see Chapter 19), which includes a succession of dive through moves.

Inside couple In a formation of three or four couples "stacked" so that all are facing in the same or opposite directions and none are side by side, a couple that has other couples both in front of and behind it. In a three-couple formation there is one inside couple; in a four-couple formation there are two.

Inside out and outside in (1) A visiting-couple figure in which the active couple ducks under the inactive couple's arch, then makes an arch and backs over the inactive couple. Introduced in 1942 by Lloyd Shaw. (2) A call to reverse a star promenade by having couples pivot either halfway or once and a half, so the dancers who were on the outside now form the star. The star changes from right-hand to left-hand or vice versa.

Inside track The inner "traffic lane" when four dancers are promenading single file and the other four are doing something (such as starring) in the center.

Institute A common term in modern square dancing, especially during the boom years, for a week-long residential event with intensive sessions for dancers and/or callers.

Jamboree In some regions, a dance event sponsored by more than one club.

Jet A gender-neutral term for the person taking the gent's role (the corresponding term for the lady's role is ruby). See **gender-free.**

Jig In 20th- and 21st-century usage, a dance tune in 6/8 meter. Jigs could originally be in a number of meters.

Jig dancing A term, common in Missouri, for **percussive dancing.**

Jig 'er down eight In Canada, a direction to **balance** or to dance **percussively** in place.

Jig figure In 19th-century quadrilles, a figure that had all couples active at once and contained a partner change. Similar to **breakdown** (definition 2). At the prompter's discretion, a jig figure could be substituted for one of the normal figures of a plain quadrille, often the last. In Michigan and parts of New York state, the third change in a set of three squares.

Jigging A term for **percussive dancing,** common in Pennsylvania and among the Métis dancers of western Canada.

Just one See **allemande left just one.**

Keeper A colloquial term for a square dance in which partners stay together with not even a temporary change.

Keno A word shouted by the caller to indicate the end of a change or a set (definition 2). It appears to have been more common in the western and southwestern traditions than in the East or the Deep South. Keno is, of course, a well-known gambling game, but no one seems to know how the word came to square dancing. Attested as early as 1898, in a poem by journalist James Barton Adams. Compare **Domino.**

King's Highway A figure used in the big circle segment of a southern mountain dance. From a couple promenade, the gents reverse direction and all walk in single file until partners meet again. Queen's Highway is the same figure with the ladies reversing.

Ladies chain* Two ladies in facing couples move forward, give right hands as for a handshake, and pass by. They join left hands with their opposite gent and execute a courtesy turn until the same couples are facing again. Originally the call "ladies chain" meant over and back; during the 1940s and 1950s, when callers began combining small portions of figures to create new figures, the call came to mean a one-way trip.

Ladies chain the (grand) square Another term for **rout(e) chain**.
Ladies chain three-quarters Ladies turn by the right hand in the center, three-quarters around, and do a courtesy turn with a gent on the right side of the square (measured from the ladies' starting place). Depending on the dance, this may be the lady's own partner (who has traveled one-quarter to his right to meet her) or the gent who is already there (who may follow the courtesy turn with a rollaway, putting this lady on his left while his own partner remains on his right). Can also be called to all four ladies, who star three-quarters by the right hand; again, the caller will indicate which gent will turn each lady.
Ladies grand chain Four ladies make a right-hand star in the center and turn it halfway; they give left hand to the opposite gent for a courtesy turn. A return to original places via a second identical chain used to be automatic. Also known as four ladies chain.
Ladies half chain See **half chain**.
Lady The member of a couple who stands on the right side to begin the dance and traditionally is led by the other member through certain movements. Anyone, irrespective of gender, may play the part of a lady.
Lancers One of the five-figure quadrilles introduced in ballrooms in the early 19th century. Probably the most popular such quadrille, and one of the most popular square dances, of all time; the fifth figure has been adapted into singing squares, and simplified versions of the same figure survive at rural dance events (see *Kitchen Lancers* in Chapter 17).
Lark A gender-neutral term for the person taking the gent's role (the corresponding term for the lady's role is robin or raven). See **gender-free**.
Lasso Another term for **do-si-do mountain style**.
Lead (noun) A gender-neutral term for the person taking the gent's role (the corresponding term for the lady's role is follow). Common in couple dancing, these terms are somewhat controversial in country dancing. See **gender-free**.
Lead* (verb) To travel as an active couple. The most common instance is "Couple 1 (or head couples) lead to the right"; that is, they move from home position to face their right-hand couple, which does not move. If the call had been "face to the right," the active couples would have stayed home and pivoted slightly to their right while the other couples pivoted to their left.
Leading patter A line of patter ending with a word that rhymes with the next direction to the dancers, in order to warn them of what is coming. An example is "Circle left in a pretty little ring, break that ring with a corner swing." The term was coined by Frank Kaltman. Compare **trailing patter**.
Lead up four (or six) Another term for "**pick up two** and make it six (or eight)."
Left allemande Same as **allemande left**. The exigencies of rhyme and scansion sometimes require this inversion of words.
Left grand chain A Canadian term for **grand left and right**.
Left hand (a)round A traditional call for a left-hand turn.
Left-hand gent (1) In a square, from a given lady's viewpoint, the gent in the couple on her left; the gent who is neither her partner, her corner, nor her opposite. To him she is the right-hand lady. A suggested term applicable to both

people is "next-door neighbor." (2) In some figures, a gent who happens to be on the lady's left; he may or may not be her original partner.

Left-hand lady (1) A gent's corner lady. (2) In some figures, a lady who happens to be on the gent's left; she may or may not be his original corner.

Left hands across See **hands across** (definition 1).

Level A term, often somewhat nebulous, for the nature of a given degree of complexity in a square dance program. In the early days of modern square dancing (about 1945 through the 1960s), the terms "fun level," "class level," and "club level" were in common use. "Club level" was especially nebulous, as the prevailing complexity of club dancing varied widely by region and even by club. "High level," equally ambiguous, was sometimes used for material done at advanced workshops. Callerlab standardized a few levels, starting in the 1970s, and later tried to substitute the term "programs," with limited success.

Line A formation of three or more dancers side by side, usually facing the same direction. If they are alternately facing in opposite directions, the formation is commonly known as an ocean wave or simply a wave.

Line dance (1) A partnerless dance, consisting of a sequence of steps and turns, done by a number of people all facing the same direction. Also known as "solo dance." (2) Occasionally used as a synonym for **longways** or **contra dance.**

Line of dance Counterclockwise around the room (used by ballroom dance and round dance instructors, and by some teachers of international folk dance). Also known as line of direction. Abbreviated "LOD." Same as promenade direction.

London Bridge A figure used in the grand march and in the big circle segment of a southern dance. A designated lead couple reverses direction, forms an arch, and extends it over the other couples. Each couple follows in turn.

Lonesome couple Same as **odd couple** (definition 2).

Lonesome gent (lady) A dancer standing alone on one side of the set, rather than in a couple or a line of three or more.

Longways (1) A formation of dancers in two parallel lines, usually with partners in opposite lines facing each other to start the dance. (2) Any dance done in this formation, whether a **whole-set longways** or a progressive longways (**contra dance**).

Mainstream In modern square dancing, the second of five programs a dancer may learn. It was originally intended to be the prevailing program at clubs worldwide, but in many areas it has been supplanted by Plus.

Maneuver A polite word for **fudge.**

March A type of dance tune in 4/4 or 6/8 meter, characterized by longer phrases, and longer and fewer notes, than jigs and reels.

Measure A small unit of musical time containing a set number of beats. (2/4, 2/2, and 6/8 meters have 2 beats to a measure, 3/4 meter has 3, and 4/4 has 4.) In written music, measures are separated by bar lines for easier reading.

Medley change A visiting-couple dance in which each couple does a different figure (or even three different figures) in its turn. It was one of the earliest forms of hash.

Mental imagery In modern square dance calling, a method of knowing where the dancers are at all times. It is similar to sight calling, but instead of relying on a few memorized "key" dancers, the caller keeps track of the set mentally. This requires extensive knowledge of how each movement changes the dancers' facing direction and their position relative to one another.

Mescolanze A progressive dance done by lines of two couples facing similar lines; may be done with the groups arranged in a circle or straight up and down the hall. Also known as four-by-four or four-face-four.

Meter The rhythm of a tune, determined by the number of beats in a measure and by their value. The usual meters in square and contra dancing are 2/4, 4/4, and 6/8. In some regions, notably Ontario and Cape Breton, it is traditional for the first change of a square set to be in 6/8. This custom surely dates back to the 19th-century quadrille, whose first figure was very often in 6/8. Not to be confused with **tempo.**

Minor set A group of two or three couples (in a contra dance) or two couples or trios (in a progressive circle) who work together during one round of the dance.

Mixer (1) A dance, usually a circle, in which every dancer receives a new partner during each round and original partners are not reunited (except by coincidence if the set is small enough). (2) Used by some callers to refer to a square with a partner change, as distinguished from a **keeper.** (3) A square dance break. Used by Joe Lewis in the early 1950s. An unfortunate usage, as a nearly universal rule for breaks is that they do not change partners.

Modal tune A fiddle tune that employs the "home" chord of the key one whole step lower than its overall key (for instance, the C major chord in a D major tune). Because this note is not part of the tune's major scale, it can make it sound as if the tune is partly in a minor key. "Model tune" in Mayo 1943 (p. 10) is a typo for "modal tune."

Modern dancing A term used in some areas to denote the local form(s) of freestyle couple dance (waltz, polka, foxtrot, swing, etc.), especially when programmed in alternation with squares. It was used in the northeastern US in the 1940s and on Cape Breton Island fairly recently.

Modern square dance A style of square dance characterized by a large number of basic movements, dance sequences assembled from those movements with no unique figures, lack of strong physical connection (giving weight), loose musical phrasing, the use of recorded music, and relatively few and short swings (walk-around or buzz-step). Also associated (usually) with formal lessons and a lack of walkthroughs and (often) with formal dress and organization. Developed starting around 1945 from a blend of traditional styles, assuming its present form in the 1970s with the advent of Callerlab. Often called "modern western" because in its early stages it was similar to traditional western style; often abbreviated "MWSD," particularly in Internet usage. Also called "club dancing" or "club style," particularly by traditionalists in an attempt to avoid confusion with western style (definition 1).

Glossary 433

Module A series of movements that modern square dance callers memorize as a unit; a caller can string several modules together and appear to be improvising the whole sequence. Important types of module are the zero and the equivalent.

Mother Used extensively by modern square dance callers, particularly in the 1950s and 1960s, to refer to a gent's partner. Also "Ma," "Mama," or "Maw."

Mountain style See **Do-si-do mountain style.**

Move or **movement** A short series of steps that the dancers do in response to a single called direction; the smallest unit of square dance choreography. A movement may be an accepted basic (such as "do-si-do") that is learned by rote, or it may be so close to plain English (such as "go around two") that it needs no special teaching.

Neighbor (1) In a contra dance, the person of opposite gender role in a minor set who is not one's partner. (2) Used by some callers, especially at one-night stands, instead of "corner" because "partner" and "corner" are alike enough in sound that the terms can easily be misheard in a reverberant hall. (3) See **next-door neighbor.**

Neo-traditional style The term used in this book for an eclectic style of dancing, calling, and choreographing squares that has emerged between the 1970s and the present. Whether intentionally or inadvertently, it incorporates characteristics of New England, southern mountain, and traditional western styles as well as modern square dance.

New England style A form of eastern style associated with prompted calls to traditional jigs, reels, and marches (as well as singing calls in some communities) and the frequent use of contras in addition to, or instead of, squares.

Next couple In a visiting-couple dance, the inactive couple counterclockwise from the inactive couple with whom the active couple is working or has just finished working. (In some 19th-century quadrilles in which the action was mainly across the set and the head couples were numbered 1 and 2, the term "next couple" was used to mean "next couple counterclockwise" when the choreographer wanted the couples to be active in that order.)

Next-door neighbor A gender-neutral term, coined by the present author, for **right-hand lady** and **left-hand gent;** the dancer of opposite gender role in a square who is not one's partner, corner, nor opposite. "Next-door neighbor" fits neatly into patter calls in place of "right-hand lady"; in certain contexts "neighbor" may be a sufficient call, as it is not commonly used in squares and is easy to distinguish from "partner" and "corner."

Ninepin An extra person, without a partner, in the square dance *Ninepin,* which is a blend of dance and game. The ninepin's goal is to take as a partner one of the four dancers of opposite gender role, whose partner becomes the new ninepin (see Chapter 22). Compare **cut in, Tucker.**

Novelty dance A term used during the height of the international folk dance hobby in the 1940s and 1950s for dance routines created using folk dance steps but not adhering to a particular national or ethnic style.

Numbering See **couple numbering.**

Ocean wave The full original name for a **wave.** The term may derive from the line's resemblance to a real-life wave or from the singing square *Life on the Ocean Wave,* in which the formation became popular. Compare **wave the ocean.**

Odd couple (1) In southern mountain circle dancing, the couple that initiates the small circle figures and travels from one even couple to the next. (2) In a square, the couple left over when three couples are working together. When Couple 1 leads the figure, Couple 3 or 4 is likely to be the odd couple and may be given a call of their own.

Old Grandmaw See **Grandmaw.**

Old-time (1) Sometimes used as a synonym for **traditional,** to distinguish older forms from modern square dancing. (2) Denoting a style of string-band music, heard in recordings from the 1920s and 1930s, in which the texture seldom varies: Everyone plays throughout a number, and the melody instruments play melody on every repetition of the tune. Compare **bluegrass.** (3) In England, a term for a repertoire that includes many sequence dances along with the *Lancers* and other formal quadrilles.

On both corners In some communities, when Couple 1 has visited Couples 2 and 3 and gets to Couple 4, a signal for Couples 2 and 3 to face each other and do the same figure that 1 and 4 are doing. Same as "Everybody dance."

Once and a half Aside from its plain English functions (e.g. "turn partner right, once and a half around"), this is another name for **elbow swing** (definition 2).

One more change A warning that a do-si-do (definition 2) is coming to an end. In most of Texas until the mid-1950s, the call had real meaning, as it was customary there to continue turning corner right and partner left until this call was heard. In regions where the number of turns in a do-si-do was fixed by custom, this call was still sometimes used, perhaps as a vestige of the old Texas practice.

One-nighter or **one-night stand** An event featuring square dancing and/or other forms of country dancing, often including ballroom dancing and/or games, geared to people who are unfamiliar with country dancing and do not intend to take it up as a hobby. The most common term used among callers for this sort of event; no disrespect or contempt is intended. See also **barn dance, fun night.**

One-step (1) A ballroom dance based on a plain walking step. (2) The most commonly used basic footwork in square dancing; dancers take one step on each downbeat of the music.

On the corner An alternative call for allemande left, common in Texas in the early to mid-20th century: "On the corner with your left hand, a right to your partner, right and left grand." It may have originated as a truncated form of "Honor the corner..."

On to the next (1) See **next couple.** (2) If a dancer or couple is clearly facing in a given direction (as after a pass through), an instruction to continue in the same direction until they meet a facing dancer or couple.

Open dance (1) A dance event that anyone may attend, with or without previous instruction or experience. (2) In modern square dancing, an event open to anyone who has learned the movements constituting the advertised level, as distinguished from a closed dance limited to members of the sponsoring club. (Closed events were common in the early days of the club system, due partly to high demand and limited dancing space.)

Open tunnel A figure used in the grand march and in the big circle segment of a southern mountain dance. A designated lead couple reverses direction and ducks under arches made by the other couples. Each couple follows in turn.

Opposite (1) From any given dancer's viewpoint, the person of opposite gender role who stands directly across from him or her at the beginning of a square dance. (2) In some complex figures, the person directly across from one at a given time. (3) In a circle of four, the person of opposite gender role who is not one's partner.

Other way When adjacent couples (e.g. #1 and #2) are dancing figures together on the diagonal, a signal for each couple to face its other adjacent couple (to switch from the right-hand to the left-hand couple, or vice versa).

Other way back A call to reverse direction. Usually given during a circle left, but can be used whenever it is easy and intuitive for the dancers to comply. If given during a promenade, the dancers wheel around and travel clockwise.

Out (1) Away from the center of a square or a big circle. (2) Occasionally, away from one's partner.

Out of sequence See **sequence** (definition 4).

Outside The area behind the dancers when all are at home facing in (as in "Couple 1 promenade around the outside").

Outside couple In a formation of three or four couples "stacked" so that all are facing in the same or opposite directions and none are side by side, a couple at the edge of the set.

Outside track The outer "traffic lane" when four dancers are promenading single file and the other four are doing something (such as starring) in the center.

Over and under Another term for **dip and dive**.

Overflow A term used by modern square dance callers to denote a sequence of movements that flows so smoothly and repetitively that the dancers perceive it as monotonous and/or dizzying, particularly one including a lot of clockwise motion.

Over the shoulder See **promenade position** (definition 3).

Own A fairly neutral one-syllable term for one's partner (as in "Meet your own with an elbow swing").

Ozark style See **southern style**.

Packsaddle A name for the **wrist hold** in a **star**.

Partner (1) In a square or a circle mixer, the person with whom one is dancing a given time through the figure. In all normal squares and many circles, one's partner in starting formation is the gent clockwise from a lady or the lady counterclockwise from a gent. Often, near the end of a figure, the person a dancer is directed to swing becomes his or her new partner. (2) In a longways or a progressive circle, the person with whom one has chosen to dance that number, no matter where he or she may be.

Pass the ocean A modern square dance term that has migrated into contra dancing and is likely to show up in neo-traditional squares. Two facing couples start a pass through; as the ladies draw adjacent, they join left hands and turn one-quarter to face left; meanwhile the gents take another step or two and face right, joining right hands with the lady who started beside them to form a wave.

Pass through* Two facing couples or lines exchange places, each dancer passing the opposite person by the right shoulder. They end back to back with the other couple or line; another call is required if they are to turn around or travel in any direction.

Patter Wording in a dance call that does not describe a movement and is inserted to provide color, to support the rhythm, and/or to help the caller time the descriptive calls properly. See **leading patter, trailing patter.**

Patter call A dance in which the caller uses patter, whether the descriptive calls are given on the phrase (cadence calls) or ahead of it (prompts).

Paul Jones A circle mixer in which the dancers do a freestyle couple dance with each new partner. There are many versions. The most common means of mixing is probably the grand right and left. In some versions the music is at square dance tempo throughout and the freestyle dance is a one-step; in others the music changes to a waltz or other ballroom dance when new partners meet. (See *Lucky Circle* in Chapter 16 for further description.)

Peel the banana A name, apparently recent in origin, for the cast off that begins the march figure in many whole-set longways dances.

Percussive dancing Any dance form in which the feet beat distinctive rhythms on the floor beyond a simple walk or two-step. At square dances, most often done solo (either in the time between set dances or by solo dancers while others are in sets), but can be done by dancers executing square dance figures (either by one dancer in the center while others are circling or by a whole set, the latter usually in performance). Terms for percussive dancing include buckdancing, clogging, flatfooting, jig dancing or jigging, and stepdancing.

Phrase A group of beats that is felt to belong together as a subset of a tune. In square and contra dance music, phrases are generally considered to be either 8 or 16 beats long.

Phrasing The practice of making the movements of a dance coincide with the phrases of the tune to which it is danced. Phrasing is fundamental to eastern style, but used sporadically or not at all in some other styles of square dancing.

Pick up two From a circle, one active dancer releases a handhold and adds a standing couple to the circle.

Pigeon wing (1) A particular percussive dance step. (2) A name for the hands-up hold for the allemande (hand turn) that is commonly used in contra dancing and New England–style square dancing.

Pivot step (1) A step in which a dancer's foot swivels on the floor as the dancer changes facing direction. (2) Sometimes used loosely to mean the **buzz step.**

Glossary 437

Plain quadrille (1) One of the most popular quadrilles (definition 1). (2) Same as quadrille (definition 2).

Play-party game A country dance performed in time with the singing of the dancers and/or onlookers, with no instrumental accompaniment. Done as a means of recreation and/or courtship at times and places where fiddle music and undisguised dancing were considered sinful.

Plus In modern square dancing, the third of five programs a dancer may learn. It was originally divided into two subgroups called Mainstream Plus One and Mainstream Plus Two. In many areas it has become the prevailing program at club dances.

Point To extend one foot and tap the toe on the floor without shifting one's weight to it. Used in some sequence dances.

Pokey waltz Same as **bouquet waltz.** Also known as pokey-o.

Polka step A dance sequence consisting of a hop and three steps (or hop-step-close-step), either while traveling forward or while turning as a couple. Incorporated into a few quadrilles and contra dances in the mid-19th century.

Positional calling A type of calling that refers to dancers by their position in the set relative to one another and the walls of the room, with no reference to gender roles even by non-gendered names. It has been used by some English and Scottish country dance groups since the 1970s and has recently been tried by some contra dance callers. Few if any have attempted it yet in squares. Also known as global terminology.

Posture In general, it seems that the faster the tempo, the more the dancers "lean into it," bending slightly forward at the waist and pushing back with their feet on each step. At slower tempos, dancers are more likely to stand erect. The exception is modern square dancing, where dancers typically maintain an erect posture no matter the tempo.

Poussette See **wheelbarrow.**

Power turn A courtesy turn in which each couple, after turning to face the opposite couple, turns another 180 degrees to face the dancers who were behind them. The term was coined by Kathy Anderson in the 1980s.

Pretty side out Same as **sunny side out.**

Program (1) The caller's plan for the sequence of dances at an event. (2) In modern square dancing, one of the standardized groups of basic movements that are taught in succession: Basic, Mainstream, Plus, Advanced 1 & 2, and Challenge 1 through 4. The term was adopted by Callerlab as a replacement for "level" in an attempt to keep more accomplished dancers from looking down on less accomplished ones, but "level" is still in wide use.

Progression (1) A change of partners in a square dance or mixer. Squares are said to have either corner progression or right-hand lady (next-door neighbor) progression, depending on whether the ladies (or occasionally the gents) progress counterclockwise or clockwise. (2) In a contra dance or a progressive circle, a change in the relative positions of the couples. In most such dances, half the couples progress up the hall (or clockwise in a circle) while the other half progress down (or counterclockwise) to meet a new couple.

Progressive An adjective used to describe a movement which one couple begins and others join in as they are able. A grand right and left may be choreographed in this way. Typically such a move is called directively and the word "progressive" is not used.

Progressive circle A formation composed of a number of subsets or "groups" forming a circle around the hall, each group made up of a couple or a line of three or four people facing a similar couple or line. Each half-group remains together throughout the dance, meeting and dancing with other half-groups. There are several methods of progression (see Chapter 16). In most such dances, the dancers face around the big circle to start; in a few, they face across (that is, they face the wall or the center). A four-by-four or mescolanze is a similar dance for lines of four facing up and down the hall.

Progressive squares One term for a dance done by a number of squares that are aligned in both directions; dancers find themselves migrating between squares. Typically the caller aims at returning all the dancers to their original partners and sets. The term was popularized by Ed Gilmore. See also **exploding square;** compare **grid square.**

Promenade* To assume a promenade position and travel as a couple, either (1) around a square or big circle, (2) along a line or longways set, or (3) across a square or longways set to change places with another couple (a "half promenade"). Originally pronounced to rhyme with "façade," as in French, and can be heard that way on some recordings from the 1940s; now generally pronounced to rhyme with "lemonade."

Promenade direction To the right (counterclockwise) unless otherwise specified. Same as line of dance.

Promenade left See **promenade right.**

Promenade position Two dancers side by side, lady to the gent's right, hands joined in one of the following ways: (1) Hands joined in front, right hands (in front of lady's waist) above left hands (in front of gent's waist). Sometimes called "skaters' " or "front skaters' position." The accepted practice in modern square dancing. (1a) Same as #1 with left hands above right hands. Formerly standard in Texas. (2) Left hands in front of gent's chest, right hands at lady's right hip with gent's right arm around lady's waist. Sometimes called "skaters' position"; could be called "back skaters' " to distinguish it from #1. The usual New England practice; also standard for courtesy turns. (3) Left hands in front of gent's chest, right hands above lady's right shoulder with gent's right arm around lady's shoulders. Called "varsovienne" (from a couple dance of that name), "over the shoulder position," or "courting promenade." (4) Gent's right arm around lady's waist, lady's left hand on gent's right shoulder; lady's right arm and gent's left arm are free. Sometimes called "half shoulder-waist position." Allows an easy transition into or out of a swing in ballroom position. Used in Quebec. (4a) Same as #4 with gents forming a left-hand star in the center. Used in northern New England and other parts of the Northeast; where this is the standard position it is called simply "promenade," not "star promenade." In the 1940s, Margot Mayo observed it in Massachusetts under the name of "promenade pokey world" (perhaps a corruption of "polka" and "whirl"). (5) Lady's left hand holds gent's bent right arm at the elbow ("escort position"). (6) In a few areas, couples assume closed ballroom (waltz) position and do a turning two-step or polka step instead of walking side by side.

Promenade right (left) Directed to one or more couples who are finishing a move that leaves them facing away from the center of the set. They are to assume promenade position and dance around the outside, starting to their right (or left) as they face out.

Promeno Used by callers to mean "promenade" in order to rhyme a line of patter with the preceding line.

Prompt As a verb, to deliver a call ahead of the musical phrase during which the dancers are supposed to execute it. As a noun, a call delivered in this way.

Prompt call (1) A dance in which the calls are given ahead of the musical phrase to which they apply. (2) A dance meeting definition 1 in which the calls are brief directions (such as "Circle left" or "Ladies chain") with no patter or extraneous wording.

Prompter A common name for a caller in the 19th century; in some regions the term lasted partway into the 20th century.

Pull by Two facing dancers join right (or left) hands, pull gently as they move forward past each other, and release the handhold quickly in order to avoid an unwanted change in facing direction.

Pull her through From a mixed-gender star or single file promenade, each gent reaches his free hand (or the hand that would be free if the other hand were starring) over his opposite shoulder and takes the same hand (e.g. right in right) of the lady behind him. Without turning, he pulls her past him (releasing the star if there is one) so that she faces him. It may help if he takes a step or two backward while pulling.

Quadrille (1) A formal square dance in five or six figures, introduced in the early 19th century. (2) In the Northeast, a term used until the mid-20th century for a set of (usually three) squares done with the same partner. (3) A term used by modern square dance callers for a square phrased and prompted in New England style. (4) In some areas, a fiddle tune in 6/8 meter (from the custom of using 6/8 music for the first figure of the 19th-century quadrille).

Queen's Highway A figure used in the big circle segment of a southern mountain dance. From a couple promenade, the ladies reverse direction and all walk in single file until partners meet again. King's Highway is the same figure with the gents reversing.

Queue du chat (French for "cat's tail," from the curving path) A 19th-century term for a two-couple promenade across the set and back (which we would now call a half promenade done twice). More recently the term has been used in Quebec to mean a half promenade followed by a half right and left.

Rag A musical composition in several parts, similar to a march but characterized by syncopation. Rags developed in the late 19th and early 20th centuries, originally as piano pieces, but rural string bands soon added them to their repertoire. Several rags have been adapted (often by omitting one or more parts) for square dance use.

Range The span between the highest and lowest notes in the melody of a song or a singing call. Compare **tessitura.**

Rat race A pejorative term for calling that the dancers have trouble keeping up with. It can be caused by too fast a tempo, clipped timing, or both.

Rattlesnake twist One of several similar figures, done from a circle of eight or a southern big circle. In one version, a leader (such as Gent 1) drops his corner's hand while all others retain their handholds; the leader then moves toward his partner and ducks under the raised arms of each pair of people in succession, the others following him, going alternately behind and in front of the line.

Raven A gender-neutral term for the person taking the lady's role (the corresponding term for the gent's role is lark). It has been supplanted in many areas by **robin.** See **gender-free.**

Red hot A square dance break, popular in the 1950s. From a couple promenade, each lady crosses in front of her partner to face the gent behind her, who is her next-door neighbor. All turn that neighbor by the right hand once, original partner by the left once and a half, corner by the right once, partner by the left, and follow the next call (which was originally to promenade the corner).

Reel (1) A dance tune in 2/4 meter, characterized by short phrases and a continuous flow of short notes. (2) A common American name for **strip the willow.** (3) The Scottish term for a **hey.** (4) Originally, in the British Isles, a dance that alternated setting or balancing in place with what we would now call a hey. (5) Sometimes used as a synonym for **whole-set longways,** perhaps because the *Virginia Reel* is the best-known such dance.

Reel a grand reel A name for the **Grange do-si-do,** used in Ohio.

Reel away four A name for the **Grange do-si-do**, used in southwestern Pennsylvania.

Reel the set A name for the **Grange do-si-do**, used in southwestern Pennsylvania.

Re-sashay (1) After a half sashay, partners again change places to regain their starting position, the lady again passing in front of the gent. If the call is "Re-sashay, go all the way around," the couple does a re-sashay, followed by a full sashay with the gent going in front, then behind. (2) Used by some 1950s recording callers to mean simply "reverse," as from a circle left to a circle right.

Resolve the square In modern square dance calling, to move the dancers from wherever they are at the moment to a formation in which the couples are in sequence with original partners. From that point, they can do an allemande left with corner or start a grand right and left with partner.

Retro-phrasing A term coined by the present author for the practice of fitting to the musical phrase a figure or break that was not necessarily written with phrasing in mind.

Reverse line of dance Clockwise around the room (used by ballroom dance and round dance instructors, and by some teachers of international folk dance). Also known as reverse line of direction. Abbreviated "RLOD."

Reverse swing A swing in which the dancers revolve counterclockwise. Rarely is this an official part of the dance, but couples sometimes indulge in it for variety or to counteract dizziness.

Reverse the chain A Canadian call for a **turn back** (definition 2) from a grand right and left.

Rhythm In country dance usage, the basic downbeat to which the dancers step. To call in rhythm with the music is to make the spoken, chanted, or sung words coincide with the musical downbeats and upbeats.

Right and left through* Two facing couples exchange places by doing a pass through and a courtesy turn to face the other couple again. In some regions, and in modern square dancing, the couples do a right-hand pull by instead of a pass through.

Right and left eight (1) Four couples in box formation travel back and forth across a square, using pass throughs and courtesy turns, until all are where they started this movement. Right hands are not given in passing. Compare **eight chain through.** (2) Occasionally used as a synonym for **grand right and left.**

Right and left grand Same as **grand right and left.** The exigencies of rhyme and scansion sometimes require this inversion of words.

Right and left six Three couples (typically the heads or sides plus an extra couple in the center) travel back and forth across a square set, each couple doing two pass throughs and a courtesy turn, until all are where they started this movement. Right hands are not given in passing.

Right end high, left end low Same as **right hand high, left hand low,** but used when a line consists of four people. The dancers on the ends travel while the two in the center stand in place.

Right hand (a)round A traditional call for a right-hand turn.

Right-hand gent (1) In a square, the gent in the couple to a given lady's right; he is her corner if all are at home. As a rule he is termed the right-hand gent only if the lady is also interacting with her opposite and left-hand gents in the same figure. (2) In some figures, a gent who happens to be on the lady's right; he may or may not be her original corner.

Right hand grand A call, observed in Iowa in the 1920s, for a **grand right and left.** Presumably used in order to fit the call to the music, as in "A left allemande and a right hand grand."

Right hand high, left hand low From a line of three, the center person makes an arch with the right-hand person. The end people cross in front of the center person, the left-hand one ducking through the arch. Usually handholds are released and the center person remains in place.

Right-hand lady (1) In a square, from a given gent's viewpoint, the lady in the couple on his right; the lady who is neither his partner, his corner, nor his opposite. To her he is the left-hand gent. A suggested term applicable to both people is "next-door neighbor." (2) In some figures, a lady who happens to be on the gent's right; she may or may not be his original partner.

Right hand over, left hand back Two facing dancers join right hands and change places with a slight pull, then join left hands and return to where they started this movement. The key move in one version of the singing square *Darling Nellie Gray*.

Right hand over, left hand under Same as **right hand high, left hand low**.

Right hands across See **hands across** (definition 1).

Right (left) shoulder round See **gypsy**.

Rights and lefts An old term for the movement the English now call a circular hey with hands; this was apparently the direct ancestor of our right and left through. See also **square through.**

Rim The perimeter of a set; specifically, the dancers on the outside of a star promenade or a thar star.

Ring up 4 (6, 8) Another term for "circle 4 (6, 8)."

Rip and snort From a circle (usually of eight people), all handholds are retained with one exception. The designated couple moves across the set, goes under an arch made by the opposite couple, drops partner's hand only, and each active person leads half the set around the outside until the active couple is reunited where they began the movement. Those making the arch must turn under their own arms.

Robin A gender-neutral term for the person taking the lady's role (the corresponding term for the gent's role is lark). It is supplanting "raven" in the contra dance world to avoid misunderstandings with indigenous peoples, particularly in the Pacific Northwest; some of the latter hold the raven as a sacred symbol, while others do not wish to identify with it. See **gender-free**.

Role Short for "gender role": one of the two possible parts, traditionally termed "lady" and "gent," that a dancer may play in any partnered dance. See **gender-free** for alternative terms for these roles.

Rollaway* Partners, side by side, change places as follows: One dancer, normally the lady, moves from right to left by doing a complete left-face turn as her partner moves sideways from left to right to take her place. For a split second halfway through the move, the lady is facing her partner and holding both of his hands. The move developed as a variation of the half sashay; it was, and is, often called as "Rollaway with a half sashay." Apparently named by Ed Gilmore in 1950; around that time some callers tried to make a distinction between "rollaway" (done from a courtesy turn) and "whirlaway" (done at arm's length), but at present both moves are known as "rollaway," with the context determining how close or far apart the dancers are.

Roll back To turn solo in a small loop, covering a bit of floor space (i.e., not turning on the spot) and ending behind one's starting point. Examples: From a star or a single file promenade, to move from a position ahead of another dancer to a new position behind that dancer; from a couple promenade or a star promenade, to move from alongside one dancer to a new position alongside the person behind that dancer.

Roll promenade From a courtesy turn, couples keep pivoting until they face promenade direction and go into a promenade. In the California style that led to modern square dancing, promenades were done with a different handhold (front skaters') than courtesy turns; "roll promenade" called before the start of a courtesy turn directed the dancers to assume front skaters' position immediately.

Roll the barrel From a circle of two couples, the active couple ducks under the inactive couple's arch. The active dancers raise their joined hands, turn away from each other, and pull the inactive couple between them. Finally, the inactives raise their hands and turn away from each other (or "unwind") so the four are in a normal circle again, all facing in. All hands remain joined throughout. Sometimes the call "Roll it back" is given, whereupon the movement is repeated with the couples reversing roles. Compare **four-leaf clover** (definition 1).

Rotate Same as **stir the bucket.**

Round and square A term used in some parts of the East for the local programming format, consisting of a series of freestyle couple dances (such as waltz, polka, and foxtrot) alternating with sets of (usually three) squares. The term has been used in areas ranging from West Virginia to upstate New York. Compare **square and round.**

Round dance (1) Same as **couple dance.** (2) A dance using the positions, steps, and rhythms of a ballroom dance (such as a waltz), but in a choreographed routine, which is either memorized by the dancers or prompted to them by a cuer. Often done in conjunction with modern square dancing, although there are also clubs that do round dances exclusively.

Roundup (1) A large dance event, often sponsored by more than one club. (2) In Australia, a procedure similar to an abbreviated grand march, used for forming squares either at the beginning of an event or before each tip.

Routine The series of movements making up: a square dance figure, break, or sequence of figures and breaks; a circle or longways dance; or a round dance.

Rout(e) chain The sequence of ladies chains from the dance *The Rout(e),* starting in facing lines of four: chain across, in line, across, in line.

Rout(e) lines Two facing lines, each made up of two couples, as in the dance *The Rout(e).*

Royal square Another name for **double square.**

Ruby A gender-neutral term for the person taking the lady's role (the corresponding term for the gent's role is jet). See **gender-free.**

Running set A name given by English ballad and dance collector Cecil Sharp to a dance form he encountered in rural Kentucky. The name appears to have no basis in folklore; it may stem from a misinterpretation of "Let's run a set" (i.e. "Let's form a square or circle and do some dancing"). Some leaders make a distinction between the "running set" as Sharp observed it and other forms of southern mountain dance; others use the term for all such forms.

Run the reel A name for the **Grange do-si-do,** used in western Pennsylvania.

Sail Sometimes used in patter as a synonym for **promenade**.

Sally Goodin In the traditional dance of that name, a gent's **right-hand lady**. In the 1950s that dance was so well known that the term was easily incorporated into other patter or singing calls (e.g. "Right hand round old Sally Goodin and a left hand round your own").

Salute An old word for **honor**. Occasionally interpreted by dancers, possibly with humorous intent, as a military salute.

Sashay A word corrupted from the French *chassez* (pronounced "shassay"), meaning "to hunt" or literally "to chase," as one foot chases the other. (1) To use a side-close step (one foot steps to the side, then the other foot catches up with it and takes the weight briefly) in traveling. The best-known example is probably "Head couple sashay down" in the *Virginia Reel*. (2) To follow the floor track of a do-si-do (definition 1) while both people are facing the center. Based on the directions for some 19th-century quadrilles, this was originally done with a side-close step, but by the 1950s it was being walked in most areas where the movement was used. The half sashay, which eventually became more common than the full sashay, was simply the first part of the latter, with the lady going in front of the gent to exchange places with him. Note that a full sashay is identical to the modern contra dance movement known as Mad Robin after the English country dance of that name. In that English dance, only one person in each pair moves, but in the contra dance version everyone moves. (3) To do a do-si-do (definition 1) or an all around or see-saw. The term was used in the 1950s in Texas, where "do-si-do" always meant a hand-turn figure.

Scatter promenade A promenade in which all the couples on the dance floor may move in any direction, without regard to formations such as circle or square. Often followed by a call to find one couple and form a circle, or to find three couples and form a square, for the next movement or sequence of movements. When there are not enough couples for a workable progressive circle, the groups of two couples may start anywhere on the floor and a scatter promenade may be used as the progression.

Schottische A European couple dance in slow duple meter (often "swung" with dotted notes), with a basic pattern of step-step-step-hop, done twice, followed by four step-hops. Done between square sets in some dance communities.

Scoot and scat When dancers are in a star promenade, a call for the four outside dancers to leave their current partner and join a star in another set. The usual call is "scoot" for the gents and "scat" for the ladies.

Scrambled eggs Another name for **hash**.

Second couple or **Couple 2** In the visiting-couple tradition and most present-day square dancing, the couple to the right of Couple 1. In some 19th-century quadrilles, the couple opposite Couple 1.

Second four A term for the side couples. Used by a few callers in the Southwest around 1950; the term "side four" appears to have been more common, even where "first four" was used for the heads.

See-saw A **do-si-do** (definition 1) passing left shoulders first. Developed during the 1950s out of **see-saw your pretty little taw**.

See-saw your pretty little taw Following **all around the left-hand lady,** the ladies again go forward and back as the gents move to the right behind their partner and continue to dance forward in a counterclockwise loop, passing in front of their partner and returning to place. During the 1950s much of this combination's unique styling was lost and the moves degenerated into a right shoulder do-si-do with corner and a left shoulder do-si-do (from then on, called simply "see-saw") with partner.

Semi-singing call A dance that is composed with a specific set of words to fit a specific tune, with the caller singing melody or harmony, but whose tune is not a song likely to be known by the dancers. Popularized by Ralph Page and Rod Linnell in the mid-20th century.

Separate To move away from an adjacent dancer, often one's partner. Can be done from home (in which case "divide" is the more common call) or after passing through or splitting a facing couple. The next call will determine how far to move and in what direction.

Sequence (1) A group of basic movements done in succession; they may be a figure or a break, or part of one. (2) The number of figures and breaks, and the order of their arrangement, in a complete square dance. (3) The order and number of "A" and "B" parts in a tune. (4) A term used primarily by modern square dance callers referring to the order of the couples in a square. A set with couples in normal order (1, 2, 3, 4 counterclockwise) is "in sequence"; if either the heads or the sides have exchanged places, so that the order is 1, 2, 3, 4 clockwise, the set is "out of sequence." Just the four ladies or gents may also be in or out of sequence.

Sequence dance A couple dance consisting of a number of steps (such as walking, sliding, touching, and pointing) done in a prescribed order, often ending with some turning two-steps or waltz steps. It may or may not be a mixer. Compare **freestyle dance.**

Set (1) A group of dancers arranged in a specific formation, as a circle, square, or longways. (2) A group of two or more dances called in succession, done in the same sets with the same partners. Known as a tip in some regional styles and in modern square dancing. (3) As a verb, to **balance** (a term formerly used in quadrilles and still used in English country dancing).

Set dance (1) Any dance done by two or more couples in a specified formation, as opposed to a **couple dance.** (2) A dance for a fixed number of couples, as opposed to a "longways for as many as will" (the English name for the dance type that became the American contra).

Set running Same as **running set.**

Sets in order Same as **square your sets.**

Set-up In modern square dance calling, a sequence of basics, usually memorized, that will move the dancers from their starting positions to a formation (such as facing lines of four) from which the caller can start the key sequence of a dance, either memorized or improvised. Compare **get-out.**

Share weight Same as **give weight.**

Shoo-fly swing In a big circle, an active couple steps slightly toward the center and does a one-sided strip the willow; that is, the active couple turns by the right, then only one member of that couple turns each inactive opposite-role dancer by the left, returning to his or her partner each time for a right-hand or right-arm turn.

Shoot the star From a thar star, the current pairs do a left-hand turn halfway. This turn functions as an allemande left, causing everyone to face in grand right and left direction.

Shoulder-waist position Partners face each other; gent places both arms around lady's waist while lady places both arms around gent's shoulders. Used in some European couple dances, such as some figures of the schottische. Half shoulder-waist position is one possible promenade position in square dancing.

Sicilian circle Originally, a specific dance in progressive circle formation; often used as a generic term for any progressive circle dance.

Side couples (or **side four** or **sides**) The couples to the right and to the left of Couple 1; the couples who are neither at the head nor the foot of the hall. In visiting-couple traditions, and in most present-day square dancing, they are Couples 2 and 4; in some 19th-century quadrilles they were Couples 3 and 4.

Sight calling In modern square dance calling, a method of keeping track of the dancers that allows the caller to improvise without relying on memorized routines. The caller notes the appearance of a few "key" dancers (often Couples 1 and 4) in one or more squares, and after improvising for a while, moves those dancers into a position from which they can do an allemande left with their original corner. Because nearly all modern square dance choreography is symmetrical, the caller knows that if Couples 1 and 4 are in a certain position relative to each other, Couples 2 and 3 are as well.

Sight timing The practice of watching the dancers to see how long it takes them to execute a movement, and giving the call for the next movement about two beats before they finish the current one.

Silent couple In some across-the-set square figures, the couple opposite the active couple.

Singing call A dance with calls that are sung to a definite melody rather than spoken or chanted; specifically, such a dance that is set to a popular song, usually one that the dancers know and like. Often the calls are arranged to allow the caller (and the dancers if they choose) to sing some of the original lyrics of the song.

Single dishrag See **dishrag turn.**

Single elbow Another name for **elbow swing** (definition 2).

Single file Of a promenade, arranged so that each dancer is traveling solo, one behind another. If all eight dancers go into a single file promenade (counterclockwise by default) when all are in original order, each lady will be ahead of her partner. A common traditional break has each gent turn around to swing the lady behind him (his corner), repeating the action three more times to reunite original partners. A break component that has become popular since around

1950, particularly in modern square dancing, has the ladies (or gents) promenade single file in the center and return home to swing partner.

Six-eight (6/8) meter Nominally, a musical time signature in which there are six beats to a measure and an eighth note is worth one beat. In practice, each measure is considered to have two beats, each beat containing three eighth notes. The odd number of sub-beats produces a pleasing effect that contrasts with the more common 2/4 and 4/4 meters. Jigs as used for traditional dancing are in 6/8, as are some marches and a few popular songs.

Skaters' position See **promenade position** (definitions 1 and 2).

Slide through A modern square dance movement: Two facing dancers pass right shoulders, then face a quarter right (if playing a gent's role) or left (if playing a lady's role). When done by one lady and one gent, it is equivalent to a star through, but avoids the problem of the two roles having different hands free (which makes several possible following moves awkward). Slide through has the additional advantage (over star through) of being danceable by any two people (though the result varies depending on their gender roles).

Slip the clutch From a thar star, each dancer releases the left hand of the current partner and immediately joins left hands with the next person facing him or her. Compare **throw in the clutch.**

Small circle In southern mountain circle dancing, a circle of two couples during what is customarily the middle part of a dance. The four people dance a figure together, then each couple moves to a new couple to dance the same or a different figure as directed by the caller. In most but not all areas, odd (traveling) and even (receiving) couples are designated before the dance begins.

Snaparoo See **star through.**

Sociable figure In 19th-century quadrilles, a figure that included a change of partners. At the prompter's discretion, a sociable figure could be substituted for one of the normal figures of a plain quadrille.

Soft In modern square dancing, denoting an approach that uses the basic movements of one of the standardized programs (lists of calls), but only from their most frequently encountered formations. The most common usage is "soft Plus," which is aimed at dancers who know the Mainstream calls more or less well but are shaky on the Plus calls.

Southern style A style of dancing, in four-couple squares and in big circles made up of two-couple circles, traditional in the southern Appalachians and the Ozark Mountains, and characterized by fast tempo, dances with unique figures (i.e., not made up of standard basics), sparing use of patter (possibly because the caller often dances), and frequent but short walk-around swings. There is considerable variation in the details of the dance from one end of the region to the other, and even from town to town.

Southwestern style A form of square dancing similar to western style (definition 1), but using noticeably slower tempos and, in many cases, a two-step as the default footwork. It was developed to a fine art in western Texas between about 1935 and 1955 (Holden 1992). It seems to have disappeared shortly thereafter as the Southwest joined the rest of the continent in adopting the style promoted in southern California in the 1950s, which evolved into modern square dancing.

Spin (1) To rotate as an individual, as some dancers do during a do-si-do (definition 1), or as a lady may do while supported by a gent's raised arm in lieu of a courtesy turn. (2) A term often used by non-dancers to mean **swing** (noun or verb).

Split To pass between the members of a standing couple. Can be done by an individual or an active couple.

Split the pot A type of raffle, held at both traditional and modern square dance events, in which the winner receives half the money collected and the sponsoring group keeps the other half. Also known as fifty-fifty.

Split the ring Sometimes used as a direction for two people to move away from the center of the set and separate, whether or not they need to split a standing couple in order to do so.

Split timing A phenomenon seen in complex figures in which, because some of the movements take unusual numbers of beats to perform, they do not always begin and end with the musical phrase in an otherwise completely phrased routine. Also known as split-phrase timing. Compare **clipped timing**.

Split your corners From home position, a pair of active couples (say the heads) go forward, then each active person moves away from partner, goes out through a side couple between corner and corner's partner (briefly alongside opposite dancer), and moves toward home, passing behind corner. The next call may direct the actives to do something with partner at home, or to stop short of home and take hands with corner in a line of four.

Spread the star A direction to dancers in a star promenade to keep the star going but change from half shoulder-waist position to holding near hands with current partner, then moving apart and often raising the joined hands in an arch. Common following calls are (1) outside people duck through their own arches to the person behind them; (2) all four couples California twirl to reverse direction; (3) one or more couples reverse direction and duck through one or more arches.

Square and round The common programming format in modern square dancing: a tip of two squares, done with the same partner in the same set, followed by one or two round dances. Compare **round and square.**

Square contra A dance routine, usually a mescolanze or four-by-four, that uses the progression and repetition of a contra but puts the dancers in a square formation for a time. Compare **contra square.**

Square dance (1) A dance in square formation, or a similar group dance (see note below). (2) An event at which square dances (and, usually, other dance forms) are done. Note: Depending on the era and local custom, "square dance" may refer only to dances in square formation, or it may be a catch-all term for any dance in which two or more couples cooperate (such as a square, a big circle, or a longways dance) as distinguished from choreographed or freestyle dances for couples acting independently.

Square dance boom See **boom years.**

Glossary 449

Square dancing The hobby of gathering for the purpose of learning and doing squares and similar group dances, as distinguished from the practice of doing such dances with friends and neighbors as part of a social event. (At least one general dictionary suggests that "square dance" was not used as a verb until well into the 20th century; that is, until people started dancing squares as a hobby. My cursory research in books of the era corroborates this.)

Square set A group of (usually) four couples, each standing on one side of an imaginary square, each facing the center of the set with backs to a wall of the room. Traditionally the lady stands on the gent's right side.

Square through A modern square dance movement, introduced in 1957 by Bill Hansen, adapted (knowingly or coincidentally) from the English "circular hey with hands." Two facing couples join right hands with the opposite, pull by, and face partner. They join left hands with partner, pull by, and face opposite (the couples have now exchanged places). They again pass opposite by the right hand and partner by the left; they do not turn after the final left-hand pass, but stay back to back with partner, ready to follow the next call. A half square through (two hand passes) or a square through three-quarters (three hand passes) may be called. In every case the dancers do not turn after the final pass; this feature distinguishes square through from its antecedents.

Square tune A tune all of whose phrases are exactly 8 or 16 beats long, as opposed to a **crooked tune.** In this context the word "square" is unrelated to the square formation of dances.

Square your sets An instruction to the dancers to check that they are all in their home positions and their set is a manageable size. Usually called before the music starts, but can be used during a number if one or more sets have broken down. Equivalent calls are "Square 'em up" and "Sets in order."

Squeeze the balloon In a big circle, without dropping hands, the dancers on two facing sides of the room move into the center while those on the other two sides remain in place or dance backward a few steps. The name appears to be of recent origin, but the movement was described in 1948 (*Let's Dance* magazine) as "heads and feet balance in; now the sides."

Stacking calls The practice of giving two or more calls before the dancers are expected to execute the first one. Most often done to let the caller (and the dancers if they choose) sing the lyrics of the original song during a singing call.

Standing couple An inactive couple who are standing still as one or more active couples move toward, around, or through them.

Star* Three or more dancers move around a hub formed by their extended right (or left) hands. There are two common holds: In a wrist star (also known as a "box star" or "packsaddle hold"), each dancer holds the wrist of the one ahead. In a hands-across star (possible only with an even number of dancers), each dancer joins right (or left) hands with the person who is directly opposite him or her if all are facing the center of the group. In modern square dancing, the default is to press palms together, fingers pointing up, except in the case of a thar star where the default is a wrist hold. Modern square dancing also allows a two-person star; the term refers to a hands-up turn as distinguished from the forearm hold that is the default for most two-person turns.

Star promenade Three or more couples promenade in half shoulder-waist position (see **promenade position,** version 4) while the innermost people form a star.

Star through* A modern square dance movement, introduced simultaneously in 1960 by Ed Michl and by Frank Lane (who named it "snaparoo" but eventually withdrew the name). Can be done only by two facing dancers of opposite gender roles. The gent raises his right arm, the lady her left. They touch their raised palms and move into each other's place, the lady going under the gent's arm. The lady has turned a quarter to her left, the gent a quarter to his right: If the gent was facing north and the lady south, both are now facing east. Called "star through" because when two couples do it, they appear to be forming a star for a moment. The movement occurs in one version of the *Spanish Dance,* a 19th-century progressive circle in waltz time; Michl and Lane may or may not have been familiar with that dance.

Static square A term used in modern square dancing for a square in which all eight dancers are in someone's home place. The term refers to the shape of the set rather than the identity of the dancers.

Station Used in some instruction books as a synonym for home position.

Step A move of the leg and foot to a new position, whereupon that foot takes the body's weight (as opposed to **touch** in couple dance footwork). The basic step in most square dance traditions is a brisk walk. Parts of Texas used a two-step until the mid-1950s; in some areas, some or all of the dancers incorporate **percussive dancing** into their group dances, although it appears more common to reserve percussive steps for freestyle solo dancing between group sets. See also **posture.**

Stepdancing A form of **percussive dancing.** The term is most often used for the styles done in Scotland, Ireland, and parts of Canada.

Step right back During a swing in ballroom position, an instruction for a couple to retain their handhold (lady's right hand, gent's left) and move out to arm's length, as in swing dancing, then resume ballroom position. A typical call is "Step right back and watch her smile, step right up and swing her awhile." The move is usually called for twice; the following lines may be "Step right back and watch her grin, step right up and swing her ag'in." The sequence may be called during a break, or it may be used as a visiting-couple figure in itself; in the latter case it is often done with the opposite in each two-couple group.

Step-swing balance A New England balance done sideways in which the free foot is swung across in front of the other leg.

Stir the bucket To rotate a square set one-quarter, so that the heads become sides and vice versa. At some times and places it has been customary to do this between the two dances of a tip. The practice was intended to give everyone an equal amount of time being active; it appears to have fallen into disuse in the modern square dance world, as in modern choreography it matters very little who the heads or sides are.

Straight "When you're straight" means "when you finish the movement you were just executing." Usually used only if that movement leaves the dancers in sequence (i.e., in normal 1-2-3-4 order).

Straight-arm hold One possible position for a buzz-step swing: Each dancer straightens the right arm and places the right hand on partner's right shoulder; left hands are joined underneath. At some times and places, this hold has been taught to children to enable them to swing without intimate contact. The hold has the advantage of putting partners in the optimum position (relative to each other) to do an effective buzz step. The chief disadvantage is that it makes it easy to swing wildly and lose control; if their hands are sweaty, the dancers may fly apart and injure themselves and/or others.

String dance A term for a contra dance, used in parts of New England in the early 20th century.

Strip the gears A variation on the **wagon wheel** (definition 2): After partners turn by the right and the ladies do their right-face solo spin, partners catch left hands or arms and start a do paso (instead of going into a star promenade).

Strip the willow In a longways dance, the head couple turns partner by the right hand, arm, or elbow, then turns each successive opposite dancer by the left, returning to partner after each opposite and again turning by the right. The name is more common in England than in North America (where it is more often called "reel") but is occasionally found in printed dance directions. See also **shoo-fly swing.**

Sunny side out Facing the walls of the room, with one's back to the center of the set. Can be said of dancers in a large formation like a square or big circle, or of ladies or gents standing back to back in the center of a set. Note that in a square or big circle, if all are facing out, each gent's corner is on his right and each lady's corner is on her left. Also known as "pretty side out."

Suzy Q A name for the **Grange do-si-do.** Introduced by Jim York in 1949, this was the most common name for this movement in the emerging modern square dance scene. The name was presumably given because the series of right- and left-hand turns forces the dancers to twist their bodies in a fashion similar to the 1930s ballroom dance step known as the Suzy Q.

Swap To exchange partners with another couple.

Swap and swing (1) A name for a common visiting-couple sequence: Couple 1 lead right and circle four, swing your opposite, swing your own, and on to the next. Many older eastern singing calls consist entirely of this sequence; in southern mountain style as danced in many areas, each small circle figure ends with it. (2) A name occasionally used for **eastern style** square dancing. The term may be pejorative, used by those who believe eastern style consists of nothing more than this sequence.

Swat the flea A left-handed **box the gnat.** The term appears to have been coined in the 1960s by modern square dance leaders to do away with dancer confusion between "box the gnat" and "box the flea."

Sweep the floor A movement done in the big circle portion of some southern mountain dances. From a promenade, couples move slightly apart and join near hands (gent's right, lady's left). The gent drops to one knee and the lady moves forward around him, passing their joined hands over his head, until she is at his right side again. Also known as "Gents kneel and do-si your lady." **Do-si-do mountain style** is similar except that the gent remains standing.

Swing* (1) To hold another dancer relatively close and revolve as a unit, almost always clockwise. The couple may use a walking step or a **buzz step,** depending on local custom, the tempo of the music, their ability, and/or their energy level. Arm positions include **ballroom hold, straight-arm hold,** and either of two **unisex holds.** (2) At some times and places (notably the Southwest in the 1950s), a synonym for "turn": There were one-hand and two-hand swings as well as waist swings. (3) Formerly, a synonym for "circle"; one version of the singing square *Pop Goes the Weasel* includes the line "Swing four hands in a circle."

Swing all eight Everyone takes a few steps forward, gives right hand to opposite and left hand to next-door neighbor, and the formation moves clockwise using a buzz step. The movement appears (without a name) in a medley in Linnell and Winston 1974; whether Rod devised it or learned it elsewhere is not known.

Swing like thunder To form a **basket** and move to the left (clockwise) using a **buzz step.**

Swing on the corner Formerly in Texas, a synonym for **allemande left.**

Swing through A modern square dance movement, introduced in 1963 by Del Coolman. From an ocean wave, those who can turn half by the right, then those who can turn half by the left. The most common occurrence is in a "right-hand wave"; i.e., a wave in which each center person is holding an end person by the right hand and the center two people have left hands joined. Included in this glossary because it was perhaps the first movement in widespread use that cannot be danced comfortably in a multiple of 4 beats (it takes 6); veteran caller Jim Mayo believes that this marked the beginning of the end of phrased calling and dancing in the modern square dance scene.

Swoopie Dorothy Shaw's name for a figure with much movement in curving paths, such as the visiting-couple figures of southern and traditional western dancing.

Tag A short musical passage, often the last 8 beats of the song, inserted at the end of the figure or break of a singing call to allow extra time to complete a movement. The last 8 beats of the song are also commonly used as an introduction to the entire square, to cue in the caller and the dancers.

Tail couple A rare synonym for foot couple in a square (Dick's 1878).

Tandem square A dance done by a square set with two couples on each side, one couple behind the other. Compare **big square, double square.**

Taw A term for a gent's partner, used in the West and Southwest and in modern square dancing. Origin obscure; may be southwestern, as the word appears in Greggerson 1939 (Texas) but not in Shaw 1939 (Colorado). Possibly named for the large shooting marble that was among a boy's most valued possessions.

Glossary 453

Teacup chain A complicated break, introduced by Pat Morrison Lewkowicz in the 1940s when modern square dancing was beginning to develop out of traditional dancing. It has often been seen as the dividing line between novice and seasoned modern square dancers. Describing it is beyond the scope of this book, but descriptions and videos can readily be found at the Square Dance History Project and other online sources.

Tempo The speed at which the music is played (as distinguished from **timing**). Sometimes used incorrectly to mean **meter.**

Tessitura A musical term (Italian for "texture") for the strongest part of a singer's range or the part of a song's range where most of the notes fall. This is a more useful measure than range alone for finding one's ideal key for a singing call, because songs with identical ranges can have very different tessituras.

Texas do-si-do From a circle of any number of couples, all face partner and turn by the left, turn corner by the right, and turn partner by the left. The call was simply "do-si-do" (not "Texas do-si-do"). In most parts of Texas, according to Rickey Holden (1951), the dancers continued the sequence of "corner right, partner left" until they heard the call "One more change and on [or home] you go." In Dallas and the rest of the Southwest (outside Texas), "do-si-do" meant only three turns: partner, corner, partner. In either case the do-si-do ended with partners doing a courtesy turn or a left-hand turn, whichever blended more smoothly into the following movement. In the mid-1950s most of Texas adopted California styling and terminology, including the term "do paso" for the Texas do-si-do and the practice of limiting it to three turns.

Texas star A square dance figure based on star promenades. The term is occasionally used as a synonym for star promenade.

Texas style See **Southwestern style.**

Thar star The four-couple star formed during the Allemande Thar break. In its default form, the gents make a right-hand star in the center, always using a wrist hold. Each gent has left hands joined with a lady, as this star is preceded by a left-hand turn. By default, the gents move backward as the ladies move forward.

Third couple or **Couple 3** In the visiting-couple tradition and most present-day square dancing, the couple opposite Couple 1. In some 19th-century quadrilles, the couple to the right of Couple 1.

Those who can A call addressed to those dancers in a set who are in position to execute the next movement in the standard way. If the call is "Those who can do a right and left through," only the dancers who are in facing couples, lady on the gent's right, will move. The term was apparently first used by Madeline Allen in 1958; it is used primarily in modern square dancing.

Three ladies chain Three couples (the heads or sides plus an extra couple in the center) do a series of ladies chains until partners are reunited. The outside couples finish each chain with a normal courtesy turn, but the center gent simply helps each lady he receives to continue in the direction she was already going.

Three-quarter chain See **ladies chain three-quarters.**

Throw in the clutch From a thar star, each dancer releases the left hand of the current partner. The ladies continue to travel forward while the gents reverse their motion from backward to forward, so that ladies and gents are moving forward past each other. The caller must specify how far the dancers are to travel, typically by telling them what to do the first or second time they meet a specific person. Introduced by Fenton "Jonesy" Jones in 1949. Compare **slip the clutch.**

Timber A word traditionally shouted by the dancers or the caller when partners are reunited near the end of a square featuring a partner change. Occasionally the word is used to refer to one's partner, as in "Swing old timber."

Timing The number of musical beats allowed by the choreographer or the caller for the dancers to execute each movement (as distinguished from **tempo**).

Tip In some regional traditions and in modern square dancing, a group of dances done in succession with the same partner. Since the 1950s the standard tip in modern square dancing has comprised one patter call and one singing call. (At some times and places, "tip" referred to each individual dance within the group of two or three; the term is so used in Shaw 1939.) The term may have its origin in the custom of paying or "tipping" the musicians a small amount, such as a nickel per couple, before or after each dance number.

Top couple In a longways dance, the couple nearest the head of the hall; in a whole-set longways, this is the only active couple. The term is occasionally used to refer to the first couple, or either head couple, in a square set.

Touch A move of the leg and foot to a new position without shifting the body's weight to that foot (as opposed to **step**). Rare in square dance traditions except for some forms of the balance, but common in couple dances and the folk dances of other nations and ethnic groups.

Traditional square dance Broadly, any square dance form that existed before the advent of modern square dancing (which developed its distinctive character after 1945), or any style that has survived or been revived since then.

Trail See **break and trail.**

Trailing patter Patter, typically following a directive call, that does not itself contain a directive call or warn the dancers of one to come. It adds color to the proceedings and may also help the caller time the directive calls. The term was coined by Frank Kaltman (Holden 1951). Compare **leading patter.**

Trail through See **cross trail.**

Transition The point at which one dance movement ends and the next one begins. The smoothness or awkwardness of the transitions can have as great an effect on the difficulty of a dance as the number and complexity of moves used.

Transitional squares A recent term for squares composed during the period, roughly 1945 to 1955, when modern square dancing was beginning to develop out of traditional dancing. These squares keep more dancers active more of the time than many traditional figures, but because they use few if any newly invented names for movements, they are accessible to traditional and neo-traditional dancers. Several such routines, such as *Ends Turn In* and *Fiddle Faddle* (both included in Chapter 21), are popular with contra dancers.

Traveling swing   A swing during which the couple moves to a different spot rather than revolving around a fixed point. In some areas this was known as a carry-o-swing.

Trio   (1) A group of three people who have chosen to dance together. (2) A dance written specifically for groups of three, such as a circle mixer or a three-face-three progressive circle. A few squares have been written for trios.

Triple Allemande   A break in which three left allemandes are done with the same corner. After the first, the ladies right-hand star while the gents promenade counterclockwise in single file until corners meet again. After the second, the gents star while the ladies promenade; the third leads into a normal grand right and left. Introduced by Vera Holleuffer in 1945. See Chapter 23 for a call chart.

Triple minor   A contra dance in which each minor set has three couples. Compare **triplet**.

Triplet   A longways dance for exactly three couples. The sets do not interact with other sets on the floor. Compare **triple minor**.

Tucker   A name for an extra gent whose task it is to secure a partner during a big circle dance. His opportunity may come during a grand right and left or a single file promenade. The dance appears to stem from the song Old Dan Tucker; it may be treated as a play-party game, with singing the only accompaniment. There is also a dance, *Tucker Waltz,* in which the music changes between a waltz (for freestyle dancing) and a march or fiddle tune (for a couple promenade). During the waltz no cutting in is allowed, but during the promenade a solo gent may insert himself in front of a couple; the gent of that couple must drop back to the next lady, setting off a chain reaction that lasts until the music changes again. Compare **cut in, ninepin.**

Turn   (1) Same as **hand turn.** (2) Any individual or couple movement to the right or left, in place or along a floor track. (3) In 19th-century quadrilles, a **two-hand turn.** Even as the swing began to replace the two-hand turn in the late 19th and early 20th centuries, many prompters still called "Turn partners."

Turn alone   To turn 180 degrees on the spot, reversing one's facing direction. Often called "U turn back." During a walkthrough, the caller may specify whether a right-face or left-face turn will flow more smoothly, depending on the preceding and following movements.

Turn back or **turn right back**   (1) To reverse one's direction of travel by making a 180-degree solo turn, but covering some ground rather than turning on the spot. As an example, from a single file promenade, the ladies may "turn back on the outside track" while the gents keep going, or vice versa. (2) Upon meeting partner in a grand right and left, to turn halfway by the right hand and start a grand right and left in the opposite direction.

Turn your corner under   A mirror-image **California twirl,** done by two people side by side with the lady on the left. Also called "California whirl."

Twirl   A move in which a lady spins as she goes under a gent's raised arm, his hand supporting hers. Substituting a twirl for a courtesy turn to complete a ladies chain or right and left through is an increasingly common practice in contra dancing and neo-traditional squares. In modern square dancing, a twirl is customary during the transition from a grand right and left or a swing to a promenade, and also at the end of a promenade home.

Twirl to swap* A generic term, used in present-day contra dancing, for any move in which the lady goes under the gent's raised arm. The most commonly used specific moves are box the gnat (and box the flea / swat the flea), California twirl, and star through. Callers in styles other than modern square dancing sometimes refer to all these moves loosely as "box the gnat."

Two by two or **two plus two** An abbreviation, common in dance publicity, for a common programming format in modern square dancing: a tip of two squares followed by two round dances.

Two-faced line A line of four formed by two couples facing in opposite directions. Used primarily in modern square dancing.

Two-four (2/4) meter The most-used time signature for square dance music: There are two beats to a measure, and a quarter note is worth one beat. Reels and breakdowns (hoedowns) are in 2/4, as are hornpipes as played in the USA, Canada, and Scotland.

Two-hand turn Two dancers join both hands (usually with arms straight across, but sometimes with arms crossing each other at the hands), give weight, and move forward (usually clockwise) around each other.

Two-step (1) A type of couple dance, done to music in 2/4 or 4/4 meter, consisting of repeated units of step-close-step; like a polka without the initial hop. (2) The step-close-step footwork, used either sporadically or continuously in place of a dance-walk in squares and similar group dances. It was a trademark of the local square dance style in western Texas between the 1930s and the 1950s (Holden 1992). (3) A name, common in Canada, for a tune type similar to a polka and intermediate in character between a reel and a march.

Two-two (2/2) meter See **cut time.**

Unique figure A movement or series of movements that has a call, usually traditional, that is not descriptive (i.e. uses neither accepted basics nor everyday English) and occurs in only one dance. Most visiting-couple figures, such as *Bird in the Cage,* are unique. Also known as "dominant figure."

Unisex hold A hand and arm hold for swinging in which the two dancers assume identical positions. There are two chief variants: (1) Each dancer puts right arm around the other's back (as the gent would do in a ballroom hold) and rests left arm on the other's right arm (as the lady would do in a ballroom hold). (2) Each dancer puts right arm around the other's waist; left hands are joined underneath. (The straight-arm hold is also a unisex hold but is not generally referred to as such.)

Upbeat The musical impulse that occurs just after the downbeat and inspires dancers to dance "up" off their heels. Music played with too weak an upbeat can have the effect of making dancers feel pounded into the floor like tent pegs.

U turn back In modern square dancing, the standard call for dancers to turn 180 degrees on the spot. Same as "turn alone." The name was apparently coined by Jim York in 1954.

Varsovienne (1) A couple dance in triple time, once commonly done between square sets in some regions. (2) The hand position used in this dance, which is also used for square dance promenades in some areas (see **promenade position,** definition 3).
Veer To move diagonally, forward and to the right (or left) at the same time.
Venus and Mars A figure in which the ladies form a right-hand star and the gents form an adjacent left-hand star. Partners exchange places, one couple at a time, the lady crossing in front of the gent. Typically partners cross again to restore the original stars, then each lady joins her partner in a star promenade.
Virginia Reel The best-known whole-set longways dance. The name is sometimes used loosely to mean any whole-set longways.
Visiting couple A couple that travels from one standing couple to another, doing the same or a similar figure with each.
Visiting-couple figure A figure consisting entirely of one couple (or a pair of opposite couples) visiting their way around the set. Traditionally, most such figures are unique figures, but a visiting-couple sequence may be constructed using standard basics such as circle, do-si-do (definition 1), swing, and ladies chain. In some regions, each visit of an active couple to an inactive couple ends with a do-si-do (definition 2) before the actives go "on to the next."

Wagon wheel (1) A version of the traditional figure *Forward Six*. In its distinctive move, the facing lines of three join hands or arms in one of several possible ways to form an attached group of six people and circle left halfway, then back up into lines of three on the opposite side. (2) A break devised by Lloyd Shaw in 1939 and released to the public in 1947. All allemande left corner, turn partner by the right once, and each gent helps his partner into a right-face spin once and a half (or just half) around. The lady takes her partner's right arm with her left hand ("escort position"), the gents form a left-hand star, and everyone travels counterclockwise in a star promenade. At the next call, "The hub flies out and the rim flies in," the gents release the star and the couples pivot counterclockwise about once around; partners join right hands and pull by in grand right and left direction. All pull by the next person with the left hand, then repeat with the next (original opposite) the sequence they just did with partner. One more left-hand pass (with original corner) will reunite partners.
Waist swing A swing in ballroom hold. Not used in calling, but used in dance directions in areas where "swing" could also mean a one- or two-hand turn.
Walk-around swing A swing in which the dancers use a normal dance-walk rather than a buzz step.
Walkthrough A dance figure or break, done without music and generally not in rhythm or up to tempo, as a means of instructing the dancers.
Waltz (1) A couple dance in 3/4 meter with a pattern of step-step-close, often done between squares and nearly always at the end of an evening. (2) As a verb,

can mean to do a standard waltz or, loosely, to travel as a couple counterclockwise around the hall, regardless of the footwork or the type of music, especially if the couple is rotating clockwise while traveling.

Waltz position (1) The face-to-face ballroom hold used for the waltz, known as closed position in ballroom dancing. (2) Loosely, the modified ballroom hold (with partners slightly offset to the side) used for the square dance swing.

Waltz quadrille A type of phrased square in 3/4 meter using waltz steps and sometimes a turning waltz for the promenade. First introduced in the mid-19th century; revivals were attempted by Ed Durlacher in the 1940s and by several western leaders in the 1950s.

Waltz swing (1) A square dance swing using the ballroom hold. (2) A name for the **bouquet waltz.**

Warm walkthrough The teaching of a dance movement, figure, or break while the music is playing.

Wave Same as **ocean wave.**

Wave the ocean Any of several figures involving a back-and-forth motion. One such figure is identical to **inside out and outside in** (definition 1); another has the active couple splitting the inactive couple (who move apart without making an arch) and either backing up to place or being split by the inactives. Compare **ocean wave.**

Weave the ring A grand right and left without the handholds: Dancers pass right shoulders with partner, left shoulders with the next person they meet, and so on around the set. Everyone moves forward at all times.

Weight See **give weight.**

Western style (1) A style of square dancing characterized by relatively fast tempo, many dances with unique figures, liberal use of patter, and infrequent, short, walk-around swings. Also known as "cowboy style" or "old western" (to distinguish it from modern square dancing). (2) A common name for modern square dancing, especially in its formative years (1945 through the 1960s).

Wheel and deal A modern square dance movement introduced by Clarence Watson in 1960. From a line of two couples, each couple wheels toward the center of the line to end facing the opposite direction. From a two-faced line, the couples end facing each other; if the line was all facing the same way, the couples end with one behind the other (the original left-hand couple moves forward before wheeling to let the other couple go in front).

Wheel around* To pivot as a couple, usually 180 degrees, either with near hands joined or in promenade position depending on the preceding move. Most often the couple consists of a lady on the right side of a gent, and they do a left-face pivot with the lady moving forward and the gent backing up. Introduced as a modern square dance call by Bill Castner in 1950, though of course the movement is much older. Compare **backtrack** (definition 2).

Wheelbarrow Two couples, each with both hands joined, move around each other by alternately pushing and pulling their partner, never changing their facing direction. This is the movement known in English country dancing as "poussette."

Glossary 459

Wheel chain Similar to a two ladies chain, except that the ladies turn each other once around by the right hand before going to their opposite gent. Popular for a brief time in the 1950s.

Whirlaway See **rollaway**.

Whole-set longways A dance in longways formation in which only one couple at a time is active and there are no subsets, as distinguished from a typical contra dance. *Virginia Reel* is the best-known example.

Wind up the ball of yarn From a big circle, a designated dancer releases the corner's handhold and leads the other dancers into the center on a spiral track. The dance may end when the leader is in the center, or the leader may double back, spiral outward, and form the circle again.

Working couple Same as **active couple** or **visiting couple**.

Workshop In modern square dancing, an event or a series of events at which dancers are taught more complex moves and concepts than those they already know. The term is sometimes used to mean a complete class taking dancers from one standardized program to the next (e.g. from Plus to Advanced).

Wring the dishrag To execute a **dishrag turn,** often a double dishrag.

Wrong way Contrary to the standard or expected direction. A wrong way promenade is clockwise (to the left if the dancers are facing the center when the call is given).

Wrong way grand A grand right and left with the gents traveling clockwise and the ladies counterclockwise. Also known as "grand right and wrong."

Wrong way thar A thar star with the gents forming a left-hand star in the center and joining right hands with the ladies. As in a normal thar, the gents move backward and the ladies forward unless otherwise instructed.

You turn back A spelling of **U turn back,** used occasionally in the 1950s.

Zero A movement or series of movements that returns all dancers to the places where they began it (or at least to the same positions relative to one another, even if they are facing a different wall of the room). There are also fractional zeroes, which must be called twice or three times in a row to achieve the zero effect. The term was first used widely by modern square dance callers, but it is useful for a neo-traditional caller to understand how various movements and combinations affect the dancers' positions.

Zig and zag One method of progressing to the next couple in a progressive circle: Without changing their facing direction, each couple veers right for 4 beats, then veers left for 4 beats, to face a new couple.

Zig-zag In a square, the members of an active couple separate at one end of the set, and each member travels alternately behind and in front of the inactive dancers (who are probably standing in a line of three) until the couple is reunited at the other end of the set.

Resources

We are living in a new Golden Age of information about all subjects, including dance. There is more information readily available about all forms of social dance than there has ever been. Thanks to modern technology, many video clips are free for the downloading – and of course, video is the only way (other than being there in person) to see and hear exactly what was being danced, and how, at a given place and time. In the case of dance forms that were in fashion before the development of video, there are many excellent reenactments.

In addition, it is easier than ever to read books and magazines and to listen to audio recordings. Many resources have been uploaded to the Web, including complete runs of several important square dance magazines. And if a book or recording is not available online, a used copy can often be purchased readily through such websites as ABEBooks, Alibris, and eBay.

Advice on Buying

Before you spend serious money, watch auction listings for a while. I have seen different sellers offer copies of the same book in similar condition for $5 and $50. I have seen asking prices above $30 for single issues of national square dance magazines that may be viewed free online. On eBay, after you have entered a search term and gotten results, you can check a box in the left-hand column to view only sold items; this is a quick and easy way to discover the actual selling prices, and therefore the actual market value, of any given item.

Using Books and Recordings

Don't assume a dance in a book or on a recording is correct. I am bemused by the number of authors who appear not to have double-checked their dance descriptions, which made it into print with too many or too few beats allowed for some movements. Similarly, many recordings were obviously not made with live dancers, as the movements cannot be done comfortably in the time allowed by the caller. If you like a figure, by all means use it, but work it out on paper first and make sure the timing is correct.

Remember when reading books and articles that the writer may be relying on outdated information. Also, different writers may use the same names to mean different things. "Cotillion" and "quadrille" were used interchangeably for a time in the early 19th century; "cotillion" often meant the "German" in the later 19th century; "western style" may mean either traditional calls and figures or modern square dancing.

TUNE TITLES

Listed here are some of my favorite tunes for squares and similar group dances. Each of them appears in at least one of the most widely used tune books.

Reels and reel-like tunes (2/4 meter)

Angeline the Baker	FF	Lady of the Lake (G)	PC
Angus Campbell	FF	Lamplighter's Hornpipe	NE
Arkansas Traveler	FF	Leather Britches	FF
Bastringue, La	FF, NE	Levantine's Barrel	NE, PC
Batchelder's	NE, PC	Liberty	FF
Bay of Fundy	PC	Little Liza Jane	FF
Big John McNeil	NE	Mason's Apron	FF, NE, PC
Bill Cheatham	FF	Mississippi Sawyer	FF, PC
Billy in the Lowground	FF, PC3	Nail That Catfish to the Tree	PC
Bull at the Wagon (3-part)	FF	North Carolina Breakdown	PC
Cripple Creek	FF, PC3	Old French	FF, NE
Crooked Stovepipe	NE	Old Joe Clark	FF
Cumberland Gap	PC3	Paddy on the Turnpike	FF, NE, PC3
Dailey's Reel	FF, PC3	Pays de Haut	NE, PC
Devil's Dream	FF, NE	Possum up a Gum Stump	PC
Dominion Reel	PC	Quince Dillon's High D	FF
Dubuque	FF, PC3	Quindaro Hornpipe	NE
Durang's Hornpipe	FF, NE, PC	Ragtime Annie (3-part version)	FF
East Tennessee Blues	FF, PC2	Rakes of Mallow	NE
Eighth of January	FF, PC3	Richmond Cotillion	FF, PC
Far from Home	NE, PC	Rickett's Hornpipe	FF, NE
Fiddler's Dream	PC3	Road to California	PC
Fireman's Reel	NE	Rock the Cradle Joe	FF, PC
Fisher's Hornpipe	FF, NE	Round the Horn	PC
Forked Deer	PC	Saint Anne's Reel	FF, NE
Glise a Sherbrooke	NE, PC	Saturday Night Breakdown	PC
Golden Slippers	FF	Seneca Square Dance	PC
Golden Wedding Reel	PC2	Shoes and Stockings	PC
Goodbye Liza Jane	FF	Soldier's Joy	FF
Green Willis	FF, PC3	Speed the Plough	FF, NE, PC
Growling Old Man	FF, NE	Walker Street	NE, PC
Joys of Quebec	FF	Waynesboro	PC
Juliann Johnson	PC	White Cockade	FF, NE
Kansas City Reel	PC	Woodchopper's Reel	FF, NE
Lady of the Lake (D)	PC		

Jigs (6/8 meter)

Atholl Highlanders (4-part)	FF, PC	Larry O'Gaff	FF, NE
Belfast Jig	PC2	Little Burnt Potato	FF, NE
Blackberry Quadrille	NE	Maggie Brown's Favorite	FF, NE
Coleraine	FF, NE	Mug of Brown Ale	PC
Frost Is All Over	PC	Off She Goes	FF, NE
Haste to the Wedding	FF, NE	Rock Valley Jig	NE, PC2
Hundred Pipers	NE, PC	Shandon Bells	NE
Irishman's Heart	NE, PC	Smash the Windows	FF, NE
Kitty McGee	FF, NE, PC	Tobin's Jig	FF

Marches and march-like tunes (2/4 or 4/4 meter; the line is fuzzy)

Bonaparte Crossing Rhine	FF, PC3	Miss Murray of Lintrose	PC2
Earl of Mansfield	NE	My Love Is But a Lassie	NE
Gallopede	FF, NE	O'Donnell Abu	NE
Girl I Left Behind Me	FF, PC	Pete's March	PC2
Girl with the Blue Dress On	PC2	Road to Boston	NE
Guizer's March, Da	PC2	Scotland the Brave	FF
March of St. Timothy	PC	Scotty O'Neil	PC2
Meeting of the Waters	NE, PC2		

References for the lists above (see under "Tune Books" below):
FF   *Fiddler's Fakebook*
NE   *New England Fiddler's Repertoire*
PC   *Portland Collection*
PC2   *Portland Collection, Volume 2*
PC3   *Portland Collection, Volume 3*

Songs for Singing Calls

All of these songs have been used for singing square dances (or, in a few cases, prompted quadrille-style squares) at one time or another. All have entered the public domain in the United States. As discussed in Chapter 3, I would not necessarily use all of them, but I leave it to you to decide which ones you are comfortable with. Songs in waltz time (3/4 meter) were either stretched into 4/4 or sped up to 6/8.

Music for many of these songs appears in collections of singing squares (see below under "Books"). Copies of public domain sheet music for most titles can be ordered from **pdinfo.com** (the source for most of the dates shown here).

After They've Seen Paree (1919)
Ain't We Got Fun (1921)
Alabama Jubilee (1915)
Alexander's Ragtime Band (1911)
Alice Blue Gown (1919)
Animal Fair (1898)
Avalon (1920)
Ballin' the Jack (1913)
Battle Hymn / John Brown's Body (1861)
Bill Bailey (1902)
Buffalo Gals (1844)
Bye Bye Blues (1925)
California Here I Come (1924)
Camptown Races (1850)
Can't You Hear Me Calling, Caroline (1914)
Captain Jinks (1868)
Casey Jones (1909)
Charley, My Boy (1924)
Chinatown (1910)
Cielito Lindo (1882)
Climbing Up the Golden Stairs (1884)
Colonel Bogey March (1916)
Crawdad Song (1917)
Daisy Bell / Bicycle Built for Two (1892)
Darling Nellie Gray (1856)
Down Yonder (1921)
Five Foot Two (1925)
Floatin' Down to Cotton Town (1919)
Freight Train (1912)
Gilbert & Sullivan melodies (1871–1896)
Girl I Left Behind Me (1810)
Give My Regards to Broadway (1904)
Golden Slippers (1879)
Goodbye My Lady Love (1904)
Grandfather's Clock (1876)
Hard Hearted Hannah (1924)
Henery the Eighth (1910)
Hinky Dinky Parley-Voo (1915)
Hot Time in the Old Town (1896)
If You Knew Susie (1925)
I'm Nobody's Baby (1921)
Indiana (1917)
In the Good Old Summertime (1902)
It's a Long Way to Tipperary (1912)
I Want a Girl (1911)
I Want to Be Happy (1924)
Lady Be Good (1924)
Last Night on the Back Porch (1923)
Let the Rest of the World Go By (1919)
Life on the Ocean Wave (1851)
Listen to the Mocking Bird (1855)
Little Brown Jug (1869)
Little Old Log Cabin in the Lane (1871)
Loch Lomond (1841)

Lucy Long (1842)
Ma! He's Making Eyes at Me (1921)
Marching Through Georgia (1865)
McNamara's Band (1889)
Melancholy Baby (1912)
Mountain Dew (1920)
My Gal Sal (1907)
My Little Girl (1915)
My Old Kentucky Home (1853)
Nelly Bly (1850)
Nobody's Baby (1921)
No, No, Nora (1923)
Oh, Johnny (1917)
Oh Susanna (1848)
Old Folks at Home / Swanee River (1851)
On the Old Fall River Line (1913)
Original Dixieland One-Step (1917)
Pack Up Your Troubles (1915)
Pony Boy (1909)
Pop Goes the Weasel (1853)
Prisoner's Song (1924)
Put On Your Old Grey Bonnet (1909)
Puttin' On the Style (1925)
Put Your Arms Around Me, Honey (1910)
Ramblin' Wreck (1919)
Red River Valley (1896)
Red Wing (1907)
Reuben and Rachel (1871)
Roamin' in the Gloamin' (1911)
Sailing Down the Chesapeake Bay (1913)
Sheik of Araby (1921)
Smiles (1918)
Solomon Levi (1887)
Somebody Stole My Gal (1918)
Some of These Days (1910)
Spanish Cavalier (1881)
Stars and Stripes Forever (1897)
Sweet Georgia Brown (1925)
Take Me Out to the Ball Game (1908)
Tarara Boom-de-ay (1891)
Tea for Two (1924)
That Old Gang of Mine (1923)
There'll Be Some Changes Made (1921)
Trail of the Lonesome Pine (1913)
Vive la Compagnie (1844)
Wabash Cannonball (1904)
Waiting for the Robert E. Lee (1912)
Wait Till the Sun Shines, Nellie (1905)
Washington and Lee Swing (1910)
Wearing of the Green (1841)
When Johnny Comes Marching Home (1863)
When the Saints Go Marching In (1923)
When the Work's All Done This Fall (1910)
When You Wore a Tulip (1914)
Whispering (1920)
World Is Waiting for the Sunrise (1919)
Wreck of the Old 97 (1924)
Yankee Doodle Boy (1904)
Yellow Rose of Texas (1853)
Yes Sir That's My Baby (1925)
Yes, We Have No Bananas (1923)
You're a Grand Old Flag (1906)

BOOKS

NOTE: To conserve space, I have omitted from this bibliography dozens of books and booklets that are primarily or entirely compilations of standard square dance figures. Any such volume is worth acquiring if the price is reasonable. A few books that are mainly compilations appear below, usually because they contain unusual dance material or worthwhile thoughts on calling.

If you are interested in dance history, it will help to keep in mind that the more recent a book, the more likely it is to be affected by regional and national cross-currents. This can be true even of successive editions of the same book (see, for instance, Writers' Program 1940 and Bol 1950).

Musical scores are not included in these books (except perhaps for an occasional example) unless otherwise noted. Unless "piano music" is mentioned, printed music consists of melody lines, possibly with chord symbols. Books that consist entirely of music are listed separately under "Tune Books," but several titles in the main list include a tune for every dance.

The star (☆) denotes a book that is both excellent of its kind and likely to be of more than average interest to the neo-traditional caller.

Anderson, Virginia C., ed. *Square and Circle*. Woodbury, NJ: American Squares, 1950. Contains dances published in the second year (1946–47) of *American Squares*: 51 squares, 11 other dances. Like Burgin 1949, includes many unusual figures. To my knowledge, the plan of issuing yearbooks was abandoned after this second volume.

Armstrong, Don. *Square Dance Workbooks*. New Port Richey, FL: The author, 1955 and 1956. Three mimeographed letter-size volumes. The first has full definitions of most basic movements and well-known breaks then in use, along with tips on styling and etiquette, but no dance figures. The second has 100 patter and singing figures, the third 53 more. There are no descriptions, but Armstrong was a master at re-wording calls to make them nearly self-explanatory (and improve word metering – putting the actual commands in the right place). His milieu at the time was the square dance club scene, but he eschewed the more advanced calls; just about every dance in these books is suitable for (or easily adaptable to) neo-traditional style. All three volumes are available free at **https://squaredancehistory.org/items/show/1834**.

☆Bol, Lawrence "Bud," ed. *The Square Dance*. Chicago: Chicago Park District, 1950. This large-format paperback of nearly 300 pages is a revision of Writers' Program 1940. Squares are no longer referred to as "quadrilles," and the dances are no longer characterized as fast or slow, easy or difficult. Interestingly, the use of live music is still assumed: Suggested tune titles are given but not record numbers, and the section on sound presupposes an orchestra, not a turntable. There are 60 patter calls, 20 singing calls, 18 couple dances, and several mixers. Cross-currents have been at work since 1940; several squares hail from outside the Midwest. This revision is much easier to find than the 1940 original; all but the regional purist will be happy with it.

Borggreen, Jørn, ed. *Right to the Helm: Cape Breton Square Dances.* Jyllinge, Denmark: The author, 2002. A careful documentation of the local style of this isolated Nova Scotia island where folk traditions have survived or been revived. Contains about 15 multi-figure square sets, each ascribed to a specific town and informant. Variations on the styling of basic movements are assiduously notated.

Boyd, Neva L., and Tressie M. Dunlavy. *Old Square Dances of America.* Chicago: Recreation Training School of Chicago, 1925. Reprinted 1932 by H.T. FitzSimons Co., Chicago. A seminal work; contains 42 squares collected from callers in Taylor County, Iowa, who were old in 1925. Presumably these figures were called and danced in this form in the late 1800s. To my knowledge, this is the earliest printed source for most of them. Each dance has calls (in patter style but without much trailing patter), brief but clear descriptions, and titles of suggested tunes. The text mentions a companion book, *Country Dance Tunes,* compiled by Boyd; I have never seen a copy.

Burgin, Dorothy "Dot," ed. *America Square Dances.* Woodbury, NJ: American Squares, 1949. Contains dances published in the first year (1945–46) of *American Squares,* at the time a national magazine covering all regional styles: 61 squares, 10 contras, 8 other dances. Includes many unusual dances you won't find elsewhere. See also Anderson 1950.

Campbell, Calvin, Ken Kernen, and Bob Howell. *Dancing for Busy People.* Castle Rock, CO: Calvin Campbell, 1995. A complete handbook for an ongoing program for people who want to dance regularly with a minimum of commitment to lessons. Explains how to create simple square dance "hash" using only 25 basic movements and gives dozens of drills and dances arranged by difficulty; also contains 19 "quadrilles" (phrased, prompted squares) and 52 contras, with a clear explanation of prompt calling, and about 90 trios, Sicilians, four-face-fours, mixers, and line (solo) dances. Assumes the use of recorded music; each dance has a recommended record, though some may be hard to find and there are no clear guidelines for choosing substitute music. All in all, a valuable assemblage of material that would otherwise require an extensive search. Available free online at **archive.org/details/dancing-for-busy-people.**

Cazden, Norman. *Dances from Woodland.* 2nd edition. Bridgeport, CT: The author, 1955 (preface mentions a smaller first edition of 1945). A valuable snapshot of the Catskill Mountain region of New York state. Contains 42 dances, mostly squares, mostly singing or semi-singing calls, with piano music for each (plus a few extra tunes). Informants are named; preface discusses the challenges of transcription. There is a brief glossary but no real dance descriptions; however, most of the calls should be self-explanatory to a reader with some experience, and there are occasional clarifying notes. Cross-currents are acknowledged; there is a southern "running set" as well as some local quadrilles that were probably shaped over many decades. Noteworthy are a visiting-couple medley and a "hashed" progressive circle, both with all calls written out.

Chase, Ann Hastings. *The Singing Caller*. New York: Association Press, 1944. By the mid-1940s it was rare to find a square dance book unaffected by crosscurrents, but this appears to be one. It contains 15 singing calls, apparently collected in Connecticut, each with simple piano music and calls for all figures and breaks. Singing squares were reportedly the fashion in many New England communities between the 1920s (when they took over from prompted quadrilles and contras) and the 1950s (when western squares gained favor). Cadence calls are the norm: "Note that, usually, the figure is executed *during* – not *after* – the call" (emphasis in original). A link to a scanned copy is at **squaredancehistory.org/items/show/1809.**

Clossin, Jimmy, and Carl Hertzog. *West Texas Square Dances*. El Paso, TX: Carl Hertzog, 1948; revised 1949, 1950. "A revised and enlarged edition of *Honor Your Partner*, the original Texas cowboy square dance book by Buck Stinson, edited and published by Carl Hertzog in 1938 [and revised in 1940]." Contains 29 figures (1950 edition); notable for its beautifully engraved diagrams, its inclusion of variations of several figures, and its focus on exhibition dancing. Issued in Great Britain as *The American Cowboy Square Dance Book* (London: G. Bell and Sons, Ltd, 1951). A scanned copy of *Cowboy Square Dances of West Texas* by Carl Hertzog, which appears to be the 1940 edition mentioned above although it makes no mention of Stinson, is available at **squaredancehistory.org/items/show/1634.** It contains 10 complete dances and brief descriptions of a few others.

Dalsemer, Robert G. [Bob]. *West Virginia Square Dances*. New York: Country Dance & Song Society of America, 1982. The author visited five West Virginia communities where group dancing had survived and documented the social details of each as well as the dance figures. Don't you wish someone had done this in every part of the continent? (See Fahs 1939, Lippincott 1984, and Borggreen 2002 for other examples.) This book is now available as a free download at **cdss.org.**

Damon, S. Foster. *The History of Square Dancing*. Barre, MA: Barre Gazette, 1957. For years this was the only book devoted entirely to the history of the group dances that developed into square dancing as we know it. It is valuable for its many quotations, chiefly from primary sources, though Damon often jumps to unwarranted conclusions. Strongest on the 18th and 19th centuries, sketchy on the 20th. The book is a reprint from the proceedings of the American Antiquarian Society in 1952, so is not as up to date as might be guessed; even for a 1952 work, it says relatively little about the great square dance revival that started in most areas around 1940. Available online at **https://www.americanantiquarian.org/proceedings/44807230.pdf** or **https://archive.org/stream/historyofsquared00damo#page/n5/mode/2up.**

Dick's Quadrille Call-Book and Ball-Room Prompter. New York: Dick & Fitzgerald, 1878; later issued by Fitzgerald Publishing Corp. and Behrens Publishing Co.; revised 1923. One of the easiest to find of the late 19th-century dancing master's manuals (others are French 1893 and Schell 1890). Contains fewer figures than some of its contemporaries, but they are described more fully: 18 five-figured quadrilles, 10 "fancy figures," 5 longways and progressive circles, a section on couple dances, and 116 figures for the "German" (a type of party mixer for small groups).

Durlacher, Ed. *Honor Your Partner*. New York: Devin-Adair Co., 1949. Reprinted shortly thereafter by Bonanza Books, a division of Crown Publishers, New York; reprint corrects some typos and adds tune titles (which were omitted from first printing). One of the easiest books to find from the boom years, this large-format hardcover was intended to be "the square dance book to end all square dance books." It contains 15 patter squares, 6 prompted squares, 42 singing squares (including 4 in waltz time), and 18 circles, longways, and other dances. Each dance is given a two-page spread, with piano music on one page and calls and descriptions on the other. Each is presented "as if it were the only one in the book": The definitions of the basics are given in full for every dance. There is also a glossary, as well as a few tips on calling, a few samples of patter, and a bibliography and discography. The most distinctive feature is a set of photographic "flip movies" illustrating 23 basics, a real innovation in the days before home video.

Durlacher, Ed. *Square Dance Calling Course Manual*. Freeport, NY: Square Dance Associates, 1960. This hard-to-find book was made to accompany the author's audio course (issued on long-playing 12" vinyl records and never reissued in any other format). It contains several pages of drills (corresponding to audio drills on the records) and 25 complete squares (most can be found on the author's "Honor Your Partner" recordings). Much of the material also appears in Durlacher's big 1949 book, but this manual includes quite a few personal observations from a working caller that appear nowhere else.

Edelman, Larry. *Square Dance Caller's Workshop*. Denver: Piggysnout Productions; fourth edition 1996. Produced as a workbook for the author's in-person calling classes; contains much good theory and practical tips, plus 32 figures from New England, southern, and western traditions. Available online at **squaredancehistory.org/items/show/1192**.

Everett, Bert. *Fifty Canadian Square Dances*. Toronto: Can-Ed Media, 1977, 1983. A large-format book with call charts of prompted and patter squares. Each dance is given in full, with all figures and breaks in correct order. You could read a dance aloud to live dancers without knowing what the calls mean (but please don't).

Fahs, Lois S. *Swing Your Partner: Old Time Dances of New Brunswick and Nova Scotia*. Sackville, NB: The author, 1939. This large-format mimeographed book leaves me in awe of the author and wishing the dances of every region had been so carefully and lovingly documented. (See Dalsemer 1982, Lippincott 1984, and Borggreen 2002 for more recent examples.) Contains 27 dances, many of them multi-figure quadrilles; each is credited to a specific informant and town and described in detail. Included are 5 contras, rarely seen outside New England between the late 1800s and the 1950s. There is a comprehensive section on steps and basic movements, with attention paid to local styling, as well as piano music for 14 tunes.

Flood, Jessie B., and Cornelia F. Putney. *Square Dance U.S.A.* Dubuque, IA: Wm. C. Brown Company, 1955. A revision of the authors' self-published *Square Dance Revival in Lincoln [Nebraska] 1940–1950* (which is available at **squaredancehistory.org/items/show/1171**), this large-format book provides a fascinating look at a period when hobbyists were dancing routines from every part of the continent and leaders hoped the trend would continue and this eclectic style would become the Great American Folk Dance. Contains about 30 patter calls, 20 singing calls, and 20 couple dances and mixers, with piano music for most. Includes a short glossary, tips for callers, and essays on the history and current state of the activity.

Ford, Mr. & Mrs. Henry [actually by Benjamin B. Lovett and Charlotte Lovett]. *Good Morning.* Dearborn, MI: Dearborn Publishing Co., 1926 (some advance copies are dated 1925). The most lasting evidence of Ford's grand plan to sweep jazz from Americans' collective consciousness and replace it with formal 19th-century dances and their music. Contains calls and explanations for 25 multi-figure quadrilles, 16 contras and progressive circles, and about 20 couple dances and mixers. Illustrated with line drawings and a few photographs of the Lovetts. Includes piano music for many dances, though small format makes it hard to read. Larger-format 1941 edition (some copies are marked "Second Edition," some "Third") omits most of the quadrilles and couple dances and adds 17 singing squares; fourth edition (1943) makes a few more alterations and includes catalog numbers of matching Ford recordings.

Foster, C.D. *Learn to Dance and Call Square Dances the Foster Way.* Denver: Foster's Folkway Features. For an item as ephemeral as a stack of 3x5 cards in a slipcase, this series turns up surprisingly often. Part 1 (1942) has 23 squares, a grand march, and the *Virginia Reel,* plus a few cards of calling tips, definitions, and patter. Part 2 (1947) has 25 more squares plus a few couple dances and mixers. Part 3 (1949) has about 30 singing calls contributed by Charley Thomas, then editor of *American Squares,* with some of his thoughts on using the genre. Part 4 (*Play Party Games the Foster Way,* 1950) has a dozen singing games with their music plus a few party stunts. The author learned the games, and presumably some of the dances, as a boy in Nebraska. These packs are well worth grabbing if the price is right.

Fredland, Nils, ed. *New River Train: Singing Squares from the Collection of Keith Blackmon.* Easthampton, MA: Country Dance and Song Society, 2013. A selection of 40 figures from more than 300 in this New York state caller's repertoire (he self-published them all in 2008). Dances are classified as easy or intermediate. Music is provided; editor suggests calling the figures in patter style if your musicians are not inclined to play singing squares. Includes an essay on the dancing of the region, a glossary, and tips for callers.

French, J.A., ed. *The Prompter's Hand Book.* Boston and New York: Oliver Ditson Co., 1893. One of the most frequently encountered late 19th-century manuals (others are Dick's 1878 and Schell 1890). Contains 22 quadrilles, each with 4 or 5 figures – the direct ancestors of present-day New England squares. Notable for including quadrilles as called by several leading prompters of Massachusetts and New Hampshire. There is at least one example of a call deliberately designed to mislead the dancers; that sort of playfulness was a trademark of Ralph Page, who studied this book when he was learning to call.

Gowing, Gene. *The Square Dancers' Guide*. New York: Crown Publishers, 1957. One of two large-format books by Gowing issued in the same year. This one is a hardcover with elaborate diagrams of some figures and very clear cartoon-style drawings of the basic movements. Text is addressed to the caller in a fairly formal style; there is a large section on theory and practical tips. Contains 28 squares, 12 contras, and 6 circles, plus sections on the Kentucky "running set" (big circle dance) and the five-figure *Lancers*. Gowing was a contemporary and friend of Ralph Page, and many of the dances here have a New England flavor.

Gowing, Gene. *Square Dancing for Everyone*. New York: Grosset & Dunlap, 1957. This is a large-format paperback, originally selling for $1, illustrated with clear black and white photographs (in which the couples are distinguished by the patterns of their shirts and skirts – light, dark, stripes, and plaid). In contrast to Gowing's other book, text is addressed to the beginning dancer and tone is folksy, as if the caller were speaking from the platform. Contains 2 circles, 10 squares, 4 contras, and a couple dance; most of these are also in Gowing's larger book.

Greggerson, H[erbert] F. Jr. *Herb's Blue Bonnet Calls*. [El Paso, TX]: The author, 1939. Square dancing as done in western Texas before the Lloyd Shaw style swept the country. Contains 52 square dance figures, with calls and explanations, plus several pages of patter for various situations and a glossary. Ilustrated throughout with photographs and diagrams. Available online at **archive.org/details/herb-greggerson-s/**.

Gunzenhauser, Margot. *Square & Fair*. Virum, Denmark: Square Dance Partners, 1996. I have not included many recent single-author collections of dances in this bibliography. I make an exception for Margot because she has a deep understanding of New England style, firmly believes that squares belong in the repertoire, and puts her money where her mouth is by including 22 original squares in this book (along with 19 contras and 14 other dances). Dances are graded by difficulty; there is a brief glossary but no musical recommendations.

☆Gunzenhauser, Margot. *The Square Dance and Contra Dance Handbook*. Jefferson, NC: McFarland & Company, 1996. By far the best of several books on folk and country dancing produced for the wider educational market; the author (who taught hundreds of callers in Denmark) really knows her stuff and explains things articulately. Contains 20 square figures, 18 breaks, 36 figures for southern "big sets," 14 contras, 11 mixers, 9 other dances, and music for 35 tunes, plus a well-done glossary and a huge bibliography and discography with extensive comments on each title. Diagrams and drawings are used to advantage throughout.

Harris, Jane A., Anne Pittman, and Marlys Swenson. *Dance a While: Handbook of Folk, Square and Social Dance*. Minneapolis: Burgess Publishing Co., 1950; revised periodically and issued by various publishers. In its tenth edition at press time, this is the standard college text for those who plan to teach social dance, either full-time or as part of a broader teaching career (music, phys. ed., etc.). It has grown in size and scope over the years; recent editions include a chapter on contra dance. It must be nearly impossible to compile a book of this magnitude without errors; I have noticed some, factual and technical. The square dance section has varied in style and quality from one edition to the next; after a flirtation with modern "western" style, the authors have reverted to a more traditional repertoire. Any edition is worth acquiring if available for a few dollars, though I wouldn't buy the current one at its $150 catalog price.

Hendrix, David B. *Smoky Mountain Square Dances*. Sevierville, TN: The author, 1941. This small, slim booklet could have been issued on bulkier paper in larger format at several times its price, and it would still be a bargain. Contains general advice on organizing a southern style dance, plus 17 small circle figures, 7 big circle figures, and three pages of patter. A scanned copy is available at **squaredancehistory.org/items/show/1296** (scroll down to "Additional Files"); an expanded version with 35 big circle figures and 43 small circle figures, edited by Bob Dalsemer after Hendrix's death, is at **squaredancehistory.org/items/show/1701.**

Hinds, Tom. *Calling New England Squares*. Faber, VA: The author, [2005]. Contains 17 phrased figures intended to be prompt-called, plus 7 breaks, interspersed with brief but pithy comments on analyzing and adapting material, teaching, and programming.

Hinds, Tom. *Give Me a Break!* [Faber, VA]: The author, 1997. Contains 64 breaks, most of them phrased and intended for use in New England–style squares, with brief advice on how and when to use them.

☆Holden, Rickey. *The Square Dance Caller*. San Antonio, TX: The author, 1951. No praise is too high for this slim volume; in 48 pages, Holden touches on every aspect of the caller's art and has important things to say about most of them. No dance material (save a couple of examples), but the book is more valuable than any single dance collection you will find.

Holden, Rickey. *Square Dances of West Texas*. Austin, TX: The Society of Folk Dance Historians, 1992. An attempt to preserve, and if possible renew interest in, square dancing as done in western Texas and New Mexico from 1935 to 1955. Contains 19 figures plus an explanation of how a dance is assembled from figures and breaks.

Holden, Rickey, and Lloyd Litman. *Instant Hash*. Cleveland: Lloyd Litman, 1962. Written when western square dancing was in the throes of its transition from traditional to modern; perhaps the first comprehensive attempt to catalog the possible permutations of square dance figures and break every figure down into its component parts. Uses the concept of modules (set-ups, conversions, get-outs) without the name. Contains more than 230 complete and partial figures, with hints on how to alter and expand them.

Howard, Carole. *Just One More Dance: A Collection of Old Western Square Dance Calls*. [Mt. Pleasant, MI]: The author, 1989. No dance figures, only patter, about 50 pages of it, collected over a lifetime by a caller (and instructor of thousands of callers) who knew many of the old-timers (Grace Ryan was a mentor). Many of these couplets are sexist, a few are racist, but some are quite usable and most are entertaining.

Hunt, Paul, and Charlotte Underwood. *Eight Yards of Calico: Square Dance Fun for Everyone*. New York: Harper & Brothers, 1952. One of the easiest books of the era to find, due to its issue by a major trade publisher. Next to Shaw 1939, it may well be the most literate square dance book ever (Underwood was a professional writer). It is addressed to small groups with beginning callers. The material is organized into 8 programs, as for a weekly class that becomes a club. Basic movements are introduced when needed for a particular dance, rather than being grouped in a glossary; this can be inconvenient, though there is an index of basics as well as one of dance titles. Contains 50 figures, nicely balanced between patter and singing calls, eastern and western styles. Some of the basics are illustrated by charming photos of pipe-cleaner dolls with painted faces. (The authors followed this title with a similar book on basic couple dances, *Calico Rounds*.)

☆Jamison, Phil. *Hoedowns, Reels, and Frolics: Roots and Branches of Southern Appalachian Dance*. Urbana, Chicago, and Springfield, IL: University of Illinois Press, 2015. This is a book of history, not a treatise on calling or a collection of dance material, but it is required reading for anyone who wants to understand the essence of country-style square dancing. Jamison, who is both a scholar and a working caller and musician, has done extensive primary research into the roots of the southern dance; he explodes some widely held myths, such as that Appalachia was an isolated and insular region and that its dance tradition is a pure form of an ancient English dance. He finds not only various European strains in these dances, but also Native American and African-American influence (although he occasionally goes beyond his sources in formulating theories). There are chapters on couple dances, the cakewalk, percussive dancing, and the nationwide square dance boom; a glossary of dance terms, figures, and steps; and a discography of 95 recordings with calls from the 1920s and '30s (Jamison has made the recordings available for listening at **philjamison.com**).

Jennewein, J. Leonard. *Dakota Square Dance Book and Instructor's Manual*. Huron, SD: The author, 1950. Contains 26 figures and 33 breaks, an outline for a 6-lesson class, some theory, and a bibliography of the important books available at the time, with extensive (and opinionated) comments. The author completely misinterprets the traditional call "once and a half"; he does better in his attempt to sort out the various movements that have been given the name of "do-si-do." Tone is very folksy throughout.

Jones, Fenton "Jonesy." *Singing Calls for Square Dancing*. Los Angeles: Sets in Order, [1951]. Part of a series of "slim jim" pamphlets (see Osgood and Hoheisal for the others); contains 33 square dance figures with calls set to the tunes of popular songs from the mid-19th century to the mid-20th. Jonesy was a prolific recording caller; recommended records are listed for each dance (of course, many tunes have been reissued since then, often with better musicianship and sound quality).

King, Jay. *The Fundamentals of Hash Calling.* 4th edition. Lexington, MA: The author, 1972. Explains the "mental image" method for keeping track of dancers in the modern style in which the caller creates the choreography in real time. Even though I do very little improvising, this book led me to a greater understanding of what each call accomplishes; this has helped me in creating set routines. I endorse the author's recommendation to draw diagrams of every sequence before using it.

Kirkell, Miriam H., and Irma K. Schaffnit. *Partners All – Places All!* New York: E.P. Dutton & Co., 1949. One of the first books of the boom years to come from a major trade publisher, this attractive volume contains 22 squares, 9 circles, 3 longways, and several couple and no-partner dances. Descriptions are brief but well-written. Easy piano arrangements are furnished for most dances; format is large enough to make the music scores legible. There are a few clear drawings and a short glossary.

Kraus, Richard. *Recreation Leader's Handbook.* New York: McGraw-Hill, 1955. Sections on theory, games, songs, dramatics, plus 29 squares and 19 other dances, many with piano music. As always with Kraus, there are many good thoughts for callers and other leaders, here including a section on group dynamics and the philosophy of leadership. (Unfortunately, Folk Dancer Album 39, which was to have featured Kraus calling several of the squares in this book, was never released; I have no idea whether the masters exist.)

☆Kraus, Richard. *Square Dances of Today and How to Teach and Call Them.* New York: A.S. Barnes and Co. (some copies show Ronald Press as the publisher), 1950. One of the best collections of squares for general recreational use; author was more concerned with usability than regional authenticity, though he credits some informants by name. Contains 26 patter squares, 15 singing squares, and 14 other dances, plus well-thought-out advice for callers. Simple piano music is provided for dances that have their own tunes; five tunes for patter squares are included. Exceptionally clear drawings in realistic "adventure" comic-book style illustrate the glossary and many of the dances.

Leifer, Fred. *The Li'l Abner Official Square Dance Handbook.* [New York]: Toby Press, 1953; reprinted the same year by A.S. Barnes and Co., New York. Not as hokey as the name might suggest. Abner and Daisy Mae appear on the cover, but inside, the dance movements are illustrated with generic cartoons. The Dogpatch characters' names are associated with certain dances, but the 26 dances themselves are very usable standard singing and patter squares, plus the *Virginia Reel* and a few couple dances and mixers. Piano music is provided for each dance. The Toby Press version was a paperback on cheap pulp paper, selling for 35 cents; the back pages touted the author's "National Dance Club of America," which sold memberships, dance books and records, and such essential items as straw hats, bandannas, sheriff's badges, and rubber masks of Li'l Abner and Daisy Mae. The A.S. Barnes version was a hardcover at several times the price (but still on high-acid paper), with the type completely reset and all mention of mail-order commerce deleted.

Linnell, Rod, and Louise Winston. *Square Dances from a Yankee Caller's Clipboard*. Norwell, MA: The New England Square Dance Caller [magazine], 1974; reprinted 2002 by New England Folk Festival Association. Contains about 50 phrased squares and half a dozen contras, most original with this Maine caller, a few collected and/or adapted. Included are the five "Rod's Quads" (eight-couple squares), probably Linnell's best-known creations. Winston finished the book after Linnell's untimely death and included a few figures that he might well have discarded or insisted on polishing, but as it is, the book gives us a fascinating glimpse of a choreographic genius at work.

Lippincott, Peter, and Marget Lippincott. *Traditional Dance in Missouri, Volume One: Southern Missouri Jig Dancing*. St. Louis: Childgrove Country Dancers, 1984. Squares as done in Douglas and Wayne counties at the time; contains a detailed description of the social aspects of the gatherings, an essay on the music, and descriptions of 18 figures. The call wording is not supplied; according to the authors, calls are delivered in as few words as possible because the caller typically dances (in both communities each set has its own caller). A scanned copy is at **squaredancehistory.org/items/show/1502.**

Litchman, William M., and Kristin E. Litchman. *Rocky Mountain Caller: Bill Litchman's Calling Book*. Albuquerque, NM: Medley Publications, 2005. A veteran caller in the traditional western style shares his repertoire. Contains a good discussion of the basic skills of calling, along with 33 figures from the traditional and "transitional" eras, with explanations as needed.

Lunsford, Bascom Lamar, and George Myers Stephens. *It's Fun to Square Dance: Southern Appalachian Calls and Figures*. Asheville, NC: The Stephens Press, 1942. This widely circulated little booklet has explanations of half a dozen figures to be done by two-couple circles within a big circle, illustrated with diagrams and photographs of formally dressed dancers. A scanned copy is available at **squaredancehistory.org/items/show/1527.** The booklet, along with additional photos of big circle figures, is incorporated in *Bascom Lamar Lunsford: "Minstrel of the Appalachians,"* a short biography by Pete Gilpin and George Stephens (1966).

Lyman, Frank L., Jr., ed. *One Hundred and One Singing Calls*. Fort Madison, IA: The editor, 1949; revised 1951 (distributed by American Squares, Woodbury, NJ). Singing squares were the prevailing country-dance form in much of the Northeast before the contra revival. In 1949 they were coming into their own across the country, and Lyman attempted to collect a representative sample – some traditional, some newly written (and credited to their authors); most set to folk and popular songs from the 19th and early 20th centuries, a few to more recent hits. There are multiple figures for some tunes, from different callers and regions. It is assumed that the reader is familiar with square dance choreography, though there is a short glossary; there are also short lists of tune books and of instrumental records for callers to use. A standout is an extended semi-singing call by Ralph Page to the tune of Old Joe Clark, beginning "Join your hands and all around, Eight hands once around; Guess you've got the rheumatiz, Don't believe you'll ever get round."

Maddocks, Durward. *Swing Your Partners: A Guide to Modern Country Dancing.* Brattleboro, VT and New York: Stephen Daye Press, 1941; revised 1950. Contains 38 square figures, 7 progressive circles, 5 contras. Squares are mainly the prompted type that was dominant in New England before singing calls; book is old enough to be free from the western cross-currents that influenced later eastern works. Revised edition differs merely in expanded book and record lists, and in notes in the front and back in which the author makes it explicit that "separating the dance from the tune" means not only doing away with special tunes for certain dances, but also disregarding the musical phrase and giving the next call when the dancers are ready for it. Fortunately, the material is usable whether one goes with Maddocks or with long tradition. An interesting feature: The squares are not grouped by type (visiting-couple, across the set, all active) but printed in rotating order so that any three consecutive figures make a nicely contrasting set.

Marron, Graeme, and Anna Marron. *Square Dancing for Young and Old.* New York: Padell Book Co., 1945. This fascinating pulp pamphlet is a cover-to-cover ripoff of Margot Mayo's classic 1943 book. Every sentence is re-worded, presumably to keep just on the right side of the law, but the sentiments are nearly identical – except that the Marrons occasionally lapse into bad taste, both in their prose and in their sample patter. The dancers in the illustrations are dressed to the nines, in jacket and tie, heels and hose; they must be indulging in square dancing at a nightclub, as was fairly common in the 1940s. Several of the ladies are allowing their stocking tops to show.

Mayo, Margot. *The American Square Dance.* New York: Sentinel Books, 1943; revised and enlarged 1948; reprinted 1964 by Oak Publications, New York. Mayo founded the American Square Dance Group, a New York City recreational and performing society. Her tastes were eclectic: Both in this book and in several record albums, she collected dances in varying formations from many parts of the US. The book contains 13 dances, described in detail with attention paid to regional styling points, and 11 tunes, most arranged for piano, plus tips on calling, playing the tunes, and using recorded music.

McNair, Ralph J. *Square Dance!* Garden City, NY: Garden City Books, 1951. One of the easiest-to-find books from the boom years (it was published by a unit of Doubleday and presumably had a large print run). Contains 39 figures, each with calls and explanations, most illustrated with at least one cartoon-style drawing. Throughout the book, the dancers are given names instead of numbers: Andy and Amy, Bill and Bess, Cal and Cora, Dan and Dot. The drawings are consistent: Andy is bald and portly, Bill lean and overalled, etc. Much of the patter is unique to this book, undoubtedly created by the author, a Colorado caller. McNair cites many 19th-century sources but ignores most 20th-century writers, mentioning Henry Ford, Cecil Sharp, and Lloyd Shaw only in passing. A charming feature is the recounting of many 19th-century anecdotes of dances in the Old West. An earlier mimeographed edition (*Western Square Dances,* Denver: Oran V. Siler Co., 1941) has 30 figures and omits the anecdotes; its drawings are rough sketches.

McVicar, Wes. *Wes McVicar's 75 Favorite Square Dance Calls* and *Wes McVicar's 75 More Square Dances.* Niagara Falls, NY and Toronto: Gordon V. Thompson, Ltd., 1949 and 1953. Eclectic compilations of material that was popular at the peak of the North American square dance craze. Some of the patter is unique to Canada; a few of each 75 are couple dances and mixers.

Mills, Bob. *All Mixed Up: A Guide to Sound Production for Folk and Dance Music.* Princeton, NJ: The author, 1994; revised 1996, 2004, 2008. Everything you need to know about choosing and operating a sound system. Second edition is available for purchase as a paperback (including a quick reference card); fourth edition is available free at **bobmills.org.**

Muller, "Allemande" Al. *All-American Square Dances.* New York: Paull-Pioneer Music Corp. (or Delaware Water Gap, PA: Shawnee Press), 1941. One of a dozen or more books issued from the 1920s to the 1940s in folio (sheet-music) size. Most of them are primarily music, with perhaps a few dance calls for each tune. This one gives more space and attention to the dances, with simple piano arrangements for most of the figures. It is listed here because, like several other entries, it provides a snapshot of a particular time and place – in this case, New York's Adirondack Mountains. The author warns "Don't be too determined in forcing your interpretation of the 'calls' upon the dancers," but he can get pretty dogmatic ("You can never allemande your partner"). As seen in other regions (Michigan, Ontario), the figures are grouped into first change, second change, and breakdown; some of the breakdowns can be done in a big circle of couples.

Napier, Patrick E. *Kentucky Mountain Square Dancing.* Berea, KY: The author, 1960 (reprinted several times with new copyright dates but no apparent revisions). Group dancing as done in eastern Kentucky in the 1930s. Contains a general discussion, 21 large and small circle figures for the "big set," and 6 additional figures for a four-couple square (here termed the "running set"). Descriptions are concise but clear. Some tune titles are suggested, but no music is included. This book is available as a free download at **cdss.org.**

Nevell, Richard. *A Time to Dance: American Country Dancing from Hornpipes to Hot Hash.* New York: St. Martin's Press, 1977; reprinted 2017 by Bauhan Publishing, Peterborough, NH. The author interviewed practitioners of contra dancing, southern mountain big circle dancing, and modern square dancing; their comments are naturally opinionated but give interesting "snapshot" views of several dance communities of the time. The chapter on history mixes documented evidence with conjecture but is one of the better overviews. Dance descriptions, diagrams, and glossary are replete with errors; bibliography classifies all books on four-couple squares, including some New England classics, as "western."

Nielsen, Erica M. *Folk Dancing*. Santa Barbara, CA: Greenwood, an imprint of ABC-CLIO, 2011. Although marred by sloppy editing and proofreading, this book gives the best layperson's overview I've seen of the history of folk dancing as a social recreation in 20th-century America. Nielsen covers English country, international folk, traditional and modern square, and contra dance forms, seeing them as equally valid expressions of the human urge to move to music and connect with other people.

Osgood, Bob, ed. *The Caller/Teacher Manual for the Basic Program of American Square Dancing*. Los Angeles: Sets in Order, 1969. One of several attempts to re-establish a recreational square dance program not requiring a year-long class. The SIO Basic Program was intended to be taught in 10 lessons; it lists 50 "basics," but some are minor variations (right- and left-hand stars are listed separately, as are two and four ladies chain). Most of the basics will be familiar to tradition-minded callers, who will therefore find most of the dances and drills useful. Includes several singing calls arranged by master caller Ed Gilmore for proper timing. This edition is a large-format 96-page softcover; later, more elaborate versions incorporate Mainstream movements and are worth acquiring by the traditionalist only if the price is low.

☆Osgood, Bob, ed. *Five Years of Sets in Order* (cover title is *5 Years of Square Dancing*). Los Angeles: Sets in Order, 1954. A compilation of more than 300 square dance figures and breaks published during the first five years of the leading national magazine of western square dancing. SIO issued yearbooks in subsequent years, but this first collection is particularly valuable to the neo-traditionalist, as it documents the transition from more or less traditional figures to the beginnings of modern grid-type squares. Searchable scans of this and the next few yearbooks are at **sdfne.org/caller-note-services-periodical-magazines/** (scroll to the bottom and click on Sets-in-Order, then Yearbook).

Osgood, Bob, and Jack Hoheisal. *Square Dancing for Beginners*. Los Angeles: Sets in Order, 1949. A "slim jim" (4" x 9") pamphlet with 23 relatively easy figures and 4 breaks, as danced in southern California in the early days of the nationwide square dance boom. Some but not all of these calls made it into regular issues of *Sets in Order* and therefore appear in the "Five Year" book.

Osgood, Bob, and Jack Hoheisal. *Square Dancing for Intermediates*. Los Angeles: Sets in Order, 1949. Another "slim jim" with 38 figures and 4 breaks. Again, not all of them are in the monthly magazines or the "Five Year" book.

Osgood, Bob, and Jack Hoheisal. *Square Dancing: The Newer and Advanced Dances*. Los Angeles: Sets in Order, 1950. The third "slim jim" from SIO, with 46 figures and 6 breaks. Most are fairly complex, but a few are easy.

Owens, Lee. *American Square Dances of the West and Southwest*. Palo Alto, CA: Pacific Books, 1949. An interesting attempt to codify traditional western calling and dancing along the lines of the 19th-century quadrille, with strict timing and phrasing. This means the dance descriptions are dogmatic at times, but they are also unusually thorough. All the basic movements and 33 figures are described in detail, many with very clear line drawings. Seven tunes are included (see Owens and Ruth 1950 for more music). Available online at the Internet Archive; a link is at **squaredancehistory.org/items/show/867**.

Owens, Lee, and Viola Ruth. *Advanced Square Dance Figures of the West and Southwest.* Palo Alto, CA: Pacific Books, 1950. A companion volume to Owens 1949, with material suitable for workshops and exhibition groups. Ruth, the music consultant for Owens' first book, gets co-author billing here because there's much more music: Each of 29 figures has its own tune. There are also 10 breaks ("trimming or chorus figures"), some very flashy. The basic movements are described briefly; the reader is referred to Owens 1949 for a fuller treatment. A link is at **squaredancehistory.org/items/show/868**.

Page, Ralph. *An Elegant Collection of Contras and Squares.* Denver: Lloyd Shaw Foundation, 1984. This was Page's working repertoire toward the end of his career. He had discarded many dances along the way; presumably he felt these were the cream of the crop. Contains 10 Lancers figures, 9 other squares, and 47 contras, plus melody lines for a few tunes.

Parkes, Tony. *Contra Dance Calling: A Basic Text.* Bedford, MA: Hands Four Books, 1992; revised 2010. A companion to the present volume; although it deals primarily with contra dances, the book is listed because it treats certain aspects of calling in more depth than is done here. Not primarily a book of material, but contains 4 square figures and 4 breaks with call charts in addition to 14 circle and longways dances.

Parkes, Tony. *Shadrack's Delight.* Bedford, MA: Hands Four Books, 1988. A booklet containing descriptions (no actual calls) of 17 squares, 25 contras, and a progressive circle, all devised or adapted by the author.

Parkes, Tony. *Son of Shadrack.* Bedford, MA: Hands Four Books, 1993. Similar to *Shadrack's Delight;* contains 11 squares, 26 contras, 3 circle mixers, and 2 progressive circles.

Piper, Ralph, and Zora Piper. *Developing the Creative Square Dance Caller.* Minneapolis: The authors, 1956. This large-format mimeographed book anticipates the present volume by combining a section on theory with a large amount of dance material. Intended for use in callers' classes, it includes 29 suggested "creative projects," from writing a break to arranging a singing square. About 20 basic movements are discussed in depth (with many examples of patter), followed by 36 visiting figures, 35 other patter calls, 13 singing calls, and 36 contras and progressive circles. Traditional and recent dances are intermingled, with no author credit for the latter. Much attention is given to word metering and to checking published dances for proper timing. (If you think I overanalyze the art of calling, you should see what the Pipers do.) The book concludes with a thorough discussion of the elements of good calling: clarity, rhythm, voice quality, etc.

Riley, Milly, ed. *Western Square Dancing.* Jacksonville, IL: The author, 1989. About 130 dances, nearly all squares, from the syllabi of the annual Lloyd Shaw Dance Fellowship (1955–1970). Many of these dances are difficult if not impossible to find elsewhere. The Fellowship was a close-knit group that emphasized the joy of dancing rather than complexity for its own sake. This focus is evident in the many comments, most by Dorothy Shaw, the Fellowship's guiding light.

Rohrbough, Lynn, ed. *Handy Country Dance Book* or *Handy Square Dance Book* (depending on edition). Delaware, OH: Cooperative Recreation Service, various dates (final edition 1955). A small-format (3.5" x 7") book reprinting several pamphlets from the 1930s and '40s, dealing with square dancing as done in various regions: Mississippi, Kentucky, Pennsylvania, Ohio. Particularly valuable for traditionalists, as most of the material was collected directly from informants and is relatively unaffected by cross-currents.

Ryan, Grace L. *Dances of Our Pioneers*. New York: A.S. Barnes and Co., 1926; revised 1939. First edition comprises a letter-size hardbound book with 27 tunes arranged for piano and a smaller paperbound book in a back pocket with 59 dances. Second edition is smaller in format and integrates the tunes with the dances, the latter numbering 82. Most of the dances are square figures, intended to be danced in sets of three (first change, second change, and "jig"); a few are printed in sets, followed by many single figures for assembling one's own sets. Format is similar to *Good Morning,* with spare quadrille-style calls, but among the figures are many I would classify as "country style." The author worked in Michigan; presumably her informants (some of whom she acknowledges by name) lived in the North Central states. A caller could survive for years using only the squares in this book.

☆Sannella, Ted. *Balance and Swing*. New York: Country Dance and Song Society, 1982. The first of two dance collections from a master caller; contains 20 squares, 25 contras, and 10 triplets (three-couple longways), most by the author, with copious notes. Includes printed music for every dance, a glossary, and a detailed account of Boston-area square and contra dance history from the 1930s through the early 1980s.

☆Sannella, Ted. *Calling Traditional New England Squares*. Haydenville, MA: Country Dance and Song Society, 2005. This unassuming booklet is worth several times its price: It comes with a CD of Ted calling 14 different squares with improvised breaks, including two versions of his signature *Merry-Go-Round*. The text contains a clear, concise explanation of how a prompted square is constructed and an extensive discussion of breaks, with more than 80 examples. There are transcriptions of the *Merry-Go-Round* recordings, but not of the other squares, most of which are treated fully in Ted's other books. Note: Make sure your copy has the CD in a back pocket; I once saw the book offered for sale at full price without the CD (it was an honest mistake).

☆Sannella, Ted. *Swing the Next*. Northampton, MA: Country Dance and Song Society, 1996. A follow-up to Sannella 1982; contains 25 squares, 35 contras, 10 triplets, and 10 circles, most by Ted, along with his always valuable thoughts on various aspects of dancing and calling. (An extended discussion of squares, intended for this book, was published separately as Sannella 2005.) Printed music is included for every dance.

Schell, John M. *Prompting: How to Do It.* [Boston: J. White, 1890]; New York: Carl Fischer, reprinted 1948. One of the easiest to find of the late 19th-century dancing master's manuals, thanks to a relatively late reissue (others are Dick's 1878 and French 1893). Contains 19 five-figured quadrilles (the direct ancestors of present-day New England squares), several miscellaneous square figures, and 130 contra dances (though some are duplicates under different names; Rickey Holden suggests that Schell lifted his contra section from Elias Howe and neglected to check two of Howe's editions against each other).

☆Shaw, Lloyd. *Cowboy Dances: A Collection of Western Square Dances.* Caldwell, ID: The Caxton Printers, Ltd., 1939. Reprinted several times, with minor changes in text and increasingly large discographies; most printings include as an appendix *Cowboy Dance Tunes* (33 tunes arranged for piano), originally published separately. The bible of the 1940s square dance revival in the West; contains 76 squares, supposedly collected from old-time callers in and around Colorado. Some of the dances and the method of classifying them bear a strong resemblance to Boyd and Dunlavy 1925, but there are many more dances here, and each is treated more fully; most are illustrated with diagrams and/or photographs. There is a fair amount of patter, both incorporated in the dances and in a separate section. A few couple dances are included; there are many more in Shaw's equally large and influential *Round Dance Book* (Caxton, 1948). Note: Contrary to persistent myth, Shaw did not "invent" modern square dancing, which did not assume its present distinctive form until after his death. The figures in this book are strictly traditional in feel. Available online at **archive.org/details/square-and-contra-dances-for-leaders.**

Smith, Frank H. *The Appalachian Square Dance.* Berea, KY: Berea College, 1955. This is one of the most literate and best organized works on southern sets, and no wonder: Smith founded the Berea Country Dancers and the Christmas Dance School at Berea College. Calls and descriptions are given for 10 big circle figures, 15 small circle figures, and 5 figures particularly suited to four-couple sets. (Smith acknowledges that the latter have come to be known as "running sets" but admits that the distinction is arbitrary: "Whether the formation is 4, 6, 8, or 50 couples, the dancing style is exactly the same.") Photographs and sketches are used to good effect. There are sections on the separate skills of calling and teaching. Fiddle and piano scores are included for 19 tunes; a back pocket contains an insert with fiddle-only scores for the same tunes.

Smith, Raymond H. *Raymond Smith's Square Dance Hand Book.* Dallas: The author, 1947; revised 1948. Contains 37 figures (1948 edition) as danced in eastern Texas, a dozen breaks (termed "fill-ins or mixers"), and 3 pages of patter. Explanations are brief but clear.

☆Spalding, Susan Eike. *Appalachian Dance: Creativity and Continuity in Six Communities.* Urbana, Chicago, and Springfield, IL: University of Illinois Press, 2014. The best evocation I have seen of a region and its dance traditions. Based on the author's extensive visits and interviews, it gives the reader a feeling of "being there." The South is not a monolith; neither are its dances. The communities explored here differ in many respects; what they share is the desire and ability to use and adapt their dances to meet their social needs.

☆Spalding, Susan Eike, and Jane Harris Woodside, eds. *Communities in Motion: Dance, Community, and Tradition in America's Southeast and Beyond.* Westport, CT: Greenwood Press, 1995. Scholarly but readable essays on squares, contras, clogging, and other forms including Native American and African-American dance. Essential reading for anyone interested in traditional dance history and sociology.

Sumrall, Bob. *Do-Si-Do: Thirty-Five Square Dance Calls with Explanations.* Abilene, TX: The author, 1942. Revised in 1948 (with 51 calls) and 1949 (with 55 calls). Square dance figures as done in western Texas in the 1940s, with little or no influence from the Lloyd Shaw style that was sweeping the rest of the US. Patter is incorporated in the dances; there is also a section with examples of patter to be used in various situations.

Sweet, Ralph. *Let's Create "Olde Tyme" Square Dancing.* Hazardville, CT: The author, 1966. At a time when traditional dancing in New England was on the wane (this was before the great contra dance revival) and modern square dancing appeared to be running out of people willing to take a year's worth of lessons, Sweet argued for what might be termed a neo-traditional program, incorporating the best of the old dances and some of the simpler new ones. Book contains 20 patter squares, 14 prompted squares (plus the 5-figure *Lancers*), 21 singing squares, 11 contras, plus an outline for a 12-lesson class. Assumes the use of recorded music (dance musicians were scarce at the time).

☆Sweet, Ralph, and Nils Fredland. *On the Beat with Ralph Sweet.* Haydenville, MA: Country Dance and Song Society, 2010. The life's work of a master caller from Connecticut who was influenced by both traditional New England dancing and the 1950s square dance boom, this large-format book contains directions and calls for 34 singing squares, 56 patter squares, and two dozen breaks. Printed music is included for the singing calls and half a dozen hoedowns. I find the typeface curiously small and hard to read, but that shouldn't dissuade you from getting the book, currently the easiest place to find the standard 1950s repertoire.

Tolman, Beth, and Ralph Page. *The Country Dance Book.* Weston, VT: The Countryman Press jointly with Farrar & Rinehart, New York, 1937. Reprinted by A.S. Barnes and Co., New York; reprinted 1976 by Stephen Greene Press, Brattleboro, VT. Written by a *Yankee* magazine editor and an influential caller (based on a series of articles in the then-new *Yankee*), this was the bible of the 1940s square and contra dance revival in New England. Contains more than 70 dances, along with many enjoyable stories about the dances, the music, and the people who kept them alive. A promotional booklet with a handful of dances from the book is at **squaredancehistory.org/items/show/1662**.

Waudby, Marion, and George Waudby. *Square Your Sets*. Woodbury, NJ: American Squares, 1949; revised 1950. A booklet of dances as done in the Tucson, AZ area at the time, including several from other regions. Contains 40 patter calls, 8 singing calls, a few couple dances and mixers, all with brief explanations.

Waudby, Marion, and George Waudby. *Square Your Sets, Vol. II: Advanced Dances*. Tucson, AZ: The authors, 1950. More than 100 figures and breaks, as done "from Texas to California."

Welsch, Roger L., ed. *A Treasury of Nebraska Pioneer Folklore*. Lincoln, NE: University of Nebraska Press, 1966. Much of this book, including "Square Dances" (pp. 80–137), is compiled from pamphlets produced by the Federal Writers' Project, a WPA program, in the late 1930s. Some of the material is unusual enough to suggest that before standardization there was more variety in the heartland than we'll ever know. Alas, there is very little explanation of the calls. The original pamphlets are available free online, though the mimeographed text is hard to read in spots. The first of three pamphlets is at **squaredancehistory.org/items/show/1625;** the others are 1626 and 1627.

☆Writers' Program of the Work Projects Administration of the State of Illinois. *The Square Dance*. Chicago: Chicago Park District, 1940. A magnificent example of a government agency's getting something right. This large-format book contains as complete a treatment as you're likely to see of the way squares were actually called and danced in a given area, in this case Chicago circa 1940. (According to the text, each set of squares in an evening was termed a "quadrille" and consisted of one fast and one slow dance.) Each fundamental movement is defined and illustrated with drawings and/or diagrams, as are the 56 figures and 23 couple dances and mixers that follow. Each square is classified as fast or slow, and as easy or difficult. (My copy has a 1943 appendix bound into the back, with 6 more dances and an apology for not revising the entire book in wartime.) Three tunes are recommended for each non-singing square; a companion volume of music arranged for violin and piano (*Folk Tunes*) was issued in 1942. Note: This book is much easier to find in its revised edition; see Bol 1950 for a description.

Especially for Children and First-Timers

I always encourage callers to add dances other than contras and four-couple squares to their repertoire, for variety's sake and because those two popular forms are not always the best choices for a group or an occasion. The following books and recordings include both square and non-square dances.

All of the material from these producers (all experienced callers) is excellent. They are listed together for convenience, as many leaders are looking specifically for dances suitable for children, families, and first-time dancers. The books include thoughtful tips on teaching, calling, and organizing.

Hulsether, Sue. *Join Up Hands*. Book with directions for 23 dances; CD of 12 southern-style tunes plus sample calls and a waltz. **suehulsether.com**

New England Dancing Masters. Several books and recordings (CD or download) of easy dances and singing games, plus 2 albums of all-purpose tunes and a DVD on teaching dance to children. **dancingmasters.com**

Rose, Marian. Several book/CD (or download) sets of easy dances, singing games, and traditional Canadian and French dances. **marianrose.com**

Rosenberg, Paul. *Peel the Banana*. Book/CD set with 19 American and international dances. **homespun.biz**

Silveria, Paul. *Old Time Dance Party*. Book and recording (CD or download) of 5 southern-style dances with and without calls. Uses gender-neutral terminology ("birds" and "crows"). **paulsilveria.com/dance-calling-guide**

Tune Books

Brody, David. *The Fiddler's Fakebook.* New York: Oak Publications, 1983. A monumental collection: about 465 tunes from northern, southern, and Celtic traditions. (The number is approximate because multiple tunes have the same title.) Many are transcribed from recordings; these may be hard for a beginning fiddler to read, but there are quite a few "plain vanilla" versions too. Many reels are incorrectly notated in 4/4; trust your ear, not the notation.

Miller, Randy, and Jack Perron. *New England Fiddler's Repertoire.* East Alstead, NH: Fiddlecase Books, 1983 (second edition 2003; third edition, by Randy Miller and Robert Bley-Vroman, 2008). Contains 168 time-tested tunes; book is aimed at contra dance musicians, but many tunes are suitable for squares, especially phrased squares in New England style. **fiddlecasebooks.com**

Sky, Patrick, ed. *Ryan's Mammoth Collection.* Pacific, MO: Mel Bay, 1995. A reprint of an 1883 classic, which was the New England fiddler's bible until the newer books on this list came along. Many musicians know it as Cole's *One Thousand Fiddle Tunes,* a 1940 edition that sold for 75 cents.

Songer, Sue, and Clyde Curley. *The Portland Collection: Contra Dance Music in the Pacific Northwest.* Portland, OR: The authors, 1997; revised 2011. Don't let the title put you off: Although a few of the 318 tunes are by Northwest composers and the book was obviously inspired by the contra dance revival, there are dozens of tunes suitable for squares of all regional styles, including many fine southern tunes. (See "Tune Titles" earlier in this section for some of my favorites.) A masterpiece of tune collecting, editing, and formatting; includes extensive commentary and a resource list. Companion recordings are available. **theportlandcollection.com**

Songer, Sue, and Clyde Curley. *The Portland Collection, Volumes 2 and 3.* Portland, OR: The authors, 2005 and 2015. Identical in format to the first volume; contain 322 and 314 tunes respectively. Multiple genres are represented, including New England, Appalachian, and Québécois. All three volumes are now available in iOS format for musicians who use iPads.

RECORDINGS

Recordings with calls (see also under "Videos" below)

A series of audio recordings to accompany this book, with calls by the author, is planned. Some will be complete dances; others will illustrate various points made in the book, such as the various types of tune. See **hands4.com** for a listing of currently available titles.

From the hundreds of callers who have recorded commercially, I have chosen a few who display excellence in delivery, good usable material, or (usually) both. Most were active during the peak of square dance activity in the 1950s.

> **Special mention:**
> Santa Monica Diamond Jubilee. This is a nearly complete audio record of a 1950 street dance that is still the largest single-day event in square dance history: 15,000 dancers, 35,000 spectators. Most of the material is solidly traditional. Not all the callers are great, but this is a unique snapshot of square dancing at the height of its popularity in southern California. Available at **buddyweavermusic.podbean.com** (in five parts; scroll to January 2021).

Square Dance – Live Recordings   Nearly 300 field recordings of prominent callers from the mid-1950s to the early 1990s, mostly in the evolving modern "western" style. Those from the 1950s are of particular interest to the tradition-minded caller, as the material being danced in that scene remained largely tradition-based for years after the club structure was set up. Part of the Internet Archive; available at **archive.org/details/Square_Dance-Live_Recordings** or **squaredancehistory.org/items/show/1826.**

Don Armstrong (Florida/Colorado)   A prominent caller in the 1950s, hosting a large open dance near Tampa and traveling nationally, Armstrong recorded several popular singing squares for Folk Dancer and Windsor. In the 1960s, unhappy with the direction the modern square dance was taking, he began specializing in contras and became their leading advocate in the modern network. He was active in the Lloyd Shaw Foundation, recording many called contras and supervising most of the group's recordings of folk dances for the educational market. Some of his calls are available as inexpensive downloads at **lloydshaw.org** under the "Store" tab; at Square Dance – Live Recordings (see above) there is a 1960 dance featuring Don and his wife Marie, ending with their signature number *Trail of the Lonesome Pine* called in harmony.

Sandy Bradley (Washington)   This Seattle-based caller fell in love with traditional and transitional western squares in the 1970s and sparked interest in squares in the Pacific Northwest in an era when most folk-revival groups elsewhere were focused on contras. Perhaps her most lasting contribution has been to inspire many women to take up calling.

Potluck and Dance Tonight (Fretless/Alcazar). Issued on LP and later on cassette. Contains 9 patter calls (in some cases two figures are done consecutively to the same music, as was Sandy's practice), plus three songs and a short instrumental polka. Figures are Lloyd Shaw–style western (not modern "western"); music is mainly old-time southern. Calls and music alike are hard-driving. Downloadable music files and complete liner notes, including dance descriptions, are at **stickerville.org/potluck**.

Bob Dalsemer (Maryland/North Carolina) spreads the joy of traditional dance wherever he goes. He helped start regular dancing in Baltimore and Washington, DC and headed the music and dance programs at the John C. Campbell Folk School for 22 years. He collected and published surviving traditional dance material of West Virginia (see Dalsemer 1982 under "Books").

Smoke on the Water and *When the Work's All Done*. Rousing renditions of 19 classic singing and patter squares from the 1940s and 1950s, with an all-star band. Currently available as downloads (**dosadomusic.com/brands/trad**); each purchase includes called and instrumental versions of one dance and a PDF file of calls and music notation.

Ed Durlacher (New York) was the all-time greatest popularizer of square dancing; he strove for simplicity and called to thousands every year (sometimes thousands a night) in the New York City parks. His *Honor Your Partner* series on his own label (which eventually became Educational Activities) has remained in print for 70 years, on 78 rpm, LP, cassette, and CD; the label was recently acquired by Smithsonian Folkways (**folkways.si.edu**). Some may find his teaching and calling style a bit stilted, but this was the most comprehensive series ever to include spoken instruction. Durlacher also recorded much of his repertoire (60 dances) for an archival project; these recordings are now available at **squaredance.podbean.com** (scroll to Nov. 2016 through Jan. 2017). The dances often sound rushed, especially compared with his commercial releases, but otherwise give a good idea of his style. Most of his early Decca and Sonora sides can be found on YouTube.

Ed Gilmore (California) started calling in the late 1940s and quickly rose to the top during the boom that led to the development of modern square dancing. He was among the first full-time traveling callers and caller coaches. Although some of his timing is very tight by New England standards, his calling and choreography are exemplary for their smoothness. He recorded a graduated series with spoken instruction, plus a number of intermediate-level dances, for Decca (later absorbed into MCA) and later issued several well-crafted singing squares with and without calls on his own Balance label. Some of his Decca releases are currently available on YouTube. Square Dance – Live Recordings (see above) includes some complete evenings by Gilmore, as well as a lecture to budding callers. Just as this book was going to press, Buddy Weaver started uploading a series of talks by Gilmore from a multi-session callers' class (**buddyweavermusic.podbean.com;** scroll to November 2021, where the series begins).

Les Gotcher (Texas/California) was famous for his high opinion of himself, but he appears to have actually been a very competent caller. His early recordings on the Capitol and MacGregor labels are of traditional material, called with good diction and energy (and more attention to phrasing than some other Texas-bred callers). His later releases on his own Black Mountain and Square-N-Round labels (and his field recordings available online) are of modern hash and will be of less interest to most tradition-based callers.

Jerry Helt (Ohio) was not only a club caller but worked extensively with casual dancers, particularly senior citizens. Many of his recordings, especially his videos, feature extremely easy material. His walkthroughs are laced with artificial enthusiasm that some will find annoying; his calling style is surprisingly gentle by contrast. There is a field recording of Helt at Square Dance – Live Recordings (see above); excerpts from his videos are available on YouTube.

Rickey Holden (Texas/Delaware) studied calling in both New England and Texas, and it shows. In his Folkraft album (8 dances) and his MacGregor singles (4 dances) he calls traditional and transitional Texas squares with precise timing and phrasing (plus a bit of twang). A few segments of workshops from much later in his career are available on YouTube.

Bruce Johnson (California), who started calling as a college student during the square dance boom, was one of the all-time greats, for his enthusiasm, his precision, his choice of material, and his impressive patter style: He could keep up a seemingly endless stream of rhyming couplets, always putting the command words in the right place. His singing calls on the Windsor label have never been surpassed for energy (standouts: *Alabama Jubilee, Crawdad Song*). His patter style can (and should) be heard at Square Dance – Live Recordings (see above); look under his name and also under "Funstitute."

Fenton "Jonesy" Jones (California) was in on the ground floor of the square dance boom that hit California in the 1940s. For years he was the house caller for the MacGregor label, recording all the standard singing squares plus many new ones (several are on YouTube). His style was deceptively low-key compared with a Bruce Johnson; it is easy to overlook his smoothness, precision, confidence, and all-around competence. His patter style, heard on albums for Black & White (reissued on Imperial) and Capitol, is less pleasing: He repeatedly used little four-beat melodies regardless of what the band was playing.

Richard "Dick" Kraus (New York)   A driving force in the academic study of recreation, first at Teachers College, Columbia and later at Temple University, Kraus was an inspiring caller with a lifelong love for square dancing; several of his textbooks on recreation devote space to squares. I did most of my early practice calling at his weekly Columbia dance in the 1960s, with Dick's generous encouragement.

Let's Square Dance! Volumes 1–5. Originally released by RCA Victor in 1955 and 1956 on vinyl in all three speeds, this is in some ways the finest graduated series ever made. Officially it was aimed at school grades 3–4 through 11–12, although the placement is somewhat arbitrary; Kraus never talks down to his listeners, although he uses "girls" and "boys" in the early grades, shifting to "ladies" and "gents" partway through the series. Both music and calling are upbeat and assured; patter is dated ("Swing right around with the pretty little thing"), but Kraus's energy is infectious. Each volume contains a circle dance, half a dozen squares, a longways, and an instrumental track. The squares include both singing and patter calls; the latter are generally phrased 1–4 but not 1–64. There are no spoken walkthroughs, and the printed leaflets appear to be unavailable, but most dances are in Kraus's 1950 book, which is easy to find. After a long hiatus, these albums are once again available, this time as downloads from **amazon.com.** Prices are barely higher than they were in the 1950s, and for the first time the tracks may be purchased individually. (In a later series on the Rec-o-Dance label, Kraus calls many favorite dances omitted from the RCA series but is hampered by a shaky orchestra.)

Dick Leger (Rhode Island) made a career out of calling relatively easy material, with New England–style timing and phrasing, to modern music for club square dancers. His singing call recordings on Folkraft, Top, and Grenn were always in demand; he also recorded several albums for school use on the Kimbo educational label (still available at **www.kimboed.com**). Several field recordings of his club dances are at Square Dance – Live Recordings (see above).

Phrase Craze Squares for Good Times! Grenn 43014, LP only. A dozen squares, 6 patter and 6 singing, delivered with impeccable timing and phrasing. Music varies from Dixieland to Latin (the selections had been previously issued as instrumentals at 45 rpm). Backbeat is a bit heavy, as was common in the modern square dance world of the 1960s and 1970s, but the overall feel is fairly traditional. Choreography is smooth; difficulty is just above "one-nighter" level. Never reissued, but well worth seeking out.

Ralph Page (New Hampshire) was the most prominent of the callers who kept square and contra dancing alive in New England during the 1930s and 1940s, paving the way for the boom of 1950 (and, indirectly, the contra revival of 1970). His contra recordings show a surprising amount of cadence calling as opposed to prompting (presumably he expected his dancers to be familiar with the material), but these and his square dance recordings on the Disc and Folk Dancer labels are well worth hearing. He nearly always calls on a musical pitch, sometimes improvising little countermelodies to the tune, and shows how to use rhyming patter without going overboard. Field recordings of two Page events are available at Square Dance – Live Recordings (see above); clips from his commercial records and a couple of field recordings are at **squaredancehistory.org.**

Ted Sannella (Massachusetts) Upon Ralph Page's demise, Sannella became the undisputed dean of New England's traditional-revival callers, not just for his calling and creative choreography but also for his mentorship of newer callers and his leadership in organizations such as the New England Folk Festival Association. He never recorded commercially, but several field recordings exist. Sannella 2005 (see "Books") includes a CD of several squares, including two versions of his signature *Merry-Go-Round,* and there are a few clips at **squaredancehistory.org.**

Marvin Shilling (Colorado) was active in the 1950s, traveling, operating a dude ranch, and recording on the Western Jubilee and later his own Lightning S label. In his patter calls he harmonized with the music while remaining clear and easy to follow. There are field recordings of him at Square Dance – Live Recordings (misspelled "Schilling") and at **squaredancehistory.org;** several of his commercial sides can be downloaded at **lloydshaw.org.**

Ralph Sweet (Connecticut) began dancing and calling in the 1940s, embraced the "western" style that captivated New England in the 1950s, then abandoned it when he felt it was not serving the needs of the average dancer and became an icon in the contra and traditional square dance revival scene. He converted an old barn into a dance hall and founded a company making wooden flutes.

Shindig in the Barn. A CD with 12 of the singing calls that were Ralph's trademark. A seven-piece band includes two saxophones. No dance directions are included, but the figures should be accessible to anyone familiar with present-day contras or the squares commonly done with them. A book is available with transcriptions of the calls and three-part arrangements of the tunes. **cdss.org**

Recordings without calls

As mentioned in Chapter 12, instrumental recordings have several uses in addition to the obvious one. They can be used for calling practice at home, or played for musicians to teach style or repertoire.

Most vendors, especially of single tracks, now allow you to hear at least a sample of each track before purchasing. I encourage you to listen and choose tracks that appeal to you. Different playing styles are appropriate for different dance material and situations: straight-ahead playing for continuous calling, flashier arrangements for prompted dances.

Suggested recordings for some of the dances in this book:

Atlantic Mixer	Crooked Stovepipe (Shane Cook)
Bird in the Cage #1	Durang's Hornpipe (Lloyd Shaw Foundation)
Birthday Contra Square	Reel de Rimouski (Any Jig or Reel)
Crooked Stovepipe	Weaver's Reel (LSF)
Dip and Dive Six	Early Bird Jig (Calvin Vollrath)
Do-si-do and Face the Sides	Texas Gals (Join Up Hands)
Duck Through and Swing	Growling Old Man (LSF)
Ends Turn In	Kansas City Reel (LSF)
Fiddle Faddle	Durang's Hornpipe (LSF)
Grapevine Twist	Sam and Elzie (Bluegrass Hoedown)
Heel and Toe Mixer	Jenny Lind Polka (Bluegrass Hoedown)
Hofbrau Square	Quindaro Hornpipe (Pure Quill)
Joys of Wedlock	Blarney Pilgrim (Listen to the Mockingbird)
Swing Two Ladies	Blarney Pilgrim (as above)
Three Against One	Spotted Pony (Join Up Hands)

Albums (many tracks can be purchased singly)

> **Special Mention:**
> *Tommy Jackson: Nashville Fiddler* (And More Bears AMB 71002, 6 CDs). One of the first and greatest Nashville "session men," playing backup for many famous country singers, Jackson also recorded many instrumental tracks of old and new fiddle tunes. This 2020 boxed set collects them all, along with a few vocals and two albums with calls. Recording quality varies, as some tracks date back to 1949, but most are quite good. Playing is uniformly excellent, with supreme confidence and wonderful tone and energy. Most tracks are short, averaging 5x, but many are easily looped. My favorites include Ragtime Annie, Tennessee Wagoner, Chinese Breakdown, Golden Slippers, Rachel, and Saint Anne's Reel. Available in the US from **countysales.com**.

Any Jig or Reel. Three fine New England musicians play 9 all-purpose medleys and 3 waltzes. **dancingmasters.com**

Bluegrass Hoedown (Voyager CD 359). Fiddle, banjo, and mandolin swap leads on over a dozen single-tune tracks, many 9 or 10 x 32 measures. Tempos are medium for southern-style dancing. **voyagerrecords.com**

Chimes of Dunkirk. A small but tight band plays a jig medley and a reel medley (10 x 32 each) plus several tunes that normally go with specific dances but can be used for others. **dancingmasters.com**

Full Swing. A multi-fiddle band plays 5 long medleys plus 2 squares and a contra with calls (instructions included). **greatmeadowmusic.com**

Join Up Hands. A dozen tunes in old-time string band style, including a 48-bar (AABBCC) selection. Tempos are slow for southern dancing, which can be an advantage in some situations. **suehulsether.com**

Listen to the Mockingbird. Five long medleys (all 10 x 32): Quebec reels, New England jigs, Southern reels, and 2 of Irish reels, plus a 6 x 48 track, 4 easy squares with calls, and other goodies. **dancingmasters.com**

Old Time Dance Party. A southern-style string band plays 5 single-tune tracks. Tempos are slow for the genre. The same tunes with gender-neutral calls are also included. **paulsilveria.com/dance-calling-guide**

Pure Quill. New England icons Rodney Miller and Bob McQuillen play several jig and reel medleys, including 2 outstanding 4-tune (8 x 32) tracks ideal for double-length square figures. **greatmeadowmusic.com**

Sashay the Donut. Long medleys: Quebec reels (10 x 32), old-time (southern) reels (15 x 32), Irish jigs and Irish reels (each 9 x 32), plus several shorter tracks and 2 squares with calls. **dancingmasters.com**

Shane Cook. A self-titled album from a flamboyant Canadian fiddler. Has a few dance-length tracks. **shanecook.com**

Square Dance Tunes (Without Calls). Calvin Vollrath, a Canadian fiddler and teacher/organizer, plays 12 long jig and reel tracks (11 or 12 x 32). No medleys or lead instrument swaps; many callers find this makes their job easier. **calvinvollrath.com** (look for Vollmart/mp3 tab, then scroll down to "traditional recordings")

Step Lively. The standout is a southern medley that runs 11 x 32 measures (the same track is repeated with gender-neutral calls for two-couple figures, using a scatter promenade for the progression). Also included are a reel medley and a jig medley (8 x 32 each) played with enthusiasm but fairly slowly (proving that it can be done), plus a nearly 7-minute march medley and several easy folk dances. **marianrose.com**

Step Lively 2. Includes one of my favorite reel medleys, starting with the classic St. Anne's (12 x 32), plus several 6x and 7x tracks. **marianrose.com**

Single recordings (all can be sampled before purchase)

Buddy Weaver Music. Remastered tracks from 1950s and later. Most are too "modern" for my taste (electronic instruments, heavy drum backbeat), but a few are more traditional in feel. Favorites: Chinese Breakdown, Earl's Hoedown, Just Walkin' (correct title: Blue Mountain Rag). The Ragtime Annie is irregular; Lloyd Shaw (below) has the same track "corrected" to 8 x 32. **buddyweavermusic.com** (click on Rawhide, then scroll down to Classic Hoedowns)

Lloyd Shaw Foundation. An extensive collection of instrumental tracks in various styles. Some were created recently, others date from the 1950s and have been cleaned up and extended. The following are my favorites; there are many more. **lloydshaw.org** (click on Store, then Recordings)

    Old-time southern:
        Black Mountain Rag (15 x 32)
        Booth Shot Lincoln/Briarpicker Brown (12 x 32)
        Brandywine/Three Forks of Reedy (12 x 32)
        Dinah/Wake Up Susan (12 x 32)
        Forked Deer/Doctor, Doctor (12 x 32)
        Granny, Will Your Dog Bite? (12 x 32)
        John Brown's March/Waiting for the Federals (slow, 12 x 32)
        Julianne Johnson/Grub Springs (14 x 32)
        Kansas City Reel (12 x 32)
        Sadie at the Back Door/Waiting for Nancy (12 x 32)
        Year of Jubilo/Yellow Rose of Texas (12 x 32)
    Sets in Order 1950s hoedowns extended to 9 minutes:
        Chinese Breakdown (banjo lead, 12 x 48)
        Durang's Hornpipe (18 x 32)
        Dusty Roads (= My Love Is But a Lassie; banjo, 18 x 32)

New Chinese Breakdown (fiddle lead, 18 x 32)
Rubber Dolly (banjo lead; irregular)
Steve Green (18 x 32)
Other LSF tracks:
Aw Shucks (Combination Rag, 9 x 32)
Balancing Billy (New Brunswick Hornpipe, 7 x 32)
Circassian Circle version 1 (Montreal Breakdown, 6 x 32)
Fisher's Hornpipe (banjo lead, 7 x 32)
Growling Old Man (7 x 32)
Inflation Reel (Ragtime Annie, 8 x 32)
Weaver's Reel (Topsy-Turvy = Crooked Stovepipe, 8 x 32)
Yucca Jig (Major Mackey's Jig, 6/8, 7 x 32)

Square Dance Music.com. Downloads of 1950s and 1960s singles. Noteworthy are hoedowns on Sets in Order (including some not available from Lloyd Shaw) and Sunny Hills labels, plus some good singing call music on Grenn label. **squaredancemusic.com**

Vintage recordings

I have listed a few of my favorite tracks from the 1950s, in case you acquire the record case of a retired or deceased caller. The recordings can be cleaned up digitally (if they are not too worn) and even made longer or shorter.

Capitol: A&E Rag / Rakes of Mallow, Hornet's Nest, Jackson's Breakdown, Late for Supper, Silver Lake / Grandma's Favorite
Folk Dancer: Glise a Sherbrooke / Wright's Quickstep (6/8), St. Anne's Reel / Reel de Ti-Jean, Garfield's Hornpipe, Come Up the Back Stairs (6/8), Lamplighter's Hornpipe, Old Joe Clark / Up Jumped the Devil, Maple Leaf Jig (6/8) / Indian Reel, Reel de Montreal / La Bastringue, Mount Gabriel Reel (perfect for *Kitchen Lancers*)
Folkraft: Aunt May's Canadian Jig (6/8), Cincinnati Hornpipe, Crooked Stovepipe, Father O'Flynn (6/8), My Love Is But a Lassie Yet
MacGregor: Six Mix or Virginia Reel (the same instrumental: Haste to the Wedding [6/8])
RCA Victor: Blackberry Quadrille (6/8) / Soldier's Joy (from 1940s; one of the first usable instrumental records)
Sets in Order: Jackson's Breakdown (never reissued); many others now available as downloads from two vendors (see above)
Sunny Hills: Blue Mountain Rag / Roanoke, Rag Time Annie, Romping Molly / Dill Pickle Rag, Up Jumped the Devil, Wake Up Susie / Old Joe Clark
Western Jubilee: Gray Eagle / Braying Mule, Raggin' Up Annie / Shaw's Reel, Soldier's Joy / Cripple Creek (all ideal for Texas-style dances)

Non-dance recordings

Total Warm-Up with Shelley Kristen. My favorite vocal warm-up recording of several I've bought. Has 20 exercises that let you ease into your full singing or speaking voice. *Total Work Out* has 20 more exercises for strengthening the voice. Both are available as CDs or downloads. **singingvoicelessons.com**

VIDEOS

Dance to the Music and Listen to the Calls. A documentary of traditional caller Jerry Goodwin, made by Larry Edelman who apprenticed with him in 1987. Goodwin was a West Virginia native who moved to southwestern Pennsylvania, where this film was made. He called in both patter and singing styles, mostly visiting-couple figures; a variety of couple dances was also done. This is a valuable look at a genre that used to be widespread in the Northeast and can still be found here and there. 29 minutes. A link to the YouTube page is at **squaredancehistory.org/items/show/913,** where there is also a companion booklet with some of the calls.

Square Dance History Project YouTube Channel. Individual videos of about 80 squares and big circles presented by six veteran callers at the 2011 Dare To Be Square weekend at the John C. Campbell Folk School in Brasstown, NC. While there is no such thing as a "definitive" version of a traditional dance, a version refined over the years by an experienced caller is well worth seeing and hearing – and perhaps emulating. Note that regardless of regional style (several were presented), the dancers always move smoothly and display enthusiasm. This, I submit, is the result that a good caller hopes and tries for. **youtube.com/user/SquareDanceHistory/videos**

Square Dance Interviews YouTube Channel. Segments from interviews with several long-time callers, including the six staff members of the 2011 Dare To Be Square weekend. **youtube.com/user/SquareDanceInterview/videos**

Sweet Talk. An interview with Ralph Sweet, who became first a modern square dance caller and then an elder statesman of the traditional square and contra dance scene, famous for preserving many classic singing calls. Includes audio and video clips from the square dance boom of the 1950s. 73 minutes. **davidmillstonedance.com** (click on Video tab; website offers other videos, dealing primarily with contras but providing valuable insights into recent dance history)

COMPUTER SOFTWARE

SqView. A music player; can vary pitch and tempo independently, has looping feature. The program is freeware; users must supply their own music tracks (purchased or created). **sqview.se** (a Swedish website in English)

Resources 495

ORGANIZATIONS

Canadian Olde Tyme Square Dance Callers Association. Dedicated to preserving traditional square and couple dances. Website includes dance directions, videos, sample music with and without calls, a directory of callers and one of dance events. **sca.uwaterloo.ca/cotsdca/**

Country Dance and Song Society. Runs camps, workshops, and symposia; produces books, recordings, and periodicals and sells those of others; acts as a clearinghouse of dance information and an umbrella organization with benefits for local dance groups. Primary focus is English country and ritual dance and contemporary contra dance, but much of its how-to information applies to squares; a few of the books and articles housed on its website deal specifically with squares. **cdss.org**

Folk Arts Center of New England. A leading nonprofit dance organization based in the Boston area. Primary focus is international folk dance, but a good source for tune books and recordings of square and contra dance music and family-oriented dance material. **facone.org**

Lloyd Shaw Foundation. Dedicated to preserving "the folk dances of America," including contras, couple dances and mixers, easy squares, and some international folk dance. Runs camps and workshops; produces and sells recordings singly and in kits for various age and ability groups. Website has some dance directions as well as links to items for sale. **lloydshaw.org**

National Folk Organization. Provides resources and networking for people and groups in folk dance and related arts; runs the annual Pourparler (see "Events" below). Currently the cheapest source for liability insurance (it's included in membership). **nfo-usa.org**

New England Folk Festival Association. Co-founded by Ralph Page in 1944; runs one of the largest weekly contra dances in the Boston area, a spring festival in Massachusetts, and a winter weekend in New Hampshire (see "Events" below). **neffa.org**

RETAILERS

See also the entities listed under "Organizations" above, many of which produce their own items and/or sell those of others. Many items are produced by independent artists; you can support them by purchasing directly from them (their Web addresses, where known, appear in the reviews above).

Anglo-American Dance Shop. Based in Belgium, serves all of Europe with dance books, recordings, and paraphernalia. Website is in English; sometimes has copies of out-of-print items that are unavailable in the US. **www.aads.be**

Great Meadow Music. Produces and sells CDs of contra dance music, much of which is suitable for phrased squares. Sells items from other producers, including David Millstone's documentary videos. **greatmeadowmusic.com**

EVENTS

At press time many events are on hiatus due to the Covid-19 pandemic; some groups are running online symposia instead. Those listed here are well-established and expected to resume running in person as soon as feasible. There are also many local and regional dance weekends; check **cdss.org** and **contradancelinks.com** for up-to-date information.

Ashokan Center. Weekend and week-long events in New York state. Of particular interest are Northern Week (New England and Québécois dance and its music) and Southern Week (old-time string band music and southern squares and circles). **ashokancenter.org**

Augusta Heritage Center. Week-long camps and weekend conferences in central West Virginia, focusing primarily on the music and dance of the Appalachian Mountains. **augustaartsandculture.org**

Berea Christmas Country Dance School. A winter week of traditional music and dance in Kentucky, featuring English and American forms. **bereaccds.org**

Brasstown. The John C. Campbell Folk School, at the western tip of North Carolina, runs dance weeks and weekends as part of a huge and varied folk arts curriculum. Believes strongly in dance as a means of bringing people together. **folkschool.org**

Country Dance and Song Society. Summer weeks at the historic Pinewoods Camp in Massachusetts and sometimes in other locations. There is often a track for callers, allowing them to study in the morning and try out their skills on the campers at night. **cdss.org**

Dance Flurry. Held in February in central New York state; one of the largest contra dance weekends in the East. Often includes workshops on squares and family dances. **danceflurry.org**

Dare To Be Square DMV. A fall weekend devoted to traditional square dance and old-time music, held near Washington, DC. **daretobesquaredmv.com**

Dare To Be Square West. A fall weekend, similar to the one above, held in Washington state. **daretobesquarewest.org**

Lady of the Lake. Summer music and dance weeks and a fall weekend in northern Idaho. **ladyofthelake.org**

Mainewoods. Summer weeks in Maine. Emphasis is on international folk dance; staff often includes a specialist in contra/square, English, or Scottish dance. **mainewoodsdancecamp.org**

New England Folk Festival. Held in April in eastern or central Massachusetts; includes contra, square, English country, and international folk dance, plus ethnic food and folk crafts for sale. **neffa.org**

Pinewoods. A former Girl Scout camp between Boston and Cape Cod; one of the first rustic venues to be devoted to dance, with four open-air pavilions. Home to weeks and weekends run by the Country Dance and Song Society (**cdss.org**) and several other groups; see **pinewoods.org** for a complete schedule.

Pourparler. A yearly gathering of folk dance leaders who teach in schools and at community events. Includes networking, discussion, and sharing of material. Location changes from year to year. **nfo-usa.org**

Ralph Page Dance Legacy Weekend. Held in January at the University of New Hampshire; features evening dances and workshops for square and contra dancers, callers, and musicians. Mission includes focusing on older (pre-1970) dance forms as well as newer ones. Information on upcoming events is at **neffa.org;** links to syllabi from past years (a particularly good source of usable squares) are at **https://library.unh.edu/find/archives/collections/ralph-page-dance-legacy-weekend-rpdlw-1988-2017.**

Stockton. The oldest (1948) and largest international folk dance camp in the US. Two identical summer weeks in northern California. Staff always includes a square/contra caller (Jerry Helt for an amazing 58 years, the present author more recently) and often an English or Scottish country dance specialist as well. Syllabi from prior years are available free online; many early ones contain much square dance material (1957 is especially good for Ralph Page's "town hall squares"). **folkdancecamp.org**

PERIODICALS

American Dance Circle (1979–present). The voice of the Lloyd Shaw Foundation; contains dance material and articles on dance history as well as news of people and events connected with the Foundation. Back issues are available at **lloydshaw.org** under the Education tab.

American Squares (1945–present). The first square dance magazine to be truly national in scope. Covered all regional forms as well as the evolving "modern" style until October 1959, when a new owner focused solely on the latter. Earlier issues are of interest to the tradition-minded reader; the best in terms of scholarship and writing style are those edited by Rickey Holden (April 1952 to June 1956; for a few more months he was a figurehead and wrote occasional pieces). Issues from the first year through 2009 (eventual title: *American Square Dance*) are available at **newsquaremusic.com/ASDindexUNH.html.** At press time this magazine is scheduled to be revived; I have been asked to write a column on dance history and other matters from the viewpoint of a tradition-based caller. The new address is **americansquaredance.com.**

Foot 'n Fiddle (1946–1957). Founded and edited by several prominent Texas callers, this magazine did for the Lone Star State what *Northern Junket* did for New England folklore. Copies are hard to come by, but three issues are available online at **squaredancehistory.org/items/show/1064.**

Let's Dance! (1944–present). Published by the Folk Dance Federation of California. In the 1940s and early 1950s most international folk dance clubs in the Golden State programmed some squares, and issues from that period contain much square dance material. **folkdance.com/resources/archives**

Northern Junket (1949–1984). Ralph Page's home-printed labor of love, issued whenever he had time for it. In addition to feature articles, every issue includes a square, a contra, a circle or couple dance, a folk song, some recipes, and reprints of old (mainly 19th-century) news items that mention dance. Available online at **https://scholars.unh.edu/northern_junket/**.

Promenade (1940–1952). Produced by Margot Mayo, a Texan who lived in New York City for many years and founded the American Square Dance Group there, this is the first known periodical to devote significant space to country-style square dance (it also covered folk music in general). Most issues are at the Internet Archive; a link is at **squaredancehistory.org/items/show/1047**.

Rosin the Bow (1945–1957). Begun as the club newsletter of the Ramapo Rangers square dance group, this elaborately produced magazine was the work of New Jersey caller and dance historian Rod La Farge and his wife Helen. It focused on the New York City area but contained articles on the dances and other folklore of various countries in addition to squares. Volume 1 is available at **squaredancehistory.org/items/show/1941;** Volume 2 is item 1980. Later issues are worth obtaining; some have elaborate hand-painted covers.

Sets in Order (1948–1985). The voice of the "modern" square dance style that began as Lloyd Shaw's flamboyant version of traditional western dancing and evolved into a very different form. Issues up to the mid-1950s contain material usable by neo-traditional callers (much of it is also in the titles by Bob Osgood listed under "Books" above), along with various leaders' thoughts on the state of the hobby. Available online at **newsquaremusic.com/SIOindex.html**.

MAILING LISTS

Shared Weight. A group of discussion lists for callers, musicians, and organizers of traditional dance and song events. **sharedweight.net**

ARCHIVES

New Hampshire Library of Traditional Music & Dance. One of the two most important repositories of square dance artifacts, and the largest in the East. Strongest on New England squares and contras and English country dance, but covers all regions. Contains thousands of books, letters, papers, and audio and video recordings, including the archives of several dance organizations and the personal collections of many influential callers.
https://library.unh.edu/find/special/subject/new-hampshire-library-traditional-music-dance

University of Denver Archives. One of the two largest square dance collections; focuses on modern square dancing and its roots in traditional western style. Includes several personal collections and the archives of *Sets in Order* magazine and the Lloyd Shaw Foundation. **https://duarchives.coalliance.org** (search for "square dancing")

WEBSITES

An American Ballroom Companion: Dance Instruction Manuals, ca. 1490 to 1920. Just what the title says: more than 200 manuals selected and uploaded by the Library of Congress, most of them readable and even searchable online. Many include descriptions of quadrilles and other forerunners of the square dance. **loc.gov/collections/dance-instruction-manuals-from-1490-to-1920**

Contra Dance Links. The best organized and most complete directory of its kind, listing regular series and special events worldwide. Has a page devoted to old-time square dance events. Don't overlook the Resources link (almost hidden under Sites and Pages near the top of the home page); it leads to 300 essays including many on calling. Some of the calling articles deal specifically with squares. **contradancelinks.com**

Internet Resources for Contra Dance Callers. A short but pithy set of links, including handouts from several calling workshops. **quiteapair.us/calling/**

Introduction to the Various Styles of American Square Dancing. A page on the Country Dance and Song Society website that collects various articles and other resources on square dancing and calling in various styles. (Note: What I term "neo-traditional," this page refers to as " 'traditional style' modern squares.") **cdss.org** (go to Resources, then Callers, then Reflections on the History and Evolution of Calling)

A Look at Southern Squares. Created by the late Bill Martin, mentor to many southern-style callers, this site gives a brief orientation and describes about 30 small circle figures, 30 big circle figures, 20 figures suited to four-couple squares, and a handful of mixers. All are taken from the existing literature, with full credit; Martin urges the reader to obtain the original books. **bubbaguitar.com/squaredance/index.html**

Michael Dyck's Contradance Index. Attempts to list, by title and author, every contra dance ever published. Cites the source (book or website) of each dance; if the source is a website, the citation is a live link. At press time the total dance count is more than 8,000. About 900 squares are listed under the notations "C 4x2" and "C 4x2 mixer"; most circle mixers are under "Cm 1x2 mixer." **ibiblio.org/contradance/index/**

Square Dance History Project. A searchable online collection of nearly 2,000 audio and video recordings, photographs, newspaper and magazine articles, monographs, syllabi, callers' repertoire lists, and even complete books, documenting the history of both traditional and modern square dancing. The pages for many items include links to other items that are related in various ways. Highly recommended. (Note: I am a "core consultant" to this project but derive no financial benefit from it.) **squaredancehistory.org**

Vintage Dance Manuals. A monumental list of more than 6,000 books and other publications on all types of dance, including squares, contras, mixers, and similar group dances. About 2,000 of them are available as free downloads. Dates range from around 1450 to the present. Contents of many books are listed by dance title. **libraryofdance.org/manuals/**

Index

See also the discussion of various terms in the Glossary, which is not indexed.

AABB tune sequence, 49
adapting dances, 161–66
   to be gender-neutral, 157
Advanced (modern program), 24
African-Americans, 9, 13, 18
   and origins of calling, 15–16
   calling to, 151
Alamo Style, 213
alcohol, and dancing, 21, 27, 42
All Mixed Up (Mills), 85
Allemande Alphabet, 88, 173, 214
allemande left
   importance in hash, 172–73
Allemande O, 214
Allemande Thar, 214
allemande, defined, 197–200
Anderson, Kathy, 222
arch and dive, defined, 233–34
Armstrong, Don, 122, 292
Autry, Gene, 20
Away You Go, 215
backtrack, 240
balance, defined, 217–18
ballroom swing, 201
band styles, 135
barn dance radio shows, 20
Basic (modern program), 24
basic movement, defined, 63
Beck, Don, 166
bend the line, defined, 232
Benny, Buck, 360
big circle formation, 249–50
Black people. *See* African-Americans
Bland, James A., 331
bluegrass music, 27
Bowling Alone (Putnam), 34
box formation, 170

box the gnat, 219
Boyd, Neva, 19, 205, 244
Bradley, Sandy, 27, 316, 358, 369
breakdown (figure type), 64
breaks
   defined, 63
   history of, 87–88
   improvising, 91
   in dance construction, 70–71
   learning to call, 90
   pairing with figures, 92
   sample, 93–95
Buhler, Mildred, 199
Bunny, Bugs, 376
Burchenal, Elizabeth, 190
buzz step, 201
cadence calls, 75–77, 179
California twirl, 219
call-and-response songs, 15
Callerlab, 24, 28, 220, 247
calling, origins of, 14–16
Canterbury Country Orchestra, 26
care of voice, 86
catch all eight, 212
chain. *See under specific types*
Challenge (modern program), 24
Chambers, Don, 308
change, defined, 64
changing tunes, 137
checkers, using, 166
Cheyenne Mountain Dancers, 20
children, 148–49
   and race, 151
choosing material, 119
choreographic management, 175–78
circle (basic move)
   defined, 186–87

circle dances
Atlantic Mixer, 262
Circassian Circle, 258
discussion, 249–56
Heel and Toe Mixer, 264
Lucky Circle, 260
Pattycake Polka, 264
Paul Jones, 260
Sanita Hill Circle, 266
circle to a line, defined, 230–31
clipped timing, 53
command call, 101
constructing a sequence, 69–71
contests, 21
contra dancers, calling squares to, 152–55
contra dances, revival of, 25–26
copyright, and square dances, 162
corn-shuckings, 16
costumes, 17, 21, 22, 24, 26, 40, 42
cotillion
 18th-century, 11, 64
 and two-key tunes, 132
 German, 12
Country Dance and Song Society, 19, 27
Country Dance Book (Tolman & Page), 200
courtesy, 183
courtesy turn, 221, 225
Cowboy Dances (Shaw), 20, 192, 244
cowboy, image of, 17, 20, 21
creating original dances, 167–72
crooked tunes, 50, 137
cross trail, defined, 246–47
dance (figures and breaks)
 defined, 64
dance-walk, 183
Dare To Be Square movement, 27
Dart, Mary, 35
de Garmo, William, 367
demonstrations, 123–24
diagrams, using, 166, 178
Dick's Quadrille Call-Book, 337

diction, 83
difficulty level
 assessing, 111
 should peak in middle, 110
disabilities, dancers with, 149–50
dive through, defined, 233–34
do paso, 242
docey-doe, 242
do-si-do (back to back)
 defined, 190–92
do-si-do (hand turns)
 defined, 242–45
double elbow, 212
drive (musical quality), 133
Drucker, Peter, 33
Dunlavy, Tressie, 19, 205, 244
Durlacher, Don, 314, 342, 344, 348, 350
Durlacher, Ed, 20, 33, 122, 266, 270, 314, 344
Ecclesiastes, 161
Edelman, Larry, 34, 314
ending break, 89
English Dancing Master (Playford), 10, 238
English language learners, 150
enunciation, 83
equivalents, 163, 177
ethical decisions, 41–42
etiquette, 19th-century, 337
exercises, warm-up, 86
exploding squares, 370
exploitive behavior, 45–46
face right, 229
fatigue, as programming factor, 110
feedback, acoustic, 84
figure
 defined, 63
 in dance construction, 69–70
 types of, 66–67
first-timers, 144–48
 arriving late, 111
 no pre-dance lesson, 121
flow, 91, 169

Index

folk dancing, international, 18, 24, 25, 109
Ford, Henry, 19, 151, 205
forward and back
   defined, 188–89
Foster, Stephen, 41, 331
four ladies chain, 222
four-by-four dances, 110, 154, 255
free jobs, 41–42
French, J.A., 368
frontier whirl, 219
gender-neutral calling, 155–58
gents chain, 223
Georgia rang tang, 243
German cotillion, 12
get-out (module), 177
Gilbert, Gib, 324, 377
Gilmore, Ed, 23, 24, 99, 111, 166, 167, 169, 173, 174, 220, 228, 290, 296, 346, 352, 358, 360, 362, 364, 369, 394, 398, 400
giving weight, 184
global terminology, 157
Good Morning (Lovett), 19
Goodwin, Jerry, 34, 314
Gotcher, Les, 23
Gowing, Gene, 298
grand allemande, 212
grand chain (grand right and left), 211
grand left and right, 213
grand march, 250–53
grand right and left
   defined, 211–16
grand right and wrong, 213
Grand Sashay, 212
grand slide, 237
grand square, defined, 235–39
Grange do-si-do, 242
grapevine step, 186
Greggerson, Herb, 191, 244, 398
grid squares, 369
griots, 15
guest calling, 6, 112
Guthrie, Woody, 192

half promenade, 208
half sashay, 228
Hanby, Benjamin R., 331
hand turn, defined, 197–200
Hansen, Bill, 232
harassment, 45–46
hash, 172–80
   history of, 172–74
Helt, Jerry, 164, 166, 282, 294, 300, 338, 369
Hendrickson, Chip, 237, 266
Herman, Mary Ann, 201
Hildenbrand, A.J., 262
history, 9–31
Hoheisal, Jack, 88, 215
Holden, Rickey, 161, 232, 243, 380
   on phrasing, 56
Holleuffer, Vera, 215, 384
Howe, Elias, 367
humility, 42–43
infatuation, dealing with, 46
international folk dancing, 18, 24, 25, 109
introductory break, 89
Irish dance, 13
Irish immigration, 13, 18
Isaacs, Bob, 369
Jamison, Phil, 13, 20, 26, 190
Jennings, Larry, 36
jig (tune type), 18, 129
Johnson, Bruce, 37, 101
Jones, Fenton, 214
Kaltman, Frank, 99, 322
Kanter, Rosabeth Moss, 34
keeping track in hash, 175–78
Kemble, Fanny, 15
key words
   emphasizing, 83
   placement of, 78–79
keys, musical
   of singing calls, 335
   personality of, 131
King, Jay, 166
Kipling, Rudyard, 98
Kraus, Dick, 322

Kristen, Shelley, 86
La Farge, Rod, 199
ladies chain, defined, 221–23
ladies grand chain, 222
Lane, Frank, 220
Laufman, Dudley, 25
lead right, defined, 229
leadership, 35–36
leading patter, 100
Leger, Dick, 118, 282, 340, 394
lesson, pre-dance, 120
LGBTQ groups, 155–58
lift (musical quality), 132
Linnell, Rod, 334, 356
live music, 21
   in teaching sessions, 123
   working with, 133–39
long figures (AABBCC), 57
looping of recorded music, 140
Louis XIV, 11
Lovett, Benjamin, 19, 205
Mainstream (modern program), 24
management, choreographic, 175–78
march (tune type), 130
Mark, gospel of, 43
marketing, 6
Martin, Bill, 27
material, choosing, 119
McKay, Jack, 221
McNair, Ralph, 244, 369
medley change, 174
medleys of tunes, 137
Melish, John, 310
memorizing calls, 175
mental image calling, 177
mescolanzes. *See* four-by-four dances
Métis people, 27
Meyers, Dick, 342
Michl, Ed, 220
microphone technique, 84
middle break, 89
Mills, Bob, 85
Millstone, David, 26

mistakes, 7, 36–37
mixers. *See* circle dances
modern square dancers, calling to, 158–59
modern square dancing
   evolution of, 22–24
modernizing figures, 67–68
modifying dances, 161–66
   to be gender-neutral, 157
modules, 177
money, and calling, 38
Moody, Ed, 286
Mormons, 17
Morris dance, 11
movies, western, 20
musical pitch, 82
musicians
   finding, 138
   working with, 133–39
naming and numbering, 64–66, 184–85
National Square Dance Convention, 24
Native Americans, 13
neo-traditional style
   defined, 29
New England
   modernization of style, 25
new movements, writing, 171
nomenclature, of set, 64–66, 184–85
Old-Time Herald, 26
old-time music, 18, 27
old-time squares
   revival of, 26–27
once and a half, 212
one-nighters. *See* first-timers
orientation, of set, 64–66, 184–85
original dances, writing, 167–72
Osgood, Bob, 23, 24
Page, Ralph, 19, 25, 88, 89, 97, 112, 172, 199, 274, 286, 292, 294, 302, 304, 308, 334, 356, 368, 370, 371, 373, 374, 386
   advice to callers, 257

Index

pass through, defined, 195–96
patter, 97–107
   leading, 100
   questionable, 99
   sexist, 98
   trailing, 99
   vs. prompting and singing, 100
   with 6/8 music, 101
Pattison, Pat, 246
people of color
   calling to, 151
percussive dancing, 50
perfectionism, 43
phrasing, 56–62, 82
Piper, Ralph, 218
pitch, musical, 82
Playford, John, 10, 11, 13, 238
play-party games, 18, 20
Plus (modern program), 23, 24
positional calling, 157
positions in set, 64–66, 184–85
power turn, 222
practicing, 5
pre-dance lesson, 120
professionalism, 37–39
programming, 109–15
progressive circle formation, 253–55
progressive squares, 369
projection, vocal, 83
promenade
   defined, 207–10
   judging length of, 91–92, 168
   positions, 207
prompt, then patter, 77, 179
prompting, 74–75, 179
Protestants, conservative, 17
Putnam, Robert, 34
quadrille
   19th-century, 11, 64
   modern, 334
radio shows, barn dance, 20
Ralph Page Dance Legacy Weekend, 152
rap, 16, 98

reading calls, 6, 175
recorded music, 21, 59, 62, 70, 139–42
   looping, 140
reel (tune type), 18, 129
regional tune structure, 136
religion, and dancing, 17
retro-phrasing, 61
rhythm, 50, 81
Ricciotti, Chris, 157
right and left through
   defined, 224–26
rinncí fighte (Irish dance), 13
Rogers, Roy, 20
roll back, 240
rollaway, defined, 227–28
Rose and the Thorn, 376
round dancing, 30, 109
running set, 18
Ryan, Grace, 19, 205, 331
safety, at dances, 46
Saletan, Tony, 373
same-sex couples, 155–58
Sannella, Ted, 25, 58, 88, 166, 172, 288, 308, 371, 373, 386, 390
Santa Monica Diamond Jubilee, 22
Scots-Irish, 13
Scott, Edward, 205
Scottish recordings, 60
seated square dances, 150
semi-singing call, 334
seniors, 149
   and gender imbalance, 155
sequence, in and out of, 169
set of dances, defined, 64
Sets in Order magazine, 23, 24
set-up (module), 177
sexist patter, 98
sexual harassment, 45–46
Sharp, Cecil, 13, 18
Shaw, Lloyd, 20, 22, 23, 30, 33, 88, 171, 173, 174, 190, 192, 214, 243, 244, 322, 324, 382, 398
Sheldon, George T., 286
showmanship, 39–40

shuffle step, 22, 159
shyness, 40
sight calling, 176
signals, for band, 135
singing call figures
  Around One to a Star, 340
  Crosstown, 342
  Don's Easy Star, 344
  Ed's Grand Chain, 346
  In the Good Old Summertime, 348
  Jingle Bells, 350
  Queen's Quadrille in 4/4, 338
  Whispering, 352
singing calls, 17, 18, 20, 21, 52, 59, 83, 130, 165, 174
  appropriateness of lyrics, 41
  discussion, 331–36
  history, 331
  keys of, 335
  with live band, 139
single file promenade, 209
slip the clutch, 214
slipped phrases, 59, 144
  with live band, 137
Smith, Ray, 88, 215
snaparoo (star through), 220
sound systems, using, 84
southern sets, 18, 58, 61, 110, 255–56
spatial sense, 4
split timing, 52
square breaks
  Alamo Style, 380
  Allemande Thar, 382
  Double Turn Back, 398
  No Promenade, 388
  Other Four Star, 390
  Promenade First, 392
  Pull the Corner By, 400
  Rip and Snort, 375
  Single File Twice, 394
  Sound Check, 386
  Stars and Turns, 396
  Triple Allemande, 384

Square Dance Caller (Holden), 161
square figures
  Bird in the Cage #1, 314
  Bird in the Cage #2, 316
  Birdie Fly Out, 368
  Birthday Contra Square, 356
  Cheat or Swing, 369
  Crooked Stovepipe, 274
  Cumberland Square, 276
  Deer Park Lancers, 286
  Dip and Dive Six, 318
  Do-si-do and Face the Sides, 288
  Duck for the Oyster, 320
  Duck Through and Swing, 290
  Ends Turn In, 358
  Fiddle Faddle, 360
  Gents and Corners, 292
  Grapevine Twist, 322
  Heads and Sides, 270
  Heads Arch, 272
  Hofbrau Square, 294
  Indiana, 296
  Joys of Wedlock, 298
  King's Quadrille, 300
  Kitchen Lancers, 278
  Ladies Chain, 280
  Ladies' Whirligig, 370
  Lady Round Two, 324
  Lazy H, 362
  Length of the Hall, 371
  Merry-Go-Round, 373
  Ninepin, 373
  Queen's Quadrille, 300
  Right and Left Five, 302
  Right Hand High, Left Hand Low, 326
  Rout(e), The, 304
  Six Pass Through, 282
  Squareback Reel, 306
  Starline, 364
  Step Right Back, 376
  Swing Like Thunder, 328
  Swing Two Ladies, 308
  Three Against One, 310
square set, defined, 64–66, 184–85

stacking calls, 51
star promenade, 209
star through, 219
star, defined, 193–94
starting a dance series, 6
stepdancing, 50
stereotypes, 17, 42, 151
straight-ahead tunes, 130, 136
straight-arm swing, 202
Suzy Q, 244
swing, defined, 201–6
table, timing of movements, 54–55
talents, list of, 3
teaching, 117–28
   order for first-timers, 126
   order for series, 126
   pre-dance lesson, 120
tempo, 49, 51, 125, 144
   distinguished from timing, 52
   in boom years, 22
Texas do-si-do, 242
throw in the clutch, 214
Thurston, Hugh, 13
timing, 51–52, 82
   distinguished from tempo, 52
   table of movements, 54–55
tip (dance term), defined, 64
tips (money), accepting, 39
Tolman, Beth, 97
tone production, 83
Total Warm-Up (Kristen), 86
toxic behavior, 45–46
traditional dances
   survival of, 27
trail through, 246
trailing patter, 99
transitional era, 61
transitions, 184

Triple Allemande, 215
tune structure, regional, 136
tunes that tell a story, 130, 136
turn back (from grand right and left), 213
turn, one-hand, defined, 197–200
twirl to swap, defined, 219–20
twirl, in lieu of courtesy turn, 222
two-hand swing, 202
two-key tunes, 132
two-step, 50, 51
uneven numbers, dealing with, 68
unisex swings, 201
unpaid jobs, 41–42
visiting-couple figures, 22, 64, 313
vocal projection, 83
voice, care of, 86
Wade, George, 19
walk, as dance step, 183
walkthroughs, 121–23
   of breaks, 90
   warm, 123
warm walkthrough, 123
warm-up exercises, 86
Watson, William, 111
weave the ring, 212
weight, giving, 184
western movies, 20, 23
wheel around
   defined, 240–41
whirlaway, 228
Whittemore, Tod, 166
Whynot, Roger, 306, 394
Winston, Louise, 356
workshops, 110
writing original dances, 167–72
York, Jim, 220, 244, 360
zero movements, 162, 177